Analytical Methods in Economics

Analytical Methods in Economics

Akira Takayama

Ann Arbor

The University of Michigan Press

ISBN 0-472-10162-5
ISBN 0-472-08135-7
Published in the United States of America by
The University of Michigan Press
Manufactured in the United States of America

1998 1997 1996 1995 6 5 4 3

A CIP catalogue for this book is available from the British Library.

To Carl Kreider and Lionel McKenzie,
who first taught me
Economics

Preface

This monograph provides an introduction to the analytical approach to economics. It presents an exposition of what I think are the basic analytical tools in economics today (nonlinear programming, uncertainty, differential equations, and optimal control theory) and illustrates their applications to selected economic problems. The applications cover both micro and macro economics (although such a dichotomy may be unfortunate). In so doing, I hope to clarify the unifying analytical structure of economic theory and elucidate the basic mathematical tools that underlie it. It has been said that economics is an amalgam of poetry and precise logic (analytics) as well as a wide knowledge of facts. Even so, the analytical approach to the study of economics has become very important only during the last four or five decades.

This book is addressed to economists, graduate students, and advanced undergraduates in economics who want an introduction to some of the analytical foundations of economics with nontrivial economic applications. The book emphasizes motivation, explanation, and economic illustrations. It thus avoids the "definition-axiom-theorem" approach, although the author is fully aware of its importance. The book is not intended as a state-of-the-art handbook for researchers. Some important topics are thus regretfully omitted. Additionally, my emphasis is not to present the most general theorems or propositions. Rather, there is a special effort to make the exposition as simple as possible and to minimize the prerequisites for reading this book, although the reader will be brought pretty much to the frontier of all basic tools of analysis in economics today. It often happens in economics that the analytical structure of a particular problem is unfortunately not made clear even among some who write on the topic. Once the analytical structure is clarified, extensions to more general cases are usually straightforward. Thus, my emphasis in discussing economic problems is to clarify their analytical structure. Also, this book is *not* like textbooks on "engineering mathematics," which typically emphasize the question of "how-to." Although such books are useful at times, this book rather addresses questions of "why."

In terms of prerequisites, a rigorous second- or third-year undergraduate economic theory sequence should provide the reader with sufficient economics background to undertake this study. Two or three semesters of calculus and a basic knowledge of linear algebra (such as the rules of matrix multiplication) should provide a sufficient background in mathematics. For the convenience of some readers, the elements of linear algebra are also exposited in appendix A.

This book, in large measure, is a record of my lectures given on various subjects over the years to undergraduate and first- and second-year graduate students at Purdue University, Texas A&M University, University of Tokyo, Australian National University, University of Kyoto, Doshisha University, Tulane University, and Southern Illinois University at Carbondale. This book also represents some of my research efforts that have been published in professional journals such as *American Economic Review, Economics Letters, Journal of Economic Theory, Journal of Macroeconomics, Metroeconomica, Quarterly Journal of Economics, Southern Economic Journal, Economics Studies Quarterly, Zeitschrift für die gesamte Staatswissenschaft*, *Osaka Economic Papers*, *Keio Economic Studies*, and *Journal of International Economic Integration*, and also in *The New Palgrave: A Dictionary of Economics* (London, Macmillan 1987). This book is also written as a companion to my *Mathematical Economics* (2d ed., New York, Cambridge University Press, 1985). Thanks are due to these journals and the *New Palgrave* for permission to include in this book some materials by the author originally published in the above journals and the book. I am also indebted to Cambridge University Press for permission to use some materials published in *Mathematical Economics.* John Wiley & Sons, Inc. kindly gave me permission to use a diagram in the *Mathematical Theory of Optimal Processes* by L. S. Pontryagin, V. G. Boltyanskii, R. V. Gamkrelidze, and E. F. Mishchenko (tr. by K. N. Trirogoff), 1962. The precise source of each reference is given in its respective place.

While I owe intellectual debts to numerous distinguished members of our profession, among the many I would like to mention Professors Carl Kreider, Lionel W. McKenzie, Ronald W. Jones, Richard N. Rosett, Edward Zabel, Alan Gleason, Kiyoshi Kojima, Masao Hisatake, Yasukichi Yasuba, the late David Bryn-Jones, S. C. Tsiang, Takao Fukuchi, Miyohei Shinohara, Hugo Sonnenschein, Takashi Negishi, William A. Brock, Edward Sieper, Sydney Afriat, John D. Pitchford, James W. Friedman, Seiji Naya, Robert L. Basmann, Murray C. Kemp, Maurice McManus, James P. Quirk, Mohamed El-Hodiri, Yasuo Uekawa, Koichi Hamada, Winston W. Chang, Takeshi Amemiya, James B. McDonald, Michihiro Ohyama, Yashuhiro Sakai, Masayoshi Hirota, Yutaka Horiba, John Z.

Drabicki, Richard K. Anderson, Tatsuo Hatta, David Kleykamp, and Chi-Chur Chao for their long friendship. They have constantly provided me with a great deal of intellectual stimulation.

I also feel fortunate to live in this period of history in which many fine economists, such as the late Sir John R. Hicks, Paul A. Samuelson, Kenneth J. Arrow, Lionel W. McKenzie, Leonid Hurwicz, Gerard Debreu, James Tobin, Franco Modigliani, Robert M. Solow, and Takuma Yasui have been active, and the economics of Marshall, Walras, Keynes, and von Neumann is very much alive in present refinements of basic economics paradigm. Thus, I have not felt an urgent need for "breakaway" changes of "paradigms" or "research programs." At the minimum, the overwhelming superiority of some of the new, proposed "paradigms" has not been clearly demonstrated.

Some sections in the book are based on papers coauthored with John Z. Drabicki (University of Arizona), Richard K. Anderson (Texas A&M University), and Toyonari Ide (Fukuoka University). I am indebted to them for giving permission to include the materials that were jointly written. I am also indebted to John and Toyo, and to Jess Benhabib (New York University), Christopher Bliss (University of Oxford), Yasuhiro Sakai (University of Tsukuba), Jack Meyer (Michigan State University), Rulon Pope (Brigham Young University), Myoungjae Lee (Pennsylvania State University), and Peter Coughlin (University of Maryland) for useful comments on parts or all of the manuscript. Specifically, John as usual provided a generous share of comments, but all were to the point. Finally, I am indebted to the many students in various universities who took my courses, provided useful comments on the content, and remained cheerful after my long classes. Needless to say, none of the people above are responsible for any possible shortcomings of the book.

In preparing this book, I am indebted to Gertrudes Castillo-Holder, Toyonari Ide, and Doh-Joon Bhak for their excellent research assistance. I am also greatly indebted to Kathy Elders for her excellent stenographic services in typing the entire manuscript and to Don Stribling for his perseverance in reproducing it with a typesetting program. I am, as well, very grateful for the last-minute efforts of Don and Doh-Joon at the time of publication. I also wish to thank Mary Mertz who cheerfully typed part of the first drafts and also to Dr. T. C. Lin who set up the word processing and typesetting system for our computers. The book would not have been completed without the patience of all these people in going through numerous revisions (though, in this regard, there are others at my University to whom I am not particularly indebted.)

All this assistance was made possible through the funding of the Vandeveer Chair of Economics at Southern Illinois University—Carbondale, which I wish to gratefully acknowledge. I am also indebted to Colin Day and his staff at the University of Michigan Press for their help and patience in bringing out this book.

May 1993 A. T.

Contents

Preface vii

Contents xi

Introduction xvii

Part 1 Preliminaries 1

1 Some Basic Mathematics 3

1.1 Preliminary Concepts and Notations 4
1.1.1 Sets 4
1.1.2 Logical Statements 8
1.1.3 Functions 10
1.1.4 Real Numbers 13
1.2 Euclidian Space 13
1.3 A Little Topology 25
1.3.1 Convergence 25
1.3.2 Continuity 28
1.3.3 Some Topological Concepts and Results 32
1.4 Quadratic Forms 36
1.5 Differentiation, Concave and Quasi-Concave Functions . . 40
1.5.1 Differentiation 40
1.5.2 Some Important Results 45
1.5.3 Higher Order Derivatives and Hessians 49
1.5.4 Concave and Convex Functions 52
1.5.5 Quasi-Concave Functions 60
Exercises 65
References 70

Part 2 Nonlinear Programming and Microeconomics 73

2 Nonlinear Programming 75

2.1 Introduction . . . 75
2.2 Characterization of Optimum by First-Order Condition . 85
2.3 Saddle-Point Characterization of Optimum . . . 103
2.4 Classical Optimization and Nonlinear Programming . . . 111
2.4.1 Classical Optimization . . . 111
2.4.2 Comparison to Nonlinear Programming . . . 117
Exercises . . . 120
References . . . 122

3 Sensitivity Analysis and Elements of Microeconomics 125

3.1 Comparative Statics: Conventional Procedure . . . 125
3.2 The Envelope Theorem . . . 131
3.3 Elements of Microeconomic Theory . . . 139
3.4 Elasticity of Factor Substitution and Its Estimation . . . 151
3.5 On the Concept of Returns to Scale . . . 157
3.6 The Le Châtelier-Samuelson Principle . . . 163
Exercises . . . 171
References . . . 181

4 Other Topics in Microeconomic Theory 187

4.1 Inferior Inputs, Marginal and Average Costs . . . 187
4.1.1 Inferior Inputs . . . 187
4.1.2 Factor Prices and Shifts of the Average Cost Curve 193
4.2 Marginal Cost Pricing . . . 196
4.3 Factor Prices and the Shape of Average Cost Curves . . . 201
4.4 Supply of Labor: Income-Leisure Choice . . . 206
4.4.1 The Case without Nonwage Income . . . 206
4.4.2 The Case with Nonwage Income . . . 210
4.5 Behavior of the Firm under Regulatory Constraint . . . 212
4.6 The Peak-Load Problem . . . 219
4.6.1 Introduction . . . 219
4.6.2 The Case of a Welfare-Maximizing Monopoly . . . 221
4.6.3 The Case of a Profit-Maximizing Monopoly . . . 230
4.7 On the Coase Theorem . . . 235
4.7.1 Introduction . . . 235
4.7.2 Externality and the Pigouvian Scheme . . . 237
4.7.3 The Coase Theorem . . . 242

References . . . 247

Part 3 Economics of Uncertainty 255

5 Economics of Uncertainty 257

5.1 The Expected Utility Hypothesis . . . 257
5.2 Expected Utility and Behavior toward Risk . . . 271
5.2.1 Behavior toward Risk . . . 271
5.2.2 Arrow-Pratt Measures of Risk Aversion . . . 273
5.2.3 Examples . . . 278
5.2.4 Indifference Curves . . . 280
5.3 Applications . . . 281
5.3.1 Insurance . . . 281
5.3.2 The Theory of the Firm . . . 286
5.3.3 Portfolio Choice . . . 290
5.3.4 Consumption and Savings Decision . . . 296
5.4 Economics of Information . . . 305
5.4.1 Asymmetry of Information, the Lemon Principle, and Signaling . . . 305
5.4.2 Preventive Activity and Asymmetry of Information in Insurance . . . 307
5.4.3 Adverse Selection . . . 312
5.5 Concluding Remarks . . . 315
References . . . 316

Part 4 Differential Equations and Economic Analysis 323

6 Elements of Differential Equations and Economic Applications 325

6.1 Basic Concepts and Existence of a Solution . . . 325
6.2 Stability . . . 333
6.3 Economic Applications . . . 345
6.3.1 The Stability of Competitive Equilibrium: the Walrasian Process . . . 345
6.3.2 The Stability of Macroeconomic Equilibrium . . . 350
6.3.3 Neoclassical Growth Model . . . 355
6.3.4 On the Phillips Curve . . . 358

6.3.5 Tobin's "Walras-Keynes-Phillips" Model:An Application of the Routh-Hurwitz Theorem 365
6.4 Competitive Equilibrium for the Three-Commodity Case . 370
References 376

7 Linear Differential Equations on the Plane and Elements of Nonlinear Systems 383

7.1 Linear Systems 383
7.2 Homogeneous Linear Systems on the Plane 385
7.3 Dynamic Behavior of the Solution on the Plane 395
7.4 Nonlinear Systems 407
7.4.1 Local Behavior of the Trajectories on the Plane . . 407
7.4.2 Stability of the Nonlinear System: Liapunov's Direct Method 411
7.4.3 Local Asymptotic Stability 414
Exercises 415
References 416

8 Macroequilibrium and Neoclassical Growth Models 419

8.1 Static Macroequilibrium and Its Stability 419
8.2 Money and Growth—Part 1 423
8.2.1 Model 423
8.2.2 Steady State 427
8.2.3 Stability and Instability 430
8.2.4 The Source of Instability 434
8.3 Money and Growth—Part 2 436
8.3.1 Introduction 436
8.3.2 Model and Momentary Equilibrium 438
8.3.3 Long-Run Analysis 440
8.3.4 The Source of Stability 444
8.3.5 Appendix to Section 8.3 445
References 447

Part 5 Optimal Control Theory and Applications 449

9 Elements of Optimal Control Theory and Applications 451

9.1 Pontryagin's Maximum Principle 451
9.2 Various Cases 461
9.3 Two Illustrations 468

9.3.1 Calculus of Variations 468
9.3.2 An Illustrative Problem by Pontryagin *et al.* . . . 472
9.4 Optimal Growth Problem 475
References 488

10 Infinite Horizon Optimization Control Problem and Applications **493**

10.1 A General Theorem 493
10.2 Optimal Monetary Policy 498
10.3 Savings: Permanent Income Hypothesis 504
10.4 Investment 514
10.4.1 The "Neoclassical" Theory 515
10.4.2 The Adjustment Cost Approach 522
10.4.3 Tobin's q, the Value of the Firm, and Keynes's Rule of Marginal Efficiency of Capital 525
References 535

11 Extensions of Optimal Control Themes **541**

11.1 The Main Theorem 541
11.2 Consumer's Lifetime Allocation Process: Finite Horizon Case 547
11.3 Isoperimetric Problem 553
11.4 Spatial Pricing Problem 557
Appendix to Section 11.4: Spatial Pricing Problem and Nonlinear Programming 564
References 568

Appendices **571**

A Elements of Linear Algebra **573**

A.1 Matrices and Basic Operations 573
A.2 Transposes, Vectors, Simultaneous Equations, and Nonsingular Matrices 576
A.3 Linear Independence, Rank, and Linear Subspaces 581
Linear Subspaces and Ranks 582
A.4 Matrices as Linear Transformations 585
A.5 Determinants and Partitioned Matrices 590
A.5.1 Determinants, Laplace Expansion, and Cramer's Rule 590
A.5.2 Partitioned Matrices and Determinants 594

A.6 Eigenvalues, Eigenvectors, and Symmetric Matrices 595
A.7 Negative or Positive Definite Matrices 600
References 603

B Seven Kinds of Concavity and Quasi-Concave Programming: A Survey of Some Results and Extensions 605

B.1 Seven Kinds of Concavity 605
B.2 The Role of Nonvanishing Gradients 611
B.3 Quasi-Concave Programming 615
References 619

C Consumer's Surplus 621

C.1 Introduction 621
C.2 Some Basics 626
C.3 Computing the Hicksian Measures 627
C.4 The Correct Welfare Measure 630
C.5 Hicksian Measures under Constancy of Marginal Utility of Income 640
Concluding Remarks 643
References 644

Indices 649

Name 651
Subject 657

Introduction

This book is divided into five parts. The first part (chap. 1) provides the background material in mathematics necessary for reading the rest of the book and for further research in economics. The second, third, and fourth parts constitute the core of the book. The second part (chaps. 2 through 4) is concerned with nonlinear programming and its applications to economics. Many applications to microeconomics are discussed. The third part (chap. 5) is concerned with the economics of uncertainty. The fourth part (chaps. 6 through 8) deals with differential equations and optimal control theory with a number of applications to economic theory. The fifth part (chaps. 9 through 11) are concerned with optimal control theory and its applications to economic theory. The book is completed with three appendices.[1]

Chapter 2 surveys the major results of nonlinear programming theory. Chapter 3 discusses sensitivity analysis and its applications. Here, I first exposit the conventional approach to comparative statics that has been popularized by Hicks and Samuelson. I then develop the envelope theorem, which allows sensitivity results for certain problems to be obtained with greater ease. As an illustration, I show that many of the major results of basic micro theory can be obtained as a simple application of this theorem. I also discuss the Allen elasticities of factor substitution and their estimation via the specification of cost functions. Chapter 3 ends with the clarification of some important concepts of returns to scale and of the Le Châtelier-Samuelson principle. Some confusions in the literature on the returns to scale are corrected. Chapter 4 discusses other selected topics in microeconomics. Here, I examine such topics as inferior inputs, marginal cost pricing, the sensitivity of average cost curves

[1] In this book, those results mainly in mathematics are called "theorems," and those mainly in economics are called "propositions" (although the distinction between the two is sometimes ambiguous). The proofs of virtually all theorems are regretfully omitted (with some exceptions, such as the expected utility theorem in chap. 5). Most of these proofs are available in my *Mathematical Economics* (2d ed., New York: Cambridge University Press, 1985) and, if not, in the sources indicated in the respective chapter references.

with respect to a change in factor prices, the problem of income-leisure choice, the regulatory constraint (the Averch-Johnson effect), the peak-load problem, and the Coase theorem. In the applications, my emphasis is to clarify the basic analytical structure of these problems rather than to generalize the known results: extensions of the known results should be easy once the analytical structure is clarified. In fact, this is an important theme underlying this book. Also, our conclusion in section 3.3 that the shape of average cost curves can be very sensitive to factor price changes casts some (even serious) doubt on the plausibility of analysis in terms of such curves that pervades the literature.

Part III consists only of chapter 5. Here, I discuss the economics of uncertainty and information, a topic that has been attracting a great deal of attention since the 1970s, and I attempt to offer a self-contained, clear exposition of the expected utility hypothesis and its applications.

Chapters 6, 7, and 8 constitute Part IV. These are concerned with the topic of differential equations. Chapter 6 deals with basic concepts and stability properties in the theory of differential equations and some economic applications. Applications include such topics as the stability of competitive equilibrium, the stability of macroequilibrium, the neoclassical aggregate growth model, the Phillips curve, and Tobin's discussion of the "Walras-Keynes-Wicksell" model. In the last section of this chapter, I illustrate the phase diagram technique by considering the stability question of competitive equilibrium for the three commodity case. Chapter 7 exposits the theory of linear differential equations on the plane. This provides a background for the discussion of the dynamics for the two-dimensional case, which has been widely used in economics. Even with linearity, the extension of the dimension from one to two generates various patterns of trajectories. The Poincaré theorem provides the justification for approximating the behavior of the two-dimensional nonlinear case by the corresponding linear system. Chapter 8 offers some macroeconomic applications of the theory of differential equations. In section 8.1, I illustrate the trajectory leading to the IS-LM equilibrium: it is shown that the equilibrium is a node or a spiral point, depending on whether one is inclined to be a Keynesian or a monetarist. Section 8.2 of this chapter exposits Tobin's "money and growth" model; many papers have been written on this topic, especially during the 1960s and 1970s. Section 8.3 extends the usual assumption (in this literature), that there are only two assets in the economy, money and physical assets. I introduce a third asset, interest yielding securities. Whereas the steady state is a saddle-point and, hence, unstable for the usual two-asset economy, we show that it can be stable for the three-asset economy.

Chapters 9, 10, and 11 constitute Part V. These are concerned with optimal control theory and its applications. Chapter 10 exposits the basic results of optimal control theory. Various results obtained by Pontryagin and his associates are developed. A number of applications and illustrations are provided to help the understanding of various theorems. Economic applications include the regional allocation of investment and the optimal growth problem. Chapter 10 considers one mathematical theorem for the infinite horizon optimal control problem, which is developed in section 10.1. In the subsequent sections, I illustrate its applications to a number of economic problems. Section 10.2 considers the problem of optimal monetary policy for economic growth. Whereas the usual optimal growth literature deals with a centralized economy in which money is not explicitly introduced, here I introduce money in the context of a decentralized framework. Among other things, I show that the usual Cass-Koopmans rule holds for a decentralized economy with money. Section 10.3 discusses the permanent income hypothesis using the optimal control framework. This hypothesis is now a classical proposition in macroeconomics concerning the consumption-saving behavior of an individual. Section 10.4 is concerned with the dynamic behavior of the firm, or the theory of investment with adjustment costs. Tobin's q is discussed in this context. Chapter 11 deals with optimal control theory for the finite horizon case. Section 11.1 develops an important mathematical theorem from which a number of its applications can be taken. Section 11.2 is again concerned with the consumption-saving behavior of an individual whose life is finite. Sections 11.3 and 11.4 illustrate the application of optimal control theory to the case in which "t" does not signify "time." Section 11.3 is concerned with a classical calculus of variations problem, or more specifically the isoperimetric problem. Section 11.4 deals with the spatial pricing problem.

The book is completed with three appendices. Appendix A surveys the major results of linear algebra. Appendix B develops seven concepts of quasi-concavity, clarifies the relationship among them, and obtains an important theorem on quasi-concave programming. Appendix C discusses the concept of consumer's surplus, a topic which has been heavily debated in the literature and which has produced a lot of confusion. Appendices A, B, and C, in some sense, may be considered appendices to chapters 1, 2, and 3, respectively. On the other hand, each of the topics discussed in these three appendices is important by itself, and these can also be read as independent chapters. The book omits recent developments in game theory and in nonlinear dynamics (such as chaos theory). Excellent expositions on these topics are available elsewhere.

Part 1

Preliminaries

CHAPTER 1

Some Basic Mathematics

This chapter presents some basic materials in mathematics that are widely used and often taken for granted in economic analysis. Some of the material exposited here will be used in later discussions in the book. Some topics, when they are deemed important in themselves, are also discussed in this chapter, even though they will not be utilized in subsequent chapters. It is hoped that the reader who is not familiar with some or all of the topics discussed here will find this chapter useful in understanding the current literature of economic analysis. The material assembled here is typically covered in several courses in mathematics. Every effort has been made to make the exposition of this chapter simple, so that even the reader who has never confronted such material should be able to understand it without too much difficulty. Our emphasis is not in proving all results presented, but rather in facilitating the understanding of these results and aiding the reader in applying them.

On the other hand, it has become increasingly more common, at least in the United States, to require entering graduate students in economics to have some knowledge of matrix algebra, advanced calculus, etc. It is hoped that even those students who already have a background in these topics will still find the exposition of this chapter useful in refreshing their memory by summarizing the basic mathematical material. (The elements of matrix algebra are contained in appendix A). Though such students should be able to go through the material here fairly quickly, they still find the exposition of the material helpful.

Finally, in spite of the fact that the material presented here is basic (and even elementary to a certain extent) and that our exposition sometimes stresses an intuitive understanding of the material, an effort has been made to convey some of the atmosphere of modern mathematics, such as the reduction of basic concepts to axioms, which, in turn, facilitates rigorous logical deductions. To appreciate such a method will be useful when the student studies the analytical approach to economics at a more sophisticated level. Thus, the present chapter is intended to be something more than a simple collection of mathematical material.

1.1 Preliminary Concepts and Notations

1.1.1 Sets

Intuitively, a **set** is a collection of objects (of any kind). For example, the collection of all human beings on earth (who live, say, today) is a set, all of the laptop computers made in Japan during 1992 would be a set, the collection of all real numbers is a set, and the collection of all positive integers is a set. Instead of axiomatizing what the word "set" means, we shall assume that what is meant by a set is intuitively clear. Words such as *family, collection*, and *class* are often used synonymously with the word *set.* If x is a member of a set S, we denote that by $x \in S$ where "$\in$" is the notation for "is an element of." If x is not a member of S, we denote that by $x \notin S$. A set is often denoted by braces $\{\}$. A set can be described by enumerating its members. For example, the set consisting of three numbers, say 1, 6, and 28, may be written as $\{1, 6, 28\}$. A set can also be described by

$$\{x : P(x)\}, \quad \text{or} \quad \{x \mid P(x)\},$$

where the colon or the bar separates two descriptions: the first denotes a typical element x of the set and the second, $P(x)$, denotes the properties that a typical element must satisfy in order to belong to the set. (For consistency, we use the colon rather than the bar throughout this book.) That any set can be written in this form is sometimes called the **axiom of specification**. Throughout this book we denote the *set of all real numbers* by R. Thus

$$R \equiv \{x : x \text{ is a real number}\}.$$

The set of points on the unit radius circle in the two-dimensional plane can be denoted by

$$\{(x, y) : x \in R,\ y \in R,\ x^2 + y^2 = 1\}.$$

An element of a set is often also called a"point" in the set. When the number of elements of a set is finite, it is called a **finite set**. Otherwise, it is called an **infinite set**.

Given two sets A and B, if every element of A is an element of B, we say that A is a set in B or A is a **subset** of B, and we denote this by

$$A \subset B.$$

Note that $A \subset A$. We say that two sets A and B are **equal** if they have the same elements, and we write $A = B$ or $B = A$ (which is often called the **axiom of extension**). (Similarly, by $x = y$ we mean that x and y are symbols for the same object.) Note that $A \subset B$, A being a subset of B, does not preclude the possibility that $A = B$. In fact, if $A = B$, it is true that both $A \subset B$ and $B \subset A$. Conversely, if $A \subset B$ and $B \subset A$, then $A = B$. If $A \subset B$ *and* $A \neq B$, then A is called a **proper subset** of B.

Given two sets A and B, the collection of all the elements that belong to both sets A and B is called the **intersection** of A and B, and is denoted by $A \cap B$:

$$A \cap B \equiv \{x : x \in A \text{ and } x \in B\}.$$

It is possible that two sets A and B have no common elements, in which case the set $A \cap B$ has no elements. To take care of such a situation, we introduce a special convention; the "set having no elements," which we call the **empty set**, and denote it by $\emptyset$. Therefore, when $A \cap B$ has no common elements, $A \cap B = \emptyset$, in which case A and B are said to be **disjoint** or **nonintersecting**. Given two sets A and B, the **difference** between two sets A and B (which we denote by $A \setminus B$) is defined by

$$A \setminus B \equiv \{x : x \in A \text{ and } x \notin B\}.$$

Again $A \setminus B$ can be an empty set.

Given two sets A and B, the collection of elements that belong to set A *or* set B is called the **union** of A and B, and is denoted by $A \cup B$:

$$A \cup B \equiv \{x : x \in A \text{ or } x \in B\}.$$

Here, by convention, "or" includes the possibility of $x \in A$ *and* $x \in B$ (as well as of $x \in A$ but $x \notin B$, and $x \in B$ but $x \notin A$). Since the empty set is only a convention, we further make the convention that for each object x, the relation"$x \in \emptyset$" does *not* hold. Similarly, we have

$$A \cap \emptyset = \emptyset, \text{ and } A \cup \emptyset = A.$$

When S is a subset of set X, the set of elements that belong to X but not to S is called the **complement** of S, and it is denoted by S^c:

$$S^c \equiv \{x : x \in X, x \notin S\}.$$

The union (or intersection) can be taken over a finite or infinite collection of sets. For example, if $S_1, S_2, \ldots, S_k, \ldots$, are sets, we can consider:

$$\bigcup_{i=1}^{k} S_i, \text{ or } \bigcup_{i=1}^{\infty} S_i.$$

In fact, the symbol i need not be an integer. For example, letting T be the set of all real numbers between (and including) 0 and 1, we may consider the union

$$\bigcup_{t \in T} S_t.$$

If S_t is the set of all human beings on earth at time t, $\cup_{t \in T} S_t$ is the set of all human beings on earth during the period T. Analogously, the reader should easily be able to understand the notation

$$\bigcap_{i=1}^{k} S_i, \bigcap_{i=1}^{\infty} S_i, \text{ and } \bigcap_{t \in T} S_t.$$

Given two sets X and Y, consider an *ordered pair* (x, y), where $x \in X$ and $y \in Y$. The collection of all those ordered pairs is called the **Cartesian product** of X and Y and is denoted by $X \times Y$. The ordinary two-dimensional plane can be written as $R \times R$, which is abbreviated as R^2. Similarly, R^n denotes the set of n-tuples of real numbers;

$$R^n \equiv \{(x_1, x_2, \ldots, x_n) : x_i \in R, i = 1, 2, \ldots, n\}.$$

In general, suppose that $\{X_1, X_2, \ldots, X_n\}$ is a collection of sets indexed with the positive integers from 1 to n, and let

$$X \equiv X_1 \bigcup X_2 \bigcup \cdots \bigcup X_n.$$

The *Cartesian product* of this indexed collection of sets, denoted by

$$X_1 \times X_2 \times \ldots \times X_n \text{ or } \mathop{\times}_{i=1}^{n} X_i,$$

is defined to be the set of all n-tuples $(x_1, x_2, \ldots, x_n)$ of elements such that $x_i \in X_i$ for each i, that is,

$$x = (x_1\ x_2, \ldots, x_n) \in \mathop{\times}_{i=1}^{n} X_i.$$

x_i is called the ith **coordinate** of point x, and the set X_i is called the ith **coordinate set**. The set of indices $\{1, 2, \ldots, n\}$ is called an **index set**. The index set need not be a finite set. It can be an infinite set $\{1, 2, \ldots, n, \ldots \infty\}$, or a set of continuum, say $T = [0, 1]$, or $T = [0, \infty]$, etc.

The cartesian product of these can be written as

$$\mathop{\times}_{i=1}^{\infty} X_i \quad \text{and} \quad \mathop{\times}_{t \in T} X_t.$$

Given two points a and b in R with $a < b$, the notation (a, b) is also used to denote

$$(a, b) \equiv \{x : x \in R,\ a < x < b\},$$

which is called an **open interval**. (The distinction between this and an ordered pair of a and b should be apparent from the context.) Similarly, the set $[a, b]$ is defined by

$$[a, b] \equiv \{x : x \in R,\ a \leqq x \leqq b\}$$

is called a **closed interval**. Analogously we may define

$$(a, b] \equiv \{x : x \in R,\ a < x \leqq b\}, \quad \text{and}$$

$$[a, b) \equiv \{x : x \in R,\ a \leqq x < b\}.$$

Similarly, we may define the sets (a, ∞) and $[a, \infty)$ by

$$(a, \infty) \equiv \{x : x \in R,\ x > a\},\ [a, \infty) \equiv \{x : x \in R,\ x \geqq a\}.$$

The following examples may be useful in illustrating the concepts of set intersection and union:

$$[0, 2] \cap (1, 2) = (1, 2),\quad (0, 1) \cap (1, 2) = \emptyset,$$

$$[0, 2] \cup (1, 2) = [0, 2],\quad [0, 1] \cup [1, 2] = [0, 2],$$

$$\bigcap_{i=1}^{\infty}(0,\ 1/i) = \emptyset, \quad \bigcap_{i=1}^{\infty}(-1/i,\ 1/i) = \{0\}.$$

1.1.2 Logical Statements

Let P and Q are two statements. Then the statement "if P, then Q" means that if P is true, then Q is true, and that is all it means. Note that if P is false, Q may be true or false. In everyday English, the meaning of "if P, then Q" can be ambiguous. Munkres (1975, p. 7) gives the following example:

> "Mr. Jones, if you get below 70 on the final, you are going to flunk this course."

In this context, Mr. Jones knows that if he gets a grade below 70, he will flunk the course, and he *also* knows that if he gets a grade of at least 70, he will pass. Namely, in this example, "if P, then Q" means not only "if P is true, then Q is true," but also it means that "if P does not hold, then Q does not hold." In mathematics, the latter possibility is disallowed.

As a shorthand notation of "if P, then Q," the following notation is often used:

$$P \Rightarrow Q,$$

which is read "P implies Q." Then the above discussion may be summarized as

$$(P \Rightarrow Q) \text{ does not necessarily imply } (\text{not } P \Rightarrow \text{not } Q).$$

If a number can be expressed as a ratio of two integers it is called a **rational number**. Hence, the statement "if x is a positive integer, then x is a rational number" is correct. However, the statement "if x is not a positive integer, then x is not a rational number" is *not* correct (consider $x = -1,\ 1/2$, etc., for example). In the statement $(P \Rightarrow Q)$, P is called the **hypothesis** of the statement, and Q is called the **conclusion** of the statement. It is possible that in the statement $(P \Rightarrow Q)$, the hypothesis P will not hold under any circumstances. In this case the statement $(P \Rightarrow Q)$ is said to be **vacuously true**. For such an example of P, consider "$x \in R$ and $x^2 < 0$," in which case *any* statement Q concerning $x \in R$ is vacuously true.

Given the statement $(P \Rightarrow Q)$, we may form another statement,

$$(Q \Rightarrow P),$$

which is called the **converse** of $(P \Rightarrow Q)$. Even if the statement $(P \Rightarrow Q)$ is true, its converse may or may not be true. For example, the converse of the statement "if x is a positive integer, then x is a rational number," that is, "if x is a rational number, then x is a positive integer," is not correct.

If the statement $(P \Rightarrow Q)$ is true, then P is called a **sufficient condition** for Q, and Q is called a **necessary condition** for P. Or more simply, P is said to be sufficient for Q, and Q is said to be necessary for P. If both statements $(P \Rightarrow Q)$ and $(Q \Rightarrow P)$ are true, then P is called a **necessary and sufficient condition** for Q, and Q is called a **necessary and sufficient condition** for P. We denote such a case by

$$P \Leftrightarrow Q \quad (\text{or } Q \Leftrightarrow P), \quad \text{or} \quad P \text{ iff } Q,$$

where "iff" is the abbreviation for *if and only if*. In this case, two statements P and Q are said to be **(logically) equivalent**.

Given the statement $(P \Rightarrow Q)$, we may form the following statement:

$$\text{not } Q \Rightarrow \text{not } P,$$

which is called the **contrapositive** of $(P \Rightarrow Q)$. For example, the contrapositive of the statement "if x is a positive integer, then x is a rational number" is the statement "if x is not a rational number, then x is not a positive integer." If the statement $(P \Rightarrow Q)$ is true, its contrapositive (not $Q \Rightarrow$ not P) is always true. Conversely, if the statement (not $Q \Rightarrow$ not P) is true, then its contrapositive $(P \Rightarrow Q)$ is also true. Thus a statement and its contrapositive are two ways of saying the same thing; they are logically equivalent, that is,

$$(P \Rightarrow Q) \Leftrightarrow (\text{not } Q \Rightarrow \text{not } P).$$

The above is often used to prove certain statements. Namely, to prove the statement $(P \Rightarrow Q)$, we may equivalently prove (not $Q \Rightarrow$ not P). More specifically, suppose that Q does not hold. Then assuming that P holds, we obtain a contradiction if and only if the statement $(P \Rightarrow Q)$ is valid. This method of proving a statement by contradiction is called a **contrapositive argument**. Such an argument is often useful in proving an "intuitively obvious" statement.

In order to use the contrapositive argument, we have to know how to form the statement (such as "not P"), which is called the **negation** of P. In many cases this causes no difficulty. However, confusion can occur when P is a statement that involves "for all" or "for some." The phrases "for all" and "for some" can, respectively, be replaced by "for every" and "for at least one." These phrases are called **logical quantifiers** or simply **quantifiers**. The *negation* of the statement

"P holds, for *all* x in X"

is formed as

"P does not hold, for *some* x in X."

Here the quantifier "for all" is replaced by "for some." The *negation* of the statement

"P holds, for *some* x in X"

is formed as

"P does not hold, for *all* x in X."

1.1.3 Functions

Given two sets X and Y, if we can associate each member of X with an element of Y in a certain manner, then we say that f is a **function** from X into Y. This is denoted by

$$f : X \to Y,$$

and the rule of associating an element in Y with an element in X is denoted by $f(x)$. The following are some well-known examples of function $f\colon R \to R$.

$$f(x) = x^3, \ f(x) = e^x, \ \text{and} \ f(x) = \sin x.$$

When $Y \subset R$, the function is said to be a **real-valued function**. Given the function $f\colon X \to Y$, X is called the **domain** of f, and the set $f(X)$, defined by

$$f(X) \equiv \{f(x) : x \in X\},$$

is called the **range** of f, where $f(x)$ is called the **value** or the **image** of x under f. When $f(X) = Y$, the function f is said to be **onto**. The function $f(x) = x^3$ is onto, while function $f(x) = e^x$ and $f(x) = \sin x$ are *not* onto. The range of e^x is $(0, \infty)$ and the range of $\sin x$ is $[-1, 1]$. The terms **mapping, transformation, operator**, and **function** are often used synonymously. Thus "$f: X \to Y$" can also be read as "f is a mapping from X into Y," "f maps X into Y," etc.

If we can associate more than one point in Y for each x in X under the function f, namely if $f(x)$ is a set of points in Y, then f is called a **multivalued function**, or a **set-valued function**. When only one point in Y is associated with each point of X, we call it a **single-valued function** or simply a **function**. In this book, unless otherwise specified, "function" always refers to a single-valued function. Even if a function is single-valued, it is possible that more than one point in X is associated with the same value in Y under this function. A simple example would be

$$f: R \to R, \ f(x) = a \ (= \text{constant}) \text{ for all } x \text{ in } R,$$

which is called a **constant function**. The function $f(x) = \sin x$ provides another such example, unless the domain is restricted, for example, to $[0, \pi/2]$. Given a function $f: X \to Y$, the set defined by

$$\{(x, y) : (x, y) \in X \times f(X), \ y = f(x)\}$$

is called the **graph** of f. The graph on R^2 is useful in facilitating a diagrammatical exposition of certain real-valued functions such as $f(x) = a$, $f(x) = x^2$, $f(x) = x^3$, $f(x) = \log x$, $f(x) = \sin x$, etc.

Given a function $f: X \to Y$ where $y = f(x)$, we may define the function f^{-1} by

$$f^{-1}: Y \to X, \quad \text{where } x \in f^{-1}(y) \text{ iff } y = f(x).$$

The function f^{-1} is called the **inverse function** of f. Note that the function f^{-1} thus defined can be either single-valued or multivalued (even under the current assumption that f is single-valued). For example, if $f: R \to R$ and $f(x) = x^2 + 1$, then $f^{-1}(2) = \{-1, 1\}$. When both functions f and f^{-1} are single-valued, f is said to be **one-to-one** or an **injection**. In addition, if $f(X) = Y$, that is, if f is *onto* as well as one-to-one, it is called a **one-to-one correspondence**, or simply a **bijection**.

Given a function $f: X \to Y$, and given a subset A of X, the set $f(A)$, defined by

$$f(A) \equiv \{y : y = f(x), \ x \in A\},$$

is called the **image** of A under the function f. On the other hand, if B is a subset of Y, the set $f^{-1}(B)$, defined by

$$f^{-1}(B) \equiv \{x : x \in X,\ f(x) \in B\},$$

is called the **inverse image** of B under the function f, which is the same as the image of B under the inverse function f^{-1}.

If B consists of only one point, the inverse image of B is one point. That is, if $B = \{y\}$, then the inverse image of B under f is simply denoted by $f^{-1}(y)$. For example, if f is defined by

$$f\colon R \to R, \quad \text{where} \quad f(x) = 3 \quad \text{for all } x \text{ in } R,$$

then $f^{-1}(3) = R$. Also, if $f(x) = x^2 + 1$, then $f^{-1}(2) = \{-1,\ 1\}$ as mentioned above.

Note that it is *not* generally true that

$$f^{-1}[f(A)] = A \quad \text{and} \quad f[f^{-1}(B)] = B.$$

For example, consider the function f, defined by

$$f\colon R \to R, \quad \text{where} \quad f(x) = x^2 + 1.$$

Then we may observe:

$$f^{-1}(f([0,1])) = f^{-1}([1,2]) = [-1,\ 1] \neq [0,\ 1],$$

$$f(f^{-1}([0,\ 2])) = f([-1,\ 1]) = [1,\ 2] \neq [0,\ 2].$$

Given functions f and g,

$$f\colon X \to Y, \quad g\colon f(X) \to Z, \quad \text{where} \quad f(X) \subset Y,$$

we may define a function h by

$$h\colon X \to Z, \quad \text{where} \quad h(x) \equiv g[f(x)].$$

Function h is obtained by first applying f, and then g. We call h the **composite function** of f and g and denote it by $h \equiv g \circ f$. For example, let f and g be defined by

$$f\colon R \to R \text{ where } f(x) = x^2 + 1, \quad \text{and}$$
$$g\colon R \to R \text{ where } g(x) = 2x.$$

Then the composite function $h(x) = (g \circ f)(x) = 2(x^2 + 1)$. Note that this is quite different from $(f \circ g)(x) = (2x)^2 + 1$.

1.1.4 Real Numbers

Consider the set of all real numbers, R, and let S be a subset of R. If there exists a real number b such that $x \leqq b$ for all x in S, then S is said to be **bounded above**, and b is called an **upper bound**. In general, S may not have an upper bound. However, if it has one, it has infinitely many. For example, the interval, $(0, \infty)$ has no upper bound, while $(0, 1)$ has 1 as an upper bound (and, in fact, any $x \geqq 1$ is an upper bound of $(0, 1)$). Let S be a subset of R that is bounded above. An upper bound of S is called a **supremum** or a **least upper bound** ($l.u.b.$) of S, if it is less than any other upper bound of S. The supremum of S is denoted by sup S or $l.u.b.$ S. A fundamental property of the real number system is that every nonempty subset of real numbers having an upper bound also has a supremum (which is called the **supremum principle**).

Similarly, a subset S of R is said to be **bounded below**, if there exists a real number a such that $a \leqq x$ for all $x \in S$. Such a number a is called a **lower bound** of S. (If S is bounded both above and below, then S is simply called **bounded** and if S lacks either upper or lower bound, it is called **unbounded**). If it is greater than any other lower bound of S, a lower bound of S is called an **infimum** or the **greatest lower bound** ($g.l.b.$) of S. The infimum of S is denoted by inf S or $g.l.b.$ S. In parallel to the supremum principle, we can assert that every nonempty subset of real numbers having a lower bound also has an infimum.

Given a bounded subset S of R, both sup S and inf S always exist. However, sup S may or may not be in S. Similarly, inf S may or may not be in S. For example, let S be the open interval $(0, 1)$; then inf $S = 0$ and sup $S = 1$, so that neither inf S nor sup S is in the set S. Given an arbitrary subset S of R (which may not be bounded), if sup S exists *and* if it is in S, then it is called the **maximum element** of S, and is denoted by max S. Similarly, if inf S exists *and* if it is in S, then it is called the **minimum element** of S, which we denote by min S. Namely,

$$\alpha = \min S \text{ means that } \alpha \in S \text{ and } \alpha \leqq x \text{ for all } x \text{ in } S,$$

$$\beta = \max S \text{ means that } \beta \in S \text{ and } x \leqq \beta \text{ for all } x \text{ in } S.$$

1.2 Euclidian Space

Let R be the set of all real numbers. Then an ordered n-tuple x of real numbers, $x = (x_1, x_2, \ldots, x_n)$, is called a **vector**. The number n is referred to as the **dimension** of x. As mentioned earlier, R^n denotes the set of all (ordered) n-tuples of real numbers, $R^n = \{(x_1, x_2, \ldots, x_n) : x_i \in R, i = 1, 2, \ldots, n\}$. The ith element x_i of $x \in R^n$ is called the ith **coordinate** of x. When $n = 1$, x is obviously a real number and is also referred to as a **scalar**. The **addition** of two n-dimensional vectors x and y is defined by coordinate-wise addition; that is,

$$x + y = (x_1 + y_1, x_2 + y_2, \ldots, x_n + y_n). \tag{1}$$

Clearly, $x + y$ is also in R^n. In other words R^n is "closed" under the above addition, operation. Given an arbitrary scalar $\alpha \in R$, the multiplication of a vector $x \in R^n$ by α (called **scalar multiplication**) is defined by coordinate-wise multiplication; that is,

$$\alpha x \equiv (\alpha x_1, \alpha x_2, \ldots, \alpha x_n) \tag{2}$$

αx in (2) can also be written as $x\alpha$. Clearly $x \in R^n$ and $\alpha \in R$ imply $\alpha x \in R^n$. That is, R^n is also closed under scalar multiplication. The **difference** of two vectors x and y, denoted by $x - y$, is defined by $x + (-1)y$. Thus, by (1) and (2), we have

$$x - y = (x_1 - y_1, x_2 - y_2 \ldots, x_n - y_n).$$

Note that $x + y$ and $x - y$ cannot be defined unless x and y are vectors of the same dimension. Assuming $n = 2$, we may illustrate the concepts of coordinates, addition, and scalar multiplication as in figure 1.1. The diagram should be well-known to the reader. From this diagram, the reader can also easily see that (x_1, x_2) is, generally, different from (x_2, x_1). Similarly, R^n is the set of all *ordered* n-tuples of real numbers. Given the above rule of addition and scalar multiplication in R^n, we can readily check that the following eight properties hold for arbitrary elements x, y, and z of R^n and scalars $\alpha, \beta \in R$:[1]

(L1) $x + (y + z) = (x + y) + z$,

(L2) There exists an element called 0 such that $x + 0 = 0 + x$,

(L3) There exists an element $(-x)$ for every x such that $x + (-x) = 0$,

---

[1]Properties (L1) and (L5) are called the **associative laws**, (L4) is called the **commutative law**, and (L7) and (L8) are called the **distributive laws**. Fig. 1.1 is borrowed from Takayama (1985, p. 9).

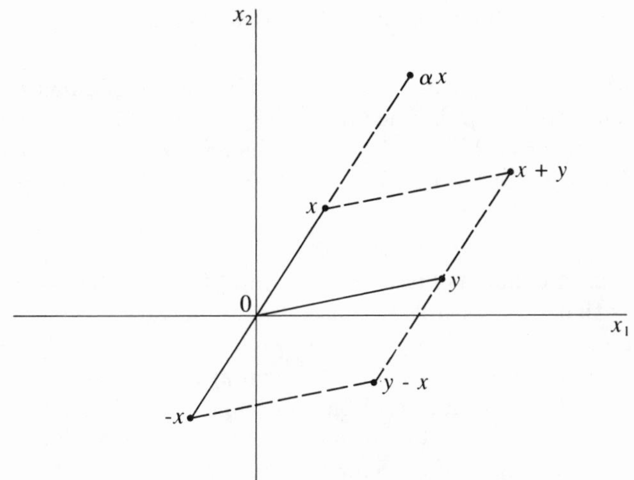

Figure 1.1: An illustration of addition and scalar multiplication

(L4) $x + y = y + x$,

(L5) $\alpha(\beta x) = (\alpha\beta)x$,

(L6) $1x = x$,

(L7) $\alpha(x + y) = \alpha x + \alpha y$, and

(L8) $(\alpha + \beta)x = \alpha x + \beta x$.

A little notational caution is needed here about the symbol 0, which can mean the scalar zero or the n-tuple of 0's. The latter is called the **zero vector**, or the **origin** (because of the obvious geometric reason, see fig. 1.1).

Given an arbitrary set X (not necessarily R^n), if "addition" and "scalar multiplication" are defined, if X is closed under these two operations, and if properties (L1) to (L8) are satisfied, then X is called a (real) **linear space** or (real) **vector space**, and an element of X is called a **vector**.

Thus properties (L1) to (L8) are of fundamental importance, as they contribute the *defining* properties of the linear space.[2] Clearly, R^n, with the rules of addition and scalar multiplication (equations 1 and 2), is one example of a linear space. However there are many other examples of linear spaces. One such example is given below.

Example 1.1. Consider the set S of all real-valued functions defined on the interval [0, 1]. Define "addition" $f + g$ for all f and g in S by $f(x) + g(x)$ for each x in [0, 1], and define "scalar multiplication" by $\alpha f(x)$ for each x in [0, 1]. Then the set S under these two operations is a linear space.

The concept that is of fundamental importance in the theory of linear spaces is that of a "basis." Because of its importance, we will brieflyex-posit the gist of this theory. It is also relevant to linear algebra, which is exposited in appendix A. Let X be an arbitrary linear space (which may not be R^n), so that addition and scalar multiplication are defined in X and so that X is closed under such operations. Given k vectors, $x^1, x^2, \ldots, x^k$, in X, the vector z, defined by

$$z \equiv \sum_{j=1}^{k} \alpha_j x^j, \ \alpha_j \in R, \ j = 1, 2, \ldots, k,$$

is called a **linear combination** of these k vectors. The k vectors, $x^1, x^2, \ldots, x^k$ in a linear space are called **linearly independent** if, for $\alpha_j \in R$, $j = 1, 2, \ldots, k$,

$$\sum_{j=1}^{k} \alpha_j x^j = 0 \text{ implies } \alpha_j = 0 \text{ for every } j.$$

An arbitrary (finite or infinite) collection of vectors, S, is said to be **linearly independent** if every finite subset is linearly independent.

The collection of vectors S is said to be **linearly dependent** if it is not linearly independent; thus S is linearly dependent if and only if there exists a linear combination of a finite number of vectors in S, say

[2]In defining the properties of a linear space, scalar multiplication is confined to multiplication by real numbers. In general, we do not have to restrict the scalars to real numbers. If a linear space is defined over complex numbers, we call X, with properties (L1) to (L8) (where α and β are arbitrary complex numbers) a **complex linear space** or a **linear space with complex field**.

$x^1, x^2, \ldots, x^k$, such that[3]

$$\sum_{j=1}^{k} \alpha_j x^j = 0, \quad \text{for some } \alpha_j \neq 0, \; j = 1, 2, \ldots, k.$$

Let X be a linear space. A linearly independent set S in X, with the property that every vector x in X can be expressed as a linear combination of the vectors in S, is called a **basis** for X. A basis S may consist of a finite or infinite number of members. If it is finite, X is said to be **finite dimensional**; otherwise X is said to be **infinite dimensional**, as is the case in example 1.1 above. There can be *many* bases for a given linear space X. However, it can be shown that any two bases of a given linear space are related by one-to-one correspondence. Hence the number of elements in any basis of a *finite* dimensional space is the same as in any other basis. Hence we can define the number of elements of a basis of a finite dimensional space as the **dimension** of the space.

---

[3]Hence, if S is a *finite* set consisting of k vectors, $x^1, x^2, \ldots, x^k$, S is **linearly independent** if and only if for any $\alpha_i \in R$, $i = 1, 2, \ldots, k$,

$$\alpha_1 x^1 + \alpha_2 x^2 + \ldots + \alpha_k x^k = 0 \text{ implies } \alpha_1 = \alpha_2 = \ldots = \alpha_k = 0,$$

and S is **linearly dependent** if and only if

$$\alpha_1 x^1 + \alpha_2 x^2 + \ldots + \alpha_k x^k = 0 \text{ for some } \alpha_j \neq 0, \; j = 1, 2, \ldots, k.$$

To consider the concepts of linear independence and linear dependence, consider R^3. The vectors, $e^1 \equiv (1, 0, 0)$, $e^2 \equiv (0, 1, 0)$ and $e^3 \equiv (0, 0, 1)$ are linearly independent, since, for any $\alpha_1, \alpha_2, \alpha_3 \in R$,

$$\alpha_1 e^1 + \alpha_2 e^2 + \alpha_3 e^3 = 0 \text{ implies } \alpha_1 = \alpha_2 = \alpha_3 = 0.$$

Also, the two vectors e^1 and e^2 are linearly independent in R^3, since

$$\alpha_1 e^1 + \alpha_2 e^2 = 0 \text{ implies } \alpha_1 = \alpha_2 = 0.$$

On the other hand, the three vectors, $x^1 = (1, 1, 0)$, $x^2 = (0, 0, 1)$ and $x^3 = (3, 3, 3)$ are linearly dependent since

$$\alpha_1 x^1 + \alpha_2 x^2 + \alpha_3 x^3 = (\alpha_1 + 3\alpha_3, \alpha_1 + 3\alpha_3, \alpha_2 + 3\alpha_3) = 0,$$

if we let, for example, $\alpha_1 = \alpha_2 = -3$ and $\alpha_3 = 1$. Note that any three vectors, x^1, x^2, and x^3 in R^3 are linearly dependent if any one of the three (say x^3) is the zero vector [like $x^3 = (0, 0, 0)$]. In general, k vectors ($k \leqq n$), $x^1, x^2, \ldots, x^k$, are linearly dependent in R^n if any one of these k vectors is the zero vector, $(0, 0, \ldots, 0)$. From the definition of linear dependence, it can be shown easily that k vectors are linearly dependent if and only if one vector of these k vectors can be expressed as a linear combination of the other $k - 1$ vectors. From this it also follows that k vectors in R^n are always linearly dependent if $k > n$.

For R^n, the usual Cartesian coordinate system, that is n vectors, $(1, 0, \ldots, 0), (0, 1, \ldots, 0), \ldots, (0, 0, \ldots, 1)$, each consisting of n elements, form a *basis* for R^n, since any vector in R^n can be expressed as a linear combination of these n vectors. Hence the dimension of R^n is equal to n. This justifies our earlier definition of the dimension of R^n being equal to n.The fundamental result in the theory of a basis is that *every linear space has a basis.*[4] Without this result, the discussion on basis would be vacuous.

To simplify the exposition, we now return to R^n. Given any two arbitrary members $x = (x_1, x_2, \ldots, x_n)$ and $y = (y_1, y_2, \ldots, y_n)$ of R^n, we may define the rule of multiplication of x and y as follows:

$$x \cdot y = \sum_{i=1}^{n} x_i y_i, \tag{3}$$

which is called the **(Euclidian) inner product** or the **dot product** of x and y;[5] where $x \cdot y$ is a real number and the above rule of multiplication defines, for arbitrary elements x, y, and z, a real-valued function with the following properties,

(I1) $x \cdot y = y \cdot x$,

(I2) $(\alpha x + \beta y) \cdot z = \alpha(x \cdot z) + \beta(y \cdot z)$, for any $\alpha,\ \beta \in R$, and

(I3) $x \cdot x \geqq 0$, and $x \cdot x = 0$, if and only if $x = 0$.

In general, if we can define a real-valued function $f(x, y) \equiv x \cdot y$ on $X \times X$, where X is a linear space with the properties (I1), (I2), and (I3), then X is called an **inner product space**. Namely, properties (I1) to (I3) are the *defining properties* of an inner product space. Our R^n with the rule of vector multiplication (3) is only one example of an inner product space. The requirement that X be a linear space (rather than an arbitrary set) stems from the rules concerning addition and scalar multiplication. The choice of an inner product is not necessarily unique.

In R^n, the Euclidian inner product can be used to define the well-known geometric concept of "distance." More precisely, for any two elements $x = (x_1, x_2, \ldots, x_n)$ and $y = (y_1, y_2, \ldots, y_n)$ in R^n, we define

---

[4]The proof of this result is not elementary when a linear space is infinite dimensional. See, for example, Wilansky (1964, pp. 16–17) for the proof.

[5]At this stage, we need not distinguish between column vectors and row vectors. On the other hand, if we let x be a column vector and x' be its transpose, then we have $x \cdot y = x'y = y'x$.

$d(x, y)$ by

$$d(x, y) \equiv [(x - y) \cdot (x - y)]^{1/2} = [\sum_{i=1}^{n} (x_i - y_i)^2]^{1/2}. \tag{4}$$

The quantity $d(x, y)$ is called the **(Euclidian) distance** between x and y. For $n = 2$, the $d(x, y)$ defined by (4) corresponds to the usual concept of distance as illustrated in figure 1.2. We can show that the

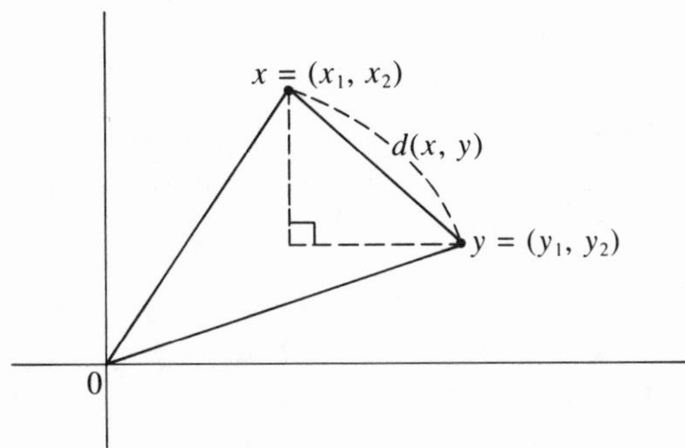

Figure 1.2: An illustration of Euclidian distance

Euclidian distance defined above is a real-valued function that satisfies the following properties for all x and y:

(M1) $d(x, y) = 0$, if and only if $x = y$.

(M2) $d(z, x) \leqq d(x, y) + d(y, z)$. **[triangular inequality]**

From (M1) and (M2), the following properties also follow:

(M3) $d(x, y) \geqq 0$, and

(M4) $d(x, y) = d(y, x)$. **[symmetry]**

Given an arbitrary set X, if we can define a real-valued function with properties (M1) and (M2) for any x and y in X, then X is called a **metric space** (and d is called a **metric**). Properties (M1) and (M2) are thus the *defining properties* of a metric space. The set R^n with the Euclidian distance defined by (4) is only one example of a metric space. Note that the abstract concept of "metric space" defined by properties (M1) and (M2) need *not* be a linear space, since no vector addition and scalar multiplication are used in these two properties. The following example of a metric space is often used to show that certain properties that hold in R^n (with the Euclidian distance) do not necessarily hold in an arbitrary metric space with a different concept of distance.

Example 1.2. Consider an arbitrary nonempty set X, and define $d(x, y)$ for arbitrary elements x and y in X by

$$d(x, y) = 0 \text{ if } x = y, \text{ and } d(x, y) = 1 \text{ if } x \neq y.$$

It can be easily shown that $d(x, y)$, thus defined, satisfies properties (M1) and (M2), and hence X is a metric space. Needless to say, X does not have to be a linear space at all.

We now return to R^n. Given a point $x = (x_1, x_2, \ldots, x_n)$ in R^n, the Euclidian distance between x and the origin, $d(x, 0)$, is called the **(Euclidian) norm** of x, and it is denoted by $\| x \|$. Namely,

$$\| x \| \equiv d(x, 0) = (x \cdot x)^{1/2} = [\sum_{i=1}^{n} x_i^2]^{1/2}. \tag{5}$$

Similarly, $d(x, y) = \| x - y \|$. It can be shown that the Euclidian norm satisfies the following three properties for all x and y:

(N1) $\| x \| \geqq 0$, and $\| x \| = 0$, if and only if $x = 0$,

(N2) $\| x + y \| \leqq \| x \| + \| y \|$, and [**triangular inequality**]

(N3) $\| \alpha x \| = | \alpha | \| x \|$, for any $\alpha \in R$.

Given an arbitrary *linear space* X (not necessarily R^n), if we define the real-valued function, called a **norm**, satisfying properties (N1) to (N3), we call X a **normed linear space** (or a **normed vector space**). Properties (N1) to (N3) are the defining properties of a normed linear space. The requirement that X be a linear space (rather than an arbitrary set) again stems from the rules concerning vector addition and scalar multiplication used in properties (N2) and (N3).[6] The choice of

[6]Given an arbitrary inner product space X (not necessarily R^n) with the inner

a norm is not necessarily unique. For example, R^n is a normed linear space with the Euclidian norm, but it can also be a normed linear space with the following norms:

$$\| x \| \equiv \max | x_i |, \ 1 \leqq i \leqq n, \quad \text{or} \quad \| x \| \equiv \sum_{i=1}^{n} | x_i |.$$

In R^n, the Euclidian inner product thus induces the concepts of the Euclidian distance and the Euclidian norm, where the latter is the distance between a point and the origin. Thus we have:

$$\| x \| = (x \cdot x)^{1/2} = d(x, \ 0),$$

$$\| x - y \| = [(x - y) \cdot (x - y)]^{1/2} = d(x, \ y), \tag{6}$$

where $d(x, \ y)$ denotes the Euclidian distance between x and y. Keeping this in mind, and confining our attention to the two-dimensional case, R^2, we may recall the cosine law in trigonometry which may be expressed as

$$\| x - y \|^2 = \| x \|^2 + \| y \|^2 - 2\| x \| \, \| y \| \cos \theta, \ 0 \leqq \theta \leqq \pi, \tag{7}$$

where θ signifies the angle between the two vectors, x and y, and π denotes $180°$. This relation may be illustrated by figure 1.3. Two vectors $x = (x_1, \ x_2)$ and $y = (y_1, \ y_2)$ are illustrated by OA and OB in this diagram, where point A, for example, represents the coordinate of $(x_1, \ x_2)$. $\|x\| = (x_1^2 + x_2^2)^{1/2}$ is measured by OA. Similarly, $\|y\|$ is measured by OB. The line segment AB measures $\|x - y\|$ where $x - y = (x_1 - y_1, \ x_2 - y_2)$. The vector $x - y$ is represented by OC. The length of OC is equal to $\|x - y\|$, which is also equal to the length of AB. From (7) we can easily obtain the following relation:

$$x \cdot y = \| x \| \, \| y \| \cos \theta, \ 0 \leqq \theta \leqq \pi, \tag{8}$$

where θ signifies the angle between the two vectors x and y.

---

product $x \cdot x$ satisfying the axioms (I1) to (I3), suppose we define $\| x \|$ by

$$\| x \| = (x \cdot x). \tag{5'}$$

It might be natural to conjecture that $\| x \|$ satisfies the axioms for norms, (N1) to (N3), and thus $\| x \|$ as defined by (5′) is a norm so that X also becomes a normed vector space. Such a conjecture can be shown to be in general false.

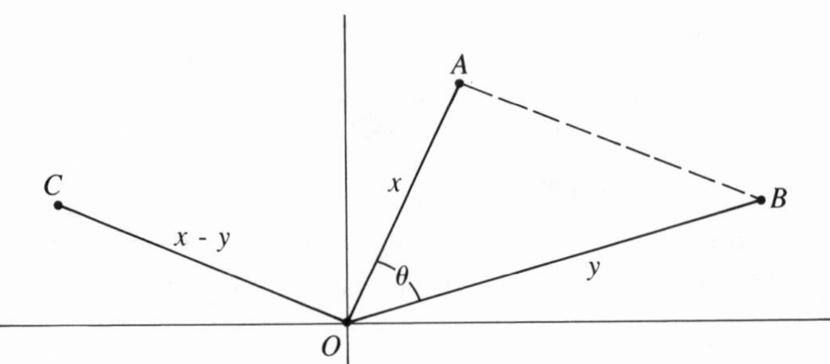

Figure 1.3: The cosine law of trigonometry

Equations (7) and (8) are obtained for the two-dimensional case. For the n-dimensional case, we can show

$$\|x - y\|^2 = \|x\|^2 + \|y\|^2 - 2(x \cdot y), \quad \text{for } x,\ y \in R^n. \tag{9}$$

Define the **angle** θ between x and y in R^n by (8). Then by virtue of (9), it is easy to see that if (7) holds for arbirary n (which need not be equal to 2), then (8) holds for such an n, and the converse also holds.[7] The definition of angle θ between x and y in R^n introduced above can be more precisely defined by

$$\cos\theta \equiv (x \cdot y)/(\| x \| \, \| y \|) \text{ or } \theta \equiv \cos^{-1}[(x \cdot y)/(\| x \| \, \| y \|)]. \tag{8'}$$

Here (8), a theorem for the two-dimensional case, is now used as a definition for the n-dimensional case. Since $\cos\theta$ ranges from -1 to 1, it would be necessary to show

$$(x \cdot y)^2 \leqq \| x \|^2 \| y \|^2, \quad \text{for all } x,\ y \in R^n, \tag{10}$$

in order to make the definition of θ in (8′) meaningful. Inequality (10) is known as the **Cauchy-Schwartz inequality**. To prove this, let α

[7]Substituting (9) into (7), we obtain

$$2\| x \| \| y \| \cos\theta = \| x \|^2 + \| y \|^2 - \| x - y \|^2 = 2(x \cdot y),$$

which in turn establishes (8), where n need not be restricted to 2. Conversely, substituting (9) into (8), we at once obtain (7).

be any real number, and observe

$$\| x - \alpha y \|^2 = \| x \|^2 - 2\alpha(x \cdot y) + \alpha^2 \| y \|^2.$$

Since (10) holds trivially when $\| y \| = 0$ (which implies $y = 0$), we may assume $\| y \| \neq 0$. Then letting $\alpha = (x \cdot y)/\| y \|^2$ in the right-hand side of the above equation, we obtain

$$0 \leqq \| x - \alpha y \|^2 \leqq [\| x \|^2 \| y \|^2 - (x \cdot y)^2]/\| y \|^2,$$

which in turn establishes (10).[8]

In the two-dimensional case, vectors x and y have obvious geometric representations. Hence for such a case, we may easily assert, from (7), that

(*a*) $x \cdot y > 0$, if the angle between x and y is sharp (acute, i.e., less than 90°),

(*b*) $x \cdot y = 0$, if $\theta = \frac{\pi}{2}$, that is, if x and y are orthogonal (i.e., equal to 90°), and

(*c*) $x \cdot y < 0$, if the angle between x and y is obtuse (i.e., between 90° and 180°).

In general, we say that two vectors x and y in R^n are **orthogonal** if $x \cdot y = 0$. The following are examples of two vectors in R^3 that are orthogonal:

(*a*) $x = (1, 0, 0)$, $y = (0, 1, 0)$, and

(*b*) $x = (1, 2, 3)$, $y = (5, 2, -3)$.

---

[8] The Cauchy-Schwartz inequality is also useful in proving the triangular inequality (N2). To this end, recalling (9), it can simply be observed that

$$\begin{aligned} \| x + y \|^2 &= \| x \|^2 + \| y \|^2 + 2(x \cdot y) \\ &\leqq \| x \|^2 + \| y \|^2 + 2 \| x \| \| y \| = [\| x \| + \| y \|]^2, \end{aligned}$$

which in turn establishes the triangular inequality

(N2) $\| x + y \| \leqq \| x \| + \| y \|,$

since $\| x + y \|$ and $\| x \| + \| y \|$ are both nonnegative. Using inequality (N2), we can easily show the triangular inequality (M2) for the Euclidian distance.

In R^n, any two vectors of the n vectors, $(1, 0, \ldots, 0)$, $(0, 1, 0, \ldots, 0)$, ..., $(0, 0, \ldots, 0, 1)$, are orthogonal. Recall that these n vectors form a basis for R^n. If every pair of vectors of a basis is orthogonal, then such a basis is called an **orthogonal basis**.

The concept of the (Euclidian) inner product appears quite often in economics. For example, in the conventional theory of consumer's choice, a consumer is supposed to maximize his or her satisfaction (utility) subject to the budget condition. Let p be the price vector that is exogenously given to the consumer, and let x be the consumption vector (commodity bundle), where $p = (p_1, p_2, \ldots, p_n)$ and $x = (x_1, x_2, \ldots, x_n)$. Then letting Y be income, the budget condition can be written as $p \cdot x \leqq Y$, where $p \cdot x$ denotes the Euclidian inner product of p and x, $\sum p_i x_i$. Assuming that the consumer spends all his or her income (for buying goods and services, and financial assets for saving, etc.), this can be written as $p \cdot x = Y$. Fixing x at a particular bundle x° and letting $p \cdot x^\circ = Y$, and if we take any other bundle x that satisfies $p \cdot x = Y$, then $(x - x^\circ)$ is orthogonal to the price vector p, since $p \cdot (x - x^\circ) = 0$.

In concluding this section, we may observe that we have derived here various important concepts from R^n, the set of all n-tuples of real numbers. More specifically, we have derived "linear space" via the rules of addition (1) and scalar multiplication (2), "inner product space" via the Euclidian inner product, "metric space" by the Euclidian distance, and "normed space" via the Euclidian norm. When we define these concepts on R^n, we call it (the collection of all n-tuple real numbers) the **Euclidian space**. Since the Euclidian space is a linear space, we may also define such concepts as linear independence (or dependence) of vectors, bases, and dimensions in the usual manner on R^n.

It is also important to observe that R^n induces these concepts in an abstract manner. These concepts can be defined abstractly in terms of their respective defining properties ("axioms"), and such abstract concepts can be quite different from R^n, from which such concepts are obtained. For example, the concept of "linear space" as defined in terms of properties (L1) to (L8) is derived from R^n, and yet example 1.1 illustrates a linear space that is quite different from R^n. Similarly, the concepts of "inner product space," "metric space," and "normed linear space" are defined in terms of properties (I1) to (I3), (M1) to (M2), and (N1) to (N3), respectively. The pursuit of the implications and the relations of such abstract concepts leads to many extremely interesting, fertile, and useful studies that form a crucial aspect of modern mathematics. In this book, however, we shall not go into such. Instead, we simply confine our attention to the Euclidian space R^n.

1.3 A Little Topology

1.3.1 Convergence

Let S be a subset of R^n. A **sequence** in the set S is a function defined on the set of all positive integers whose range is in S, and it is denoted by

$$x^1,\ x^2,\ \ldots,\ x^q,\ \ldots,$$

or more compactly by $\{x^q\}$, where $x^1,\ x^2,\ \ldots,\ x^q,\ \ldots$ are the images of the function (called the **values** or the **terms** of the sequence). Given a point x° in R^n and a subset S of R^n (x° may or may not be in S), a sequence $\{x^q\}$ is said to **converge** to x°, denoted by

$$x^q \to x^\circ \text{ (as } q \to \infty\text{), or } \lim_{q\to\infty} x^q = x^\circ,$$

if for any real number $\varepsilon > 0$, there exists a positive integer $\bar{q}$ such that

$$d(x^q,\ x^\circ) < \varepsilon \text{ (or equivalently, } \| x^q - x^\circ \| < \varepsilon\text{), for all } q \geqq \bar{q},$$

where $d(x^q,\ x^\circ)$ is the Euclidian distance between x^q and x°, and $\| x^q - x^\circ \|$ signifies the Euclidian norm of $(x^q - x^\circ)$. The "point" x° is called the **limit** of $\{x^q\}$, and such a sequence is called a **convergent sequence** in S if x° is also in the set S. Intuitively this means that if the terms of a sequence approach a limit, they get "extremely" close together. Note again that x° does not have to be in S. For example, let S be the interval $(0,\ 1)$, a subset of R. The sequence $\{1/q\}$, where the q's are positive integers, is a sequence whose values are in S. The point 0 is the limit of this sequence, but it is not in S.

An arbitrary sequence in S, $\{x^q\}$, may or may not have a limit (in which case, $\{x^q\}$ is called a **nonconvergent sequence**). However, if the limit exists, it can be easily shown that it is *unique*. For the limit of a sequence (or sequences), we can easily prove the following relations:

(i) $x^q \to x^\circ$ implies $\alpha x^q \to \alpha x^\circ$ for any $\alpha \in R$,

(ii) $x^q \to x^\circ$ and $y^q \to y^\circ$ imply $x^q + y^q \to x^\circ + y^\circ$,

(iii) $x^q \to x^\circ$ implies $\| x^q \| \to \| x^\circ \|$, and

(iv) $x^q \to x^\circ$ and $y^q \to y^\circ$ imply $(x^q,\ y^q) \to (x^\circ,\ y^\circ)$.

Let $\{x^q\}$ be a sequence in $S \subset R^n$, and consider a sequence $\{x^{q_s}\}$, where $q_1 < q_2 < \ldots < q_s < \ldots$. Then the sequence $\{x^{q_s}\}$ is called a

subsequence of $\{x^q\}$. There can be infinitely many subsequences of a sequence. Examples of subsequences of the sequence $\{1, 2, 3, \ldots, q, \ldots\}$ are:

$$\{1,\ 3,\ 5,\ \ldots\},\ \{1,\ 3,\ 5,\ 7,\ \ldots\},\ \{1,\ 5,\ 8,\ 9,\ \ldots\}.$$

As stated earlier, an arbitrary sequence $\{x^q\}$ in S might not converge. But, if it converges, it has a unique limit. In this case, *every* subsequence of the sequence is convergent, and thus has the same limit, which is the original sequence $\{x^q\}$. When a sequence has no limit, its subsequence may or may not converge. For example, $\{0,\ 1,\ 0,\ 1,\ \ldots\}$ has no limit, but its subsequences $\{0,\ 0,\ 0,\ \ldots\}$ and $\{1,\ 1,\ 1,\ \ldots\}$ both converge with limits 0 and 1, respectively. Needless to say, there are also many nonconvergent subsequences such as $\{0,\ 0,\ 1,\ 1,\ 0,\ 0,\ \ldots\}$.

A concept that is often confused with the limit of a sequence is a "limit point."

Definition 1.1. Let $S \subset R^n$. Then a point x° in R^n is called a **limit point** of S, if there exists a sequence $\{x^q\}$ in $S\backslash\{x^\circ\}$ such that

$$x^q \to x^\circ \quad \text{as} \quad q \to \infty.$$

REMARK: Note that x° in definition 1.1 does not have to be in the set S, and that the sequence $\{x^q\}$ is taken from the set $S\backslash\{x^\circ\}$; that is, the set obtained from S by deleting the point x° (in case that x° is in S). Thus, letting S be an open interval $(0,\ 1)$, 0 is a limit point of S with $x^q = 1/q$, for example. On the other hand, $x^q \to x^\circ$ with $\{x^q\}$ in S does not necessarily mean that x° is a limit point of S. For example, let S be the set that consists of a single point 1; then a sequence $\{1,\ 1,\ 1,\ \ldots\}$ is a convergent sequence whose values are in S, with the limit 1. But the point 1 is *not* a limit point of S. Since S consists of a single point, it cannot have any limit points. The crucial distinction between a limit point and a limit is that the former is a concept associated with a set, while the latter is a *function* defined on integers $\{q = 1,\ 2,\ \ldots\}$ with values on the set (i.e., $x^q \in S$). As mentioned above, the limit of a sequence in S may not even be a limit point of the set S.

A sequence $\{x^q\}$ is said to be **bounded**, if there exists a (nonnegative) real number α such that $\| x^q \| \leqq \alpha$ for all q. If a sequence $\{x^q\}$ is convergent, then it is bounded. However, the converse does not hold. There can be bounded sequences that are not convergent.

When $n = 1$, that is, $S = R$, $\{x^q\}$ is called a **sequence of real numbers**. Such a sequence $\{x^q\}$ is convergent if it is bounded *and* either

(i) $x^1 \leqq x^2 \leqq x^3 \leqq \ldots \leqq x^q \leqq \ldots$, or

(ii) $x^1 \geqq x^2 \geqq x^3 \geqq \ldots \geqq x^q \geqq \ldots$.

Let $\{x^q\}$ be a bounded sequence of real numbers and let α^1 be its least upper bound (*l.u.b.*). Consider a sequence x^2, x^3, ..., which is obtained by deleting x^1 from $\{x^q\}$. Such a sequence is obviously bounded since $\{x^q\}$ is bounded. Denote its *l.u.b.* by α^2. In general, consider a sequence, x^q, x^{q+1}, ..., and denote its *l.u.b.*'s by α^q, α^{q+1}, ... Then, clearly

$$\alpha^1 \geqq \alpha^2 \geqq \ldots \geqq \alpha^q \geqq \ldots.$$

Since the sequence $\{\alpha^q\}$ is obviously also bounded, it is convergent. Denote its limit by α°. Then α° is called the **limit superior** of $\{x^q\}$, and it is denoted by

$$\lim\sup x^q \quad \text{or} \quad \overline{\lim}\, x^q.$$

Similarly, let β^q be the greatest lower bound (*g.l.b.*) of $\{x^q\}$: for example, β^3 is the *g.l.b.* of x^3, etc. Then, clearly

$$\beta^1 \leqq \beta^2 \leqq \beta^3 \leqq \ldots \leqq \beta^q \leqq \ldots.$$

Since the sequence β^q is obviously also bounded, it is convergent. Denote its limit by β°. Such a number β° is called the **limit inferior** of $\{x^q\}$, and it is denoted by

$$\lim\inf x^q \quad \text{or} \quad \underline{\lim}\, x^q.$$

Returning to R^n, let $\{x^q\}$ be a sequence in R^n. Then it can be shown that the sequence $\{x^q\}$ is convergent if and only if for any real number $\varepsilon > 0$ there exists a $\overline{q}$ such that

$$\| x^q - x^r \| < \varepsilon, \quad \text{for all } q,\ r \geqq \overline{q}, \quad \text{or simply,}$$

$$\lim \| x^q - x^r \| = 0 \quad \text{as} \quad q,\ r \to \infty.$$

Such a sequence is called a **Cauchy sequence**. Using this property we can also show that if the series

$$\| x^1 \| + \| x^2 \| + \ldots + \| x^q \| + \ldots$$

for a given sequence, $\{x^q\}$, converges, then the series $(x^1 + x^2 + \ldots + x^q + \ldots)$ also converges.[9] The converse of this statement does not hold

[9]Given a sequence $\{x^q\}$ in R^n, the sum

$$s^q \equiv x^1 + x^2 + \ldots + x^q,$$

in general. Namely, it is possible that $(x^1 + x^2 + \ldots + x^q \ldots)$ converges, and yet $(\| x^1 \| + \| x^2 \| + \ldots + \| x^q \| + \ldots)$ does not converge. The series $(x^1 + \ldots + x^q + \ldots)$ is said to be **absolutely convergent** if $(\| x^1 \| + \ldots + \| x^q \| + \ldots)$ converges. If the series $(x^1 + \ldots + x^q + \ldots)$ is absolutely convergent, then it is convergent, and any series obtained from it by "rearranging" terms is also convergent.[10]

1.3.2 Continuity

An important concept that is closely related to the concept of the convergence of a sequence is that of "continuity," to which we now turn. We first define the concept of the "limit of a function."

Definition 1.2. Let $f: X \to R^m$, where $X \subset R^n$, and let x° be a limit point of X. We say that $f(x)$ **converges** to y° in R^m as x approaches x°, and we write

$$f(x) \to y^\circ \text{ (as } x \to x^\circ\text{), or } \lim_{x \to x^\circ} f(x) = y^\circ,$$

if for every $\varepsilon > 0$, there exists a $\delta > 0$ such that

$$d(x,\ x^\circ) < \delta \text{ implies } d[f(x),\ y^\circ] < \varepsilon,$$

where $d(x,\ x^\circ)$ is the Euclidian distance between x and x°.

REMARK: Note that in the above definition, x° need not be in X (recall the definition of a limit point). Also, even if $x^\circ \in X$, it is possible to have

$$\lim_{x \to x^\circ} f(x) \neq f(x^\circ).$$

REMARK: It can be shown that the above definition can equivalently be recast in terms of limits of sequences. Namely,

$$f(x) \to y^\circ, \text{ as } x \to x^\circ, \text{ if and only if } f(x^q) \to y^\circ, \text{ as } x^q \to x^\circ,$$

is called a **series**. The symbolic expression

$$x^1 + x^2 + x^3 + \ldots,$$

is called an **infinite series**. s^q is called a **partial sum** of the series. The infinite series, $x^1 + x^2 + \ldots$, is said to be **convergent** if the sequence $\{s^q\}$ is convergent. The limit of this sequence is called the **sum** of the infinite series.

[10]The term *rearranging* is obviously rather loose, and it can be defined rigorously. We omit its formal definition, as its meaning should intuitively be obvious.

for every sequence $\{x^q\}$ in $X \backslash \{x^\circ\}$.

We now define the concept of continuity.

Definition 1.3. Let $f\colon X \to R^m$, where $X \subset R^n$, and let x° be a point in X. The function f is said to be **continuous** at a point x° if for any real number $\varepsilon > 0$ there exist a real number $\delta > 0$ such that

$$d(x,\ x^\circ) < \delta \ \text{implies}\ d[f(x),\ f(x^\circ)] < \varepsilon.$$

If this does not hold, f is said to be **discontinuous** at x°. The function f is called a **continuous function in X**, if it is continuous at every point in X.[11] If f is discontinuous even at one point in X, f is said to be a **discontinuous function**.

REMARK: In terms of the previous remark, it can be easily shown that the above definition of continuity (at x°) is equivalent to the following statement:

$$x^q \to x^\circ \ \text{as}\ q \to \infty \ \text{implies}\ f(x^q) \to f(x^\circ) \ \text{as}\ q \to \infty.$$

Namely, function f is *continuous* at x° if, as x approaches x°, $f(x)$ approaches x°. In short, continuity preserves convergence. For example, the function $f\colon R \to R$ defined by $f(x) = a$ (constant) is obviously continuous in R. Using the definition of continuity, the reader should easily be able to prove (as an exercise) that the function $f\colon R \to R$ defined by $f(x) = x^2$ is continuous.

Intuitively, the continuity of a function at a point x° may also be interpreted as the one in which the graph of $f(x)$ has no "hole" at x°. However, such an interpretation may be misleading. In figure 1.4, we illustrate three kinds of discontinuities (at point x°) where $f\colon R \to R$. In figure 1.4*a* and *b*, both lim $f(x)$ for $x \to x^\circ$ with $x > x^\circ$ (called the **right-hand limit**) and lim $f(x)$ for $x \to x^\circ$ with $x < x^\circ$ (called the

---

[11] It is important to note that the δ here, in general, depends both on x and ε. If we can choose δ *independent* of any x and x°, then $f(x)$ is said to be **uniformly continuous** in X. For example, if $f\colon R \to R$ is defined by $f(x) = 2x$, then

$$|f(x) - f(x^\circ)| = 2|x - x^\circ|.$$

For any $\varepsilon > 0$, we choose δ as $\delta = \varepsilon/2$. Then,

$$|x - x^\circ| < \delta \ \text{implies}\ |f(x) - f(x^\circ)| < \varepsilon,$$

so that the choice of δ is independent of x and x°. Hence $f(x) = 2x$ is uniformly continuous.

left-hand limit) exist and are finite, while in figure 1.4*c*, neither the right-hand nor the left-hand limit is finite. The former is called the **discontinuity of the first kind**. It is possible that a function is *nowhere*

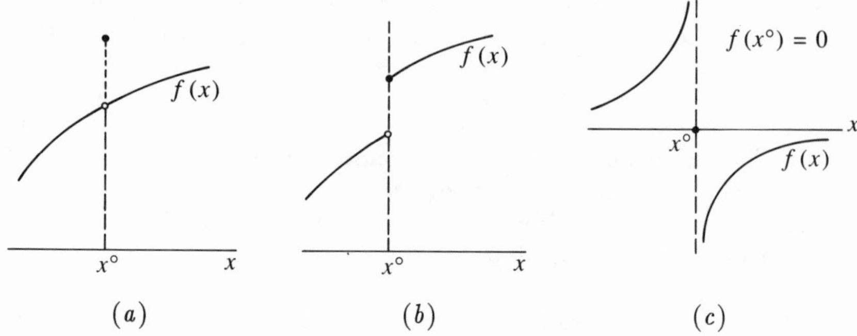

Figure 1.4: Examples of discontinuities

continuous. The following function (called **Dirichlet's discontinuous function**) is known to provide such an example, in which we may recall that a rational number is defined as any number obtained as a ratio of two integers:

$$f(x) = 1 \text{ if } x \text{ is rational, and } f(x) = 0 \text{ if } x \text{ is irrational.}$$

Let $f, g : R^n \to R^m$, and define $f + g$, $f - g$, αf $(\alpha \in R)$, and $f \cdot g$ (inner product), respectively, by

$$f(x) + g(x),\ f(x) - g(x),\ \alpha f(x), \text{ and } f(x) \cdot g(x).$$

When $m = 1$, we may define f/g (quotient) by

$$f(x)/g(x),$$

where we assume $g(x) \neq 0$. Furthermore, define $\| f \|$ and $f \circ g$, respectively, by

$$\| f(x) \| \text{ and } f[g(x)].$$

Then the following theorem readily follows from the definition of continuity.

Theorem 1.1.

(i) If f and g are continuous *at a point*, then the algebraic combinations

$$f + g,\ f - g,\ \alpha f,\ f \cdot g, \text{ and } f/g,$$

are all continuous at that point, where $\alpha \in R$ and $g(x) \neq 0$ for f/g.

(ii) If f and g are continuous at a point, then $\| f \|$ and $(f \circ g)$ are also continuous at that point.

REMARK: From the above theorem, we may assert that if f and g are continuous *in* S, a subset of R^n, then

$$f + g,\ f - g,\ \alpha f,\ f \cdot g,\ f/g,\ \| f \|, \text{ and } f \circ g$$

are all continuous in S. Note that $(f \circ g)$ is continuous means that *the continuous function of a continuous function is also continuous.*

From theorem 1.1, the following statements also follow at once.

Corollary.

(i) The norm $\| x \|$ is a continuous, real-valued function in R^n. The inner product $x \cdot y$ and the distance function $d(x, y)$ are continuous, real-valued functions in R^{2n}.

(ii) Let A be an $m \times n$ matrix and define $f\colon R^n \to R^m$ by $f(x) = Ax$. Then $f(x)$ is a continuous function.

(iii) Let $f_i : R^n \to R^m$ and $\alpha_i : R^n \to R$, $i = 1, 2, \ldots, k$, be continuous functions in R^n. Then $f(x) = \sum_{i=1}^{k} \alpha_i(x) f_i(x)$ is also continuous in R^n.

(iv) Every polynomial is a continuous function.

(v) The "Cobb-Douglas function,"

$$f(x) \equiv x_1^{\alpha_1} x_2^{\alpha_2} \ldots x_n^{\alpha_n},\quad \alpha_i > 0,\quad i = 1, 2, \ldots, n,$$

is a continuous function.

1.3.3 Some Topological Concepts and Results

Let S be a subset of R^n, and consider a sequence x^q in S. The sequence x^q may or may not converge. If, however, the sequence converges, then it has a unique limit, which we denote by x°. The point x° is in R^n, but it may or may not be in S. If it is in S, then S is called a "closed set."

Definition 1.4. Let S be a subset of R^n and let x^q be a sequence in S. S is said to be a **closed set** if

$$x^q \to x^\circ \quad (\text{as } q \to \infty) \text{ implies } x^\circ \in S.$$

A closed set is a set in which every convergent sequence in the set has the limit in the set; that is, a *closed set is a set that is closed under the limit operation.* For example, every closed interval $[a, b]$ is a closed set in R. On the other hand, an open interval $(0, 1)$ is not a closed set. To see this, consider the sequence $1/q$ (q: positive integers). It is a sequence in $(0, 1)$, and it has the limit 0, which is *not* in the set.

Note that the set consisting of only one point x°, where $x^\circ \in R^n$, is a closed set. Also, the whole set R^n and the empty set $\emptyset$ are (trivially) closed sets.

The following fundamental properties follow from the definition of closed sets.

(i) A finite or infinite intersection of closed sets is also closed; that is, if S_α is closed for $\alpha \in A$, then $\bigcap_{\alpha \in A} S_\alpha$ is closed.

(ii) A finite union of closed sets is also closed; that is, if S_i is closed for $i = 1, 2, \ldots, k$, then $\bigcup_{i=1}^{k} S_i$ is closed.

Since the set consisting of only one point is a closed set, the set consisting of a finite number of points, $\{x^1, x^2, \ldots, x^k\}$, is also closed by property (ii). Also, an infinite union of closed sets may not be closed. It can be shown that a set S is closed if and only if it contains all its limit points. From this, it can also be trivially seen that the set consisting of only one point is a closed set, since such a set contains no limit points. We now define an open set.

Definition 1.5. Let S be a subset of R^n. S is called an **open set**, if its complement is a closed set; that is, if S^c is closed where $S^c \equiv R^n \backslash S$.

For example, every open interval $(a,\ b)$ is an open set in R, as its complement $\{x : x \in R,\ x \leqq a \text{ or } x \geqq b\}$ is a closed set (exercise: show why). Notice also that the intervals $(0,\ 1]$ and $[0,\ 1)$ are neither closed nor open.

Now consider the collection of all open sets in R^n. Note that R^n itself and the empty set $\emptyset$ are open sets, while these two sets are also closed sets. We denote the *collection* of open sets in R^n by τ. Also, we denote R^n by X. Then from the properties of closed sets discussed above, we can easily show that τ satisifies the following properties:

(T1) $X \in \tau,\ \emptyset \in \tau,$

(T2) $S_i \in \tau,\ i = 1,\ 2,\ \ldots,\ k$ implies $\bigcap_{i=1}^{k} S_i \in \tau.$

(T3) $S_\alpha \in \tau$ for all $\alpha \in A$ implies $\bigcup_{\alpha \in A} S_\alpha \in \tau.$

Property (T2) states that every finite intersection of open sets is also open, and property (T3) states that a finite or infinite union of open sets is also open. Note that an infinite intersection of open sets may not be open. For example, if $\{q\}$ is the set of positive integers, then

$$\bigcap_{q=1}^{\infty} (-1/q,\ 1/q) = \{0\},$$

which is a closed set.

Given an arbitrary set X (it need not be R^n, nor a linear space, nor a metric space), if we can define a collection of subsets τ that satisfies properties (T1) through (T3), we call it a **topological space** with **topology** τ, and it is denoted by $(X,\ \tau)$. A member of τ in such an abstract topological space is called an "open set." A "closed set" is then defined as a set whose complement is an open set.

Earlier, we defined a set as open if its complement is closed, where a closed set is defined as the one that is closed under a limit operation in R^n. Extracting some essential characteristics of such open sets, axioms (T1) through (T3) for topological space are obtained, and an open set can now be defined in terms of such axioms. Clearly, the open sets defined earlier in terms of closed sets via convergence in R^n satisfy these axioms. However, many *other* sets would satisfy these axioms and, thus, are topological spaces. Note that these axioms do not even require the set to be in R^n. Also, convergence need not be defined. In fact, any set can be a topological space for either one of the following topologies:

(i) $\tau \equiv \{X, \emptyset\}$ (known as the **indiscrete topology**), or

(ii) $\tau \equiv$ all the subsets of X (called the **discrete topology**).

Also, many other kinds of topologies can be defined on an arbitrary set X. Starting from the axioms of a "topological space," (T1) through (T3), many interesting and rich results have been obtained, and such a study constitutes an important branch of mathematics. We shall not go into such studies here. Rather, for the purposes of this book, it suffices to confine ourselves to R^n with open sets and closed sets as defined in terms of convergence.

Given a point x° in R^n, define the set N, which may alternatively be denoted by $N(x^\circ)$, by

$$N \equiv \{x : x \in R^n, \ d(x, x^\circ) < \varepsilon\},$$

where $d(x, x^\circ)$ is the Euclidian distance between x and x°. The set N is called an **open ball** about x° with **radius** ε, or simply a **neighborhood** of x°. We interpret the word "neighborhood" freely, so that N can be the *entire* space R^n (i.e., $\varepsilon \to \infty$), or N can be quite small (i.e., ε is small). It can be easily shown that every neighborhood is an open set. In fact, a "neighborhood" of a point x° in R^n is often (alternatively) defined as any *open set* containing x°.

Given an arbitrary set S in R^n, a point x° in S is called an **interior point** of S, if there exists a neighborhood of x° that is contained in S. It can be shown that *if every point in S is an interior point, then S is an open set.* Furthermore, it can be shown that *every point in an open set is an interior point.* The collection of all the interior points of S is called the **interior** (or the **open kernel** of S).[12]

Using the concept of an open set or a closed set, we may obtain an important characterization of continuous functions. Let X and Y, respectively, be subsets of R^n and R^m and consider the function f :

[12]Given S in R^n, the set of all the limit points of S is called the **derived set** of S. The union of S and its derived set is called the **closure** of S. If a point is in the closure of S but not in the interior of S, it is called a **boundary point** of S. The collection of all the boundary points of S is called the **boundary** of S. For example, if $S = (0, 1)$, the derived set of S is $[0, 1]$, which is also the closure of S. The boundary of S is $\{0, 1\}$. If $S = (0, 1) \cup \{2\}$, then the derived set of S is $[0, 1]$, since the set consisting of only one point $\{2\}$ has no limit points. The closure of S is $[0, 1] \cup \{2\}$, and the boundary of S is $\{0, 1, 2\}$.

$X \to Y$ with $f(x) = y$. Let B be a subset of Y. The inverse image of B under f, denoted by $f^{-1}(B)$, is (as defined earlier):

$$f^{-1}(B) \equiv \{x : x \in X,\ f(x) \in B\}.$$

Clearly, $f^{-1}(B)$ is a subset of X. On the other hand, B may not be a subset of the range set, $f(X)$. The following properties of a continuous function are fundamental.[13]

(i) The function f is continuous in X if and only if $f^{-1}(B)$ is open in X whenever B is open in R^m.

(ii) The function f is continuous in X if and only if $f^{-1}(B)$ is closed in X whenever B is closed in R^m.

REMARK: Namely, continuous functions are precisely those which pull open sets (resp. closed sets) back to open sets (resp. closed sets). Note also that these properties provide *global* characterization of a continuous function, as opposed to the continuity of f at a point in the domain, and this is facilitated by topological concepts such as open sets and closed sets.

We now proceed with another fundamental topological concept, a "compact set." We first define a bounded set. A subset S of R^n is said to be **bounded** if there exists some number M such that

$$d(x^1,\ x^2) \leqq M,$$

for every pair $(x^1,\ x^2)$ of points in S. Using this, we now define a compact set.

Definition 1.6. A subset S of R^n is said to be **compact** if S is closed and bounded.

For example, the closed interval $[0, 1]$ is compact in R, while $(0, 1)$, $(0, 1]$ and $[0, \infty\}$ are not. Some important properties of compact sets are summarized as follows.

---

[13] The proof is again omitted. Note that "f is continuous in X and B is an open set" does not necessarily imply that $f(B)$ is an open set. Similarly, "f is continuous in X and B is a closed set" does not necessarily imply that $f(B)$ is a closed set. Namely, the continuous image of an open set (resp. a closed set) is *not* necessarily open (resp. closed).

Theorem 1.2.

(i) The set S in R^n is compact *if and only if* every sequence in S has a convergent subsequence whose limit is in S (which is known as **sequential compactness**).

(ii) The continuous image of a compact set in R^n is also compact. Namely, if $f\colon S \to R^m$ is a continuous function in S, a compact subset of R^n, then $f(S)$ is also compact in R^m.

(iii) (**Weierstrass theorem**): A continuous real-valued function on a compact set S achieves a minimum and a maximum in S. Namely, if $f\colon S \to R$ is continuous and if S is a compact subset of R^n, then there exists a and b in S such that

$$f(x) \geqq f(a) \text{ for all } x \text{ in } S, \text{ and } f(x) \leqq f(b) \text{ for all } x \text{ in } S.$$

REMARK: To illustrate the concept of sequential compactness, consider the set S consisting of only two points in R, 0 and 1; that is, $S \equiv \{0, 1\}$. Clearly, S is closed and bounded, and hence it is compact. Consider an infinite sequence $\{0, 1, 0, 1, \ldots\}$ in S.

Clearly, this sequence is not convergent, but it has convergent subsequences such as $\{0, 0, \ldots\}$ or $\{1, 1, \ldots\}$. This property of a compact set, the sequential compactness, is useful for proving many important results in R^n.

REMARK: Statement (iii) of theorem 1.2, the Weierstrass theorem, plays an important role in obtaining the *existence* of a maximum and a minimum in certain constrained optimization problems. It would be a useful exercise for the reader to verify that the continuity of f and the closedness and the boundedness of S are essential in obtaining the conclusion that a maximum or a minimum exists.

1.4 Quadratic Forms

The bulk of the exposition on linear algebra is contained in appendix A. Here we only discuss quadratic forms. Let $A \equiv [a_{ij}]$ be an $n \times n$ matrix (over the real field), not necessarily symmetric, and let $x \in R^n$ be a column vector. Then consider a real-valued function $Q(x)$ defined on R^n by

$$Q(x) \equiv x'Ax (= \sum_{i=1}^{n} \sum_{j=1}^{n} a_{ij} x_i x_j), \tag{11}$$

where x denotes a column vector and x' denotes its transpose, a row vector. The function $Q(x)$ is called a **(real) quadratic form**. For example, if A is a 2×2 matrix, then (11) can be written as

$$Q(x) = a_{11}x_1^2 + a_{22}x_2^2 + a_{12}x_1x_2 + a_{21}x_2x_1.$$

If, in particular, $a_{12} = a_{21}$, then this becomes

$$Q(x) = a_{11}x_1^2 + a_{22}x_2^2 + 2a_{12}x_1x_2.$$

Note that a_{ij} and a_{ji} in (11) are both coefficients of x_ix_j when $i \neq j$ (since $x_ix_j = x_jx_i$), so that the coefficient of x_ix_j is $(a_{ij} + a_{ji})$, when $i \neq j$. If $a_{ij} \neq a_{ji}$ (i.e., if A is not symmetric), then we can define new coefficients uniquely by

$$b_{ij} \equiv (a_{ij} + a_{ji})/2, \quad \text{for all } i \text{ and } j,$$

so that $b_{ij} + b_{ji} = a_{ij} + a_{ji}$ and $B \equiv [b_{ij}]$ is a symmetric matrix. Furthermore,

$$Q(x) = x'Ax = x'Bx, \quad \text{for all } x.$$

This redefinition of the coefficients does not change the value Q for any x. Hence, we can develop the theory of quadratic forms by assuming that the matrix A associated with the quadratic form $Q(x) = x'Ax$ is *symmetric*.

The following definition is fundamental in the theory of quadratic forms.

Definition 1.7. Let $Q(x) = x'Ax$ be a quadratic form.

(i) $Q(x)$ is said to be **positive definite**, if $Q(x) > 0$ for all x except for $x = 0$, and $Q(x)$ is said to be **negative definite**, if $Q(x) < 0$ for all x, except for $x = 0$. Matrix A is said to be **positive definite** (resp. **negative definite**) if $Q(x)$ is positive definite (resp. negative definite).

(ii) $Q(x)$ is said to be **positive semidefinite** if $Q(x) \geqq 0$ for all x, and $Q(x)$ is said to be **negative semidefinite**, if $Q(x) \leqq 0$ for all x. Matrix A is said to be **positive semidefinite** (resp. **negative semidefinite**) if $Q(x)$ is positive semidefinite (resp. negative semidefinite).

Clearly, if $Q(x)$ is positive definite (resp. negative definite), it is always positive semidefinite (resp. negative semidefinite). The converse does not hold. Also, the zero matrix is (trivially) both positive and negative semidefinite.

Example 1.3.

(*a*) If $x' = (x_1, x_2)$ and $A = \begin{bmatrix} 1 & 0 \\ 0 & 1 \end{bmatrix}$, then $Q(x) = x'Ax = x_1^2 + x_2^2$. Hence $Q(x) > 0$ for all $x \neq 0$.

(*b*) If $x' = (x_1, x_2)$ and $A = \begin{bmatrix} 0 & 1 \\ 1 & 0 \end{bmatrix}$, then $Q(x) = x'Ax = 2x_1x_2$. Hence $Q(x)$ can be negative, positive, or zero depending on the values of x_1 and x_2.

(*c*) If $x' = (x_1, x_2)$ and $A = \begin{bmatrix} 0 & 0 \\ 0 & 1 \end{bmatrix}$, then $Q(x) = x'Ax = x_2^2$. $Q(x) \geqq 0$ for all x but $Q(x) = 0$ if $x' = (1, 0)$, for example.

In example 1.3, matrix A in statement (*a*) is positive definite, matrix A in statement (*b*) is neither positive (semi)definite nor negative (semi)definite, and matrix A in statement (*c*) is positive semidefinite but *not* positive definite. Also, by the above definition, the following relations hold immediately.

$(A + B)$ is positive (resp. negative) definite, if A and B are positive (resp. negative) semidefinite. (12a)

$(A + B)$ is positive (resp. negative) semidefinite, if A and B are positive (resp. negative) semidefinite. (12b)

We now describe a useful method to determine the definiteness of a particular matrix in terms of minors. Given an $n \times n$ matrix $A = [a_{ij}]$, we define the following $k \times k$ determinants, for $k \leqq n$:

$$D_k \equiv \begin{vmatrix} a_{11} & a_{12} & \dots & a_{1k} \\ a_{21} & a_{22} & \dots & a_{2k} \\ \dots & \dots & \dots & \dots \\ \dots & \dots & \dots & \dots \\ a_{k1} & a_{k2} & \dots & a_{kk} \end{vmatrix}, \quad k = 1, 2, \dots, n. \tag{13}$$

The determinants, D_1, D_2, ..., D_n are called the **successive principal minors** of A. Given A, we may also define the following $k \times k$ determinant:

$$\tilde{D}_k \equiv \begin{vmatrix} a_{ii} & a_{ij} & \cdots & a_{ik} \\ a_{ji} & a_{jj} & \cdots & a_{jk} \\ \cdots & \cdots & \cdots & \cdots \\ \cdots & \cdots & \cdots & \cdots \\ a_{ki} & a_{kj} & \cdots & a_{kk} \end{vmatrix}, \quad k = 1,\ 2,\ \ldots,\ n, \tag{14}$$

where $(i,\ j,\ \ldots,\ k)$ is any permutation of k integers from the set of integers $\{1,\ 2,\ \ldots,\ n\}$. The determinant $\tilde{D}_k$ is called a **principal minor** of A with order k. Note that every $\tilde{D}_n$ has the same sign as the determinant of A, since *both* rows and columns are interchanged in the process of permutation.

Example 1.4.

$$A = \begin{bmatrix} a_{11} & a_{12} \\ a_{21} & a_{22} \end{bmatrix};$$

$$D_1 = a_{11},\ D_2 = \begin{vmatrix} a_{11} & a_{12} \\ a_{21} & a_{22} \end{vmatrix}:$$

$$\tilde{D}_1 = a_{11},\ a_{22},\ \text{and}\ \tilde{D}_2 = \begin{vmatrix} a_{11} & a_{12} \\ a_{21} & a_{22} \end{vmatrix},\ \begin{vmatrix} a_{22} & a_{21} \\ a_{12} & a_{11} \end{vmatrix}.$$

The following theorem provides a complete characterization of definiteness in terms of principal minors.

Theorem 1.3. Let A be an $n \times n$ symmetric matrix with its quadratic form $Q(x) \equiv x'Ax$. Then

(i) A is positive definite if and only if

$$D_1 > 0,\ D_2 > 0,\ D_3 > 0,\ \ldots,\ D_n > 0.$$

(ii) A is negative definite if and only if

$$D_1 < 0,\ D_2 > 0,\ D_3 < 0,\ \ldots,\ (-1)^n D_n > 0.$$

(iii) A is positive semidefinite if and only if

$$\tilde{D}_1 \geqq 0,\ \tilde{D}_2 \geqq 0,\ \tilde{D}_3 \geqq 0,\ \ldots,\ \tilde{D}_n \geqq 0.$$

(iv) A is negative semidefinite if and only if

$$\tilde{D}_1 \leqq 0,\ \tilde{D}_2 \geqq 0,\ \tilde{D}_3 \leqq 0,\ \ldots,\ (-1)^n \tilde{D}_n \geqq 0.$$

REMARK: Since D_n = determinant of A, statements (i) and (ii) of theorem 1.3 confirm that a positive or negative definite matrix must be nonsingular.

REMARK: The determinants $\tilde{D}_k$ all have the same signs if $\{i, j, \ldots, k\}$ is the same index set, since both rows and columns are interchanged in the process of permutation.

REMARK: The $\tilde{D}_k$'s in statements (iii) and (iv) in theorem 1.3 *cannot* be replaced by D_k. For example, in (c) of example 1.3,

$$A = \begin{bmatrix} 0 & 0 \\ 0 & 1 \end{bmatrix},\ D_1 = 0,\ D_2 = 0,\ \text{ but } \tilde{D}_1 = 0 \text{ and } 1.$$

A is *not* negative semidefinite (while it is positive semidefinite but not positive definite), where we may note $Q(x) = x'Ax = x_2^2$.

1.5 Differentiation, Concave and Quasi-Concave Functions

1.5.1 Differentiation

We begin our discussion here by reminding the reader of the definition of a derivative on the real line from elementary calculus.

Definition 1.8. Let X be an open set in R and let x° be a point in X. The function $f\colon X \to R$ is said to be **differentiable at x°** if there exists a real number a such that

$$\lim_{h \to 0} \frac{f(x^{\circ} + h) - f(x^{\circ})}{h} = a, \quad \text{or}$$

$$\lim_{h \to 0} \frac{f(x^{\circ} + h) - f(x^{\circ}) - ah}{h} = 0, \tag{15}$$

where $h \neq 0$ and $x^{\circ} + h \in X$. We call a **the derivative of f at x°** and denote it by $f'(x^{\circ})$. If f is differentiable at every x in X, then f is called a **differentiable function in X**.

The limit in (15), in general, depends on x°. When x° changes in X, the value of $f'(x^{\circ})$ also changes in R. Hence f' is a function of x in

X, and we may denote it by $f'(x^\circ)$. Also, the derivative is essentially a local concept, since it is concerned with a particular point x° and that the set X can be small. Since X is an open set, x° is an interior point of X. This is important, since equation h in (15) can be either postive or negative. Namely, $x^\circ + h$ is allowed to approach x° from any direction. The approach does not have to even be monotone: it can oscillate around x°. We illustrate the concept of derivatives in figure 1.5*a*. As is well-known and as is clear from the diagram, the derivative

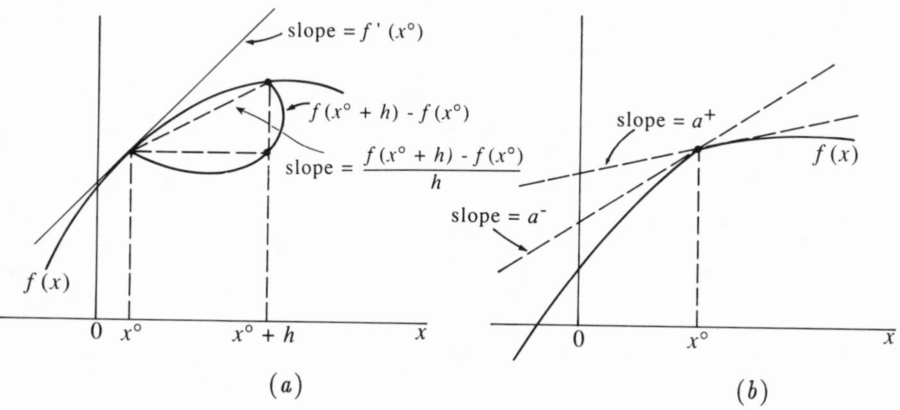

Figure 1.5: Illustrations of derivatives

signifies the slope of the line which is tangent to the graph of $f(x)$ at the point x°. Notice that the above definition, in particular, requires that both of the limits

$$\lim_{\substack{h\to 0\\ h>0}} \frac{f(x^\circ + h) - f(x^\circ)}{h} = a^+,$$

$$\lim_{\substack{h\to 0\\ h<0}} \frac{f(x^\circ + h) - f(x^\circ)}{h} = a^-$$

exist, and that they are equal, $a^+ = a^-$.[14] [It can be shown that the converse is also true: i.e., if a^+ and a^- in the above exist and if

[14]If the limits a^+ and a^- exist, a^+ is called the **right-hand derivative** and a^- is called the **left-hand derivative**.

$a^+ = a^-$, then f is differentiable at x° and $f'(x^\circ) = a^+ = a^-$.] Figure 1.5b illustrates the case in which a^+ and a^- both exist, but are not equal, and hence $f(x)$ is not differentiable at x°.

Another simple example in which both a^+ and a^- exist, but are not equal would be

$$f(x) = |x|, \quad \text{where } a^- = -1 \text{ and } a^+ = 1 \text{ at } x = 0.$$

Hence $f(x) = |x|$ is not differentiable at the origin ($x = 0$). Thus, a continuous function may *not* be differentiable. It is also clear from the above definition that if a function is discontinuous at a point x°, then it cannot be differentiable at this point.

Continuity is necessary for differentiability, but not sufficient. In fact, one may construct examples of a continuous function that is *nowhere differentiable.*[15]

Now if f is defined on R^n, or on a subset of R^n, then definition 1.8 needs to be modified, for h must now be a vector as x° is a vector in R^n. Letting $\| h \|$ be the Euclidian norm of h, the following definition is a natural extension of Definition 1.8.

Definition 1.9. Let X be an open set in R^n and let x° be a point in X. The function $f: X \to R$ is said to be **differentiable at x°**, if there exists an n-dimensional vector a such that

$$\lim_{h \to 0} \frac{f(x^\circ + h) - f(x^\circ) - a \cdot h}{\| h \|} = 0, \tag{16}$$

where h is also an n-dimensional vector with $h \neq 0$, and $x^\circ + h \in X$. Vector a is (again) denoted by $f'(x^\circ)$ and it is called the **derivative of f at x°**. If f is differentiable at every point of X, then f is called a **differentiable function in X**.

REMARK: In the above definition of derivatives, the distinction between column and row vectors has no important consequences. We thus use the dot "$\cdot$" to denote the Euclidian inner product. The notation $a \cdot h$ may be preferred to $a'h$ because the transpose notation in a' can be confused with the derivative notation.

---

[15] Such an example was first constructed by Weierstrass, and it was published by du Bois Reymond in 1875. Since then, simpler examples have been constructed. A systematic discussion of nowhere differentiable functions is given in Hobson (1926, pp. 401–12).

In defining derivatives, the concept of "Landau's o" is quite useful. Definition 1.9 may be recast in the following equivalent form: f is said to be **differentiable at x°**, if there exists an a in R^n such that

$$f(x^\circ + h) - f(x^\circ) = a \cdot h + o(\| h \|), \tag{16'}$$

where $o(\| h \|)$ is an infinitesimal of higher order than h, defined by

$$\lim_{h \to 0} \frac{o(\| h \|)}{\| h \|} = 0, \quad \text{for } h \neq 0.$$

This $o(\cdot)$ is often called **Landau's o-symbol**. More precisely, $o(\| h \|)$ is the symbol that collectively signifies any scalar or vector that is "infinitesimally small," in the sense that $r(h) = o(\| h \|)$ means

$$\lim_{h \to 0} \frac{\| r(h) \|}{\| h \|} = 0, \quad \text{for } h \neq 0,$$

where $r(h)$ can be scalar or a vector. Similarly, $r(h) = o(\| h \|^2)$ means

$$\lim_{h \to 0} \frac{\| r(h) \|}{\| h \|^2} = 0, \quad \text{for } h \neq 0.$$

For example, if $h \in R$, $h^2 = o(\| h \|)$, $h^3 = o(\| h \|^2)$, and $1/h \neq o(\| h \|)$. Therefore, (16′) may also be written as

$$f(x^\circ + h) - f(x^\circ) = a \cdot h + r(h),$$

where $r(h) = o(\| h \|)$, and where $r(h)$ signifies the **remainder term**. This may also be interpreted as the $f(x)$ (where $x = x^\circ + h$) that may be approximated by $f(x^\circ)$ when h is sufficiently small, and that the approximation error is equal to $r(h)$ whose magnitude is measured by $o(\| h \|)$.

Definition 1.10. A real-valued function f on an open set in R^n is said to have a **partial derivative with respect to x_i at x°**, where $x^\circ \in X$, if there exists a real number a_i such that

$$\lim_{h \to 0} \frac{f(x^\circ + e_i h) - f(x^\circ) - a_i h}{h} = 0, \tag{17}$$

where h is a scalar with $h \neq 0$, and where e^i is an n-dimensional vector whose i^{th} element is equal to 1 and all other elements are equal to 0

$(i = 1, 2, \ldots, n)$. The scalar a_i is the *partial derivative of f with respect to x_i at x°* and is denoted by $\partial f(x^{\circ})/\partial x_i$.

Let $f: X \to R$, where X is an open set in R^n, and x° is a point in X. Then the following results are fundamental:

(i) If a real-valued function $f(x)$ defined on an open set in X of R^n is differentiable at $x^{\circ} \in X$, then it is continuous at x°, and has partial derivatives with respect to each of its coordinate variables, where $f'(x^{\circ}) = a = (a_1, a_2, \ldots, a_n)$ can be written as

$$f'(x^{\circ}) = \left[\frac{\partial f(x^{\circ})}{\partial x_1}, \frac{\partial f(x^{\circ})}{\partial x_2}, \ldots, \frac{\partial f(x^{\circ})}{\partial x_n}\right].$$

(ii) The function f is differentiable and its derivative $f'(x)$ is continuous in an open set D in X, if and only if f has continuous partial derivatives for all x in D with respect to each of its coordinate variables.

REMARK: The function f is said to be **continuously differentiable** in D, if it is differentiable *and* if $f'(x)$ is continuous for all x in D. The vector $f'(x^{\circ})$, expressed as in (i), is often called the **gradient vector** of f at x°. It is also denoted by f_x°, $f_x(x^{\circ})$, or $\nabla f(x^{\circ})$. The notation f_x is useful when f depends on some other variables, say $f(x, y)$, where $y \in R^m$. In this case, f_x means the gradient vector of f with respect to x (with y being kept constant).

In these definitions of derivatives, we assumed that f is a real-valued function. We can extend the concept of derivatives, in a natural way, to the case in which f is a vector-valued function.

Definition 1.11. Let X be an open set in R^n, and let x° be a point in X. The function $f: X \to R^m$ is said to be **differentiable at x°** if there exists an $m \times n$ matrix A with real number entries such that

$$f(x^{\circ} + h) - f(x^{\circ}) = Ah + o(\| h \|),$$

$$\text{for } h \in R^n \text{ with } x^{\circ} + h \in X. \quad (18)$$

The matrix A is denoted by $f'(x^{\circ})$ and it is called the **derivative of f at x°**. If f is differentiable at every point of X, then f is called a **differentiable function in X**. (Matrix A in equation 18 can be shown to be unique.)

REMARK: In (18), the h in Ah is taken to be a column vector in order to make the product Ah meaningful. However, in the definition of derivatives, the distinction between column and row vectors should not play any important role. Hence one may prefer $A \cdot h$ to Ah. Writing $f(x) = [f_1(x), \ldots, f_m(x)]$, we can easily show that $f(x)$ is differentiable at x° if and only if $f_i(x)$ is differentiable at x° for all i. Matrix A, called the **Jacobian (matrix)** of f at x°, can be written in the following form:

$$A = \begin{bmatrix} \dfrac{\partial f_1(x^\circ)}{\partial x_1} & \cdots\cdots & \dfrac{\partial f_1(x^\circ)}{\partial x_n} \\ \vdots & & \vdots \\ \dfrac{\partial f_m(x^\circ)}{\partial x_1} & \cdots\cdots & \dfrac{\partial f_m(x^\circ)}{\partial x_n} \end{bmatrix}$$

By notation, $A = f'(x^\circ)$. The Jacobian matrix is also denoted by f_x° or $f_x(x^\circ)$. Again, the notation f_x is useful when f depends on variables other than x, say, $f(x, y)$. In this case f_x signifies the Jacobian matrix of f with respect to x (with y being kept constant).

Note that all the definitions of differentiability or derivatives in terms of (15), (16), or (16′), and (18), etc., are really the same. The first definition is concerned with the case $n = m = 1$, the second definition is concerned with $n \geqq 1$, $m = 1$, and the third definition is concerned with $n \geqq 1$, $m \geqq 1$.

1.5.2 Some Important Results

We now list some important results that involve derivatives. The first of these extends an important theorem (called the **chain rule**) of elementary calculus.

Theorem 1.4 (composite function theorem). Let $f \colon X \to R^m$, where X is an open set in R^n, and let $g : Y \to R^k$, where Y is an open set in R^m with $f(X) \subset Y$. Suppose that f is differentiable at x° in X and g is differentiable at $f(x^\circ)$. Then the function $h = g \circ f : X \to R^k$, defined by $h(x) = g[f(x)]$ is differentiable at x° and $h'(x^\circ) = g'[f(x^\circ)]f'(x^\circ)$, where the product $g'f'$ simply follows the usual rule of matrix multiplication. f' is an $m \times n$ matrix and g' is a $k \times m$ matrix, so that $g'f'$ is a $k \times n$ matrix.

Example 1.5.

(a) Let $n = k = 1$ and $m > 1$. In this case, writing $f(x) = [f_1(x), \ldots, f_m(x)]$ and $y_i = f_i(x)$, we have

$$h'(x) = \sum_{i=1}^{m} \frac{\partial g}{\partial y_i} \frac{\partial f_i}{\partial x}.$$

In particular, if $f(x) = a + bx$, $x \in R$ and $a, b \in R^m$, then we have:

$$h'(x) = g'(y) \cdot b.$$

(b) Let $n = m = 2$ and $k = 1$, and let $z = g(x, y)$, and $x = r \cos\theta$, $y = r \sin\theta$ (i.e., the polar coordinate system).

$$\partial x/\partial r = \cos\theta, \quad \partial x/\partial\theta = -r \sin\theta,$$

$$\partial y/\partial r = \sin\theta, \quad \text{and} \quad \partial y/\partial\theta = r \cos\theta.$$

Hence, letting $h(r, \theta) \equiv g(r \cos\theta, r \sin\theta)$, we have

$$\partial h/\partial r = (\cos\theta)g_x + (\sin\theta)g_y,$$

$$\partial h/\partial\theta = (-r \sin\theta)g_x + (r \cos\theta)g_y,$$

where $g_x \equiv \partial g/\partial x$ and $g_y \equiv \partial g/\partial y$.

Let $f(x, z) = 0$, where f is a continuously differentiable function on $R \times R$. If we can obtain function ϕ such that $x = \phi(z)$ and $f[\phi(z), z] = 0$, then we say that $f(x, z) = 0$ is "solved for x." Simply differentiating $f(x, z) = 0$, we obtain $f_x dx + f_y dy = 0$, where f_x and f_y are the partial derivatives of f with respect x and y, respectively. Hence, $dz/dx = \phi' = -f_z/f_x$. Thus, to solve $f(x, z) = 0$ for x, it is crucial to have $f_x \neq 0$. This can be generalized to the case where x is an n-vector and z is an m-vector. In other words, we may obtain theorem 1.5. Theorems 1.4 and 1.5 are probably the most important theorems in advanced calculus.

Theorem 1.5 (implicit function theorem). Let $f\colon D \to R^n$ be a continuously differentiable function, where D is an open set in $R^n \times R^m$.

Let $(x^\circ,\ z^\circ)$ be a point in D for which $f(x^\circ,\ z^\circ) = 0$. If $f_x(x^\circ,\ z^\circ)$, the Jacobian matrix of f with respect to x evaluated at $(x^\circ,\ z^\circ)$, is nonsingular, then there exists a unique continuously differentiable function ϕ such that $x^\circ = \phi(z^\circ)$, *and*

$$f[\phi(z),\ z] = 0, \quad \text{for all } z \text{ in some neighborhood of } z^\circ.$$

REMARK: Theorem 1.5 provides only a *sufficient* condition for the *local* existence of the function $\phi\,[= (\phi_1,\ \ldots,\ \phi_n)]$, or the "solvability" of $f(x,\ z) = 0$ for x as $x = \phi(z)$, since $f[\phi(z),\ z] = 0$ holds only in a neighborhood of z°. The function $\phi(z)$ is implicitly defined by $f[\phi(z),\ z] = 0$; hence the name of the theorem. The nonsingularity of the Jacobian matrix f_x provides only a part of sufficient condition, not a *necessary* condition, for the existence of function ϕ.

By totally differentiating $f(x,\ z) = 0$ to obtain

$$f_x dx + f_z dz = 0,$$

where f_x and f_z are the Jacobian matrices of f with respect to x and z, respectively, we obtain $dx = -(f_x^{-1} f_z)dz$. This equation gives, $dx_1,\ dx_2,\ \ldots,\ dx_n$ and hence all partial derivatives, $\phi_1,\ \phi_2,\ \ldots,\ \phi_n$ of the unknown function ϕ. Clearly, in order for this equation, $dx = -(f_x^{-1} f_z)dz$, to be meaningful, f_x must be nonsingular.

Similarly, let $f(x,\ z)$ be a linear system

$$f(x,\ z) \equiv Ax + z = 0,$$

where A is an $n \times n$ matrix, and x and z are n-dimensional (column) vectors, in order for this system to have a unique solution x, matrix A must be nonsingular, in which case x is uniquely determined as $x = -A^{-1}z$. Since matrix A corresponds precisely to the Jacobian matrix of f with respect to x, this example also shows that the nonsingularity of the Jacobian matrix in theorem 1.5 plays a crucial role for the existence of the implict function.

The following example may illustrate the importance of theorem 1.5 in economics.

Example 1.6. Let f_i denote the excess demand (i.e., demand minus supply) for the ith commodity and let the equilibrium conditions be written as

$$f_i(p_1,\ p_2,\ \ldots,\ p_n,\ \alpha_1,\ \alpha_2,\ \ldots,\ \alpha_m) = 0, \text{ for } i = 1,\ 2,\ \ldots,\ n,$$

or more compactly, $f(p, \alpha) = 0$, where p_i signifies the price of the ith commodity and α is the vector of parameters which affect excess demands. If f is continuously differentiable and if the Jacobian matrix of f with respect to p, f_p, is nonsingular, then there exists a unique continuously differentiable function ϕ such that $p = \phi(\alpha)$. The quantity $\partial\phi_i/\partial\alpha_j$ measures the effect of a change in the jth parameter on the ith price. As is well-known, this is an exercise in **comparative statics.**

The previous theorem is closely related to the so-called inverse function theorem.

Theorem 1.6 (inverse function theorem). Let $f\colon X \to R^n$ be a continuously differentiable function, where X is an open set in R^n. If the Jacobian $f'(x^\circ)$ is nonsingular at some point x° in X, then there exists a unique continuously differentiable function ϕ such that

$$\phi[f(x)] = x, \quad \text{for all } x \text{ in some neighborhood } x^\circ,$$

where the domain of ϕ is an open set $Y \subset f(X)$ for which $f(x^\circ) \in Y$.

The function ϕ is the **inverse function** of f, which is denoted by f^{-1}. This theorem states, roughly speaking, that a continuously differentiable function f is invertible in a neighborhood of x° at which the (Jacobian) matrix $f'(x^\circ)$ is nonsingular.

While its proof may not be well known, the following result is well known to economists and has been extensively used in the economics literature.[16]

Theorem 1.7 (Euler's theorem). Let $f(x)$ be a differentiable real-valued function defined on an open set X in R^n. Then $f(x)$ is homogeneous of degree m, if and only if $f'(x) \cdot x = mf(x)$ for all x in X; that is,

$$f_1(x)x_1 + f_2(x)x_2 + \ldots + f_n(x)x_n = mf(x),$$

$$\text{for all } x \text{ in } X, \text{ where } f_i \equiv \partial f/\partial x_i,\ i = 1, 2, \ldots, n. \tag{19}$$

---

[16] For the proof of this theorem, see Takayama (1972, pp. 31–35).

REMARK: The function f is said to be **homogeneous of degree m** if for any real number $\alpha \neq 0$,[17]

$$f(\alpha x) = \alpha^m f(x), \quad \text{for all } x. \tag{20}$$

Equation (19) provides a complete characterization of homogeneous functions, and it is called **Euler's equation** (for homogeneous functions).

Example 1.7. Let $f(x)$ be a production function. By a popular definition, the function f is said to exhibit **constant returns to scale** if f is homogeneous of degree one. In this case, Euler's equation can be written as

$$f_1(x)x_1 + f_2(x)x_2 + \ldots + f_n(x)x_n = f(x), \quad \text{for all } x,$$

where $f_i(x) \equiv \partial f/\partial x_i$, signifying the marginal product of the ith factor. One of the important problems in marginal productivity theory is whether or not the output is distributed to all the participating factors without either surplus or shortage when each factor is rewarded according to its marginal productivity. This question, known as the **exhaustion-of-product problem**, can be solved trivially when the production function exhibits constant returns to scale, due to the above equation.[18]

1.5.3 Higher Order Derivatives and Hessians

Let $f(x)$ be a differentiable real-valued function defined on an open set X in R^n. Its derivative $f'(x)$ depends on a particular point x for which the limit is taken, so that it is, in general, a function of x. Given the function $g(x) \equiv f'(x)$, we may define its derivative $g'(x)$ (when it exists). We denote this by $f''(x)$, and we call $f''(x)$ the **second-order derivative** of f at x. Corresponding to this, $f'(x)$ is also called the **first-order derivative** of f at x. Again, in general, $f''(x)$ depends on x and thus it is a function of x. Repeating this process we may analogously define the **k^{th} order derivative** of f at x (when it exists), and we denote it

---

[17] When α is assumed to be positive, as in many applications in economics, $f(x)$ is said to be **positively homogeneous of degree m**.

[18] The marginal productivity theory of distribution has an established importance in economics. For an excellent study of its history, see Stigler (1941). Chapter XII of Stigler's book discusses the exhaustion-of-product problem. George Stigler was the 1982 Nobel laureate in Economic Science for his work on government regulation in the economy and functioning of industry.

by $f^{(k)}(x)$. If $f''(x)$ exists, f is said to be **twice differentiable** at x. Similarly, if $f^{(k)}(x)$ exists, f is **k-times differentiable** at x. $f'(x)$ and $f''(x)$ are the conventional notations for $f^{(1)}(x)$ and $f^{(2)}(x)$, respectively. If $f^{(k)}(x)$ is differentiable *and* its derivative $f^{(k+1)}(x)$ is continuous for each x in X (i.e., if $f^{(k)}$ is continuously differentiable), then f is said to be a **function of class** $C^{(k+1)}$ (on the domain X). Thus if $f \in C^{(1)}$, f is continuously differentiable. If $f \in C^{(2)}$, f is said to be a **twice continuously differentiable function.**[19]

Recall that $f'(x) = [\partial f(x)/\partial x_1, \ldots, \partial f(x)/\partial x_n]$ when $f: X \to R$, $X \subset R^n$. Note that $g_i(x) \equiv \partial f(x)/\partial x_i$ is also a real-valued function. Then define its partial derivatives in a similar fashion (if they exist), and denote these partials by $\partial g_i(x)/\partial x_j = \partial^2 f(x)/\partial x_i \partial x_j$, etc. They are called the **second-order partial derivatives** of f at x. For example, if $f(x, y) = xy^2$, $x, y \in R$, then $\partial f/\partial x = y^2$, $\partial^2 f/\partial x^2 = 0$, $\partial f/\partial y = 2xy$, $\partial^2 f/\partial x \partial y = \partial^2 f/\partial y \partial x = 2y$, $\partial^2 f/\partial y^2 = 2x$. The partial derivatives of higher orders, $k = 3, 4, \ldots$, can be defined analogously.

In the above, we have defined higher order derivatives. Here we focus on the second-order derivatives. To this end, it would be illuminating to recast its definition in the following equivalent form.

Definition 1.12. Let X be an open set in R^n and let x° be a point in X. The function $f: X \to R$ is said to be **twice differentiable at**

[19] There are a number of important results that involve higher order derivatives. Here, confining ourselves to the case in which x is a scalar, we may record one such result, known as "Taylor's expansion formula." Let $f: X \to R$, where X is an open set in R. Assume that f has continuous partial derivatives of order k for every point in X where $f \in C^{(k)}$. Then for every x in X, $f(x)$ may be expanded in the following form, for some x° in X,

$$f(x) = f(x^\circ) + f'(x^\circ)h + \frac{1}{2} f''(x^\circ)h^2 + \cdots + \frac{1}{(k-1)!} f^{(k-1)}(x^\circ)h^{k-1} + r(h), \qquad \text{(T)}$$

where $h \equiv x - x^\circ$, and $r(h) = o(\| h \|^k)$. The remainder term $r(h)$ can be more precisely written as

$$r(h) = \frac{1}{k!} f^{(k)}(\overline{x})h^k$$

for some point $\overline{x}$ interior to the interval joining x and x°. Equation (T) is called the **Taylor expansion formula**, and it gives the formula for approximating $f(x)$. Taylor's formula can be extended to the case in which X is an open set in R^n, rather than R.

x° if there exists an $a \in R^n$ and an $n \times n$ matrix A with real number entries such that

$$f(x^\circ + h) - f(x^\circ) = a \cdot h + (1/2)h \cdot (Ah) + o(\| h \|^2). \tag{21}$$

The n-vector a is called the **first-order derivative** of f at x° and A is called the **second-order derivative of f at x°**, where a is denoted by $f'(x^\circ)$ and A is denoted by $f''(x^\circ)$. The function f is said to be a twice differentiable function in X, if $f(x)$ is twice differentiable at each point in X.

REMARK: In (21), the h in (Ah) is taken to be a column vector in order to make the product Ah meaningful. Thus, letting $A = [a_{ij}]$, $h \cdot (Ah)$ means

$$h \cdot (Ah) = \sum_{i=1}^{n} \sum_{j=1}^{n} a_{ij} h_i h_j.$$

If we denote the transpose of h by h', then $h \cdot (Ah)$ can also be written as $h'Ah$.

REMARK: If f is twice differentiable at x°, then $\partial f(x^\circ)/\partial x_i$ and $\partial^2 f(x^\circ)/\partial x_i \partial x_j$ exist for all i and j, and a and A can be written as, $a = [\partial f(x^\circ)/\partial x_1, \ldots, \partial f(x^\circ)/\partial x_n]$, and

$$A = \begin{bmatrix} \dfrac{\partial^2 f(x^\circ)}{\partial x_1^2} & \dfrac{\partial^2 f(x^\circ)}{\partial x_1 \partial x_2} & \cdots & \dfrac{\partial^2 f(x^\circ)}{\partial x_1 \partial x_n} \\ \dfrac{\partial^2 f(x^\circ)}{\partial x_2 \partial x_1} & \cdots & \cdots & \dfrac{\partial^2 f(x^\circ)}{\partial x_2 \partial x_n} \\ \cdots & \cdots & \cdots & \cdots \\ \cdots & \cdots & \cdots & \cdots \\ \cdots & \cdots & \cdots & \cdots \\ \dfrac{\partial^2 f(x^\circ)}{\partial x_n \partial x_1} & \cdots & \cdots & \dfrac{\partial^2 f(x^\circ)}{\partial x_n^2} \end{bmatrix}.$$

Matrix A is called the **Hessian (matrix)** of f at x°. The function $f''(x)$ is continuous at x° if and only if the second partial derivatives $\partial^2 f(x)/\partial x_i \partial x_j$, $i, j = 1, 2, \ldots, n$, are all continuous at x°, in which case we have

$$\frac{\partial^2 f(x^\circ)}{\partial x_i \partial x_j} = \frac{\partial^2 f(x^\circ)}{\partial x_j \partial x_i}, \; i, j = 1, 2, \ldots, n,$$

which is known as **Young's theorem**. Hence if $f(x)$ is twice continuously differentiable in X, then its Hessian matrix $f''(x)$ is symmetric for all x in X. It is important to note the continuity assumption of $f''(x)$ here.

If $f''(x)$ is not continuous at x°, then $f''(x^{\circ})$ may not be symmetric. Many such examples are given in calculus or advanced calculus textbooks. The following example is found in Apostol (1957, p. 120):

$$f(x_1, x_2) = x_1 x_2 (x_1^2 - x_2^2)/(x_1^2 + x_2^2), \text{ if } (x_1, x_2) \neq 0,$$

and $f(0,0) = 0$. A routine computation reveals $\partial^2 f(0, 0)/\partial x_1 \partial x_2 \neq \partial^2 f(0, 0)/\partial x_2 \partial x_1$.

Finally, we may note some simple well-known formulas on the differentiation of inner products and quadratic forms. Let a be a constant vector in R^n and let A be an $n \times n$ constant matrix. Then we have

$$f(x) = a \cdot x \text{ implies } f'(x) = a \text{ and } f''(x) = 0, \tag{22}$$

$$f(x) = x \cdot (Ax) \text{ implies } f'(x) = 2Ax \text{ and } f''(x) = 2A, \tag{23}$$

where the 0 of $f''(x) = 0$ in (22) is the $n \times n$ zero matrix.

1.5.4 Concave and Convex Functions

Definition 1.13. Given x and y in R^n, the z defined by $z \equiv \theta x + (1 - \theta)y$, $0 \leqq \theta \leqq 1$, is called a **convex combination** of x and y.[20]

The concept of a convex combination can be illustrated by figure 1.6, where we may note that $z = x$ if $\theta = 1$, and $z = y$ if $\theta = 0$.

Definition 1.14. Let S be a subset of R^n. The set S is called a **convex set** if an arbitrary convex combination of any two points of S is in S. That is, S is convex if

$$x, y \in S \text{ implies } \theta x + (1 - \theta)y \in S, \; 0 \leqq \theta \leqq 1.$$

[20] Similarly, given k points, $x^1, x^2, \ldots, x^k$ in R^n, the z defined by

$$z \equiv \theta_1 x^1 + \theta_2 x^2 + \ldots + \theta_k x^k,$$

$$0 \leqq \theta_i \leqq 1, \; i = 1, 2, \ldots, k, \; \sum_{i=1}^{k} \theta_i = 1$$

is called a **convex combination** of these k points.

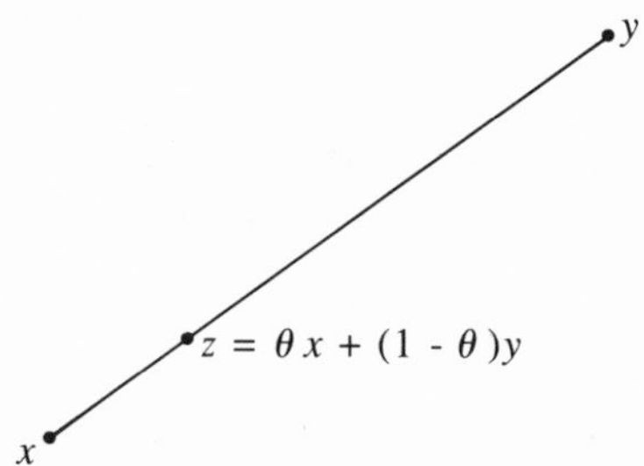

Figure 1.6: An illustration of a convex combination

Thus, for example, a circle is not a convex set, but a disk that includes all the interior points of a circle is a convex set. The area covered by the Chinese character 凸 (translation "convex") is not convex. A convex set is one of the most important concepts in economic analysis.

The following properties of convex sets are useful:

(i) Any intersection (finite or infinite) of convex sets is also convex.

(ii) If S_i, $i = 1, 2, \ldots, k$, are convex sets in R^n, then their **linear sum** is defined by,

$$S \equiv \{z : z = \alpha_1 x^1 + \alpha_2 x^2 + \ldots + \alpha_k x^k,$$

$$x_i \in S_i,\ \alpha_i \in R,\ i = 1, 2, \ldots, k\},$$

is also convex.

(iii) If S_i, $i = 1, 2, \ldots, k$, are convex sets in R^n, then their Cartesian product, $S_1 \times S_2 \times \ldots \times S_k$ is also convex.

We now introduce the concept of a concave function.

Definition 1.15. Let f be a real-valued function defined on a convex (not necessarily open) set X in R^n. The function f is called a **concave function** if for all x, $y \in X$ and $0 \leqq \theta \leqq 1$,

$$f[\theta x + (1 - \theta)y] \geqq \theta f(x) + (1 - \theta)f(y).$$

If the inequalities in the above definition are strict for all $x,\ y \in X$ with $x \neq y$ and $0 < \theta < 1$, then f is called a **strictly concave function**. On the other hand, f is called a **convex** (or **strictly convex**) **function** if $-f$ is concave (or strictly concave).

Note that X, the domain of f, is restricted to be a convex set. This is necessary to ensure $\theta x + (1 - \theta)y$ is also in X whenever x and y are in X, for otherwise $f[\theta x + (1 - \theta)y]$ has no meaning. An often seen confusion is a "concave set." Concave and convex functions designate certain classes of functions, not of sets, whereas a convex set designates a certain class of sets, and not a class of functions. A "concave set" confuses sets with functions, unless the researcher wishes to create such a concept.

Clearly, if a function is strictly concave (or strictly convex), it is automatically concave (or convex). A (strictly) concave function is illustrated in figure 1.7 (where $X = R$). Intuitively, f is a concave function if the chord joining any two points on the function lies on or below the function. The set X on which f is defined must be convex, for otherwise $\theta x + (1 - \theta)y$ may not be in X, the domain of the function f.

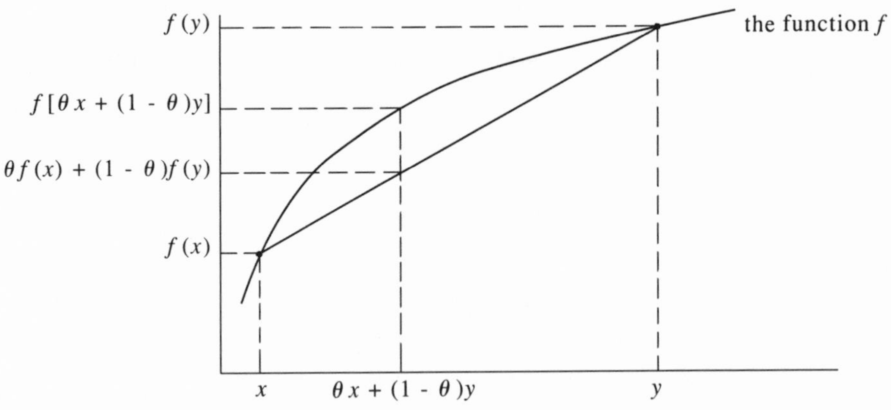

Figure 1.7: An illustration of a concave function

In particular, the function $f\colon R^n \to R$, defined by $f(x) = a \cdot x + a_0$ (where a is a constant vector in R^n and a_0 is a scalar) is both concave and convex (but neither strictly concave nor strictly convex). Also, there are many real-valued functions that are neither strictly concave nor strictly convex. The concept of concave (or convex) functions is a global concept in the sense that the defining property is concerned with all the points of the domain. On the other hand, it is possible to consider a function that is locally concave (or convex), that is, a function that is concave (or convex) on certain subsets of the domain X. For example, the trigonometric function

$$f(x) = \sin x, \; x \in X = [0, \, 2\pi]$$

is a concave function on $[0, \, \pi]$, while it is a convex function on $[\pi, \, 2\pi]$.

Some useful properties of concave functions are summarized in theorem 1.8.

Theorem 1.8.

(i) Let $f\colon X \to R$ be a concave function, where X is a convex set in R^n. Then the set L defined by

$$L \equiv \{x : x \in X, \; f(x) \geqq \alpha\},$$

is convex for any $\alpha \in R$.

(ii) Every nonnegative linear combination of concave functions is also concave. That is, if $f_i : X \to R, \; i = 1, 2, \ldots, k$, are concave and X is a convex set in R^n, then

$$f(x) \equiv \alpha_1 f_1(x) + \alpha_2 f_2(x) + \ldots + \alpha_k f_k(x),$$

$$\alpha_i \geqq 0, \; i = 1, 2, \ldots, k$$

is also a concave function on X.

(iii) The function $f\colon X \to R$, where X is convex in R^n, is concave if and only if, for every integer $k \geqq 1$,

$$f(\theta_1 x^1 + \theta_2 x^2 + \ldots + \theta_k x^k) \geqq \theta_1 f(x^1) + \ldots + \theta_k f(x^k),$$

for all $x^i \in X, \; \theta_i \in R, \; \theta_i \geqq 0, \; i = 1, 2, \ldots, k$, with $\theta_1 + \theta_2 + \ldots + \theta_k = 1$.

(iv) The function $f\colon X \to R$, where X is convex in R^n, is concave if and only if

$$\{(x, \, \alpha) : x \in X, \; \alpha \in R, \; f(x) \geqq \alpha\}$$

is convex in R^{n+1}.

(v) Every concave function is continuous in the *interior* of the domain of the function.

REMARK: The converse of statement (i) in the above theorem is not necessarily true. A weaker property than the concavity of f will ensure the convexity of the set. Such a property, called "quasi-concavity," will be discussed later. The set L in statement (i) is often called an **upper level set** or an **upper contour set**. This is illustrated in figure 1.8 by the shaded area, where it is assumed that $f(x)$ increases as any coordinate variable x_i increases (or $\partial f/\partial x_i > 0$). In the theory of consumer's choice, $f(x)$ is taken to be the utility function of a particular consumer, and the set L^*, defined by

$$L^* \equiv \{x : x \in X, \ f(x) = \alpha\},$$

is known as an **indifference curve (surface)** or a **level set**. In the theory of production, $f(x)$ is taken to be the production function of a particular product, and set L^* is known as a **production isoquant**, where α is usually taken as a positive real number.

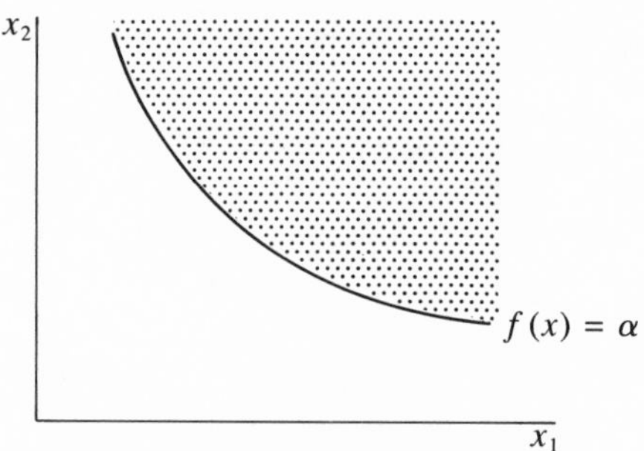

Figure 1.8: An upper contour set

REMARK: Often the domain X of a concave function f is taken to be the entire space R^n, in which case f is always continuous if it is concave (or convex) by statement (v) of theorem 1.8. On the other hand, if X

is a closed set, a concave function can be discontinuous at a boundary point. An example of such a function is, $f: X \to R$, $X = (0, \infty)$, defined by

$$f(x) = 1, \; x \neq 0, \; \text{and} \; f(0) = 0.$$

Theorem 1.9 provides a complete characterization of *differentiable* concave or strictly concave functions, and it is very useful in economic analysis.

Theorem 1.9. Let f be a differentiable real-valued function defined on an open convex set X in R^n. Then f is concave if and only if

$$f_x^\circ \cdot (x - x^\circ) \geqq f(x) - f(x^\circ), \quad \text{for all } x, \, x^\circ \text{ in } X, \tag{24}$$

where f_x° is the gradient vector of f evaluated at x°. Also, f is strictly concave if and only if the above inequality is strict: i.e., if and only if

$$f_x^\circ \cdot (x - x^\circ) > f(x) - f(x^\circ), \quad \text{for all } x, \, x^\circ \text{ in } X \text{ with } x \neq x^\circ.$$

REMARK: Theorem 1.9 is illustrated in figure 1.9. Since the function f is convex (or strictly convex), if and only if $-f$ is concave (or strictly concave), we obtain the complete characterization of differentiable convex or strictly convex functions by reversing the inequalities in theorem 1.9.

Example 1.8. Let $y = f(x)$ be a production function (which we assume to be differentiable), where x signifies a vector of n factor inputs and y signifies the output (of a single product). Suppose that $f(x)$ is concave, then by (24) of theorem 1.8, we have, for any two points x° and x^1,

$$f_x^\circ \cdot (x^1 - x^\circ) \geqq f(x^1) - f(x^\circ) \; \text{ and}$$

$$f_x^1 \cdot (x^\circ - x^1) \geqq f(x^\circ) - f(x^1).$$

Summing these two inequalities, we obtain

$$(f_x^\circ - f_x^1) \cdot (x^1 - x^\circ) \geqq 0, \quad \text{for all } x^\circ \text{ and } x^1.$$

Setting $x_j^1 = x_j^\circ$ for all j except for $j = i$, we then have

$$\left[\frac{\partial f(x^\circ)}{\partial x_i} - \frac{\partial f(x^1)}{\partial x_i} \right] (x_i^1 - x_i^\circ) \geqq 0, \quad \text{for all } x^\circ \text{ and } x^1.$$

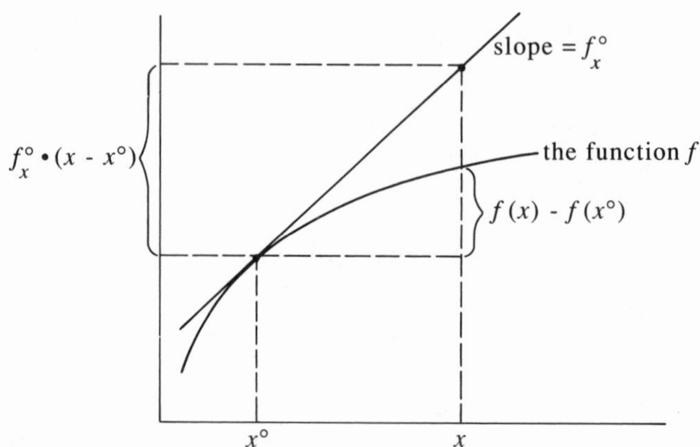

Figure 1.9: An illustration of theorem 1.9

Namely,

$$\partial f(x^1)/\partial x_i \leqq \partial f(x^\circ)/\partial x_i, \text{ if } x_i^1 > x_i^\circ.$$

Since the choice of i is arbitrary, this inequality holds for any $i = 1, 2, \ldots, n$. Hence we may conclude that if $f(x)$ is concave, then the marginal product of any factor $(\partial f/\partial x_i)$ is nonincreasing if the input of that factor is increased. The above discussion indicates that this fundamental law in economics is closely related to the concavity of the production function. A similar discussion can be cast in the context of the theory of consumer's choice by taking $f(x)$ to be the utility function of a consumer. For example, we may conclude that if the utility function is concave, then the marginal utility of any commodity $(\partial f/\partial x_i)$ is nonincreasing as the consumption of such a commodity increases.

Theorem 1.10 provides the important characterization of concave and strictly concave functions in terms of Hessians.

Theorem 1.10. Let f be a twice differentiable real-valued function defined on an open convex set X in R^n, and let $f''(x)$ be its Hessian matrix. Then:

(i) The function f is concave on X if and only if $f''(x)$ is negative semidefinite for all x in X,

(ii) The function f is strictly concave on X if $f''(x)$ is negative definite for all x in X,

(iii) The function f is convex in X if and only if $f''(x)$ is positive semidefinite for all x in X, and

(iv) The function f is strictly convex if $f''(x)$ is positive definite for all x in X.

REMARK: Obviously, statements (iii) and (iv) follow at once from statements (i) and (ii), respectively, since f is (strictly) convex if $-f$ is (strictly) concave.

REMARK: Concavity or convexity is a global concept. Hence, in each statement of theorem 1.10, the phrase "for all x in X" is needed. If $f(x)$ is concave or convex in a convex subset S of its domain X, set X in theorem 1.10 would be replaced by S.

REMARK: The converse of statement (ii) and the converse of statement (iv) do not necessarily hold. For example, $f(x) = -(x-1)^4$, $x \in R$, is strictly concave, but $f''(1) = 0$.

Now recall theorem 1.3, which characterizes the "definiteness" of a (square) matrix in terms of its principal minors. Let $f''(x) = [a_{ij}]$ and define the determinants D_k's and $\tilde{D}_k$'s as in (13) and (14). Then combining theorem 1.10 with theorem 1.3, we obtain theorem 1.11.

Theorem 1.11. Let $f(x)$ be a twice continuously differentiable real-valued function defined on an open convex set X in R^n. Then:

(i) The function f is concave if and only if

$$\tilde{D}_1 \leqq 0,\ \tilde{D}_2 \geqq 0,\ \ldots,\ (-1)^n \tilde{D}_n \geqq 0, \text{ for all } x \text{ in } X,$$

(ii) The function f is strictly concave if

$$D_1 < 0,\ D_2 > 0,\ \ldots,\ (-1)^n D_n > 0, \text{ for all } x \text{ in } X,$$

(iii) The function f is convex if and only if

$$\tilde{D}_1 \geqq 0,\ \tilde{D}_2 \geqq 0,\ \ldots,\ \tilde{D}_n \geqq 0, \text{ for all } x \text{ in } X, \text{ and}$$

(iv) The function f is strictly convex if

$$D_1 > 0,\ D_2 > 0,\ \ldots,\ D_n > 0, \quad \text{for all } x \text{ in } X.$$

REMARK: Again, the converse of statement (ii) and the converse of statement (iv) are not necessarily true.

Example 1.9. Let $y = f(x_1, x_2)$ be a concave function with $\partial^2 f/\partial x_1^2 < 0$ and $\partial^2 f/\partial x_2^2 < 0$ for all (x_1, x_2) (diminishing returns or diminishing marginal utility). If f is homogeneous of degree one, then it can be easily shown by using theorem 1.11 that f is concave (but not strictly concave). In particular, if f is of the "Cobb-Douglas form,"

$$f(x_1, x_2) = x_1^\alpha x_2^\beta, \quad 0 < \alpha,\ \beta < 1,$$

then f is concave when $\alpha + \beta = 1$. Also, it can be shown by theorem 1.11 that f is strictly concave if $\alpha + \beta < 1$.

1.5.5 Quasi-Concave Functions

It was stated in section 1.5.4, in connection with theorem 1.8, that although the concavity of the relevant function ensures the convexity of the level set, the converse does not necessarily hold. Indeed, a weaker concept is sufficient to ensure the convexity of the level set. We now define such a concept and closely related concepts.

Definition 1.16. Let f be a real-valued function defined over a convex set X in R^n. The function f is called **quasi-concave** if, for all x, x° in X,

$$f(x) \geqq f(x^\circ) \text{ implies}$$

$$f[\theta x + (1 - \theta)x^\circ] \geqq f(x^\circ),\ 0 \leqq \theta \leqq 1.^{21} \tag{25}$$

The function f is called **strictly quasi-concave**, if for all x, x° in X with $x \neq x^\circ$,

$$f(x) \geqq f(x^\circ) \text{ implies}$$

[21] We say that the function f is **quasi-convex** if $-f$ is quasi-concave, **explicitly quasi-convex** if $-f$ is explicitly quasi-concave, and **strictly quasi-convex**, if $-f$ is strictly quasi-convex.

$$f[\theta x + (1 - \theta)x^{\circ}] > f(x^{\circ}),\ 0 < \theta < 1. \tag{26}$$

The function f is called **explicitly quasi-concave** if it is quasi-concave *and* if, for all x, x° in X with $x \neq x^{\circ}$,

$$f(x) > f(x^{\circ}) \text{ implies}$$

$$f[\theta x + (1 - \theta)x^{\circ}] > f(x^{\circ}),\ 0 < \theta \leqq 1.\text{[22]} \tag{27}$$

It can be easily shown that the upper level set,

$$L \equiv \{x : x \in X,\ f(x) \geqq \alpha\},$$

is convex for each $\alpha \in R$ if and only if the function f is quasi-concave. It can also be shown that every concave function is quasi-concave, but the converse does not necessarily hold.[23]

Some quasi-concave functions that are not concave are the following:

(*a*) $f(x) = x^2$, where $X \equiv \{x : x \in R,\ x \geqq 0\}$,

(*b*) $f(x) = x_1^{\alpha} x_2^{\beta}$, where $\alpha,\ \beta > 0$, $\alpha + \beta > 1$, and $X \equiv \{x : x \in R^2,\ x_1,\ x_2 \geqq 0\}$.

---

[22] The two properties required to define explicit quasi-concavity, namely, quasi-concavity and (27), are independent. For example, consider $f(x)$, $x \in R$, defined by

$$f(x) = -1 \text{ if } x = 0, \text{ and } f(x) = 0 \text{ if } x \neq 0.$$

Then f is not quasi-concave, but it satisfies (27). However, in economics it is often assumed that f is continuous. In this case (27) implies the quasi-concavity of f, so that quasi-concavity becomes a superfluous additional requirement for explicit quasi-concavity.

[23] As we pointed out in statement (ii) of theorem 1.8, every nonnegative linear combination of concave functions is concave. Unfortunately, a similar statement does not hold for quasi-concave functions. A nonnegative linear combination of quasi-concave functions may not be quasi-concave. For example, consider a competitive firm that produces a single output by using the production function $f(x)$, where x is an n-dimensional vector. Let p and w, respectively, denote the price of the output and the factor price vector, both of which are given to the firm. Then the profit function $\pi(x)$ may be defined as

$$\pi(x) = pf(x) - w \cdot x\,[= pf(x) + (-w \cdot x)].$$

If $f(x)$ is concave, then $\pi(x)$ is also concave. However, if $f(x)$ is quasi-concave, $\pi(x)$ may not be quasi-concave.

In fact, it can be shown that any monotone increasing (or decreasing) function is strictly quasi-concave if $X \subset R$. Also, from definition 1.16, it is clear that every explicitly quasi-concave function is quasi-concave, and that every strictly quasi-concave function is explicitly quasi-concave. Furthermore, it can be shown that every concave function is explicitly quasi-concave, and that every strictly concave function is strictly quasi-concave. The relations among the various concepts of concavity and quasi-concavity may be schematically summarized in fig. 1.10, where the arrow ($\Rightarrow$) reads "implies." The converse statement of the direction of the arrow need not hold.[24]

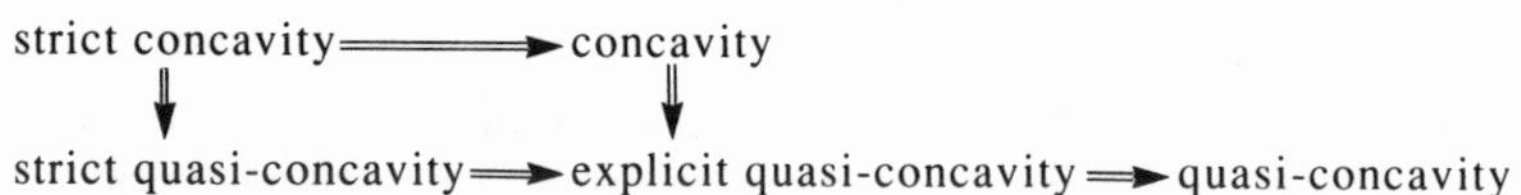

Figure 1.10: Relations among concavity and quasi-concavity

An interesting example in this context would be the *Cobb-Douglas function*, defined by

$$f(x) = x_1^{\alpha_1} x_2^{\alpha_2} \dots x_n^{\alpha_n},$$

$$0 < \alpha_i < 1, \quad i = 1, 2, \dots, n, \qquad \sum_{i=1}^{n} \alpha_i = 1.$$

This function can be shown to be strictly quasi-concave, and concave on $X \equiv \{x : x \in R^n, x > 0\}$, but *not* strictly concave. In definition 1.16, we defined three concepts of quasi-concavity. The distinction among these three concepts may best be illustrated in terms of a level set (an indifference curve),

$$L^* \equiv \{x : x \in X, f(x) = \alpha\}, \ \alpha \in R.$$

[24]All the logical relations in fig. 1.10 are more or less obvious from the definitions of various concepts. The only exception may be the one that states that every concave function is explicitly quasi-concave. To show this, we use the **arithmetic mean theorem**; i.e., min $\{a, b\} \leqq \theta a + (1 - \theta)b \leqq$ max $\{a, b\}$, where $a, b, \theta \in R$, $0 < \theta < 1$, and where the equalities hold if and only if $a = b$. Let $a = f(x)$ and $b = f(x^\circ)$, and apply the left inequality. Note that the converse of the statement does not necessarily hold.

Strict quasi-concavity means that indifference curves are strictly "bowed-in" toward the origin (see fig. 1.11*a*). Explicit (but not strict) quasi-concavity means that each indifference "curve" can contain a "flat" or linear segment (see fig. 1.11*b*), and quasi-concavity (but neither explicit nor strict quasi-concavity) means that each indifference "curve" can contain a thick region (see fig. 1.11*c*).

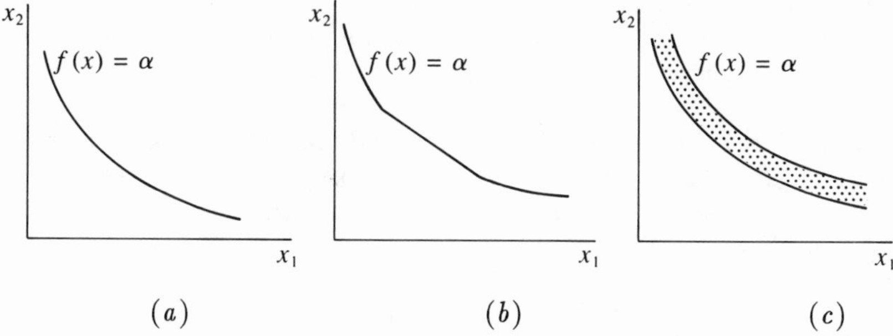

Figure 1.11: Indifference curves for three quasi-concave functions

The economic implication of the three kinds of quasi-concavity is not hard to understand. This may be illustrated in terms of the usual theory of consumer's choice in which a consumer chooses a consumption bundle $x \in R^n$ so as to

(UM) Maximize $u(x)$, subject to: $p \cdot x \leqq Y$ and $x \geqq 0$,

where $u(x)$ = utility function, Y = income, and p = the price vector, and where p and Y are given parameters to the consumer. The solution of this problem may be written as $x^* = x(p, Y)$. By adding the budget line $p \cdot x = Y$ into the three diagrams of figure 1.11, the reader should easily be able to see that if the utility function is quasi-concave or explicitly quasi-concave, then the demand function $x(p, Y)$ can be multivalued (i.e., there can be more than one, in fact, infinitely many x^* that solve this utility maximization problem). On the other hand, if $u(x)$ is strictly quasi-concave, the solution of the utility maximization problem is unique, and hence the demand function is single-valued. The strict quasi-concavity of the utility function means that the consumer prefers to consume a *variety* of commodities rather than to consume any one commodity: a convex combination (with positive weights) of any two indifferent commodity bundles is preferred to either one of those bundles. A thick indifference "curve" (or band) means that the consumer may not experience a change in the level of utility when the consumption of commodities increases "slightly." In this book, we shall not worry about the case of multivalued functions. Many results can be obtained in a simple and straightforward way without losing much economic insight if we assume that $f(x)$ is strictly quasi-concave, or that the solution of the relevant constrained maximization or minimization problem is single-valued.

Finally, we may note the characterization of quasi-concave functions in terms of derivatives.

Definition 1.17. Let f be a real-valued function defined on an open set X in R^n. Assume it is twice differentiable in X. Then the following matrix B is called the **bordered Hessian matrix of f** (the Hessian of f bordered by the f_i's):

$$B \equiv \begin{bmatrix} 0 & f_1 & f_2 & \cdots & f_n \\ f_1 & f_{11} & f_{12} & \cdots & f_{1n} \\ f_2 & f_{21} & f_{22} & \cdots & f_{2n} \\ \vdots & \vdots & \vdots & & \vdots \\ \vdots & \vdots & \vdots & & \vdots \\ f_n & f_{n1} & f_{n2} & \cdots & f_{nn} \end{bmatrix},$$

where $f_i \equiv \partial f/\partial x_i$ and $f_{ij} \equiv \partial^2 f/\partial x_i \partial x_j$, $i, j = 1, 2, \ldots, n$. Clearly, matrix B depends on the x at which these derivatives are evaluated. Let the $(k+1)^{\text{th}}$ successive principal minor of B, which we call the **k^{th} bordered Hessian determinant**, be denoted by B_k, where

$$B_k \equiv \begin{vmatrix} 0 & f_1 & f_2 & \cdots & f_k \\ f_1 & f_{11} & f_{12} & \cdots & f_{1k} \\ f_2 & f_{21} & f_{22} & \cdots & f_{2k} \\ \vdots & \vdots & \vdots & & \vdots \\ \vdots & \vdots & \vdots & & \vdots \\ f_k & f_{k1} & f_{k2} & \cdots & f_{kk} \end{vmatrix}, \quad k = 1, 2, \ldots, n.$$

Clearly, matrix B_k also depends on x. We conclude this chapter with the following theorem.

Theorem 1.12: Let $f(x)$ be a twice continuously differentiable real-valued function on R^n. Then the following holds:

(i) If $f(x)$ is quasi-concave in R^n, then

$$B_1 \leqq 0,\ B_2 \geqq 0,\ B_3 \leqq 0,\ \ldots (-1)^n B_n \geqq 0,$$

for all $x \geqq 0$ (where $B_1 \leqq 0$ holds trivially).

(ii) Conversely, if

$$B_1 < 0,\ B_2 > 0,\ B_3 < 0,\ \ldots,\ (-1)^n B_n > 0,$$

for all $x \in R^n$, then $f(x)$ is strictly quasi-concave in R^n.

REMARK: This theorem follows by redoing the proof of theorem 5 of Arrow and Enthoven (1961).

Exercises

Part A

(1) Let A_n, B_n and C_n be the intervals in R defined by

$$A_n = [0,\ 1/n],\ \ B_n \equiv (0,\ 1/n],\ \text{and}\ C_n \equiv (-1/n,\ n),$$

where n is a positive integer. Obtain

$$\bigcup_{n=1}^{\infty} A_n\,,\ \bigcap_{n=1}^{\infty} A_n\,,\ \bigcup_{n=1}^{\infty} B_n\,,\ \bigcap_{n=1}^{\infty} B_n\,,\ \bigcup_{n=1}^{\infty} C_n\,,\ \text{and}\ \bigcap_{n=1}^{\infty} C_n.$$

(2) Define the following items.

(a) inner product

(b) norm

(c) sequence, subsequence

(d) limit

(e) limit point
(f) interior point
(g) neighborhood
(h) closet set, open set
(i) continuous function
(j) compact set
(k) sequential compactness
(l) linear function, affine function
(m) gradient vector
(n) Landau's "o"
(o) Jacobian matrix
(p) concave function
(q) strictly quasi-concave function
(r) homogeneous function of degree m
(s) Hessian matrix
(t) negative semidefinite

(3) State the following theorems.

(a) Weierstrass' theorem on the existence of maximum and minimum
(b) composite function theorem
(c) implicit function theorem
(d) Euler's theorem on homogeneous functions

(4) Give an example for each:

(a) A subset S of R which does not contain its supremum.
(b) An infinite union of closed sets which is not a closed set.
(c) An infinite intersection of open sets which is not an open set.
(d) A continuous function which is not differentiable.
(e) A function which is neither concave or convex.
(f) A function which is concave *and* convex.

(g) A convex function which is not continuous.

(h) A quasi-concave function which is not concave.

(i) A strictly quasi-concave function on R^2, which is not strictly concave.

(j) A non-concave function whose upper contour set is convex.

(k) A matrix which is negative semidefinite but not negative definite.

Part B

(1) Set operations

(a) Let A and B be closed sets in R^n. Show that $A \cap B$ is also closed.

(b) Let A and B be convex sets in R^n. Show that $A \cap B$ is also convex. Also show that $A + B$ is convex.

(2) Let f: $R^n \to R^m$. It is known that f is continuous in R^n if and only if $f^{-1}(T)$ is closed for any closed subsets T of R^m. Using this, prove the following statements.

(a) Let $b \in R^m$, then $f^{-1}(b)$ is closed in R^n, if f is continuous.

(b) Let f: $R^n \to R$ be continuous. Then for any $\alpha \in R$

$$S \equiv \{x : x \in R^n, \ f(x) \geqq \alpha\}$$

is closed in R^n.

(3) Let S be a set in R^n. It is known that set S is compact *if and only if* every sequence in S has a convergent subsequence, and its limit is in S (this is known as **sequential compactness**). Now let $f: R^n \to R^m$ be a continuous function in R^n, and let S be a compact subset of R^n. Using the sequential compactness, prove that $f(S)$ is also compact.

(4) Show that the conclusion of the Weierstrass theorem (on the existence of maximum and minimum) need not hold if either the continuity or the compactness assumption is eliminated.

(5) Let $S \equiv \{x \in R^n : \sum_{i=1}^{n} x_i = 1,\ x_i \geqq 0,\ i = 1, 2, \ldots, n\}$ (called a **simplex**). Show that S is a closed set.

Hint: Let $f_0(x) \equiv \sum_{i=1}^{n} x_i$ and $f_i(x) \equiv x_i$, and use the fact that sets

$$S_0 \equiv \{x \in R^n : f_0(x) = 1\} \text{ and}$$

$$S_i \equiv \{x, \in R^n : f_i(x) \geqq 0\},\ i = 1, 2, \ldots, n,$$

are closed.

(6) Let f be a real-valued function defined on a convex subset X of R^n. Show that the following set S is convex if f is concave.

$$S \equiv \{x : x \in X,\ f(x) \geqq 0\}.$$

Hint: Let $x, y \in S$. We want to show $\theta x + (1 - \theta)y \in S$, $0 \leqq \theta \leqq 1$, i.e.,

$$f[\theta x + (1 - \theta)y] \geqq 0,\ 0 \leqq \theta \leqq 1.$$

Then use the concavity of f and the fact that $x, y \in S$.

REMARK: The converse of the statement of this question need not hold. Find an example.

(7) Let $f\colon X \to R$, where X is a convex subset of R^n. Show that f is quasi-concave if and only if $S \equiv \{x \in X : f(x) \geqq \alpha\}$ is convex for each $\alpha \in R$.

Hint: Only if: we wish to show that if $x, y \in S$, $\theta x + (1 - \theta)y \in S$. Without loss of generality, we may set $f(x) \geqq f(y)$. *If* we want to show that if $x, y \in X$ and $f(x) \geqq f(y)$, then $f[\theta x + (1 - \theta)y] \geqq f(y)$. Let $\alpha = f(y)$, then we are done.

(8) Given a fixed vector a^i in R^n and a scalar b_i, define $f_i(x)$ by

$$f_i(x) \equiv a^i \cdot x + b_i,\ i = 1, 2, \ldots, m,$$

where $a^i \cdot x \equiv \sum_{j=1}^{n} a_{ij}x_j$, $i = 1, 2, \ldots, m$. Define the set S by

$$S \equiv \{x \in R^n : f_i(x) \geqq 0, \ i = 1, 2, \ldots, m\}.$$

(a) Prove that S is a convex set.

(b) Let $m = 2$, $a^1 = (-1, -2)$, $b_1 = 1$, $a^2 = (-2, -1,)$, and $b_2 = 1$. Graphically illustrate the set S.

(9) Let $f : \Omega^2 \to R$ be defined by $f(x_1, x_2) \equiv x_1^{1/2}x_2^{1/2}$, where $\Omega^2 \equiv \{(x_1, x_2) \in R^2 : x_1, x_2 \geqq 0\}$. Show that $f(x_1, x_2)$ is a concave function using its definition.

Hint: We want to show that $f[\theta x_1 + (1 - \theta)x_2] \geqq \theta f(x_1) + (1 - \theta)f(x_2)$, $0 \leqq \theta \leqq 1$, for all $x_1, x_2 \in X$. Note then $f(x) = x_1^{1/2}x_2^{1/2}$, etc., and $x_1, x_2 \geqq 0$. How would you express $f[\theta x_1 + (1 - \theta)x_2]$?

(10) Let $f : \Omega^n \to R$, where $\Omega^n \equiv \{x : x \in R^n, x \geqq 0\}$. Prove that $f(x)$ can*not* be *strictly* concave if f is homogenous of degree one.

Hint: Strict concavity requires $f(x/2 + x'/2) > f(x)/2 + f(x')/2$ for all $x, x' \in \Omega^n$, with $x \neq x'$ (Why ?). Let $x' = 2x$ and note $x' \in \Omega^n$ if $x \in \Omega^n$. Then obtain a contradiction if f is homogenous of degree one.

REMARK: This result is important because of a frequent use of linear homogenous function in economics.

(11) Let $f(x, y) = x^\alpha y^\beta$, $(x, y) \in \Omega^2$ and $\alpha, \beta, > 0$, $\alpha + \beta < 1$, where Ω^2 is the nonnegative orthant of R^2. Prove that $f(x, y)$ is strictly concave.

(12) Let $f(x)$ be a real-valued function defined on a convex subset of X of R^n. Prove that f is concave if and only if $S \equiv \{(x, \alpha) : f(x) \geqq \alpha, x \in X, \alpha \in R\}$ is convex in R^{n+1}.

(13) Let $f(x)$ be a real-valued function defined in a convex subset X of R^n. Prove that f is concave if and only if for each integer $m \geqq 1$

$$f(\theta_1 x^1 + \theta_2 x^2 + \ldots + \theta_m x^m) \geqq \theta_1 f(x^1) + \ldots + \theta_m f(x^m),$$

for all $x^j \in X$, $\theta_j \in R$, $\theta_j \geqq 0$, $j = 1, \ldots, m$, with $\sum_{j=1}^{m} \theta_j = 1$.

Hint: Use (12).

(14) Let $f(x)$ be a concave function which is homogeneous of degree one defined on a convex subset X of R^n. Then for any $x^j \in X$, $j = 1, \ldots, m$, we have

$$f(x^1 + \ldots + x^m) \geqq f(x^1) + \ldots + f(x^m).$$

Hint: Use (13).

References

Apostol, T. 1957. *Mathematical Analysis*. Reading, Mass.: Addison-Wesley.

Arrow, K. J. and A. C. Enthoven. 1961. "Quasi-Concave Programming." *Econometrica* 19 (October): 779–800.

Bartle, R. G. 1987. *The Elements of Real Analysis*. 3d ed. New York: Wiley (1st ed. 1964, 2d ed. 1976).

Berge, C. 1963. *Topological Spaces*. Trans. E. M. Patterson. New York: Macmillan.

Gantmacher, F. R. 1959. *The Theory of Matrices*. 2 vols. Trans. by K. A. Hirsch. New York: Chelsea Publishing.

Hicks, J. R. 1946. *Value and Capital*. 2d ed. Oxford: Clarendon Press (1st ed. 1939).

Hobson, E. W. 1926. *The Theory of Functions of a Real Variable*. Vol. 2. 2d ed. Cambridge: Cambridge University Press.

Kelley, J. L. 1955. *General Topology*. New York: Van Nostrand.

Munkres, J. R. 1975. *Topology: A First Course*. Englewood Cliffs, N.J.: Prentice-Hall.

Rudin, W. 1976. *Principles of Mathematical Analysis*. 3d ed. New York: McGraw-Hill (1st ed. 1953, 2d ed. 1964).

Samuelson, P. A. 1947. *Foundations of Economic Analysis*. Cambridge, Mass.: Harvard University Press (enl. ed. 1983).

Stigler, G. 1941. *Production and Distribution Theories*. New York: Macmillan.

Takayama, A. 1972. *International Trade: An Approach to the Theory*. New York: Holt, Rinehart, and Winston.

———. 1985. *Mathematical Economics*. 2d ed. New York: Cambridge University Press (1st ed. 1974).

Wilansky, A. 1964. *Functional Analysis*. New York: Blaisdell.

Part 2

Nonlinear Programming and Microeconomics

CHAPTER 2

Nonlinear Programming[1]

2.1 Introduction

Let X be a subset of R^n, where we allow the possibility of $X = R^n$.Let f be a real-valued function defined on X, and consider the problem of choosing $x = (x_1, x_2, \ldots, x_n)$ so as to

Maximize $f(x)$, subject to $x \in S$, where S is a subset of X.

The set S can be equal to X.

We call $f(x)$ the **maximand function**, or the **objective function**. The set S is called the **constraint set** or the **feasible set**. The variables x_i, $i = 1, 2, \ldots, n$, are called the **decision variables** or the **choice variables**. The point x^* which solves the problem is called a **solution** or an **optimum point**. Namely, x^* is a "solution" of the problem, if $x^* \in S$, and

$$f(x^*) \geqq f(x), \quad \text{for all } x \in S.$$

Given a particular maximization problem, the solution may or may not exist. When the solution exists, it may be unique or may not be unique. The solution x^* is said to be **unique**, if $x^* \in S$, and

$$f(x^*) > f(x), \text{ for all } x \in S \text{ whenever } x \neq x^*.$$

For example, let $S = [-1, 1]$ be a closed interval in R, and let $f\colon R \to R$ be defined by $f(x) = -x^2$. The problem of choosing x to maximize $f(x) = -x^2$ subject to $x \in S$ yields the unique solution, $x^* = 0$.

---

[1] As would be natural, this chapter is heavily indebted to Takayama (1985, chap. 2). The reader is also referred to excellent discussions of the topic by mathematicians such as Mangasarian (1969), Luenberger (1973), and Hestenes (1975). Discussions by economists such as Intriligator (1981) and Dixit (1990) may also be useful.

On the other hand, suppose $f(x) = 3$ for all x in S. Then any point in S is a solution of the problem of maximizing $f(x) = 3$ subject to $x \in S$. Also, the solution is not unique in this case; in fact, there are infinitely many solutions. The solution also may not exist. For example, let $S = (0, 1)$ be an open interval in R, and consider the function $f : R \to R$ defined by $f(x) = x$. In this case, we cannot find x^* *in* S such that $f(x^*) \geqq f(x)$ for all x in S. Similarly, if $S = [0, \infty)$ and $f(x) = x$, the problem of maximizing $f(x) = x$ subject to $x \in S$ does not have a solution. These two examples (as illustrated in fig. 2.1*a* and 2.1*b*) suggest that the compactness of the choice set S (S being closed and bounded) will play an important role in establishing the existence of a solution. In these examples, the function $f(x) = x$ is a continuous function. When $f(x)$ is not continuous, then the solution may not exist, even if the choice set is compact. Consider this example. Let $S = [0, 1]$ (which is compact), and let $f : R \to R$ be defined by

$$f(x) = x \quad \text{for all } x \in R, \text{ except for } x = 1, \text{ and } f(1) = 1/2.$$

Then the problem of maximizing $f(x)$ subject to $x \in S$ does not yield a solution (cf. fig. 2.1c).

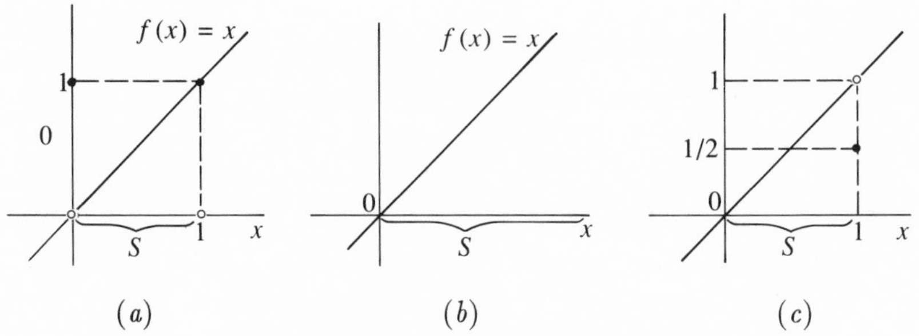

Figure 2.1: Nonexistence of a solution

This then leads to the question: Under what circumstances can we ensure the existence of a solution to a particular maximization problem? One obvious and yet powerful answer to this question is provided by the *Weierstrass theorem* (statement iii of theorem 1.2). Namely,

> If f is continuous and if S is compact, then there exists a solution x^* in S such that $f(x^*) \geqq f(x)$, for all x in S, where $f : X \to$

$$R, \; X \subset R^n, \text{ and } S \subset X.$$

Note that this provides only a set of *sufficient* (but not *necessary*) conditions for the existence of a solution. An example is the problem of maximizing $f(x) = -x^2$ subject to $x \in R$ that allows a unique solution, $x^* = 0$, although the choice set R is not compact. Needless to say, this does not imply that the compactness of S and the continuity of f are not important in ensuring the existence of a solution.

In the preceding discussion we formulated the problem in terms of maximization. Alternatively, consider the problem of choosing x so as to minimize $f(x)$ subject to $x \in S$. However, this minimization problem can easily be converted to the equivalent maximization problem of choosing x so as to maximize $-f(x)$ subject to $x \in S$. Therefore, without loss of generality, we may henceforth focus our attention on the maximization problem.

We now proceed with characterizing the nature of the choice set S. The most useful characterization of the choice set in economics would be the one in terms of specific functional relations. Letting $g_j : X \to R$, $j = 1, 2, \ldots, m$, be continuous, real-valued functions, we characterize the set S in terms of the following *inequalities*:

$$g_1(x) \geqq 0, \; g_2(x) \geqq 0, \; \ldots, \; g_m(x) \geqq 0,$$

in which case the choice set S may be defined as

$$S \equiv \{x \in X : g_j(x) \geqq 0, \; j = 1, 2, \ldots, m\},$$

which is called, as mentioned earlier, the *constraint set* or the *feasible set*. An element of S is called a **feasible point**. The functions g_j's are called the **constraint functions**. The functions f and g_j's are nonlinear in general, and the above problem is thus called **nonlinear programming** or that of **constrained maximization** (with inequality constraints). In economics, the variable x is often typically further constrained by

$$x_i \geqq 0, \; i = 1, 2, \ldots, n, \quad \text{or } x \geqq 0 \text{ in short},$$

which is called the **nonnegativity constraint**. We henceforth focus our attention on constraints in the form of

$$g_1(x) \geqq 0, \; g_2(x) \geqq 0, \; \ldots, \; g_m(x) \geqq 0, \; x \geqq 0,$$

where $g_j : X \to R$, $j = 1, 2, \ldots, m$, and $X \subset R^n$. (For a discussion of the case in which the nonnegativity constraint is absent, see Takayama

1985, chap. 1.) Then the constraint set S can now be defined as

$$S \equiv \{x \in X : \ g_j(x) \geqq 0, \ j = 1, 2, \ldots, m, \ x \geqq 0\}.$$

We consider the *nonlinear programming* problem (**NLP**) of choosing x so as to

(NLP) Maximize $f(x)$,
subject to $g_j(x) \geqq 0, \ j = 1, 2, \ldots, m$, and $x \geqq 0$,

where $f, \ g_j : \ X \to R, \ j = 1, 2, \ldots, m$, and where $X \subset R^n$.

Economics, by its very nature, is full of applications of such a constrained maximization or minimization problem. This is natural, since economics is traditionally concerned with the problem of "scarcity," in which the scarcity can be expressed in terms of some constraint functions g_j's.

Example 2.1.

(i) Consumer's Choice. Consider a consumer who chooses a commodity bundle of consumption $x \in R^n$ so as to maximize $u(x)$ subject to $p \cdot x \leqq Y$, and $x \geqq 0$, where $u(x)$, p, and Y are, respectively, his or her utility (indicator) function, price vector, and income, and where p and Y are given. In this case, the constraints can be written as $g(x) = Y - p \cdot x \geqq 0$, and $x \geqq 0$.

(ii) Cost Minimization. Consider a firm that chooses a combination of factor inputs $x \in R^n$ so as to minimize $w \cdot x$ (= maximize $-w \cdot x$) subject to $f(x) \geqq y$, and $x \geqq 0$, where w = factor price vector, y = target level of (a single) output, $f(x)$ = production function, and where w and y are given. The constraints can then be written as $g(x) \equiv f(x) - y \geqq 0$, and $x \geqq 0$.

(iii) Planning Model. Let a_{ij} be the amount of ith resource necessary to produce one unit of the jth commodity ($i = 1, 2, \ldots, m$, $j = 1, 2, \ldots, n$), and let r_i be the amount of the ith resource available in the country under consideration. Let p be the evaluation vector of a commodity bundle x by the planning agency, where p may be interpreted as a "price vector." Then we may consider the problem of choosing x so as to maximize $p \cdot x$ subject to $\sum_{j=1}^{n} a_{ij}x_j \leqq r_i, \ i = 1, 2, \ldots, m$, and $x \geqq 0$, where we assume that the a_{ij}'s, r_i's and p_j's are constants. Let a_i be an n-dimensional vector whose j^{th} component is a_{ij}. Then the constraints can be written as $g_i(x) \equiv r_i - a_i \cdot x \geqq 0$, $i = 1, 2, \ldots, m$, and $x \geqq 0$.

In the "planning problem," both the maximand function $p \cdot x$ and the constraint functions are linear. In general, if the maximand function $f(x)$ and the constraint functions, $g_j(x)$, $j = 1, 2, \ldots, m$, are all linear, such a constrained maximization problem is called the problem of **linear programming**. This is often abbreviated as **LP**. The term *nonlinear programming* may be somewhat misleading since it includes linear programming as a special case.

We now return to the general nonlinear programming problem defined by problem (NLP) above. A functional relation $g_j(x) = 0$, whether it is linear or nonlinear, may define a surface (or curve) on the x-space (or plane). It divides the space R^n into two regions, the regions where $g_j(x) \geqq 0$ and the region where $g_j(x) \leqq 0$. The surface $g_j(x) = 0$ serves as the common boundary of these two regions. For example, in figure 2.2, $g_j(x) = 1 - x_1 - 2x_2 = 0$ defines a straight line on the x-plane, and divides R^2 into two regions. In the region that contains the origin (the shaded region), we can easily show that $1 - x_1 - 2x_2 \geqq 0$, while in the other region we have $1 - x_1 - 2x_2 \leqq 0$.

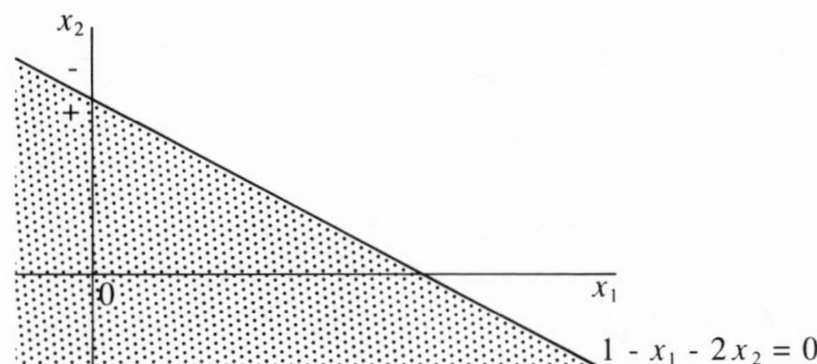

Figure 2.2: The division of the space

In figure 2.3, the shaded region satisfies the four functional relations, $g_1(x) \geqq 0$, $g_2(x) \geqq 0$, $g_3(x) \geqq 0$, and $x \geqq 0$ *simultaneously* on R^2, where it is assumed that the region satisfying $g_j(x) \geqq 0$, for all j, lies below the corresponding depicted $g_j(x) = 0$ locus. Note that the number of constraints, or m, can be greater than, less than, or equal to the number of decision variables, n (x_i, $i = 1, 2, \ldots, n$). Note also that it is possible that the constraint set,

$$S \equiv \{x \in X : g_j(x) \geqq 0, \ j = 1, 2, \ldots, m, \ x \geqq 0\},$$

is empty. An example is $g_1(x) = 1 - x_1 - 2x_2 \geqq 0$ and $g_2(x) = x_1 + 2x_2 - 3 \geqq 0$ do not allow for any (x_1, x_2) that satisfies these two relations *simultaneously* in R^2. In such cases, we say that these constraints are **inconsistent**.

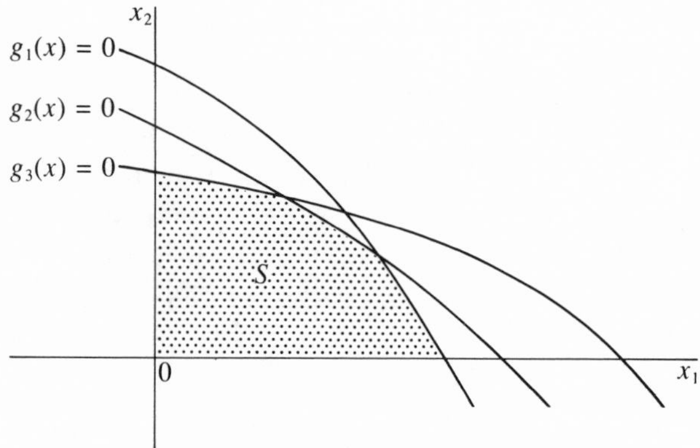

Figure 2.3: The constraint set

Define the sets S_j, $j = 1, 2, \ldots, m$, and Ω^n by

$$S_j \equiv \{x \in X : g_j(x) \geqq 0\}, \ \Omega^n \equiv \{x \geqq R^n : x \geqq 0\},$$

where Ω^n is called the **(n-dimensional) nonnegative orthant** from its obvious geometric interpretation. Then the constraint set S may be expressed as

$$S = S_1 \times S_2 \times \ldots \times S_m \times \Omega^n.$$

Since Ω^n is convex and since any intersection of convex sets is always convex, the constraint set S is convex if S_j is convex for each j. As mentioned in Chapter 1, S_j is convex if and only if g_j is quasi-concave and X is convex. From this we may conclude: A sufficient condition for the constraint set S to be convex is that $g_j(x)$ is quasi-concave for each $j = 1, 2, \ldots, m$, where X is convex. In particular, if the constraint functions g_j's are all concave, then the constraint set S is always convex, since every concave function is always quasi-concave. Note also that the quasi-concavity of the function g_j's is only a sufficient condition and not a necessary condition for the convexity of the set S. The convexity of the constraint set often plays an important role in economics, especially in establishing the global characterization of a solution of a given optimization problem.

Turning now to the objective function f, the locus of x such that $f(x) = \alpha$ defines a curve or a surface on R^n when α is a given scalar. Such a locus is a contour curve for the level α. As mentioned in chapter 1,

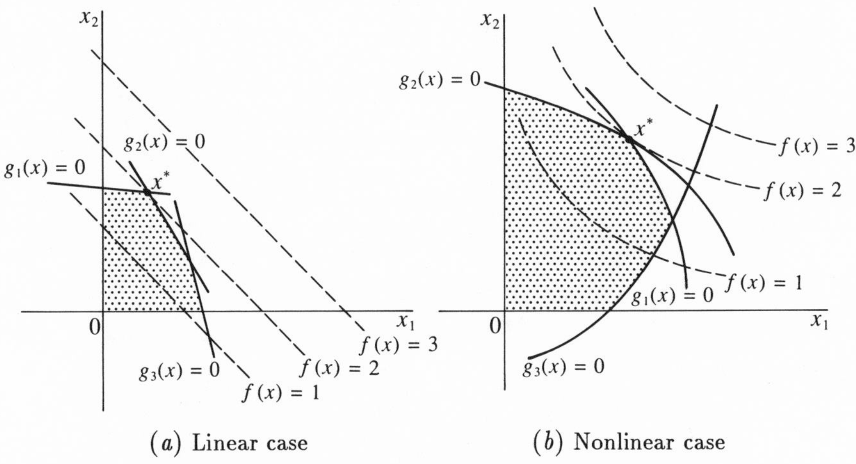

Figure 2.4: The optimum point

it is called a *level set* or an *indifference curve* (*surface*). When the value of α changes, we obtain a *family* of indifference curves. The problem is then to choose x which enables us to reach the indifference curve that represents the highest contour level (the highest value of f) subject to the constraint that x be in the set S. Two diagrams in figure 2.4 illustrate such problems, where figure 2.4*a* illustrates the case in which f and the g_j's are all linear, and figure 2.4*b* illustrates the case in which these functions are all nonlinear. The optimum point, denoted by x^*, is the solution of a given constrained maximization problem. Note that in both cases, the optimum point x^* is strictly inside the region of the constraints, $g_3(x) \geqq 0$ and $x \geqq 0$. We say that these constraints are **ineffective** at x^*, while the constraints $g_1(x) \geqq 0$ and $g_2(x) \geqq 0$ are **effective** at x^* in both cases shown in figure 2.4. In general, we say that the jth constraint $g_j(x) \geqq 0$ is **effective** at a point x^* if $g_j(x^*) = 0$, and **ineffective** at x^* if $g_j(x^*) > 0$. The nonnegativity constraint $x \geqq 0$ is said to be **ineffective** at x^* if $x_i^* > 0$, for all i.

The conventional formulation of consumer's choice mentioned in example 2.1.(i) illustrates the nonlinear programming problem described above. In this example, the constraint set is written as

$$B \equiv \{x \in R^n\colon\ p \cdot x \leqq Y,\ x \geqq 0\}.$$

Set B is known as the **budget set**. The consumer's problem is to maximize his or her utility function $u(x)$ subject to $x \in B$. This is illustrated in figure 2.5 for the two-dimensional case. Here the locus

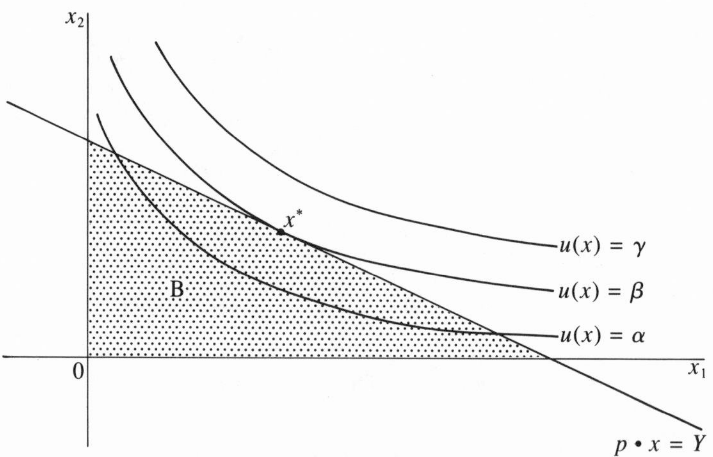

Figure 2.5: An illustration of consumer's choice

of x in which $u(x) =$ constant defines an indifference curve, and by changing values of such a constant (say from α to β, and to γ, etc.) we obtain a family of indifference curves. In figure 2.5, the optimum point is illustrated by x^*. Note that the budget set, represented by the shaded triangular area is closed and bounded, and hence compact. Then assuming $u(x)$ is continuous, the solution to this consumer's choice problem exists due to the Weierstrass theorem.

Returning to the general nonlinear programming problem (NLP) stated earlier, we may naturally ask the following questions, whereas the set $S \equiv \{x \in X : g_j(x) \geqq 0, j = 1, 2, \ldots, m, x \geqq 0\}$ signifies the constraint set.

Question 1 Is the set S nonempty? If not, the solution does not exist.

Question 2 Assuming S is nonempty, does a solution x^* exist? Namely, does there exist an x^* that maximizes $f(x)$ subject to $x \in S$?

Question 3 What are the characteristics of the solution x^*, if it exists?

Question 4 Is the solution x^*, if it exists, unique?

Question 5 What is the algorithm to find all the solutions?

One simple answer to question 2 is provided by the Weierstrass theorem. Namely, if the set S is compact and the function f is continuous, there exists a solution x^* for (NLP). In subsequent sections, we shall study question 3. In particular, we shall discuss the first-order and the saddle-point characterizations of the solution x^*. The differentiability of the functions f and g_j's are needed to obtain the first-order characterization.

In the case of linear programming, both the objective funtion f and the constraint functions g_j's are all linear. In this case, it would not be hard to see from figure 2.4a that for R^2 the solution must be either on the **vertex** in which the "constraint line" (i.e., the locus of x in which $g_j(x) = 0$ for some j) intersects another constraint line (or one of the axes), *or* any convex combination of two vertices. The latter possibility arises when the slope of the indifference curve is equal to the slope of the line connecting two vertices. From this it follows that we may find a solution for the linear programming problem by evaluating the value of $f(x)$ at each of these vertices and comparing the values thus obtained. Since there are only a finite number of constraints, there are only a finite number of vertices. Thus, we can, in principle, find a solution in a finite number of steps. This is the gist of the algorithm known as the **simplex method**, which seeks the solution by trying various vertices in an *efficient* way. (Why this method is so efficient has not been known until recently. See, for example, Smale 1983). The software for the simplex method is now widely available for computers. Given this, our attention can mostly be focused on the case in which the objective and/or the constraint functions are *not* linear. We may note that the discovery of this algorithm aroused a strong interest in linear programming and, at least in its earlier stage, provided a stimulus to the development of related mathematics such as the theory of linear inequalities (see, for example, Kuhn and Tucker 1956). This, together with other things, prompted the development of nonlinear programming, for example.

At this point, a comment on the *classical* theory of optimization is necessary. A marked feature of the classical theory, as opposed to the theory of nonlinear programming, is that the former is concerned with the case in which all the constraints are in the *equality form*,

$$g_1(x) = 0,\ g_2(x) = 0,\ \ldots,\ g_m(x) = 0,$$

and where the nonnegativity constraint ($x \geqq 0$) is ignored. In this case, the constraint set S^* may be defined by

$$S^* \equiv \{x \in R^n : g_j(x) = 0,\ j = 1, 2, \ldots, m\}.$$

If $m = n$, then S^*, except for uninteresting cases (such as $S^* = \emptyset$), consists of only one point (say, x^*), in which case the maximization problem becomes trivial. For example, if the g_j's are all linear, we may write the constraints in the form of

$$g(x) \equiv Ax + b = 0,$$

where $A = [a_{ij}]$ is an $n \times n$ matrix since $m = n$. Assuming A is nonsingular, the set S^* consists of one point, $x^* = -A^{-1}b$, and hence x^* becomes a unique solution of the problem regardless of the objective function f. On the other hand, if $m > n$, or if the number of constraints exceeds the number of decision variables, then these equality constraints need not be satisfied simultaneously at points x^*. Namely, they need not be *consistent*. Then, the constraint set is empty and the solution does not exist (see also fn 18). Hence in classical theory, it is assumed that $m < n$, that is, the number of constraints is less than the number of decision variables. This assumption is not necessary in the nonlinear programming formulation. Assuming $m < n$, classical theory obtains the well-known characterization of the optimum in terms of Lagrangians.

In the subsequent sections of this chapter, we shall first exposit the main results of nonlinear programming without going into their proofs. In particular, we shall exposit the characterization of the optimum by the first-order condition and also by the saddle-point condition for the case in which the constraints are stated in the form of *inequalities*. However, this does not mean that the classical optimization theory with equality constraints has lost its importance. We shall therefore briefly exposit it in section 2.4, although we shall also indicate some important advantages in economics of using the nonlinear programming approach with inequality constraints.

On the other hand, it may so happen that certain constraints may have to take the form of equalities (rather than inequalities) by the nature of a given problem, such as the case in which the constraints are definitional equations. To cope with this problem, it may be desirable to extend the discussion to the case in which *both* equality and inequality constraints are present (the case of **mixed constraints**). Namely, we may wish to consider the problem of choosing x so as to maximize $f(x)$ subject to $g_j(x) \geqq 0$, $j = 1, 2, \ldots, m$, $h_k(x) = 0$, $k = 1, 2, \ldots, l$. For simplicity, we omit such a consideration. The interested reader is referred to Mangasarian (1969, chap. 11).

Notational Convention on Vector Inequalities

We make the following notational convention regarding the relative size of two vectors:

(*a*) $x \geqq y$ to denote $x_i \geqq y_i$ for all i,

(*b*) $x > y$ to denote $x_i > y_i$ for all i,

(*c*) $x \geq y$ to denote $x_i \geqq y_i$ for all i, and $x_i > y_i$ for some i,

where x_i and y_i, respectively, signify the ith element of x and y. Needless to say, $x = y$ means $x_i = y_i$ for all i, and $x \geq y$ means $x \geqq y$ and $x \neq y$. Note that in our notation $x \geqq 0$ is consistent with the above convention, where we may recall that $x \geqq 0$ means $x_i \geqq 0$ for all i. Note also that in terms of this convention, the constraints, $g_j(x) \geqq 0$, $j = 1, 2, \ldots, m$, can more compactly be written as $g(x) \geqq 0$, where $g(x) \equiv [g_1(x), \ldots, g_m(x)]$.

2.2 Characterization of Optimum by First-Order Condition

In the above, we assumed that the functions f and the g_j's are defined on X, as a subset of R^n. To ease the exposition, we henceforth assume that $X = R^n$. Assume further that these functions f and the g_j's are continuously differentiable in R^n. The differentiability assumption is required because the "first-order condition" is concerned with the characterization of the optimum in terms of the first-order derivatives.

If $X \neq R^n$, but rather if X is a proper subset of R^n, then we need to assume that X is an open set. Given such functions defined on R^n, we consider the problem of choosing $x \in R^n$ so as to maximize $f(x)$ subject to $g_j(x) \geqq 0$, $j = 1, 2, \ldots, m$, and $x \geqq 0$. Hence the constraint set S can be written as

$$S \equiv \{x \in R^n : g_j(x) \geqq 0, \ j = 1, 2, \ldots, m, \ x \geqq 0\}.$$

Subsequent discussions can easily be extended, with proper qualification, to the case in which the domain of the functions f and the g_j's is a subset X of R^n, not necessarily Ω^n. The reader interested in such an extension is referred to Takayama (1985, chapter 1), for example.

First, we wish to distinguish two concepts of the solution for this maximization problem. One furnishes a maximum of $f(x)$ over the entire constraint set, and the other furnishes a maximum of $f(x)$ in a certain neighborhood of a point in the constraint set. The former is referred to as a (constrained) global maximum, and the latter as a (constrained) local maximum. More specifically, we define the following two conditions, where (**M**) and (**LM**), respectively, signify the (constrained) **global maximum** condition and the (constrained) **local maximum** condition:

(M) There exists an x^* in S such that $f(x^*) \geqq f(x)$ for all $x \in S$.

(LM) There exists an x^* in S and a neighborhood $N_r(x^*)$ such that $f(x^*) \geqq f(x)$ for all $x \in S \cap N_r(x^*)$.

Here the neighborhood, $N_r(x^*)$, about x^* with radius r in condition (LM) is defined as $N_r(x^*) \equiv \{x \in R^n : d(x, x^*) < r\}$, where $d(x, x^*)$ signifies the Euclidian distance between x and x^*. Note that in condition (LM), the radius r of the neighborhood $N_r(x^*)$ can be very small.

The concepts of (LM) and (M) are illustrated in figure 2.6. The points, x^1, x^2, x^3, and x^4 in figure 2.6*a* are the local maximum points, and x^3 is the global maximum point, where $S \equiv \{x \in R : x \geqq 0\}$. In figure 2.6*b*, any point of x in the interval between x^1 and x^2 furnishes a global maximum. Analogous to conditions (M) and (LM), we may define the (constrained) **global minimum** condition (**m**) and the (constrained) **local minimum** condition (**lm**), respectively, as

(m) There exists an x^* in S such that $f(x^*) \leqq f(x)$ for all $x \in S$.

(lm) There exists an x^* in S and a neighborhood $N_r(x^*)$ such that $f(x^*) \leqq f(x)$ for all $x \in S \cap N_r(x^*)$.

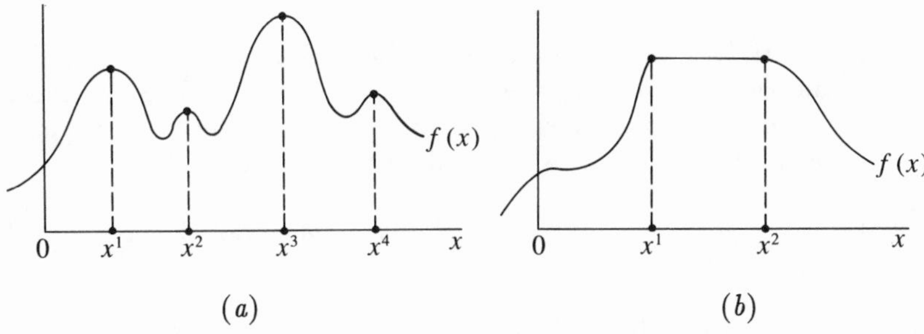

Figure 2.6: Local and global maximum points

Clearly, condition (M) implies condition (LM): that is, every global maximum point is a local maximum point. Needless to say, the converse does not necessarily hold. However, assuming that the constraint set S is convex and $f(x)$ is *properly* constrained, the converse statement (LM $\Rightarrow$ M) and other interesting results follow. The convexity of the constraint set S is ensured if the g_j's are all quasi-concave. One important result in this context is that every local maximum point is a global maximum point [i.e., (LM) $\Rightarrow$ (M)] if $f(x)$ is a *concave function* and S is a convex set.[2] If in addition, f is *strictly* concave, then the maximum point is *unique*, that is,

$$f(x^*) > f(x) \text{ for all } x \in S,$$

where S is convex, and $x \neq x^*$.[3]

The assumption of the concavity of f is often regarded as too restrictive. Theorem 2.1 indicates the extent to which this assumption can be relaxed.

---

[2]We prove this by contradiction. Suppose that x^* furnishes a local maximum but *not* a global maximum. Since x^* does not furnish a global maximum, there exists an $\bar{x}$ in S so that $f(\bar{x}) > f(x^*)$. By concavity, $f[\theta\bar{x} + (1-\theta)x^*] \geqq \theta f(\bar{x}) + (1-\theta)f(x^*)$, $0 \leqq \theta \leqq 1$. Since $f(\bar{x}) > f(x^*)$, this implies $f[\theta\bar{x} + (1-\theta)x^*] > f(x^*)$, $0 < \theta \leqq 1$. Let $\tilde{x} \equiv \theta\bar{x} + (1-\theta)x^*$, $0 < \theta \leqq 1$. Since x^* furnishes a local maximum by assumption $f(x^*) \geqq f(x)$ for all x in $S \cap B_r(x^*)$ for some radius r. Choose θ close enough to zero, so that $\tilde{x} \in S \cap B_r(x^*)$. Then we have $f(\tilde{x}) > f(x^*)$ and yet $\tilde{x} \in S \cap B_r(x^*)$, which is a contradiction.

[3]To show the uniqueness, suppose the contrary and assume $f(x^*) = f(\hat{x}) \geqq f(x)$ for all $x \in S$, where $\hat{x} \in S$ *and* $\hat{x} \neq x^*$. Let $\tilde{x} \equiv (x^* + \hat{x})/2$. Then $\tilde{x} \in S$, but $f(\tilde{x}) > f(x)$ by the strict concavity of f, which is a contradiction.

Theorem 2.1. Assume that the constraint set is convex.

(i) Every local maximum is also a global maximum; that is, (LM) implies (M), if $f(x)$ is explicitly quasi-concave.[4] Since every concave function is explicitly quasi-concave, the explicit quasi-concavity of f can be replaced by the concavity of f.

(ii) Every local maximum furnishes a *unique* global maximum if $f(x)$ is strictly quasi-concave.[5]

REMARK: It may be worthwhile to recall that strict quasi-concavity implies explicit quasi-concavity but not vice versa, and that concavity implies explicit quasi-concavity but not vice versa. Strict concavity implies both concavity and strict quasi-concavity, but not vice versa. Strict quasi-concavity means that the indifference curves (or surfaces) are strictly convex ("bowed-in") toward the origin, whereas explicit quasi-concavity allows flat portions of the indifference curves (but disallows "thick" indifference curves, recall figure 1.11 in chapter 1).

We may now proceed with the main discussion of this section. We discuss the characterization of the optimum in terms of the "first-order condition." To this end, the concept of the Lagrangian plays a key role. Define the real-valued function $\Phi(x, \lambda)$ by

$$\Phi(x, \lambda) \equiv f(x) + \sum_{j=1}^{m} \lambda_j g_j(x) \quad [\equiv f(x) + \lambda \cdot g(x)]. \tag{1}$$

The function $\Phi(x, \lambda)$ is called the **Lagrangian**, and the λ_j's are called **Lagrangian multipliers**. Since f and g_j's are assumed to be continuously differentiable, so is $\Phi(x, \lambda)$. The following characterization of an optimum point, (LM) or (M), by the Lagrangian is called the **first-order condition** (**FOC**), and it is a characterization of an optimum point in terms of the first-order derivatives of the Lagrangian.

---

[4] Again, we prove by contradiction. Suppose that x^* is a local maximum point in S that is not a global maximum. Then there exists an $\overline{x} \in S$ so that $f(\overline{x}) > f(x^*)$. Due to the explicit quasi-concavity of f, this means $f[\theta\overline{x} + (1 - \theta)x^*] > f(x^*)$ for all θ, such that $0 < \theta \leqq 1$. Choosing θ close enough to zero, we get a contradiction that x^* furnishes a local maximum of $f(x)$ in S.

[5] Since every strictly quasi-concave function is explicitly quasi-concave, x^* achieves a global maximum in S from statement (i) of theorem 2.1. To show the uniqueness, suppose the contrary: $f(x^*) = f(\hat{x}) \geqq f(x)$ for all $x \in S$, where $x^* \neq \hat{x}$. Letting $\tilde{x} \equiv (x^* + \hat{x})/2$, we have $f(\tilde{x}) > f(x^*)$ and $x \in S$, which is a contradiction.

(FOC) There exists an $(x^*, \lambda^*) \geqq 0$ with $\lambda^* \in R^m$ such that

$$\partial\Phi^*/\partial x_i \leqq 0, \ (\partial\Phi^*/\partial x_i)x_i^* = 0, \ i = 1, 2, \ldots, n, \tag{2a}$$

$$g_j(x^*) \geqq 0, \ \lambda_j^* g_j(x^*) = 0, \ j = 1, 2, \ldots, m. \tag{2b}$$

Here $\partial\Phi^*/\partial x_i$ is the partial derivative of Φ with respect to x_i evaluated at (x^*, λ^*). Namely,

$$\partial\Phi^*/\partial x_i = \partial f(x^*)/\partial x_i + \sum_{j=1}^{m} \lambda_j^* \partial g_j(x^*)/\partial x_i.$$

As can be seen below, (FOC) becomes necessary and sufficient for (LM) or (M) *under certain assumptions.* Without such conditions (FOC) is neither necessary nor sufficient for (LM) or (M).

Some readers may wonder why the inequalities occur in (2a), since such is not the case in classical theory in which (2a) is typically stated as

$$\partial\Phi(x^*, \lambda^*)/\partial x_i = 0, \ i = 1, 2, \ldots, n.$$

The reason why inequalities appear in (2a) is that we, in our maximization problem, allow the possibility of $x_i^* = 0$ for some or even all i (which is called a **corner solution**), whereas such a possibility is ruled out *a priori* in classical optimization. To illustrate our condition (2a), assume $g_j(x) \equiv 0$, $j = 1, 2, \ldots, m$, for simplicity, so that $\Phi(x) = f(x)$. Also assume that x is a scalar. Figure 2.7*a* through 2.7*c* illustrate the cases in which $(x^* > 0, f'(x^*) = 0)$, $(x^* = 0, f'(x^*) < 0)$, and $(x^* = 0, f'(x^*) = 0)$, respectively. Figure 2.7*a* corresponds to the case of classical optimization.

In some cases, it is possible that the maximand function f and the constraint functions g_j are such that we can ascertain $x_i^* > 0$ for all $i = 1, 2, \ldots, n$, from the nature of the problem. Then (FOC) can be simplified to the following familiar form (**FOC′**), which is equivalent to (2) under the assumption of $x_i^* > 0$ for all i (which is called an **interior solution**).

(FOC′) There exists an $(x^*, \lambda^*) \geqq 0$, $\lambda^* \in R^m$, $x^* > 0$, such that

$$\partial\Phi(x^*, \lambda^*)/\partial x_i = 0, \ i = 1, 2, \ldots, n, \tag{3a}$$

$$g_j(x^*) \geqq 0, \ \lambda_j^* g_j(x^*) = 0, \ \lambda_j^* \geqq 0, \ j = 1, \ldots, m. \tag{3b}$$

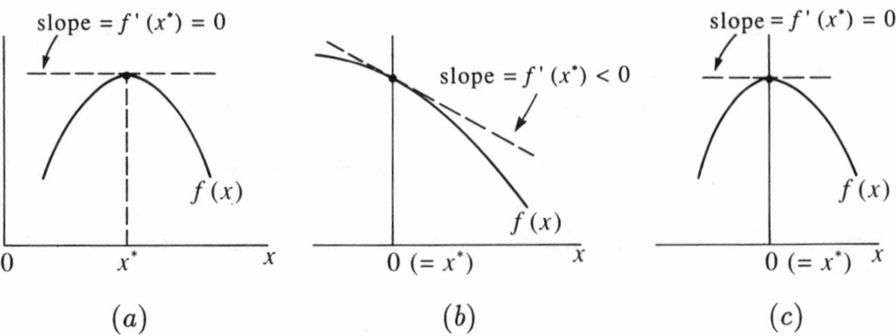

Figure 2.7: An illustration of (FOC)

Example 2.2. Consider the problem of choosing $(x_1, x_2) \in R^2$ so as to

$$\text{Maximize } f(x_1, x_2) = x_1^{\alpha} x_2^{1-\alpha}, \; 0 < \alpha < 1,$$

$$\text{subject to } p_1 x_1 + p_2 x_2 \leqq Y, \; x_1 \geqq 0, \; x_2 \geqq 0,$$

where p_1, p_2, and Y are positive constants. This problem can be interpreted as the usual problem of consumer's choice, where f, p_i, and Y, respectively, signify the consumer's utility function, the price of the ith commodity ($i = 1, 2$), and his or her nominal income. The Lagrangian of this problem is defined by

$$\Phi(x, \lambda) \equiv x_1^{\alpha} x_2^{1-\alpha} + \lambda(Y - p_1 x_1 - p_2 x_2).$$

Then we may compute

$$\partial\Phi/\partial x_1 = \alpha x_1^{\alpha-1} x_2^{1-\alpha} - \lambda p_1, \; \partial\Phi/\partial x_2 = (1 - \alpha) x_1^{\alpha} x_2^{-\alpha} - \lambda p_2.$$

Omitting the star (*) to denote the optimum for simplicity, (2) or (FOC) can be written as:

$$\alpha x_1^{\alpha-1} x_2^{1-\alpha} - \lambda p_1 \leqq 0, \; (1 - \alpha) x_1^{\alpha} x_2^{-\alpha} - \lambda p_2 \leqq 0, \tag{4a}$$

$$(\alpha x_1^{\alpha-1} x_2^{1-\alpha} - \lambda p_1) x_1 = 0, \; \{(1 - \alpha) x_1^{\alpha} x_2^{-\alpha} - \lambda p_2\} x_2 = 0, \tag{4b}$$

$$Y - p_1 x_1 - p_2 x_2 \geqq 0, \; \lambda(Y - p_1 x_1 - p_2 x_2) = 0, \tag{4c}$$

where $x_1 \geqq 0$, $x_2 \geqq 0$, and $\lambda \geqq 0$. Since we can show that $x_1 > 0$ and $x_2 > 0$ at the optimum (see fn. 7 below), (4a) and (4b) can equivalently be rewritten as

$$\alpha x_1^{\alpha-1} x_2^{1-\alpha} = \lambda p_1, \ (1 - \alpha) x_1^{\alpha} x_2^{-\alpha} = \lambda p_2, \tag{4'a}$$

which in turn implies $\lambda > 0$, so that (4c) can equivalently be rewritten as

$$p_1 x_1 + p_2 x_2 = Y. \tag{4'b}$$

Namely, (4) can be simplified to the equivalent and familiar form of (4′). From (4′), the optimum values of x_1, x_2, and λ can now be easily obtained.

One of the most important problems in the theory of constrained maximization is the relation between the optimality condition, (LM) or (M), and the (FOC) condition. As mentioned earlier, (*FOC*) is, in general, *neither necessary nor sufficient* for an optimum. For example, the usual contention that (FOC) is *necessary* for (LM) is false, in general. This can be seen in terms of example 2.3, which is known as **Slater's counterexample**.

Example 2.3. Consider the problem of choosing x to

$$\text{Maximize } f(x) = x, \quad \text{subject to } g(x) = -x^2 \geqq 0, \ x \geqq 0, \ x \in R.$$

Clearly, the constraint set consists of only one point 0, $S = \{0\}$. Hence $x^* = 0$ is trivially a unique solution of the problem; $x^* = 0$ satisfies condition (M). On the other hand, letting $\Phi(x, \lambda) \equiv f(x) + \lambda g(x) = x - \lambda x^2$, we have

$$\partial\Phi(x^*, \lambda^*)/\partial x = 1 - 2\lambda x^* = 1 > 0, \quad \text{for } x^* = 0.$$

Therefore, (FOC) is *not* satisfied at $x^* = 0$.

That (FOC) may not be a sufficient condition for (LM) is well known. We shall illustrate this in terms of the following two cases in example 2.4.

Example 2.4. Let $S \equiv \{x \in R : x \geqq 0\}$, and consider $f(x) = (x - 1)^3$. Clearly, $f(x)$ is also the Lagrangian ($f \equiv \Phi$) in this case, and

$$f'(x^*) = 3(x^* - 1)^2 = 0, \quad \text{if } x^* = 1.$$

Thus, (FOC) is satisfied at $x^* = 1$, and yet $x^* = 1$ furnishes neither (LM) nor (M). The point of $x^* = 1$ is known as an **inflection point**. Alternatively, consider $f(x) = (x - 1)^2$ for $S \equiv \{x \in R : x \geqq 0\}$. Again $f(x)$ is also the Lagrangian, and

$$f'(x^*) = 2(x^* - 1) = 0, \quad \text{if } x^* = 1.$$

Thus, (FOC) is satisfied at $x^* = 1$, and yet $x^* = 1$ furnishes neither (LM) nor (M). The point $x^* = 1$ instead furnishes the *minimum* value of $f(x)$ for all x in S.

Given that (FOC) is neither necessary nor sufficient for (LM), the natural question is: Under what circumstances can we ascertain that (FOC) is necessary for (LM), and that (FOC) is sufficient for (LM)? Theorem 2.2, which in essence states that (FOC) is necessary and sufficient for (M) (*global maximum*) under concavity, has powerful applications in economics.

Theorem 2.2. Let f, g_j, $j = 1, 2, \ldots, m$, all be concave functions defined on R^n. Then,[6]

(i) (FOC) implies condition (M);

(ii) (M) implies (FOC), provided that the following condition holds:

$$\text{There exists an } \bar{x} \geqq 0 \text{ such that } g_j(\bar{x}) > 0, \quad j = 1, 2, \ldots, m. \tag{5}$$

REMARK: Condition (5) is known as the **Slater condition**. From theorem 2.2, we can at once assert that (FOC) is *necessary and sufficient* for (M), provided that f, g_j, $j = 1, 2, \ldots, m$, are all concave *and*

[6]Statement (i) is not too difficult to prove. Since f and the g_j's are concave in x and since the λ_j's are nonnegative, $\Phi(x, \lambda)$ is concave in x. Hence, by theorem 1.9, we have: $\Phi(x, \lambda^*) - \Phi(x^*, \lambda^*) \leqq \Phi_x(x^*, \lambda^*) \cdot (x - x^*)$, where $\Phi_x(x^*, \lambda^*)$ is the gradient vector of Φ in x evaluated at (x^*, λ^*). Since $\Phi_x^* \cdot x^* = 0$ by (2a) of (FOC), this implies $\Phi(x, \lambda^*) - \Phi(x^*, \lambda^*) = \Phi_x^* \cdot x$, where $\Phi_x^* \cdot x \leqq 0$ for all $x \geqq 0$ by $\Phi_x^* \leqq 0$ in (2a). Using $\lambda^* \cdot g(x^*) = 0$ in (2b), $\Phi(x, \lambda^*) - \Phi(x^*, \lambda^*) \leqq 0$ for all $x \geqq 0$ implies $f(x^*) - f(x) \geqq \lambda^* \cdot g(x)$ for all $x \geqq 0$. From this, we may conclude $f(x^*) \geqq f(x)$ for all x with $x \geqq 0$ and $g(x) \geqq 0$, and this completes the proof. Statement (ii) is much harder to prove. For its proof, see Takayama (1985, pp. 70–73, and p. 91).

the Slater condition holds. Note that example 2.3 violates the Slater condition, although both f and g are concave. Example 2.3 thus illustrates the crucial importance of the Slater condition in statement (ii) of theorem 2.2.

REMARK: Recall example 2.2. In this problem, $f(x_1, x_2)$ is concave, and $g(x_1, x_2) = Y - p_1x_1 - p_2x_2$ is linear (and hence concave). Slater's condition is satisifed (trivially) as long as $Y > 0$, since $Y > 0$ allows an interior point in the budget set $\{(x_1, x_2) \geqq 0 : p_1x_1 + p_2x_2 \leqq Y\}$. Hence, condition (4) is *necessary and sufficient* for a global maximum. This in particular means that under concavity, a cumbersome discussion of the second-order condition in classical optimization theory can be dispensed with completely. Furthermore, (FOC) in classical theory provides only a characterization of a *local* maximum. In example 2.2, we can show $x_1 > 0$ and $x_2 > 0$ at the optimum, so that (4′) becomes necessary and sufficient for a global maximum.[7] From (4′), a routine computation (by using $x_1 > 0$, $x_2 > 0$, and $\lambda > 0$) yields:

$$x_1 = \alpha Y/p_1, \quad x_2 = (1 - \alpha)Y/p_2,$$

$$\lambda = \alpha^{\alpha}(1 - \alpha)^{1-\alpha} p_1^{-\alpha} p_2^{-(1-\alpha)}. \tag{4''}$$

In theorem 2.2, we asserted that the concavity of f and the g_j's and Slater's condition will ensure that (FOC) is necessary for (M). It turns out that the concavity of the maximand function f can completely be dispensed with to ensure that (FOC) is necessary for (LM), and hence for (M). It can be shown that some restrictions only on the *constraints* (known as **constraint qualifications**) would in general ensure that (FOC) is necessary for (LM). The following theorem (Arrow, Hurwicz, and Uzawa 1961), which we call the **Arrow-Hurwicz-Uzawa theorem** provides such a proposition. (See also Takayama 1985, pp. 102–7, for an exposition of the theorem and its proof.)

Theorem 2.3. (FOC) is necessary for (LM), provided that any one of the following conditions is satisfied.

---

[7]Recall $f(x) = x_1^{\alpha}x_2^{1-\alpha}$ in example 2.2. If $x_1 = 0$, then $f = 0$, while we can have $f(x) > 0$ by choosing $x_1 > 0$ and $x_2 > 0$ satisfying $p_1x_1 + p_2x_2 \leqq Y$. Hence f cannot reach a constrained maximum if $x_1 = 0$. Thus $x_1 > 0$ at the optimum. Similarly, $x_2 > 0$ at the optimum. In general, under the Cobb-Douglas form of utility function as in example 2.2, an interior solution is ensured. Also, note that $f(x) = x_1^{\alpha}x_2^{1-\alpha}$ is strictly quasi-concave as well as concave, so that by statement (ii) of theorem 2.1, the maximum point is unique.

(i) The functions $g_j(x)$, $j = 1, 2, \ldots, m$, are all convex functions.

(ii) The functions $g_j(x)$, $j = 1, 2, \ldots, m$, are all linear.

(iii) The functions $g_j(x)$, $j = 1, 2, \ldots, m$, are all concave functions and Slater's condition (5) holds.

(iv) The constraint set S is convex and possesses an interior point, and $g_j'(x^*) \neq 0$ for all $j \in E$, where E is the set of all the effective constraints at x^*.

(v) The rank of $[g_j'(x^*)]_{j \in E}$ equals the number of effective constraints at x^*, where it is assumed that $m < n$ (**rank condition**).

REMARK: We may call these conditions the **Arrow-Hurwicz-Uzawa** (or the **A-H-U**) **conditions**. Condition (ii) is obviously a special case of condition (i). In example 2.2, the constraint is linear, and hence by condition (ii), the previous discussion of Slater's condition can be dispensed with. Also, condition (ii) plays an obviously important role in linear programming.

In theorem 2.3, the rank condition (v) may require a further explanation. To illustrate this, let the constraints be given by

$$g_j(x) \geqq 0, \ j = 1, 2, \ldots, 11,$$

and let

$$g_j(x^*) = 0, \ j = 3, 7, 8, \ \text{and}$$

$$g_j(x^*) > 0 \ \text{for} \ j \neq 3, 7, 8,$$

so that $E = \{3, 7, 8\}$. Then

$$A \equiv \left[\frac{\partial g_j(x^*)}{\partial x_i}\right]_{j \in E} = \begin{bmatrix} \partial g_3^*/\partial x_1 & \ldots & \partial g_3^*/\partial x_n \\ \partial g_7^*/\partial x_1 & \ldots & \partial g_7^*/\partial x_n \\ \partial g_8^*/\partial x_1 & \ldots & \partial g_8^*/\partial x_n \end{bmatrix},$$

where $\partial g_j^*/\partial x_i$ signifies $\partial g_j/\partial x_i$ evaluated at x^*. The rank of the rectangular matrix is defined as the number of its linearly independent rows (which is equal to the number of linearly independent columns).[8] Since it is assumed that $m < n$, the rank condition states that matrix A has "full rank." In classical optimization theory, it is required that $g_j(x^*) = 0$ for all $j = 1, 2, \ldots, m$, where m is assumed to be less than n. In this case all the constraints are effective at x^*, and the rank condition requires that the rank of the Jacobian matrix $g'(x^*)$ is equal to m. That is, $g'(x^*)$ is also required to have full rank. Thus, the rank condition of theorem 2.3 corresponds precisely to the rank condition of classical optimization theory. Note also that in the classical maximization problem, it is presupposed that $m < n$: if $m > n$, then there is no way that the rank condition can be satisfied.[9]

Theorem 2.3 is concerned with conditions that ensure that (FOC) is necessary for (LM). We may then ask under what circumstances (FOC) is sufficient for an optimum. The following theorem, which is due to Arrow and Enthoven (1961), provides useful conditions in this context.

Theorem 2.4. Let f and g_j, $j = 1, 2, \ldots, m$, be quasi-concave functions. Then condition (FOC) is sufficient for condition (M) if any one of the following conditions is satisfied

(i) $\partial f(x^*)/\partial x_i < 0$, for at least one variable x_i.

(ii) $\partial f(x^*)/\partial x_i > 0$ for some "relevant variable" i, where x_i is said to be a **relevant variable** if there exists an $\overline{x}$ in $S \equiv \{x \in R^n\colon x \geqq 0, g_j(x) \geqq 0, j = 1, 2, \ldots, m\}$ such that $\overline{x}_i > 0$.

(iii) $f'(x^*) \neq 0$, and $f(x)$ is twice continuously differentiable in a neighborhood of x^*.

(iv) The function $f(x)$ is a concave function.

REMARK: The requirement that the functions g_j are all quasi-concave can be relaxed to the assumption that the constraint set $S \equiv \{x \in R^n : x \geqq 0, g_j(x) \geqq 0, j = 1, 2, \ldots, m\}$ is convex. Condition (iv) weakens statement (ii) of theorem 2.2 as the g_j's are only required to be quasi-concave rather than concave. The "relevant variable" in

[8]The number of linearly independent rows of any (possibly rectangular) matrix is equal to the number of its linearly independent columns. This is known as the *rank theorem* (see theorem A.3 in appendix A).

[9]The interested reader may also be referred to the proof of the classical optimization theorem that is sketched in footnote 18 below, where the nonsingular Jacobian matrix condition in the implicit function theorem plays a key role.

condition (ii) is a variable "which can take on a positive value without necessarily violating the constraint" (Arrow and Enthoven 1961, p. 783). In many economic applications, the variables are typically all relevant variables, so that condition (ii) is very useful in economics. If $f(x)$ is a utility function in the theory of consumer's choice, condition (ii) states that there exists at least one commodity with which the consumer is not satiated at least in a neighborhood of x^*. If $f(x)$ is a production function as in the theory of production, condition ii states that the marginal product of at least one factor is positive at x^*. We call theorem 2.4 the **Arrow-Enthoven theorem**. An extension of this theorem is obtained in appendix B.

We now illustrate some of the above discussions, especially those concerning theorems 2.3 and 2.4, in terms of the following example.

Example 2.5. We consider the problem of choosing $(x_1, x_2) \in R^2$ so as to maximize $f(x) = x_1 + x_2$ subject to $x_1^2 + x_2^2 \leqq 1$, $x_1 \geqq 0$, and $x_2 \geqq 0$. The solution of this problem can easily be obtained graphically as $x_1 = x_2 = 1/\sqrt{2}$ without invoking the mathematical discussions of (FOC), etc. (see fig. 2.8).

We shall now illustrate how such a solution can be obtained mathematically via (FOC). The purpose of doing this is only to illustrate the preceding discussion in terms of a simple example. The reader then should be able to analyze more complex problems whose solutions cannot be obtained readily from diagrams. Write the Lagrangian for the present problem as, $\Phi(x, \lambda) \equiv (x_1 + x_2) + \lambda(1 - x_1^2 - x_2^2)$. We omit the (*) to denote the optimum for simplicity, and write the (FOC) of the above problem as: there exist $x_1 \geqq 0$, $x_2 \geqq 0$, and $\lambda \geqq 0$ such that

$$\partial\Phi/\partial x_1 = 1 - 2\lambda x_1 \leqq 0,\ \partial\Phi/\partial x_2 = 1 - 2\lambda x_2 \leqq 0, \tag{6a}$$

$$(1 - 2\lambda x_1)x_1 = 0,\ (1 - 2\lambda x_2)x_2 = 0, \text{ and} \tag{6b}$$

$$1 - x_1^2 - x_2^2 \geqq 0,\ \lambda(1 - x_1^2 - x_2^2) = 0. \tag{6c}$$

Clearly, $f(x)$ is linear, and hence concave. It can also be shown that $g(x) \equiv 1 - x_1^2 - x_2^2$ is strictly concave.[10] Since both the maximand function and the constraint functions are concave, and hence quasi-concave,

[10] The Hessian matrix $g''(x)$ is easily computed as

$$g''(x) = \begin{bmatrix} -2 & 0 \\ 0 & -2 \end{bmatrix}.$$

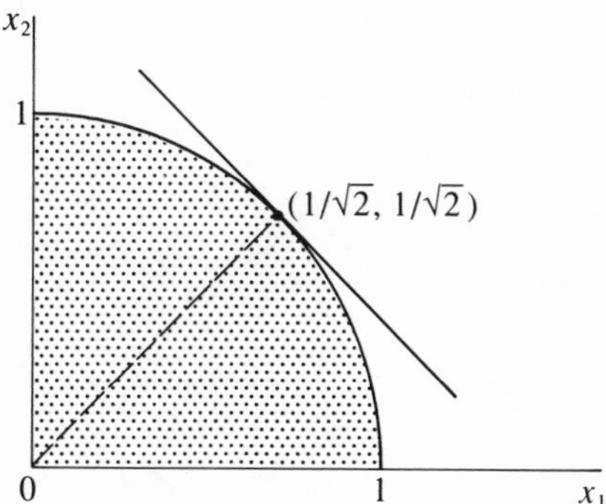

Figure 2.8: Illustration of example 2.5

we may utilize the Arrow-Enthoven theorem (theorem 2.4). Using condition (iv) of this theorem, we may at once conclude that (FOC) is a sufficient condititon of a global maximum (M). Noting that Slater's condition is satisfied in the present problem, we may conclude that (FOC) is necessary for a local maximum (LM) by the Arrow-Hurwicz-Uzawa theorem (theorem 2.3). Thus, we may conclude that (FOC), or condition (6), is *necessary and sufficient* for global maximum as (M) obviously implies (LM), where we may note

$$\text{(FOC)} \Rightarrow \text{(M)} \Rightarrow \text{(LM)} \Rightarrow \text{(FOC), so that (FOC)} \Leftrightarrow \text{(M)}.$$

Note that $x_1 = 0$ cannot furnish an optimum, since by condition (6a), $1 \leqq 2\lambda x_1$, and $x_1 = 0$ implies a contradiction. Similarly, $x_2 = 0$ cannot furnish an optimum. Therefore we must have $x_1 > 0$ and $x_2 > 0$ at the optimum. Then (6a) and (6b) are simplified as

$$1 = 2\lambda x_1 = 2\lambda x_2, \tag{6'a}$$

which in turn *implies* $\lambda > 0$, so that (6c) is simplified as

$$1 - x_1^2 - x_2^2 = 0. \tag{6'b}$$

Hence $x \cdot g''(x) \cdot x = -2x_1^2 - 2x_2^2 < 0$ for all $(x_1, x_2) \neq 0$, which shows the strict concavity of $g(x)$ (recall theorem 1.10 in chap. 1).

From (6′a) and (6′b), we may easily obtain

$$x_1 = x_2 = 1/\sqrt{2} \ (\text{also } \lambda = 1/\sqrt{2}\,), \tag{6''}$$

which furnishes the solution for the original problem.

In the remainder of this section, we consider two well-known problems in microtheory, the problem of consumer's choice and the problem of cost minimization. We use these two problems to illustrate our discussions concerning the relation between (M) and (FOC).

Consumer's Choice. As before, we consider a consumer who chooses a commodity bundle of consumption, $x \in R^n$, so as to maximize $u(x)$ subject to $p \cdot x \leqq Y$, and $x \geqq 0$, where $u(x)$, p, and Y are, respectively, his or her utility function, price vector, and income. The price vector p is assumed to be given to him or her, and Y is assumed to be a positive constant. The Lagrangian of this problem may be written as $\Phi(x, \lambda) \equiv u(x) + \lambda(Y - p \cdot x)$. Then letting $u_i \equiv \partial u/\partial x_i$, condition (2) or (FOC) for this problem can be written as

$$u_i(x^*) \leqq \lambda^* p_i,\ [u_i(x^*) - \lambda^* p_i]x_i^* = 0,\ i = 1, 2, \ldots, n, \tag{7a}$$

$$Y - p \cdot x^* \geqq 0,\ \lambda^*(Y - p \cdot x^*) = 0, \tag{7b}$$

where $x^* \geqq 0$ and $\lambda^* \geqq 0$. Since the constraint function $g(x) \equiv Y - p \cdot x$ is linear, (7) provides a set of *necessary* conditions for a local maximum due to theorem 2.3. Assuming that $u(x)$ is strictly quasi-concave, and that $u_i(x^*) > 0$ for some relevant variable i, (7) is also *sufficient* for a unique global maximum by statement (ii) of theorem 2.4 and by statement (ii) of theorem 2.1. Condition $u_i(x^*) > 0$ means that the consumer is not satiated, at least for one commodity, in a neighborhood of the optimum. And we may call it **local nonsatiation**. In short, under the strict quasi-concavity of u and local nonsatiation, (7) is *necessary and sufficient* for a unique global maximum. Note that a rather cumbersome discussion of the second-order condition via bordered Hessians in the traditional exposition is dispensed with completely in this discussion. It is replaced, in essence, by the strict quasi-concavity of u, which in turn facilitates an easier economic interpretation than bordered Hessians.[11] Furthermore, the quasi-concavity of u facilitates

[11] The strict quasi-concavity of the utility function means that the indifference curves are strictly "bowed-in" toward the origin. In other words, the consumer prefers to consume a *variety* of commodities rather than to consume any one commodity: a convex combination of any two "equally satisfying" commodity bundles (with positive weights) is preferred to those bundles. Also recall subsection 1.5.4 of chap. 1.

a *global* characterization of an optimum by way of (FOC), whereas in classical theory, the first- and the second-order conditions characterize the optimum only *locally*.

Since $u_i(x^*) > 0$ for some i, $u_i(x^*) \leqq \lambda^* p_i$ in (7a) implies that $\lambda^* > 0$ and p_i must be positive for such a commodity. With $\lambda^* > 0$, (7b) can be rewritten in the following equivalent form:

$$Y - p \cdot x^* = 0. \tag{7'b}$$

Namely, if the consumer is not satiated with at least one commodity at the optimum, λ^* must be positive and the consumer will spend all his or her income, as can be expected.

If in addition we assume that $x_i^* > 0$ for all i (an *interior solution*), then (7a) is simplified as

$$u_i(x^*) = \lambda^* p_i, \; i = 1, 2, \ldots, n. \tag{7'a}$$

From the $(n+1)$ equations in (7′a) and (7′b), the conventional procedure will determine the $(n + 1)$ variables, $x_i^* = x_i(p, Y)$, $i = 1, 2, \ldots, n$, and $\lambda^* = \lambda(p, Y)$, via the implicit function theorem. The functions $x_i(p, Y)$, $i = 1, \ldots, n$, are known as the (**Marshallian**) **demand functions**.

In the above case, we assumed that $x_i^* > 0$ for all i. In general this need not be the case. It is possible to have $x_i^* = 0$ for some i (a *corner solution*). For instance, such a case would be observed if a particular commodity is too expensive relative to a consumer's taste and income. If $x_i^* = 0$, then we have

$$u_i(x^*) \leqq \lambda^* p_i, \quad \text{for such an } i.$$

Since $u_i(x^*) < \lambda^* p_i$ is possible in this case, the price line may *not* be tangent to the indifference curve (or surface) at such a corner point x^*. This is illustrated in figure 2.9, where the dotted line signifies the tangent line at x^*, and its slope is different from that of the budget line.

In the traditional exposition of consumer's theory, (FOC) is stated in the form of (7′a). Not only does this imply that the consumer purchases every commodity *regardless of* his price income structure, but also it disallows the case of negative marginal utility. Namely, with (7′a) and the assumption that $p_i > 0$ for all i, it is not possible to have

$$u_i(x^*) < 0, \quad \text{for some } i.$$

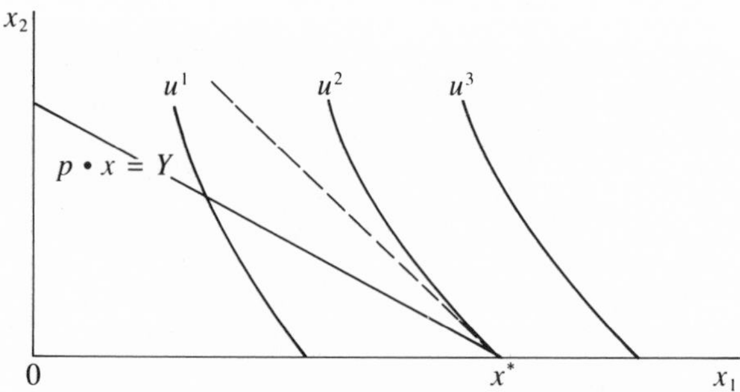

Figure 2.9: An illustration of a corner solution

On the other hand, this can readily be incorporated into analysis in the nonlinear programming formulation. It is perfectly consistent to have a positive price ($p_i > 0$), *and* $x_i^* = 0$: that is, if the consumer has a negative marginal utility (at least at the optimum) for a certain commodity whose price is positive, then he will simply not consume such a commodity. Meat products for vegetarians and alcoholic beverages for Mormons may be such an example; in fact, in this case we may have, for such an i,[12]

$$u_i(x) < 0, \quad \text{for } all\ x \text{ (not only at } x^*).$$

Also note that our formulation allows for negative prices for certain commodities. It is possible that the consumer has to pay a positive (negative) price to dispose of (or acquire) a certain commodity. Trash

[12]It is also possible that the marginal utility is positive until the consumption of a particular commodity becomes too "excessive." In this case, $u_i(x) > 0$ up to a certain level of consumption of the ith commodity. For example, consider the utility function (on the nonnegative orthant of R^2) defined by

$$u(x_1, x_2) \equiv x_1^{\alpha}(x_2 - ax_1)^{1-\alpha}, \text{ if } x_2 \geqq ax_1, \text{ and } u = 0 \text{ otherwise},$$

where $0 < a < 1$ and a is a positive constant. We may compute:

$$u_1(\equiv \partial u/\partial x_1) = x_1^{\alpha-1}(x_2 - ax_1)^{-\alpha}(\alpha x_2 - ax_1),$$

which is positive if $x_1/x_2 < \alpha/a$, but becomes negative for $x_1/x_2 > \alpha/a$. Such a possibility is closely related to the concept of "weak disposability," which is studied by R. Färe and others, especially in the context of production.

and rubbish may be examples of such commodities. If $p_i < 0$, then (7a) requires $u_i(x^*) < 0$ (since $\lambda^* > 0$), but it is still possible to have $x_i^* > 0$ for such an i (in which case $u_i(x^*) = \lambda^* p_i < 0$).

The theory of nonlinear programming as exposited above has some important features (as compared to classical optimization theory).[13] For example, we may consider the following features.

(1) The discussion of the necessity and sufficiency of (FOC) becomes much simpler and clearer, as it does not involve (often tedious) discussions in terms of bordered Hessians.

(2) (FOC) is obtained as a necessary and sufficient characterization for a global optimum, whereas in classical theory it is obtained only as a characterization of a local optimum.

(3) Unlike the classical theory, it is *not* necessary to assume that the constraint must always be effective (for example, in utility maximization the consumer need not spend all his or her income; that is, $p \cdot x < Y$ is allowed, while we can show that he or she will spend all his or her income $p \cdot x^* = Y$, if he or she is not satiated with at least one commodity at the optimum).

(4) A corner solution is allowed.

Next, we consider the familiar problem of cost minimization.

Cost Minimization. We consider a firm that chooses a combination of factor inputs, $x \in R^n$, so as to minimize $w \cdot x$ [= maximize $-(w \cdot x)$] subject to $f(x) \geqq y$, and $x \geqq 0$, where w = factor price vector, y = target level of output, $f(x)$ = production function, and where w and $y\,(> 0)$ are given. To ease the exposition, assume $w_i > 0$ for all i (the reader should easily be able to relax this assumption). The Lagrangian of this problem may be defined by $\phi(x, \lambda) \equiv -w \cdot x + \lambda[f(x) - y]$. Then, (FOC) for the present problem can be written as

$$-w_i + \lambda^* f_i(x^*) \leqq 0, \quad [-w_i + \lambda^* f_i(x^*)]x_i^* = 0, \quad \text{for all } i, \tag{8a}$$

$$f(x^*) - y \geqq 0, \ \lambda^*[f(x^*) - y] = 0, \tag{8b}$$

$x^* \geqq 0$, and $\lambda^* \geqq 0$, where $f_i \equiv \partial f / \partial x_i$. These conditions determine

[13] The reader should have some familiarity with the classical optimization theory through the works of Hicks (1946) and Samuelson (1947), or through textbooks on microtheory.

the factor demand functions $x_i^* = x_i(w, y)$, $i = 1, 2, \ldots, n$, as well as $\lambda^* = \lambda(w, y)$.

Assume that there exists an $\bar{x} \geqq 0$ such that $f(\bar{x}) > y$ (Slater's condition). If the production function f is concave, then by condition (iii) of theorem 2.3 (the Arrow-Hurwicz-Uzawa theorem), (8) is necessary for a local optimum and hence for a global optimum. Since $(-w \cdot x)$ is linear and hence concave, and since $\{f(x) - y\}$ is concave (and hence quasi-concave) under the concavity of f, (8) is also sufficient for a global optimum by condition (iv) of theorem 2.4 (the Arrow-Enthoven theorem). Thus (8) is *necessary and sufficient* for a global optimum if f is concave (and if Slater's condition is satisfied). On the other hand, the concavity of the production function may be too strong. So instead, we may consider the case in which f is required to be only quasi-concave. Note that the constraint set S for the present problem can be written as

$$S \equiv \{x \in R^n\colon\ x \geqq 0,\ f(x) \geqq y\}.$$

If f is quasi-concave, the set S is convex. Hence, again by condition (iv) of theorem 2.4, (8) is sufficient for a global optimum. Here we may again note that $(-w \cdot x)$ is linear and hence concave. To establish the necessity of (8) we may use condition (iv) of theorem 2.3.

Assume $x_i^* > 0$ for some i, that is, at least one factor is used for production. Condition (8a) then requires $\lambda^* f_i(x^*) = w_i$ so that $\lambda^* > 0$ as well as $f_i(x^*) > 0$. We assume $f_i(x^*) > 0$, that is, if the ith factor is used for production, its marginal product is positive. $\lambda^* > 0$ implies $f(x^*) = y$ by (8b). Note that we did not assume *a priori* $f(x) = y$ for all x. We obtained $f(x^*) = y$ *as a result of* the optimization and assuming $x_1^* > 0$ for some i. Note also that in (8a) it is perfectly possible to have $f_i(x^*) > 0$ and $\lambda^* f_i(x^*) < w_i$ for some i, in which case $x_i^* = 0$. If a certain factor is "too expensive" for the firm given its technology, such a factor will not be used at the optimum. Namely, a corner solution is perfectly possible.

If, in particular, we have $x_i^* > 0$ for all i (an interior solution), that is, if all factors are used by production at the optimum as in the conventional theory, then (8a) can equivalently be rewritten as $\lambda_i^* f_i(x^*) = w_i$, for all i. Hence recalling $f(x^*) = y$ for such a case, (8a) and (8b) can be written in the following familiar form:

$$\lambda^* f_i(x^*) = w_i,\ i = 1, 2, \ldots, n, \ \text{ and } f(x^*) = y. \tag{8'}$$

The $(n + 1)$ equations in (8′) determine the $(n + 1)$ variables, $x_i^* = x_i(w, y)$, $i = 1, \ldots, n$, and $\lambda^* = \lambda(w, y)$, in the usual way via the implicit function theorem.[14] The function $x_i(w, y)$ signifies the demand function for the ith factor.

2.3 Saddle-Point Characterization of Optimum

Let $X \subset R^n$ and $Y \subset R^m$, where we allow the possibility of $X = R^n$ and $Y = R^m$. The following concept plays a key role in this section.

Definition. Let $\Phi(x, y)$ be a real-valued function defined on $X \times Y$, where $x \in X$ and $y \in Y$. A point (x^*, y^*) in $X \times Y$ is called a **saddle-point** of $\Phi(x, y)$, if

$$\Phi(x, y^*) \leqq \Phi(x^*, y^*) \leqq \Phi(x^*, y), \quad \text{for all } x \in X \text{ and } y \in Y.$$

REMARK: A saddle-point may not exist, and when it exists, it need not be unique. Note that

$$\Phi(x^*, y^*) = \max_x \Phi(x, y^*), \quad \text{for all } x \in X, \text{ and}$$

$$\Phi(x^*, y^*) = \min_y \Phi(x^*, y), \quad \text{for all } y \in Y.$$

Namely, for a fixed value of y^*, x^* achieves the *maximum* of $\Phi(x, y^*)$; and for a fixed value of x^*, y^* achieves the *minimum* of $\Phi(x^*, y)$. Intuitively, the saddle-point may then be illustrated by a picture resembling a horse saddle (fig. 2.10).[15]

REMARK: On the other hand, it is not true that the saddle-point can always be illustrated by a saddle-like picture. Consider the following

---

[14] Needless to say, functions $\lambda(w, y)$ and $x_i(w, y)$ can also be obtained directly from (8) without going through (8′). Similarly, functions $\lambda(p, Y)$ and $x_i(p, Y)$ defined in terms of (7′) can also be defined in terms of (7).

[15] Consider, for example, $\Phi : R^2 \to R$, defined by

$$\Phi(x, y) \equiv y^2 - x^2.$$

Then the origin is a saddle-point, since

$$\Phi(x, 0) \leqq \Phi(0, 0) \leqq \Phi(0, y), \quad \text{for all } (x, y) \in R^2,$$

where $\Phi(0, 0) = 0$. The origin $(0, 0)$ may be illustrated by a horse saddle-like picture. Note also that $\Phi'(x, y) = (-2x, 2y)$, so that $\Phi'(0, 0) = (0, 0)$. Hence, this example also illustrates (in a rather spectacular way) that the satisfaction of (FOC) alone does not ensure the maximum: here it is *not* the case that $\Phi(0, 0) \geqq \Phi(x, y)$ for all $(x, y) \in R^2$. Fig. 2.10 is borrowed from Takayama (1985, p. 67).

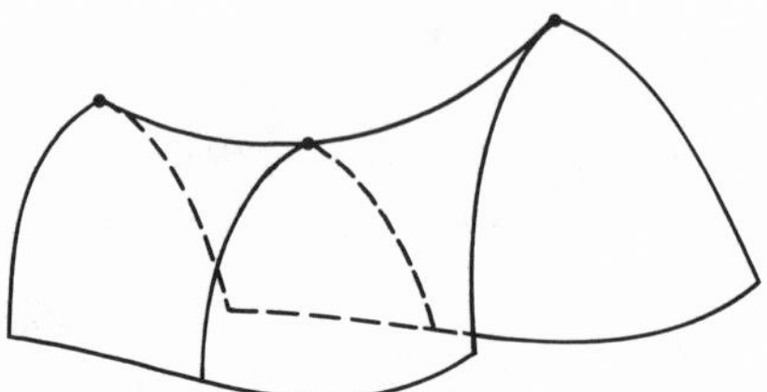

Figure 2.10: An illustration of a saddle-point

example (from Nikaido 1961, pp. 142–43):

$$\Phi(x,\ y) \equiv 1 - x + y,\ 0 \leqq x \leqq 1,\ 0 \leqq y \leqq 1.$$

Point (0, 0) is a saddle-point of $\Phi(x,\ y)$, but it cannot be illustrated by a saddle-like picture. The reader should easily be able to illustrate the saddle-point of this case.

The saddle-point provides a nice characterization of the optimum. Let f and g_j, $j = 1, 2, \ldots, m$, be real-valued functions, where we at this stage need *not* assume the differentiability of these functions. Consider the problem of choosing $x \in R^n$ to maximize $f(x)$ subject to $g_j(x) \geqq 0$, $j = 1, 2, \ldots, m$, and $x \geqq 0$. The constraint set of this problem is again denoted by S; that is, $S \equiv \{x \in R^n\colon\ g_j(x) \geqq 0,\ j = 1, 2, \ldots, m,\ x \geqq 0\}$. Define the Lagrangian by

$$\Phi(x,\ \lambda) \equiv f(x) + \lambda \cdot g(x),$$

where $\lambda = (\lambda_1, \ldots, \lambda_m) \geqq 0$. Let $\Omega^n \equiv \{x \in R^n : x \geqq 0\}$: i.e., Ω^n denotes the nonnegative orthant of R^n.

We distinguish between the following two conditions:

(M) There exists an x^* in R^n such that $f(x^*) \geqq f(x)$, for all $x \in S$.

(SP) There exists an $(x^*,\ \lambda^*)$ in $\Omega^n \times \Omega^m$ such that

$$\Phi(x,\ \lambda^*) \leqq \Phi(x^*,\ \lambda^*) \leqq \Phi(x^*,\ \lambda),$$

for all $x \in \Omega^n$ and $\lambda \in \Omega^m$, where $\Phi(x,\ \lambda) \equiv f(x) + \lambda \cdot g(x)$.

Condition (M) is the global maximum condition (under the constraints) used in the previous section. Condition (SP) is called the **saddle-point condition**. In terms of the above concepts, we have theorem 2.5.

Theorem 2.5. Suppose that condition (SP) holds. Then:

(i) Condition (M) holds, and

(ii) $\lambda^* \cdot g(x^*) = 0$.

REMARK: Note that theorem 2.5 requires no assumptions on the nature of the functions, f and g_j's (unlike previous theorems). Yet, the proof of the theorem is elementary. See, for example, Takayama (1985, p. 74).

The converse of the above theorem is not so easy to prove, and it probes rather deeply into the basic nature of a convex set. Theorem 2.6 is from Kuhn and Tucker (1951) and Uzawa (1958). See also Takayama (1985, pp. 70–73).

Theorem 2.6. Suppose that the functions f and the g_j's are all concave, and that Slater's condition is satisfied, that is,

(S) There exists an $\overline{x} \geqq 0$ such that $g_j(\overline{x}) > 0$, $j = 1, 2, \ldots, m$.

Then condition (M) implies condition (SP).

Combining theorems 2.5 and 2.6, we at once obtain theorem 2.7.

Theorem 2.7. Assume that f and g_j, $j = 1, 2, \ldots, m$, are all concave, and that Slater's condition (S) holds. Then condition (M) holds if and only if (SP) holds, in which case $\lambda^* \cdot g(x^*) = 0$.

In theorems 2.5, 2.6, and 2.7, we require no differentiability of the functions f and g_j's. Now assume that these functions are continuously differentiable. This in turn enables us to relate the saddle-point condition (SP) to some of the results obtained in the previous section. Noting that (SP) provides the global maximum condition for $\Phi(x, \lambda^*)$ with respect to x for an unconstrained maximization problem, except for the nonnegativity constraint $x \geqq 0$, we may easily obtain theorem 2.8. See, for example, Takayama (1985, pp. 91–92).

Theorem 2.8.

(i) Condition (SP) implies (FOC).

(ii) (FOC) implies condition (SP) if f and g_j, $j = 1, 2, \ldots, m$, are all concave.

REMARK: Since condition (SP) always implies (FOC) and since the converse does not necessarily hold (requiring additional conditions), (FOC) is often referred to as the **quasi–saddle–point condition (QSP)**. It is also known as the **Kuhn-Tucker-Lagrange condition.**

REMARK: The saddle-point characterization of optimum can be useful in a number of ways. An obvious advantage is that it does not require the differentiability of any functions. Takayama-El-Hodiri (1968, also Takayama 1985, pp. 285–94) applied it to obtain the characterization of a competitive equilibrium. In its application to comparative statics questions, we can allow discrete jumps in shift parameters, if we use the (SP) characterization. See Anderson-Takayama (1979).

At this juncture, it may be worthwhile to summarize some of the results obtained with respect to the characterization of a solution of a nonlinear programming problem. First, we remind ourselves of the problem and the various conditions. Our problem is to choose $x \in R^n$ to maximize $f(x)$ subject to $x \in S$, where $S \equiv \{x \in R^n : g_j(x) \geqq 0,\ j = 1, 2, \ldots, m,\ x \geqq 0\}$. Various conditions are listed below.

Condition (M) There exists an x^* in S such that $f(x^*) \geqq f(x)$ for all $x \in S$.

Condition (LM) There exists an x^* in S and a neighborhood $N_r(x^*)$ such that

$$f(x^*) \geqq f(x) \text{ for all } x \in S \cap N_r(x^*).$$

Condition (SP) There exists an $(x^*, \lambda^*) \geqq 0$ such that (x^*, λ^*) is a saddle-point of the Lagrangian, $\Phi(x, \lambda) \equiv f(x) + \lambda \cdot g(x)$.

Condition (FOC) There exists an $(x^*, \lambda^*) \geqq 0$ such that conditions (2a) and (2b) hold.

Condition (A-H-U) The constraint functions g_j satisfy any one of the following Arrow-Hurwicz-Uzawa conditions.

(i) The g_j's are all convex or linear.

(ii) The g_j's are all concave and satisfy the Slater condition:

(S) There exists $\overline{x} \geqq 0$ such that $g_j(\overline{x}) > 0$ for all j.

(iii) The rank condition is satisfied.

Condition (A-E) The functions f and the g_j's are all quasi-concave and any one of the four conditions of the Arrow-Enthoven theorem is satisfied. For example,

(i) $\partial f(x^*)/\partial x_i > 0$ for some relevant variable i,

(ii) The function $f(x)$ is concave.

Condition (Conc) The functions f and g_j, $j = 1, 2, \ldots, m$, are all concave.

Condition (Conv) Set S is convex, and the function f is explicitly quasi-concave or concave.

Note that condition (Conv) is always satisfied if condition (Conc) is satisfied. We are now ready to present a diagram that shows the logical connections among the above conditions (fig. 2.11). In figure 2.11, the arrow reads "implies" under the conditions stated with the arrow. If no conditions are stated, then no conditions are necessary to obtain the given implication. Whenever (FOC) appears, the differentiability of f and the g_j's are assumed.

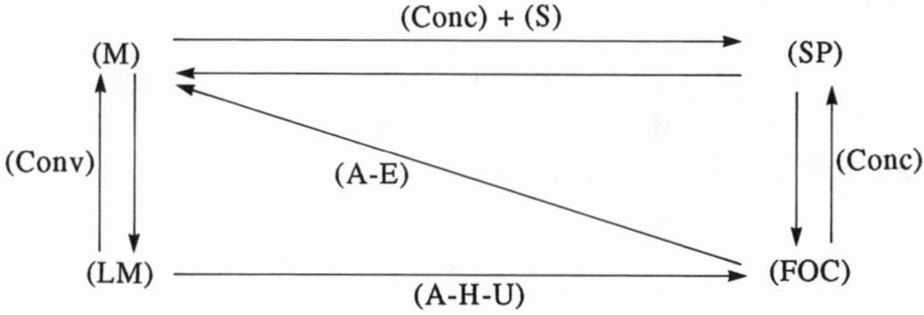

Figure 2.11: Characterization of x^*

In many practical applications of nonlinear programming theory to economics, either of the following conditions is satisfied.

(N1) The functions f and the g_j's are all concave and satisfy condition (S), or

(N2) The function f is concave and the g_j's are all linear.

In such a "nice" situation, we can easily see that figure 2.11 is considerably simplified to figure 2.12, in which (M), (LM), (FOC), and (SP) are all equivalent. In linear programming, condition (N2) is satisfied; hence all these conditions become equivalent. In summary, we obtain the following result.

Theorem 2.9. In general, we have the implications among various conditions as illustrated in figure 2.11 to characterize x^*, a solution of the nonlinear programming problem. In addition, if either condition (N1) or (N2) is satisfied, then (M), (LM), (FOC), and (SP), are all equivalent as illustrated in figure 2.12. Linear programming provides a special case of such a "nice" situation.

$$(M) \rightleftarrows (LM) \rightleftarrows (FOC) \rightleftarrows (SP)$$

Figure 2.12: Characterization of x for a "nice" case

Linear Programming

Let p be a given vector in R^n and let r be a given vector in R^m, and let A be an $m \times n$ matrix. Then a typical *linear programming* problem may be stated as the problem of choosing $x \in R^n$ to

(M_{LP}) Maximize $p \cdot x$, subject to $Ax \leqq r$ and $x \geqq 0$.

The vector p is called the **evaluating vector**. As an example of linear programming, we may interpret symbols in problem (M_{LP}) as follows: p = price vector, x = output vector, r = resource vector, a_{ij} = the amount of the ith resource that is required to produce one unit of the jth commodity, where a_{ij} is the i–j element of matrix A.

The Lagrangian of the above maximization problem ($\mathrm{M_{LP}}$) may be defined as

$$\Phi(x,\ w) \equiv p \cdot x + w \cdot (r - Ax), \tag{9}$$

where $w \in R^m$ denotes the Lagrangian multiplier. Then by theorem 2.9, there exists a solution x^* of the maximization problem ($\mathrm{M_{LP}}$) if and only if there exists an $(x^*,\ w^*) \geqq 0$ such that $(x^*,\ w^*)$ is a saddle-point of $\Phi(x,\ w)$, that is,

$$\Phi(x,\ w^*) \leqq \Phi(x^*,\ w^*) \leqq \Phi(x^*,\ w),\ \forall\, x \geqq 0 \text{ and } w \geqq 0, \tag{10}$$

where $\forall$ reads "for all." Define the function Ψ by

$$\begin{aligned} \Psi(w,\ x) \equiv -\Phi(x,\ w) &= -p \cdot x - w \cdot (r - Ax) \\ &= -w \cdot r + x \cdot (A'w - p), \end{aligned} \tag{11}$$

where A' is the transpose of matrix A. Then from (10) we have

$$\Psi(w,\ x^*) \leqq \Psi(w^*,\ x^*) \leqq \Psi(w^*,\ x),\ \forall\, w \geqq 0 \text{ and } x \geqq 0. \tag{12}$$

Thus, there exists a solution of x^* of the problem ($\mathrm{M_{LP}}$) if and only if there exists a $(w^*,\ x^*) \geqq 0$ such that $(w^*,\ x^*)$ is a saddle-point of $\Psi(w,\ x)$.

Now consider the problem of choosing $w \in R^m$ to

$$(\mathrm{m_{LP}}) \quad \begin{aligned} &\text{Minimize } w \cdot r\,(= \text{Maximize } - w \cdot r), \\ &\text{subject to } A'w \geqq p, \text{ and } w \geqq 0, \end{aligned}$$

where p and r are given vectors. Here w is the decision variable and not the Lagrangian multiplier. Denote the Lagrangian multiplier of this minimization problem ($\mathrm{m_{LP}}$) by x. Then the Lagrangian can be written as

$$\Psi(w,\ x) \equiv -w \cdot r + x \cdot (A'w - p), \tag{11'}$$

which is formally the same as (11). By theorem 2.9, there exists a solution $w^* \geqq 0$ of the minimization problem $\mathrm{m_{LP}}$ if and only if there exists a $(w^*,\ x^*) \geqq 0$ such that $(w^*,\ x^*)$ is a saddle-point of $\Psi(w,\ x)$. Hence (12) holds. On the other hand, the existence of such a saddle-point $(w^*,\ x^*)$ for $\Psi(w,\ x)$ is necessary and sufficient for the existence of a solution x^* for the maximization problem ($\mathrm{M_{LP}}$). Thus we may conclude the following.

Theorem 2.10.

(i) There exists a solution x^* for the maximization problem (M_{LP}) if and only if there exists a solution w^* for the minimization problem (m_{LP}).

(ii) There exists a solution x^* for (M_{LP}) and a solution w^* for (m_{LP}) if and only if there exists a $(w^*,\ x^*) \geqq 0$ which is a saddle-point of $\Psi(w,\ x)$, or equivalently, there exists an $(x^*,\ w^*) \geqq 0$ which is a saddle-point of $\Phi(x,\ w)$, in which case we have

$$w^* \cdot (r - Ax^*) = x^* \cdot (A'w^* - p) = 0, \quad \text{and} \tag{13}$$

$$p \cdot x^* = w^* \cdot r. \tag{14}$$

REMARK: (13) holds by statement (ii) of theorem 2.5. Also, noting $\Phi(x^*,\ w^*) = -\Psi(w^*,\ x^*)$, where $p^* \cdot x^* + w^* \cdot (r - A \cdot x^*) = w^* \cdot r - x^* \cdot (A'w^* - p)$, we obtain (14) by using (13).

REMARK: The maximization problem (M_{LP}) is called the **dual problem** of the minimization problem (m_{LP}). Similarly, (m_{LP}) is called the dual problem of (M_{LP}).

In the two problems (M_{LP}) and (m_{LP}), which are dual for each other, one should note the following:

(i) the evaluating vector p in (M_{LP}) appears in the constraint of (m_{LP}), and the evaluating vector r in (m_{LP}) appears in the constraint of (M_{LP}),

(ii) the constraint matrices are each other's transposes, and

(iii) except for the nonnegativity condition, the inequality in the constraint is reversed.

REMARK: Statement (i) and (13) and (14) are at the heart of an important result in linear programming, which is called the **LP Duality theorem**. Statement (ii) is known as the **Goldman-Tucker theorem**. It was first obtained by Goldman and Tucker (1956) by using the LP duality theorem, and plays an important role in the development of linear and nonlinear programming. There are a variety of direct proofs of the LP duality theorem, which do not rely on the theory of nonlinear programming. For these, see any standard textbook on linear programming. Two proofs that are among the simplest and most interesting may be the one by Dantzig (1963, pp. 129–34) and the other by Nikaido (1970, pp. 120–30), where the former proves the theorem as an application of the LP simplex method. The preceding proof of theorem 2.10 was obtained by Takayama (1985, pp. 156–57).

2.4 Classical Optimization and Nonlinear Programming[16]

Classical optimization theory has become well known to economists since the works of Hicks (1939, 1946) and Samuelson (1947). It has been very heavily used in economics even after the development of nonlinear programming. Hence, it would be useful to provide a short summary of the results of classical optimization and compare these results with those in nonlinear programming. In our exposition we shall use some familiar problems in economics for illustration. We shall also point out some common mistakes made by economists.

2.4.1 Classical Optimization[17]

Let f and g_j, $j = 1, 2, \ldots, m$, be real-valued, twice continuously differentiable functions defined on R^n and consider the following classical maximization problem (**CM**), which chooses $x \in R^n$ to

(CM) Maximize $f(x)$, subject to $g_j(x) = 0, j = 1, 2, \ldots, m$.

As discussed in section 2.1, it is assumed that $m < n$, where the number of constraints is less than the number of choice variables. Also, all the constraints are stated in the form of *equalities* (rather than inequalities). The **local maximum condition** (**LM** *) is written as:

(LM *) There exists an x^* such that f achieves local maximum at x^* subject to the constraints.

---

[16]Section 2.4 is adapted from Takayama (1981).

[17]For an exposition of classical optimization theory, see, for example, Hestenes (1975, chap. 3) and Takayama (1985, chap. 1) and references cited there such as Bliss (1946) and Carathéodory (1967).

This condition is analogous to (LM*) conditions discussed in section 2.2.

The **first-order condition** (**FOC** *) is written as:

(FOC *)There exists an $x^* \in R^n$ and a $\lambda \in R^m$ such that

$$\Phi_x^* = 0; \text{ that is,}$$

$$\partial f(x^*)/\partial x_i + \sum_{j=1}^{m} \lambda_j^* \partial g_j(x^*)/\partial x_i = 0, \ i = 1, \ldots, n, \quad (15a)$$

$$g_j(x^*) = 0, \ j = 1, 2, \ldots, m, \quad (15b)$$

where $\Phi(x, \lambda) \equiv f(x, \lambda) + \lambda \cdot g(x)$ (the Lagrangian), and where Φ_x signifies the gradient vector of Φ evaluated at (x^*, λ^*).

The following result is fundamental in classical optimization.

Theorem 2.11 (Euler, Lagrange):[18] Let B be the Jacobian matrix

---

[18]The proof of this theorem is facilitated by the implicit function theorem and the composite function theorem (theorems 1.5 and 1.4). Since the proof is, in essence, elementary and since it will facilitate a better understanding of the nature of the classical theorem and of the use of theorems 1.5 and 1.4, it may be worthwhile to sketch the proof here. To this end, first partition an n-vector x into an $(n-m)$-vector y and an m-vector z, and assume that the Jacobian matrix of $g(x) \equiv g(y, z)$ with respect to z (which we denote by g_z) is nonsingular at $x^* = (y^*, z^*)$. Due to the rank condition (R), such a nonsingularity assumption is possible, where the variables x_i's can be renumbered if necessary. Then, by the implicit function theorem, there exists a unique continuously differentiable function $z(y)$ such that

$$z^* = z(y^*), \text{ and } g[y, z(y)] = 0 \text{ for all } y \in N(y^*),$$

where $N(y^*)$ is some neighborhood of y^*. Substituting $z(y)$ into $f(x)$, we may define the function h by

$$f(x) = f[y, z(y)] \equiv h(y).$$

By condition (LM*), $x^* = (y^*, z^*)$ furnishes a local maximum of f under the constraint $g(x) = 0$. Hence $h(y)$ achieves an (unconstrained) local maximum at y^*. Thus, we have

$$(*) \qquad h_y^* = f_y^* + f_z^* z_y^* = 0,$$

where the subscript denotes the variable with respect to which derivatives are taken, and where the asterisk (*) signifies that these derivatives are evaluated at $x^* = (y^*, z^*)$. Also, differentiation of $g[y, z(y)] = 0$ yields

$$g_y^* + g_z^* z_y^* = 0.$$

Substituting this into $(*)$, we obtain

$$f_y^* + \lambda^* g_y^* = 0, \text{ where } \lambda^* \equiv -f_z^*(g_z^*)^{-1},$$

of g evaluated at x^*,

$$B \equiv [\partial g_j(x^*)/\partial x_i] \quad (\equiv g_x^*),$$

where $m < n$, assume that the following **rank condition** (**R**) holds:

(R) Rank $B = m$.

Then (LM*) implies (FOC*).

Since B is an $m \times n$ matrix and since $m < n$, condition (R) states that the matrix B must have full rank. As is well known, theorem 2.11 has been utilized extensively in economics, and it is known to be very useful. In spite of this, there is a common mistake in applying the theorem to economics. Namely, it is often asserted that condition (LM*) automatically implies (FOC*) without the additional condition (R). As a result, there are many papers and textbooks in which condition (R) is *not* checked to infer (FOC*) from (LM*). This is rather unfortunate since condition (R) plays a key role in establishing theorem 2.11 (as shown in fn. 18).

Note that (15) is quite comparable to (2), (FOC), for *nonlinear programming*. However, it may be worthwhile to point out some differences.

(i) λ^* in (2) is restricted to $\lambda^* \geqq 0$, while λ^* in (15) can be positive, negative, or zero.

(ii) In (2), Φ_x^* is required to only be nonpositive, while in (15) we must have $\Phi_x^* = 0$. This difference stems from the nonnegativity constraint $x \geqq 0$ in nonlinear programming. On the other hand, if $x^* > 0$ (an interior solution) in nonlinear programming, then we also have $\Phi_x^* = 0$, as we discussed in (3).

(iii) In (2), some constraints are allowed to be ineffective at the optimum, that is, $g(x^*) \geqq 0$, while in (15), *all* constraints must

---

and where we may note λ^* is a $1 \times m$ vector since f_z is a $1 \times m$ vector and g_z^{-1} is an $m \times m$ matrix. Since we (trivially) have

$$f_z^* + \lambda^* g_z^* (= f_z^* - f_z^*) = 0,$$

we also obtain

$$f_x^* + \lambda^* g_x^* = 0, \text{ or } \Phi_x^* = 0,$$

where $\Phi \equiv f + \lambda \cdot g$. This completes the proof for the statement that (LM) and (R) imply (FOC). (Q.E.D.)

be effective at the optimum, $g(x^*) = 0$. In fact, in classical optimization it is required that $g(x) = 0$ for all x, that is, *all* the constraints must *always* be effective.

(iv) While it is possible to have $g_j(x^*) > 0$ for some j in nonlinear programming, we must have $g_j(x^*) = 0$ if $\lambda_j^* > 0$. Hence, if $\lambda^* > 0$ (i.e., $\lambda_j^* > 0$ for all j), then we must have $g_j(x^*) = 0$, for all j. Thus if $x^* > 0$ *and* $\lambda^* > 0$, then (FOC) for nonlinear programming looks identical to the one for classical optimization.

We now proceed to the second-order conditions. To this end, we define the $m \times n$ matrix A by

$$A = [\partial^2 \Phi(x^*, \lambda^*)/\partial x_i \partial x_j] \, (\equiv \Phi_{xx}^*).$$

A is the Hessian matrix of Φ in x evaluated (x^*, λ^*). The **second-order necessary condition** (**SONC**) and the **second-order sufficient condition** (**SOSC**) are, respectively, written as

(SONC) $\quad \xi' A \xi \leqq 0$, for all ξ such that $B\xi = 0$;

(SOSC) $\quad \xi' A \xi < 0$, for all $\xi \neq 0$ such that $B\xi = 0$,

where ξ' is the transpose of ξ (and ξ' is a row vector).[19]

We are now ready to state the second-order characterization of an optimum under classical theory.

Theorem 2.12.

(i) Conditions (LM*) and (R) imply (SONC).

(ii) (FOC*) and (SOSC) imply (LM*), in which the optimum point is unique.

---

[19] If the original optimization problem is stated as a minimization problem rather than a maximization problem, then (SONC) and (SOSC) should, respectively, be rewritten as

(SONC) $\quad \xi' A \xi \geqq 0$ for all ξ such that $B\xi = 0$;

(SOSC) $\quad \xi' A \xi > 0$ for all $\xi \neq 0$ such that $B\xi = 0$.

By statement (i), (SONC) as well as (FOC*) is *necessary* for (LM*) provided that (R) holds. Statement (ii) says that a *sufficient* condition for a unique local maximum is (SOSC) provided that (FOC*) holds.

A common confusion is the assertion that (SOSC) is *required* (or necessary) for (LM*), given condition (R).[20] This is a confusion between (SONC) and (SOSC), that is, between a necessary condition and a sufficient condition. A simple example that (SOSC) is *not* required for (LM*) would be obtained by simply using an example similar to example 2.4.

Example 2.4′. Consider the problem of choosing $x \in R$ to maximize $f(x) = -(x - 1)^4$. Clearly, $f(x)$ achieves its maximum at $x^* = 1$. Note that (FOC*), $f'(x^*) = 0$, is satisfied if and only if $x^* = 1$, where condition (R) is not needed since there are no constraints. (SONC) is $f''(x^*) \leqq 0$ and (SOSC) is $f''(x^*) < 0$. Clearly, $f''(x^*) = -12(x^* - 1)^2$, which is equal to 0 when $x^* = 1$, so that (SONC) is satisfied, *but*(SOSC) is violated.

Write the elements of A and B, respectively, by a_{ij} and b_{ij}, where $A \equiv [a_{ij}]$ and $B \equiv [b_{ij}]$. Define the $(m + k) \times (m + k)$ determinant $|C_k|$ by,

$$|C_k| \equiv \begin{vmatrix} 0 & 0 & \cdots & 0 & b_{11} & b_{12} & \cdots & b_{1k} \\ 0 & 0 & \cdots & 0 & b_{21} & b_{22} & \cdots & b_{2k} \\ \cdot & \cdot & & \cdot & \cdot & \cdot & & \cdot \\ \cdot & \cdot & & \cdot & \cdot & \cdot & & \cdot \\ 0 & 0 & \cdots & 0 & b_{m1} & b_{m2} & \cdots & b_{mk} \\ b_{11} & b_{21} & \cdots & b_{m1} & a_{11} & a_{12} & \cdots & a_{1k} \\ b_{12} & b_{22} & \cdots & b_{m2} & a_{21} & a_{22} & \cdots & a_{2k} \\ \cdot & \cdot & & \cdot & \cdot & \cdot & & \cdot \\ \cdot & \cdot & & \cdot & \cdot & \cdot & & \cdot \\ \cdot & \cdot & & \cdot & \cdot & \cdot & & \cdot \\ b_{1k} & b_{2k} & \cdots & b_{mk} & a_{k1} & a_{k2} & \cdots & a_{kk} \end{vmatrix} .$$

Let H^* be the $(m + n) \times (m + n)$ matrix definead by,

$$H \equiv \begin{bmatrix} 0 & b \\ b^T & A \end{bmatrix} = \begin{bmatrix} 0 & g_x^* \\ g_x^{*T} & \Phi_{xx}^* \end{bmatrix} .$$

[20]For example, Hicks (1946, p. 306) asserts, in the context of the consumer choice problem, "In order that u should be the maximum, it is *necessary* to have not only $du = 0 \ldots$ but also $d^2u < 0 \ldots$" (italics added).

where B^T and g_x^{*T} are, respectively, the transpose matrices of B and g_x^*. The matrix H is called the **bordered Hessian matrix** (the Hessian Φ_{xx}^* being bordered by g_x^*) for the given optimization problem. Note that the $|C_k|$'s are the successive principal minors of H. Now recalling a well-known result in linear algebra (cf. theorem A.10 in appendix A), we may rewrite condition (SOSC)[21] as

(BHC) $\quad (-1)^k|C_k| > 0, \; k = m + 1, \ldots, n,$

which is known as the **bordered Hessian condition (BHC)**.[22] By theorem 2.12, (BHC) provides a *sufficient* condition for a unique local maximum, provided that conditions (FOC*) and (R) hold.

An error similar to that of confusing (SOSC) with (SONC) also appears in the context of (BHC). Namely, it is often asserted that condition (LM*) *requires* (BHC), or that (BHC) is necessary for (LM), where (BHC) is often referred to simply as a "second-order condition." This is wrong. For a simple counterexample, recall example 2.4′. Since there are no constraints, $\Phi_{xx} = f''(x) = -12(x - 1)^2$, and (BHC) would simply be $f''(x^*) < 0$. However, $f''(x^*) = 0$ as $x^* = 1$; that is, (BHC) is violated, and yet $x^* = 1$ furnishes a unique global maximum of f. We may also note $H = f''(x^*)$.

---

[21] We assume that condition (R) holds. We may note that by statement (i) of theorem A.10 in appendix A we have the following. Let A be an $n \times n$ symmetric matrix and let B be an $m \times n$ matrix with $m < n$ and rank $B = m$. Then $\xi' A \xi < 0$ for all $\xi \neq 0$ such that $B\xi = 0$, if and only if

$$(-1)^k |C_k| > 0, \; k = m + 1, \ldots, n,$$

where $|C_k|$ is the $(m + k)^{\text{th}}$ successive principal minor or the matrix defined by

$$\begin{bmatrix} 0 & B \\ B^T & A \end{bmatrix}$$

where 0 is the $m \times m$ zero matrix.

[22] If the original optimization problem is stated as a minimization problem, the bordered Hessian condition should be rewritten as

(BHC) $\quad (-1)^m |C_k| > 0, \; k = m + 1, \ldots, n,$

where $|C_k|$ denotes the $(m + k)^{\text{th}}$ successive principal minor of H. The result is obtained through statement (ii) of theorem A.10.

2.4.2 Comparison to Nonlinear Programming

Classical optimization theory and its comparisons with nonlinear programming may best be illustrated in terms of some well-known examples. Here, using the problem of consumer's choice, we shall illustrate how the classical optimization theory is applied to economics and compare it with the nonlinear programming approach. We may recall that some comparisons were already made and summarized in section 2.2.

In the classical formulation, the consumer is to choose $x \in R^n$ so as to maximize $u(x)$ subject to $p \cdot x = Y$. The consumer is assumed a priori to spend all his or her income. Writing the Lagrangian as $\Phi(x, \lambda) = f(x) + \lambda(Y - p \cdot x)$, (FOC*) or (15) for this problem can also be written as

$$u_i(x^*) = \lambda^* p_i,\ i = 1, 2, \ldots, n, \quad \text{and } p \cdot x^* = Y, \tag{16}$$

where $u_i \equiv \partial u / \partial x_i$. If $p_i > 0$ for all i and $u_i(x^*) > 0$ for *some* i in (16), then we must have $u_i(x^*) > 0$ for *all* i as well as $\lambda^* > 0$. This disallows the possibility that the consumer has a negative marginal utility of certain commodity, ($u_i(x^*) < 0$), whose price is positive.

Also, as mentioned earlier, very little is said about corner solutions in the classical optimization condition. From (16), we cannot obtain much information about whether the consumer would or would not purchase certain commodities relative to the price-income structure. On the other hand, such information plays a key role in obtaining the condition similar to (16).

Since the constraint function may be written as $g(x) = Y - p \cdot x$, we have $g'(x) = -p$. Hence assuming $p_i > 0$, or $u_i(x^*) > 0$, for all i, the rank condition (R) is satisfied, where the rank of $g'(x)$ is equal to 1. Thus (FOC*), or (16), is the necessary condition for a local maximum by theorem 2.11. This classical rank condition corresponds to condition (v) of theorem 2.3 (the Arrow-Hurwicz-Uzawa theorem). However, in the nonlinear programming formulation, a simple observation of the linearity of the constraint function suffices to conclude that (FOC) is necessary for LM without invoking the rank condition.

Recalling the expression for the Lagrangian for this problem, we may at once observe $\Phi_{xx} = u''(x)$, the Hessian of u. Then recalling $g'(x) = -p$, we may define the bordered Hessian as

$$H = \begin{bmatrix} 0 & -p \\ -p^T & u''(x^*) \end{bmatrix},$$

where p^T is the transpose of p. Thus, (BHC) can be written as

$$\begin{vmatrix} 0 & -p_1 \\ -p_1 & u^*_{11} \end{vmatrix} < 0, \begin{vmatrix} 0 & -p_1 & -p_2 \\ -p_1 & u^*_{11} & u^*_{12} \\ -p_2 & u^*_{21} & u^*_{22} \end{vmatrix} > 0 \ldots, \tag{17}$$

where $u^*_{ij} \equiv \partial^2 u(x^*)/\partial x_i \partial x_j$, $i, j = 1, 2, \ldots, n$. This can equivalently be written as

$$\begin{vmatrix} 0 & p_1 \\ p_1 & u^*_{11} \end{vmatrix} < 0, \begin{vmatrix} 0 & p_1 & p_2 \\ p_1 & u^*_{11} & u^*_{12} \\ p_2 & u^*_{21} & u^*_{22} \end{vmatrix} > 0 \ldots. \tag{17'}$$

Given (17′), (FOC*) or (16) is sufficient for a unique local maximum. Note that with (16), (17′) can also be written as

$$\begin{vmatrix} 0 & u^*_1 \\ u^*_1 & u^*_{11} \end{vmatrix} < 0, \begin{vmatrix} 0 & u^*_1 & u^*_2 \\ u^*_1 & u^*_{11} & u^*_{12} \\ u^*_2 & u^*_{21} & u^*_{22} \end{vmatrix} > 0 \ldots. \tag{18}$$

In nonlinear programming, (FOC) under the quasi-concavity of $u(x)$ is sufficient for a *global* maximum. Furthermore, (FOC) ensures a *unique* global maximum if $u(x)$ is *strictly* quasi-concave. As mentioned earlier, the economic interpretation of (strict) quasi-concavity is transparent (cf. fn. 9), whereas that of (BHC) is quite hard.

On the other hand, from (ii) of theorem 1.11 in chapter 1, we may also conclude that if

$$\begin{vmatrix} 0 & u_1(x) \\ u_1(x) & u_{11}(x) \end{vmatrix} < 0, \begin{vmatrix} 0 & u_1(x) & u_2(x) \\ u_1(x) & u_{11}(x) & u_{12}(x) \\ u_2(x) & u_{21}(x) & u_{22}(x) \end{vmatrix} > 0 \ldots, \tag{19}$$

for *all* x, then $u(x)$ is strictly quasi-concave. This condition may be contrasted with (BHC) or (18). (19) requires that the inequalities in the form of (18) hold for all x, where the inequalities in (18) are required only at the optimum point. In other words, the strict quasi-concavity provides a *global* characterization of $u(x)$, while (BHC) provides a *local* characterization. Given this, it may not then be surprising that the classical theory in terms of (BHC) provides a sufficient condition only for a local optimum. Also, given (FOC*), (BHC) means the *local* strict quasi-concavity of $u(x)$, which in turn facilitates the economic interpretation of (BHC). On the other hand, it is not clear from the classical theory that requiring the inequalities in the form of (BHC) for *all* x or (19) ensures that (FOC*) is sufficient for a (unique) global maximum. Recall that the quasi-concavity part of the strict quasi-concavity of $u(x)$ plays a central role in establishing a global maximum. By statement (i) of theorem 1.11, we may assert that if $u(x)$ is quasi-concave, then

$$\begin{vmatrix} 0 & u_1(x) \\ u_1(x) & u_{11}(x) \end{vmatrix} \leqq 0, \begin{vmatrix} 0 & u_1(x) & u_2(x) \\ u_1(x) & u_{11}(x) & u_{12}(x) \\ u_2(x) & u_{21}(x) & u_{22}(x) \end{vmatrix} \geqq 0 \ldots, \tag{20}$$

for *all* x. Condition (20) is weaker than (18), in the sense that (20) allows equalities and (18) requires strict inequalities. On the other hand, (20) is stronger than (18) in the sense that (20) is required for all x, and (18) is required only at the point x^*. The former is because (18) is concerned with uniqueness and (20) is not, and that the latter is because (18) is concerned with the *local* maximum and (20) is not.

We may now summarize some important points of comparison between the classical theory (**CT**) and nonlinear programming theory (**NPT**).

(i) (NPT) incorporates the nonnegativity constraint $x \geqq 0$ explicitly, while (CT) has no such provision.

(ii) (CT) requires that the constraint be satisfied for all x, while (NPT) has no such requirement.

(iii) Hence, in particular, (CT) requires $m < n$, that is, the number of constraints should be less than the number of choice variables, while (NPT) has no such requirement.

(iv) (CT) is concerned with the characterization of a local optimum, while (NPT) has useful provisions for the characterization of a global optimum.

(v) (SOSC) or (BHC) is required only for a *particular point* x, while the quasi-concavity condition pertains to *all* x. This corresponds to the fact (SOSC) or (BHC) is concerned with a *local* optimum, while the quasi-concavity condition is concerned with a *global* optimum.

(vi) For the classical theory, (SOSC), which is stated in the form of (BHC), requires the bordered Hessians determinant to alternate in sign with *strict* inequalities as it pertains to a *unique* optimum. Corresponding to this, the *strict* quasi-concavity of the maximand function plays a central role in establishing the uniqueness of the optimum in (NPT).

(vii) The quasi-concavity condition used in (NPT) enables us to obtain a more transparent economic interpretation than does (SOSC) or (BHC) in (CT).

Exercises

(1) Consider the problem of choosing $(x,\ y) \in R^2$ so as to maximize $u(x,\ y) \equiv x^{1/2}y^{1/2}$ subject to $x/a + y/b \leqq 1$ and $x,\ y \geqq 0$, where a and b are positive constants.

(i) Let $(x^*,\ y^*)$ be a solution of the above problem. Show that $x^* > 0$ and $y^* > 0$.

Hint: Assume $x^* = 0$ and obtain the contradiction. Similarly, assume $y^* = 0$ and obtain the contradiction.

(ii) Write out the first-order condition (FOC) of the above problem.

(iii) Obtain the values of x^* and y^* as functions of a and b.

REMARK: This question corresponds to the problem considered by John Stuart Mill, where he introduced the demand condition in the Ricardian theory of comparative advantage. Equation $(x/a + y/b = 1)$ signifies the production possibility lie of a particular country under constant cost.

Reference: Takayama, A. 1972. *International Trade: An Approach to the Theory.* New York: Holt, Rinehart, and Winston, Chapter 5.

(2) Determine whether the origin is a saddle-point of the following $\Phi(x,\ y)$

(a) $\Phi(x,\, y) = 1 - x + y,\;\; 0 \leqq x \leqq 1,\;\; 0 \leqq y \leqq 1,$

(b) $\Phi(x,\, y) = x^2 + y^2,\;\; -1 \leqq x \leqq 1,\;\; -1 \leqq y \leqq 1.$

(3) Kelvin Lancaster in his *Mathematical Economics* states (pp. 74–75),

(a) "The general maximum problem max $f(x)$ S. T. $g^i(x) \leqq 0$, $i = 1, 2, \ldots, n$, $x \geqq 0$ always possess a solution if: (a) $f(x)$ is concave and every $g^i(x)$ is convex, (b) the feasible set $K = \{x \mid g^i(x) \leqq 0,\, i = 1, 2, \ldots, n;\, x \geqq 0\}$ is bounded and nonempty."

(b) "Under these conditions the Lagrangian $L(x, \lambda) = f(x) - \sum \lambda_i g^i(x)$ possesses a saddle-point x^*, λ^*, where x^* is optimal in the maximum problem."

Lancaster also states,

(c) "The optimal point x^* of the problem max $f(x)$ S.T. $g_i(x) \leqq 0$ satisfies the following conditions

$$\frac{\partial L(x^*,\, \lambda^*)}{\partial x_j^*} = f_j - \sum \lambda_i g_j^i \leqq 0, \ldots \text{" (p. 64)},$$

where $f_j \equiv \partial f / \partial x_j$ and $g_j^i \equiv \partial g^i / \partial x_j$.

(d) "If $f(x)$ is strictly convex (concave), its Hessian is positive (negative) definite." (p. 333).

Questions:

(i) States (b), (c), and (d) are all wrong. Give a counter-example for each statement and explain.

(ii) Statement (a) is also wrong in the sense that condition (a) is basically irrelevant and that condition (b) is incomplete. To guarantee the existence of a solution, what condition would you impose in addition to that K be nonempty and compact, and why?

Hint: For (b) and (c) of question (i), recall Slater's example.

Reference: Lancaster, K. 1968. *Mathematical Economics*. New York: Macmillan.

(4) Discuss the relevance of the bordered Hessian condition to economic theory.

References

Anderson, R. K. and A. Takayama. 1979. "Comparative Statics with Discrete Jumpts in Shift Parameters, or How to Do Economics on the Saddle (-Point)." *Journal of Economic Theory* 21, December: 491–509.

Arrow, K. J. and A. C. Enthoven. 1961. "Quasi-Concave Programming." *Econometrica* 29 (October): 779–800.

Arrow, K. J. L. Hurwicz, and H. Uzawa. 1961. "Constraint Qualifications in Maximization Problems." *Naval Research Logistics Quarterly* 8 (June): 175–191.

Bliss, G. M. 1946. *Lectures on the Calculus of Variations.* Chicago: University of Chicago Press.

Carathéodory, C. 1967. *Calculus of Variations and Partial Differential Equations of the First Order.* Trans. R. Dean. Part 2, especially chap. 11. San Francisco: Holden-Day.

Dantzig, G. B. 1963. *Linear Programming and Extensions.* Princeton, N.J.: Princeton University Press.

Dixit, A. K. 1990. *Optimization in Economic Theory.* 2d ed. New York: Oxford University Press (1st ed. 1976).

El-Hodiri, M. A. 1971. *Constrained Extrema: Introduction to the Differentiable Case with Economic Applications.* New York: Springer-Verlag.

Goldman, A. J., and A. W. Tucker. 1956. "Theory of Linear Programming." In *Linear Inequalities and Related Systems*, ed. by H. W. Kuhn and A. W. Tucker, 53–97. Princeton, N.J.: Princeton University Press.

Hestenes, M. R. 1966. *Calculus of Variations and Optimal Control Theory.* New York: Wiley.

———. 1975. *Optimization Theory: The Finite Dimensional Case.* New York: Wiley.

Hicks, J. R. 1946. *Value and Capital.* 2d ed. Oxford: Clarendon Press (1st. ed. 1939).

Intriligator, M. 1981. "Mathematical Programming with Applications to Economics." In *Handbook of Mathematical Economics*, ed. K. J. Arrow and M. D. Intriligator, 1: 53–81. Amsterdam: North-Holland.

Kuhn, H. W, and A. W. Tucker 1951. "Non-Linear Programming." In *Proceedings of the Second Berkeley Symposium on Mathematical Statistics and Probability*, ed. J. Neyman. Berkeley, Calif.: University of California Press.

Kuhn, H. W, and A. W. Tucker, eds. 1956. *Linear Inequalities and Related Systems.* Princeton, N.J.: Princeton University Press.

Luenberger, N. G. 1973. *Introduction to Linear and Nonlinear Programming.* Reading, Mass.: Addison-Wesley.

Mangasarian, O. L. 1969. *Nonlinear Programming.* New York: McGraw-Hill.

Nikaido, H. 1961. *Linear Mathematics for Economics* (in Japanese). Tokyo: Baifu-kan.

———. 1970. *Introduction to Sets and Mappings in Modern Economics.* Trans. K. Sato. Amsterdam: North-Holland, (Japanese original).

Samuelson, P. A. 1947. *Foundations of Economic Analysis.* Cambridge, Mass.: Harvard University Press (enl. ed. 1983).

Slater, M. 1950. "Lagrange Multipliers Revisited: A Contribution to Non-Linear Programming." *Cowles Commission Discussion Paper*, Math. 403 (November).

Smale, S. 1983. "On the Average Number of Steps." *Mathematical Programing* 27: 241–62.

Takayama, A. 1981. "Classical Optimization and Nonlinear Programming," Lecture notes, Texas A & M University (October).

———. 1985. *Mathematical Economics.* 2d. ed. New York: Cambridge University Press, (1st. ed. Dryden Press, 1974).

Takayama, A. and M. A. El-Hodiri. 1968. "Programming, Pareto Optimum, and the Existence of Competitive Equilibria." *Metroeconomics* 20 (Gennaio-Aprile): 1–10.

Uzawa, H. 1958. "The Kuhn-Tucker Theorem in Concave Programming." In *Studies in Linear and Non-Linear Programming.* ed. K. J. Arrow, L. Hurwicz, and H. Uzawa: 32–37. Stanford, Calif.: Stanford University Press.

CHAPTER 3

Sensitivity Analysis and Elements of Microeconomics

3.1 Comparative Statics: Conventional Procedure[1]

Many important problems in economics can be formulated in terms of nonlinear programming. When a certain problem is expressed as that of maximizing or minimizing a certain function subject to certain constraints for given parameters, the next question then is to consider the effect of a change in these parameters. The producer's factor demand function can be obtained by such a procedure, as can the consumer's demand function.[2] Such a method, known as **sensitivity analysis** in the literature of constrained maximization, is known in economics by the name of **comparative statics** in the case of statics, and as **comparative dynamics** in the case of dynamics. Its importance in economics is well known and cannot be overemphasized. In fact, it is a main theme of Hicks's *Value and Capital* and Samuelson's *Foundations*.[3]

To illustrate sensitivity analysis, we may consider the following two familiar problems.

Example 3.1 (cost minimization). Consider a competitive firm that chooses a factor input combination $x \in R^n$ to

---

[1]The discussion here is adapted from Takayama (1985, pp. 159–68). Although the best effort is made to ease the exposition of the Hicks-Samuelson theory of comparative statics, it is inherently tedious. The reader may then wish to skip the bulk of the discussion of this section.

[2]By taking a discrete time formulation (as opposed to continuous time formulation), many dynamic problems can be analyzed by using the ordinary nonlinear programming techniques as described in chap. 2. For an exposition of the discrete time formulation of the optimal growth problem for an aggregate neoclassical economy, see Takayama (1985, pp. 468–85; 1977, pp. 33–35).

[3]Paul Samuelson was the 1970 Nobel Prize laureate in Economic Science. Sir John Hicks won the award in 1972.

(CM) Minimize $w \cdot x$, subject to $f(x) \geqq y$, and $x \geqq 0$,

where w = factor price vector, y = the target level of output, and $f(x)$ = the production function, and where $w > 0$ and $y > 0$ are given parameters. The solution of this cost minimization problem x^*, in general, depends on the parameters w and y, and hence can be expressed as $x^* = x(w, y)$. The sensitivity analysis for the problem is then concerned with ascertaining the magnitudes and the signs of $\partial x_i/\partial w_j$, $\partial x_i/\partial y$, etc. Let $C(w, y) \equiv w \cdot x(w, y)$, which then signifies the (minimum total) cost function. Then $\alpha(w, y) \equiv C(w, y)/y$ and $\mu(w, y) \equiv \partial C(w, y)/\partial y$, respectively, signify the average cost and the marginal cost. The usual U-shaped average cost curve in intermediate price-theory textbooks depicts the locus of $\alpha(w, y)$ for changes in y for a given value of w. Similarly, the marginal cost curve depicts the locus of $\mu(w, y)$ for changes in y for a given value of w. Hence, studies of the shapes of average and marginal cost curves are exercises in sensitivity analysis.

Example 3.2 (utility maximization). Consider a consumer who chooses his (or her) consumption bundle $x \in R^n$ so as to

(UM) Maximize $u(x)$, subject to $p \cdot x \leqq Y$, and $x \geqq 0$,

where $u(x)$ = utility function, p = price vector, and Y = income, and where $p > 0$ and $Y > 0$ are given parameters. The solution of the problem x^* depends on the parameters p and Y, and hence can be expressed as $x^* = x(p, Y)$. The sensitivity analysis is concerned with problems such as ascertaining the magnitudes and the signs of $\partial x_i/\partial p_j$ and $\partial x_i/\partial Y$.

In general, let f and g_j, where $j = 1, 2, \ldots, m$, be real-valued, continuously differentiable functions defined on R^n and consider the problem of choosing $x \in R^n$ to

$$\text{Maximize } f(x, \alpha^*), \quad \text{subject to } g_j(x, \alpha^*) \geqq 0, \quad j = 1, 2, \ldots, m, \text{ and } x \geqq 0,$$

where $\alpha^* = (\alpha_1^*, \ldots, \alpha_\ell^*)$ is a given vector of parameters. In the cost minimization problem, $\alpha \equiv (w, y)$, and in the utility maximization problem, $\alpha \equiv (p, Y)$. In general, the solution of this maximization problem x^* depends on the values of the parameters, α_k^*'s, and hence can be expressed as $x^* = x(\alpha^*)$. To proceed with our analysis, assume for the sake of simplicity that $x_i^* > 0$, $i = 1, 2, \ldots, n$ (an interior solution) and $\lambda_j^* > 0$, $j = 1, 2, \ldots, m$. Then the first-order condition (FOC) for the above maximization problem can be written as

$$\partial f(x^*, \alpha^*)/\partial x_i + \sum_{j=1}^{m} \lambda_j^* \partial g_j(x^*, \alpha^*)/\partial x_i = 0, \quad i = 1, 2, \ldots, n, \tag{1a}$$

$$g_j(x^*, \alpha^*) = 0, \quad j = 1, 2, \ldots, m. \tag{1b}$$

Assume that (1) provides a necessary and sufficient condition for $x^* > 0$ to be a solution of this nonlinear programming problem for a given α^*.

Define the Lagrangian function of the above problem as

$$\Phi(x, \lambda, \alpha) \equiv f(x, \alpha) + \lambda \cdot g(x, \alpha).$$

Let the Φ_x be the gradient vector of Φ with respect to x, then (1) can equivalently be written as

$$\Phi_x(x^*, \lambda^*, \alpha^*) = 0, \; g(x^*, \alpha^*) = 0. \tag{1'}$$

Let $A = [a_{ij}]$ and $B = [b_{ij}]$, respectively, be $(n \times n)$ and $(m \times n)$ matrices defined by

$$A \equiv \Phi_{xx}(x^*, \lambda^*, \alpha^*); \text{ that is, } a_{ij} \equiv \partial^2 \Phi(x^*, \lambda^*, \alpha^*)/\partial x_i \partial x_j$$

$$B \equiv g_x(x^*, \lambda^*, \alpha^*); \text{ that is, } b_{ij} \equiv \partial g_i(x^*, \lambda^*, \alpha^*)/\partial x_j$$

Let B' be the transpose of B, and assume rank $B = m$ and also

$$\det \begin{bmatrix} 0 & B \\ B' & A \end{bmatrix} \neq 0. \tag{2}$$

Then by the implicit function theorem, we may assert that there exist unique, continuously differentiable functions $x(\alpha)$ and $\lambda(\alpha)$ such that $x^* = x(\alpha^*)$ and $\lambda^* = \lambda(\alpha^*)$, and

$$\Phi_x[x(\alpha), \lambda(\alpha), \alpha] = 0, \; g[x(\alpha), \alpha] = 0, \tag{3}$$

for all α at least in some neighborhood of α^*, say $N(\alpha^*)$.

The comparative static analysis or the sensitivity analysis, in the context of optimization, is to establish the effect of changes in α_k's on the values of $x(\alpha)$ and $\lambda(\alpha)$, by using (3). Differentiating (3) with respect to α_k yields (for each $k = 1, 2, \ldots, \ell$),

$$\begin{bmatrix} \Phi_{xx} & \Phi_{x\lambda} \\ \Phi_{\lambda x} & 0 \end{bmatrix} \begin{bmatrix} \partial x(\alpha)/\partial\alpha_k \\ \partial\lambda(\alpha)/\partial\alpha_k \end{bmatrix} + \begin{bmatrix} \Phi_{x\alpha_k} \\ \Phi_{\lambda\alpha_k} \end{bmatrix} = 0, \tag{4}$$

for all $\alpha \in N(\alpha^*)$, where all the second partials of Φ are evaluated at α; that is, $\Phi_{xx} \equiv \Phi_{xx}[x(\alpha), \lambda(\alpha), \alpha]$. Obviously, $\Phi_{x\lambda} = \Phi_{\lambda x} = g_x[x(\alpha), \alpha]$. Equation (4) can equivalently be rewritten as

$$\begin{bmatrix} 0 & \Phi_{\lambda x} \\ \Phi_{x\lambda} & \Phi_{xx} \end{bmatrix} \begin{bmatrix} \partial\lambda(\alpha)/\partial\alpha_k \\ \partial x(\alpha)/\partial\alpha_k \end{bmatrix} + \begin{bmatrix} \Phi_{\lambda\alpha_k} \\ \Phi_{x\alpha_k} \end{bmatrix} = 0. \tag{4'}$$

Define the $(m + n) \times (m + n)$ matrices H and H^* by

$$H \equiv \begin{bmatrix} 0 & \Phi_{\lambda x} \\ \Phi_{x\lambda} & \Phi_{xx} \end{bmatrix}, \quad H^* \equiv \begin{bmatrix} 0 & B \\ B' & A \end{bmatrix}.$$

By (2), H^* is nonsingular, and hence H is also nonsingular for all α in some neighborhood of α^*, say, $\overline{N}(\alpha^*)$ where $\overline{N}(\alpha^*) \subset N(\alpha^*)$, since H is continuous in α by the continuity of the functions $x(\alpha)$ and $\lambda(\alpha)$ and the continuous differentiability of the functions f and g_j's. Therefore, from (4'), we obtain theorem 3.1.

Theorem 3.1. Under the above specification, we have

$$\begin{bmatrix} \partial\lambda(\alpha)/\partial\alpha_k \\ \partial x(\alpha)/\partial\alpha_k \end{bmatrix} = -\begin{bmatrix} 0 & \Phi_{\lambda x} \\ \Phi_{x\lambda} & \Phi_{xx} \end{bmatrix}^{-1} \begin{bmatrix} \Phi_{\lambda\alpha_k} \\ \Phi_{x\alpha_k} \end{bmatrix},$$

$$\text{for } k = 1, 2, \ldots, \ell. \tag{5}$$

Equation (5) is called the **fundamental equation of comparative statics**. Since Φ_{xx} is the Hessian matrix of Φ with respect to x, H is the bordered Hessian matrix of Φ (bordered with $\Phi_{\lambda x} = g_x$). Equation (5) involves the inverse of such a bordered Hessian matrix.

In theorem 2.12 in section 2.4 of chapter 2, we stated that conditions (LM) and (R) imply (SONC). From (SONC) and condition (2), we may assert

$$\xi' A \xi < 0 \text{ for all } \xi \neq 0 \text{ such that } B\xi = 0.^4 \tag{6}$$

Namely, (SOSC) is satisfied, which in turn implies the bordered Hessian condition (BHC); that is, the last $(n - m)$ successive principal minors of H^* alternate signs. Since every element of H is continuous in α, the last $(n - m)$ successive principal minors of H alternate in signs for each α in $\overline{N}(\alpha^*)$. In other words, letting H_i be the ith successive principal minor of H, we have

$$(-1)^i H_i > 0,\ i = 2m + 1, \ldots, m + n, \quad \text{for all } \alpha \in \overline{N}(\alpha^*). \tag{7}$$

From this we may at once conclude

$$\text{sign } (\det H) = (-1)^{m+n}. \tag{8}$$

Also, let h_{ii} be the cofactor of the ith diagonal $(i - i)$ element of H, then $h_{m+n,\ m+n}$ is the $(m + n) - (m + n)$ cofactor of H. From (7) it has the sign opposite of $\det H$ so that

$$\text{sign } h_{m+n,\ m+n} = (-1)^{m+n-1}.$$

Since a simultaneous permutation of rows and columns does not alter the sign and the value of a determinant, this implies

$$\text{sign } h_{ii} = (-1)^{m+n-1}, \quad \text{for all } i. \tag{9}$$

Recall that the inverse of H may be obtained as

$$H^{-1} = \frac{1}{\det H}[h_{ji}],$$

where h_{ji} is the cofactor of the $j - i$ element of H(i.e., $[h_{ji}]$ is the transpose of $[h_{ij}]$). Then combining (8) and (9), we may conclude

$$h_{ii}/\det H < 0, \quad \text{for all } i. \tag{10}$$

Next decompose the matrix H as

$$H^{-1} = \begin{bmatrix} K_1 & K_2 \\ K_3 & K_4 \end{bmatrix}, \quad \text{for all } \alpha \in \overline{N}(\alpha^*). \tag{11}$$

Here, K_1, K_2, K_3, and K_4 are, respectively, $m \times m$, $m \times n$, $n \times m$, and $n \times n$ matrices. We may note that K_1, K_2, K_3, and K_4, respectively, correspond to the $m \times m$ zero matrix, $\Phi_{\lambda x}$, $\Phi_{x\lambda}$, and Φ_{xx} in the matrix

---

[4]This follows from the fact that if A is negative semidefinite and nonsingular, then A is negative definite.

H. Since H is symmetric, so is H^{-1}, and K_1 and K_4 are also symmetric. Furthermore, we may conclude that K_4 is negative semidefinite, where we may note rank $B = m$ by assumption, and that (6) holds.[5] In summary, we have theorem 3.2.

Theorem 3.2. Partition the matrix H^{-1} in the form of (11). Then K_1 and K_4 are symmetric. Furthermore, K_4 (the $n \times n$ southeast matrix of H^{-1}) is symmetric, negative semidefinite and its diagonal elements are all negative.

Example 3.3. Consider the problem of utility maximization of example 3.2. The Lagrangian for this problem may be defined as

$$\Phi(x, \lambda, p^*, Y^*) \equiv u(x) + \lambda(Y^* - p^* \cdot x),$$

for given values of price vector p^* and income Y^*. Assuming $x^* > 0$ and $\lambda^* > 0$ at the optimum, the first-order condition (FOC) for this problem may be written as

$$Y^* - p^* \cdot x^* = 0; \; u_i(x^*) - \lambda^* p_i^* = 0, \; i = 1, 2, \ldots, n,$$

where $u_i \equiv \partial u / \partial x_i$, which corresponds to (1) above. The bordered Hessian matrix H for the present problem may be written as

$$H = \begin{bmatrix} 0 & -p \\ -p' & (u_{ij}) \end{bmatrix},$$

where $u_{ij} \equiv \partial^2 u / \partial x_i \partial x_j$, and (u_{ij}) is the $n \times n$ array of the u_{ij}'s. Evaluate these u_{ij}'s at x^* and set $p = p^*$ in H, and denote it by H^*.

---

[5] In general we have the following theorem on matrix algebra, which may be called the **Carathéodory-Samuelson theorem**. *Let H be any $(m + n) \times (m + n)$ symmetric matrix with real entries. Assume that H is decomposed in the form of H^* in the text. Assume also that rank $B = m$ and that A is negative definite subject to $Bh = 0$. Then H^{-1} exists and K_4 of H^{-1} [where H^{-1} is decomposed as (11)] is symmetric and negative semidefinite.* See Carathéodory (1967, pp. 195–96), and Samuelson (1947, pp. 378–79). Hence a part of the assertions made so far (such as the nonsingularity of H and the negative semidefiniteness of K_4) may also be obtained as a direct application of the Carathéodory-Samuelson theorem. Note that the condition of rank $B = m$ corresponds to the rank condition (R) of classical optimization, whereas equation (6) corresponds to the second-order sufficiency condition (SOSC) for local maximum, where we may recall the discussion of conditions (R) and (SOSC) in chapter 2. In the literature, (R) and (SOSC) are often outrightly assumed in the optimization procedure. Such an outright assumption then enables the researcher to utilize the Carathéodory-Samuelson theorem from which one may obtain the nonsingularity of the bordered Hessian matrix and the negative semidefiniteness of K_4.

Assume $\det H^* \neq 0$, which corresponds to (2) above. By this, we may apply the implicit function theorem to obtain

$$Y - p \cdot x(p,\ Y) = 0,\ u_i[x(p,\ Y)] - \lambda(p,\ Y)p_i = 0,$$
$$i = 1,\ 2,\ \ldots,\ n,$$

for all $(p,\ Y)$ in some neighborhood of $(p^*,\ Y^*)$. Then using theorem 3.1, we may obtain the Hicks-Slutsky equation, and using theorem 3.2, we may obtain the major properties of the (net) substitution matrix (see Takayama 1985, pp. 163–66 for details). We shall obtain such properties in a much simpler fashion in section 3.3.

The procedure described above via theorems 3.1 and 3.2 is the one utilized in obtaining the classical results of consumer's choice and producer's choice as developed in Hicks (1939, 1946) and Samuelson (1947). However, this procedure is, as mentioned earlier, often quite tedious and cumbersome. Fortunately, some simpler methods to cover important aspects of sensitivity have been developed. Although the usefulness of the general procedure and the classical treatises of Hicks and Samuelson on consumption and production cannot by any means be underrated, we shall now turn to the discussion of this important simple procedure.

3.2 The Envelope Theorem

As in the previous section, we consider the problem of choosing x, for a given α, to

$$\text{Maximize } f(x,\ \alpha), \text{ subject to } g_j(x,\ \alpha) \geqq 0,$$
$$j = 1,\ 2,\ \ldots,\ m, \text{ and } x \geqq 0,$$

where $\alpha \in R^\ell$. The *sensitivity analysis* is concerned with the effect of a change in α_k's upon x_i's. There is one result known as the "envelope theorem," which enables us to carry out sensitivity analysis in a remarkably simple manner. In this section, we discuss this theorem. To this end, assume $x_i(\alpha) > 0$ for all i (an interior solution) and $\lambda_j(\alpha) > 0$ for all j. Then letting $\Phi(x,\ \lambda,\ \alpha) \equiv f(x,\ \alpha) + \lambda \cdot g(x,\ \alpha)$ be the Lagrangian, we may write (FOC) for this problem as follows:

$$\Phi_x[x(\alpha),\ \lambda(\alpha),\ \alpha] = 0,\quad g[x(\alpha),\ \alpha] = 0. \tag{12}$$

Assume further that (12) is necessary and sufficient for optimum. Conditions that ensure this are discussed in chapter 2. Under such circumstances, the $x(\alpha)$ that satisfies (12) is a solution of this maximization problem, and $\lambda(\alpha)$ is the vector of its associated Lagrangian multipliers. We assume that $x(\alpha)$ and $\lambda(\alpha)$ are continuously differentiable. Needless to say, (12) can equivalently be rewritten as

$$f_x[x(\alpha),\ \alpha] + \lambda(\alpha) \cdot g_x[x(\alpha),\ \alpha] = 0, \tag{12$'$a}$$

$$g[x(\alpha),\ \alpha] = 0, \tag{12$'$b}$$

where f_x and g_x are, respectively, the gradient vector of f and the Jacobian matrix of g, each with respect to x. We assume that (12′) holds for all α in a certain region D of R^ℓ, and we further assume that $x(\alpha)$ and $\lambda(\alpha)$, which satisfy (12′), are continuously differentiable for all α in D.

Given the solution $x(\alpha)$ of the above maximization problem, we define the function $F(\alpha)$ and $\Psi(\alpha)$ by

$$F(\alpha) \equiv f[x(\alpha),\ \alpha], \tag{13}$$

$$\Psi(\alpha) \equiv f[x(\alpha),\ \alpha] + \lambda(\alpha) \cdot g[x(\alpha),\ \alpha]\ (\equiv \Phi[x(\alpha),\ \lambda(\alpha),\ \alpha]). \tag{14}$$

The function $F(\alpha)$ is called the **maximum value function**. We then have theorem 3.3, which is known as the **envelope theorem.**[6]

Theorem 3.3. Assume that F and Φ are continuously differentiable. Then $F_\alpha = \Phi_\alpha = \Psi_\alpha$: that is,

$$\frac{\partial F(\alpha)}{\partial \alpha_k} = \frac{\partial \Phi(x,\ \lambda,\ \alpha)}{\partial \alpha_k} = \frac{\partial \Psi(\alpha)}{\partial \alpha_k},\ k = 1,\ 2,\ \ldots,\ \ell, \tag{15}$$

where $\Phi(x,\ \lambda,\ \alpha) \equiv F(x,\ \alpha) + \lambda \cdot g(x,\ \alpha)$, so that

$$\partial \Phi(x,\ \lambda,\ \alpha)/\partial \alpha_k = \partial f(x,\ \alpha)/\partial \alpha_k + \sum_{j=1}^{m} \lambda_j \partial g_j(x,\ \alpha)/\partial \alpha_k.$$

---

[6]The result of $F_\alpha = \Phi_\alpha$ is from Afriat (1971, pp. 355–57). The basic idea of this theorem is found in Samuelson (1947). The present formulation is also found in Takayama (1985, pp. 137–53).

Proof. Using the chain rule, simply observe that[7]

$$\Psi_\alpha = \Phi_x \cdot x_\alpha + \Phi_\lambda \cdot \lambda_\alpha + \Phi_\alpha = \Phi_x \cdot x_\alpha + g \cdot \lambda_\alpha + \Phi_\alpha$$

$$= \Phi_\alpha \qquad \text{[by using (12)]}$$

$$F_\alpha = f_x \cdot x_\alpha + f_\alpha$$

$$= -\lambda \cdot g_x \cdot x_\alpha + f_\alpha \qquad \text{[since } f_x = -\lambda \cdot g_x \text{ from (12'a)]}$$

$$= \lambda \cdot g_\alpha + f_\alpha \qquad \text{[since } g_x \cdot x_\alpha + g_\alpha = 0 \text{ by (12'b)]}$$

$$= \Phi_\alpha . \qquad \text{(QED)}$$

REMARK: Notice that $\partial\Psi/\partial\alpha_k$ measures the *total* effect of a change in α_k on the Lagrangian, while $\partial\Phi/\partial\alpha_k$ measures the *partial* effect of a change in α_k on the Lagrangian with x and λ being held constant.

REMARK: It is possible that F and Φ are *not* continuously differentiable. See Samuelson (1958), for example.

We now show some examples of the application of the envelope theorem. We hope that these examples will illustrate the use of this theorem.

Example 3.4 (consumer's choice). Consider the problem of utility maximization (UM) discussed earlier. Assume $p > 0$ and $u_i(x)$ ($\equiv \partial u/\partial x_i$) > 0 for all i at optimum, let $x(p, Y) > 0$ be its solution, and let $\lambda(p, Y)$ be the corresponding multiplier. Here $\alpha = (p, Y)$. Define the function U by

$$U(p, Y) \equiv u[x(P, Y)] \text{ (indirect utility function)}. \tag{16}$$

Then by the envelope theorem, and $\Phi \equiv u(x) + \lambda(Y - p \cdot x)$,

$$\partial U/\partial Y = \partial\Phi/\partial Y = \lambda(p, Y). \tag{17}$$

Thus the Lagrangian multiplier signifies the **marginal utility of income**. We also obtain

$$\partial U/\partial p_j = \partial\Phi/\partial p_j = -\lambda x_j, \; j = 1, 2, \ldots, n. \tag{18}$$

---

[7] Here the dot is used to make the nature of matrix (or vector) multiplication clear, as opposed to simple scalar multiplication. For example, Φ_x, x_α, Φ_λ, λ_α, and Φ_α are, respectively, a $1 \times n$ vector, an $n \times \ell$ matrix, a $1 \times m$ vector, an $m \times \ell$ matrix, and a $1 \times \ell$ vector; thus the multiplications, $\Phi_x \cdot x_\alpha$ and $\Phi_\lambda \cdot \lambda_\alpha$ are well defined, and its meaning should be clear.

This means that an increase in any price will lower the consumer's satisfaction (as can be expected). Also combining (17) and (18) yields

$$\partial U/\partial p_j + x_j \partial U/\partial Y = 0,\ j = 1, 2, \ldots, n, \tag{19}$$

which is known as **Roy's identity** (Roy 1942, pp. 18–19). Note that (17) through (19) are identities as they hold for all (p, Y) in the relevant range.

Example 3.5 (the interpretation of the multiplier). In general, consider the problem of choosing $x \in R^n$ to maximize $f(x)$ subject to $g_j(x) \leqq b_j$, $j = 1, 2, \ldots, m$, and $x \geqq 0$. Let $x(b)$ and $\lambda(b)$ be its solution and the vector of Lagrangian multipliers, where $b \equiv (b_1, b_2, \ldots, b_m)$. Define $F(b) \equiv f[x(b)]$ and

$$\Phi(x, \lambda, b) \equiv f(x) + \lambda \cdot [b - g(x)].$$

Then by the envelope theorem, we obtain

$$\frac{\partial F(b)}{\partial b_j} = \partial \Phi / \partial b_j = \lambda_j(b),\ j = 1, 2, \ldots, m. \tag{20}$$

Thus the jth Lagrangian multiplier signifies the marginal rate of change of the optimal value of the objective function with respect to a change in the jth constraint. Equation (17) of example 3.4 is clearly a special case of this. Interpreting b_j as the amount of the jth resource supply, λ_j measures the loss of the maximum value $F(b)$ when one unit of the jth resource is withdrawn. Namely, λ_j signifies the **shadow price** of the jth resource as expressed in Carl Menger's *opportunity cost* theory based on the "loss principle" (see Samuelson 1958 and Takayama 1977, pp. 22–24).

Example 3.6 (cost minimization). Consider the problem of cost minimization (CM) that was discussed earlier. Assume $w > 0$ and $f_i(x)$ $(\equiv \partial f / \partial x_i) > 0$ for all i at optimum, and let $x(w, y)$ be the optimal input vector and $\lambda(w, y)$ be the corresponding multiplier. Define the minimal total cost function by

$$C(w, y) \equiv w \cdot x(w, y) \tag{21}$$

and the Lagrangian by

$$\Phi(x, \lambda, w, y) \equiv -w \cdot x + \lambda[f(x) - y].$$

Then by the envelope theorem, we may obtain

$$\frac{\partial C}{\partial y} = \lambda(w,\ y) > 0,\ \frac{\partial C}{\partial w_i} = x_i(w,\ y) > 0,\ i = 1, 2, \ldots, n. \tag{22}$$

That is, the multiplier signifies the marginal cost and an increase in a factor price will always increase the total cost. The result $\partial C/\partial w_i = x_i$ is known as the **Shephard (-McKenzie) lemma** (see Shephard 1953 and McKenzie 1957).[8]

Assume that the cost function $C(w,\ y)$ is twice continuously differentiable, so that its Hessian matrix is symmetric. Then using (22), we may readily obtain

$$\frac{\partial x_j}{\partial w_i} = \frac{\partial x_i}{\partial w_j},\ \text{ and }\ \frac{\partial x_i}{\partial y} = \frac{\partial \lambda}{\partial w_i},\ \text{ for all } i \text{ and } j, \tag{23}$$

which is known as **Samuelson's reciprocity relation**. The first result of (23) states that the change in the jth factor input with respect to a change in the ith factor price, output being constant, must be equal to the change in the ith factor input with respect to a change in the jth factor price, output being constant (Samuelson 1947, p. 64). Our derivation of (23) is greatly simplified thanks to the use of the envelope theorem.

Example 3.7 (profit maximization). Consider a competitive firm that produces a vector of outputs y using input vector x, where the output price vector $p > 0$ and the input price vector $w > 0$ are given to the firm. Assume that the production function constraint of the firm is written as $g(x,\ y) \geqq 0$. If y is a scalar and $f(x)$ is the production function as in the previous cost minimization problem, $g(x,\ y) \equiv f(x) - y$. The firm is supposed to choose $x \in R^n$ and $y \in R^m$ to

(PM) Maximize $p \cdot y - w \cdot x$,

subject to $g(x,\ y) \geqq 0$, $x \geqq 0$, and $y \geqq 0$.

Let $x(p,\ w)$ and $y(p,\ w)$ be the solution of the above problem, and define

[8] We obtained $x_i = \partial C/\partial w_i$ by presupposing the production function $f(x)$ and invoking the envelope theorem. This is different from the approach taken by Shephard and McKenzie, who begin directly from the function C. We shall discuss this later in this section.

the maximum profit function by

$$\pi(p,\ w) \equiv p \cdot y(p,\ w) - w \cdot x(p,\ w) \tag{24}$$

and the Lagrangian by

$$\Phi(x,\ y,\ \lambda,\ p,\ w) \equiv p \cdot y - w \cdot x + \lambda g(x,\ y).$$

Then by the envelope theorem, we at once obtain

$$\frac{\partial \pi}{\partial p_i} = y_i > 0,\ i = 1,\ 2,\ \ldots,\ m, \tag{25a}$$

$$\frac{\partial \pi}{\partial w_i} = -x_i < 0,\ i = 1,\ 2,\ \ldots,\ n. \tag{25b}$$

Namely, an increase in the price of any output increases the maximum profit, while an increase in the price of any input lowers the maximum profit. The relations in (25) are known as **Hotelling's lemma** (1932, p. 594).[9]

Assume that the profit function $\pi(p,\ w)$ is twice continuously differentiable, so that its Hessian matrix is negative semidefinite. Then using (25), we may readily obtain

$$\frac{\partial y_j}{\partial p_i} = \frac{\partial y_i}{\partial p_j},\ \frac{\partial x_j}{\partial w_i} = \frac{\partial x_i}{\partial w_j},\ \frac{\partial x_i}{\partial p_i} = -\frac{\partial y_i}{\partial w_j},\quad \text{for all } i \text{ and } j. \tag{26}$$

Note that the first relation of (26) is the same as the first relation of (23), and it is also known as **Hotelling's symmetry relation** (1935,

[9]The cost minimization problem discussed earlier assumes Y is a scalar. It can readily be extended to the joint output case in which y is a vector. Writing the production function constraint for such a case as $g(x,\ y) \geqq 0$ (as in the present profit maximization problem), the cost minimization problem can be stated as the one of choosing $x \in R^n$ so as to minimize $w \cdot x$ subject to $g(x,\ y) \geqq 0$ and $x \geqq 0$, where $w > 0$ and $y > 0\,(y \in R^m)$ are given vectors. Write the solution of this problem as $x(w,\ y)$, and define $C(w,\ y) \equiv w \cdot x(w,\ y)$. Then the application of the envelope theorem readily yields

$$\partial C/\partial w_i = x_i,\ i = 1,\ 2,\ \ldots,\ n,\ \partial C/\partial y_j = \partial g/\partial y_j,\ j = 1,\ 2,\ \ldots,\ m,$$

where the first relation corresponds to the Shephard lemma obtained earlier for the single output case. From the second relation, we may at once obtain the following result,

$$\frac{\partial C/\partial y_i}{\partial C/\partial y_j} = \frac{\partial g/\partial y_i}{\partial g/\partial y_j},\ i,\ j = 1,\ 2,\ \ldots,\ m,$$

since $\lambda > 0$ at the optimum. See Hall (1973) and Takayama (1977, p. 22).

p. 69). Since profit maximization presupposes cost minimization for the present problem, it is not surprising to obtain the same reciprocity result, $\partial x_j/\partial w_i = \partial x_i/\partial w_j$. Note that this relation holds for the joint output case, in which y is a vector as in the present case, as well as for the single output case (as is the case in the previous cost minimization problem).

REMARK: The traditional comparative statics results as obtained in this section are concerned with the effect of an "infinitesimal" shift in a parameter or parameters. The effect of discrete jumps in the parameters can also be analyzed in a simple fashion (see Anderson and Takayama 1979). As mentioned earlier, the saddle-point characterization of the optimum plays a crucial role in obtaining the comparative statics results that allow discrete jumps in parameters.

A Note on Duality

In the preceding discussion, we obtained Roy's identity, Shephard's lemma, Hotelling's lemma, and Hotelling's symmetry relation as applications of the envelope theorem. It is important to note, however, that these authors do not obtain these relations by presupposing the existence of the utility function $u(x)$ or the production function $f(x)$. They rely on what is now known as **duality relations** (see Diewert 1982, for an excellent survey). Hence the results obtained via the envelope theorem should be distinguished from the original results obtained by Roy (1942), Shephard (1953 and 1970), McKenzie (1957), and Hotelling (1932 and 1935) referred to above. On the duality theory, Diewert (1982, p. 548) remarks, "The English language literature on duality theory seems to have started with two papers by Hotelling (1932 and 1935).... The next important contribution to duality theory was made by Roy." As surveyed in Diewert (1982), various forms of duality theorems are now available, where the modern rigorous development of duality theorems is due to Shephard (1953 and 1970). Here it may be useful to briefly explain the distinction between envelope results and duality results.

The point in question may best be illustrated in terms of production theory using $\partial C/\partial w_i = x_i$ in (22). This relation was obtained as an application of the envelope theorem by presupposing a production function $f(x)$ and assuming rational behavior (cost minimization). In contrast to this, $\partial C/\partial w_i = x_i$ in the original formulation by Shephard (1953) relies on dual information. It assumes only the existence of a cost function and does not rely on the production function information. In this context, the **duality theorem** asserts that given the cost function $C(w, y)$ and rational behavior, we can, under certain regularity conditions, derive a unique production function that generates the cost function. Since this cost minimization procedure obtains the cost function given the production function, we now have, under the regularity condition, the two-way relations between production and cost functions.[10] Thus, as Shephard states (1953, p. 9), "the production function and minimum cost function are equivalent specifications of the technology of production." The real Shephard lemma, $\partial C/\partial w_i = x_i$, as originally obtained by Shephard from the cost function information, then coincides with the envelope result (22). If such regularity conditions hold, then the duality theorem holds.[11] On the other hand, if the duality theorem does not hold, the (true) Shephard lemma should sharply be distinguished from the envelope result. Thus, it is not really correct to call $\partial C/\partial w_i = x_i$ in (22) obtained from the envelope theorem, "Shephard's lemma," since the latter relies on cost function information and the former relies on production function information.[12] These two do not coincide when the duality theorem does not hold. From an empirical viewpoint the latter may be more significant as Shephard (1953) noted.

In the remainder of this section, we briefly sketch the Shephard duality theorem (1953 and 1970). In Shephard's formulation, the concept of a "distance function" plays a key role. The distance function D is defined as

$$D(y,\ x) \equiv \max_{k}\ \{k \in R : f(\frac{x}{k}) \geqq y,\ k > 0\}. \tag{27}$$

In these terms, the production function and the cost function can be

---

[10]Although there are alternative specifications of the "regularity conditions," one such specification of the production function $f(x)$ is that it is continuous, monotone increasing, and quasi-concave with $f(0) = 0$. See Diewert (1982, pp. 537–56).

[11]In this context, we may also note that McKenzie (1957), in his discussion of consumer's choice, similarly begins with the "minimum expenditure function" (which corresponds to the cost function) without postulating the utility function and obtains the relation that corresponds to the Shephard lemma, through which he derives all the basic properties of the Hicks-Slutsky substitution matrix.

[12]Furthermore, information on one side of the dual relations can imply the other. For example, Saijo (1983) shows that, under the assumption of strict monotonicity of the production function, differentiability of the cost function is equivalent to strict quasi-concavity of the production function. Namely, "the assumption of differentiability determines the production structure" (Saijo 1983, p. 135). Although there are obviously many interesting and important economic problems that we need to analyze before we indulge in questions of differentiability, it would be important to understand its implications.

written as

$$f(x) = \max_{y} \{y : D(y, x) \geqq 1, y \geqq 0\}, \tag{28}$$

$$C(w, y) = \max_{x} \{w \cdot x : D(y, x) \geqq 1, x \geqq 0\}, \tag{29}$$

where we may note that $D(y, x) \geqq 1$ corresponds to $f(x) \geqq y$. Furthermore, we also have

$$D(y, x) = \max_{w} \{w \cdot x : C(w, y) \geqq 1, w \geqq 0\}. \tag{30}$$

Equations (29) and (30) constitute the heart of the Shephard duality theorem (see Shephard 1953, p. 22; 1970, p. 159). Note the chain of determination, $f \Rightarrow D \Rightarrow C \Rightarrow D \Rightarrow f$ by way of (27), (29), (30), and (28). Alternatively, one may start the chain from the cost function C and end it with C, namely $C \Rightarrow D \Rightarrow f \Rightarrow D \Rightarrow C$ by (30), (28), (27), and (29). Also, one may consider the chain starting from the distance function D and ending with D (see Blackorby, Primont, and Russell 1978, p. 39).[13]

3.3 Elements of Microeconomic Theory

The preceding discussion is useful in obtaining some well-known results in microeconomic theory. The derivation of such results would further illuminate the usefulness and the importance of sensitivity analysis. We shall illustrate the derivation of some well-known results in microeconomic theory by using familiar examples. It is hoped that the reader can, in this not so long section, realize that the analytics of basic microtheory are really simple and straightforward.

Before we embark on our discussion, we impose the following **regularity condition (RC)**.

(RC) $f(x)$ is positive, finite, twice continuously differentiable, strictly monotone, and strictly quasi-concave,

where $x \in R^n$. Function $f(x)$ can be interpreted as a production function. (RC) is, implicitly or explicitly, imposed in the usual cost

[13] The usefulness of the distance function has been explored by R. Färe and others. For a recent, succinct discussion of Shephard's duality theory, see Färe and Primont (1990). See also Afriat (1980).

minimization and profit maximization problems. Then the *strict* quasi-concavity ensures the uniqueness of the solution for cost minimization problems. Similarly, we may interpret $f(x)$ as the utility functions $u(x)$. Again, (RC) is imposed in the usual expenditure minimization and utility maximization problems. We first consider the cost minimization problem.

Cost Minimization. We again consider the problem of a firm that chooses $x \in R^n$ to

$$\text{(CM)} \quad \text{Minimize } w \cdot x, \quad \text{subject to } f(x) \geqq y \text{ and } x \geqq 0,$$

where y is a scalar, and $w > 0$ is assumed to be a given vector to the firm. Again, let $x(w, y) > 0$ be the solution of the above problem, and let $C(w, y) \equiv w \cdot x(w, y)$ be the minimum total cost function. Then we obtain (22) and (23) as discussed earlier. Let $x_{ij} \equiv \partial x_i / \partial w_j$ and consider the $n \times n$ matrix $S \equiv [x_{ij}]$. S is called the **substitution matrix.** Condition (23) states that S is symmetric. *For a fixed* y, S is a function of w, $S(w)$, since $x_{ij} = x_{ij}(w, y)$. Note that $x(w, y)$ is homogeneous of degree zero in w by the structure of the cost minimization problem (CM). Hence by Euler's equation,

$$\sum_{j=1}^{n} x_{ij} w_j = 0, \quad \text{or} \quad S(w)w = 0, \text{ for all } w,$$

where w is a column vector, which in turn implies $w'S(w) = 0$ as $S(w)$ is symmetric, where w' is the transpose of w.

Also, $C(w, y)$ is homogeneous of degree one in w, and concave in w. The homogeneity is obvious since $C(w, y) \equiv w \cdot x(w, y)$ and x is homogeneous of degree zero in w. To show concavity,[14] let $x^\circ \equiv x(w^\circ, y)$, $x^* \equiv x(w^*, y)$ and $x^\theta \equiv x(w^\theta, y)$, where $w^\theta \equiv \theta w^\circ + (1 - \theta)w^*$, $0 \leqq \theta \leqq 1$. Then,

$$w^\circ \cdot x^\circ \leqq w^\circ \cdot x^\theta \text{ and } w^* \cdot x^* \leqq w^* \cdot x^\theta,$$

by cost minimization, where we have $f(x^\circ) \geqq y$, $f(x^*) \geqq y$, and $f(x^\theta) \geqq y$ by definition of x°, x^* and x^θ. Hence,

$$\theta w^\circ \cdot x^\circ + (1 - \theta)w^* \cdot x^* \leqq \theta w^\circ \cdot x^\theta + (1 - \theta)w^* \cdot x^\circ = w^\theta \cdot x^\theta,$$

[14] The method of proof here is from McKenzie (1957).

where $0 \leqq \theta \leqq 1$. Namely, $\theta C(w^\circ, y) + (1 - \theta)C(w^*, y) \leqq C(w^\theta, y)$, $0 \leqq \theta \leqq 1$, which establishes the concavity of C in w. Thus the Hessian of C with respect to w is negative semidefinite, so that S is negative semidefinite since $x_{ij} = \partial^2 C/\partial w_i \partial w_j$. We have $z'S(w)z \leqq 0$ for all z. With S being negative semidefinite, we can easily show that $x_{ii} \leqq 0$ for all i. In addition, if we assume $z'S(w)z < 0$ for all z *not proportional to* w, then we can show that the rank of S is equal to $(n - 1)$.[15] This in turn implies (by a well-known theorem in matrix algebra) that the $(n - 1) \times (n - 1)$ matrix obtained from S by deleting the kth row and the kth column is negative definite. This in turn implies $x_{ii} < 0$, $i = 1, 2, \ldots, n$. In summary, we have the following proposition in economics.

Proposition 3.1. Let $S \equiv [x_{ij}]$ be the substitution matrix of the cost minimization problem (CM).

(i) $C(w, y)$ is homogeneous of degree one and concave in w with $\partial C/\partial w_i = x_i > 0$.

(ii) S is symmetric and negative semidefinite with $x_{ii} \leqq 0$ for all i. Also $S(w)w = 0$ and $w'S(w) = 0$ (w is a column vector so that w' is a row vector).

(iii) In addition, if we assume that $z'S(w)z < 0$, for all $z \neq 0$ not proportional to w, then the rank of S is $(n - 1)$, and $x_{ii} < 0$, for all $i = 1, 2, \ldots, n$.

REMARK: Statement (i) of proposition 3.1 exhausts all the basic properties of the cost function $C(w, y)$. Statements (ii) and (iii) exhaust all the basic properties of the substitution matrix S. The condition that $z'S(w)z < 0$ for all z not proportional to w in statement (iii) is known as **Samuelson's regularity condition** (see Samuelson 1947, p. 68). This condition will also be discussed in example A.7 in appendix A.

REMARK: $x_{ij} (\equiv \partial x_i/\partial w_j)$ measures a change in the ith factor demand with respect to a change in the jth factor price, when the level of

[15] To show this, let $N \equiv \{z : Sz = 0\}$: i.e., N is the null space of S. Since $Sw = 0$ and since $z'Sz < 0$ for all z not proportional to w, $N = \{z : z = tw,\ t \in R\}$, so that the rank of N is equal to one. Then by a well-known theorem in matrix algebra on the rank of a null space, the rank of S is $n - 1$. See (25) of appendix A. The restriction on the values of z is necessary because the homogeneity property (as observed earlier) requires $Sw = 0$.

output (y) is held constant. Factor i is said to be a **(Hicks-Allen) substitute** for factor j if $x_{ij} > 0$, and factor i is said to be a **(Hicks-Allen) complement** to factor j if $x_{ij} < 0$ ($i \neq j$) (see Hicks 1946, chap. 7). Since $x_{ij} = x_{ji}$, this definition is perfectly symmetric. Namely, if i is a substitute for (resp. complement to) j, then j is also a substitute for (resp. complement to) i. If the price of factor j increases, then the use of factor j decreases with $x_{jj} < 0$. If the use of factor i ($\neq j$) increases when the jth factor price increases (with output being constant), then factor i is a substitute for j, and if the use of i decreases, i is a complement of j. For example, suppose that w_1 is the wage rate (the price of labor employment), then an increase in w_1, *ceteris paribus*, lowers the demand for labor x_1, with $x_{11} < 0$. If x_2 is the amount of capital employed, and if labor and capital are substitutes for each other ($x_{12} > 0$), then this causes an increase in the demand for capital. On the other hand, if w_1 denotes the wage rate of skilled labor and if skilled labor and capital are complements for each other ($x_{12} < 0$), then an increase in w_1 causes a fall in the demand for skilled labor x_1 and also a *fall* in the demand for capital x_2. Recall $Sw = 0$, that is, $x_{i1}w_1 + x_{i2}w_2 + \ldots + x_{in}w_n = 0$, $i = 1, 2, \ldots, n$. With $x_{ii} < 0$, this means that at least one pair of factors must be substitutes (i.e., it is not possible that all factors are complements). If $n = 2$, $x_{ii} < 0$ implies $x_{12} = x_{21} \geqq 3$, complementarity can arise.

The usual profit maximization problem in intermediate-price-theory textbooks may be considered a two stage problem in which $x(w, y)$ is obtained by solving the cost minimization problem (where y is a scalar), and then y is chosen so as to maximize $py - C(w, y)$, where $C(w, y) \equiv w \cdot x(w, y)$. The solution of the second problem yields the familiar result for a competitive firm, $p = \partial C / \partial y$ or price = marginal cost.

Proposition 3.1 and the preceding discussion do *not* require the homogeneity of the production function $f(x)$. We now consider the case in which $f(x)$ is homogeneous of degree one (constant returns to scale). In this case, we may observe (assuming an interior solution, $x_i > 0$ for all i, and $\lambda > 0$):

$$C = w \cdot x = \lambda \sum_{i=1}^{n} f_i x_i = \lambda f(x) = \lambda y, \quad \text{where } f_i \equiv \partial f / \partial x_i,$$

by using the first-order conditions, $w_i = \lambda f_i$ and $f(x) = y$, and also the homogeneity of $f(x)$. From this we may at once assert $\lambda = C/y$, which in turn implies $\partial C/\partial y = C/y$ by (22). From this, we may observe

$$\frac{\partial \lambda}{\partial y} = \frac{1}{y^2}(\frac{\partial C}{\partial y}y - C) = \frac{1}{y}(\frac{\partial C}{\partial y} - \frac{C}{y}) = 0,$$

which means that λ is independent of y, so that λ can be written as $\lambda = c(w)$, a function of w alone. Recalling $\lambda = C/y$, we then have $C = c(w)y$. In summary, we have the results in proposition 3.2, which we call the **Shephard-Samuelson theorem** (Shephard 1953 and Samuelson 1953).

Proposition 3.2. If the production function exhibits constant returns to scale, then for the cost minimizing firm, we have

$$C/y = \partial C/\partial y = \lambda, \text{ and } C = c(w)y.$$

Namely, the average cost C/y is equal to the marginal cost $\partial C/\partial y$, and both of these are independent of output y.[16] We now turn to the problem of consumer's choice.

Consumer's Choice. Consider the following "expenditure minimization problem" (**EM**), in which a consumer chooses his or her consumption bundle $x \in R^n$ to

$$\text{(EM)} \quad \text{Minimize } p \cdot x, \text{ subject to } u(x) \geqq u, \text{ and } x \geqq 0,$$

where p = price vector, $u(x)$ = utility function, and u = the target level of utility, and where $p > 0$ is a given vector to the consumer. The consumer minimizes his or her expenditure subject to the condition that he or she achieves the utility level not less than u. Let $x^*(p, u)$ be the solution of this problem, which is known as the **compensated demand function** (or the **Hicksian demand function**). Let $E(p, u) \equiv p \cdot x^*(p, u)$. Function E is called the **minimum expenditure function**, and it signifies the minimum expenditure level that ensures the consumer at the same utility level u when p changes. The word "compensated" for the function $x^*(p, u)$ thus signifies the movement along the same indifference curve or surface when p changes.

---

[16]Taking y in the horizontal axis, this means that the average cost curve and the marginal cost curve coincide, and such a curve is a straight line that is parallel to the horizontal axis. This consequence of a constant returns to scale production function should be contrasted to the usual exposition of cost curves in intermediate price-theory textbooks, in which the average cost curve is U-shaped, and the marginal cost curve passes through its minimum point and is rising at such a point.

Now, compare the above expenditure minimization problem (EM) with the cost minimization problem (CM) of a firm, and note that these two problems are completely parallel to each other, where p, $u(x)$, and u in problem (EM) correspond to w, $f(x)$, and y in problem (CM), respectively. Then we may at once realize that proposition 3.1 holds as in the present expenditure minimization problem. Let $x^*_{ij} \equiv \partial x^*_i / \partial p_j$ and $S^* \equiv [x^*_{ij}]$, an $n \times n$ matrix. Since $x^*_{ij} = x^*_{ij}(p, u)$, S^* is a function of p *for a fixed value of* u; $S^* = S^*(p)$. We may now state a proposition that is completely parallel to proposition 3.1.

Proposition 3.3. For the previous expenditure minimization problem of a consumer, we have

(i) $E(p, u)$ is homogeneous of degree one and concave in p with $\partial E / \partial p_i = x^*_i$ for all i.

(ii) S^* is symmetric and negative semidefinite with $x^*_{ii} \leqq 0$ for all i. Also, $S^*(p)p = 0$ and $p'S^*(p) = 0$ (where p' is the transpose of the column vector p).

(iii) If we, in addition, assume that $z'S^*(p)z < 0$ for all z not proportional to p, then the rank of S^* is $(n - 1)$, and $x^*_{ii} < 0$ for all $i = 1, 2, \ldots, n$.

We now obtain the Hicks-Slutsky equation. To achieve this end, we recall the utility maximization problem, in which a consumer chooses his or her consumption bundle $x \in R^n$ to

(UM) Maximize $u(x)$, subject to $p \cdot x \leqq Y$, and $x \geqq 0$,

where $p > 0$ is a given vector to the consumer. Write the solution of this problem as $x(p, Y)$, and let $U(p, Y) \equiv u[x(p, Y)]$, be the maximum utility that the consumer can achieve when his or her income is Y and he or she faces a price vector p. Then we may observe the following dual relations:

$$E(p, U) = Y \quad \text{and} \quad x(p, Y) = x^*(p, U), \tag{31}$$

where $U = U(p, Y)$.[17] Namely, the minimum expenditure to reach utility U is Y, if U is the maximal attainable utility under (p, Y). The

[17]The understanding of (31) may be facilitated by drawing the conventional two-dimensional diagram of indifference curves and the budget line. Although (31) may thus be intuitively obvious, it requires a proof that is often glossed over in the text-

utility maximizing demand at income Y is the same as the compensated demand at utility U when $U = U(p, Y)$. From (31), we may assert

$$x[p, E(p, U)] = x^*(p, U). \tag{32}$$

Differentiating this with respect to p_j, we obtain the **Hicks-Slutsky equation**, or the **fundamental equation in value theory**,

$$\partial x_i / \partial p_j = x^*_{ij} - x_j(\partial x_i / \partial Y), \; i, j = 1, 2, \ldots, n, \tag{33}$$

where we may recall $\partial E / \partial p_j = x^*_j$.[18] The term x^*_{ij} is the **net substitution term** whose properties were already obtained in proposition 3.3, while $x_j(\partial x_i / \partial Y)$ represents the **income effect**. Virtually all textbooks on price theory contain graphic exposition of (33). Recalling $S \equiv [x^*_{ij}]$, we may at once obtain the following proposition from (33).

Proposition 3.4. Let $x(p, Y)$ (> 0) be a vector of demand functions that was obtained as a solution to (UM). Then we have the Hicks-Slutsky equation (33) and the matrix S^* satisfying properties (ii) and (iii) of proposition 3.3.

REMARK: The matrix S^* is called the (**net**) **substitution matrix**, and properties (ii) and (iii) of proposition 3.3 exhaust all the basic properties of the net substitution matrix.

---

book exposition. To prove $Y = E(P, U)$, first observe that $E(p, U) \leqq p \cdot x$ for all x such that $u(x) \geqq U$ (by definition of EM). Letting $x = x(p, Y)$, we then have $E(p, U) \leqq p \cdot x(p, Y) = Y$. Now suppose $E(p, U) < Y$, or $p \cdot x^* < Y$ where $x^* = x^*(p, U)$. Then there exists an x^1 such that $p \cdot x^* < p \cdot x^1 < Y$, and $x^1 \geqq x^*$. Then $u(x^1) > u(x^*) = U$, assuming the monotonicity of u. But since $U = u[x(p, Y)]$, $u(x^1) > u[x(p, Y)]$. Thus x^1 furnishes a higher utility than $x(p, Y)$ and yet it is affordable at income Y. This contradicts that $x(p, Y)$ is a utility maximizing point at income Y. Hence, $E(p, U) < Y$ is impossible, which in turn establishes $E(p, U) = Y$.

[18] In essence, the proof here follows McKenzie (1957), which was repeated by Karlin (1959, pp. 271–273); Takayama (1977; 1985, pp. 142–43); Varian (1984, pp. 130–31); Okuno-Suzumura (1985, pp. 196–97); and Silberberg (1990, pp. 329–32), for example. Eq. (33) is often referred to as the *Slutsky equation*. However, this particular form was obtained by Hicks (1939, 1946), and it is slightly different from that of Slutsky (1915). For a discussion on the conceptual distinction between Slutsky and Hicks on compensations involved on the net substitution term, see Silberberg (1990, pp. 351–53). The decomposition of $\partial x_i / \partial p_j$ into the substitution effect and the income effect is due to Slutsky (1915, 1952). It was rediscovered by Hicks and Allen (1934). Hicks' *Value and Capital* (1939, 1946) contains a classic discussion of (33) and related topics, which in turn is instrumental to many important studies.

REMARK: Commodity i is said to be **Giffen** if $\partial x_i(p,\ Y)/\partial p_i > 0$, and **inferior** if $\partial x_i(p,\ Y)/\partial Y < 0$.[19] Hence from (33) it is clear that every Giffen commodity is inferior, but not vice versa. It has generally been accepted among economists that, although inferior goods can occasionally be seen (e.g., use of Greyhound/Trailway bus lines vs. airlines), the Giffen paradox is very exceptional.[20] Hence we may safely rule out such a paradox, and conclude that a relative increase in the price of a commodity lowers the demand for that commodity (i.e., $\partial x_i/\partial p_i < 0$). This is called the **law of demand.**

Note that $x^*_{ij}(\equiv \partial x^*_i/\partial p_j)$ measures a change in the demand for commodity i when p is changed to keep the level of utility u fixed (i.e., a **compensated change in income**). Two commodities $i \neq j$ are said to be **substitutes** if $x^*_{ij} > 0$, and **complements** if $x^*_{ij} < 0$. Since $x^*_{ij} = x^*_{ij}$, the definitions of substitutes and complements are symmetric. If i is a substitute for (resp. complement to) j, then j is also a substitute for (resp. complement to) i. The definitions of substitutes and complements in consumption are completely analogous to the ones in the theory of production.

For example, if p_1 is the price of coffee, then an increase in p_1 lowers the demand for coffee x_1 with $x^*_{11} < 0$. If commodity 2 is tea and tea is a substitute for coffee ($x^*_{12} > 0$), then this increases the demand for tea. On the other hand, if p_1 is the price of a tennis racket, an increase in p_1 lowers its demand x_1 with $x^*_{11} < 0$. If commodity 2 is a tennis ball, and tennis balls are complements of tennis rackets ($x^*_{12} < 0$), then

---

[19] Partially differentiating the budget condition, $p_1x_1(p,\ Y) + p_2x_2(p,\ Y) + \ldots + p_nx_n(p,\ Y) = Y$, with respect to Y, we obtain

$$p_1\partial x_1/\partial Y + p_2\partial x_2/\partial Y + \ldots + p_n\partial x_n/\partial Y = 1.$$

Thus, it is not possible that all goods are inferior.

[20] The Giffen paradox is first pointed out by Marshall in the third edition (1895) of his *Principles*, where he gave credit to Sir Robert Giffen. However, Stigler (1947 and 1963) asserts that no one, including Giffen, has ever discovered any example of Giffen goods. More recently, Negishi (1989, pp. 45–46) offers the following argument that clarifies the *un*usual nature of Giffen goods. If a number of goods is large, and if the share of consumption of any one good in the individual's budget is small, then the income effect of each good would be small. On the other hand, the magnitudes of substitution effects need not get smaller as the number of goods increases (or the classification of goods becomes finer). In fact, the latter can increase as the number of goods increases. For example, the substitutability between Java and Columbian coffee would be greater than that between coffee and tea. Incidentally, it is possible to argue that the use of long-distance bus lines is not a case of inferior goods, but simply a case of *time* (which is required for traveling by such means) being too expensive for some people.

this causes a *fall* in the demand for tennis balls.

REMARK: As in the case of the cost minimization problem, we can easily make the following assertions. Since $S^*p = 0$, we have

$$x^*_{i1}p_i + x^*_{i2}p_2 + \ldots + x^*_{in}p_n = 0, \; i = 1, 2, \ldots, n.$$

With $x^*_{ii} < 0$, this means that at least one pair of commodities must be substitutes (that is, it is not possible that all commodities are complements). If $n = 2$, $x^*_{ii} = 0$ implies $x^*_{21} = x^*_{12} > 0$, so that the two commodities are necessarily substitutes, while if $n \geqq 3$, complementarity can arise.

An important concept in production theory as well as in consumption theory is *homothetic functions*, which is attributed to Shephard (1953).

Definition 3.1. The function $f(x)$ is said to be **homothetic** if there exists continuous and positive monotone increasing transformations $\phi(f)$ such that $g(x) \equiv \phi[f(x)]$ is homogeneous of degree one.[21]

Clearly if $f(x)$ is homogeneous of degree one (linear homogeneous) then it is a homothetic function, since $\phi(f) = f$. Thus, the class of homothetic functions is a wider class of functions than linearly homogeneous functions. Assume that f is well-behaved, that is, (RC) is satisfied. Then, the following proposition summarizes the important features of homothetic functions. Here, we use the cost minimization problem (CM) to illustrate basic results, where $f(x)$ is interpreted as a production function. By interpreting $f(x)$ as a utility function, we can obtain the parallel results for the theory of consumer's choice.

Proposition 3.5.

(i) $f(x)$ is homothetic *if and only* if it is "separable" in the sense that

$$C(w, y) = h(w)\phi(y), \text{ for any } w > 0 \text{ and } y > 0, \tag{34}$$

where h and ϕ are the same as the ones used in the defini-

[21] Alternatively, $f(x)$ is said to be **homothetic** if it is expressed as a continuous, monotone increasing transformation ψ of a function $g(x)$ which is homogeneous of degree one: i.e., $f(x) = \psi[g(x)]$ where $g(x)$ is homogeneous of degree one (Shephard 1953, p. 41). Needless to say, these two definitions of homotheticity are identical.

tion of homotheticity, $g(x) = \phi[f(x)]$.[22] In this case, we have $\lambda(w, y) = h(w)\phi'(y)$.

(ii) $f(x)$ is homothetic *if and only if*

$$x_i(w, y) = h_i(w)\phi(y), \text{ for all } w > 0 \text{ and } y > 0, \tag{35}$$

where $h_i \equiv \partial h(w)/\partial w_i$, $i = 1, \ldots, n$.

(iii) $f(x)$ is homothetic *if and only* if every expansion path is a ray from the origin for all input price vectors $w > 0$.

REMARK: Statement (ii) follows at once from statement (i) and Shephard's lemma, $\partial C/\partial w_i = x_i$. We may readily assert that if $f(x)$ is homothetic, then (35) holds so that the ratio x_i/x_j is independent of y for each i and j: the expansion path is a straight line from the origin. This then establishes the "only if" part of statement (iii). The proofs of the "if" part of statement (iii) typically make use of partial differential equations (Lau 1969 and Førsund 1975), or utilizes a rather lengthy set-theoretic argument (Färe and Shephard 1977a and 1977b). A simple and elementary proof is provided by Ide and Takayama (1989b).[23]

---

[22] To prove (34), it suffices to show $\partial(C/\phi)/\partial y = 0$, or $(\partial C/\partial y) - C\phi'/\phi = 0$. Since $\partial C/\partial y = \lambda$ by (22), it then suffices to show $C\phi'/\phi = \lambda$. To this end, simply observe that the following relations hold at optimum.

$$C = \sum w_i x_i = \sum \lambda f_i x_i = \sum \lambda(g_i/\phi')x_i = (\lambda/\phi')\sum g_i x_i$$

$$= \lambda g(x)/\phi' = \lambda\phi[f(x)]/\phi'.$$

where $f_i \equiv \partial f/\partial x_i$ and $g_i \equiv \partial g/\partial x_i$.

[23] Ide and Takayama (1989b) obtain both "if" and "only if" parts simultaneously. Since their proof is short, it can be reproduced here. Define the expansion path determined by a given $w > 0$, by

$$S(w) \equiv \{x > 0 : f_i(x)/f_j(x) = w_i/w_j,\ i, j = 1, 2, \ldots, n,\ i \neq j\},$$

which is fixed as long as w is fixed. We prove statement (iii) by showing the equivalence of the following two statements for any arbitrarily fixed $w > 0$.

(A) The *EP* is a ray from the origin; i.e., $\bar{x} \in S(w)$ implies $k\bar{x} \in S(w)$ for all $k > 0$.

(B) The minimum cost function is "separable," $C(w, y) = h(w)\phi(y)$, for $y > 0$.

We first show statement (A) implies statement (B). Let $y \equiv f(k\bar{x})$. By the strict monotonicity and continuity of f, we can solve this for k to obtain, $k = k(y, \bar{x}) \equiv \phi(y)$, as $\bar{x}$ is fixed. By statement (A), $\bar{x} \in S(w)$ and $k\bar{x} \in S(w)$ for all $k > 0$.

REMARK: Note that the Shephard-Samuelson theorem (proposition 3.2) is a special case in which $\phi(y) = y$, for if $\phi(y) = y$, then $C/y = \partial C/\partial y = h(w) = \lambda$. In this case, $w_i x_i / y = w_i h_i(w)$ is independent of output y. Namely, if $f(x)$ is homogeneous of degree one, the ith relative share (which is also equal to the ith cost share under the linear homogeneity of f) is independent of y.

REMARK: Statement (iii) of proposition 3.4 indicates a remarkable feature of homothetic functions, stating that any ray through the origin will cut the isoquants in the input space at points where the slopes are the same (namely, w is given), and that if we join the points at which isoquants are tangent to iso-cost curves for any fixed $w > 0$, then such curves are all straight lines from the origin.

Given this property (iii), homothetic functions have been widely used in the theory of production and consumption. Linear homogeneous functions, a special class of homothetic functions, have also been widely used in economics, producing many interesting and useful results. However, since every expansion need not be a ray from the origin, in general, the homotheticity assumption can also be considered too restrictive. In fact, in the theory of consumption, the assertion that every Engel curve (which is an expansion path) is a ray from the origin is sometimes considered rather outlandish, as it appears to contradict virtually all empirical evidence.

To explore this point a little further, let μ_i be defined by

$$\mu_i \equiv [\partial x_i(w,\ y)/\partial y](y/x_i),\ i = 1,\ 2,\ \ldots,\ n. \tag{36}$$

Namely, μ_i signifies the output elasticity of the demand for factor i. If $f(x)$ is homothetic, we may readily obtain from (35)

$$\mu_1 = \mu_2 = \ldots = \mu_n\ [= \phi'(y)y/\phi(y)]. \tag{37}$$

Conversely, if (37) holds, $f(x)$ is homothetic. Thus, function $f(x)$ is homothetic if and only if the output elasticities of factor demands are

---

Hence we may observe $C(w,\ y) \equiv w\cdot\phi(y)\overline{x} = \phi(y)w\cdot x[w,\ f(\overline{x})] = \phi(y)h(w)$, where $h(w) \equiv w\cdot x[w,\ f(\overline{x})]$. This establishes statement (B). To show the converse, assume statement (B), $C(w,\ y) = h(w)\phi(y)$. By the strict monotonicity and continuity of f and hence of ϕ, we may choose $\overline{y}$, such that $\phi(\overline{y}) = 1$. Accordingly, we may choose $\overline{x} \in S(w)$ so that $w\cdot\overline{x} = h(w)$ for such a $\overline{y}$. Multiplying through $\phi(y)$, we obtain $C(w,\ y) = \phi(y)h(w) = \phi(y)(w\cdot\overline{x}) = w\cdot\phi(y)\overline{x}$. Hence $\phi(y)\overline{x} \in S(w)$. This establishes statement (A). Thus (A) and (B) are equivalent. Since the choice of w is arbitrary, the equivalence of statements (A) and (B) holds for any $w > 0$. Hence this completes the proof of statement (iii) of proposition 3.4.

equal over all factors. If $f(x)$ is homogeneous of degree one, then $\phi(f) = f$, so that we have

$$\mu_1 = \mu_2 = \ldots = \mu_n = 1. \tag{38}$$

Namely, the output elasticities of factor demands are equal to unity for all factors.

Let θ be defined by

$$\theta \equiv [\partial C(w,\ y)/\partial y](y/C). \tag{39}$$

Then θ signifies the cost elasticity of output, and it is also equal to the ratio of the marginal cost over the average cost. Let $\theta_i \equiv w_i x_i / C$, the ith cost share. Then we can readily show that

$$\theta = \theta_1\mu_1 + \theta_2\mu_2 + \ldots + \theta_n\mu_n. \tag{40}$$

Namely, θ is a convex combination of the μ_i's. The parameter θ is often used as a measure for returns to scale in recent literature. We may say that **increasing returns to scale** prevail if $\theta < 1$, **decreasing returns to scale** prevail if $\theta > 1$, and **constant returns to scale** prevail if $\theta = 1$. (For further discussions of the concepts of returns to scale, see sec. 3.5). If $f(x)$ is homogeneous of degree one, then we can show $\theta = 1$ for all y.

Equation (37) can be used as a null hypothesis for empirically testing the homotheticity of $f(x)$. If this is rejected, then $f(x)$ fails to be homothetic. Also (40) can be used to compute the returns to scale measure θ, once we estimate the μ_i's. Using a data set from the U.S. manufacturing industry, Chao and Takayama (1991) attempt such an empirical study, in which they show that the output elasticity of factor demand (μ_i) differs by factors and that $\theta < 1$ (increasing returns to scale).[24]

---

[24] The empirical procedure of Chao and Takayama (1991) emphasizes a distinction between variable factors and quasi-fixed factors (or fixed factors), which in turn incorporates the Marshallian distinction between "short-run" and "long-run" into empirical analysis. Some studies on this topic *a priori* assume homotheticity. Such an assumption is avoided in Chao and Takayama (1991) both in the short-run and in the long-run, as they purportedly derive an empirical procedure to obtain estimates of returns to scale and elasticities of factor substitution. Their study attempts to mark a departure from related studies by Brown and Christensen (1981); Morrison and Berndt (1981); and Morrison (1986), for example.

3.4 Elasticity of Factor Substitution and Its Estimation

In recent empirical studies, the concept of elasticities of factor substitution has increasingly become important. In this section, we briefly exposit this and related issues. Micro theory is very relevant to empirical studies, and the present section would provide one example of such studies.

Consider the usual cost minimization problem, and let $x_i(w, y)$ be the demand for the ith factor. Let $x_{ij} \equiv \partial x_i / \partial w_j$. As mentioned earlier, factors i and j are substitutes for each other if $x_{ij} > 0$, and factors i and j are complements to each other if $x_{ij} < 0 (i \neq j)$. Define the price elasticity of factor demand in the conventional way as

$$e_{ij} \equiv (\partial x_i / \partial w_j)(w_j / x_i) (= x_{ij} w_j / x_i),\ i,\ j = 1,\ 2,\ \ldots,\ n,$$

which signifies the percentage change in the ith factor demand per percentage change in the jth factor price. An important feature of this definition is that e_{ij} is *not* symmetric. Namely, $e_{ij} \neq e_{ji}$, $i \neq j$, in general. To overcome this problem, we may define σ_{ij} by

$$\sigma_{ij} \equiv e_{ij} / \theta_j, \text{ where } \theta_j \equiv w_j x_j / (w \cdot x),\ i,\ j = 1,\ 2,\ \ldots,\ n. \quad (41)$$

Here, θ_j signifies the cost share of the jth factor (at the cost minimizing optimum). It would be easy to show that $\sigma_{ij} = \sigma_{ji}$, that is, the σ_{ij}'s are symmetric. The σ_{ij}'s are called the **(Allen- partial) elasticities of factor substitution (ES)**.[25]

Clearly $\sigma_{ij} > 0$ (or < 0) if factors i and j are substitutes (or complements) for each other. Thus, the sign of ES can then be used to determine whether a particular pair of factors are substitutes or complements.

A succinct feature of ES is that not only is it symmetric, but also it has important implications for the underlying production function. For example, the Cobb-Douglas production function results in $\sigma_{ij} = 1$ for all $i \neq j$, and vice versa. For the two factor case, we may easily obtain, from (41) and $x_{i1} w_1 + x_{i2} w_2 = 0 (i = 1,\ 2)$, the following well-known relation *under homotheticity*:

$$dz/z = -\sigma(d\omega/\omega),\ z \equiv x_1/x_2,\ \omega \equiv w_1/w_2,$$

[25] The concept of the elasticity of substitution was first developed by Hicks (1932) for the two factor case. When $n \geq 3$, alternative concepts are possible. These alternative concepts are important. The present concept is along the line of Allen's (1938) work.

where $\sigma \equiv \sigma_{12} = \sigma_{21}$. A one percent increase in ω results in a σ percent fall in z. ES thus measures the "curvature" of the isoquants for the two factor case. Also, since $\theta_1/\theta_2 = (w_1x_1)/(w_2x_2)$, an increase in ω results in a fall (or a rise) in the relative share ration θ_1/θ_2 if $\sigma > 1$ (or $\sigma < 1$) (see Hicks 1932). If σ is constant all along the isoquant, the production function takes the following **CES** form, which is due to Arrow, Chenery, Minhas, and Solow (1961),

$$y = f(x_1, x_2) = (ax_1^\rho + bx_2^\rho), \text{ where } \rho \equiv (\sigma - 1)/\sigma.$$

The CES form has inspired a large number of empirical and theoretical studies, although extension to the multifactor case has encountered some important difficulties (see, for example, Fuss, McFadden, and Mundlak 1978).

Thus the Allen elasticities reduce to the usual Hicksian elasticity of factor substitution (σ) for the two-factor case. This occurs provided that the production function is homothetic (prove it). In the two-factor case, we may obtain "nice features" such as the interpretation of the elasticities in terms of the curvature of isoquants and its implication for income distribution or the relative share. On the other hand, for the general n-factor case, these nice features mostly disappear when we use the Allen elasticities. It appears that the only useful information that we can obtain from the Allen elasticities are that these can tell us whether two particular factors (i and j) are substitutes or complements for each other (see Blackorby and Russell 1989). Blackorby and Russell then advocate the use of "Morishima elasticities."

Let $C(w, y)$ be the (minimum) total cost function as before. Letting $C_i \equiv \partial C/\partial w_i$ and $C_{ij} = \partial^2 C/\partial w_i \partial w_j$ and recalling Shephard's lemma, we can easily show

$$\sigma_{ij} = CC_{ij}/C_iC_j, \; i, \; j = 1, 2, \ldots, n, \quad \text{for all } w \text{ and } y. \tag{42}$$

A similar relation is obtained by Uzawa (1962) in a more tedious manner. In addition, he assumed that the production function $f(x)$ is homogeneous of degree one. If $f(x)$ is homogeneous of degree one, then $C(w, y) = c(w)y$ by proposition 3.2 so that (42) can readily be reduced to Uzawa's formula (1962, p. 293):

$$\sigma_{ij} = cc_{ij}/c_ic_j, \quad \text{where } c_i \equiv \partial c/\partial w_i, \; c_{ij} \equiv \partial^2 c/\partial w_i \partial w_j. \tag{43}$$

As Brown and Christensen (1981, p. 209) write, "the widespread application of duality theory to economic analysis and the concommitant development of flexible functional forms" have attracted a great deal of attention in the empirical literature, especially since the 1970s. To illustrate this, we focus our attention on the case of production theory, in particular the problem of estimating factor demand functions, $x(w,\ y)$. The conventional procedure, which is to specify an explicit form for the production function f and then solve the cost minimization problem, either imposes quite restrictive assumptions regarding such key parameters as ES,[26] or yields difficult questions from the point of view of empirical estimation. More specifically, the latter problem stems from the difficulty of obtaining an algebraic expression for $x(w,\ y)$ in terms of empirically manageable (unknown) parameters that characterize the production function f. This occurs especially when we require f to be flexible in the sense that it provides a second-order differentiable approximation to an arbitrary twice continuously differentiable function.[27]

However, there is an alternative approach that has recently been attracting a great deal of attention. The alternative approach is to utilize the Shephard duality (which ensures the existence of a unique production function given the existence of a unique cost function with certain regularity conditions) and Shephard's lemma ($\partial C/\partial w_i = x_i$). Shephard's lemma, as originally obtained by Shephard (1953), postulates only such a cost function, and does not require the specification of a production function. The second approach also enables us to avoid the sometimes painful algebra in deriving $x(w,\ y)$ by the conventional approach via Lagrangian multipliers. In summary, the second approach specifies a (flexible) form of the cost function with the appropriate regularity conditions, utilizes the Shephard duality and Shephard's lemma, and then estimates the relevant parameters by simple regression.

More concretely, we specify the cost function by the following translog (transcendental logarithmic) function introduced by Christensen, Jorgenson, and Lau (1971 and 1975) and others. The translog form is shown to be flexible, and it is popular in current empirical studies.[28]

---

[26]The Cobb-Douglas function restricts $\sigma_{ij} = 1$ for all i and j. The CES function for the two-factor case assumes that relation ES is constant, while there is no apparent technological justification for such a restriction. Extension of the CES function to more than two factors restricts, "with unimportant exceptions," the ES of every pair of factors to be equal and constant. See Fuss, McFadden, and Mundlak (1978, p. 240).

[27]The function $\overline{f}$ is said to provide a **second-order approximation** of an arbitrary twice continuously differentiable function f at a point x°, if $f(x^\circ) = \overline{f}(x^\circ)$, $f'(x^\circ) = \overline{f}'(x^\circ)$, $f''(x^\circ) = \overline{f}''(x^\circ)$. See, for example, Diewert (1982, p. 574) and Fuss, McFadden, and Mundlak (1978).

[28]Note that if $a_{ij} = b_i = 0$ and $a_i > 0$ for all i and j with $c_1 = 0$ and $c_2 = 0$, then $C(w,\ y)$ defined by (44) reduces to a Cobb-Douglas cost function, from which

The translog function can be specified as follows:

$$\log C(w,\ y) = a_o + \sum_{i=1}^{n} a_i \log w_i + \frac{1}{2}\sum_{i=1}^{n}\sum_{j=1}^{n} a_{ij} \log w_i \log w_j + \sum_{i=1}^{n} b_i \log w_i \log y + [c_1 \log y + \frac{1}{2} c_2 (\log y)^2], \tag{44}$$

where

$$\sum_{i=1}^{n} a_i = 1,\ \sum_{j=1}^{n} a_{ij} = 0 \text{ for all } i,$$

$$a_{ij} = a_{ji} \text{ for all } i \text{ and } j, \text{ and } \sum_{i=1}^{n} b_i = 0. \tag{45}$$

Conditions in (45) are imposed to ensure that $C(w,\ y)$ is homogeneous of degree one with respect to w and that the Hessian $\partial^2 C/\partial w_i \partial w_j$ is symmetric.[29] The translog function may be viewed as a quadratic logarithmic approximation of an arbitrary function.[30]

---

we can construct a Cobb-Douglas production function. Needless to say, another flexible functional specification of the cost function other than the translog function is possible.

[29]Note that $\partial^2 C/\partial w_i \partial w_j = a_{ij}$, so that the symmetry of the Hessian matrix means $a_{ij} = a_{ji}$. Imposing the linear homogeneity on (44), $C(\alpha w,\ y) = \alpha C(w,\ y)$ for all $\alpha > 0$ (which holds irrespective of the form of the production function), we obtain the rest of (45).

[30]Viewing the translog function as an approximation of the true function, one may then question the plausibility of imposing various restrictions such as concavity since not all properties of the underlying true function can be inherited by the approximating function. However, as Lau (1978, pp. 418–19) argues,

> if we restrict our attention to those second-order approximating functions which agree with the first and second derivatives at the point of approximation, then all approximating functions to underlying monotonic, convex, or quasi-convex functions will exhibit behavior similar to the function they are approximating at the point of approximation . . . non-convexity of the approximating function at the point of approximation necessarily implies nonconvexity of the underlying function.

Differentiating (44) with respect to w_i and applying Shephard's lemma, we obtain

$$\theta_i(w,\ y) \equiv w_i x_i / C(w,\ y)$$

$$= a_i + \sum_{j=1}^{n} a_{ij} \log w_j + b_i \log y,\ i = 1, \ldots, n, \tag{46}$$

where θ_i signifies the ith factor share (the cost of the ith factor over the total cost).[31] Notice that in (46), θ_i is linear in the unknown parameters a_i, a_{ij}'s, and b_i. Since the θ_i's are observable, (46) allows the estimation of these parameters by ordinary linear regression. In performing the regression, we need to be cautious such that only $(n - 1)$ of n equations in (46) can be statistically independent since $\sum_i \theta_i = 1$. By appending (44) to these $(n - 1)$ equations, we may estimate all of the parameters, given data on the cost shares, factor prices, and output. In addition, if the underlying production function is known to be homothetic, then C is separable, $C(w,\ y) = h(w)\phi(y)$, as mentioned earlier, which in turn implies $b_i = 0$ for all i. This then means that we can statistically test the homotheticity of the production function by checking the parameters b_i's, estimated from (46), to see if they are significantly different from zero.[32] Note that if we can assume *a priori* that the production function is homothetic, then the estimation (46) is simplified as

$$\theta_i \equiv w_i x_i / C = a_i + \sum_{j=1}^{n} \log w_j,\ i = 1,\ 2,\ \ldots,\ n, \tag{47}$$

since θ_i is independent of y by (34) and (35). Namely, in estimating the a_i's and the a_{ij}'s, we need no data for y (output), which can be useful

---

[31] In the differentiation of (44), use the following well-known result in matrix algebra. Let $Q(x) \equiv x \cdot A \cdot x$, where $A = [a_{ij}]$ is an $n \times n$ matrix. Then we have $\partial Q / \partial x_i = 2 \sum_j a_{ij} x_j$, $i = 1,\ 2,\ \ldots,\ n$. Thus differentiating (44) with respect to w_i yields

$$(\partial C / \partial w_i)/C = a_i / w_i + \sum_j a_{ij} \ \log w_j \ (1/w_i) + b_i \ \log y \ (1/w_i).$$

[32] If we can reject $H_0 : b_i = 0$ for all i, then we can reject homotheticity. When we cannot reject this null hypothesis, we need to examine necessary and sufficient conditions for homotheticity since $[b_i = 0$ for all $i]$ is only a necessary condition for homotheticity. For such a test, see Berndt-Christensen (1973).

in some empirical studies.[33] In addition, if the production function is homogeneous of degree one, we have $C(w, y) = h(w)y$, so that we must have $c_1 = 1$ and $c_2 = 0$ as well as $b_i = 0$ for all i in (44).

Next, note from (44)

$$a_{ij} = \frac{\partial^2 \log C(w, y)}{\partial \log w_i \partial \log w_j} = w_i w_j \frac{\partial}{\partial w_i} (\frac{1}{C} \frac{\partial C}{\partial w_j}), \quad \text{if } i \neq j;$$

$$a_{ii} = w_i^2 \frac{\partial}{\partial w_i} (\frac{1}{C} \frac{\partial C}{\partial w_i}) + (\frac{1}{C} \frac{\partial C}{\partial w_i})\, w_i.$$

Then recalling $\partial C / \partial w_i = x_i$ (Shephard's lemma) and (41), we may obtain the following formula to compute the Allen elasticities of factor substitution (the σ_{ij}'s) using the values of the a_{ij}'s estimated from (47):

$$\sigma_{ij} = (a_{ij} + \theta_i \theta_j)/(\theta_i \theta_j), \; i \neq j,$$

$$\sigma_{ii} = (a_{ii} - \theta_i + \theta_i^2)/\theta_i^2. \tag{48}$$

This formula can also be obtained by applying (44) to (43). Note that since θ_i can change from time to time, the σ_{ij}'s need not be constant (unlike the case of CES production functions). Using the aggregate data for U.S. manufacturing during 1947–71 in terms of the four factor model, Berndt and Wood (1975) obtain the result that capital (K) and energy (E) are complements and labor (L) and energy are substitutes with $\sigma_{KE} = -3.2$ and $\sigma_{LE} = 0.65$ (while labor and capital are substitutes with $\sigma_{LK} = 1.01$). This implies that a rise in the energy price (as in late 1973, for example) lowers the use of capital (due to the E-K complementarity) and increases the use of labor (due to the E-L substitutability). This is often taken as being consistent with a sharp decrease in the growth rate of U.S. labor productivity after 1973. Berndt and Wood's study inspired many others to empirically ascertain E-K complementarity. Although these studies seem to be rather inconclusive, more seem to support the E-K complementarity (as opposed to

[33] For example, the output data may not be available or the definition of "output" becomes ambiguous when these refer to such things as monetary services, transportation services, medicare services, and research output. As an example of such an estimation, see Sims, Takayama, and Chao (1987). Since many transactions of financial assets can be completed quickly by telephone calls, etc., the distinction between variable and quasi-fixed factors in production models is not important in some studies of financial assets. Using this view, Sims, Takayama, and Chao (1987) estimate the degree of substitutability and complementarity among different assets that are called "near monies." They use Allen elasticities to measure such degrees, which can be updated in view of Blackorby and Russell (1989).

the E-K substitutability). One weakness in many studies on this topic is that they ignore the distinction between quasi-fixed factors and variable factors. For example, capital, being slow to adjust, is a quasi-fixed factor. A number of empirical attempts have been made to incorporate this distinction in the 1980s (e.g., the literature cited in fn. 24). For a recent study, see Chao and Takayama (1991), in which they develop a theoretical formula to estimate the long-run elasticities.[34]

3.5 On the Concept of Returns to Scale

In the literature, the terms such as increasing returns to scale (scale economies), decreasing returns to scale (scale diseconomies), and constant returns to scale have very often been used. However, the various definitions of these concepts and the relationship among them often remain ambiguous. In this section,[35] we shall clarify such definitions and the relationship among them. It goes without saying that an understanding of these issues is important in any serious studies involving scale economies and diseconomies.

Let $f(x)$ be a production function, and let $C(w,\ y)$ be the cost function that is obtained by the usual cost minimization procedure. Let $w > 0$ be a *fixed* factor price vector. Then $\theta(y) \equiv (\partial C/\partial y)/(C/y) = MC/AC$, which also signifies the cost elasticity of output, serves as a measure for returns to scale as observed in connection with (40). **Increasing returns to scale** (**IRS**) can be defined in terms of θ.

Definition 3.2. **IRS**(θ) is said to prevail if $\theta < 1$, where IRS(θ) means that IRS in terms of θ.

This means that IRS(θ) prevails if a 1 percent increase in output results in less than 1 percent increase in the total cost. Similarly, decreasing returns to scale (DRS) and constant returns to scale (CRS) are defined

---

[34] Using essentially the same data as Berndt and Christensen (1975), but distinguishing quasi-fixed factors from variable factors, Chao and Takayama (1991) obtain the following estimates for U.S. manufacturing, where M stands for materials: $\sigma_{KE} = -0.57$, $\sigma_{LK} = 0.41$, $\sigma_{LM} = 0.31$, $\sigma_{LE} = 1.59$, $\sigma_{KM} = -0.08$, and $\sigma_{EM} = -0.07$. Scale economies prevail (the cost elasticity of output is less than unity), and technical change explains approximately 28 percent of output growth for the period of observation. The own-price elasticities are all negative as theory indicates.

[35] This section summarizes a part of the results contained in Ide and Takayama (1987 and 1991). To avoid clutter, here we simply ignore such well-known factors as "fixed costs" and "indivisibility." The introduction of these should not be difficult, and is left to the interested reader.

in terms of θ as follows: (i) **DRS**(θ) prevails if $\theta > 1$ and (ii) **CRS**(θ) prevails if $\theta = 1$.

Alternatively, we may define returns to scale in terms of the shape of average cost curves. To this end, let $\beta(y) \equiv C(w, y)/y$, where w is assumed to be a fixed vector, and $\beta(y)$ signifies the average cost. Then we obtain the following definition, where IRS(β) signifies IRS in terms of β.

Definition 3.3. **IRS**(β) is said to prevail if $\beta'(y) < 0$, whereas **DRS**(β) prevails if $\beta'(y) > 0$. **CRS**(β) prevails if $\beta'(y) = 0$.

Namely, IRS(β) prevails if the AC curve is falling with an increase in output. The definitions 3.2 and 3.3 of returns to scale are equivalent. Namely, we have the following result.

Proposition 3.6. IRS(θ) prevails if and only if IRS(β) prevails.

Proof: Simply observe

$$\frac{\partial}{\partial y}\left(\frac{C}{y}\right) = \frac{1}{y}\left(\frac{\partial C}{\partial y} - \frac{C}{y}\right) = \frac{C}{y^2}(\theta - 1).$$

From this we may at once conclude that $\beta' < 0$ if and only if $\theta < 1$.[36]

(QED)

Analogously, we can show that $\theta > 1$ if and only if $\beta' > 0$. We may then obtain $\theta = 1$ if and only if $\beta' = 0$.

In the theory of production, it is often useful to restrict the defining properties of returns to scale to a certain range of output levels. For example, in the usual U-shaped AC curve, the AC curve is decreasing to a certain level of output (in which $\beta' < 0$ and $\theta < 1$), and then increases as output increases (in which $\beta' > 0$ and $\theta > 1$). It would then become important to restrict the concepts of returns to scale to a certain range of output levels. This is simply facilitated by restricting the range of y in the definitions of returns to scale. However, since this is rather obvious, we shall not modify our definitions, thereby avoiding chatter in exposition.

Now note that the "most widely used" (Hanoch 1975, p. 492) concept of returns to scale is different from the preceding. It goes as follows. IRS is said to prevail if output increases more than k times when all factors

---

[36] A similar relation is obtained in connection with the proof of proposition 3.2.

are increased by k times ($k > 1$). Define parameter α by

$$\alpha(k,\ \overline{x}) \equiv f(k\overline{x})/[kf(\overline{x})], \tag{49}$$

where $\overline{x}$ is a fixed (reference) input vector. Then the most widely used concept of increasing returns to scale, IRS in terms of α, denoted by IRS(α), runs as follows.

Definition 3.4. **IRS**(α) is said to prevail, if

$$\alpha(k,\ \overline{x}) > 1 \text{ for all } k > 1, \text{ and} \tag{50a}$$

$$\alpha(k,\ \overline{x}) < 1 \text{ for all } k \text{ such that } 0 < k < 1, \tag{50b}$$

where $\alpha(k,\ \overline{x}) = 1$ for $k = 1$. The scalar k is known as the **scale coefficient** or the **scale factor**.[37] If the inequalities for α in (50) are reversed, then we say that **DRS**(α) prevails. If $\alpha(k,\ \overline{x}) = 1$ for all k, namely if f is homogeneous of degree one, then **CRS**(α) prevails.

Another popular definition of returns to scale is obtained in terms of **scale elasticity**, ε, which is defined by

$$\varepsilon(k\overline{x}) \equiv \frac{k}{f(k\overline{x})}\frac{\partial f(k\overline{x})}{\partial k}, \tag{51}$$

where $w > 0$ is assumed to be constant.[38] The parameter ε measures the percentage increase in output per percentage increase in the scale coefficient k. Then we may define IRS in terms of ε, denoted by IRS(ε), as follows.

Definition 3.5. **IRS**(ε) is said to prevail if

$$\varepsilon(k,\ \overline{x}) > 1 \text{ for all } k > 0.$$

Similarly, **DRS**(ε) prevails if $\varepsilon < 1$ for all $k > 0$, and **CRS**(ε) prevails if $\varepsilon = 1$ for all k.

The following proposition relates IRS(α) to IRS(ε).

---

[37] Although (50a) and (50b) are not independent (as one is implied by the other), it may be useful to mention both conditions.

[38] The parameter ε corresponds to Frisch's (1965, p. 65) "passus coefficient." Frisch points out that this concept has been used by a number of prominent economists.

Proposition 3.7. IRS(α) prevails if and only if IRS(ε) prevails.

We show this by proving lemmas 3.1 and 3.2.

Lemma 3.1. $\partial\alpha(k,\bar{x})/\partial k > 0$ for all $k > 0$ if and only if $\varepsilon(k, \bar{x}) > 1$ for all $k > 0$.

Proof. Simply recall the definitions of α and β, and observe:

$$\frac{\partial\alpha(k, \bar{x})}{\partial k} = \frac{1}{k^2 f(\bar{x})}[k \frac{\partial f(k\bar{x})}{\partial k} - f(k\bar{x})]$$

$$= \frac{f(k\bar{x})}{k^2} f(\bar{x}) \ [\varepsilon(k\bar{x}) - 1]. \qquad \text{(QED)}$$

Lemma 3.2. $\partial\alpha(k, \bar{x})/\partial k$ is equivalent to IRS in terms of α. More specifically, we have

(i) For $k > 1$, $\alpha(k, \bar{x}) > 1$ if and only if $\partial\alpha(k, \bar{x})/\partial k > 0$, and

(ii) For $0 < k < 1$, $\alpha(k, \bar{x}) < 1$ if and only if $\partial\alpha(k, \bar{x})/\partial k > 0$.

Proof. To prove statement (i), simply observe that for $k > 1$,

$$\alpha(k, \bar{x}) \equiv f(k\bar{x})/\{kf(\bar{x})\} > f(\bar{x})/f(\bar{x}) = 1,$$

if and only if $\partial x(k, \bar{x})/\partial k > 0$. Simply noting that the inequality is reversed for $0 < k < 1$, statement (ii) follows at once. (QED)

Combining these two lemmas, proposition 3.7 follows at once. Analogously, we can show that DRS(α) prevails if and only if DRS(ε) prevails. Thus, we may also assert that CRS(α) prevails if and only if CRS(ε) prevails.

Proposition 3.8 relates various concepts of constant returns to scale.

Proposition 3.8. CRS(α), CRS(ε), CRS(θ), and CRS(β) are mutually equivalent.

Proof. By proposition 3.6 and 3.7, it suffices to show that CRS(θ) prevails if and only if $f(x)$ is homogeneous of degree one, where the latter is equivalent to CRS(α). If $f(x)$ is homogeneous of degree one, then by the Shephard-Samuelson theorem (proposition 3.5), we have

$C/y = \partial C/\partial y$, or $\theta = 1$, so that CRS(θ) prevails. Conversely if CRS(θ) prevails, $C/y = \partial C/\partial y (= \lambda)$. Then observe

$$\lambda y = C = \sum_{i=1}^{n} w_i x_i = \lambda \sum_{i=1}^{n} f_i x_i, \quad \text{where } f_i \equiv \partial f/\partial x_i,$$

so that we must have $y = \sum_{i=1}^{n} f_i x_i$. This relation holds (Euler's equation for homogeneous functions) if and only if f is homogeneous of degree one. (QED)

If we depart from CRS, we are not able to obtain the result such as proposition 3.8. Though IRS(θ) and IRS(β) are mutually equivalent, they are not equivalent to IRS(α), nor to IRS(ε). The reason for this is straightforward. Both concepts, IRS(α) and IRS(ε), are defined in terms of a proportional increase in all factor inputs, that is, in terms of a *ray* from the origin in the isoquant map, and consequently these concepts ignore the configuration of factor prices. On the other hand, IRS(θ) and IRS(β) are defined in terms of cost function, which is obtained via the cost minimization procedure. Namely, IRS(θ) and IRS(β) are defined in terms of an *expansion path* (EP). Then it would be natural to conclude that the concepts of IRS(θ) and IRS(β) are, in general, different from those of IRS(α) and IRS(ε). The precise relationship among these concepts is obtained in Ide and Takayama (1987 and 1989a). It is possible that a firm enjoys IRS or scale economies by its expansion along an EP, but it suffers from DRS or scale diseconomies by its expansion along a ray from the origin. *Since the firm does not expand its scale of operation mechanically along a ray from the origin but rather along an EP, the concepts of IRS(α) and IRS(ε), though they are widely used in the literature, need not be consistent with the rational behavior of the firm.*

However, by statement (iii) of proposition 3.5, we know that every EP is a ray from the origin if and only if the production function $f(x)$ is homothetic. Then, it would not be surprising when we obtain the following result.[39]

Proposition 3.9. If and only if $f(x)$ is homothetic, IRS in terms of an EP is equivalent to IRS in terms of a ray from the origin.

We may now schematically illustrate the relationship among the four

[39] A rigorous discussion of this is seen in Ide and Takayama (1989a).

different concepts in figure 3.1.

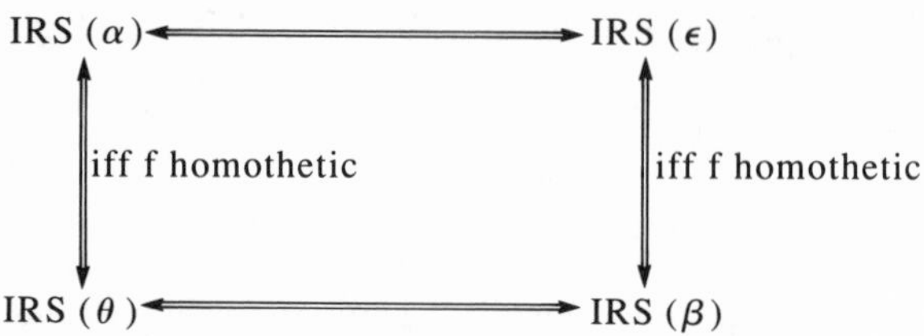

Figure 3.1: Different concepts of IRS

In the literature, "local" measures of IRS are often used. To understand this, define

$$\alpha \equiv \lim_{k \to 1} \alpha(k,\ \bar{x}), \qquad \varepsilon_1 \equiv \lim_{k \to 1} \varepsilon(k\bar{x}),$$

$$\theta_1 \equiv \lim_{y \to y_1} \theta(y), \qquad \beta_1 \equiv \lim_{y \to y_1} \beta(y),$$

where $y_1 \equiv f(\bar{x})$. Then we may obtain the following result.

Proposition 3.10. All local measures are equivalent, that is,[40]

$$\alpha_1 = \varepsilon_1 = \theta_1 = \beta_1.$$

This proposition is the source of the recent popularity of using θ_1 as a measure of returns to scale (e.g., Varian 1984; Helpman 1984; Helpman and Krugman 1985). The difficulty of using θ_1 is that it only provides a *local* measure. In fact, (52) means that all four measures of returns to scale are local measures and they are equal *if* they are evaluated at the point in which the relevant ray intersects with the EP, that is, at the point in which the scale factor k is equal to 1 (*no* expansion or shrinkage of factors).[41] It is surprising that such concepts have even been accepted in the literature.

[40] $\theta_1 = \varepsilon_1$ is obtained by Ohta (1974, p. 64) and Hanoch (1975, p. 493). For the proof of (52) under a unified framework, see Ide and Takayama (1989a).

[41] For a diagrammatical exposition of the local nature of (52) and of the distinction between the concepts defined along a ray from the origin and those defined along an EP, see Ide and Takayama (1989, p. 377).

3.6 The Le Châtelier-Samuelson Principle[42]

In 1844, the French chemist H. L. Le Châtelier, upon his study of thermochemical equilibrium, formulated a heuristic principle,

> If a system is in stable equilibrium, and one of the conditions is changed, then the equilibrium will shift in such a way as to tend to annul the applied change of the conditions.[43]

Samuelson (1947) formulated this mathematically to obtain an important general result in the comparative statics question, and introduced it into economics. He called it the "Le Châtelier Principle." It has subsequently been further elaborated by Samuelson and others. Even confining ourselves to relatively recent contributions, we have Pollak (1969), Eichhorn and Oettli (1972), Silberberg (1971, 1974, and 1990), Hatta (1980 and 1987), and Otani (1982), for example. The principle is now often called the **Le Châtelier-Samuelson (LeS) principle**.

Specifically, Samuelson (1947) showed that (*a*) the elasticities of factor demand and commodity supply are larger in the long-run than in the short-run, and (*b*) the elasticity of (compensated) consumer demand for a product is lower with rationing than without. Namely, suppose that a "just binding" constraint is added to an optimization problem, where the phrase *just binding* means that the addition of this constraint does not displace the original solution. The LeS principle thus obtained states that the (compensated) effect of a shift in a parameter upon the optimum value of a decision variable is smaller with such an additional constraint than without.[44]

In this section, we examine this principle in such a way that its important aspects will be revealed. Our discussion is considerably simplified by the use of the envelope theorem (theorem 3.3). Unlike other methods

---

[42] The discussion in this section is based on Anderson and Takayama (1991).

[43] See Eichhorn and Oettli (1972, p. 711). Samuelson (1960a) states this in a somewhat colorful way by saying, "Squeezing a balloon will decrease its volume more if you keep its temperature constant than it will if (by insulating it) you let the squeezing warm it up." (p. 368). For clear expositions of these heuristic statements, see Samuelson 1966 and Eichhorn and Oettlli (1972). As these authors explain, there are really two forms of the Le Châtelier principle, i.e., the "weak form" and the "strong form." Its weak form can be explained in terms of an example. Let $x_i(w,\ y)$ be the demand function of factor i (example 3.6). Then the weak form simply states $\partial x_i/\partial w_i \leqq 0$, which we obtained in proposition 3.1. In this section, we are concerned with the strong form. For global extensions of the weak form, see Eichhorn and Oettli (1972), Takayama (1977), and Anderson and Takayama (1979).

[44] This paragraph is adapted from Hatta (1987, p. 157).

used to obtain the LeS principle, including Hatta (1980), our method also provides an easy access to the effect of a shift parameter on the *Lagrangian multipliers* (or the shadow prices of resources), as well as on the optimum values of decision variables. In the context of the usual cost minimization problem, this means that the long-run marginal cost (MC) curve is flatter than its short-run counterpart (when MC is rising), and that the long-run supply price is greater than its short-run counterpart.

Let x and z, respectively, denote the vectors of variable and quasi-fixed factors, where $x \in R^n$ and $z \in R^m$. Let $f(x, z)$ be a production function, which is assumed to satisfy the regularity condition (RC). Let $w > 0$ be the price vector of variable factors, and let $r > 0$ be the vector of the user's cost of quasi-fixed factors. The firm's "short-run" problem is written as:

$$\underset{x}{\text{Minimize}} \quad w \cdot x, \text{ subject to } f(x, z) \geqq y \text{ and } x \geqq 0.$$

Let $x^\circ(w, y; z) > 0$ be the unique solution to this problem, and let $\lambda^\circ(w, y; z) > 0$ be the Lagrangian multiplier associated with it. Define $C^\circ(w, y; z) \equiv w \cdot x^\circ(w, y; z)$, which we assume to be twice continuously differentiable in w and y. Then, via the envelope theorem, we obtain

$$\partial x_i^\circ / \partial w_j = \partial x_j^\circ / \partial w_i, \quad \partial x_i^\circ / \partial y = \partial \lambda^\circ / \partial w_i, \; i, j = 1, \ldots, n,$$

as we obtained in (23).

To ease the exposition, we first suppose that $m = 1$, or z is a scalar, signifying the "plant" of the firm, and write the firm's "long-run" problem as

$$\underset{x,\, z}{\text{Minimize}} \quad w \cdot x + rz, \quad \text{subject to } f(x, z) \geqq y, \; x \geqq 0, \text{ and } z \geqq 0.$$

Let $x^1(w, r, y) > 0$ and $z^1(w, r, y) > 0$ be the unique solution to this problem, $\lambda^1(w, r, y)$ be the Lagrangian multiplier associated with it, and define $C^1(w, r, y) \equiv w \cdot x^1(w, r, y) + rz^1(w, r, y)$. Assume that C^1 is twice continuously differentiable in (w, r, y), then, via the envelope theorem, we obtain[45]

$$\partial x_i^1 / \partial r = \partial z^1 / \partial w_i, \; \partial z^1 / \partial y = \partial \lambda^1 / \partial r, \; i = 1, 2, \ldots, n, \qquad (52a)$$

[45] Since C^1 is concave in w and r, its Hessian is negative semidefinite. Then noting $\partial C^1/\partial w_i = x_i^1$, $\partial C^1/\partial r = z^1$, and $\partial C^1/\partial y = \lambda^1$ by way of the envelope theorem, we obtain (52a) and (52b). (52a) corresponds to (23), and (52b) corresponds to the property that the diagonal elements of the substitution matrix are non-positive.

$$\partial x_i^1/\partial w_i \leqq 0,\ i = 1, 2, \ldots, n,\ \partial z^1/\partial r \leqq 0. \tag{52b}$$

Next, assume the following identities, which are crucial to obtain the LeS principle.[46]

$$x_i^1(w, r, y) \equiv x_i^{\circ}[w, y; z^1(w, r, y)],\ i = 1, 2, \ldots, n, \tag{53a}$$

$$\lambda^1(w, r, y) \equiv \lambda^{\circ}[w, y; z^1(w, r, y)]. \tag{53b}$$

For example, (53a) states that the short-run and the long-run demands for variable factors are identical when the optimal value of z in the long-run, $z^1(w, r, y)$, is substituted into the short-run demand function x_i°. Differentiation of (53a) with respect to w_i, and (53b) with respect to y, yields

$$\partial x_i^1/\partial w_i = \partial x_i^{\circ}/\partial w_i + (\partial x_i^{\circ}/\partial z)(\partial z^1/\partial w_i),\ i = 1, 2, \ldots, n, \tag{54a}$$

$$\partial \lambda^1/\partial y = \partial \lambda^{\circ}/\partial y + (\partial \lambda^{\circ}/\partial z)(\partial z^1/\partial y). \tag{54b}$$

Next recall $\partial z^1/\partial w_i = \partial x_i^1/\partial r$ from (52a). Then, noting $\partial x_i^1/\partial r = (\partial x_i^{\circ}/\partial z)(\partial z^1/\partial r)$ from (53a), we may rewrite (54a) as

$$\partial x_i^1/\partial w_i = \partial x_i^{\circ}/\partial w_i + (\partial x_i^{\circ}/\partial z)^2(\partial z^1/\partial r),\ i = 1, 2, \ldots, n.$$

The second term on the RHS of this equation signifies the "adjustment effect." Since $\partial z^1/\partial r \leqq 0$ by (52b), the adjustment effect is non-positive, and we may conclude

$$\partial x_i^1/\partial w_i \leqq \partial x_i^{\circ}/\partial w_i (\leqq 0),\ i = 1, 2, \ldots, n. \tag{56}$$

(55) relates the long-run input demand function to its short-run counterpart with respect to own price changes, where the adjustment effect will never be positive. Also, recall $\partial z^1/\partial y = \partial \lambda^1/\partial r$ from (52a). Then, noting $\partial \lambda^1/\partial r = (\partial \lambda^{\circ}/\partial z)(\partial z^1/\partial r)$ from (53b), we may rewrite (54b) as:

$$\partial \lambda^1/\partial y = \partial \lambda^{\circ}/\partial y + (\partial \lambda^{\circ}/\partial z)^2(\partial z^1/\partial r).$$

---

[46]See Samuelson (1947, p. 36). For this assumption, he writes, "the short-run condition holds in the long-run as well ... since long-run total costs cannot be at a minimum unless short-run total costs are as low as possible."

Since $\partial z^1/\partial r \leqq 0$ by (52b), we then obtain

$$\partial\lambda^1/\partial y \leqq \partial\lambda^\circ/\partial y. \tag{57}$$

We assume $\partial\lambda^1/\partial y > 0$ at the optimum.[47] Since λ is equal to the marginal cost (MC), we may then obtain the following relation from (56).

$$0 < \partial MC^1/\partial y \leqq \partial MC^\circ/\partial y. \tag{58}$$

Corresponding to the effect of a change of w_i on x_i° and x_i^1, we may obtain the following relation.

$$\partial MC^1/\partial y = \partial MC^\circ/\partial y + \text{(adjustment effect)} \leqq 0,$$

$$\text{[where (adjustment effect)} = (\partial\lambda^\circ/\partial z)^2(\partial z^1/\partial r)],$$

which again relates the long-run effect to the short-run effect.

Assume that the firm is a competitive firm, so that its output price $p > 0$ as well as factor price vector $w > 0$ are given exogenously. Then the firm's supply response is obtained by solving $p = MC$ for y. This implies that the firm's supply response is the reciprocal of the marginal cost output response. Namely, (57) implies

$$\partial y^1/\partial p \geqq \partial y^\circ/\partial p. \tag{59}$$

If we impose *Samuelson's regularity condition* (Samuelson 1947, p. 68) introduced earlier, then the own-price effects are obtained in strict inequalities. In other words,

$$\partial x_i^\circ/\partial w_i < 0,\ \partial x_i^1/\partial w_i < 0,\ \partial z^1/\partial r < 0,\ i = 1, 2, \ldots, n.$$

In this case (55), (57), and (58) can, respectively, be rewritten as

$$\partial x_i^1/\partial w_i < \partial x_i^\circ/\partial w_i < 0,\ i = 1, 2, \ldots, n, \tag{55'}$$

$$0 < \partial MC^1/\partial y < \partial MC^\circ/\partial y, \tag{57'}$$

$$\partial y^1/\partial p > \partial y^\circ/\partial p > 0. \tag{58'}$$

[47] This is the usual assumption in the literature. It can also be shown that $\partial\lambda^1/\partial y \geqq 0$ for *all* y if and only if f is concave. Namely, the marginal cost curve is nondecreasing if and only if the underlying production function is concave. See Marino, Otani, and Sicilian (1981).

Relations (55), (57), (58), (55′), (57′), and (58′) constitute the LeS principle for the present problem. Relation (55′) states that *the long-run input demand functions will be more responsive to own-price changes than will be their short-run counterparts.* Relation (57′) states that *the long-run marginal cost curve is flatter than its short-run counterpart.* Relation (58′) states that *the long-run supply response is greater than the short-run response.* In terms of elasticities, (55′) means that *the long-run price elasticities of variable input demands are greater than their short-run counterparts*, and (58′) means that *the long-run supply elasticity is greater than its short-run counterpart.*

Hatta (1980 and 1987) derives the LeS results via the "gain function." Noting that it achieves an extremum with respect to parameters, the first-order and the second-order necessary conditions enable him to obtain the LeS results concerning the effect of parameter changes on decision variables (such as $\partial x_i / \partial w_i$). Although this method is clever, it is not as natural as ours. In fact, it is round-about and more complicated than ours. Also, it is not obvious, though possible, from his method that we can obtain the LeS results for the effect of parameter changes on the Lagrangian multiplier such as $(\partial \lambda^1 / \partial y)$, (57), and (58).

We can easily relax the assumption that z is a scalar, and we suppose $z \in R^m$. To this end, we define the following notations. Let $z^s = (z_1, \ldots, z_s)$, $z_{(s)} = (z_{s+1}, \ldots, z_m)$, $r^s = (r_1, \ldots, r_s)$, and $r_{(s)} = (r_{s+1}, \ldots, r_m)$, where $0 \leqq s \leqq m$. Obviously, $z = (z^s, z_{(s)})$ and $r = (r^s, r_{(s)})$. We then consider the following minimization problem.

$$\underset{x,\, z^s}{\text{Minimize}} \; w \cdot x + r^s \cdot z^s,$$

$$\text{subject to } f(x, z) \geqq y, x \geqq 0, \text{ and } z^s \geqq 0.$$

Let $x^s(w, r, y; z_{(s)})$ and $z^s(w, r, y; z_{(s)})$ be the unique solution of this problem, and let $\lambda^s(w, r^s, y; z_{(s)})$ be its associated Lagrangian multiplier. Define C^s by $C^s(w, r^s, y; z_{(s)}) \equiv w \cdot x^s(\cdot) + r^s \cdot z^s(\cdot)$, where $z_{(s)}$ is a constant vector. Then, $(C^s + r_{(s)} \cdot z_{(s)})$ signifies the minimum total cost. We may call this problem "problem s" and interpret the distinction between problems "$(s - 1)$" and "s" as caused by "time." Namely, in problem s, the $(m - s)$ quasi-fixed factors are fixed, whereas in problem $(s - 1)$, the $(m - s + 1)$ quasi-fixed factors are fixed because time is not long enough to allow the adjustment of the sth quasi-fixed factor. Needless to say, x°, λ°, and C°, respectively, signify the optimal values of x, λ, and C when $r^s \cdot z^s = 0$ in the minimand function. Assume that C^s is twice continuously differentiable with respect to (w, r^s, y).

Note that from the envelope theorem, we at once obtain

$$\partial C^s/\partial w_i = x_i^s,\ \partial C^s/\partial r_k = z_k^s,\ \partial C^s/\partial y = \lambda^s.$$

Since C^s is concave in $(w,\ r^s)$, its Hessians with respect to $(w,\ r^s)$ is negative semidefinite, so that we have

$$\partial z_k^s/\partial w_i = \partial x_i^s/\partial r_k,\ \partial z_k^s/\partial r_j = \partial z_j^s/\partial r_k,$$

$$\partial z_k^s/\partial y = \partial \lambda^s/\partial r_k, \tag{59a}$$

$$\partial x_i^s/\partial w_i \leqq 0,\ \partial z_k^s/\partial r_k \leqq 0, \tag{59b}$$

Corresponding to (53), we have the following identities for $i = 1, 2, \ldots, n$ and $1 \leqq s \leqq m$.[48]

$$x_i^s[w,\ r^s,\ y;\ z_{(s)}] \equiv x_i^{s-1}[w,\ r^{s-1},\ y;\ z_s(\cdot),\ z_{(s)}], \tag{60a}$$

$$z_j^s[w,\ r^s,\ y;\ z_{(s)}] \equiv z_j^{s-1}[w,\ r^{s-1},\ y;\ z_s(\cdot),\ z_{(s)}], \tag{60b}$$

$$\lambda^s[w,\ r^s,\ y;\ z_{(s)}] \equiv \lambda^{s-1}[w,\ r^{s-1},\ y;\ z_s(\cdot),\ z_{(s)}], \tag{60c}$$

where $z_s(\cdot) \equiv z_s^s[w,\ r^s,\ y;\ z_{(s)}]$. Differentiating (60a) with respect to w_i, (60b) with respect to r_j, and (60c) with respect to y, we obtain for $i = 1, 2, \ldots, n$ and $1 \leqq s \leqq m$,

$$\partial x_i^s/\partial w_i = \partial x_i^{s-1}/\partial w_i + (\partial x_i^{s-1}/\partial z_s)(\partial z_s^s/\partial w_i), \tag{61a}$$

$$\partial z_j^s/\partial r_j = \partial z_j^{s-1}/\partial r_j + (\partial z_j^{s-1}/\partial z_s)(\partial z_s^s/\partial r_j), \tag{61b}$$

$$\partial \lambda^s/\partial y = \partial \lambda^{s-1}/\partial y + (\partial \lambda^{s-1}/\partial z_s)(\partial z_s^s/\partial y), \tag{61c}$$

Also, using (59a), (60a), (60b), and (60c), we obtain, for $1 \leqq s \leqq m$

$$\partial z_s^s/\partial w_i = \partial x_i^s/\partial r_s = (\partial x_i^{s-1}/\partial z_s)(\partial z_s^s/\partial r_s),\ i = 1, 2, \ldots, n,$$

$$\partial z_s^s/\partial r_j = \partial z_j^s/\partial r_s = (\partial z_j^{s-1}/\partial z_s)(\partial z_s^s/\partial r_s),$$
$$j = 1, 2, \ldots, s-1,$$

[48]The demand function $x_i^s(w,\ r^s,\ y;\ z_{(s)})$ corresponds to Pollak's (1969) "conditional demand function." His formulation is a special case of ours.

$$\partial z_s^s/\partial y = \partial \lambda_i^s/\partial r_s = (\partial \lambda^{s-1}/\partial z_s)(\partial z_s^s/\partial r_s).$$

Combining this with (61), we obtain for $1 \leqq s \leqq m$

$$\partial x_i^s/\partial w_i = \partial x_i^{s-1}/\partial w_i + (\partial x_i^{s-1}/\partial z_s)^2(\partial z_s^s/\partial r_s),$$
$$i = 1,\ 2,\ \ldots,\ n,$$

$$\partial z_j^s/\partial r_j = \partial z_j^{s-1}/\partial r_j + (\partial z_j^{s-1}/\partial z_s)^2(\partial z_s^s/\partial r_s),$$
$$j = 1,\ 2,\ \ldots,\ s-1,$$

$$\partial \lambda^s/\partial y = \partial \lambda^{s-1}/\partial y + (\partial \lambda^{s-1}/\partial z_s)^2(\partial z_s^s/\partial r_s).$$

Since $\partial z_s^s/\partial r_s \leqq 0$, we obtain the following relations from this.

$$0 \geqq \partial x_i^0/\partial w_i \geqq \partial x_i^1/\partial w_i \geqq \ldots. \geqq \partial x_i^m/\partial w_i,$$
$$i = 1,\ 2,\ \ldots,\ n, \tag{62a}$$

$$0 \geqq \partial z_j^{s-1}/\partial r_j \geqq \partial z_j^s/\partial r_j,$$
$$j = 1,\ 2,\ \ldots,\ s-1,\ 1 < s \leqq m, \tag{62b}$$

$$\partial \lambda^0/\partial y \leqq \partial \lambda^1/\partial y \leqq \ldots. \leqq \partial \lambda^m/\partial y > 0. \tag{62c}$$

Again, assume that the firm is a competitive firm, so that its output price and factor price vector are given exogenously. Since the firm's supply response is then the reciprocal of the marginal cost, (62c) implies

$$0 < \partial y^0/\partial p \leqq \partial y^1/\partial p \leqq \ldots. \partial y^m/\partial p. \tag{63}$$

Assume again Samuelson's regularity condition. Then we have, for $s = 0,\ 1,\ 2,\ \ldots,\ m$,

$$\partial x_i^s/\partial w_i < 0,\ i = 1,\ 2,\ \ldots.,\ n,$$

$$\partial z_k^s/\partial r_k < 0,\ k = 1,\ 2,\ \ldots,\ s. \tag{59'b}$$

Then (62) and (63) can be sharpened as

$$0 > \partial x_i^0/\partial w_i > \partial x_i^1/\partial w_i > \ldots. > \partial x_i^m/\partial w_i,\ i = 1,\ldots,\ n, \tag{62'a}$$

$$0 > \partial z_j^{s-1}/\partial r_j > \partial z_j^s/\partial r_j,$$
$$j = 1, 2, \ldots, s-1, \; 1 < s \leqq m, \qquad (62'\mathrm{b})$$

$$\partial MC^{\circ}/\partial y > \partial MC^1/\partial y > \ldots > \partial MC^m/\partial y > 0, \qquad (62'\mathrm{c})$$

$$0 < \partial y^*/\partial p < \partial y^1/\partial p < \ldots < \partial y^m/\partial p. \qquad (63')$$

The economic interpretation of (62′a) and (62′c) and (63′) can be obtained in a similar manner as that of (55′), (57′), and (58′), respectively, whereas (62′b) means that the "longer-run" demand for quasi-fixed factors will be more responsive to own price changes than will be its shorter-run counterpart.[49] Clearly, (62′) and (63′) constitute a generalization of the LeS principle in the form of (55′), (57′), and (58′).

The above method of obtaining the LeS principle results can also be applied to the theory of consumption. To this end, let $u(x)$ be an individual's utility function, where $x = (x_1, \ldots, x_n)$ is his (or her) consumption bundle. Let $p = (p_1, \ldots, p_n)$ be the price vector, and let $p^s = (p_1, \ldots, p_s)$ and $p_{(s)} = (p_{s+1}, \ldots, p_n)$. Similarly, partition x by $x = (x^s, x_{(s)})$, where $x^s = (x_1, \ldots, x_s)$ and $x_{(s)} = (x_{s+1}, \ldots, x_n)$. We then consider the problem of choosing x^s so as to

$$\text{Minimize } p^s \cdot x^s, \quad \text{subject to } u(x) \geqq u \text{ and } x^s \geqq 0,$$

where $x_{(s)}$ is a fixed vector. In the theory of rationing, this is a form of "point rationing" in which $x_{(s)}$ is a vector of rationed commodities.[50] There are other instances in which $x_{(s)}$ is fixed. As Pollak (1969, p. 63) writes

> "consumers, like firms, have commitments which are fixed in the short-run. For example, if an individual signs a lease

[49] This result corresponds to the following by Samueslon (1947, pp. 38–39): "A lengthening of the time period to permit new factors to be varied will result in *greater* changes in the factor whose price has changed, ...," However, as Pollak (1969, p. 76) remarks, "Samuelson's proof of the theorem requires the manipulation of cumbersome Jacobian and the use of Jacobi's theorem."

[50] Reflecting the war-time experience, rationing has been discussed extensively in the 1940's and in the early 1950's. For a survey, see Tobin (1952). A definitive work on this topic may be Tobin and Houthakker (1951). Their analysis is quite tedious as it is carried out in terms of bordered Hessians (naturally reflecting the state of the art in those days). Yet their analysis provides a further insight into the problem of the LeS principle. See, for example, Pollak (1969) and Hatta (1980)

to rent an apartment for twelve months, his consumption of housing services during any month is fixed. ..."

Let $x^s(p^s, u; x_{(s)}) > 0$ be the unique solution of the above problem, and let $\lambda^s(p^s, u; x_{(s)}) > 0$ be the Lagrangian multiplier associated with it. Note that this problem is formally identical to the cost minimization problem discussed earlier by considering the change of notations, $r \to p$ and $z \to x$. Then, the results which correspond to (62) and (63) follow at once. In particular, from (62b), we obtain

$$0 \geqq \partial x_i^{s-1}/\partial p_i \geqq \partial x_i^s/\partial p_i, \quad i = 1, 2, \ldots, s-1, \; 1 < s \leqq n. \tag{64}$$

This then generalizes (6.4), the LeS result obtained by Pollak (1969), where he assumes $s = n$. Under the Samuelson regularity condition, (64) is sharpened as

$$0 > \partial x_i^{s-1}/\partial p_i > \partial x^s/\partial p_i, \quad i = 1, 2, \ldots, s-1, \; 1 < s \leqq n. \tag{64'}$$

In particular, if $s = n$ as in Pollack (1969), we obtain

$$0 > \partial x_i^{n-1}/\partial p_i > \partial x_i^n/\partial p_i, \quad i = 1, 2, \ldots, n-1. \tag{64''}$$

Thus, if the n-th commodity is rationed, then the own price elasticity of (compensated) demand for commodity i is lower with rationing than without.[51]

Now we can readily obtain the Le Châtelier-Samuelson results for a general formulation that encompass the above results on the theories of production and consumption. For such a discussion, see Anderson-Takayama (1991).

Exercises

(1) Sketch the proof of the envelope theorem and show three economic applications.

(2) Consider the usual problem of consumer's choice of choosing x so as to

Maximize $u(x)$ subject to $p \cdot x \leqq Y$ and $x \geqq 0$.

[51] See Samuelson (1947, p. 168). See also Pollak (1969).

Let $x = x(p, Y)$ be the consumer's demand function obtained from this utility maximization hypothesis. Let

$$U(p, Y) \equiv u[x(p, Y)]$$

be his or her indirect utility function. Suppose that it is known that the function U takes the following "addilog form" à la Houthakker:

$$U(p, Y) = \sum_{i-1}^{n} c_i(p_i/Y)^{-\alpha_i},$$

where $\beta_i \equiv c_i\alpha_i(i = 1, 2, \ldots, n)$ are positive constants.

(i) Recalling Roy's identity

$$(\partial U/\partial p_i)/(\partial U/\partial Y) = -x_i, \; i = 1, 2, \ldots, n,$$

show that his or her demand function can be obtained as

$$x_i(p, Y) = [\beta_i(p_i/Y)^{\gamma_i}]/[\sum_{i=1}^{n} \beta_i(p_i/Y)^{-\alpha_i}],$$

where $\gamma_i \equiv -(1 + \alpha_i)$.

(ii) Let $v_i \equiv p_i/Y$ $(i = 1, 2, \ldots, n)$, and write the indirect utility function as

$$U(p, Y) = \phi(v) \equiv \phi(v_1, v_2, \ldots, v_n),$$

where we may recall that $U(p, Y)$ is homogeneous of degree zero in p and Y. Define $\psi(v)$ by $\psi(v) \equiv 1/\phi(v)$, and show that Roy's identity can be written as

$$x_i = \psi_i/[\sum_{i=1}^{n} \psi_i v_i], \; i = 1, 2, \ldots, n,$$

where $\psi_i \equiv \partial\psi/\partial v_i$, i.e. $x = \psi'/(\psi' \cdot v)$.

REMARK: Houthakker's addilog indirect utility function is found in Houthakker (1960). More recently, there has been a number of empirical studies on consumer's demand. Such studies are concerned with the derivaton of the demand functions by the specification of indirect utilitly function and by using Roy's identity.

For references of the present topic, see papers cited in Berndt-Darrough-Diewert (1977) and Christensen-Jorgenson-Lau (1975), for example. These two papers advocate the "translog reciprocal utility function," which specifies the function $\psi(v)$ in question (2) as

$$\psi(v) = \alpha_o + \sum_i \alpha_i \log v_i + \frac{1}{2} \sum_i \sum_j \beta_{ij} \log v_i \log v_j.$$

As a further exercise, you may derive the demand function $x(p, Y)$ from such a specification of the indirect utility function. The answer to this question is found in Berndt-Darrough-Diewert (1977) and Christensen-Jorgenson-Lau (1975).

References

Berndt, E. R., M. N. Darrough, and W. E. Diewert. 1977. "Flexible Functional Forms and Expenditure distribution: An Application to Canadian Consumer Demand Functions." *International Economic Review* 18, October: 651–675.

Christensen, L. R., D. W. Jorgenson, and L. J. Lau. 1975. "Transcendental Logarithmic Utility Functions." *American Economic Review* 65, June: 367–383.

Houthakker, H. S. 1960. "Additive Preferences." *Econometrica* 28, April: 244–257.

(3) Consider the usual cost minimization problem of choosing x so as to

$$\text{Minimize } w \cdot x \text{ subject to } f(x) \geqq 0, \text{ and } x \geqq 0,$$

where $f(x)$ signifies the production function and y is a positive scaler signifying the target leval of output. Let $x(w, y)$ be the firm's optimum input vector, and let $C(w, y) = w \cdot x(w, y)$ be its (total) minimum cost function. Assume that the firm uses two factors: i.e., $x = (x_1, x_2)$. Let $w = (w_1, w_2)$ be its price vector. Suppose that the cost function is estimated econometrically as

$$C(w, y) = w_1^{\alpha} w_2^{1-\alpha} y^{\beta}, \quad 0 < \alpha < 1, \ \beta > 0, \tag{1}$$

where α and β are estimated constants.

(i) Recalling Shephard's lemma show that the production function of the firm can be obtained as

$$f(x) = (Ax_1^{\alpha} x_2^{1-\alpha})^{1/\beta}, \text{ where } A \equiv \alpha^{-\alpha}(1-\alpha)^{\alpha-1}.$$

Hint: To simplify the computation, take the logarithm of the computed expression for the Shephard lemma and eliminate $\omega \equiv w_1/w_2$ from the two equations.

(ii) Suppose that $\beta = 1$. Observe that the Shephard-Samuelson theorem holds for the above cost function (1), i.e.

$$\partial C/\partial y = C/y = \lambda(w, y), \text{ and } \partial\lambda/\partial y = 0,$$

where we may recall $\partial C/\partial y = \lambda$ obtained from the envelope theorem.

(4) Consider an individual who consumes two commodities (1 and 2) and his utitlity function is given by

$$u(x_1, x_2) = \alpha \log x_1 + \beta \log x_2, \tag{2}$$

where α and β are positive constants. The person chooses (x_1, x_2) so as to maximize u subject to his budget constraint $p_1x_1 + p_2x_2 \leqq Y$, and the non-negativity constraints $x_1 \geqq 0$, $x_2 \geqq 0$, where p_i = the price of the i-th commodity ($i = 1, 2$) and Y = income, where p_1, p_2 and Y are positive constants. Clearly, u is defined on the interior of the non-negative orthant of R^2: i.e., on $X \equiv \{x \in R^2, x_i \geqq 0, i = 1, 2\}$.

(i) Show that function u is strictly concave.

Hint: Show that Hessian matrix u'' is negative definite.

(ii) Omitting (*) to denote the optimum, write out the first-order condition (FOC) of our problem, where we note $x_1 > 0$ and $x_2 > 0$ at the optimum. You are not required to show $x_1, x_2 > 0$ (as it is obvious). But do show that $\lambda > 0$ at optimum (although this is also obvious).

(iii) Show that the (FOC) obtained above is necessary *and* sufficient for *global* maximum.

Hint: Recall the Arrow-Hurwicz-Uzawa and the Arrow-Enthoven theorems.

(iv) Show that the solution of the above problem is obtained as,

$$x_1(p, Y) = \frac{\alpha}{\alpha + \beta} \frac{Y}{p_1}, \tag{3a}$$

$$x_2(p, Y) = \frac{\beta}{\alpha + \beta} \frac{Y}{p_2}, \tag{3b}$$

$$\lambda(p, Y) = \frac{\alpha + \beta}{Y}. \tag{3c}$$

REMARK: Hence if the utility function is given by (2), we have

$$\partial x_1/\partial p_2 = \partial x_2/\partial p_1 = \partial \lambda/\partial p_1 = \partial \lambda/\partial p_2 = 0.$$

(v) The Hicks-Slutsky equation is written as

$$\partial x_i/\partial p_j = S_{ij} - x_j \partial x_i/\partial Y.$$

Let $S \equiv [S_{ij}]$ be the net substitution matrix for the present problem.

(a) Compute the expressions for S_{ij}, $i, j = 1, 2$ (in terms of p_1, p_2, and Y) using the Hicks-Slutsky equation.

REMARK: This provides a method to obtain S_{ij} from observed data.

(b) Show that S is symmetric ($S_{12} = S_{21}$) with $S_{11} < 0$ and $S_{22} < 0$. Using the definition of negative semidefinite matrices, also show that S is negative semidefinite.
Hint: To show that S is negative semidefinite, it suffices to show that the following matrix A is negative semidefinite.

$$A = \begin{bmatrix} -1/p_1^2 & 1/p_1 p_2 \\ 1/p_1 p_2 & -1/p_2^2 \end{bmatrix}$$

(c) Show that

$$\begin{bmatrix} S_{11} & S_{12} \\ S_{21} & S_{22} \end{bmatrix} \begin{bmatrix} p_1 \\ p_2 \end{bmatrix} = \begin{bmatrix} 0 \\ 0 \end{bmatrix}.$$

(d) The indirect utility function is defined by $U(p, Y) = u[x(p, Y)]$. Show that $U(p, Y)$ for the present problem can be written as

$$U(p, Y) = A + \alpha \log \frac{Y}{p_1} + \beta \log \frac{Y}{p_2}, \tag{4}$$

where

$$A \equiv \alpha \log \frac{\alpha}{\alpha + \beta} + \beta \log \frac{\beta}{\alpha + \beta}.$$

(vi) Using (4) and (3), show that

$$\partial U / \partial Y = \lambda, \ \partial U / \partial p_i = -\lambda x_i, \ i = 1, 2. \tag{5}$$

REMARK: (5) confirms the envelope relations in the context of the theory of consumer's choice. (5) obviously implies Roy's identity

$$\frac{\partial U}{\partial p_i} + x_i \frac{\partial U}{\partial Y} = 0, \ i = 1, 2.$$

(5) Consider the following usual cost minimization problem:

$$\underset{x}{\text{Minimize}} \ \ w \cdot x \text{ subject to } f(x) \geqq y, \ x \geqq 0, \ x \in R^n,$$

where $w > 0$ is a given factor price vector, $y > 0$ is the target level of output, and $f(x)$ is the production function of a given firm. We assume that $f(x)$ is continuously differentiable and $f_i(x) \equiv \partial f(x)/\partial x_i > 0$, $i = 1, 2, \ldots, n$, for all x. Assume that the following conditions are necessary and sufficient for optimum.

$$w_i = \lambda f_i(x), \ i = 1, 2, \ldots, n, \ f(x) = y.$$

These conditions in turn determine the $(n + 1)$ values, $x_i(w, y)$, $i = 1, 2, \ldots, n$, and $\lambda(w, y)$. Functions $x(w, y)$ and $\lambda(x, y)$ are assumed to be continuously differentiable. Let $C(w, y) \equiv w \cdot x(w, y)$ be the minimum cost function. We assume that it is twice continuously differentiable.

(i) Show that if $f(x)$ is homogeneous with ϕ, then $C(w, y)$ is written in a "separable" form

$$C(w, y) = h(w)\phi(y). \tag{6}$$

(ii) The converse of (6) also holds. Using this, show that $f(x)$ is homothetic with ϕ if

$$\lambda(w,\ y) = h(w)\phi'(y),$$

where we assume, for the sake of simplicity, $C(w,\ 0) = 0$ and $\phi(0) = 0$.

(iii) Show that if $f(x)$ is homothetic, then the MRS (marginal rate of substitution) of any pair of factors is independent of y :, i.e., show that if $f(x)$ is homothetic, then $x_i(w,\ y)/x_j(w,\ y)$ is independent of y for all i and j.

Hints:

(a) To show (6), it suffices to show $\partial(C/\phi)/\partial y = 0$, or $(\partial C/\partial y) - C\phi'/\phi = 0$ (why?). Since $\partial C/\partial y = \lambda$, it then suffices to show $C\phi'/\phi = \lambda$. To this end, simply observe that the following relations hold at optimum.

$$C = \sum w_i x_i = (\lambda/\phi') \sum g_i x_i = \lambda\phi/\phi',$$

where $g_i \equiv \partial g/\partial x_i$.

(b) The *only if* part of (ii) follows at once from (i). The *if* part of (ii) can be restated as $\partial C/\partial y = h(w)\phi'(y)$ implies $C = h(w)\phi(y)$. (Why?) Then fixing w and integrating $\partial C(w,\ z)/\partial z = h(w)\phi'(z)$ with respect to z from 0 to y yield $C(w,\ y) = h(w)\phi(y)$. There can be other proofs.

(c) You need to show that $\partial(x_i/x_j)/\partial y = 0$ if $f(x)$ is homothetic. To this end, recall $C = h\phi$ if and only if f is homothetic, and use Shephard's lemma.

REMARKS:

(a) It is evident from the proof that the converse of (i) also holds.

(b) From the converse of (i), the converse of (ii) also holds at once.

(c) Statement (iii) says that *if* function f is homothetic, every expansion path (EP) is a ray from the origin. The converse of this statement is also true as discussed in the text.

(6) Consider the cost minimization problem of choosing $x = (x_1, x_2)$ so as to

$$\text{Minimize } w \cdot x \quad \text{subject to } f(x) \geqq y, \ x \geqq 0.$$

Let $x_i > 0$ ($i = 1, 2$) be its solution and assume $f(x) = y$ at optimum. The (minimum) total cost function is defined by $C(w, y) \equiv w \cdot x(w, y)$. The (Allen partial) elasticities of factor substitution (σ_{ij}) may be defined by

$$\sigma_{ij} = \frac{w_j x_{ij}}{x_i \theta_j}, \quad \text{where } x_{ij} \equiv \frac{\partial x_i}{\partial w_j} \text{ and } \theta_j \equiv \frac{w_j x_j}{C}, \quad i, j = 1, 2. \tag{7}$$

If the production function is homothetic, we have

$$x_i(w, y) = h_i(w)\phi(y). \tag{8}$$

(i) Show that the following relation holds when the production function is homothetic, where $z \equiv x_1/x_2$.

$$\frac{dz}{z} = \frac{1}{x_1}(x_{11}dw_1 + x_{12}dw_2) - \frac{1}{x_2}(x_{21}dw_1 + x_{22}dw_2) \tag{9}$$

Hint: Use $\hat{z} = \hat{x}_1 - \hat{x}_2$, where $\hat{z} \equiv dz/z$, etc.

(ii) Show that (9) can be written as,

$$\hat{z} = -\sigma\hat{\omega}, \text{ where } \omega \equiv w_1/w_2 \text{ and } \sigma_{12} = \sigma_{21} \equiv \sigma. \tag{10}$$

Hint: Recall that we have,

$$x_{i1}w_1 + x_{i2}w_2 = 0, \ i = 1, 2,$$

by the homogeneity of $x(w, y)$ in w, and use (7). Also, note $\hat{\omega} = \hat{w}_1 - \hat{w}_2$, and show that $\theta_1 + \theta_2 = 1$.

REMARK: Equation (10) is the well-known relation in the two-factor model.

(7) Let the cost function $C(w, y)$ be specified in the following translog form:

$$\log C(w,\ y) = a_\circ + \sum_{i=1}^{n} a_i \log w_i$$
$$+ \frac{1}{2} \sum_{i=1}^{n} \sum_{j=1}^{n} a_{ij} \log w_i \log w_j + \sum_{i=1}^{n} b_i \log w_i \log y$$
$$+ c_1 \log y + \frac{1}{2} c_2 (\log y)^2, \tag{11}$$

where

$$\sum_{i=1}^{n} a_i = 1,\ \sum_{j=1}^{n} a_{ij} = 0,\ \sum_{i=1}^{n} b_i = 0,$$
$$\text{and } a_{ij} = a_{ji} \text{ for all } i \text{ and } j. \tag{12}$$

(i) Let $\theta_i \equiv w_i x_i / C(w,\ y)$ (the i-th cost share). Then obtain the following relation from (11).

$$\theta_i = a_i + \sum_{j=1}^{n} a_{ij} \log w_j + b_i \log y. \tag{13}$$

(ii) Show the following relations.

$$\sigma_{ij} = (a_{ij} + \theta_i \theta_j)/\theta_i \theta_j, \text{ for } i \neq j, \tag{14a}$$

$$\sigma_{ii} = (a_{ii} - \theta_i + \theta_i^2)/\theta_i^2,\ i = j. \tag{14b}$$

Hints:

(a) To answer (i), let $z_i \equiv \log w_i$ and $u \equiv \log y$. Then $C(w,\ y)$ can be rewritten as $C(e^{z_1} \ldots,\ e^{z_n},\ e^{u}) \equiv C^*(z,\ u)$, and (11) can be rewritten as

$$\log C^*(z,\ u) = a_\circ + \sum_{i=1}^{n} a_i z_i + \frac{1}{2} \sum_{i=1}^{n} \sum_{j=1}^{n} a_{ij} z_i z_j$$
$$+ \sum_{i=1}^{n} b_i z_i u + c_1 u + \frac{1}{2} c_2 u^2, \tag{11'}$$

where

$$C^*(z,\ u) = C(e^{z_1},\ \ldots,\ e^{z_n}, e^u)$$

$$= C(w_1,\ w_2,\ \ldots,\ w_n,\ y).$$

Here we may note $dz_i = dw_i/w_i$, so that $dw_i/dz_i = w_i$. For the LHS, we may then observe

$$\frac{\partial \log C^*}{\partial z_i} = \frac{1}{C^*}\frac{\partial C^*}{\partial z_i} = \frac{1}{C}\frac{\partial C^*}{\partial z_i}$$

$$= \frac{1}{C}\frac{dw_i}{dz_i}\frac{\partial C}{\partial w_i} = \frac{1}{C}w_i\frac{\partial C}{\partial w_i} = \theta_i,$$

where we may recall Shepherd's lemma. For the RHS, first note $\partial(a \cdot z)/\partial z_i = a_i$, and then recall the formula for the differentiation of quadratic form. Namely, writing a quadratic form as

$$Q(z) = z'Az \equiv \sum_{i=1}^{n}\sum_{j=1}^{n} a_{ij}z_i z_j,$$

we have

$$\partial Q/\partial z_i = 2\sum_{j=1}^{n} a_{ij}z_j.$$

(b) To answer (ii), note from (11)

$$a_{ij} = \frac{\partial^2 \log C(w,\ y)}{\partial \log w_i\, \partial \log w_j} = \frac{1}{\partial \log w_j}\frac{dw_j}{d\log w_i}\frac{\partial \log C}{\partial w_i}$$

$$= \frac{\partial}{\partial \log w_j}\left(\frac{w_i}{C}\frac{\partial C}{\partial w_i}\right) = \frac{dw_j}{d\log w_j}\frac{\partial}{\partial \omega_j}\left(\frac{w_i}{C}\frac{dC}{dw_i}\right).$$

Then recall Shephard's lemma and

$$\sigma_{ij} \equiv \frac{1}{\theta_j}\frac{\partial x_i}{\partial w_j}\frac{w_j}{x_i}.$$

REMARK: Formula (13) can be used to estimate the values of the a_{ij}'s under restriction (12) by using Zellner's method of seemingly unrelated regression. The a_{ij}'s thus estimated can be used to compute the Allen partial elasticities of factor substitution (σ_{ij}'s) by utilizing (14).

REMARK: If $f(x)$ is homothetic, it can be shown that $b_i = 0$ for all i. Furthermore, if $f(x)$ is homogeneous of degree one, then $c_1 = 1$ and $c_2 = 0$ as well as $b_i = 0$ for all i. (Also, try to prove these statements by yourself. It is straightforward.)

References

Afriat, S. N. 1971. "Theory of Maxima and the Method of Lagrange." *SIAM Journal of Applied Mathematics* 20 (May): 343–57.

———. 1980. *Demand Functions and the Slutsky Matrix.* Princeton: Princeton University Press.

Allen, R. G. D. 1938. *Mathematical Analysis for Economists.* London: Macmillan.

Anderson, R. K., and A. Takayama. 1979. "Comparative Statics with Discrete Jumps in Shift Parameters, or, How to Do Economics on the Saddle (-Point)." *Journal of Economic Theory* 21 (December): 491–509.

———. 1991. "On the Le Châtelier-Samuelson Principle." To appear in *Keio Economic Studies.*

Arrow, K. J., H. B. Chenery, B. Minhas, and R. M. Solow. 1961, "Capital-Labor Substitution and Economic Efficiency." *Review of Economics and Statistics* 43 (August): 225–50.

Berndt, E. R., and L. R. Christensen, 1973. "The Translog Function and the Substitution of Equipment, Structures, and Labor in U. S. Manufacturing 1929–68." *Journal of Econometrics* 1 (February): 81–114.

Berndt, E. R., and D. O. Wood. 1975. "Technology, Prices and the Derived Demand for Energy." *Review of Economics and Statistics* 62 (February): 259–68.

Bernstein, B., and R. A. Toupin. 1962. "Some Properties of the Hessian Matrix of a Strictly Convex Function." *Journal für die reine und angewandte Mathematik* 210: 65–72.

Blackorby, C., and R. R. Russell. 1989. "Will the Real Elasticity of Substitution Please Stand Up?" *American Economic Review* 79 (September): 882–88.

Blackorby, C., D. Primont, and R. R. Russell. 1978. *Duality, Separability and Functional Structure: Theory and Economic Applications.* New York: North-Holland.

Brown, R. S., and D. O. Christensen. 1981. "Estimating Elasticities of Substitution in a Model of Partial Static Equilibrium: An Application of U.S. Agriculture, 1947–1974." In *Modeling and Measuring Natural Resource Substitutions*, ed. E. R. Berndt and B. C. Field: 209–29. Cambridge, Mass.: MIT Press.

Carathéodory, C. 1967. *Calculus of Variations and Partial Differential Equations of the First Order.* Trans. R. Dean. Part 2, especially chap. 11. San Francisco: Holden Day (German original 1935).

Chao, C. C., and A. Takayama. 1991. "Long-Run Output Elasticities of Factor Demands, Non-Homotheticity, and Scale Economies in U. S. Manufacturing." To appear in *Zeitschrift für die gesamte Staatswissenschaft.*

Christensen, L. R., D. W. Jorgensen, and L. J. Lau. 1971. "Conjugate Duality and the T ranscendental Logarithmic Production Function." *Econometrica* 39 (July): 206 (Abstract).

———. 1975. "Transcendental Logarithmic Utility Function." *American Economic Review* 65 (June): 367–83.

Diewert, W. E. 1974. "Applications of Duality Theory." In *Frontiers of Quantitative Economics.* ed. M. D. Intriligator and D. A. Kendrick, 106–71. Amsterdam: North -Holland. See also "Comments by S. E. Jacobson, L. J. Lau, and R. W. Shepherd, 2: 171–203.

———. 1982. "Duality Approaches to Microeconomic Theory." In *Handbook of Mathematical Economics*, ed. K. J. Arrow and M. D. Intriligator, vol. 2, chap. 12, 535–99. Amsterdam: North-Holland.

Eichhorn, W., and W. Oettli. 1972. "Generalized Formulation of the Le Châtelier-Samuelson Principle." *Econometrica* 40 (July): 711–19.

Epstein, L. G. 1981. "Generalized Duality and Integrability." *Econometrica* 49 (May): 655–78.

Färe, R., and D. Primont. 1990. "The Completion of Ronald W. Shephard's Duality Theory." Presented at the Midwest Mathematical Economics Meeting at the University of Illinois, November.

Färe, R., and R. W. Shephard. 1977a. "Ray-Homothetic Production Functions." *Econometrica* 45 (January): 133–46.

———. 1977b. "On Homothetic Scalar Valued Production Functions." *Scandinavian Journal of Economics* 79 (1): 131–32.

Førsund, F. R. 1975. "The Homothetic Production Function." *Scandinavian Journal of Economics* 77 (2): 234–44.

Frisch, R. 1965. *Theory of Production.* Dordrecht, Holland: Reidel.

Fuss, M., D. McFadden, and Y. Mundlak. 1978. "A Survey of Functional Forms in Economic Analysis of Production." In *Production Economics*, ed. M. Fuss and D. McFadden, 1: 219–68. Amsterdam: North-Holland: 219–68.

Fuss, M. and D. McFadden, eds. 1978. *Production Economics: A Dual Approach to Theory and Applications.* 2 vols. Amsterdam: North-Holland.

Gorman, W. M. 1976. "Tricks with Utility Functions." In *Essays in Economic Analysis*, ed. by M. J. Artis and A. R. Nobay. Cambridge: Cambridge University Press.

Hanoch, G. 1975. "The Elasticity of Scale and the Shapes of Average Costs." *American Economic Review* 65 (June): 492–97.

Hall, R. E. 1973. "The Specification of Technology with Several Kinds of Output." *Journal of Political Economy* 81 (July/August): 878–92.

Hatta, T. 1980. "Structure of the Correspondence Principle at an Extreme Point." *Review of Economic Studies* 47 (October): 987–97.

———. 1987. "Le Chatelier Principle." In *The New Palgrave: A Dictionary of Economics*, ed. J. Eatwell, M. Milgate, and P. Newman, 3: 155–57. London, Macmillan.

Helpman, E. 1984. "Increasing Returns, Imperfect Markets and Trade Theory." In *Handbook of International Economics*, 1: 325–65. Amsterdam: North-Holland.

Helpman, E., and P. R. Krugman. 1985. *Market Structure and Foreign Trade*. Cambridge, Mass.: MIT Press.

Hicks, J. R. 1932. *Theory of Wages*. London: Macmillan.

———. 1946. *Value and Capital*. 2d ed. Oxford: Clarendon Press (1st ed. 1939).

———. 1970. "Elasticities of Substitution Again: Substitutes and Complements." *Oxford Economic Papers* 22 (November): 289–96.

Hicks, L. R., and R. G. D. Allen. 1934. "A Reconsideration of the Theory of Value, I, II." *Economica* 1 (February, May): 52–75, 196–219 ("Part I" and "Part II" are, respectively, written by Hicks and Allen).

Hotelling, H. 1932. "Edgeworth's Taxation Paradox and the Nature of Demand and Supply Function." *Journal of Political Economy* 40 (October): 577–616.

———. 1935. "Demand Functions with Limited Budgets." *Econometrica* 3 (October): 66–78.

———. 1938. "The General Welfare in Relation to Problems of Taxation and of Railway and Utility Rates" *Econometrica* 6 (July): 242–269.

Ide, T., and A. Takayama. 1987. "On the Concepts of Returns to Scale." *Economics Letters* 23 (4): 329–34.

———. 1989a. "Returns to Scale under Non-Homotheticity and Homotheticity, and the Shape of Average Cost." *Zeitschrift für die gesamte Staatswissenschaft* 145 (December): 367–88.

———. 1989b. "On Homothetic Functions." *Scandinavian Journal of Economics* 91 (3): 621–23.

Karlin, S. 1959. *Mathematical Methods and Theory in Games, Programming, and Economics*, Vol. I. Reading, Mass.: Addison-Wesly

Lau, L. J. 1969. " Duality and the Structure of Utility Functions." *Journal of Economic Theory* 1 (December): 374–96.

———. 1976. "Characterization of the Normalized Restricted Profit Function." *Journal of Economic Theory* 12 (January): 131–63.

———. 1978. "Testing and Imposing Monotonicity, Convexity and Quasi-Convexity Constraints." In Fuss and McFadden (1978), 1: 409–53.

McKenzie, L. W. 1957. "Demand Theory without a Utility Index." *Review of Economic Studies* 24 (June): 184–89.

Marino, A., Y. Otani, and J. Sicilian, 1981. "Rising Marginal Cost and Concavity of the Production Function." *Economics Letters* 8 (3): 293–99.

Marshall, A. 1920. *Principles of Economics.* 8th ed. London: Macmillan (1st ed. 1890).

Morrison, C. J. 1986. "Structural Models of Dynamic Factor Demands with Static Expectations: An Empirical Assessment of Alternative Expectation Specifications." *International Economic Review* 27 (June): 365–86.

Morrison, C. J., and E. R. Berndt 1981. "Short-Run Labor Productivity in a Dynamic Model," *Journal of Econometrics* 16 (August): 339–65.

Negishi, T. 1989. *Lectures on Microeconomics* (in Japanese). Tokyo: University of Tokyo Press.

Newman, P. 1982. "Mirrored Pairs of Optimization Problems." *Economica* 49 (May): 109–19.

Ohta, M. 1974. "A Note on Duality between the Lost Functions: Rate of Returns to Scale and Rate of Technological Progress." *Economic Studies Quarterly* 25 (December): 63–65.

Okuno, M., and K. Suzumura, K. 1985. *Microeconomics I* (in Japanese). Tokyo: Iwanami.

Otani, Y. 1982. "A Simple Proof of the Le Châtelier-Samuelson Principle and the Theory of Cost and Production." *Journal of Economic Theory* 27 (August): 430–38.

Pollak, R. A. 1969. "Conditional Demand Functions and Consumption Theory, *Quarterly Journal of Economics* 83 (February): 60–78.

Roy, R. 1942. *De l'utilité.* Paris: Hermann.

Saijo, T. 1983. "Differentiability of Cost Functions is Equivalent to Strict Quasiconcavity of the Production Functions." *Economics Letters* 12 (2): 135–39.

Samuelson, P. A. 1947. *Foundations of Economic Analysis.* Cambridge, Mass.: Harvard University Press (enl. ed.).

———. 1953. "Prices of Factors and Goods in General Equilibrium," *Review of Economic Studies* 21: 1–20.

———. 1958. "Frank Knight's Theorem in Linear Programming." *Zeitschrift für Nationalökonomie* 18 (August): 310–17.

———. 1960a. "An Extension of the Le Chatelier Principle." *Econometrica* 28, April: 368–79.

———. 1960b. "Structure of a Minimum Equilibrium System." In *Essays in Economics and Econometrics: A Volume in Honor of Harold Hotelling*, ed. R. W. Phouts, 1–33. Chapel Hill, N.C.: University of North Carolina Press.

———. 1966. "The Le Chatelier Principle in Linear Programming." In *Collected Scientific Papers of Paul A. Samuelson*, ed. J. E. Stiglitz, 1: 638–50. Cambridge, Mass.: MIT Press. See also "1965 Postscript." 684–86.

Shephard, R. W. 1953. *Cost and Production Functions*. Princeton, N.J.: Princeton University Press.

———. 1970. *Theory of Cost and Production Functions*. Princeton, N.J.: Princeton University Press.

Silberberg, E. 1971. "The Le Chatelier Principle as a Corollary to a Generalized Envelope Theorem." *Journal of Economic Theory* 3 (June): 146–55.

———. 1974. "A Revision of Comparative Statics Methodology in Economics, or, How to Do Comparative Statics on the Backof an Envelope." *Journal of Economic Theory* 7 (February): 159–72.

———. 1990. *The Structure of Economics*. 2d ed. New York: McGraw-Hill (1st ed. 1978).

Sims, G. E., A. Takayama, and C. C. Chao. 1987. "A Dual Approach to Measuring the Nearness of Near-Monies." *Review of Economics and Statistics* 69 (February): 118–27.

Slutsky, E. 1915. "Sulla Teoria Del Bilancio Del Consumatore." *Giornale Degli Economisti* 51: 1–26. [1952] "On the Theory of the Budget of the Consumer." T rans. O. Ragusa. In *Readings in Price Theory*, ed. G. J. Stigler and K. E. Boulding, 27–56. Homewood, Ill.: Richard D. Irwin.

Stigler, G. 1947. "Notes on the History of the Giffen Paradox." *Journal of Political Economy* 55 (April): 152–56.

———. 1966. *The Theory of Price*. 3d ed. New York: Macmillan.

Takayama, A. 1977. "Sensitivity Analysis in Economic Theory." *Metroeconomica* 29 (January–December): 9–37.

———. 1982. "On Theorems of General Competitive Equilibrium of Production and Trade: A Survey of Some Recent Developments in the Theory of International Trade." *Keio Economic Studies* 19: 1–37.

———. 1985. *Mathematical Economics*. 2d ed. New York: Cambridge University Press.

Tobin, J. 1952. "A Survey of the Theory of Rationing." *Econometrica* 20 (October): 521–53.

Tobin, J. and H. S. Houthakker, 1951. "The Effects of Rationing on Demand Elasticities." *Review of Economic Studies* 18(3): 140-53.

Uzawa, H. 1962. "Production Functions with Constant Elasticities of Substitution." *Review of Economic Studies* 29 (October): 291–99.

———. 1964. "Duality Principles in the Theory of Cost and Production." *International Economic Review* 5 (May): 216–20.

Varian, H. R. 1984. *Microeconomic Analysis.* 2d ed. New York: Norton (1st ed. 1978).

CHAPTER 4

Other Topics in Microeconomic Theory

In this chapter, we assemble some other important topics in microeconomic theory. Discussion of these topics would be helpful in illustrating the use of techniques developed in the previous chapters (nonlinear programming and sensitivity analysis). These topics also capture some important aspects of microtheory; thus they are not merely simple illustrations of mathematical techniques. We may note that some of these topics are not necessarily well understood in the literature. Since the relevant mathematical techniques were explained in detail in the previous chapters, our emphasis here is more on economics rather than the details of how particular mathematical theorems are or should be applied to the economic problems being considered.

4.1 Inferior Inputs, Marginal and Average Costs[1]

4.1.1 Inferior Inputs

Since Jacob Viner's (1931) classic discussion describing the gist of partial equilibrium analysis, marginal and average cost curves abound in intermediate price theory textbooks, and the power and usefulness of such a technique has been well demonstrated (see, for example, Stigler 1966, and Friedman 1962). A more rigorous formulation of such cost curves was developed in classic treatises by Hicks (1946) and Samuelson (1947), modern versions of which were presented in our previous chapters. In spite of all of this, some confusion still remains. In particular, it is often asserted that:

(a) an increase in a factor price always increases marginal cost;

[1] This section is adapted from Takayama (1979b).

(*b*) there is a perfect analogy between the theory of consumption and the theory of the firm in that the substitution effect and the income or scale effect can move in opposite directions, so that the Giffen paradox also applies to the theory of firm.

Subsequently, it has been shown that both statements are false. In addition, a number of related issues have been clarified. Some of the important works in this context are Ferguson and Saving (1969), Syrquin (1970), Portes (1971), Puu (1971), Sakai (1973), and Nagatani (1978). The purpose of the present section is to exposit the main results in this line of literature in the simplest possible way. Unlike many papers on this topic, we shall avoid the use of bordered Hessians that vexes students unnecessarily. The key idea is to utilize Shephard's lemma (alternatively, the envelope theorem), and thus follow the idea developed by Portes (1971) and Nagatani (1978). Recall the usual cost minimization problem for a competitive firm, that is, choose an input vector $x \in R^n$ to

$$\text{Minimize } w \cdot x, \quad \text{subject to } f(x) \geqq y, \text{ and } x \geqq 0,$$

where y signifies a target level of output that is a positive scalar and where w and $f(x)$, respectively, denote the input price vector and the production function. We assume that $w > 0$ is exogeneously given to the firm. Let $x(w, y)$ be a solution of this problem, and let $\lambda(w, y)$ be the Lagrangian multiplier associated with it. Let $C(w, y) \equiv w \cdot x(w, y)$ be the minimum cost function. We assume $x_i > 0$ for all i (an interior solution) and $\lambda > 0$ at optimum. $\lambda(w, y) > 0$ implies $f(x) = y$. We may recall $\lambda(w, y) = \partial C(w, y)/\partial y$.

Next we recall the usual profit maximization problem of choosing (a single) output y for a competitive firm so as to maximize the profit, $py - C(w, y)$, subject to $y \geqq 0$, where $p > 0$ and $w > 0$ are given to the firm. The optimality condition for this problem, for a positive output, can be written as

$$p = \lambda(w, y), \quad \text{where } \lambda(w, y) \equiv \partial C(w, y)/\partial y \text{ [marginal cost]}. \tag{1}$$

This is the well-known condition that the price of output is equal to the marginal cost (MC), where we assume

$$\partial\lambda(w, y)/\partial y \; [= \partial^2 C(w, y)/\partial y^2] > 0, \quad \text{at the optimum,} \tag{2}$$

to ensure a unique maximum. Condition (2) states that the MC curve is upward sloping at the optimal value of output. This is a standard assumption in intermediate-price-theory textbooks. We write the optimal output, that is, the y that satisfies (1), as $y(p, w)$.

In proceeding with our analysis, assume the desired continuous differentiability of all the relevant functions. Differentiation of (1) yields

$$dp = \sum_{i=1}^{n} \frac{\partial \lambda}{\partial w_i} dw_i + \frac{\partial \lambda}{\partial y} dy. \tag{3}$$

From this, we may determine the partial derivatives of $y(p, w)$ with respect to the w_i's as

$$\frac{\partial y}{\partial w_i} = -\frac{\partial \lambda}{\partial w_i} / \frac{\partial \lambda}{\partial y},\ i = 1, 2, \ldots, n. \tag{4}$$

Since $\partial\lambda/\partial y > 0$ at the optimum by assumption, we may at once obtain the following result.

Lemma 4.1. We have the following relation:

$$\partial y/\partial w_i \gtreqless 0 \text{ according to whether } \partial\lambda/\partial w_i \lesseqgtr 0,\ i = 1, 2, \ldots, n \tag{5}$$

Here $\partial y/\partial w_i < 0$ means that an increase in an input price lowers the profit maximizing output. While $\partial y/\partial w_i < 0$ may be more in accordance with the conventional wisdom, this need not be the case (as we shall show later).

Next recall that the optimal input vector for cost minimization is written as $x(p, w)$. We then define the function $x^*(p, w)$ by

$$x = x[w, y(p, w)] \equiv x^*(p, w). \tag{6}$$

Namely, $x^*(p, w)$ signifies the minimal cost input vector that achieves the optimal output, y, when the price vector (p, w) prevails. Differentiation of (6) with respect to w_i yields[2]

$$\partial x_i^*/\partial w_i = (\partial x_i/\partial w_i) + (\partial x_i/\partial y)(\partial y/\partial w_i),\ i = 1, 2, \ldots, n. \tag{7}$$

The first term of the right-hand side of (7) signifies the **(own) substitution effect**, while the second term signifies the **scale effect** (or the **expansion effect**). The **total effect** of a change in the price of any

---

[2]It is important to note that x and x^* in (7), respectively, signify the cost minimizing and the profit maximizing input vectors. The properties of the matrix $S \equiv [\partial x_i/\partial w_j]$ are summarized in theorem 3.2 of chap. 3. Namely S is symmetric and negative semidefinite with $\partial x_i/\partial w_i < 0$ for all i (assuming the Samuelson regularity condition). Also we have $\sum_j x_{ij} w_j = 0$ for all i and $\sum_i w_i x_{ij} = 0$ for all j, where $x_{ij} \equiv \partial x_i/\partial w_j$.

factor can be decomposed into the substitution effect and the scale effect. This decomposition of the total effect is observed by Ferguson and Saving (1969), Syrquin (1970), Puu (1971), Sakai (1973), and Nagatani (1978). We now wish to determine the signs of these three effects: the substitution, the scale, and the total effects. Recalling theorem 3.2, we may assert that the (own) substitution effect, $\partial x_i/\partial w_i$, is negative for each i, where we assume Samuelson's regularity condition.

What about the sign of the scale effect? This question naturally leads to an inquiry concerning the sign of $(\partial x_i/\partial y)$, where we now recall the following important classification of factors of production in intermediate price theory.

Definition 4.1. The ith factor is said to be **normal** (resp. **inferior**) if $\partial x_i/\partial y > 0$ (resp. $\partial x_i/\partial y < 0$), that is, if an increase in the output results in an increase (resp. a fall) in the usage of the ith factor (in order for the firm to achieve cost minimization).[3]

Inferior factors can easily be illustrated diagrammatically by using isoquant maps in the input space. In figure 4.1*a*, factor 1 is inferior and in figure 4.1*b*, factor 2 is inferior. Clearly, factor 2 is normal in fig. 4.1*a* and factor 1 is normal in figure 4.1*b*.

At this stage it might be useful to review some price theory. As pointed out by Nagatani (1978, p. 521), there seems to be two answers in basic textbooks:

(*a*) If the factor is strongly inferior, the perverse effect may outweigh the normal substitution effect so that $\partial x^*/\partial w_i$ can be positive (cf. Ferguson 1969, p. 197).

(*b*) There is only a substitution effect in factor demands, that is, $\partial x_i^*/\partial w_i = \partial x_i/\partial w_i$: hence there is no such thing as a "Giffen input" in the sense that $\partial x_i^*/\partial w_i > 0$ (cf. Henderson and Quandt 1958, p. 75; 1971, p. 70; 1980, p. 81; and Burstein 1968, p. 103).

Neither of these statements is correct. This was pointed out by Syrquin (1970). Note that (7) already indicates that the scale effect does exist. In what follows, we show that both statements (*a*) and (*b*)

[3]Since profit maximization presupposes cost minimization in the present case, the phrase *cost minimization* can be replaced by *profit maximization*. Hicks calls an inferior factor a **regressive factor**, whereas he discarded such an input regressivity as anomalous, improbable, and perverse (Hicks 1946, pp. 93–96). Puu (1971) offers some justifications why this may not be the case.

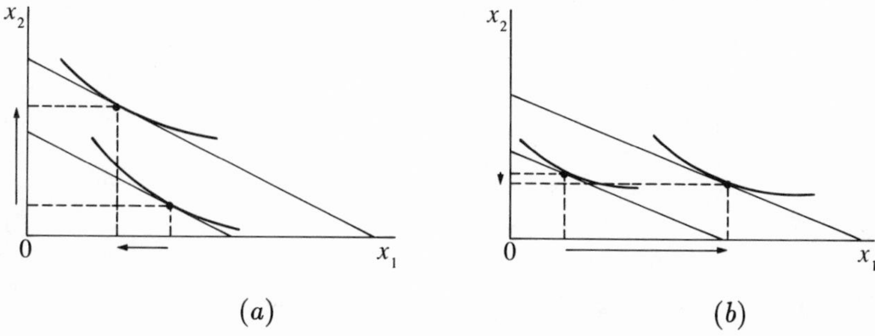

Figure 4.1: Illustration of inferior inputs

are false and, in fact, we can obtain the following results, where statement (iii) specifically negates both statements (a) and (b).

Proposition 4.1. Assume $x_i > 0$ for all i at the optimum, and assume also that the function $C(w, y)$ is twice continuously differentiable. Then we have:

(i) An increase in a factor price shifts the marginal cost curve up or down depending on whether the factor in question is normal or inferior. More precisely,

$$\frac{\partial \lambda}{\partial w_i} = \frac{\partial x_i}{\partial y}, \; i = 1, 2, \ldots, n.^4 \tag{8}$$

(ii) An increase in a factor price lowers or increases the optimum output depending on whether the factor in question is normal or inferior. More specifically,

$$\text{sign}\,(\frac{\partial y}{\partial w_i}) = -\ \text{sign}\,(\frac{\partial x_i}{\partial y}), \; i = 1, 2, \ldots, n.^5 \tag{9}$$

---

[4] Equation (8) was already obtained in the previous chapter (see eq. 23 in chap. 3).

[5] As can be seen below, statement (ii) follows immediately from statement (i). In fact, anybody who is familiar with elementary price theory can assert statement (ii)

(iii) The scale effect is always negative regardless of whether the factor in question is normal or inferior, so that the total effect is always negative,

$$\frac{\partial x_i}{\partial y}\frac{\partial y}{\partial w_i} < 0 \text{ always, so that}$$

$$\frac{\partial x_i^*}{\partial w_i} < 0, \text{ always, } i = 1, 2, \ldots, n. \tag{10}$$

Proof. Differentiating $C(w, y)$ twice, we observe

$$\frac{\partial^2 C}{\partial y \partial w_i} = \frac{\partial}{\partial y}\left(\frac{\partial C}{\partial w_i}\right) = \frac{\partial x_i}{\partial y}, \tag{11}$$

where the last equality follows from Shephard's lemma, $\partial C/\partial w_i = x_i$. Since $C(w, y)$ is twice continuously differentiable, we may switch the order of differentiation so that

$$\frac{\partial^2 C}{\partial y \partial w_i} = \frac{\partial^2 C}{\partial w_i \partial y} = \frac{\partial}{\partial w_i}\left(\frac{\partial C}{\partial y}\right) = \frac{\partial \lambda}{\partial w_i}, \tag{12}$$

where the last equality follows from $\lambda \equiv \partial C/\partial y$. Combining (11) and (12), we obtain (8).

To prove statement (ii), use (5) and (8), and simply observe

$$\text{sign}\left(\frac{\partial y}{\partial w_i}\right) = -\text{sign}\left(\frac{\partial \lambda}{\partial w_i}\right) = -\text{sign}\left(\frac{\partial x_i}{\partial y}\right). \tag{13}$$

To prove statement (iii), use (9), which indicates that

$$\text{sign}\left(\frac{\partial x_i}{\partial y}\frac{\partial y}{\partial w_i}\right) = -\text{sign}\left(\frac{\partial x_i}{\partial y}\right)^2 < 0. \tag{14}$$

By virtue of (7), this implies $\partial x_i^*/\partial w_i < 0$. (QED)

Statement (iii) of proposition 4.1, which was obtained by Syrquin (1970), Puu (1971), and Sakai (1973), states that the derived factor demand function is always inversely related to its own factor prices. That the substitution and the scale effects always go in the same direction (so that there are no such things as "Giffen inputs") creates a marked

from statement (i) instantaneously by drawing the MC curve and the price line.

contrast with consumption theory. Statement (ii) is an immediate consequence of statement (i). It is explicitly noted by Ferguson and Saving (1969). Statement (i) is shown by Mosak (1938), Samuelson (1947), and Syrquin (1970). All the proofs of these statements in the literature involve considerable use of matrix algebra (such as the use of bordered Hessians). The preceding proof does not require any such discussions. It is a simple application of Shephard's lemma. It is an extension of Nagatani (1978), in which he also provides a diagrammatic illustration of statement (iii).

Statement (i) of proposition 4.1 states that a fall in the price of an input will always increase the marginal cost if the input in question is inferior. Hence the existence of an inferior input falsifies some statements contained in the literature. For example, in Friedman's *Provisional Text* (1962, p. 179), it is stated that:

> If the price of A falls and output is kept constant, A will be substituted for other factors, . . . The reduction in the price of A has, however, . . . , increased the number of units of output attainable by spending an additional dollar, that is, *it has reduced marginal cost.* (italics added).

Friedman's statement is true if and only if the factor in question is normal. By statement (ii), $\partial y/\partial w_i < 0$ if and only if the ith factor is normal. Hence we may also conclude that the "conventional wisdom," $\partial y/\partial w_i < 0$, *fails* to hold if and only if the factor is inferior.

4.1.2 Factor Prices and Shifts of the Average Cost Curve

We now shift our attention to the effect of a change in factor prices on the average cost (AC) curve. In particular, we obtain the following results.

Proposition 4.2. Assume $x_i > 0$ for all i at the optimum and assume further that the function $C(w, y)$ is continuously differentiable. Then we have:

(i) an increase in a factor price always shifts the AC curve up regardless of whether the factor in question is normal or inferior;

(ii) an increase in the ith factor price lowers the level of output at the minimum point of the AC curve if and only if the output elasticity of the demand for the ith factor (μ_i) exceeds unity, that is, if and only if

$$\mu_i \equiv \frac{\partial x_i}{\partial y} \frac{y}{x_i} > 1, \; i = 1, 2, \ldots, n. \tag{15}$$

Proof. To show statement (i), simply note that the average cost function, α, is defined by $\alpha(w, y) \equiv C(w, y)/y$. Then simply observing

$$\frac{\partial \alpha}{\partial w_i} = \frac{1}{y} \frac{\partial C}{\partial w_i} = \frac{x_i}{y} > 0, \; i = 1, 2, \ldots, n, \tag{16}$$

we may at once obtain statement (i), where the second equality utilizes Shephard's lemma,

$$\partial C/\partial w_i = x_i.$$

Assume that the AC curve is U-shaped, as is often done in the literature. The minimum point of the AC curve is characterized by the point at which the MC and the AC curves intersect. It is determined by

$$\lambda(w, y) = C(w, y)/y, \tag{17}$$

which in turn defines the minimum point of the AC curve as

$$y = y^*(w).$$

To obtain the expression for $\partial y^*/\partial w_i$, we differentiate (17), keeping all the w_j except for w_i constant,

$$\lambda_i dw_i + \lambda_y dy = \frac{x_i}{y} dw_i + \left(\frac{\partial C}{\partial y} - \frac{C}{y} \right) \frac{dy}{y} = \frac{x_i}{y} dw_i, \tag{18}$$

where $\lambda_i \equiv \partial \lambda/\partial w_i$ and $\lambda_y \equiv \partial \lambda/\partial y$, and where $\partial C/\partial w_i = x_i$. The last equality of (18) follows from (17). From (18) we at once obtain

$$\frac{\partial y^*}{\partial w_i} = -\left(\frac{\partial x_i}{\partial y} - \frac{x_i}{y} \right)/\lambda_y, \tag{19}$$

where we recall (8). Since the choice of i is arbitrary, (19) holds for any i. Hence we may conclude:

$$\frac{\partial y^*}{\partial w_i} < 0 \text{ if and only if } \frac{\partial x_i}{\partial y} \frac{y}{x_i} > 1, \; i = 1, 2, \ldots, n, \tag{20}$$

where we may recall $\lambda_y > 0$ by assumption. (QED)

Proposition 4.2 corresponds to a similar result obtained by Ferguson and Saving (1969) using the bordered Hessian technique,[6] in which they characterize the sign of $\partial y^*/\partial x_i$ in terms of the "expenditure elasticity" of the ith factor.[7] When $\partial y^*/\partial w_i < 0$, Ferguson and Saving (1969) call the ith factor "superior." Following the spirit of such a definition we may call the ith factor **superior** when the output elasticity of its demand (μ_i) exceeds unity. Proposition 4.2 and statement (i) of proposition 4.1 completely summarize the effect of a change in factor price upon the AC and MC curves. We may illustrate this in figure 4.2 (a similar diagram was also presented in Ferguson and Saving 1969, p. 779).[8]

---

[6]Ferguson and Saving (1969, p. 775), at the outset of their analysis, made the assumption that the number of factors must be *even*. Such an assumption is unnecessary.

[7]The expenditure elasticity (of the ith factor) is defined as the percentage change in the usage of the ith factor per percentage change in the total cost of production when all factor prices are kept constant. Denote such an elasticity by e_i, and observe

$$e_i \equiv \frac{C}{x_i}\frac{dx_i}{dC}\bigg|_{w=\text{const.}} = \frac{C}{x_i}\left[\frac{\partial x_i}{\partial y} \bigg/ \frac{\partial C}{\partial y}\right],$$

where $x_i = x_i(w, y)$ and $C = C(w, y)$. Evaluating e_i at the output level that corresponds to the minimum point of the AC curve (in which $\partial C/\partial y = C/y$), we obtain

$$e_i = \mu_i = \partial x_i/\partial y.$$

Thus, e_i is the same as our output elasticity of the ith factor demand (μ_i). The same result is obtained by Portes (1971, p. 434). Statement (ii) of our theorem 4.2 corresponds precisely to Ferguson and Saving's conclusion (1969, p. 777) that $\partial y^*/\partial w_i \gtreqless 0$ according to whether $e_i \lesseqgtr 1$. Portes (1971) gave the idea of utilizing Shephard's lemma to obtain the same results as well as to avoid bordered Hessians.

[8]In the preceding discussion, we observe that $\partial x_i^*/\partial w_i$ is always negative. It might be of some interest to obtain the effect of a change in the ith factor price on the usage of the ith factor in the "long-run situation" for a competitive industry. In this case, the equilibrium occurs at the minimum point of the AC curve, in which the output level is determined by y^* in (18). We now define the function $\bar{x}$ by

$$x = x[w, y^*(w)] \equiv \bar{x}(w).$$

Then, simply observe

$$\partial \bar{x}_i/\partial w_i = \partial x_i/\partial w_i + (\partial x/\partial y)(\partial y^*/\partial w_i).$$

Substituting (20) into this, we obtain

$$\partial \bar{x}_i/\partial w_i = \partial x_i/\partial w_i - \mu_i(\mu_i - 1)x_i^2/y^2,$$

where we may recall the definition of μ_i in (15). From this, we may conclude $\partial \bar{x}_i/\partial w_i$ can be either positive or negative. This corresponds to the conclusion obtained by

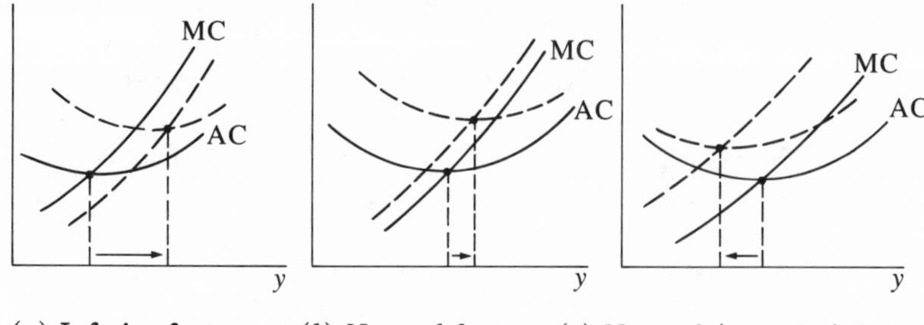

(*a*) Inferior factor (*b*) Normal factor (*c*) Normal (superior) factor

Figure 4.2: The effects of a rise in factor price

REMARK: In the preceding discussion, we considered the case in which the firm is a competitive firm and where p is an exogeneously given constant to the firm. If the firm is a monopoly, we let $p(y)$ be its inverse demand function and assume $p'(y) < 0$. The firm chooses y to maximize $R(y) - C(w, y)$, where $R(y) \equiv p(y)y$. The first-order condition can be written as $R'(y) = \lambda(w, y)$, which is the usual rule of $MR = MC$. This condition determines y as a function of w, where $y = y^\circ(w)$. Clearly, y° corresponds to the function $y(p, w)$ obtained from (2). Carrying out an analysis similar to the preceding one, we may conclude that the statements of propositions 4.1 and 4.2 also hold for a monopolistic firm. The proof is left to the interested reader.

REMARK: In figure 4.2, we assumed the usual U-shaped AC curve, which is by far the most accepted shape of AC curves. In section 4.3 below, we shall obtain a skeptical note on such a shape, in which the effect of a factor price change will play a key role.

4.2 Marginal Cost Pricing

Corporations such as public utilities and railways are often *complete monopoly* firms in certain regions. If the price is set in such a way as

---

Ferguson and Saving (1969, p. 782) that "an increase in factor price *may* result in an increase in the usage of the factor in question" (italics added). A similar result is obtained by Portes (1971, p. 431) via Shephard's lemma. Note that if $\mu_i \geqq 1$, then $\partial \overline{x}_i / \partial w_i$ is always negative.

to maximize a firm's profit, such a price may not be optimal from a social viewpoint. What then is the price that is optimal from a social viewpoint? This is a very difficult question since we cannot find any meaningful index that would indicate the level of social welfare.[9] Setting aside the difficult question of what can be used to measure social welfare, a simple pricing rule has long been discussed in the literature. The classic papers on this topic are Dupuit (1844) and Hotelling (1938). The pricing rule that is "optimal" from a social viewpoint is known as **marginal cost pricing**. Roughly speaking, it states that the price should be set at the level that is equal to the marginal cost. In this section, we shall exposit this in the *simplest* possible manner. In so doing, we omit some useful aspects of the problem.

Consider a complete monopoly firm that produces a single product y using n inputs. The production function is again written as $f(x)$, where $x = (x_1, x_2, \ldots, x_n)$. Let the industry's inverse demand function be given by $p(y)$, where p denotes the price of the product. The profit-maximizing monopoly will choose x and y to maximize $p(y)y - w \cdot x$ subject to $f(x) \geqq y$, $x \geqq 0$ and $y \geqq 0$, where $w = (w_1, w_2, \ldots w_n)$ is an exogenously given input price vector. This problem may be decomposed into two problems. One is the problem of cost minimization. The firm first chooses x to minimize $w \cdot x$ subject to $f(x) \geqq y$ and $x \geqq 0$, for a given level of y. Let $x(w, y)$ be the solution of this problem. Define the (minimum) total cost function by $C(w, y) \equiv w \cdot x(w, y)$. To ease the notation, suppress w, and replace $C(w, y)$ by $C(y)$ for simplicity, where w is held constant throughout the section. The firm is to choose y to maximize $p(y)y - C(y)$. This gives us the usual rule of $MR = MC$; that is,

$$R'(Y^\circ) = C'(Y^\circ), \tag{21}$$

where $R(y) \equiv p(y)y$, the total revenue function, and where Y° signifies the profit-maximizing output level. The profit-maximizing price is then obtained by $p^\circ = p(Y^\circ)$.

We now consider the problem of determining the price that would maximize social welfare. Following the usual practice in applied economics, we define "social welfare" as the sum of consumers' surplus plus total revenue minus total cost.[10] Although this definition of social welfare can lead to well-known difficulties that are clarified in social choice

[9] For a succinct and brief summary on Arrow's impossibility theorem (Arrow 1951, 1963) and the problem of social choice, see Sen (1987). Kenneth Arrow was a 1972 Nobel laureate in Economic Science.

[10] As is well known, the concept of consumer surplus contains some difficult prob-

theory, we follow such a definition. Our purpose is simply illustrative. It is assumed that the firm is a usual cost minimizer. We write its cost function as $C(y)$.

The magnitude of consumers' surplus (CS) plus total revenue (TR) can be illustrated by the shaded area in figure 4.3. When the firm's output level is determined by Y, the price of the product is obtained by $p(Y)$. "Social welfare" is then defined by

$$W(Y) = \int_0^Y p(y)dy - C(Y). \tag{22}$$

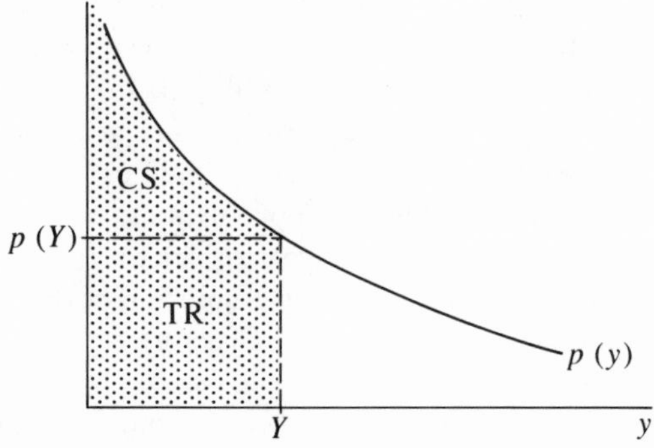

Figure 4.3: Consumers' surplus plus total revenue

Suppose that the firm is to choose Y to maximize W. The first-order condition is given by $W'(Y^*) = 0$, where we assume $Y^* > 0$. Using the rule on the differentiation of integrals (which shall explain shortly), condition $W'(Y^*) = 0$ can be written as

$$p(Y^*) = C'(Y^*). \tag{23}$$

---

lems. Even confining ourselves to a single individual, or to a society that consists of only one individual, this concept has been controversial. In the 1940s, J. R. Hicks made a series of important contributions on this topic, which was then criticized by Samuelson (1947, pp. 195–202). For recent developments on this topic, see Takayama (1984 and 1987) and appendix C.

This states that price is equal to MC, and this is the **MC pricing** rule. The second-order sufficient condition for an optimum is given by $W''(Y^*) < 0$. This can be rewritten as

$$p'(Y^*) < C''(Y^*). \tag{24}$$

If the MC curve is increasing at the point of intersection, $C''(Y^*) > 0$, this condition is always satisfied. On the other hand, if the MC curve is falling at the point of intersection, $C''(Y^*) < 0$, this condition means that the MC curve is flatter than the (negatively sloped) inverse demand curve, at the point of intersection. We may illustrate the MC pricing rule in figure 4.4. Figure 4.4*a* is concerned with the case of $C''(Y^*) > 0$, whereas figure 4.4*b* deals with the case of $C''(Y^*) < 0$. Note that in both cases, the social welfare-maximizing price (p^*) is lower than the profit-maximizing price (p^o), where $p^* \equiv p(Y^*)$.

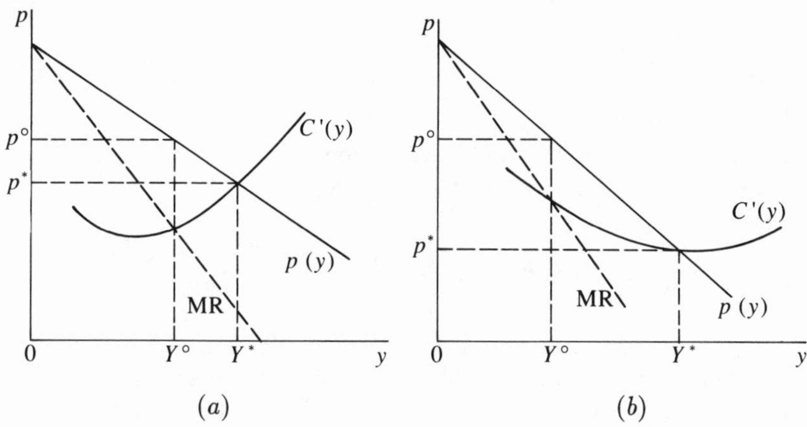

Figure 4.4: Marginal cost pricing

In summary, we may obtain the following proposition.

Proposition 4.3. Assume that social welfare is defined by (22). Then the rule that achieves the maximization of social welfare is given by (23) in which price is equated to MC, assuming (24) holds.

REMARK: Suppose that the industry in question does not consist of only one firm, but instead that it consists of a large number of firms each of which is a price taker. Each firm maximizes its profit $py - C(y)$, where p is a given constant to the firm. The profit maximization yields the usual condition $p = C'(Y^\circ)$, price = MC, assuming (in the usual way) a rising marginal cost curve at Y°. Summing this over all firms in the industry, we can see that the MC pricing rule is obtained for the industry as a whole. Namely, we obtain the well-known result that the MC pricing holds for a competitive industry.

REMARK: To obtain (23), we utilized a well-known result on the **differentiation of integrals**. It may be worthwhile to record this useful result here, as it is often used in the literature. To achieve this end, let $f(x, \alpha)$ be a real-valued differential function where $x \in R^n$ and $\alpha \in R$. Define the integral $F(\alpha)$ by

$$F(\alpha) \equiv \int_{a(\alpha)}^{b(\alpha)} f(x, \alpha)dx, \tag{25}$$

where we may note that a and b are differentiable functions of α. Then $F'(a)(\equiv dF/d\alpha)$ may be obtained as follows:

$$F'(\alpha) = \int_a^b f_\alpha(x, \alpha)d\alpha + f(b, \alpha)b'(\alpha) - f(a, \alpha)a'(\alpha), \tag{26}$$

where $f_\alpha \equiv \partial f/\partial\alpha$, $b' \equiv db/d\alpha$, and $a' \equiv da/d\alpha$. Functions f, b, and a are assumed to be differentiable in α, and that f is continuous in x. For the proof of this result, see any textbook in advanced calculus. If $b(\alpha) = \alpha$, $a(\alpha) =$ constant, and $f(x, \alpha) = f(x)$, then (26) is simplified to

$$F'(\alpha) = f(b). \tag{26'}$$

This is the rule used to obtain (23).

REMARK: Monopoly firms such as public utility corporations are often characterized by decreasing costs (scale economies). "Decreasing cost" is defined by a falling AC curve.[11] The falling AC curve means $d[C(y)/y]/dy < 0$. This can equivalently be rewritten as

$$C'(y) < C/y.$$

[11] For different concepts of increasing or decreasing returns to scale and the relationship among them, recall sec. 3.5 of chap. 3. See also Ide and Takayama (1987b and 1989a).

So the AC curve is falling if and only if the MC curve lies below the AC curve.[12] Under MC pricing, $p(Y^*) = C'(Y^*)$. Thus we may observe

$$p^*Y^* - C(Y^*) = C'(Y^*)Y^* - C(Y^*)$$
$$= [C'(Y^*) - C(Y^*)/Y^*]Y^* < 0.$$

Hence the profit must always be negative under MC pricing for the decreasing cost industry.[13] Then if the MC pricing rule is enforced upon a monopoly firm under decreasing cost, the firm would withdraw from the market unless a proper subsidy is given to the firm. Even setting aside the nontrivial question of possible distortions created by taxes that are introduced to raise revenues to finance the subsidy, this subsidy to prevent the firm from loss casts a fundamental problem. Namely, if the firm is subsidized for loss, it will then lose an important incentive to minimize its cost of production. In fact, such noncost-minimizing behavior appears to be often seen in public utilities that are operated under government subsidies.[14]

4.3 Factor Prices and the Shape of Average Cost Curves[15]

Figure 4.2 implicitly or explicitly captures the usual U-shaped AC curve, which is undoubtedly in the minds of Ferguson and Saving (1969), who use similar diagrams. In fact, the usual U-shaped AC curves abound in the literature since Viner's (1931) influential work. On the other hand, it is also a standard exercise in micro-theory courses that students are asked to obtain the cost function from a given production function via the usual cost minimization procedure. However, it is very difficult (if

---

[12] In other words, AC is falling if and only if $\theta\,(\equiv \text{MC/AC}) < 1$. This is nothing but Proposition 3.6. Namely, scale economies in terms of a falling AC curve is *equivalent* to defining scale economies in terms of $\theta < 1$.

[13] Although this proposition is easy to show, it is not necessarily well understood in the literature. See, for example, Panzar and Willig (1977), in which they obtain the following conclusion: the supposition that a "firm with economies of scale cannot recover costs with marginal cost pricing" is "in general false" (p. 481), in which they also remark that this supposition is "rarely examined" (p. 481). For critical comments on their work, see Scott (1979), and Ide and Takayama (1987a). The work by Panzar and Willig unfortunately contains elementary errors.

[14] For further discussion of marginal cost pricing, see, for example, Drèze (1964), Nelson (1964), Joskow (1976), Crew and Kleindorfer (1986), Vickery (1987), and Berg and Tschirhart (1988).

[15] This section is adapted from Ide and Takayama (1989b), which won the 1989 Daeyang Prize in 1991.

not impossible) to obtain a suitable production function that yields the usual U-shaped AC curve, unless one imposes certain *ad hoc* assumptions on the production function. Although the U-shaped AC curve may intuitively be "plausible," this appears to undermine its value considerably.

It is well known that factor prices do affect the MC and the AC curves, although there are some confusions with regard to the question of how these curves are affected. Proposition 4.2 clarifies this question. However, it is ***not*** well known that a slight change in factor prices ***can*** result in a drastic change in the shape of the AC curve, rather than a simple shift of the curve. Also, it is not well known that the concept of returns to scale is also sensitive with respect to a change in factor prices: a change in factor prices can alter technology from increasing-returns-to-scale to decreasing-returns-to-scale, and vice versa. In this section, we show these by way of simple examples. These will help us to increase our understanding of important concepts such as production functions, AC, factor prices, and returns to scale, and our clarification can have important applications to industrial organization (e.g., the determination of a particular industrial structure) and international trade (e.g., comparative advantage).

For the sake of simplicity, our examples are concerned with the case of two inputs (denoted by x_1 and x_2 and a single output, y). We denote the production function by $f(x)$, where $x = (x_1, x_2)$. Let $w = (w_1, w_2)$ be the input price vector, and let the cost function $C(w, y)$ be obtained by the usual cost minimization, where $C(w, y) = w \cdot x(w, y)$. Let the AC and the MC functions, respectively, be defined by $\alpha(w, y) \equiv C(w, y)/y$ and $\mu(w, y) \equiv \partial C/\partial y$. We assume $w_1 > 0$, $w_2 > 0$, and $y > 0$.

Example 4.1.

$$f(x) = x_1 + \log(x_2 + 0.5),$$

where $x \in \{x \geqq 0 : f(x) \geqq 0\}$.

Usual cost minimization yields

$$x_1(w, y) = y - \log q, \quad x_2(w, y) = q - 0.5,$$

$$C(w, y) = w_1(y - A), \quad \alpha(w, y) = w_1(1 - A/y), \text{ and}$$

$$\mu(w, y) = w_1,$$

where $q \equiv w_1/w_2$ and $A \equiv \log q - 1 + 1/(2q) \equiv A(q)$. Assume an interior solution, $x_1(w, y) > 0$, $x_2(w, y) > 0$, which in turn requires

$y >$ log q and $q > 0.5$, respectively. Also $C(w, y) > 0$ requires $y > A$, which is satisfied for all $q > 0.5$ (since log $q > A$ for $q > 0.5$). Note that A is determined solely by factor prices. Next we define q^* by $A(q^*) = 0$, that is, by $\log q^* = 1 - 1/(2q^*)$. Clearly such a q^* exists uniquely, and $q^* > 1$. By a simple iteration, q^* can be computed as $q^* = 2.1555\ldots$. Also, we have

$$A(q) < 0 \text{ for } 0.5 < q < q^*, \; A(q) > 0 \text{ for } q > q^*.$$

Note that the AC curve is defined for $y > a(\equiv \log q)$ if $q > 1$, whereas the AC curve is defined for all y if $0.5 < q < 1$. With these preparations, we can now illustrate the average cost (AC) and the marginal cost (MC) curves in figure 4.5, where $b \equiv A(q)$.

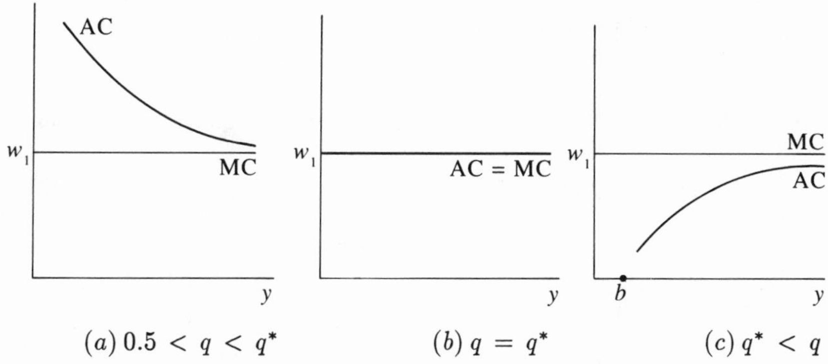

Figure 4.5: The shapes of AC and MC for example 4.1

Thus, for example 4.1, we may conclude the following.

(i) MC is constant regardless of output levels: that is, the MC line is parallel to the output axis, where MC $= w_1$.

(ii) There exists a "critical value" q^* such that if $q(\equiv w_1/w_2) < q^*$, the AC curve is always above the MC line and decreases as y increases, asymptotically approaching the MC line. On the other hand, if $q > q^*$, the AC curve is always below the MC line and increases as y increases, asymptotically approaching the MC line. Thus, the AC curve is not U- shaped, and its shape changes drastically by a slight change in the input price configuration, although $\alpha(w, y)$ is continuous in w.

(iii) Constant returns to scale (i.e., AC = MC) prevail if and only if $q = q^*$ in which case AC = w_1. Increasing returns to scale (IRS) prevail for all q, $0.5 < q < q^*$, and decreasing returns to scale (DRS) prevail for $q > q^*$. Namely, IRS changes drastically to DRS (or vice versa) in a slight move of q around q^*.

Let us take an example in international trade. Consider the world consisting of two contries, "J" and "K" (say, Japan and Korea) that have the same technology in the production of y (say, "steel"), where we call x_1 and x_2 "capital" and "labor," respectively. Since the factor price configuration is, in general, different between two countries, the shape of AC would also be different. Suppose that country K is relatively more labor abundant than J in the sense that $q^J < q^K$ where $q \equiv w_1/w_2$. If $q^J < q^* < q^K$, then for each level of output, country K can produce the commodity more cheaply than country J, where scale *economies* prevail in country J and scale *diseconomies* prevail in country K.

Example 4.2. We now consider the following production function.

$$f(x) \equiv [x_1 + \log(x_2 + 0.5)]^{1/2}, \text{ where } x \in \{x \geqq 0 : f(x) \geqq 0\}.$$

In example 4.1, $\partial^2 f/\partial x_1^2 = 0$ and $\partial^2 f/\partial x_2^2 < 0$, whereas in example 4.2, we can show by a straightforward computation, $\partial^2 f/\partial x_1^2 < 0$ and $\partial^2 f/\partial x_2^2 < 0$. Namely, example 4.2 incorporates the law of diminishing marginal productivity. The usual cost minimization yields

$$x_1(w, y) = y^2 - \log q, \; x_2(w, y) = q - 0.5,$$

$$C(w, y) = w_1(y^2 - A), \; \alpha(w, y) = w_1(y - A/y), \text{ and}$$

$$\mu(w, y) = 2w_1 y,$$

where $q \equiv w_1/w_2$ and $A \equiv \log q - 1 + 1/(2q)$ as be before. Also, $x_1(w, y) > 0$, $x_2(w, y) > 0$, $y > 0$, and $C(w, y) > 0$ require $q > 0.5$ and $y^2 > A$. The shapes of AC and MC for $w_1 = w_2 = 1$ and for $w_1 = e$, $w_2 = 1$ are illustrated in figure 4.6. Namely, when $w_1 = w_2 = 1$, AC is U-shaped containing both IRS and DRS regions. When $w_1 = e$ and $w_2 = 1$, the IRS portion vanishes and AC is always monotone decreasing. There is no intersection between AC and MC.

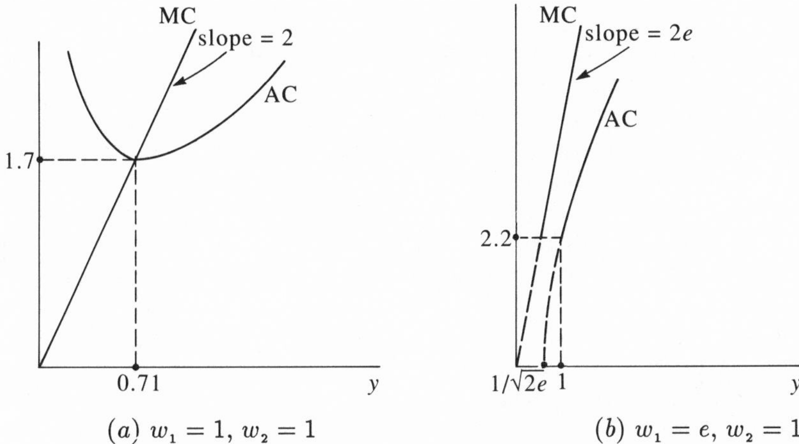

Figure 4.6: The shapes of AC and MC for example 4.2

In examples 4.1 and 4.2, we assumed away the complications due to such factors as "fixed costs" and "indivisibilities" for the sake of simplicity. The emphasis of these factors, which is often seen in the literature to obtain a falling AC curve, has an important element of truth. On the other hand, although our examples can be modified accordingly, our basic message with regard to the sensitivity of the shape of the AC curve and returns to scale with respect to factor prices would still remain. Also, we cannot overemphasize these factors, or at least, we should understand them correctly. To this end, it may suffice to recall Frank Knight's seminal paper (1921), in which he, for example, states, "There is a Fallacy in overlooking the fact that any amount of commodity *could* be made by any one of the methods available" (p. 333). Also, the following remark by Kaldor (1935, p. 34) should be of some interest: "in the long-run the supply of all factors—even the resources supplies by entrepreneur himself—can be assumed variable, and consequently there are no 'fixed costs.' "

In the literature, it is often argued that scale economies prevail up to a certain level of output (say, y^*) and they are "exhausted" beyond y^*, where scale economies are defined in terms of a falling AC curve. Then we often see empirical studies to determine such a statement for particular industries. Our examples indicate such studies based on time series data should be taken with caution, since factor prices do change overtime.

4.4 Supply of Labor: Income-Leisure Choice

The discussion on the labor supply curves in terms of an individual's rational behavior (i.e., in terms of the income-leisure choice formulation) has become familiar to us through various expositions in textbooks and articles in professional journals. As it is well known by now, the analysis of this topic can best be carried out in terms of the Hicks-Slutsky equation in the theory of consumer choice. In this section, we shall exposit the gist of such a discussion and obtain a necessary and sufficient condition for the labor supply curve to be upward sloping.[16] We first consider the simpler case in which nonwage income is ignored, and then consider the case with nonwage income. The analysis of both cases is an application of the Hicks-Slutsky equation.

4.4.1 The Case without Nonwage Income

We consider a consumer who maximizes his or her utility, $u(c,\ x)$, where c and x, respectively, measure the amount of real consumption and leisure per unit of time (say, a day). Assume he or she obtains all of his or her income from wages. The amount of his or her labor per unit of time is $(a - x)$, where a is a positive constant (say, 24 hours). Let p be the price level of consumption and w be the money wage rate per unit of time. Then his or her budget condition can be written as

$$pc \leqq w(a - x), \quad \text{or} \quad pc \leqq w\ell,$$

where $\ell \equiv a - x$, which signifies the supply of labor. This budget condition can equivalently be rewritten as

$$pc + wx \leqq wa\,(\equiv Y). \tag{27}$$

In general, c is a vector. However, the analysis for such a case is analogous to the subsequent analysis, and hence is left to the interested reader.

The problem of **income-leisure choice** (**ILC**) can now be formulated as one in which the consumer chooses $(c,\ x)$ to

---

[16] This section adapted from Takayama (1983).

(ILC) Maximize $u(c, x)$, subject to $pc + wx \leqq wa\,(\equiv Y)$,

$$c \geqq 0,\ a \geqq 0,\ \text{and } x \geqq 0.$$

Letting $q \equiv w/p$ (real wage rate), the optimum points of the above maximization problem can easily be illustrated as points A and B in figure 4.7, in which the optimum point shifts from A to B by an increase in the real wage rate q. In figure 4.7, an increase in real wage rate q reduces the amount of leisure consumption x, and hence increases the supply of labor ℓ, which results in the usual upward sloping labor supply

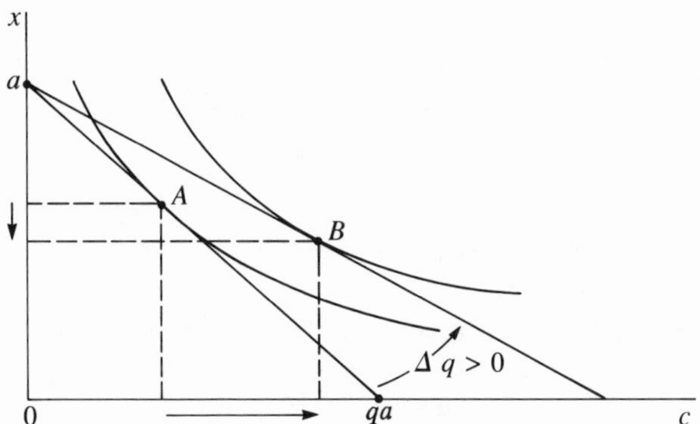

Figure 4.7: Illustration of income-leisure substitution

curve. On the other hand, the reader should easily be able to construct a diagram in which the opposite conclusion follows. By drawing a family of different shaped indifference curves, one can draw a diagram in which x increases when q increases, resulting in a "backward-bending" labor supply curve (the supply of labor decreases as real wage rate increases).

The reader may then wonder under what circumstances we obtain a usual rising labor supply curve and under what circumstances we obtain a backward-bending labor supply curve. Figure 4.8 indicates that the crux of the matter lies in the slopes of the indifference curves, that is, the **marginal rate of substitution** (**MRS**) between consumption c and leisure x. In Figure 4.8a, real wage rate q is low and the budget line is steep, so that the indifference curves are steep (at least at the points of tangency to the budget lines). When the real wage rate q is sufficiently low, the level of consumption c is quite small and the MRS between c and x is very favorable to c. (In order to obtain a one unit increase of c, the consumer is willing to sacrifice many units of x.) In

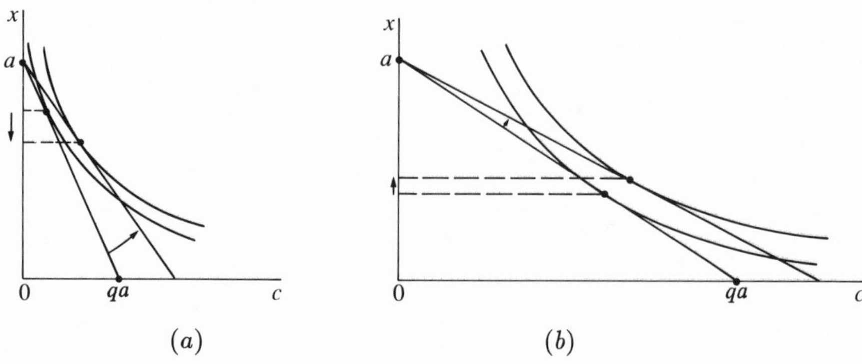

Figure 4.8: Choices behind rising/backward-bending labor supply curve

this case, x tends to decrease as q increases, so that we obtain a usual rising labor supply curve.

On the other hand, in figure 4.8*b*, the real wage rate q is high and the level of consumption c is high, in which case the budget line would be flat and the indifference curves at the point of tangency would also be quite flat. Then the MRS between c and x would be unfavorable to c. In order to obtain a one unit increase of x, the consumer is willing to sacrifice many units of c. Hence, if q is sufficiently high, we obtain a backward-bending labor supply curve.

To make the above discussion more precise and rigorous, we now proceed with a mathematical analysis. To this end, recall the preceding utility maximization problem (ILC), and assume that $c > 0$, $a > x > 0$ (an interior solution) and $pc + wx = wa$ or $pc = w\ell$ (nonsatiation) at the optimum. We may write the solution of this optimization problem as

$$c = c(p,\ w,\ Y) = c(p,\ w,\ wa) \equiv \tilde{c}(p,\ w), \tag{28a}$$

$$x = x(p,\ w,\ Y) = x(p,\ w,\ wa) \equiv \tilde{x}(p,\ w). \tag{28b}$$

That income Y depends on the (factor) price w, makes the present problem somewhat different from the conventional theory of consumer choice.

By the Hicks-Slutsky equation, we may at once obtain

$$\frac{\partial c}{\partial p} = s_{11} - c\,\frac{\partial c}{\partial Y}\,,\; \frac{\partial c}{\partial w} = s_{12} - x\,\frac{\partial c}{\partial Y} \tag{29a}$$

$$\frac{\partial x}{\partial p} = s_{21} - c\,\frac{\partial x}{\partial Y}\,,\; \frac{\partial x}{\partial w} = s_{22} - x\,\frac{\partial x}{\partial Y}, \tag{29b}$$

where s_{ij}'s are the net substitution terms. Let $S \equiv [s_{ij}]$. S is the 2×2 net substitution matrix. Recalling theorem 2.4, S is negative semidefinite, and

$$s_{11} < 0,\; s_{22} < 0,\; s_{12} = s_{21} > 0, \tag{30a}$$

$$s_{11}p + s_{21}w = 0,\; s_{21}p + s_{22}w = 0. \tag{30b}$$

Recalling $Y \equiv wa$, we may compute from (28b) and (29b),

$$\frac{\partial \tilde{x}}{\partial w} = \frac{\partial x}{\partial w} + \frac{\partial x}{\partial Y}\frac{\partial Y}{\partial w}$$

$$= (s_{22} - x\,\frac{\partial x}{\partial Y}) + \frac{\partial x}{\partial Y}\,a = s_{22} + \ell\,\frac{\partial x}{\partial Y}, \tag{31}$$

since $a - x \equiv \ell$. Define the labor supply function ℓ by

$$\ell(p,\, w) \equiv a - \tilde{x}(p,\, w). \tag{32}$$

Then from (31), we obtain

$$\partial \ell / \partial w = -s_{22} - \ell \partial x / \partial Y. \tag{33}$$

Since $s_{22} < 0$, $\partial x/\partial Y < 0$ is sufficient to obtain $\partial \ell/\partial w > 0$. Condition $\partial x/\partial Y < 0$ means that leisure is an inferior good. On the other hand, if leisure is a normal good, that is, if $\partial x/\partial Y > 0$, the sign of $\partial l/\partial w$ becomes indeterminate.

Also, from (28b), (29b), and $Y \equiv wa$, we may compute

$$\frac{\partial \tilde{x}}{\partial p} = \frac{\partial x}{\partial p} + \frac{\partial x}{\partial Y}\frac{\partial Y}{\partial p} = s_{21} - c\,\frac{\partial x}{\partial Y}\,,$$

where we may note $\partial Y/\partial p = 0$. Hence we obtain

$$\partial \ell / \partial p = -s_{21} + c\,\partial x / \partial Y. \tag{34}$$

Since $s_{21} > 0$, we have $\partial \ell/\partial p < 0$ if $\partial x/\partial Y < 0$, that is, if leisure is an inferior good. When $\partial x/\partial Y > 0$, the sign of $\partial \ell/\partial p$ again becomes indeterminate.

Using (33) and (34), and noting $s_{21} = -s_{22}w/p$ (which is obtained from $s_{21}p + s_{22}w = 0$), we have

$$\begin{aligned} d\ell &= \frac{\partial \ell}{\partial p}dp + \frac{\partial \ell}{\partial w}dw + (-s_{21} + c\frac{\partial x}{\partial Y})dp - (s_{22} + \ell\frac{\partial x}{\partial p}dw) \\ &= (s_{22}w\,dp/p - s_{22}dw) + (cdp - \ell dw)(\partial x/\partial Y) \\ &= ws_{22}(dp/p - dw/w) + (pc\,dp/p - w\ell\,dw/w)(\partial x/\partial Y) \\ &= ws_{22}(dp/p - dw/w) + w\ell(dp/p - dw/w)(\partial x/\partial Y) \\ &= [ws_{22} + w\ell(\partial x/\partial Y)]\,(dp/p - dw/w), \end{aligned}$$

where we may note $pc = w\ell$ at an optimum. Let $\ell(p, w) \equiv \ell^*(q)$, where $q \equiv w/p$. By taking note of the homogeneity of the function $\tilde{x}(p, w)$ and hence of $\ell(p, w)$, we have

$$d\ell^*/dq = -w(s_{22} + \ell\partial x/\partial Y)/q. \tag{35}$$

If leisure is an inferior good ($\partial x/\partial Y < 0$), the labor supply curve is always upward sloping ($d\ell^*/dq > 0$). On the other hand, if $\partial x/\partial Y > 0$, the labor supply curve can be either upward sloping or backward-bending ($d\ell^*/dq \gtrless 0$). In other words, the inferiority of leisure is sufficient for the upward sloping labor supply curve, and the normality of leisure is necessary for the backward-bending labor supply curve.

The necessary and sufficient condition for the upward sloping labor supply curve can easily be obtained from (35) as

$$s_{22} + \ell\partial x/\partial Y < 0, \tag{36}$$

that is, the MRS between consumption and leisure must be sufficiently favorable to consumption. If the own compensated price effect (s_{22}) exceeds any adverse income effect ($\ell\partial x/\partial Y$), then the labor supply curve is upward sloping. Namely, if the indifference curves are sufficiently steep (at least at the point of tangency to the budget line), which is likely to be the case for a sufficiently low level of c, then the labor supply curve would be upward sloping. Also, for a sufficiently high level of c, the indifference curves are likely to be sufficiently flat, in which case the inequality in (30) would be reversed to obtain a backward-bending labor supply curve.

4.4.2 The Case with Nonwage Income

In case 4.4.1, we assumed that all income comes from labor. Now we introduce nonwage income. Letting py denote the consumer's nominal nonwage income, his budget (27) will be modified as

$$pc + wx \leqq wa + py\,(\equiv Y). \tag{27$'$}$$

The consumer chooses c and x to maximize $u(c,\ x)$ subject to (27′), $c \geqq 0$, $a \geqq 0$, and $x \geqq 0$. Again assume $c > 0$ and $a > x > 0$ at the optimum (an interior solution). The demand functions for c and x can be written as

$$c = c(p,\ w,\ Y) = \tilde{c}(p,\ w,\ y), \tag{28$'$a}$$

$$x = x(p,\ w,\ Y) = \tilde{x}(p,\ w,\ y). \tag{28$'$b}$$

Note that the Hicks-Slutsky equation (29) holds as it is, and (30) also holds as it is. Recalling $Y \equiv wa + py$, we may again obtain (31) from (28b) and (29b).

Now define the labor supply function ℓ by

$$\ell(p,\ w,\ y) \equiv a - \tilde{x}(p,\ w,\ y). \tag{32$'$}$$

The rest of the analysis goes in a similar fashion. We can show that (36) also holds for the present case. The proof is left to the interested reader. In summary, we obtain the following proposition for both cases.

Proposition 4.4. The necessary and sufficient condition for the labor supply curve to be upward sloping is given by (36), i.e.

$$s_{22} + \ell \partial x / \partial Y < 0.$$

REMARK: The theory of labor supply and the possibility of a backward-bending labor supply curve have been discussed in textbooks such as Scitovsky (1951, chap. 5); Henderson and Quandt (1980, pp. 24–25); Musgrave (1959, chap. 11); Layard and Walters (1978, pp. 304–10); Deaton and Muellbauer (1980, chap. 11); and also in professional journal articles such as Hanoch (1965); Ashenfelter and Heckman (1974); and Abbott and Ashenfelter (1976). Ashenfelter and Heckman (1974) and Abbott and Ashenfelter (1976) explicitly formulated the theory in terms of the Hicks-Slutsky equation and conducted empirical investigations. The income-leisure choice is studied using experimental data on nonhuman workers (pigeons) by Battalio, Green, and Kagel (1981). They observed a backward-bending labor supply curve at higher wages. Extension of consumer theory to consider financial assets like money and bonds as well as goods and leisure is done in Morishima's (1952) classic article. The major tool of his analysis is again the Hicks-Slutsky equation. Given that (human) workers typically hold such assets, this study should be most pertinent to the problem of income-leisure choice. Unfortunately, Morishima's study has been ignored in empirical studies of income-leisure choice. Note that since nonhuman workers such as pigeons do not own assets, the experimental study by Battalio, Green, and Kagel (1981) would be quite pertinent to testing the conventional theory of income-leisure choice. As a further elaboration of the theory, Deaton and Muellbauer's (1980) book contains discussions on nonlinearities on the budget condition and on consumer's intertemporal choice. The problem of labor-leisure choice in the intertemporal context is studied by Blinder (1974, chap. 3) and others. For a more comprehensive discussion on labor supply, see Killingsworth (1983).

4.5 Behavior of the Firm under Regulatory Constraint

One of the well-known results in the economics of regulation is that the imposition of a "fair-rate-of-return" constraint (imposed on public utility industries and others) induces the profit-maximizing firm to have a larger stock of capital equipment.[17] This assertion was made by Averch and Johnson (1962) and has been discussed extensively in the literature.

It now appears even in undergraduate textbooks (see, for example, Binger and Hoffman 1988, pp. 396–99). In the course of this discussion its logical structure as well as its economic interpretation and implications have been clarified.

One such clarification is made by Takayama (1969), in which he points out that Averch and Johnson's original "proof " of the above assertion (now known as the **Averch-Johnson effect**, or the **A-J effect**) is unfortunately false, as it contains the error of confusing movements along the curve with the shift of the curve. Takayama (1969) then proposes that the A-J effect remains valid if we follow Averch and Johnson's assumption of $0 < \lambda^* < 1$, where λ^* signifies the Lagrangian multiplier of the relevant maximization problem of the regulated firm.[18]

---

[17] Section 4.5 is adapted from Takayama (1988), which follows Takayama (1969); El-Hodiri and Takayama (1973); and Takayama (1977, pp. 31–33). For the extension to a dynamic framework, see El-Hodiri and Takayama (1981).

[18] A similar proof appears in Baumol and Klevorick (1970, p. 175). They state, "Takayama asserts that this is an alternative proof of the A-J theorem, but this is simply incorrect. Neither proposition 2 nor 3 follows from his argument" (p. 175). This is false and unfair. Takayama (1969) nowhere indicates that he intends to

El-Hodiri and Takayama (1973) then provide a proof of the statement that the A-J effect holds, without assuming $0 < \lambda^* < 1$. Zajac (1972) investigates a mathematical problem associated with such a λ^*, while Zajac (1970) is concerned with a diagrammatical structure of the A-J effect. Here we shall prove the A-J effect by first proving $0 < \lambda^* < 1$. Unlike El-Hodiri and Takayama (1973), we shall *not* make any explicit use of the concavity of the revenue function $G(L, K)$.

Following Averch and Johnson (1962) and many others, we consider a monopoly that produces a single output (Y) by using two inputs, labor (L) and capital (K). The production function is specified by $F(L, K)$, where we assume that

$$F(0, 0) = 0,\ F_L \equiv \partial F/\partial L > 0,\ F_K \equiv \partial F/\partial K > 0.$$

Let p be the price of the output, and $p(Y)$ be the inverse demand function with $p'(Y) < 0$. The firm's revenue function is defined by $R(Y) \equiv p(Y)Y$, where we assume $R' > 0$, i.e., the marginal revenue product is positive. Let w and r, respectively, be the wage rate and the rental rate of capital, the firm's profit is written as

$$\pi \equiv R(Y) - wL - rK. \tag{37}$$

If the firm is subject to no regulatory constraint, the firm chooses Y, L and K so as to maximize its profit (π) subject to

$$Y \leqq F(L, K), \tag{38}$$

with $Y \geqq 0$, $L \geqq 0$, and $K \geqq 0$.

Letting $(Y^\circ, L^\circ, K^\circ)$ denote the solution to this problem and assuming an interior solution ($Y^\circ > 0$, $L^\circ > 0$, and $K^\circ > 0$), we may write the first-order necessary condition as

$$G_L(L^\circ, K^\circ) = w,\ G_K(L^\circ, K^\circ) = r, \tag{39}$$

where $G(L, K) \equiv R[F(L, K)]$, $G_L \equiv \partial G/\partial L$ and $G_K \equiv \partial G/\partial K$. We may note that at the optimum we then have $Y^\circ = F(L^\circ, K^\circ)$. In the literature, constraint (38) is often stated by the equality form

$$Y = F(L, K), \tag{38'}$$

---

prove Baumol and Klevorick's propositions 2 and 3. Baumol and Klevorick criticize assertions they alone have created. Takayama (1969) is concerned with Baumol and Klevorick's proposition 5. Furthermore, in proving their proposition 5, Baumol and Klevorick essentially follow Takayama's proof without acknowledging it.

which will yield the same conclusion as constraint (38).

Condition (39) is a familiar rule that states that the marginal revenue product of each factor is equal to its respective factor price. We assume that the second-order condition is also satisfied so that (39) is also sufficient for optimum. If we assume that $G(L, K)$ is concave,[19] then (39) provides a necessary and sufficient condition for a global optimum.

When the firm is subject to a regulatory constraint, the optimum usage of each factor would naturally be different, had such a constraint not been imposed. We now suppose that the firm is under the regulatory constraint that requires the rate of return of capital not exceed a certain "fair" value. Let s denote such a "fair rate of return." The regulatory constraint can be written as

$$(R - wL)/K \leqq s, \text{ i. e., } -(R - wL - sK) \geqq 0. \tag{40}$$

The firm's problem is now to maximize its profit, π, subject to (38) and (40) together with $Y \geqq 0$, $L \geqq 0$, and $K \geqq 0$. Let Y^*, L^*, and K^* be the solution to this problem, and assume $Y^* > 0$, $L^* > 0$, and $K^* > 0$. The regulatory constraint is now rewritten as

$$\pi^* + rK^* \leqq sK^*, \text{ or } \pi^* \leqq (s - r)K^*,$$

where π^* is the value of π evaluated at (Y^*, L^*, K^*).

Assuming $\pi^* > 0$, we can then deduce[20]

$$s > r. \tag{41}$$

Instead of deriving (41), various authors simply *assume* it. Writing the Lagrangian as

$$\Phi \equiv [R(Y) - wL - rK] + \lambda[sK - R(Y) + wL] + \mu[F(L, K) - Y],$$

[19] As pointed out by Takayama (1969, p. 260), this assumption cannot, in general, be ensured even if the underlying production function is in simple linear homogeneous Cobb-Douglas form.

[20] We may assume that the profit ratio, π/K, should not exceed a certain value $\bar{s}$, i.e.,

$$(R - wL - rK)/K \leqq \bar{s}.$$

But this constraint is equivalent to (40) where $s \equiv \bar{s} + r$. If $\pi > 0$, then $\bar{s} > 0$ so that $s > r$.

the first-order condition is obtained as

$$(1 - \lambda^*)R'^* = \mu^*, \tag{42a}$$

$$\mu^* F_L^* = (1 - \lambda^*)w, \tag{42b}$$

$$\mu^* F_K^* = r - \lambda^* s, \tag{42c}$$

$$sK^* - R^* + wL^* \geqq 0, \ \lambda^*(sK^* - R^* + wL^*) = 0, \tag{42d}$$

$$F(L^*, K^*) - Y^* \geqq 0, \ \mu^*[F(L^*, K^*) - Y^*] = 0, \ \text{ and} \tag{42e}$$

$$\lambda^* \geqq 0 \ \text{ and } \ \mu^* \geqq 0, \tag{42f}$$

where $F_L \equiv \partial F/\partial L$, $F_L^* \equiv F_L(L^*, K^*)$, $R'^* \equiv R'(Y^*)$, $R^* \equiv R(Y^*)$, etc. We assume that the second-order condition for an optimum is satisfied, and that $R' > 0$, $F_L > 0$, and $F_K > 0$ for the relevant range of (Y, L, K).

We can now assert,

$$\mu^* > 0 \ \text{ and } \ 0 < \lambda^* < 1. \tag{43}$$

To show this, we first suppose that $\mu^* = 0$. Then by (42a), we have $\lambda^* = 1$. By (42c), we then have $r - s = 0$, which contradicts (41). Hence, $\mu^* > 0$. Also, if $\lambda^* = 1$, then $\mu^* = 0$ by (42a), which contradicts $\mu^* > 0$. Hence $\lambda^* \neq 1$. Suppose $\lambda^* > 1$. Then by (42a), we have $\mu^* < 0$, which again contradicts $\mu^* > 0$, so that $\lambda^* < 1$. To show $\lambda^* \neq 0$, we only need to assume that $K^\circ \neq K^*$, that the regulatory constraint (40) is effective,[21] and that (39) has a unique solution. Indeed, if $\lambda^* = 0$, then (42a) through (42c) become $G_L^* = w$ and $G_K^* = r$. This is the same as (39) so that $K^\circ = K^*$ (and $L^\circ = L^*$), which in turn contradicts $K^\circ \neq K^*$. Thus, we have established (43). The statement of $0 < \lambda^* < 1$ shown above has been debated in the literature. Averch and Johnson's (1962, p. 1056) proof amounts to assuming it. El-Hodiri and Takayama (1973) showed that this assumption can be dispensed with if function G is concave. What we have shown above is that such a concavity assumption can be dispensed with.

---

[21] If the regulatory constraint is *not* effective, the solution is obviously the same as that obtained for the unconstrained case, i.e., $K^* = K^\circ$ and $L^* = L^\circ$.

Now using (43), we may simplify (42a) through (42e) as follows.[22]

$$G_L^* = w, \tag{44a}$$

$$(1 - \lambda^*)G_K^* = r - \lambda^* s, \tag{44b}$$

$$sK^* - G^* + wL^* = 0, \tag{44c}$$

$$Y^* = F(L^*, K^*), \tag{44d}$$

The three equations, (44a) through (44c), determine the values of L^*, K^*, and λ^*, which in turn determine Y^* by (44d). Note that L^*, K^*, and λ^* are functions of s.

From (44b), we may obtain

$$G_K^* - r = \lambda^*(G_K^* - s). \tag{45}$$

Since $\lambda^* > 0$, (45) indeed implies that $(G_K^* - r)$ and $(G_K^* - s)$ have the same sign. If $G_K^* - r > 0$ and $G_K^* - s > 0$, then $0 < \lambda^* < 1$ implies $G_K^* - s > G_K^* - r$ by (45), or $r > s$ which contradicts (41). Hence we must have[23]

$$G_K^* - r < 0 \text{ and } G_K^* - s < 0. \tag{46}$$

In this case, $0 < \lambda^* < 1$, and (45) indeed imply $r < s$, which conforms with (41).

Differentiating (44c) and noting (44a), we get

$$K^* = (G_L^* - w)\frac{dL^*}{ds} + (G_K^* - s)\frac{dK^*}{ds} = (G_K^* - s)\frac{dK^*}{ds},$$

and so

$$\frac{dK^*}{ds} = K^*/(G_K^* - s) < 0, \tag{47}$$

[22] Conditions (44a) through (44c) appear frequently in the literature on this topic, where (44d) is simply *assumed* at the outset of analysis.

[23] Alternatively, we may show $G_K^* - s < 0$ as follows. By (44b), we may observe

$$G_K^* - s = \frac{(r - \lambda^* s) - (1 - \lambda^*)s}{1 - \lambda^*} = \frac{r - s}{1 - \lambda^*}.$$

Since $0 < \lambda^* < 1$ and $r < s$, this shows $G_K^* - s < 0$.

by virtue of (46). This means that a decrease in the fair rate of return (s) increases K^*, which is the A-J effect.[24] Note that in the present proof of the A-J effect we have not made any explicit use of the concavity of the revenue function.

We may briefly mention cost minimization. Since $G_L = R'F_L$ and $G_K = R'F_K$, (44a) and (44b) imply

$$F_L^*/F_K^* = w(1 - \lambda^*)/(r - \lambda^* s) \neq w/r. \tag{48}$$

The last inequality follows from $s \neq r$. Thus the marginal rate of substitution is not equal to the factor price ratio. Under the regulatory constraint, cost minimization in the usual sense is not compatible with profit maximization. This result is obtained by Zajac (1970) using a geometric technique. Zajac (1970, p. 120) then argues, "Since a higher-than-necessary cost to the firm means the inefficient use of resources, the society is the loser." In summary, we obtain the following results.

Proposition 4.5. Under the specification of the model, the regulatory constraint induces a profit maximizing monopoly to have a larger stock of capital. The firm is not a cost minimizer in the traditional sense.

Finally, it may be worthwhile to clarify the nature of the errors in Averch and Johnson (1962), as this type of error is not uncommon in the literature. Assuming $0 < \lambda^* < 1$, Averch and Johnson rewrite (44b) as

$$G_K^* = r - \alpha, \quad \text{where } \alpha \equiv \frac{s - r}{1 - \lambda^*}\lambda^*.$$

With $s > r$ and $0 < \lambda^* < 1$, we have $\alpha > 0$. Following Averch and Johnson, assume $G_{KK} (\equiv \partial G_K/\partial K) < 0$. Since $G_K = r$ when there is no regulatory constraint and since $\alpha > 0$, Averch and Johnson argue that K must increase with the presence of the regulatory constraint. This argument is wrong. The relevant unregulated optimum condition

[24] The proof is analogous to the one found in Takayama (1969), except that he assumes the regulatory agency initially sets the value of s equal to r^o, the rate of return on capital in the nonconstrained case, and that dK^*/ds is a continuous function of s, where $r < s \leqq r^o$. If we are concerned only with a small displacement of s from r^o, we have

$$K^\circ = (G_L^\circ - w)\frac{dL^\circ}{ds} + (G_K^\circ - s)\frac{dK^\circ}{ds} = (G_K^* - s)\frac{dK^\circ}{ds}$$

by (39). Since $G_K^\circ = r$ and $r < s$, we have $G_K^\circ < s$. From this, we at once obtain $dK^\circ/ds < 0$. In this case, there is no need to show (46).

can, more precisely, be written as $G_K(L^\circ, K^\circ) = r$, and the corresponding regulated optimum condition is $G_K(L^*, K^*) = r - \alpha$. Hence we can argue that $\alpha > 0$ implies $K^* > K^\circ$ as in Averch and Johnson *when* $L^* = L^\circ$. However, a moment of reflection will reveal that it would be difficult to justify $L^* = L^\circ$, the firm's use of labor is unchanged with or without the regulatory constraint.

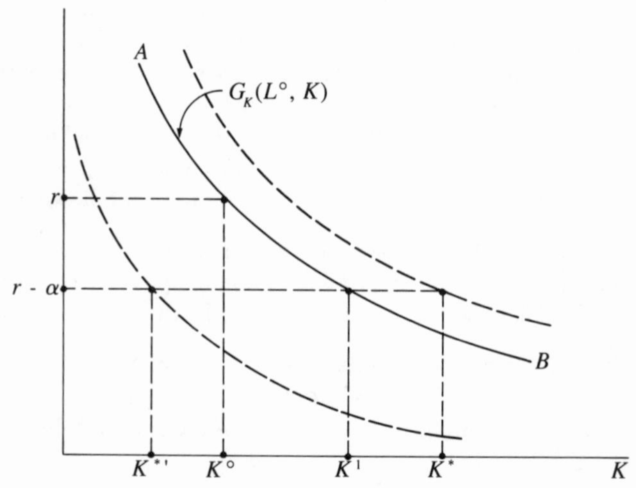

Figure 4.9: An illustration of the Averch-Johnson argument

The point at issue may be illustrated in figure 4.9, where the *AB* curve represents the marginal revenue product (G_K) curve before the fair-rate-of-return regulation is introduced. The unregulated optimum value of capital K° is illustrated for a given value of r. Under $0 < \lambda^* < 1$, we have $\alpha > 0$ and r is thus reduced to $r - \alpha$. Averch and Johnson argue that the optimum value of capital with the regulatory constraint is given by K^1 in figure 4.9. Implicitly assuming that the G_K-curve (or the AB curve in fig. 4.9) stays put, they conclude that $K^1 > K^\circ$ if the G_K-curve is downward sloping. The introduction of the rate of return constraint increases the usage of capital. This argument is false, since the *AB* curve is drawn under the assumption that L is fixed at L°, the unregulated optimum value of labor. With the introduction of the regulatory constraint, the optimum value of labor will change. This in turn would cause a shift of the G_K-curve, since the marginal product of capital at each level of capital used is, in general, a function of the labor employed. This can be illustrated in figure 4.9, if the G_K-curve were to shift downward too much, then we cannot conclude that the reduction of r to $r - \alpha$ would increase capital usage. In other words, until we can specify in which direction the G_K-curve would shift and by how much it would shift, we cannot, by the above argument, determine whether the introduction of the rate-of-return constraint would increase the amount of capital used by the firm. In short, Averch and Johnson's argument involves an error of confusing the movement along the curve and the shift of the curve, by ignoring the shift of the G_K-curve due to a change in the optimum value of labor.[25] Our proof of the A-J effect avoids such an error.

REMARK: The problem analyzed by Averch and Johnson (1962) is fairly simple, except it unfortunately contains simple but serious errors as clarified by Takayama (1969), and shown above. Although this problem now appears to be overdone in the literature, it would provide us with a simple example of an application of nonlinear programming. This section is thus written in such a spirit. For the reader who is interested in reading further on this topic, see, for example, Crew and Kleindorfer (1979 and 1986); Averch (1987); and Berg and Tschirhart (1988); as well as Westfield (1965), Kahn (1970 and 1971); Stein and Borts (1972); and Bailey (1973).

4.6 The Peak-Load Problem

4.6.1 Introduction

Consider a monopoly that produces a single *nonstorable good* (say, electricity). Suppose the output, in addition to nonstorability, has the following three additional characteristics:

---

[25] A similar flaw can be found in the literature on minimum wage legislation. The demand for labor is obtained from the marginal-revenue-product (or the value-of-the-marginal-product) curve, which is assumed to be downward sloping. It is then argued that the imposition of minimum wage regulation raises the wage rate above the equilibrium rate and thus creates unemployment. A common fallacy in this argument is that it ignores the shift of the labor demand curve due to capital-labor substitution. In general, the usages of other factors such as capital will change, as labor becomes relatively more expensive. This in turn shifts the labor demand curve. It can be shown, however, that under certain plausible conditions, a minimum wage floor, when it is effective, always reduces the employment of labor even if the adjustment via the shift of the labor demand curve is properly accounted for (see Takayama 1985, pp. 405–8).

(*a*) The demand for its output, $D(p, t)$, fluctuates over time (t) even if the price is fixed say, at $\overline{p}$ (as is illustrated in fig. 4.10).

(*b*) Its production requires an expensive "capacity" or "capital" (plant and equipment of a large size, say K).

(*c*) It is required that the firm meet the peak demand needs of its output (which is illustrated as OA in fig. 4.10).

Note that electricity typically meets all these characteristics. If we interpret condition *c* rather loosely, we can find many examples of commodities that have the above characteristics. Examples would include telephone services, transportation services (highways, railways, and airlines), restaurants, and many other service goods.

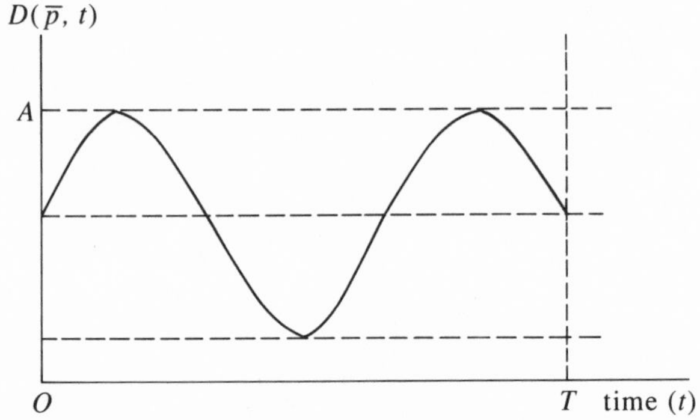

Figure 4.10: An illustration of the peak-load problem

If the firm has to have the level of capacity K to meet the peak demand OA, some of its capacity may have to be left idle for off-peak periods. Since the plant and equipment are expensive by assumption, this can lead to a large "waste." If the commodity is storable, then this problem vanishes (or, at least, becomes considerably less important) as the firm can store some of its output during the off-peak periods and sell it during the peak periods. But this is impossible as the output is not storable, by assumption.

In the literature, it has been suggested that to avoid such a waste, different prices be charged from period to period. It is proposed that the firm charges lower prices during off-peak periods so as to encourage demand for the output and charges higher prices for peak periods. The problem of devising an optimum price policy is known as the peak-load problem.[26] The peak-load problem is a problem of choosing an optimum path of prices for the periods during the given planning horizon. Although demand may change continuously over time (as illustrated in fig. 4.10), it may not be practical to change prices continuously. We then assume that prices can be changed in discrete time intervals and also that the demand for a commodity stays constant in each time interval in which the price is fixed. (For the case in which demand changes continuously over time and the price can accordingly be changed continuously, see Takayama 1985, pp. 671–84).

4.6.2 The Case of a Welfare-Maximizing Monopoly

There are two criteria for optimality. One is to maximize some sort of social welfare, and the other is to maximize profit over the prescribed time horizon. In the literature (e.g., Steiner 1957; Williamson 1966), the former criterion is typically chosen, and social welfare is defined as the sum of consumers' surplus plus total revenue minus total cost, over time. As mentioned earlier, this concept of social welfare can lead to well-known difficulties. However, we again follow such a concept. Our purpose here is again illustrative. We only wish to obtain the results in the literature (which are typically obtained diagrammatically) as a straightforward application of nonlinear programming. This would, in turn, facilitate an extension of the problem discussed here when we face complex real-world problems for which solutions are not apparent from diagrammatical techniques, or when we wish to analyze more theoretically sophisticated problems.

Thus, as in section 4.2, we assume that the social welfare for period

---

[26] The problem of peak-load pricing has been "solved" at least six times in the literature (Boiteaux 1949; Houthakker 1951 and 1958; Steiner 1957; Hirschleifer 1958; Buchanan 1966; Williamson 1966; and Panzar 1976). Boiteux (1949) and Steiner (1957) arrived at the same solution independently, where Boiteux's contribution is published in French (English translation, 1960). For recent summaries of discussions and useful expositions, see, for example, Crew-Kleindorfer (1986), Berg-Tschirhart (1988), and Starret (1988). The present section is based on Takayama (1970), which attempts to find a unified analytical framework for the problem. (Incidentally, James Buchanan was the 1986 Nobel laureate for his development of new methods for analyzing economic and political decision-making.) Since the deregulation of the airline industry in the 1970's, a complex airfare structure has emerged in the U.S. Such a structure, at least in part, reflects each airline company's effort to meet the peak-load problem compatible with profit maximization.

t is defined by

$$W_t \equiv CS_t + TR_t - TC_t, \tag{49}$$

where W_t = social welfare, CS_t = consumers' surplus, TR_t = total revenue, and TC_t = total cost, each for period t. Following the literature, we write the demand function as

$$y_t = D(p_t, t), \tag{50}$$

where Y_t and p_t, respectively, denote the output and its price for period t. The subscript t refers to period t, and hence it also signifies that the relevant variable is a function of time. Assuming that the demand function is downward sloping for each t, or that $\partial D/\partial p_t < 0$ for all p_t and t, we can rewrite (50) as

$$p_t = p(y_t, t), \text{ where } \partial p/\partial y_t < 0. \tag{51}$$

Then consumers' surplus plus the total revenue is equal to (cf. fig. 4.3):

$$CS_t + TR_t = \int_0^{Y_t} p(y_t, t)dy_t \equiv F(Y_t, t). \tag{52}$$

Since $\partial^2 F/\partial Y_t^2 = \partial p/\partial y_t < 0$, function F is strictly concave in Y_t.

Again following the usual assumption in the literature (e.g., Steiner 1957; Williamson 1966), we assume that the output Y_t depends on the size of capacity K and the vector of the variable factors, L_t. We assume that as Y_t increases, the degree of capacity utilization increases at a constant positive rate b, so that bY_t signifies the degree of capacity utilization when the output level is Y_t. Let T be the planning horizon of the firm.[27] Then the capacity constraint can be written as

$$bY_t \leqq K, \ t = 1, 2, \ldots, T, \tag{53}$$

where we may note that the suffix t is not attached to K; that is, K is not function of time. We also assume that there is a constant relation

[27] To facilitate a diagrammatical analysis, it is often assumed in the literature that $T = 2$. Namely, there are only two types of periods, "peak periods" and "off-peak periods." In the case of electricity, which is often discussed in the literature, it is assumed that T is equal to one day (say, 24 hours) and that one day can be divided into two types of periods, "day(time)" and "night." As long as we stick to the classical stationary state assumption that the planning horizon (T) is equal to two may not be as bad as it sounds. However, mathematical formulations often ease extensions considerably, and hence are important.

between L_t and Y_t in the sense that $L_t = aY_t$, where a is the vector of variable inputs required per unit of output. We assume that a is constant over time and is independent of Y_t. We assume that the production function is of a constant coefficient type. Let w be the price vector of variable inputs so that $(w \cdot a)Y_t$ signifies the total variable cost for the tth period. We assume that w is constant over time and over the relevant output levels (the firm is not a monopsony). We assume that the capital stock costs the firm r dollars per unit of capital for each t, where r is assumed to be a positive constant. Then the total cost for period t is given by

$$TC_t - (w \cdot a)Y_t + rK.$$

Combining this with (49) and (52), the total social benefit over T periods is given by

$$W(\equiv \sum_{t=1}^{T} W_t) = \sum_{t=1}^{T} [F(Y_t,\, t) - (w \cdot a)Y_t - rK].^{28} \tag{54}$$

The firm can select the policy of choosing either the time path of p_t or the time path of Y_t. However, given (50) and (51), the choice of one policy automatically implies the other, and it does not make any difference whether we suppose that the firm adopts either of the two policies. Here we suppose that the firm adopts the policy of choosing the time path of Y_t. Thus the peak-load problem can be stated as one of

---

[28]The amount r may also be viewed as the rental cost of capital. Alternatively, we may consider a firm that contemplates the construction of a new plant and equipment of size K (such as an electric power company contemplating a new hydroelectric dam). Assume that the plant lasts T periods with the same efficiency. We may then assume that the initial purchase cost of the capital stock (inclusive of installation and other associated costs) amounts to r dollars per unit of capital *for each t*. In this case, it would be proper to introduce the discount rate, as T can be quite large. Letting δ denote such a social discount rate, which is assumed to be a positive constant, we may rewrite (54) as

$$W[\equiv \sum_{t=1}^{T} W_t/(1+\delta)^{t+1}] = \sum_{t=1}^{T}[F(Y_t,\, t) - (w \cdot a)Y_t - rK]/(1+\delta)^{t+1}. \tag{54'}$$

Here it is assumed that the firm borrows the money to purchase and install the initial capital stock K, and assume that the borrowing amounts to repaying r dollars per unit of capital for each period for the T periods. The solution with the maximand function (54′) would be different from the one discussed in the present analysis. Although such an analysis may be more relevant to certain peak-load problems, it is left to the interested reader.

choosing Y_t, $t = 1, 2, \ldots, T$, and K, to maximize W defined in (54) subject to the capacity constraint (52), $Y_t \geqq 0$, $t = 1, 2, \ldots, T$, and $K \geqq 0$. Letting λ_t be the Lagrangian multiplier associated with (52), we may write the Lagrangian for this problem as

$$\Phi \equiv \sum_{t=1}^{T} [F(Y_t, t) - (w \cdot a)Y_t - rK] + \sum_{t=1}^{T} \lambda_t(K - bY_t). \tag{55}$$

Omitting a symbol such as (*) to denote the optimum for simplicity, and assuming an interior solution ($Y_t > 0$, $t = 1, 2, \ldots, T$ and $K > 0$, at the optimum),[29] the first-order condition can easily be written as

$$\partial\Phi/\partial Y_t = [F_Y(Y_t, t) - (w \cdot a)] - b\lambda_t = 0, \; t = 1, 2, \ldots, T, \tag{56a}$$

$$\partial\Phi/\partial K = -rT + \sum_{t=1}^{T} \lambda_t = 0, \tag{56b}$$

$$bY_t \leqq K, \; \lambda_t(K - bY_t) = 0, \; \lambda_t \geqq 0, \; t = 1, 2, \ldots, T, \tag{56c}$$

where $F_Y \equiv \partial F/\partial Y_t$. Since constraint (53) is linear in K and the Y_t's, (56) provides a *necessary* condition for an optimum by theorem 2.3 (the Arrow-Hurwicz-Uzawa theorem). Since the function F is strictly concave in Y_t (or $\partial^2 F/\partial Y_t^2 < 0$), the maximand function defined in (54) is strictly concave.[30] Hence by theorem 2.2, (56) is also *sufficient* for a global optimum, where we may note that the constraint functions in (53) are all linear and hence concave. By theorem 2.1, the strict concavity of the maximand function ensures uniqueness of the optimum. Conditions (56a) through (56c) completely characterize the solution of the peak-load problem.

Note that if $\lambda_t > 0$, then $K = bY_t$ (full capital utilization for such a period) by (56c). On the other hand, if $K > bY_t$, then $\lambda_t = 0$. The Lagrangian multiplier λ_t measures the *shadow price* of utilizing the capacity for period t.

---

[29] The assumption of $Y_t > 0$ for *all* t at the optimum may not be acceptable for certain commodities. It is possible that the demand for the output for some periods are so low that it would be optimal if the commodity is not produced at all for such periods. Our assumption of an interior solution is thus only made to follow the usual convention in the literature. The analysis for the corner solution case can be done analogously, and is left to the interested reader.

[30] We can show that the Hessian of the maximand function with respect to the Y_t's and K is negative definite.

From (56a), we may obtain

$$p(Y_t, t) = w \cdot a + \lambda_t b. \tag{57}$$

In particular, if $\lambda_t = 0$, the optimum pricing rule is to charge only the average variable cost $(w \cdot a)$. Summing (57) over t and using (56b), we may also obtain

$$\sum_{t=1}^{T} p(Y_t, t) = (w \cdot a + br)T. \tag{58}$$

It should be of some interest to obtain further characterizations of this solution. We consider *two cases*: the first case is concerned with the one in which the full capacity utilization is maintained for *all* periods for an optimum, and the second with full capacity not being maintained for all periods. We first consider the case in which it is optimal to maintain full capacity for all periods, that is, Y_t = constant (which is denoted by Y^*) for all t, and the optimal stock of capacity (denoted by K^*) is related to Y^* by $K^* = bY^*$. The value of such a Y^* can be determined by

$$\sum_{t=1}^{T} p(Y^*, t) = (w \cdot a + br)T. \tag{59}$$

To illustrate this solution, we suppose the following demand pattern:

$$p(Y_t, t) = P_1(Y_t), \quad \text{for } t \in T_1, \tag{60a}$$

$$p(Y_t, t) = P_2(Y_t), \quad \text{for } t \in T_2, \tag{60b}$$

where T_1 and T_2 are disjoint, nonempty subsets of $\{1, 2, \ldots, T\}$ with $T_1 \cup T_2 = \{1, 2, \ldots, T\}$. Namely, the demand shifts between the periods in T_1 and those in T_2, and yet full capacity is maintained for all periods. Using the example of electricity we may call the periods of T_1 "days" and the period of T_2 "nights." Let the number of periods of T_1 and T_2 be denoted by τ_1 and τ_2, respectively. Then we can rewrite (59) as

$$\tau_1 P_1(Y^*) + \tau_2 P_2(Y^*) = (w \cdot a + br)T, \tag{61}$$

which determines the optimum output level, Y^*, and hence the optimum prices by

$$p_1 = P_1(Y^*) \text{ for } t \in T_1, \quad \text{and } p_2 = P_2(Y^*) \text{ for } t \in T_2. \tag{62}$$

The determination of Y^* via (61) is illustrated by figure 4.11, which corresponds to Steiner's (1957, p. 588) solution for the "shifting-peak case," as generalized by Williamson (1966). The shifting peak case is the one in which it is optimal to maintain full capacity for all t. Note that in figure 4.11, the optimum output Y^* is obtained by vertically adding the demand curves. This is the famous rule in the peak-load problem.

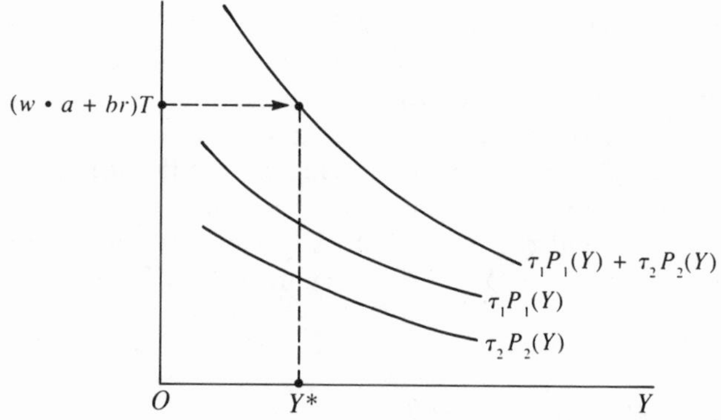

Figure 4.11: A solution when full capacity is always achieved

The second case is concerned with the case in which it is not optimal to maintain full capacity all the time. Let A be the subset of $\{1, 2, \ldots, T\}$ in which full capacity is maintained. Then for $t \in A$, Y_t is constant (which is denoted by $\hat{Y}$), and the optimum stock of capacity for this case (denoted by $\hat{K}$) is related to $\hat{Y}$ by $\hat{K} = b\hat{Y}$. It is also postulated that $bY_t < \hat{K}$ for $t \notin A$. Namely, there are periods ($t \notin A$) in which it is optimal *not* to maintain the full capacity utilization (because the demands in such periods are too "low"). In this second case, we may obtain, from (57),

$$p_t = w \cdot a, \quad \text{for } t \notin A, \tag{63}$$

from which the optimum level of output is determined by using $p_t = p(Y_t, t)$.

To obtain the solution for $t \in A$, using this concept, we can modify

(58) as

$$\sum_{t \in A} [p(\hat{Y}, t) - w \cdot a] = brT.^{31} \tag{64}$$

More concretely, assume that the demand pattern is given by

$$p(Y_t, t) = P_3(Y), \ t \in A, \ p(Y_t, t) = P_4(Y), \ t \notin A. \tag{65}$$

Let α be the number of periods in A. Then we may rewrite (64) as

$$\alpha P_3(\hat{Y}) = (w \cdot a)\alpha + brT, \ \text{ or } P_3(\hat{Y}) = (w \cdot a) + brT/\alpha, \tag{66}$$

since $Y_t = \hat{Y}$ for $t \in A$. The determination of optimum prices for this case is illustrated by figure 4.12, which corresponds to Steiner's (1957, p. 588) solution for the "firm-peak case," as generalized by Williamson (1966). The firm peak case is the one in which it is *not* optimal to maintain full capacity for *all t*.

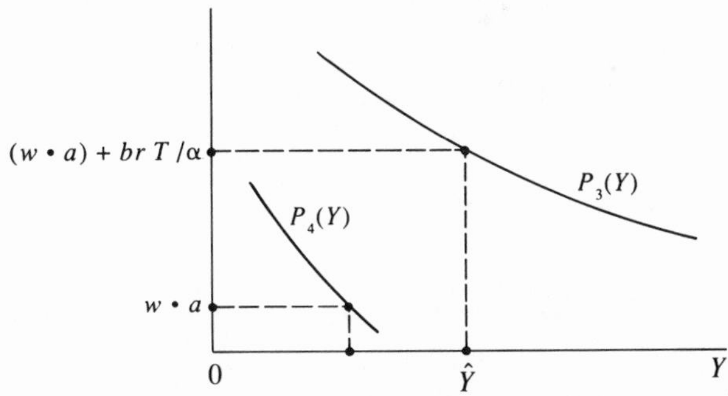

Figure 4.12: A solution when full capacity is not necessarily achieved

The profit of the firm for period t is given by

---

[31] Summing (57) for all t in A, we obtain

$$\sum_{t \in A} p(Y_t, t) = \sum_{t \in A} w \cdot a + \sum_{t=1}^{T} \lambda_t b,$$

by noting $\lambda_t = 0$ for $t \notin A$. Then, recalling (56b) and $Y_t = \hat{Y}$ for $t \in A$, we obtain (64).

$$\pi_t \equiv p_t Y_t - (w \cdot a) Y_t - rK = (p_t - w \cdot a) Y_t - rK$$
$$= \lambda_t b Y_t - rK,$$

where the last equality follows from (57). Then under the prescribed optimal policy, the total profit over the whole period is computed as

$$\pi (\equiv \sum_{t=1}^{T} \pi_t) = \sum_{t=1}^{T} \lambda_t b Y_t - rKT. \tag{67}$$

When full capacity is maintained for all periods (the shifting-peak case), we have $Y_t = Y^* = K^*/b$ for all t, so that (67) can be written as

$$\pi = \sum_{t=1}^{T} \lambda_t K^* - rK^* T = rTK^* - rK^* T = 0$$

by recalling (56b). Thus, we have $\pi = 0$.

When full capacity could not be maintained for all t (the firm-peak case), we have $\lambda_t = 0$ for $t \notin A$. Then (67) can be rewritten as

$$\pi = \sum_{t \in A} \lambda_t b\hat{Y} - r\hat{K}T = \hat{K} \sum_{t \in A} \lambda_t - r\hat{K}T$$
$$= \hat{K} \sum_{t=1}^{T} \lambda_t - r\hat{K}T = \hat{K}rT - r\hat{K}T = 0.$$

Thus, we again have $\pi = 0$. In either of the two cases, the profits over the whole planning horizon should be zero, if the pricing policy of the firm is determined so as to maximize "social welfare" over the periods in the sense of (54). This conclusion does not depend on particular demand specifications such as (60) and (65). The last discussion may be summarized as follows.

Proposition 4.6. Under this specification of the model, the pricing rule for the welfare-maximizing monopoly in the shifting-peak case of (60) is determined by (62) (i.e., by the rule of vertical summation of demand curves), and the optimum capital stock is determined by $K^* = bY^*$. In the firm-peak case of (65), the optimum price for the welfare-maximizing monopoly for peak periods ($t \in A$) is determined by (66), and the optimum capital stock is determined by $\hat{K} = b\hat{Y}$, whereas the optimum price for off-peak periods is equal to the average variable cost

$(w \cdot a)$. In either of these two cases, the profit of the welfare-maximizing monopoly over the whole period is zero.

REMARK: We may investigate whether or not the marginal cost pricing rule holds for the present problem. To this end, note that the total cost (TC) over the whole period can be obtained as

$$TC(\equiv \sum_{t=1}^{T} TC_t) = \sum_{t=1}^{T} [(w \cdot a)Y_t + rK] = \sum_{t=1}^{T} (w \cdot a)Y_t + rKT.$$

For simplicity, we focus our attention on the shifting-peak case in which full capacity output is maintained over the whole period. This is the case in which $Y_t = Y^*$ and $K^* = bY^*$ for all t. The total cost can be written as

$$TC = (w \cdot a + br)Y^*T.$$

The total output X for this case is

$$X \equiv \sum_{t=1}^{T} Y_t = Y^*T.$$

Since the term $(w \cdot a + br)$ is independent of X, the marginal cost (MC, which is also equal to the average cost) can be obtained as

$$MC = w \cdot a + br.$$

Needless to say, this is not equal to the price for each period, as the price fluctuates from time to time according to (57). On the other hand, let p be the "average price," which can be expressed (by using eq. 58) as

$$p \equiv \frac{1}{T} \sum_{t=1}^{T} p_t = w \cdot a + br. \tag{68}$$

Then p is equal to the marginal cost. Marginal cost pricing holds "on the average" for the shifting-peak case.[32]

Notice that it would be easy to see from the above discussion that the marginal cost pricing rule also holds for the conventional case in which there are no shifts in the demand function over time; that is, when

[32] It can be shown that the marginal cost pricing rule does not hold in general for the firm-peak case in which full capacity is not maintained for certain periods.

$p_t = p(Y_t)$. In this case, the optimum price (p_t) would be constant and we have

$$p_t = w \cdot a + br, \; t = 1, 2, \ldots, T, \tag{69}$$

where $(w \cdot a + br)$ again signifies the marginal cost.

4.6.3 The Case of a Profit-Maximizing Monopoly

Throughout the preceding discussion, we have confined our attention to the case in which the firm maximizes social welfare as defined by (54). Alternatively, we may consider the case in which the firm maximizes profit over time. Recalling $y_t = D(p_t, t)$, we may write the profit of the firm for the period t as

$$\pi_t = (p_t - w \cdot a)D(p_t, t) - rK.$$

The problem of the firm is now to choose $p_1, \ldots, p_t$ and K to

$$\text{Maximize } \pi \, (\equiv \pi_t) = [\sum_{t=1}^{T} (p_t - w \cdot a)D(p_t, t) - rK] \tag{70}$$

subject to $K \geqq bD(p_t, t)$, $p_t \geqq 0$, $t = 1, 2, \ldots, T$, and $K \geqq 0$. The Lagrangian of this problem may be written as

$$\Psi \equiv \sum_{t=1}^{T} [(p_t - w \cdot a)D(p_t, t) - rK] + \sum_{t=1}^{T} \lambda_t (K - bY_t). \tag{71}$$

Assuming an interior solution ($p_t > 0$, $t = 1, 2, \ldots, T$, and $K > 0$ at the optimum) and omitting the symbol to denote the optimum, such as (*) for simplicity, the first-order condition may be written as

$$\partial\Psi/\partial p_t = [D(p_t, t) + (p_t - w \cdot a)D_p] - b\lambda_t D_p = 0,$$

$$t = 1, 2, \ldots, T, \tag{72a}$$

$$\partial\Psi/\partial K = rT - \sum_{t=1}^{T} \lambda_t = 0, \tag{72b}$$

$$K \geqq bD(p_t, t), \; \lambda_t[K - bD(p_t, t)] = 0, \; \lambda_t \geqq 0,$$

$$t = 1, 2, \ldots, T, \tag{72c}$$

where $D_p \equiv \partial D(p_t, t)/\partial p_t$.[33] Define the **elasticity of demand**, $\eta_t = \eta(p_t, t)$, by $\eta_t \equiv -p_t D_p/D$. It is positive by assuming $D_p < 0$ (a downward-sloping demand curve). In terms of η_t, we may rewrite (72a) as

$$(\eta_t - 1)p_t = \eta_t(w \cdot a + \lambda_t b), \; t = 1, 2, \ldots, T, \tag{72$'$a}$$

which requires $\eta_t > 1$ for all t.[34] Define $\varepsilon_t \equiv \eta_t/(\eta_t - 1)$. Then $\varepsilon_t = \varepsilon(p_t, t)$, that is, ε_t is a function of p_t and t. Also, $\eta_t > 1$ implies

$$\varepsilon_t > 1, \; t = 1, 2, \ldots, T. \tag{73}$$

In terms of ε_t, (72$'$a) can be rewritten as

$$p_t = \varepsilon_t(w \cdot a + \lambda_t b). \tag{74}$$

Since $\varepsilon_t > 1$, (74) implies

$$p_t - w \cdot a > p_t - \varepsilon_t(w \cdot a) = \varepsilon_t \lambda_t b \geqq 0, \; t = 1, 2, \ldots, T. \tag{75}$$

Namely, the current profit, $p_t - w \cdot a$, are always positive. The total profit over the entire T periods (when it is maximized) may be computed as follows.

$$\sum_{t=1}^{T} \pi_t = \sum_{t=1}^{T} [(p_t - w \cdot a)D - rK] \tag{76}$$

$$> \sum_{t=1}^{T} [(\varepsilon_t \lambda_t b)D - rK] \qquad \text{[by (75)]}$$

$$> \sum_{t=1}^{T} (\lambda_t bD - rK) \qquad (\text{since } \varepsilon_t > 1)$$

---

[33] The discussion on the conditions that ensure that (72) is necessary and sufficient for an optimum is left to the interested reader.

[34] A similar condition is required in the theory of monopoly discussed in intermediate price-theory textbooks. In such a theory, the firm is to choose Y to maximize its profit $[p(Y)Y - C(Y)]$, where $p(Y)$ is the inverse demand function which does not shift over time, and where $C(Y)$ is the cost function in which the input prices are exogenously given constants. The first-order condition is easily obtained as $p'Y + p = C'$. The price elasticity of demand may be defined as $\eta \equiv -p/(p'Y)$. Then the first condition can be rewritten $(\eta - 1)p = \eta C'$ (which corresponds to eq. 72$'$a and where C' signifies the marginal cost). Since $C' > 0$, this requires $\eta > 1$. We may note that $\eta > 1$ holds if and only if the marginal revenue is positive.

$$= \sum_{t=1}^{T} \lambda_t bD - \sum_{t=1}^{T} \lambda_t K \qquad \text{[by (72b)]}$$

$$= \sum_{t=1}^{T} \lambda_t (bD - K) = 0. \qquad \text{[by (72c)]}$$

Thus, the profit over the whole period is always positive for the profit-maximizing monopoly. This may be contrasted with the earlier result that profits are always equal to zero for the welfare-maximizing monopoly.

Suppose that the demand elasticities, η_t, $t = 1, 2, \ldots, T$, are constant for all t. This is ensured if the demand function is written as

$$D(p_t, t) = \phi(t) p_t^{-\eta}, \tag{77}$$

where $\phi(t)$ signifies the time shift of the demand function, and where η is a constant with $\eta > 1$. In this case $\eta_t = \eta$ for all t, and ε_t = constant for all t (which we denote by ε). The total profit can be computed as

$$\sum_{t=1}^{T} \pi_t = \sum_{t=1}^{T} [(p_t - w \cdot a)D - rK] \tag{76'}$$

$$= \sum_{t=1} \{[(\varepsilon - 1)w \cdot a + \lambda_t b]D - rK\} \qquad \text{[by (74)]}$$

$$= T(\varepsilon - 1)w \cdot a + \sum_{t=1}^{T} (\lambda_t bD - \lambda_t K) \qquad \text{[by (72b)]}$$

$$= T(\varepsilon - 1)\, w \cdot a. \qquad \text{[by (72c)]}$$

Thus, the total profit is larger, the larger ε is (or the smaller η is). Namely, the total profit is larger when the demand for the output is less elastic (as can be expected).

The rest of the analysis is analogous to the case of the welfare-maximizing monopoly. Thus, omitting intermediate steps, we may summarize some of the results. For the sake of simplicity, we assume that $\varepsilon_t = \varepsilon$ (constant) for all t. First, consider the shifting-peak case in which full capacity is maintained for all periods. Specifically, we consider the demand pattern given by (60). In this case, the optimum output Y^* is determined by

$$\tau_1 P_1(Y^*) + \tau_2 P_2(Y^*) = \varepsilon(w \cdot a + br)T. \tag{61'}$$

This in turn determines the optimum capital stock by $K^* = bY^*$. The diagrammatic illustration of the determination of Y^* via (61′) is analogous to the one in figure 4.11. The optimal pricing policy is again given by

$$p_t = P_1(Y^*) \text{ for } t \in T_1, \quad p_t = P_2(Y^*) \text{ for } t \in T_2. \tag{62'}$$

Since $\varepsilon > 1$, we may also conclude from (61′) that the optimum output for the profit-maximizing monopoly would be less than the one for the welfare-maximizing monopoly, which in turn implies that the capital stock for the (profit-maximizing) private monopoly would be less than the socially optimum amount. (Here we may recall that the demand curves are downward sloping, $P_1' < 0$ and $P_2' < 0$.) Also, from this and (62′), we may conclude that the profit-maximizing monopoly always charges higher prices than the welfare-maximizing monopoly.

Next, consider the firm-peak case in which the demand pattern is given by (65). In this case, the optimum output $\hat{Y}$ for peak periods $(t \in A)$ is determined by

$$P_3(\hat{Y}) = \varepsilon[(w \cdot a) + brT/\alpha], \tag{66'}$$

and the optimum stock of capital is obtained by $\hat{K} = b\hat{Y}$. The diagrammatic illustration of the determination of $\hat{Y}$ via (66′) is analogous to the one in figure 4.12. The optimal pricing policy is given by

$$p_t = \varepsilon[(w \cdot a) + brT/\alpha],\ t \in A; \quad p_t = \varepsilon(w \cdot a),\ t \notin A. \tag{78}$$

Since $\varepsilon > 1$, the profit-maximizing monopoly always charges higher prices than the welfare-maximizing monopoly. Since the demand curves, P_3 and P_4, are both downward sloping, this implies that the profit-maximizing monopoly always produces less than the welfare-maximizing monopoly, which in turn implies that capital stock will always be less than that of the welfare-maximizing monopoly. Assuming a constant demand elasticity (or $\varepsilon_t = \varepsilon$ for all t), we may summarize some of these conclusions as follows.

Proposition 4.7. Under the preceding specification of the model, we have:

(i) the total profit of the profit-maximizing firm over the whole period is always positive, and it increases as demand becomes less elastic;

(ii) the profit-maximizing monopoly (as compared to the welfare-maximizing monopoly) always charges higher prices, produces less output, and uses less capital stock for both peak and off-peak periods; and

(iii) In the shifting-peak case, the optimal pricing policy is given by (62′), while in the firm-peak case, the optimal pricing policy is given by (78).

REMARK: From the above, it would not be difficult to see that if the profit-maximizing firm is subject to fair-rate-of-return regulation so that its profit is squeezed, then it would produce more output and use a larger stock of capital. This corresponds to the Averch-Johnson effect discussed in the previous section. A more rigorous formulation of the peak-load problem with a regulatory constraint and the computation of the optimum fair rate of return (s) is left to the interested reader as a useful exercise.

REMARK: In this discussion, we obtained our conclusion (proposition 4.6) based on a number of assumptions. These assumptions are common to a number of the mainstream analyses such as Boiteux (1949); and Steiner (1957). As mentioned earlier, our focus has been on clarifying the analytical structure of the problem, so that we can obtain useful results by altering assumptions. One conspicuous assumption is that of fixed coefficient technology. One may wish to change it to a neoclassical technology that allows substitution among factors. An excellent discussion in this direction is found in Panzar (1976). With this change, the conclusion that only users who utilize plant to capacity bear any fraction of capacity costs (as illustrated in fig. 4.12) does not hold any longer. As Panzar (1976, p. 521) states, "when a neoclassical technology is assumed . . . , it is found that *all* periods contribute to the cost of capacity; the period with largest output simply makes the greatest contribution" (see also Mohring 1970). Quite apart from this, Drèze (1964); Turvey (1968); Littlechild (1970); Michell, Manning, and Acton (1978); Sherman (1985); and Wiseman (1987); for example, provide us with interesting reading.

There are two important weaknesses in the above analysis of the peak-load problem, whether the firm is maximizing social welfare or profit over periods. One is the partial equilibrium nature of analysis. To cope with this difficulty, one may formulate a two- (or more) sector model in which one sector faces a peak-load problem (with the possibility of decreasing cost) and the other sector does not. With proper specification of the resource constraint and of the social welfare function of these commodities, one can pursue a general equilibrium analysis.

The second weakness occurs even if we confine ourselves to the partial equilibrium nature of the preceding analysis. This difficulty is due to the specification that the demand for output depends only on the price of a particular period, that is, $Y_t = D(p_t, t)$. Once the firm announces its pricing policy, $p_1, p_2, \ldots, p_T$, then consumers will naturally adjust their demand for the commodity accordingly. Then the demand function should more properly be specified as $Y_t = D(p_1, p_2, \ldots, p_T, t)$, $t = 1, 2, \ldots, T$ (e.g., Mohring 1970). Since the firm will decide its optimum pricing policy based on such consumer behavior, this would create a game-theoretic situation. Such an extension, though very important, is again assumed away here. We leave the task of pursuing these problems to the interested reader.

4.7 On the Coase Theorem[35]

4.7.1 Introduction

One of the fundamental theorems of welfare economics is that a competitive equilibrium achieves a Pareto optimum, and that, as a corollary to that proposition, a competitive equilibrium achieves productive efficiency. This constitutes a modern formulation of Adam Smith's well-known insight into the "invisible hand."[36] Although such propositions hold under a weak set of assumptions, these will break down in the presence of "externalities," external economies and diseconomies in production and consumption in which "relevant effects of production or welfare go wholly or partially unpaid" (Mishan 1964, p. 103). The presence of such externalities then constitutes a fundamental challenge to the well-accepted doctrine with the welfare implications of competitive

---

[35] This section is adapted from Takayama (1979a). Ronald Coase was the 1991 Nobel laureate in Economic Science.

[36] There are two fundamental classical propositions in welfare economics: (*a*) every competitive equilibrium realizes a Pareto optimum, and (*b*) every Pareto optimum can be supported by a competitive equilibrium with a suitable allocation of resources among individuals. The seminal work on welfare economics was by Pigou (1932). This has been criticized on the grounds that it allowed interpersonal comparisons of utility by then young economists such as Lerner, Kaldor, Hicks, and others under the apparent influence of Lionel Robbins of the London School of Economics. The Pigouvian procedure of welfare has been replaced by the concept that is now called "Pareto optimum." The classical propositions of welfare economics under such a new approach were analyzed in terms of calculus by Bergson (1938), Lange (1942), and others. In the early 1950s these propositions were reformulated in terms of a modern set theoretic framework by K. J. Arrow, G. Debreu, L. W. McKenzie, and others. See Takayama (1985, chap. 2, sec. C).

equilibrium.[37] A well-known example of external economies is that of an apple grower and a bee keeper in an adjacent field, wherein the latter obtains a benefit from the production of the former (see Meade 1952).[38] Although examples of this kind may have been taken to be rather unimportant, the question of externalities has attracted a great deal of attention more recently due to the problem of external diseconomies and the liability rules associated with it. Smoke, noise, and many forms of air and water pollution have intensified the interest in this problem.

The well-known solution to "market failure" due to externalities was proposed by Pigou (1932) and has been widely accepted. In such a case, market failure can be corrected by the governmental intervention of devising a proper tax-subsidy scheme. An important article by Coase (1960) challenged the Pigouvian solution in a fundamental way: he eloquently argues that the Pareto optimum resource allocation can be achieved via private negotiations *without* invoking governmental intervention.

The externality considered by Coase is a production externality in

---

[37]Various "deficiencies" of competitive equilibrium are known as *market failures*. For good summaries of the problem of market failures, see Imai et al. (1971), Homma (1980), Boadway and Bruce (1984, pp. 103–36), Ledyard (1987), and Stiglitz (1988, pp. 71–81); for example. For an early but excellent exposition of this problem, see Bator (1957 and 1958). For the market failures associated with incomplete markets and imperfect information, see Greenwald and Stiglitz (1986). Market failures are often used as the *prima facie* economic justification for the existence of government and government interventions. The Coase theorem is an important contribution to the antithesis of such an argument.

[38]Meade (1952) represents the first modern discussion on externalities, or nonmarket interdependence of economic agents, which is responsible for divergence between social and private costs, as well as causing an important type of market failure. (James Meade, jointly with Bertil Ohlin, was awarded the 1977 Nobel Prize in Economic Science for contributions to international economics.) A simplified variant of a production model by Meade in terms of one factor ("labor") was presented by Bator (1958). (It may be worthwhile to note the distinction with regard to different sources of market failure, one due to non-market interdependence or externalities, and the other due to economies of scale. This distinction is pointed out by Scitovsky (1954). The pioneering and classical work on the problem of divergence between private cost and social cost (and related issues) is due to Pigou (1932). In this regard, Mishan (1964, pp. 14–15) writes,

> *The Economics of Welfare* is frequently associated with the controversies of the thirties over interpersonal comparison of utility. But its enduring contribution is to be found in the continued emphasis on the vital distinction between social and private valuation of economic activities, a distinction evoked nowadays more by reference to "external effects" or "external economies and diseconomies of production and consumption."

which the production of one good becomes a negative input in the production of some other goods. A celebrated example used by Coase is the case of straying cattle; a rancher-producer raises cattle that trample a neighboring farm's crop. Another example used by Coase is the case of a confectioner and a doctor, in which the doctor, in his consulting room, is disturbed by the noise and vibrations caused by the machinery in the confectioner's kitchen.

The proposition known as the "Coase theorem" states that the Pareto optimum resource allocation (under some ideal conditions) can be achieved via private negotiation without invoking the Pigouvian tax-subsidy scheme, and that this private solution is independent of liability rules. Coase presented his proposition verbally by using interesting and eye-opening examples drawn from actual legal cases. Although this is justifiably and undoubtedly an important reason for the popularity of his proposition, here we shall present it in terms of a mathematical model. This approach should more clearly reveal the basic logical structure and assumptions involved in his proposition.[39]

4.7.2 Externality and the Pigouvian Scheme

To understand Coase's contribution properly, it is useful to first discuss the basic argument involved in the classical Pigouvian scheme. For simplicity, following Coase (1960) and others, we consider an economy consisting of two producers (1 and 2). Assume that Firm 1's production function for its output Y_1 is given by

$$Y_1 = F_1(L_1),\ F_1(0) = 0,\ F_1' > 0,\ F_1'' < 0, \tag{79}$$

where L_1 is its input (labor), while Firm 2's production function for its output Y_2 is given this,

$$Y_2 = \tilde{F}_2(Y_1,\ L_2),\ \tilde{F}_2(Y_1,\ 0) = 0, \tag{80}$$

where $\partial \tilde{F}_2/\partial L_2 > 0$, $\partial_1^2 \tilde{F}_2/\partial L_2^2 < 0$, $\partial \tilde{F}_2/\partial Y_1 < 0$, and where L_2 is its direct input (labor). Notice also that here Firm 1's output (Y_1) enters as a negative input to Firm 2's production, that is, $\partial \tilde{F}_2/\partial Y_1 < 0$.

---

[39]In many ways, Coase (1960) constitutes another significant step forward from Pigou (1932). Coase has inspired a number of works. It provides illuminating reading with many interesting legal examples, and a simple mathematical exposition as presented here may not do full justice to this important work. For a recent succinct discussion of the problem involved with this "theorem," see Cootner (1987).

Substituting (79) into $Y_2 = \tilde{F}_2(Y_1, L_2)$, we may obtain

$$Y_2 = \tilde{F}_2[F_1(L_1), L_2] \equiv F_2(L_1, L_2), \tag{81}$$

where $F_2(L_1, 0) = 0$, $\partial F_2/\partial L_1 < 0$, $\partial F_2/\partial L_2 > 0$, $\partial^2 F_2/\partial L_2^2 < 0$. Note that $\partial F_2/\partial L_1 < 0$ if and only if $\partial \tilde{F}_2/\partial Y_1 < 0$. It is assumed that Firm 2 knows function F_1.[40] The model, in terms of (79) and (81), should capture the essence of the externality considered by the Coase theorem.

A **Pareto optimum** point in production, or the efficient configuration of production, is given as a solution of the constrained maximization problem in which L_1 and L_2 are chosen so as to

$$\text{Maximize } \alpha_1 F_1(L_1) + \alpha_2 F_2(L_1, L_2),$$

$$\text{subject to } L_1 + L_2 \leqq L,\ L_1 \geqq 0, \text{ and } L_2 \geqq 0,$$

where L is the fixed amount of the resource (labor) in this economy, and α_1 and α_2 are fixed nonnegative constants with $(\alpha_1, \alpha_2) \neq 0$. Assume that $L_1 > 0$ and $L_2 > 0$ at the optimum (an interior solution), where we omit $(^*)$ to denote the optimum for simplicity. Then the first-order (necessary) conditions for optimality are given by[41]

$$\alpha_1 F_1' + \alpha_2 \partial F_2/\partial L_1 = \alpha_2 \partial F_2/\partial L_2, \tag{82}$$

$$L_1 + L_2 = L. \tag{83}$$

These two equations determine the Pareto optimum values of L_1 and L_2 for given values of the parameters, α_1 and α_2 (or, for a given value of α_1/α_2 where we assume $\alpha_2 > 0$).[42] Varying the value of α_1/α_2, we

---

[40] This presupposes that Firm 2 knows Firm 1's production function, F_1, as well as its own, i.e., $\tilde{F}_2$. Alternatively, we may suppose that the externality enters into Firm 2's production function directly in the form of L_1.

[41] Write the Lagrangian as $\Phi \equiv \alpha_1 F_1(L_1) + \alpha_2 F_2(L_1, L_2) + \lambda(L - L_1 - L_2)$. By setting $\partial\Phi/\partial L_1 = 0$ and $\partial\Phi/\partial L_2 = 0$, we at once obtain

$$\alpha_1 F_1' + \alpha_2 \partial F_2/\partial L_1 = \lambda,\ \alpha_2 \partial F_2/\partial L_2 = \lambda, \tag{82'}$$

which yields (82). The second equation of (82′) ensures $\lambda > 0$, which in turn yields (83).

[42] When $\partial F_2/\partial L_1 \equiv 0$ (no externality), the assumptions stated in (79) and (80) are sufficient to furnish a unique (globally) Pareto optimum point for a given value of α_1/α_2. Although this is not necessarily the case when the externality is present, we shall assume that such is also the case when this externality is present. The reader should be able to check the appropriate second-order condition.

obtain different Pareto optimum points.[43] Condition (82) signifies the productive efficiency condition. We may call (82) the **Pareto optimum condition** (in production).

Suppose that these two firms are immersed in a "much bigger" economy in which the prices of the two outputs (p_1 and p_2) and the factor price (w) are determined more or less independently of the two firms' levels of production, and that these two firms are "competitive" in the sense that they take these prices (p_1, p_2, and w) as exogenously given constants.[44] Under such circumstances, it is well known (and can easily be shown) that the joint profit maximization yields a Pareto optimum situation in which α_1/α_2 is set equal to p_1/p_2. To see this, consider the problem of choosing L_1 and L_2 to maximize the *joint profit* of the two firms,

$$\pi(L_1, L_2) \equiv p_1F_1(L_1) + p_2F_2(L_1, L_2) - w(L_1 + L_2),$$

subject to $L_1 \geqq 0$ and $L_2 \geqq 0$ Assuming $L_1 > 0$ and $L_2 > 0$ at the optimum, the first-order condition is given by $\partial\pi/\partial L_1 = \partial\pi/\partial L_2 = 0$, or

$$p_1F_1' + p_2\partial F_2/\partial L_1 = p_2\partial F_2/\partial L_2 (= w). \tag{84}$$

This in turn ensures the Pareto optimum (82), for $\alpha_1/\alpha_2 = p_1/p_2$. Under the given partial equilibrium situation in which each firm is able to employ any amount of labor at a fixed wage rate w, (83) is trivially satisfied.[45] Hence we may conclude that *the joint profit maximization point defined by (84) achieves a Pareto optimum* in which α_1/α_2 is taken to be equal to p_1/p_2.[46]

---

[43]Mathematically speaking, the Pareto optimum problem is formulated as the one of *vector maximization*, which can be reformulated in terms of the problem of maximizing a weighted average of the objective functions of the economic agents (producers and/or consumers) involved. For the discussion on vector maximization, see Takayama (1985, chap. 1, sec. E). Needless to say, the problem stated in the text can equivalently be reformulated as the one of choosing L_1 and L_2 so as to maximize $F_1(L_1)$ subject to $F_2(L_1, L_2) \geqq Y_2$, $L_1 + L_2 \geqq 0$, $L_1 \geqq 0$, and $L_2 \geqq 0$, where Y_2 is taken to be a parameter.

[44]Such a "partial equilibrium" set of circumstances corresponds to the situation considered by Coase (1960), as well as Meade (1952) and others.

[45]Note that (84) determines the optimum values of L_1 and L_2 as functions of p_1, p_2, and w, that is, $L_1 = L_1(q)$ and $L_2 = L_2(q)$ where $q = (p_1, p_2, w)$. Then under the partial equilibrium circumstances described here, we may define L by $L \equiv L_1(q) + L_2(q)$.

[46]This is because (82) is satisfied by (84) when $p_1 = \alpha_1$ and $p_2 = \alpha_2$. Also,

In the competitive situation, however, each firm is *not* typically interested in maximizing the joint profit or the "social profit," $\pi(L_1, L_2)$. Rather, each is interested in maximizing its own private profit. Namely, Firm 1 chooses L_1 to maximize its own profit,

$$\pi_1(L_1) \equiv p_1 F_1(L_1) - wL_1,$$

subject to $L_1 \geqq 0$, while Firm 2 chooses L_2 to maximize its own profit,

$$\pi_2(L_2, L_2) \equiv p_2 F_2(L_1, L_2) - wL_2,$$

subject to $L_2 \geqq 0$, for a given value of L_1. Assuming $L_1 > 0$ and $L_2 > 0$ at the optimum, the first-order conditions for Firms 1 and 2 are, respectively, given by

$$p_1 F_1' = w, \quad \text{and} \tag{85}$$

$$p_2 \partial F_2 / \partial L_2 = w. \tag{86}$$

This in turn implies

$$p_1 F_1' = p_2 \partial F_2 / \partial L_2. \tag{87}$$

Under such circumstances, the Pareto optimum condition (82) cannot be satisfied in general. In the presence of an externality ($\partial F_2/\partial L_1 \neq 0$), the "market solution," each firm's maximization of its own private profit, will not achieve a Pareto optimum (or a "social optimum"). This result is at the heart of the problem of market failures due to externalities.

Note that if there is no externality in this case ($\partial F_2/\partial L_1 \equiv 0$), then condition (82) is ensured by the private profit maximization (87). This is clearly an aspect of the well-known proposition by Adam Smith that "free competition" realizes a "social optimum."

A. C. Pigou proposed to remove market failure in the presence of an externality by a "tax-cum-subsidy" scheme. Suppose that Firm 1, which inflicts "damage" on Firm 2, is subject to $100 \cdot t\%$ revenue *tax*. Then Firm 1 chooses L_1 to maximize its after tax profit,

$$(1 - t)p_1 F_1(L_1) - wL_1,$$

subject to $L_1 \geqq 0$, and the given tax rate t.

---

letting λ signify the shadow price of the resource constraint, $L_1 + L_2 \leqq L$, λ is equal to the market wage rate, where we may recall (82′).

Assuming $L_1 > 0$ at the optimum, the first-order condition is given by

$$(1 - t)p_1 F_1' = w. \tag{88}$$

Suppose that Firm 2 is subject to no tax (nor subsidies). Then its profit maximization condition is given by (86). Hence, combining (86) and (88), we obtain

$$p_1 F_1' - tp_1 F_1' = p_2 \partial F_2 / \partial L_2 = w. \tag{89}$$

If the government should choose the tax rate t so that

$$-tp_1 F_1' = p_2 \partial F_2 / \partial L_1, \quad \text{that is,} \quad t = -\frac{p_2 \partial F_2 / \partial L_1}{p_1 F_1'} > 0, \tag{90}$$

then condition (89) ensures (82) with $\alpha_1 / \alpha_2 = p_1 / p_2$.[47] The Pareto optimum with $\alpha_1 / \alpha_2 = p_1 / p_2$ can be achieved via private profit maximization when the proper tax is levied on Firm 1.

The same solution can be achieved by providing *subsidies* to Firm 2. Suppose that Firm 2 receives a subsidy in the amount of $100 \cdot s\%$ of its revenue. Then Firm 2 chooses L_2 to maximize its (after subsidy) profit,

$$(1 + s)p_2 F_2(L_1, L_2) - wL_2,$$

subject to $L_2 \geqq 0$, for given values of s and L_1. Assuming $L_2 > 0$ at the optimum, the first-order condition gives

$$(1 + s)p_2 \partial F_2 / \partial L_2 = W. \tag{91}$$

Assuming that Firm 1 is subject to no taxes or subsidies, its profit maximization condition is given by (85). Combining (85) and (91), we obtain

$$p_1 F_1' - sp_2 \partial F_2 / \partial L_2 = p_2 \partial F_2 / \partial L_2. \tag{92}$$

Hence, if the government chooses s such that

$$-sp_2 \partial F_2 / \partial L_2 = p_2 \partial F_2 / \partial L_1, \quad \text{that is} \quad s = -\frac{\partial F_2 / \partial L_1}{\partial F_2 / \partial L_2} > 0, \tag{93}$$

---

[47]Note that $t > 0$ since $\partial F_2 / \partial L_1 < 0$. To compute the appropriate tax rate t, obtain the optimum values of L_1 and L_2 from (89) as $L_1 = L_1(q;\, t)$ and $L_2 = L_2(q;\, t)$, where $q = (p_1,\, p_2,\, w)$, and substitute them into (90):

$$-tp_1 F_1'[L_1(q;\, t)] = p_2 \partial F_2[L_1(q;\, t),\, L_2(q;\, t)] / \partial L_1,$$

which gives the tax rate t as $t = t(q)$, i.e., $t = t(p_1,\, p_2,\, w)$.

then the Pareto optimum (82) is ensured.

An obvious difficulty in this solution is that it is not clear how the government spends the tax revenue in the tax scheme case, or how the government obtains income to subsidize Firm 2 in the subsidy scheme case. One (possible satisfactory) answer is that since these firms are presumably very "small" in the economy, the amount (and hence the effects) of the tax revenue or the subsidy is negligible, and hence can be ignored. On the other hand, if such is the case, the significance of the problem of externalities considered here may also be small. Also, these can add up to a non-trivial amount.

4.7.3 The Coase Theorem

A remarkable feature of the Coase theorem is that a Pareto optimum can be achieved by private negotiations of the two firms without any intervention of the government. Thus, bureaucratic red tape and other (explicit or implicit) costs associated with government intervention can be dispensed with. Furthermore, the Pareto optimum can be achieved whether or not Firm 1 is liable for the damage that Firm 2 suffers. In connection with this, we may note that it is not necessarily clear why Firm 1 should always be liable to Firm 2, even if Firm 1's output is a negative input of Firm 2's production function. As an example, consider Firm 2 coming into existence after Firm 1 is already established. In such an event, it is not clear why Firm 1 should pay compensation to a newcomer, Firm 2. If Firm 1 has to pay compensation, it is possible that Firm 1 may have to cease its operation when Firm 2 is established. This may be unjustifiable.

It is often the case that the damage suffered by Firm 2 is due to the fact that Firm 1 destroys a certain "environment" (as in the case in which noise made by the confectioner inflicts damage on the doctor in the confectioner vs. doctor case). The question is then who owns the property right with regard to the environment. As in the confectioner-doctor example by Coase, if the confectioner is in operation before the doctor moves nearby, it is possible to argue that the confectioner owns the "environmental right," and hence can make noise without any compensation to the doctor. The Coase theorem asserts that the Pareto optimum can be achieved by private negotiations *regardless of* who owns the environmental right.

To begin the discussion, recall that, under private profit maximization, Firm 2's output depends on the level of Firm 1's operation. To see this, recall Firm 2's profit maximization condition,

$$p_2 \partial F_2(L_1, L_2)/\partial L_2 = w. \tag{86}$$

This in turn gives the optimum value of L_2 for a *given* level of L_1. Namely, (86) can be solved for L_2 (for a given value of w/p_2) as

$$L_2 = L_2(L_1). \tag{94}$$

The maximum profit of Firm 2, π_2^*, thus depends on L_1. In other words,

$$\pi_2^*(L_1) \equiv p_2 F_2[L_1, L_2(L_1)] - wL_2(L_1). \tag{95}$$

We now examine the two cases that arise due to two different liability rules.

Case A (Firm 1 Is Liable). When Firm 1 ceases its operation, Firm 2's maximum profit is given by $\pi_2^*(0)$. This profit is reduced to $\pi_2^*(L_1)$, when Firm 1's level of operation is given by $L_1 > 0$, where $\pi_2^*(0) > \pi_2^*(L_1)$. Hence, damage Firm 2 suffers from Firm 1 via externality is equal to $\pi_2^*(0) - \pi_2^*(L_1)$. In Case A, Firm 1 is liable for compensating this entire amount to Firm 2. Under such circumstances, Firm 1 chooses L_1 to maximize its profit after compensation,

$$p_1 F_1(L_1) - wL_1 - [\pi_2^*(0) - \pi_2^*(L_1)]. \tag{96}$$

The optimality condition is given by

$$p_1 F_1' - w + d\pi_2^*/dL_1 = 0. \tag{97}$$

Firm 2 chooses L_2 to maximize profit inclusive of the compensation from Firm 1,

$$p_2 F_2(L_1, L_2) - wL_2 + [\pi_2^*(0) - \pi_2^*(L_1)]. \tag{98}$$

Then the optimality condition is given by

$$p_2 \partial F_2/\partial L_2 - w = 0. \tag{99}$$

From (97) and (99), we obtain

$$p_1 F_1' + d\pi_2^*/dL_1 = p_2 \partial F_2/\partial L_2. \tag{100}$$

The expression for $d\pi_2^*/dL_1$ can be computed, by recalling (95), as:

$$d\pi_2^*/dL_1 = p_2[\partial F_2/\partial L_1 + (\partial F_2/\partial L_2)L_2'] - wL_2' = p_2 \partial F_2/\partial L_1 \tag{101}$$

where $L_2' \equiv dL_2/dL_1$, and where the second equality is obtained by using (99). In view of (100), (101) reduces to the Pareto optimum condition (82). Thus, we may conclude that the Pareto optimum can be achieved when Firm 1 compensates Firm 2 for the entire amount of the damage.

Case B (Firm 2 Is Liable). In this case, Firm 2 (say, a "newcomer") is responsible for compensating Firm 1. Firm 2 wishes Firm 1 reduces its production level, and is willing pay compensation for that. When Firm 1's level of production is reduced from L_1° to L_1, Firm 2's profit will increase by the amount of $\pi_2^*(L_1) - \pi_2^*(L_1^\circ)$, where $L_1 < L_1^\circ$. Let L_1° be the level of Firm 1's operation when Firm 1 receives no compensation. Since Firm 1 receives the compensation from Firm 2 by the amount of $\pi_2^*(L_1) - \pi_2^*(L_1^\circ)$, Firm 1's profit inclusive of the compensation is given by

$$p_1 F_1(L_1) - wL_1 + [\pi_2^*(L_1) - \pi_2^*(L_1^\circ)]. \tag{102}$$

Firm 1 chooses L_1 to maximize such a profit, and the optimality condition is given by

$$p_1 F_1' - w + d\pi_2^*/dL_1 = 0. \tag{103}$$

Firm 2 chooses L_2 to maximize its profit after the compensation,

$$p_2 F_2(L_1, L_2) - wL_2 - [\pi_2^*(L_1) - \pi_1^*(L_1^\circ)]. \tag{104}$$

The optimality condition for this is given by

$$p_2 \partial F_2/\partial L_2 - w = 0. \tag{105}$$

Combining (103) and (105), we get

$$p_1 F_1' + d\pi_2^*/dL_1 = p_2 \partial F_2/\partial L_2. \tag{106}$$

Then recalling $d\pi_2^*/dL_1 = p_2 \partial F_2/\partial L_1$ from (101), we can readily observe that (106) reduces to the Pareto optimum, condition (82). Thus, we may also conclude that the Pareto optimum can also be achieved when Firm 2 compensates Firm 1 for the entire amount of the damage. In summary, we obtain the following result (the **Coase theorem**). The above argument provides a formal proof of the theorem.

Proposition 4.8. In the above specification of the model, the Pareto optimum in production can be achieved by private negotiation between firms, whether Firm 1 is liable for compensation (case A) or Firm 2 is liable for compensation (case B).

Some important questions arise once the theorem is formulated. For example, what are the incentives for such negotiations and how would private negotiations result in one of the two cases considered above? Setting aside such questions, we illustrate the Coase theorem diagrammatically in figure 4.13.[48] The BB'-curve signifies the $[-d\pi_2^*(L_1)/dL_1]$-locus, where $OA = L_1^\circ$. Since $d\pi_2^*(L_1)/dL_1 = p_2\partial F_2(L_1, L_2)/\partial L_1 < 0$ by (101), the BB'-curve is above the OL_1-axis. Assume, for simplicity, $d^2\pi_2^*(L_1)/dL_1^2 < 0$.[49] Then the BB'-curve is upward sloping. In figure 4.13, the AE-curve signifies the locus of $[p_1F_1'(L_1) - w]$. Since $F_1'' < 0$, the AE-curve is negatively sloped. L_1° is the amount of labor that Firm 1 employs when the firm neither pays nor receives any compensation, and it is determined by Firm 1's profit maximization under no restrictions, that is, by $p_1F_1'(L^\circ) = w$. Denote the level of L_1 determined by the intersection of the BB'-curve and the AE-curve by L_1^*. Then, when $L_1 = L_1^*$, we have

$$p_1F_1' - w = -p_2\partial F_2/\partial L_1, \quad \text{so that} \quad p_1F_1' + p_2\partial F_2/\partial L_1 = w.$$

Recalling (84), we may at once conclude from this that L_1^* signifies the Pareto optimum level of L_1. When the level of L_1 decreases from L_1° to L_1^*, Firm 1's profit decreases by the amount of triangle ACD, while Firm 2's profit increases by the amount of trapezoid $ABCD$ in figure 4.13. There is a net increase in the "joint profit" by the amount of triangle ABC. The Coase theorem asserts that such a net increase can be achieved regardless of which firm is liable for compensation.

In Case A, Firm 1 is liable for compensation by the amount of damage that it inflicts upon Firm 2. The amount of damage $[\pi_2^*(L_1^*) - \pi_2^*(0)]$ is measured by the trapezoid area $OB'CD$. Firm 1's profit before the compensation, when its level of operation is equal to L_1^* is measured by trapezoid $OECD$, while its profit after the compensation, when $L_1 = L_1^*$, is measured by triangle $B'CE$. In Case B, Firm 2 is liable for compensating Firm 1 for restricting its production. The amount of compensation is equal to the amount of increase in profit due to Firm 1's restriction of

---

[48] We are indebted to Kudoh and Yabushita (1974) for a similar diagram and some of the subsequent discussion.

[49] Recalling (96) and (102), we may observe that condition $d^2\pi_2^*/dL^2 < 0$ ensures the second-order (sufficiency) condition for Firm 1's maximization problems for both cases A and B.

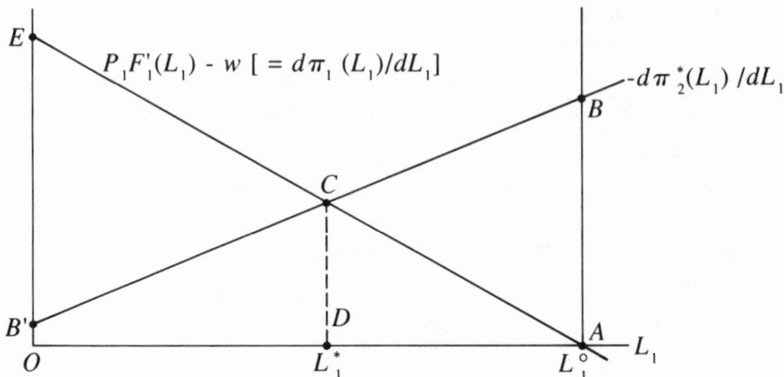

Figure 4.13: Illustration of the Coase theorem

its production, $[\pi_2^*(L_1^*) - \pi_2^*(L_1^\circ)]$, when L_1 is restricted from L_1° to L_1^*. In figure 4.13, this is measured by the trapezoid area $ABCD$. Thus in Case B, an increase in the joint profit due to Firm 1's reduction of its production level all goes to Firm 1.

Having formulated the Coase theorem mathematically, we can easily extend the analysis to more general circumstances, such as the cases (1) when the firm's production involves factors other than labor, (2) when both firms are subject to taxation (e.g., corporate profit tax), (3) when one firm is subject to some sort of governmental regulations, and (4) when one party is a consumer instead of producer, etc. Such extensions should be easy and are left to the interested reader.

Setting such generalizations aside, we may note that some important assumptions are made implicitly in the preceding formulation of the Coase theorem. One is the absence of negotiation and transaction costs. The court procedure that determines the amount of damage is very often quite costly in terms of both nominal and real costs including "time." Such costs may become inhibitively high for many typical environmental problems in which thousands of people are involved (sometimes in both parties) such as in the pollution of air and water, nuclear reactor accidents, etc. Another assumption concerns the fact that the income distribution between parties is largely influenced by the liability rule, although the final level of production after negotiation remains the same.

But the question of determining which party is liable depends on the question of which party owns the property right to the "environment," or which party has the right to harm the other. The determination of such property rights may not be easy. The third problem is that the damage may not occur with certainty, but rather occurs under a certain probability distribution (as in the case of an "accident"), and that the probability of the accident occurence depends on the cost that each party absorbs. Note that the probability of accidents depends on the position taken by both parties, which would make the concept of the "perpetrator of injury" and the "victim" even more ambiguous. On top of these economic problems, there is a well-known mathematical problem involved in externalities. The production possibility set, under even simple circumstances described by (79) and (81), is not necessarily convex.[50] This implies that the Pareto optimum is only a "local" optimum and a more careful examination of the Pareto optimum condition (82) is necessary.

A number of interesting studies have been done on all of these aspects of the problem. However, the message of the Coase theorem is clear. Using a simple framework, it clarifies a certain basic structure involved with externalities and shows that it is possible, under certain situations, to achieve the Pareto optimum by private negotiations; that is, by avoiding governmental interventions. This is a remarkable result.

References

Abbott, M., and O. Ashenfelter. 1976. "Labor Supply, Commodity Demand, and the Allocation of Time." *Review of Economic Studies* 43 (October): 389–411.

Arrow, K. J. 1963. *Social Choice and Individual Values.* 2d ed. New York: Wiley (1st ed. 1951).

Arrow, K. J. and T. Scitovsky, eds. 1969. *Readings in Welfare Economics.* Homewood, Ill.: Richard D. Irwin.

Ashenfelter, O., and J. Heckman. 1974. "The Estimation of Income and Substitution Effects in a Model of Family Labor Supply." *Econometrica* 42 (January): 73–85.

Averch, H. A. 1987. "Averch-Johnson Effect." In Eatwell, Milgate, and Newman 1987, 1: 160–63.

[50]Under the present "partial equilibrium" circumstances, the concept of the "production possibility set" may not be appropriate. It may be more proper to use the concept of the "feasible set" in the bargaining solution in the theory of cooperative games with side payments.

Averch, H. A., and L. O. Johnson. 1962. "Behavior of the Firm under Regulatory Constraint." *American Economic Review.* 52 (December): 1053–69.

Bailey, E. E. 1973. *Economic Theory of Regulatory Constraint.* Lexington, Mass.: Heath-Lexington.

Bator, F. M. 1957. "The Simple Analytics of Welfare Organization." *American Economic Review* 47 (March): 22–59.

———. 1958. "The Anatomy of Market Failure." *Quarterly Journal of Economics* 72 (August): 351–79.

Battalio, R., L. Green, and J. Kagel. 1981. "Income-Leisure Tradeoffs of Animal Workers." *American Economic Review* 69 (September): 621–32.

Baumol, W. J., and A. K. Klevorick. 1970. "Input Choices and Rate-of-Return Regulation: An Overview of the Discussion." *Bell Journal of Economics and Management Science* 1 (Autumn): 162–90.

Bear, D. V. T. 1965. "Inferior Inputs and the Theory of the Firm." *Journal of Political Economy* 73 (June): 287–89.

Berg, S. V., and J. Tschirhart. 1988. *Natural Monopoly Regulation: Principles and Practice.* New York: Cambridge University Press.

Bergson (Burk), A. 1938. "A Reformulation of Certain Aspects of Welfare Economies." *Quarterly Journal of Economics* 52 (February): 310–34.

Binger, B., and E. Hoffman. 1988. *Microeconomics with Calculus.* Glenview, Ill.: Scott, Foresman and Co.

Boadway, R., and N. Bruce. 1984. *Welfare Economics.* Oxford: Basil Blackwell.

Blinder, A. S. 1974. *Toward an Economic Theory of Income Distribution.* Cambridge, Mass.: MIT Press.

Boiteux, M. 1949. "La tarification des demandes en point: application de la theorie de la vente au cout marginal." *Revue Génerale de l'electricité.* 58 (August): 321–40. [1960] Translated as "Peak-Load Pricing." *Journal of Business* 33 (April): 157–79.

Buchanan, J. M. 1966. "Peak Loads and Efficient Pricing: Comment." *Quarterly Journal of Economics* 80 (August): 463–71.

Burstein, M. 1968. *Microeconomic Theory: Equilibrium and Change.* New York: Wiley.

Coase, R. 1960. "The Problem of Social Cost." *Journal of Law and Economics* 3 (October): 1–44.

Cootner, R. D. 1987. "Coase Theorem." In Eatwell, Milgate, and Newman 1987, 1: 457–459.

Crew, M. A., and P. R. Kleindorfer. 1979a. *Public Utility Economics.* New York: St. Martin's Press.

———. 1979b. "Marshall and Turvey on Peak Load or Joint Product Pricing." *Journal of Political Economy* 79 (November/December): 1369–77.

———. 1986. *The Economics of Public Utility Regulation.* London: Macmillan.

Deaton, A., and J. Muellbauer. 1980. *Economics and Consumer Behavior.* Cambridge: Cambridge University Press.

Drèze, J. H. 1964. "Some Postwar Contributions of French Economists to Theory and Public Policy." *American Economic Review* 54 (June): 1–64.

Dupuit, J. 1844. "On the Measurement of the Utility of Public Works." Trans. R. H. Barback. In K. J. Arrow and T. Scitovsky (1969): 255–83.

Eatwell, J., M. Milgate, and P. Newman, eds. 1987. *The New Palgrave: A Dictionary of Economics.* 4 vols. London: Macmillan.

El-Hodiri, M. A., and A. Takayama. 1973. "Behavior of the Firm under Regulatory Constraint: Clarifications." *American Economic Review* 63 (March): 235–39.

———. 1981. "Dynamic Behavior of the Firm with Adjustments Costs, under Regulatory Constraint." *Journal of Economic Dynamics and Control* 3 (February): 29-41.

Ferguson, C. E. 1969. *The Neoclassical Theory of Production and Distribution.* New York: Cambridge University Press.

Ferguson, C. E., and T. R. Saving. 1969. "Long-Run Scale Adjustments of a Perfectly Competitive Firm and Industry." *American Economic Review* 59 (December): 774–83.

Friedman, M. 1967. *Price Theory-A Provisional Text.* Rev. ed. Chicago: Aldine.

Greenwald, B. C., and J. E. Stiglitz. 1986. "Externalities in Economies with Imperfect Information and Incomplete Markets."*Quarterly Journal of Economics* 101 (May): 229–64.

Hanoch, G. 1965. "The Backward-bending Supply of Labor." *Journal of Political Economy* 73 (December): 636–42.

Henderson, J. M., and R. E. Quandt. 1980. *Microeconomic Theory: A Mathematical Approach.* 3d ed. New York: McGraw-Hill (1st ed. 1958, 2d ed. 1971).

Hicks, J. R. 1946. *Value and Capital.* 2d ed. Oxford: Clarendon Press (1st ed. 1939).

Hirschleifer, J. 1958. "Peak-Loads and Efficient Pricing: Comment." *Quarterly Journal of Economics* 72 (August): 452–62.

Homma, M. 1980. "Market Failures" (in Japanese). In *Keizaigaku Daijiten* (Great Directory of Economics) I: 247–60, Tokyo: Toyo Keizai Shimposha.

Hotelling, H. 1938. "The General Welfare in Relation to Problems of Taxation and of Railway and Utility Rates." *Econometrica* 6 (July): 242–69. Reprinted in Arrow and Scitovsky (1969), 284–308.

Houthakker, H. S. 1951. "Electricity Tariffs in Theory and Practice." *Economic Journal* 61 (March): 1–25.

———. 1958. "Peak Load and Efficient Pricing: Further Comment." *Quarterly Journal of Economics* 72 (August): 463–64

Ide, T. and A. Takayama. 1987a. "Marginal Cost Pricing and Economies of Scale." *Vandeveer Discussion Paper Series*, no. 87–20.

———. 1987b. "On the Concepts of Returns to Scale." *Economics Letters* 23 (4): 329–34.

———. 1989a. "Returns to Scale under Non- Homotheticity and Homotheticity, and the Shape of Average Costs." *Zeitschrift für die gesamte Staatswissenschaft* 145 (June): 369–88.

———. 1989b. "Factor Prices and the Shape of Average Cost Curves." *Journal of International Economic Integration*, 4, Autumn: 1–7.

Imai, K., H. Uzawa, R. Komiya, T. Negishi, and Y. Murakami. 1971. *Price Theory II* (in Japanese). Tokyo: Iwanami.

Joskow, P. L. 1976. "Contributions of the Theory of Marginal Cost Pricing." *Bell Journal of Economics* 7 (Spring): 195–248.

Kahn, A. E. 1970. *The Economics of Regulation: Principles and Institutions.* 2 vols. New York: Wiley.

Kaldor, N. 1935. "Market Imperfection and Excess Capacity." *Economica* n.s. 2 (February): 33–50.

Killingsworth, M. R. 1983. *Labor Supply.* Cambridge: Cambridge University Press.

Klevorick, A. K. 1966. "Graduated Fair Return: A Regulatory Proposal." *American Economic Review* 59 (June): 477–84.

Knight, F. H. 1921. "Cost of Production and Price over Long and Short Periods." *Journal of Political Economy* 29 (April): 304–35.

Kudoh, K. and S. Yabushita. 1974. "Economic Analysis of Pollution: A Survey" (in Japanese). *Economics Studies Quarterly* 25 (December): 1–31.

Lange, O. 1942. "The Foundations of Welfare Economics." *Econometrica* 10 1987 (July/October): 215–28. Reprinted in Arrow and Scitovsky (1969), 26–38.

Layard, P. R. G., and A. A. Walters. 1978. *Microeconomic Theory.* New York: McGraw-Hill.

Ledyard, J. O. 1987. "Market Failure" In Eatwell, Milgate, and Newman 1987: 326–29.

Littlechild, S. 1970. "Peak-load Pricing of Telephone Calls." *Bell Journal of Economics and Management Science* 1 (Autumn): 191–210.

Meade, J. E. 1952. "External Economies and Diseconomies in a Competitive Situation." *Economic Journal* 62 (March): 54–67. Reprinted in Arrow and Scitovsky 1969, 185–98.

Mishan, E. J. 1964. *Welfare Economics.* New York: Random House.

Mitchell, M., G. Manning, Jr., and J. P. Acton. 1978. *Peak Load Pricing.* Cambridge, Mass.: Ballinger.

Mohring, H. 1970. "The Peak Load Pricing Problem with Increasing Returns and Pricing Constraints." *American Economic Review* 60 (September): 693–705.

Morishima, M. 1952. "Consumer's Behavior and Liquidity Preference." *Econometrica* 20 (April): 223–46.

Mosak, J. D. 1938. "Interrelation of Production Price and Demand." *Journal of Political Economy* 46 (December): 761–87.

Musgrave, R. A. 1959. *The Theory of Public Finance.* New York: McGraw-Hill.

Nagatani, K. 1978. "Substitution and Scale Effects in Factor Demands." *Canadian Journal of Economics* 11 (April): 521–27.

Nelson, J. R., ed. 1964. *Marginal Cost Pricing in Practice.* Englewood Cliffs, N.J.: Prentice-Hall.

Panzar, J. C. 1976. "A Neoclassical Approach to Peak Load Pricing." *Bell Journal of Economics* 7 (Autumn): 521–30.

Panzar, J. C., and R. D. Willig. 1979. "Economies of Scale in Multi-Output Production." *Quarterly Journal of Economics* 91 (August): 481–93.

Pigou, A. C. 1932. *Economics of Welfare.* 4th ed. London: Macmillan.

Portes, R. D. 1971. "Long-Run Scale Adjustments of a Perfectly Competitive Firm and Industry: An Alternative Approach." *American Economic Review* 61 (June): 430–34.

Puu, T. 1971. "Some Comments on 'Inferior' (Regressive) Inputs." *Swedish Journal of Economics* 73 (June): 241–51.

Sakai, Y. 1973. "An Axiomatic Approach to Input Demand Theory." *International Economic Review* 14 (October): 735–52.

Samuelson, P. A. 1947. *Foundation of Economic Analysis.* Cambridge, Mass.: Harvard University Press (enlarged ed. 1983).

Scitovsky, T. 1951. *Welfare and Competition.* Homewood, Ill.: Richard D. Irwin.

———. 1954. "Two Concepts of External Economies." *Journal of Political Economy* 62, April: 643–51.

Scott, J. T. 1979. "Economies of Scale and Profitability of Marginal-Cost Pricing." *Quarterly Journal of Economics* 93 (November): 741–742.

Sen, A. K. 1987. "Social Choice." In Eatwell, Milgate, and Newman 1987, 4: 382–93.

Sherman, R. 1985. "The Averch and Johnson Analysis of Public Regulation Twenty Years Later." *Review of Industrial Organization* 2: 178–94.

Starrett, D. A. 1988. *Foundation of Public Economics.* New York: Cambridge University Press.

Stein, J. L., and G. H. Borts. 1972. "Behavior of the Firm under Regulatory Constraint." *American Economic Review* 62 (December): 964–70.

Steiner, P. O. 1957. "Peak-Loads and Efficient Pricing." *Quarterly Journal of Economics* 71 (November): 585-610.

Stigler, G. J. 1966. *The Theory of Prices.* 3d ed. New York: Macmillan.

Stiglitz, J. E. 1988. *Economics of the Public Sector.* 2d ed. New York: W. W. Norton.

Syrquin, M. 1970. "A Note on Inferior Inputs." *Review of Economic Studies* 37 (October): 591–98.

Takayama, A. 1969. "Behavior of the Firm under Regulatory Constraint." *American Economic Review* 59 (June): 255–60.

———. 1970. "On the Peak-Load Problem." University of Rochester. Manuscript. Revision of "On the Peak-Load Problem." *Krannert Institute Papers*, no. 251 Purdue University, 1969.

———. 1977. "Sensitivity Analysis in Economic Theory." *Metroeconomics* 29 (January-December): 9-37.

———. 1979a. "On the Coase Theorem." Lecture notes, Texas A & M University, July.

———. 1979b. "On Inferior Inputs: An Expository Note." Lecture notes, Texas A & M University, December.

———. 1983. "A Note on Labor Supply." Lecture notes, Southern Illinois University, September (also Purdue University, September 1971).

———. 1984. "Consumer's Surplus, Path Independence, Compensating and Equivalent Variations." *Zeitschrift für die gesamte Staatswissenschaft* 141 (Dezember): 594–625.

———. 1985. *Mathematical Economics.* 2d ed. New York: Cambridge University Press (1st ed. 1974).

———. 1987. "Consumer Surplus." In Eatwell, Milgate, and Newman 1987, 1: 607–13.

———. 1988. "Behavior of the Firm Under Regulatory Constraint: Revisited." Lecture notes, Southern Illinois University, June.

Turvey, R. 1968. "Peak Load Pricing." *Journal of Political Economy* 76 (January/February): 101–113.

Vickery, W. 1987 "Marginal and Average Cost Pricing." In Eatwell, Milgate, and Newman 1987, 3: 311–18.

Viner, J. 1931. "Cost Curves and Supply Curves." *Zeitschrift für Nationalökonomie* 3: 23–46. Reprinted in *Readings in Price Theory*, ed. G. J. Stigler and K. E. Boulding, 198–226, with "Supplementary Note (1950), " 227–32. Homewood, Ill.: Richard D. Irwin, 1952.

Westfield, F. M. 1965. "Conspiracy and Regulation." *American Economic Review* 55 (June): 424–43.

Williamson, O. E. 1966. "Peak-Load Pricing and Optimal Capacity," *American Economic Review* 56 (September): 810–27.

Wiseman, J. 1987. "Peak Load Pricing." In Eatwell, Milgate, and Newman 1987, 3: 822–23.

Zajac, E. E. 1970. "A Geometric Treatment of Averch-Johnson's Behavior of the Firm Model." *American Economic Review* 60 (April): 117–25.

———. 1972. "Lagrangian Multiplier Values at Constrained Optima." *Journal of Economic Theory* 4 (April): 125–31.

Part 3

Economics of Uncertainty

CHAPTER 5

Economics of Uncertainty

The foundation for the economics of uncertainty was laid by von Neumann and Morgenstern (1953). Since the important works by Arrow and Pratt in the 1960s, the topic attracted a great deal of attention in the 1970s and the 1980s, during which many important papers and books were written. Now the topic appears in virtually all microeconomics textbooks. Some useful textbooks on the subject itself, such as Hey (1979), Sakai (1982); and Laffont (1989), are also available.[1]

The major event in such a development is the use of the expected utility hypothesis. Although a number of objections have been raised against this hypothesis, it is still the most popular approach by far. One good reason for such popularity lies in its operationality. Instead of getting too philosophical about uncertainty, we note that this hypothesis provides a simple and yet powerful analytical framework to consider problems involving it. This chapter exposits the gist of the topic, and thus introduces the reader to an important field.

5.1 The Expected Utility Hypothesis

In the usual discussion of the theory of choice, no distinction is made between the act of choice, on the one hand, and its outcome on the other. However, under uncertainty, the act and its outcome depend on external circumstances, which are called **states of nature**, **states**

---

[1]Microeconomics textbooks that contain serious expositions on the topic include: Malinvaud (1977), Green (1978), Layard and Walters (1978), Deaton and Muellbauer (1980), Henderson and Quandt (1980), Varian (1984), Okuno and Suzumura (1985), Cowell (1986), Quirk (1987), Nishimura (1989), Pyndick and Rubinfeld (1989), Silberberg (1990), and Kreps (1990). Textbooks on the economics of uncertainty (and information) include: Borch (1968); Hey (1979); Sakai (1982); Ford (1983); Sinn (1983); McKenna (1986); Hosoe (1987); and Laffont (1989). Useful survey articles on the subject includes: McCall (1971), Hirschleifer and Riley (1979), Lippman and McCall (1981), and Schoemaker (1982). Diamond and Rothchild (1989) collect many important papers on this topic with useful exercises and comments.

of the world, or, simply, **states**. The set of alternatives from which a choice is made is called a **prospect**. Given s states, each prospect is defined by **outcomes**, $x_1, x_2, \ldots, x_s$, and their associated probabilities, $\pi_1, \pi_2, \ldots, \pi_s$, which are viewed as the individual's subjective probabilities.[2] We then write a prospect by $y = (\pi_1, \pi_2, \ldots, \pi_s; x_1, x_2, \ldots, x_s)$ or simply by $y = (\pi; x)$, where $\pi = (\pi_1, \pi_2, \ldots, \pi_s)$ and $x = (x_1, x_2, \ldots, x_s)$. If there are only two outcomes, we denote it simply by $y = (\pi; x_1, x_2)$, which of course means $(\pi, 1 - \pi; x_1, x_2)$. An example of a simple prospect is a bet with a probability of 0.3 of winning \$100 and a probability of 0.7 of losing \$50, that is, of receiving \$−50. This is written as (0.3; 100, −50). A more complex prospect would be the one with given probabilities of $p, p', p'', \ldots$, of receiving the prospects $y, y', y'', \ldots$, that is, $(p, p', p'', \ldots; y, y', y'', \ldots)$, called a **compound prospect** or a **compound lottery**. Here

$$y = (\pi; x),\ y' = (\pi'; x'),\ y'' = (\pi''; x''),\ \ldots,$$

where $\pi = (\pi_1, \pi_2, \ldots, \pi_s)$, $\pi' = (\pi'_1, \pi'_2, \ldots, \pi'_s)$, $\ldots$, $x = (x_1, x_2, \ldots, x_s)$, and $x' = (x'_1, x'_2, \ldots, x'_s)$, $\ldots$.

In the above formulation, we implicitly assumed that the individual can subjectively evaluate the probability that each state of nature occurs. However, we may note, as Frank Knight (1921) argued, that there is a basic distinction between "risk," where probabilities are known or at least knowable, and "uncertainty," where it is not obvious that probabilities can be meaningfully defined. An important example of uncertainty is an entrepreneur's investment decision that is unique and thus not comparable to previous decisions. However, emphasizing the subjective aspect of probability and employing the axiomatic approach, this distinction seems to have become mostly irrelevant (e.g., Savage 1954, and Anscombe and Aumann 1963). Here, therefore, we use "risk" and "uncertainty" interchangeably.

Let Y be the set of all prospects of a particular individual who is facing a certain choice problem. Assume that a binary relation "$\succsim$" can be defined on elements of Y. "$y \succsim y'$" means that y is not worse than y', that is, is a preference ordering. We assume that preference ordering is: (a) **reflexive** (i.e., $y \succsim y$ for all $y \in Y$), and (b) that **transitive** (i.e., $y \succsim y'$ and $y' \succsim y''$ imply $y \succsim y''$ for all $y, y', y'' \in Y$).

We assume that $\succsim$ is **complete**, that is, either $y \succsim y'$ or $y' \succsim y$ for all $y, y' \in Y$. If $y \succsim y'$ and $y' \succsim y$, then the individual is *indifferent* between y and y', which is denoted by $y \sim y'$. If $y \succsim y'$ but not $y' \succsim y$,

[2]To simplify the exposition here, we assume that s is finite and that probability is discrete. These are not essential assumptions and can be removed.

then the individual *prefers* y *to* y', which is denoted by $y \succ y'$. We can easily show (*a*) that $y \sim y'$ and $y' \sim y''$ imply $y \sim y''$, and (*b*) that $y \succ y'$ and $y' \succ y''$ imply $y \succ y''$. Namely, $\sim$ and $\succ$ are transitive. In summary, we impose axiom 5.1.[3]

Axiom 5.1. The individual has a preference ordering defined on Y, which is a complete ordering.

Since we trivially have $(\pi;\ x,\ x) = x$ for any $x \in X$ (where X is the set of outcomes), axiom 5.1 implies that the individual has a preference ordering $\succsim$ on X (the set of all outcomes), which is a complete ordering.

Given this background, von Neumann and Morgenstern imposed further axioms. The first may be stated as axiom 5.2.

Axiom 5.2 (Continuity). For all $y^1,\ y^2,\ y^3 \in Y,\ y^1 \succsim y^2 \succsim y^3$, there exists an $\alpha,\ 0 \leqq \alpha \leqq 1$, such that

$$\alpha y^1 + (1 - \alpha) y^3 \sim y^2. \tag{1}$$

This simply says that if $y^1 \succsim y^2 \succsim y^3$, there exists some probability α of the best of the three prospects and the corresponding probability $(1 - \alpha)$ of the worst of the three prospects that is indifferent to the one in the middle.

The following axiom is concerned with the probability calculation of compound lotteries. Let $L_1 = (\pi_1,\ \pi_2,\ \ldots,\ \pi_s;\ x_1,\ x_2,\ \ldots,\ x_s)$ and $L_2 = (\pi'_1,\ \pi'_2,\ \ldots,\ \pi'_s;\ x_1,\ x_2,\ \ldots,\ x_s)$, or $L_1 = (\pi;\ x)$ and $L_2 = (\pi';\ x)$ in short. Now consider the prospect y obtained from L_1 and L_2,

$$y \equiv (\alpha;\ L_1,\ L_2) = [\alpha;\ (\pi;\ x),\ (\pi';\ x)]. \tag{2}$$

It is a *compound lottery*, in which we begin by drawing between lottery tickets, L_1 and L_2. We now state axiom 5.3.

Axiom 5.3. For any x and $0 \leqq \alpha,\ \pi,\ \pi' \leqq 1$, consider the following compound lottery,

$$y = [\alpha;\ (\pi;\ x),\ (\pi';\ x)].$$

[3]In general, a binary relation $\succsim$ on a certain set Y is called a **partial quasi-ordering**, if it is reflexive and transitive. If either $y \succsim y'$ or $y' \succsim y$ for *all* $y,\ y' \in Y$, it is called **complete** or **total**. If $y \succsim y'$ and $y' \succsim y$ imply $y \sim y'$, it is called simply an **ordering**. The statements in the present paragraph simply make the assumption that a *complete ordering* $\succsim$ is defined on the set of prospects Y.

Then we have

$$y \sim (p;\ x), \quad \text{where } p \equiv \alpha\pi + (1 - \alpha)\pi'. \tag{3}$$

To ease the exposition, here we assume $x = (x_1,\ x_2)$. The probability of receiving x_1 via this compound lottery is

$$\begin{aligned} Pr(x_1) &= Pr(\text{of having ticket } L_1) \cdot Pr(x_1 | L_1) \\ &\qquad + Pr(\text{of having ticket } L_2) \cdot Pr(x_1 | L_2) \\ &= \alpha\pi + (1 - \alpha)\pi' \ (\equiv p), \end{aligned}$$

where $Pr(x_1|L_1)$, for example, reads as the probability of receiving x_1 given that one has ticket L_1. Similarly, the probability of receiving x_2 is given by

$$Pr(x_2) = \alpha(1 - \pi) + (1 - \alpha)(1 - \pi'),$$

so that $Pr(x_1) + Pr(x_2) = 1$. The above rule of computation simply states that the individual is indifferent between compound lottery y and simple lottery $y' \equiv (p;\ x_1,\ x_2)$, where $p \equiv \alpha\pi + (1 - \alpha)\pi'$. The two equivalent lotteries y and y' are illustrated in figure 5.1.

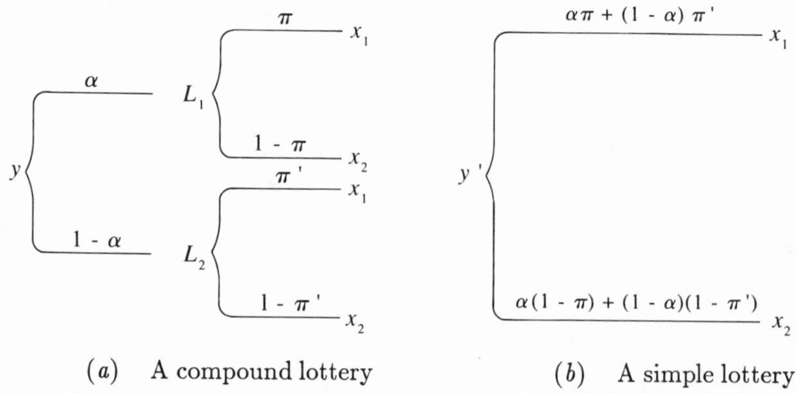

Figure 5.1: The decomposition of a compound lottery into a simple lottery

The essence of axiom 5.3 is that we can find a simple lottery that is indifferent to a compound lottery by simply following the usual probability rule. Then axiom 5.3 states more than what (3) may appear to indicate. For example, we may easily assert the following equivalence relation by way of the usual rule of probability calculation.

$$y \equiv [\alpha;\ x_2,\ (\pi;\ x_1,\ x_2)] \sim [(1 - \alpha)\pi;\ x_1,\ x_2]. \tag{4}$$

To see this, note that

$$Pr(x_1) = Pr(\pi;\ x_1,\ x_2) \cdot Pr[x_1|(\pi;\ x_1,\ x_2)] = (1 - \alpha)\pi,$$

and similarly,

$$Pr(x_2) = \alpha + (1 - \alpha)(1 - \pi) = 1 - (1 - \alpha)\pi.$$

Axiom 5.3 precludes the possibility that one can obtain a certain utility possibility from the process of reaching outcomes, though many enjoy such processes (e.g., horse races, pachinko and slot machines). An objection to axiom 5.3 using a slot machine example is raised by Alchian (1953). Axiom 5.3 means "no fun in gambling." Although this axiom may look unrealistic and dry, it enables us to avoid the question of how to measure the "fun" in the process involved in gambling, which can be arbitrary and *ad hoc*.

The axiom 5.4 runs as follows.

Axiom 5.4 (Independence).

(i) For all y^1, $y^2 \in Y$, $y^1 \succ y^2$, there exists an α, $0 < \alpha < 1$, such that

$$\alpha y^1 + (1 - \alpha)y \succ \alpha y^2 + (1 - \alpha)y, \quad \text{for any } y \in Y. \tag{5}$$

(ii) For all y^1, $y^2 \in Y$, $y^1 \sim y^2$, there exists an α, $0 < \alpha < 1$, such that

$$\alpha y^1 + (1 - \alpha)y \sim \alpha y^2 + (1 - \alpha)y, \quad \text{for any } y \in Y. \tag{6}$$

Statement (i) says the following. Assume that the individual prefers y^1 to y^2 and that y is any prospect whatever. If the lottery ticket L_1 offers outcomes y^1 and y with probabilities α and $(1 - \alpha)$, respectively, and another lottery ticket L_2 offers the outcomes y^2 and y with the same probabilities α and $(1 - \alpha)$, the individual will prefer L_1 to L_2. Namely, if $L_1 = (\alpha; y^1, y)$, $L_2 = (\alpha; y^2, y)$, and $y^1 \succ y^2$, then $L_1 \succ L_2$ for any $y \in Y$ and α with $0 < \alpha < 1$. Statement (ii) says that if the individual is indifferent between y^1 and y^2, then he or she will also be indifferent between L_1 and L_2.

Note that the following property, called the **monotonicity property**, can be obtained from the preceding axioms, including statement (i) of axiom 5.4 (the independence axiom).

Monotonicity. Let $x_1, x_2 \in X$ such that $x_1 \succsim x_2$, and let $0 < \pi, \pi' < 1$. Then we have:

(i) $\pi > \pi' \iff (\pi; x_1, x_2) \succ (\pi'; x_1, x_2)$, and

(ii) $\pi = \pi' \iff (\pi; x_1, x_2) \sim (\pi'; x_1, x_2)$.

Assume that the individual prefers x_1 to x_2, and let $y = (\pi; x_1, x_2)$ and $y' = (\pi'; x_1, x_2)$. Then the monotonicity property asserts that the individual prefers y to y' if and only if $\pi > \pi'$.[4]

We are now ready to state the major theorem in this chapter.

Theorem 5.1 (von Neumann–Morgenstern). Under the preceding set of axioms, there exists a real-valued function u defined on Y such that

(i) $y^1 \succ y^2$ if and only if $u(y^1) > u(y^2)$.

(ii) For any $x_1, x_2, \ldots, x_s \in X$, $0 \leqq \pi_i \leqq 1$, $i = 1, 2, \ldots, s$, and $\sum_{i=1}^{s} \pi_i = 1$,

$$u(\pi_1, \ldots, \pi_s; x_1, \ldots, x_s) = \pi_1 u(x_1) + \pi_2 u(x_2) + \ldots + \pi_s u(x_s). \quad (7)$$

---

[4]Let $x_1 \succ x_2$ and $1 > \pi > \pi' > 0$. Then by the independence axiom (axiom 5.4),

$$(\pi; x_1, x_2) \succ (\pi; x_1, x_2) = x_2.$$

But since $0 < \pi'/\pi < 1$, we obtain the following relation from the above by using axiom 5.4 again.

$$[1 - \pi'/\pi; (\pi; x_1, x_2), (\pi; x_1, x_2)] \succ [1 - \pi'/\pi; x_2, (\pi; x_1, x_2)].$$

Let y^1 and y^2, respectively, denote the left-hand side and right-hand side of this relation. By axiom 5.3, we can observe that

Proof. To ease the exposition, we assume $s = 2$, or $x = (x_1, x_2)$. Choose b, $w \in Y$ in such a way that $b \succsim y$ for all $y \in Y$ and $y' \succsim w$ for all $y' \in Y$.[5] If $b \sim w$, the proof is trivial, so assume $b \succ w$. Let $y \equiv (\pi; x_1, x_2) \in Y$, where x_1, $x_2 \in X$, and $0 \leqq \pi \leqq 1$. By the continuity axiom (axiom 5.2), there exists π_1 and π_2, $0 \leqq \pi_1, \pi_2 \leqq 1$, such that

$$x_1 \sim (\pi_1; b, w) \text{ and } x_2 \sim (\pi_2; b, w).$$

By statement (ii) the independence axiom (axiom 5.4), we obtain

$$(\pi; x_1, x_2) \sim [\pi; (\pi_1; b, w), (\pi_2; b, w)].$$

Using axiom 5.3, we obtain

$$[\pi; (\pi_1; b, w), (\pi_2; b, w)] \sim (p; b, w),$$

where $p \equiv \pi\pi_1 + (1 - \pi)\pi_2$. Then by the transitivity property in axiom 5.1, we have

$$y \equiv (\pi; x_1, x_2) \sim (p; b, w).$$

Let $y' \equiv (\pi'; x_1', x_2') \in Y$, where x_1', $x_2' \in X$, and $0 \leqq \pi' \leqq 1$. Repeating the same argument as above, we may obtain

$$y' \equiv (\pi'; x_1', x_2') \sim (p'; b, w),$$

$$Pr(x_1) = (1 - \pi'/\pi)\pi + (\pi'/\pi)\pi = \pi, \text{ and}$$

$$Pr(x_2) = (1 - \pi'/\pi)(1 - \pi) + (\pi'/\pi)(1 - \pi) = (1 - \pi).$$

Hence $y^1 \sim (\pi; x_1, x_2)$. For y^2, observe

$$Pr(x_1) = Pr(\pi; x_1, x_2) \cdot Pr[x_1|(\pi; x_1, x_2)] = (\pi'/\pi) \cdot \pi = \pi', \text{ and}$$

$$Pr(x_2) = (1 - \pi'/\pi) + (\pi'/\pi) \cdot (1 - \pi) = \pi'.$$

Thus we have $y^2 \sim (\pi'; x_1, x_2)$. Since $\sim$ is transitive by axiom 5.1, we obtain

$$(\pi; x_1, x_2) \succ (\pi'; x_1, x_2).$$

It is easy to show that this relation implies $\pi > \pi'$. This proves statement (i) of the monotonicity property. By switching π and π', we may obtain

$$\pi' > \pi \Longleftrightarrow (\pi'; x_1, x_2) \succ (\pi; x_1, x_2).$$

Statement (ii) of the monotonicity property follows from this.

[5]Here, b and w, respectively, signify the "best" and the "worst" outcomes.

where $p' \equiv \pi'\pi_1' + (1 - \pi')\pi_2'$, $0 \leqq \pi', \pi_1', \pi_2' \leqq 1$.

But by monotonicity, we have

$$(p;\ b,\ w) \succsim (p';\ b,\ w) \text{ if and only if } p \geqq p'.$$

Hence by the transitivity property of $\succsim$, we obtain

$$y \succsim y' \text{ if and only if } p \geqq p'.$$

Therefore, it suffices to obtain u such that

$$E[u(y)] \geqq E[u(y')] \text{ if and only if } p \geqq p'. \tag{8}$$

For certain outcomes, we let

$$u(w) = 0,\ u(b) = 1,$$

$$u(x_1) = \pi_1,\ u(x_2) = \pi_2,\ u(x_1') = \pi_1',\ u(x_2') = \pi_2'.$$

Then we have

$$E[u(y)] = \pi u(x_1) + (1 - \pi)u(x_2) = \pi\pi_1 + (1 - \pi)\pi_2 = p.$$

Similarly, we obtain

$$E[u(y')] = p'.$$

This proves (8) for $s = 2$. The above proof can readily be extended for $s > 2$. (QED)

We call the utility function obtained in theorem 5.1 a **von Neumann-Morgenstern utility function**, or simply a **NM** (or **vNM**) **utility function** or even more simply a **utility function**. The corollary to theorem 5.1 is that a "rational" individual chooses among different prospects so as to maximize the expected utility,

$$\sum_{i=1}^{s} \pi_i u_i(x_i),$$

and theorem 5.1 is known as the **expected utility theorem**. The proof of theorem 5.1 is explained in many expositions on uncertainty.[6] The preceding proof follows Bacharach (1977, pp. 26–28). Properties (i) and (ii) of theorem 5.1 are, respectively, called the **order preserving** and the **linearity properties**. These two properties combined are called the **expected utility property**.

The converse of theorem 5.1 also holds. Namely, we can easily show that if there exists a utility function u that satisfies properties (i) and (ii) of theorem 5.1, then it satisfies axioms 5.1–5.4. To illustrate this, we may show that statements (i) and (ii) imply axiom 5.3, where for simplicity we assume $s = 2$, or $x = (x_1, x_2)$. To show this, we first observe the following relation, for any $x_1, x_2 \in X$ and $0 \leqq \alpha, \pi\ \pi' \leqq 1$:

$$\begin{aligned} & u[\alpha; (\pi; x_1, x_2), (\pi'; x_1, x_2)] \\ & \quad = \alpha u(\pi; x_1, x_2) + (1 - \alpha) u(\pi'; x_1, x_2) \\ & \quad = \alpha\{\pi u(x_1) + (1 - \pi) u(x_2)\} \\ & \qquad\qquad + (1 - \alpha)\{\pi' u(x_1) + (1 - \pi') u(x_2)\} \\ & \quad = \{\alpha\pi + (1 - \alpha)\pi'\} u(x_1) \\ & \qquad\qquad + \{\alpha(1 - \pi) + (1 - \alpha)(1 - \pi')\} u(x_2) \\ & \quad = u[\alpha\pi + (1 - \alpha)\pi'; x_1, x_2]. \end{aligned}$$

By statement (i), this means that

$$[\alpha; (\pi; x_1, x_2), (\pi'; x_1, x_2)] \sim [\alpha\pi + (1 - \alpha)\pi'; x_1, x_2].$$

Similarly, we can obtain the other axioms from statements (i) and (ii) of theorem 5.1.

REMARK: Theorem 5.1 does not imply that an individual is consciously aware of his or her utility function. Theorem 5.1 simply states that given the four axioms, the individual behaves as though he or she were a maximizer of expected values of utility.

---

[6] The original proof is in von Neumann and Morgenstern (1953, sec. 3 and the appendix) who formulated the theorem, presented the axioms, and proved the theorem. There have been a number of attempts to extend or modify the standard theorems. There are also many textbook expositions of the theorem. Luce and Raiffa (1957) contains a very useful discussion of this theorem. For brief, succinct expositions of expected utility theory and related topics, see Hammond (1987), Machina (1987), and Machina and Rothchild (1987), for example.

It is easy to show that if $u(y)$ is a NM utility function, so is $v(y) \equiv a \cdot u(y) + b$, where a and b are any real numbers with $a > 0$. To show this, first observe that for any $y,\ y' \in Y$,

$$\begin{aligned} y \succ y' &\iff u(y) > u(y') \\ &\iff au(y) + b > au(y') + b \\ &\iff v(y) > v(y'). \end{aligned}$$

Namely, $v(y)$ also has the order-preserving property. Also observe

$$\begin{aligned} v(\alpha;\ y,\ y') &= au(\alpha;\ y,\ y') + b \\ &= a[\alpha u(y) + (1 - \alpha)u(y')] + b \\ &\equiv \alpha v(y) + (1 - \alpha)v(y'). \end{aligned}$$

Hence $v(y)$ has the linearity property.

The converse of the above statement is also true. Namely, if $u(x)$ is a NM utility function, then any monotonic transformation of u that has the expected utility property must be a linear (affine) transformation.[7] To show this, let $\phi(u)$ be a monotone transformation of u that has the expected utility property; that is, the order-preserving property,

$$u(y) > u(y') \text{ if and only if } \phi[u(y)] > \phi[u(y')],$$

and the linearity property,

---

[7]It may be useful to recall the definition of a "linear affine" transformation. Let $f(x)$ be a real-valued function defined on a convex set X. Then $f(x)$ is **linear affine** or simply **affine**, if it is both concave *and* convex, i.e.,

$$f[\theta x + (1 - \theta)x'] = \theta f(x) + (1 - \theta)f(x'),\ 0 \leqq \theta \leqq 1,$$

for any $x,\ x' \in X$. Equivalently, f is linear affine if and only if $f(x) - f(0)$ is **linear**, i.e., $f(x + x') = f(x) + f(x')$ for all $x,\ x' \in X$ and $f(\alpha x) = \alpha f(x)$ for $\alpha \in R$, and $x \in X$. For example, if $X = R$, a, $b \in R$, and $b \neq 0$ then $f(x) \equiv ax + b$ is a linear affine function, and $f^*(x) \equiv ax$ is a linear function. Thus, a linear function is a special class of linear affine functions. However, linear affine functions are often simply called "linear functions" in the literature. If we want to be strict about the distinction between the two, then "linear programming" should be called "linear affine programming," for example, but such would be rather pedantic.

$$\phi\{u[\alpha y + (1 - \alpha)y']\} = \alpha\phi[u(y)] + (1 - \alpha)\phi[u(y')], \quad 0 \leqq \alpha \leqq 1.$$

Since u also has the linearity property, the left-hand side of this equation is rewritten to yield

$$\phi[\alpha u(y) + (1 - \alpha)u(y')] = \alpha\phi[u(y)] + (1 - \alpha)\phi[u(y')], \quad 0 \leqq \alpha \leqq 1.$$

This is nothing but the definition of a linear (affine) transformation.

Corollary. The NM utility function is unique up to a linear (affine) transformation.

REMARK: This means the NM utility function is *cardinal* in the sense that it is unique up to a linear (affine) transformation. This is analogous to the statement that Fahrenheit temperatures (F) are a linear (affine) transformation of Centigrade temperatures (C) where we have $F = (9/5)C + 32$. Also, given that u is fixed, the difference in the NM utility function has an important implication. For example, if $u(y) = 50$, $u(y') = 20$, and $u(y'') = 0$, $u(y) - u(y') = 30 > 10 = u(y') - u(y'')$. Thus the utility increment between y' and y is greater than that between y' and y''. However, we cannot say that the former is three times larger than the latter. This is because taking $v(\cdot) = au(\cdot) + b$, we have:

$$\frac{u(y) - u(y')}{u(y') - u(y'')} = 3, \quad \frac{v(y) - v(y')}{v(y') - v(y'')} = 3a,$$

where a can be any positive number. Hence the cardinality here is not like that of, say, weight and length. The situation is similar to temperature: we cannot say that 80° Fahrenheit is four times warmer than 20° Fahrenheit, since if we convert 80° and 20° into the Centigrade scales, we cannot say the same thing.

Needless to say, the plausibility of the expected utility hypothesis depends on the validity of the four axioms that we stated above. Hence it is important to understand their meaning. Axioms 5.1 and 5.3 are usually taken as acceptable. An important objection is raised against axiom 5.2, the continuity axiom. To understand such an objection note that axiom 5.2 implies that, for $y^1 \succ y^2 \succ y^3$, there exists an $\alpha \in (0, 1)$ such that

$$\alpha y^1 + (1 - \alpha)y^3 \sim y^2.$$

Now consider an example of $x_1 = \$100$, $x_2 = \$1$, and $x_3 =$ being shot to death, where we may assume $x_1 \succ x_2 \succ x_3$. Can we say that there exists an $\alpha \in (0, 1)$ such that

$$\alpha x_1 + (1 - \alpha)x_3 \sim x_2?$$

It would be hard to imagine any person who would accept a positive probability in which he or she can be shot to death for the sake of \$1. This line of objection was raised by Alchian (1953). Although he has a point in this objection, many argue that we need not worry about this, since we are not interested in such extreme situations. We are interested in axioms that would explain human behavior under certain "normal" circumstances in which the x_i''s are bounded. Alternatively, one can avoid this problem by simply deleting such elements as x_3 from the outcome set X. Then, the problem does not arise by the definition of X.

The most serious objection is raised against axiom 5.4, the independence axiom.[8] To understand such an objection, recall that statement (i) of axiom 5.4 states that, for any y^1, $y^2 \in Y$ such that $y^1 \succ y^2$, we have

$$(\alpha;\ y^1,\ y) \succ (\alpha;\ y^2,\ y), \quad \text{for all } y \in Y \text{ and } 0 < \alpha < 1.$$

This means that the possibility of y does *not affect* the preference ordering between y^1 and y^2. Thus, if we can show that there exists a $y \in Y$ such that

$$(\alpha;\ y^2,\ y) \succ (\alpha;\ y^1,\ y), \quad \text{for some } \alpha,\ 0 < \alpha < 1.$$

then axiom 5.4 breaks down. One may then argue that we can find some such examples.

For example, consider y^1 and y^2 defined by

$$y^1 = (1;\ 3{,}000,\ 0),\ y^2 = (4/5;\ 4{,}000,\ 0).$$

[8] As mentioned earlier, expected utility theory is the most popular theory in the economics of uncertainty. It is thus important to understand this theory without losing sight of the criticisms of the available alternatives. Khaneman and Tversky (1979) present some experimental evidence that contradicts the expected utility model. Machina (1982) presents a synthesis of the literature and a more general theory than the von Neumann-Morgenstern theory in which he attempts to construct the expected utility analysis without the independence axiom (axiom 5.4). See also Loomes and Sugden (1982 and 1983), for a "regret theory." It is purportedly simpler than Khaneman and Tversky's (1982) "prospect theory." See also Machina (1987 and 1989).

Here, y^1 signifies the lottery ticket that assures \$3,000 with probability one, and y^2 signifies the ticket that assures \$4,000 with 80% probability. Suppose that the individual prefers y^1 to y^2, that is, $y^1 \succ y^2$. Let $y = (1;\ 0,\ 0)$. Then it will no become longer clear whether we can say,

$$(\alpha;\ y^1,\ y) \succ (\alpha;\ y^2,\ y), \quad \text{for all } \alpha,\ 0 < \alpha < 1.$$

For example, let $\alpha = 1/4$, i.e., $y^3 \equiv (1/4;\ y^1,\ y)$ and $y^4 \equiv (1/4;\ y^2,\ y)$. Then we can easily show

$$y^3 = (1/4;\ 3,000,\ 0) \ \text{ and } \ y^4 = (1/5;\ 4,000,\ 0).$$

The individual may then prefer y^4 to y^3, contradicting the independence axiom. Here, y^3 is obtained by reducing the probability of receiving \$3,000 from 100 percent to 25 percent, while y^4 is obtained by reducing the probability of receiving \$4,000 from 80 percent to 20 percent. Namely, when the \$3,000 is no longer certain, the individual may choose the other ticket. In short, the individual can attach a certain premium to the ticket that promises a prize with probability 1. This is the essence of what is known as **Allais's paradox**. The independence axiom precludes the possibility of such a premium for certainty.

If axiom 5.4 breaks down, then the expected utility hypothesis can also break down. Since $y^1 \succ y^2$, we may write this in the expected utility form as

$$u(y^1) = 1 \cdot u(3,000) + 0 \cdot u(0) > (4/5) \cdot u(4,000) + 0 \cdot u(0).$$

Without a loss of generality we may set $u(0) = 0$. This then means $u(3,000) > (4/5)u(4,000)$. Similarly, we may write $y^4 \succ y^3$ as

$$\begin{aligned} u(y^4) &= (1/5)u(4,000) + (4/5)u(0) \\ &> (1/4)u(3,000) + (3/4)u(0) = u(y^3), \end{aligned}$$

which means $(1/5)u(4,000) > (1/4)u(3,000)$. This contradicts $u(3,000) > (4/5)u(4,000)$.

Still another example that contradicts the independence axiom may be stated as follows. Consider y^1 and y^2 which are specified by

$$y^1 = (0.9;\ 30,000,\ 0),\ y^2 = (0.45;\ 60,000,\ 0),$$

and assume $y^1 \succ y^2$. Next consider

$$y^3 = (0.02;\ 30,000,\ 0),\ y^4 = (0.01;\ 60,000,\ 0),$$

where the 30,000 and 60,000 signify receiving \$30,000 and \$60,000. Note that the expected value of y^1 is equal to that of y^2, since

$$0.9 \cdot 30,000 = 27,000 = 0.45 \cdot 60,000,$$

and that the expected value of y^3 is equal to that of y^4 since

$$0.02 \cdot 30,000 = 60 = 0.01 \cdot 60,000.$$

Let $y = (1;\ 0,\ 0)$, and note that

$$\begin{aligned} y^3 &\equiv (0.02;\ 30,000,\ 0) \\ &= [1/450;\ (0.9;\ 30,000,\ 0)] = (1/450;\ y^1,\ 0), \text{ and} \end{aligned}$$

$$\begin{aligned} y^4 &\equiv (0.01;\ 60,000,\ 0) \\ &= [1/450;\ (0.45;\ 60,000,\ 0)] = (1/450;\ y^2,\ 0). \end{aligned}$$

By the independence axiom, $y^1 \succ y^2$ must imply $y^3 \succ y^4$. However, our individual may prefer y^4 to y^3. This is because the probability of receiving \$30,000 is only 2 percent in y^3, the probability of receiving \$60,000 is 1 percent in y^4, and the individual may prefer a larger amount of prize money when the probability of receiving it is very small. This may be called the **get-rich-quick effect.**[9]

The expected utility hypothesis will also break down in this case. To see this, express $y^1 \succ y^2$ and $y^4 \succ y^3$ in terms of expected utility as

$$u(y^1) = 0.9 \cdot u(30,000) > (0.45) \cdot u(60,000) = u(y^2),$$

$$u(y^4) = 0.01 \cdot u(60,000) > (0.02) \cdot u(30,000) = u(y^3),$$

where we set $u(0) = 0$. The first relation states $u(30,000)/u(60,000) > 0.5$, and the second relation states $u(30,000)/u(60,000) < 0.5$. These two inequalities clearly contradict each other.

---

[9]The examples and discussions of Allais's objection and the get-rich-quick effect follow Sakai (1982, pp. 74–78), which in turn follows Khaneman and Tversky (1979), and others. Maurice Allais was the 1988 Nobel laureate in Economic Science. The term *get-rich-quick effect* is from Sakai (1982).

5.2 Expected Utility and Behavior toward Risk

5.2.1 Behavior toward Risk

Let $y = (\pi_1, \pi_2, \ldots, \pi_s; x_1, x_2, \ldots, x_s)$ be a lottery with cash payoffs $x_1, x_2, \ldots, x_s$. The expected value of y can be computed as

$$E(y) = \pi_1 x_1 + \pi_2 x_2 + \ldots + \pi_s x_s.$$

An individual is said to be **risk neutral** if the utility of the expected value of the lottery equals the expected utility of the lottery, that is, if

$$u(\pi_1 x_1 + \pi_2 x_2 + \ldots + \pi_s x_s) = \pi_1 u(x_1) + \pi_2 u(x_2) + \ldots + \pi_s u(x_s), \quad (9)$$

where it is assumed that u is strictly monotone increasing. If the individual is risk neutral toward all prospects, he or she has a linear utility function $u = \alpha_1 x_1 + \alpha_2 x_2 + \ldots + \alpha_s x_s + c$, where $\alpha_i > 0$ for all i.

An individual is said to be **risk averse** if his or her NM utility function is strictly concave, that is, if

$$u(\pi_1 x_1 + \pi_2 x_2 + \ldots + \pi_s x_s) > \pi_1 u(x_1) + \pi_2 u(x_2) + \ldots + \pi_s u(x_s), \quad (10)$$

for $x_1, x_2, \ldots, x_s \in X$ and $0 < \pi_i < 1$, $i = 1, 2, \ldots, s$. Since $u(x)$ is strictly concave if $u''(x) \equiv d^2u/dx^2 < 0$, the individual is risk averse if $u''(x) < 0$.

Similarly, the individual is said to be a **risk lover** if his or her NM utility function is strictly convex. Since $u(x)$ is strictly convex if $u''(x) > 0$, the individual is a risk lover if $u''(x) > 0$. Although it may be possible to argue that $u''(x) < 0$ for some x and $u''(x') > 0$ for some other x' (i.e., the individual is a risk averter for some x and a risk lover for some other x': see Friedman and Savage 1948), we rule out such a possibility throughout this chapter.

Recall also that if $u''(x) < 0$ for all x, then u is strictly concave, but the converse does not necessarily hold, since $u''(x)$ can be zero for some x for a strictly concave u. However, barring the possibility of $u''(x) = 0$, u is strictly concave for all x (i.e., an individual is always risk averse) if and only if $u''(x) < 0$ for all x. Similarly, one may also say that an individual is a risk lover if and only if $u''(x) > 0$ for all x, assuming $u''(x) \neq 0$.

The NM utility function of a risk averter is illustrated in figure 5.2a. The expected value of prospect $y = (\pi;\ x_1,\ x_2)$ is given by $\pi x_1 + (1 - \pi)x_2$. It is measured by OA in figure 5.2a. Expected utility, $\pi u(x_1) + (1 - \pi)u(x_2)$, is measured by AB, and the utility of expected assets, $u[\pi x_1 + (1 - \pi)x_2]$, is given by AC. That point C lies above point B signifies that our individual is risk averse. Indeed, for all strictly concave functions, the function of the expectation is greater than the expectation of the function (sometimes called **Jensen's inequality**), that is,

$$u[\pi x_1 + (1 - \pi)x_2] > \pi u(x_1) + (1 - \pi)u(x_2), \tag{11}$$

for $0 < \pi < 1$ and $x_1 \neq x_2$. Thus, any individual with a strictly

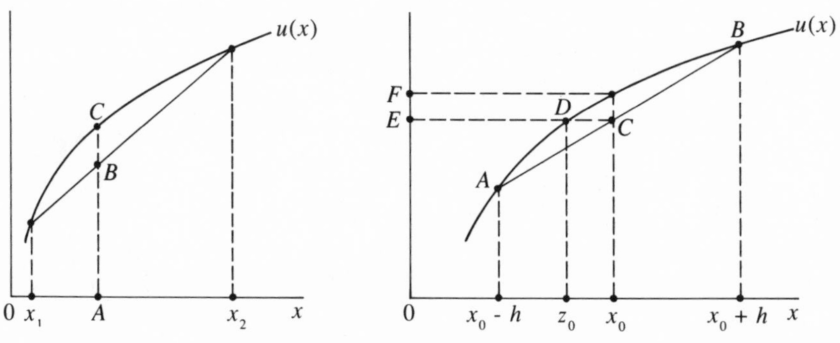

(a) Strictly concave, risk averse utility (b) Risk premium

Figure 5.2: Strictly concave utility function and risk premium

concave utility function will prefer the certainty of the expectation of a random variable to the uncertain prospect itself.

To obtain a further understanding of the last point, suppose that our individual faces the following alternatives:

(i) $\$(x_o + h)$ with probability 1/2 and $\$(x_o - h)$ with probability 1/2, where $0 < h < x_o$.

(ii) $\$x_o$ with probability 1.

The risk averse individual prefers alternative (ii) to alternative (i), that is,

$$0.5u(x_\circ + h) + 0.5u(x_\circ - h) < u(x_\circ). \tag{12}$$

The strict concavity of u means that the arc connecting $(x_\circ - h)$ and $(x_\circ + h)$ is above the cord connecting these two points. In figure 5.2*b*, the arc ADB is above the cord ACB, and $OF > OE$, where $OE = 0.5u(x_\circ + h) + 0.5u(x_\circ - h)$. Assuming that u is twice continuously differentiable, strictly concave, and increasing, there exists a unique $z_\circ(< x_\circ)$ such that

$$0.5u(x_\circ + h) + 0.5u(x_\circ - h) = u(z_\circ). \tag{13}$$

The value $z_\circ$ is called the **certainty equivalent** of the stochastic variable $x_\circ$ indicated by alternative (i). Define ρ by

$$z_\circ = x_\circ - \rho. \tag{14}$$

It is easy to see that $\rho > 0$ if the individual is risk averse, and that $\rho < 0$ if he or she is a risk lover. Assuming that he or she is risk averse, $\rho > 0$, and such a ρ is called the **risk premium**. Namely the risk premium is the maximum amount that the (risk-averse) individual is willing to pay to have the sure return rather than the expected return from the uncertain prospect. In figure 5.2*b*, ρ is equal to the length of the line segment DC. Clearly, ρ depends on $x_\circ$ and h, so that we may write $\rho = \rho(x_\circ, h)$.

5.2.2 Arrow-Pratt Measures of Risk Aversion

Often it becomes useful to compare the degree of risk aversion between different utility functions. Here we exposit important concepts and results in this connection.

From the definition of risk premium $\pi(x_\circ, h)$, we have the following identity:

$$u[x - \rho(x, h)] \equiv 0.5u(x + h) + 0.5u(x - h).$$

Performing a Taylor expansion for each of the three terms of this identity, we obtain

$$u[x - \rho(x, h)] \cong u(x) - \rho(x, h)u'(x),$$

$$u(x + h) \cong u(x) + hu'(x) + (h^2/2)u''(x), \text{ and}$$

$$u(x - h) \cong u(x) - hu'(x) + (h^2/2)u''(x).$$

Substituting these into the identity, we obtain

$$u(x) - \rho(x,\ h)u'(x) \cong u(x) + (h^2/2)u''(x),\ \text{i.e.,}$$

$$\rho(x,\ h) \cong -(h^2/2)[u''(x)/u'(x)].$$

Then defining $R_a(x)$ by

$$R_a(x) \equiv -u''(x)/u'(x), \tag{15}$$

we obtain

$$R_a(x) \cong 2\rho(x,\ h)/h^2. \tag{15'}$$

Let $u_i(x)$, $i = 1, 2$, be two different NM utility functions. Then from (15′), we may obtain, for a sufficiently small h,

$$R_{a1}(x) > R_{a2}(x) \ \text{ if and only if } \ \rho_1(x,\ h) > \rho_2(x,\ h),$$

where $R_{ai}(x)$ and $\rho_i(x,\ h)$, respectively, are the value of $R_a(x)$ and the risk premium for $u_i(x)$, $i = 1, 2$. $R_a(x)$ was introduced by Pratt (1964) and Arrow (1965), and it is called the **Arrow-Pratt measure of absolute risk aversion** or the **coefficient of absolute risk aversion.** In contrast to $R_a(x)$, the following measure of risk aversion was also introduced by Pratt (1964) and Arrow (1965):

$$R_r(x) \equiv -xu''(x)/u'(x) = x \cdot R_a(x). \tag{16}$$

$R_r(x)$ is called the **Arrow-Pratt measure of relative risk aversion** or the **coefficient of relative risk aversion.**

The monotone relation between $R_a(x)$ and $\rho(x,\ h)$ for a sufficiently small h indicated above holds **globally**. Namely, we have the following result.

Theorem 5.2 (Pratt 1964). Given two utility functions u_1 and u_2 that are twice continuously differentiable, monotone increasing, and strictly concave, the following conditions are equivalent:

(a) $R_{a1}(x) > R_{a2}(x)$,

(b) $\rho_1(x,\ h) > \rho_2(x,\ h)$, for *all* h, and

(c) u_1 is "more concave" than u_2, that is, there exists a monotone increasing, strictly concave function ϕ such that $u_1(x) = \phi[u_2(x)]$.

The proof of this theorem can be found in Pratt (1964). An alternative proof by Vernon Smith for the equivalence between (a) and (c) is provided in Kihlstrom and Mirman (1974, pp. 364–65).[10]

The coefficients of absolute and relative risk aversion are dependent only on the shape of the utility function $u(x)$, and they are directly related to the risk premium. Furthermore, they are independent of a linear transformation of u. Namely, if $u_2(x) = au_1(x) + b$, $a > 0$, then $R_{a2}(x) = R_{a1}(x)$, and $R_{r2}(x) = R_{r1}(x)$. This property is important since the NM utility function is unique only up to a linear transformation.[11] We illustrate these two measures of risk aversion by Pratt and Arrow in figure 5.3a, where OA measures x_o so that $CA = u'(x_o)$. Note that

$$R_a(x_o) \equiv -\frac{u''(x_o)}{u'(x_o)} \equiv \frac{CA/AB}{CA} = \frac{1}{AB},$$

$$R_r(x) \equiv -x_o \frac{u''(x_o)}{u'(x_o)} = \frac{OA}{AB}.$$

In figure 5.3b, $u_2(x) = au_1(x) + b$, $a > 0$. Since $u_2' = au_1'$, and $u_2'' = au_1''$, we have $C'A/AB = a \cdot (CA/AB)$, and the following relations.[12]

---

[10] Since $u_1' > 0$ and $u_2' > 0$, it readily follows that there exists a ϕ such that $u_1 = \phi(u_2)$ with $\phi' > 0$. Differentiating this, we obtain $u_1' = \phi' u_2'$ so that $u_1'' = \phi''(u_2')^2 + \phi' u_2''$. From this we can easily show $\phi'' = (R_{a1} - R_{a2})u_1'/(u_2')^2$ by utilizing $\phi' = u_1'/u_2'$ and the definition of R_a.

[11] Let a real-valued function $M_u(x)$ denote the *measure of risk aversion* associated with utility function u. Since $u(x)$ and $v(x) \equiv au(x) + c$, must yield the same measure, we must have $M_u(x) = M_v(x)$. Thus, we have simply asserted here that both $R_a(x)$ and $R_r(x)$ satisfy such a property of M. Also, we may impose the following properties for function $M_u(x)$:

(a) M_u is positive for risk *aversion*, i.e., $M_u(x) > 0$, if and only if $u''(x) < 0$. When $u''(x_o) = 0$ for some x_o, $M_u(x_o) = 0$, and vice versa.

(b) M is monotonically related to the magnitude of u''. Namely, for any utility functions $u(x)$ and $v(x)$, if $u'(x_o) = v'(x_o)$ and $u''(x_o) < v''(x_o)$, then $M_u(x_o) > M_v(x_o)$.

Clearly, both $R_a(x)$ and $R_r(x)$ satisfy these properties.

[12] In fig. 5.3a and 5.3b, it is assumed that $u'(x)$ is strictly convex, or $u'''(x) > 0$ for all x. As we shall discuss shortly, this is a necessary condition for having *decreasing absolute risk aversion*, $R_a'(x) < 0$, which is often considered a key assumption to be

$$R_{a1}(x_\circ) = \frac{CA/AB}{CA} = \frac{1}{AB} = \frac{C'A/AB}{C'A} = R_{a2}(x_\circ);$$

$$R_{r1}(x_\circ) = OA/AB = R_{r2}(x_\circ).$$

Namely, $R_a(x)$ and $R_r(x)$ are invariant under a linear transformation, $u_2(x) = au_1(x) + b$.

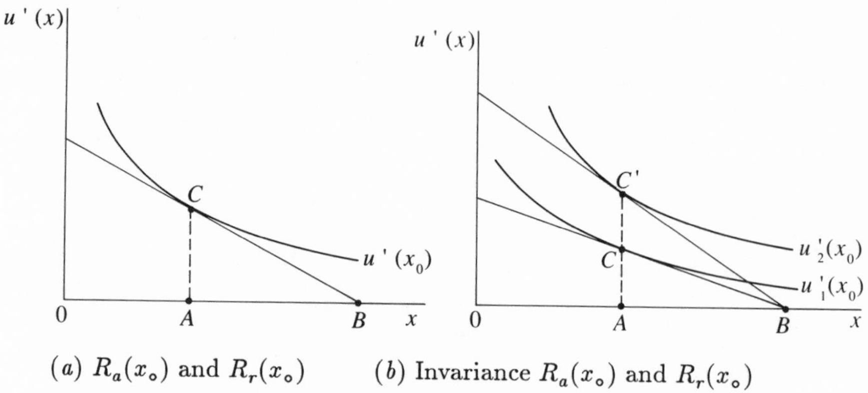

(a) $R_a(x_\circ)$ and $R_r(x_\circ)$ (b) Invariance $R_a(x_\circ)$ and $R_r(x_\circ)$

Figure 5.3: The coefficients of absolute and relative risk aversion

Now suppose that the individual faces the following alternatives:

(i′) $\$x_\circ(1 + h^*)$ with probability 1/2 and $\$x_\circ(1 - h^*)$ with probability 1/2, where $0 < h^*x_\circ < x_\circ$.

(ii) $\$x_\circ$ with probability 1.

In alternative (i) for the previous choice problem, we considered the 50/50 probability of $x_\circ + h$ and $x_\circ - h$, where h is independent of $x_\circ$. In alternative (i′) above, h is defined in relation to $x_\circ$, or $h = h^*x_\circ$. Let $z_\circ$ be the certainty equivalent of $x_\circ$ in (i′). Namely, define $z_\circ$ by

$$0.5u(x_\circ + h^*x_\circ) + 0.5u(x_\circ - h^*x_\circ) = u(z_\circ). \tag{17}$$

---

made on $R_a(x)$. In fig. 5.31b, a is assumed to be greater than unity, which of course does not lose a generality. Note that in fig. 5.3b, both tangent lines passing through points C and C' meet at point B. This follows from $u_2' = au_1'$ and $u_2'' = au_1''$. The diagrams here are also utilized by Sakai (1982, p. 97).

From this, we define $\rho^* > 0$ by

$$z_o = (1 - \rho^*)x_o, \quad \text{where} \quad \rho^* = \rho^*(x_o,\ h^*). \tag{18}$$

We call ρ^* the **relative risk premium**. In figure 5.2*b*, replace $x_o - h$, z_o, x_o, and $x_o + h$ by $(1 - h^*)x_o$, $(1 - \rho^*)x_o$, x_o, and $(1 + h^*)x_o$, respectively. Then we have

$$DC/EC = \rho^* x_o / x_o = \rho^*,$$

so that DC/EC signifies the relative risk measure.

We now state theorem 5.3, which follows readily from theorem 5.2.

Theorem 5.3. Given two utility functions u_1 and u_2 that are twice continuously differentiable, monotone increasing, and strictly concave, the following conditions are equivalent.

(a) $R_{r1}(x) > R_{r2}(x)$, and

(b) $\rho_1^*(x,\ h^*) > \rho_2^*(x,\ h^*)$, for all h^*,

where R_{ri} and ρ_i^*, respectively, denote the *coefficient of relative risk aversion* and the *relative risk premium*, when the NM utility function is given by $u_i(x)$, $i = 1,\ 2$.

Arrow (1965) and Pratt (1964) postulated the following hypotheses with regard to the individual's behavior toward risk:

Hypothesis A. The coefficient of absolute risk aversion is a monotone decreasing function, or $R_a'(x) < 0$ for all x (i.e., **decreasing absolute risk aversion**).

Hypothesis B. The coefficient of relative risk aversion is a monotone increasing function, or $R_r'(x) > 0$ for all x (i.e., **increasing relative risk aversion**).

By theorem 5.2, hypothesis A holds if and only if $\partial\rho(x,\ h)/\partial x < 0$ for any fixed h. Namely, this hypothesis is equivalent to stating that the individual's risk premium decreases as x gets larger. It suggests, in essence, that the rich are more tolerant of risks than the poor. Also, by theorem 5.3, hypothesis B holds if and only if $\partial\rho^*(x,\ h^*)/\partial x > 0$ for any fixed h^*, that is, the individual's relative risk aversion increases as x increases.[13]

Differentiating $R_a \equiv -u''(x)/u'(x)$, we obtain

$$R'_a = -[u'u''' - (u'')^2]/(u')^2,$$

where u is assumed to be three-times continuously differentiable. Hence if $R'_a < 0$, then $u'u''' > (u'')^2 > 0$, so that $u''' > 0$. Also, from this equation, we may assert that $u''' \leqq 0$ implies $R'_a > 0$. Since $R_r = xR_a$, $R'_a > 0$ implies $R'_r > 0$ provided that $x > 0$. Hence we may obtain the following relation among R_a, R_r, and u'''.

Observation. If $R'_a(x) < 0$, then $u'''(x) > 0$. On the other hand, if $u'''(x) \leqq 0$, then $R'_a(x) > 0$. If $x > 0$ in addition to $u'''(x) \leqq 0$, then $R'_r(x) > 0$.

5.2.3 Examples

In the literature, it is often assumed that the utility function takes some specific forms. Following Pratt (1964, pp. 71–74) and others, we may then examine some such examples. We require that $u(x)$ satisfy the following properties:

(i) $u'(x) > 0$, $u''(x) < 0$ for all x.

(ii) $R'_a(x) < 0$.

(iii) $R'_r(x) > 0$.

We first consider the quadratic function:

$$u(x) = a + bx - cx^2, \tag{19}$$

where $u'(x) > 0$ and $u''(x) < 0$ imply $b > 0$, $c > 0$, and $0 \leqq x \leqq b/2c$. Since $u'''(x) = 0$, we have $R'_a(x) > 0$ and $R'_r(x) > 0$ by the above observation. In fact, $R_a(x)$ and $R_r(x)$ can be computed as

$$R_a(x) = 2c/(b - 2cx),\ R_r(x) = 2cx/(b - 2cx). \tag{20a}$$

[13]With regard to hypothesis B, Arrow (1970, p. 97) writes, "the hypothesis of increasing relative risk aversion is not so easily confrontable with intuitive evidence. The assertion is that if both wealth and the size of the bet are increased in the same proportion, the willingness to accept the bet . . . should decrease."

From this, we obtain

$$R_a'(x) = 4c^2/(b - 2cx)^2 > 0, \; R_r'(x) = 2bc/(b - 2cx)^2 > 0. \quad \text{(20b)}$$

Since $R_a'(x) > 0$, the quadratic function implies that the rich are *less* tolerant of risks that the poor, and this "should be sufficient to remove quadratic utility from serious consideration" (Deaton and Muellbauer 1980, p. 400). Arrow (1970, p. 97) calls the quadratic assumptions "absurd."

Another example of a utility function is:

$$u(x) = a + b \log (x + c), \quad (21)$$

where $u'(x) > 0$, $u''(x) < 0$, and where $b > 0$ and $c \geqq 0$. For this case, we may compute

$$R_a(x) = 1/(x + c), \; R_a'(x) = -1/(x + c)^2 < 0, \quad \text{(22a)}$$

$$R_r(x) = x/(x + c), \; R_r'(x) = c/(x + c)^2 \geqq 0. \quad \text{(22b)}$$

Hence, this example satisfies conditions (i), (ii), and (iii) above.

Another example is:

$$u(x) = a - \frac{1}{(x + b)}, \quad \text{where } a \geqq 0, \; b > 0, \; a - \frac{1}{b} \geqq 0. \quad (23)$$

In this case we have:

$$R_a(x) = 2/(x + b), \; R_a'(x) = -2/(x + b)^2 < 0, \quad \text{(24a)}$$

$$R_r(x) = 2x/(x + b), \; R_r'(x) = 2b/(x + b)^2 > 0. \quad \text{(24b)}$$

Therefore, this example also satisfies conditions (i), (ii), and (iii) above.

An important, simple class of utility functions is the one in which $R_a(x) =$ constant for all x. Letting $R_a(x) = a$ (= constant), simple integration yields

$$u(x) = -e^{-ax}, \quad \text{where } a > 0, \quad (25)$$

in which case we have $u' > 0$ and $u'' < 0$. Another important, simple class is the one in which $R_r(x) =$ constant. Setting $R_r(x) = a$, simple integration yields

$$u(x) = x^{1-a} \qquad \text{if } 0 < a < 1,$$

$$u(x) = \log x \quad \text{if } a = 1,$$
$$u(x) = -x^{-(a-1)} \quad \text{if } a > 1. \tag{26}$$

These classes of functions in which $R_a(x)$ = constant or $R_r(x)$ = constant are often helpful to obtain useful conclusions in complex problems.

5.2.4 Indifference Curves

Consider a lottery ticket, $(\pi;\ x_1,\ x_2)$. The value of its expected utility is

$$EU \equiv \pi u(x_1) + (1 - \pi)u(x_2).$$

Given π, consider the locus of $(x_1,\ x_2)$ in which EU is constant, that is,

$$I^o \equiv \{(x_1,\ x_2) \in R^2 : \pi u(x_1) + (1 - \pi)u(x_2) = u^{\circ}\},$$
$$\text{where } 0 < \pi < 1. \tag{27}$$

This defines an **indifference curve under risk**. If the individual is risk averse (i.e., $u'' < 0$), then it can be shown that indifference curves are strictly convex to the origin. By differentiating $EU = u^{\circ}$, we obtain

$$dx_2/dx_1 \Big|_{u=u^{\circ}} = -\alpha u'(x_1)/u'(x_2), \tag{28a}$$

$$d^2x_2/dx_1^2 \Big|_{u=u^{\circ}} = -\alpha[u''(x_1) + \alpha u''(x_2)z^2]/u'(x_2), \tag{28b}$$

where $\alpha \equiv \pi/(1 - \pi)$ and $z \equiv u'(x_1)/u'(x_2)$.[14] Indeed, if $u'' < 0$, then $d^2x_2/dx_1^2 > 0$, so that indifference curves are strictly convex to the origin. Conversely, if $d^2x_2/dx_1^2 > 0$, then $u'' < 0$, so that the individual is risk averse.

---

[14]To obtain (28b), differentiate (28a) with respect to x_1 and note that $dx_2/dx_1 = -\alpha u'(x_1)/u'(x_2)$ for $u = u^o$ as given in (28a). A good use of indifference curves and contour sets is seen in the "state preference approach" by Yaari (1969). For useful expositions of the state preference approach, see Hirschleifer (1965) and Green (1978, pp. 249–74), for example. The latter is based on the former.

If we evaluate (28b) at (x_1, x_1), that is, on the 45° line for which x_1 and x_2 are equal, we obtain

$$d^2x_2/dx_1^2 \Big|_{u=u^\circ} = R_a(x_1)\pi/(1-\pi)^2. \tag{29}$$

This provides another interpretation of R_a, the Arrow-Pratt measure of absolute risk aversion.

In summary, we obtain proposition 5.1.

Proposition 5.1. Indifference curves are strictly convex to the origin if and only if the individual is risk averse. The curvature of an indifference curve measured at a certain point on the 45° line is equal to the coefficient of absolute risk aversion measured at that point multiplied by $\pi/(1-\pi)^2$.

5.3 Applications

5.3.1 Insurance[15]

Consider an individual who owns a certain asset (say, a house) that is worth $\$a$. Suppose this individual faces the risk that he or she will suffer a loss of $\$b$ with probability π in the case of a certain casualty (say, fire). More formally, there are two states of nature, S_1 and S_2. If S_1 (fire) occurs, the value of the asset is reduced to $a - b$, while if S_2 (no fire) occurs it remains the same. This is equivalent to the lottery $(\pi;\ a-b,\ a)$. The maximum amount that the individual is willing to pay, that is, the *risk premium* (denoted by ρ), can be defined by

$$u(a-\rho) = \pi u(a-b) + (1-\pi)u(a),$$

and $(a-\rho)$ is the certainty equivalent of this lottery. Assuming that the individual is a risk averter, ρ is positive. If $\rho = 0$ he or she is risk neutral; and if $\rho < 0$ he or she is a risk lover.

---

[15] See Arrow (1963) and Sandmo (1971). For an excellent, elementary exposition of this topic, see Hey (1979), McKenna (1986), and Sakai (1982), for example. For expositions of later developments, see, for example, Lippman and McCall (1981) and Laffont (1989). Lippman and McCall state, "the economics of insurance is the most important topic in the economics of uncertainty" (1981, p. 228, also p. 214). Their exposition of insurance is quite illuminating. For a more complete exposition of the theory of insurance, see Borch (1990).

Let $u(x) = \log x$, $a = \$90,000$, $b = \$80,000$, and $\pi = 0.01$. Then we have

$$\log(90,000 - \rho) = 0.01 \cdot \log(10,000) + 0.99 \cdot \log(90,000),$$

which yields the solution $\rho = \$1,567$. If $\pi = 0.05$, then $\rho = \$9,178$.[16]

Suppose that the individual can buy an insurance policy. Let x be the amount that the insurance company pays to that person if S_1 (casualty) occurs, and let P be the premium for that insurance. Then letting S_2 be the state in which no casuality occurs, his or her final wealth will be

$$\begin{aligned} a_1 &= a - b - P + x, \qquad &&\text{if } S_1 \text{ occurs;} \\ a_2 &= a - P, &&\text{if } S_2 \text{ occurs.} \end{aligned}$$

This is equivalent to the lottery $(\pi;\ a_1,\ a_2) = (\pi;\ a - b - P + x,\ a - P)$. The expected value of the individual's utility for this lottery is

$$\pi u(a - b - P + x) + (1 - \pi)u(a - P).$$

The individual will purchase the insurance if this exceeds the expected utility when insurance is not purchased, which is $\pi u(a - b) + (1 - \pi)u(a)$. We assume[17]

$$0 < a - b < a_1 < a_2, \text{ or}$$

$$0 < a - b < a - b - P + x < a - P.$$

It is easy to see that if the individual is risk averse, that is, if u is strictly concave, then we have

$$\pi u(a_1) + (1 - \pi)u(a_2) > \pi u(a - b) + (1 - \pi)u(a),$$

as can be seen from figure 5.4*a*. Thus, a risk averse individual will purchase the insurance.

On the other hand, if u is strictly convex (i.e., if the individual is a risk lover), the above inequality is reversed and he or she will not purchase

---

[16] In this example, $\$a$ is taken as an asset (or wealth), which is a *stock* quantity. Alternatively, we may regard it as income, which is a *flow* quantity. The present and following discussions are not altered by this change of interpretation. There are many examples in which the flow interpretation is more appropriate.

[17] $a - b < a_1$ means that $P < x$; i.e., insurance premium is less than insurance coverage. $a_1 < a_2$ means that $x < b$; i.e., the payment by the insurance company does not cover the full loss. The relaxations of these assumptions are left to the interested reader.

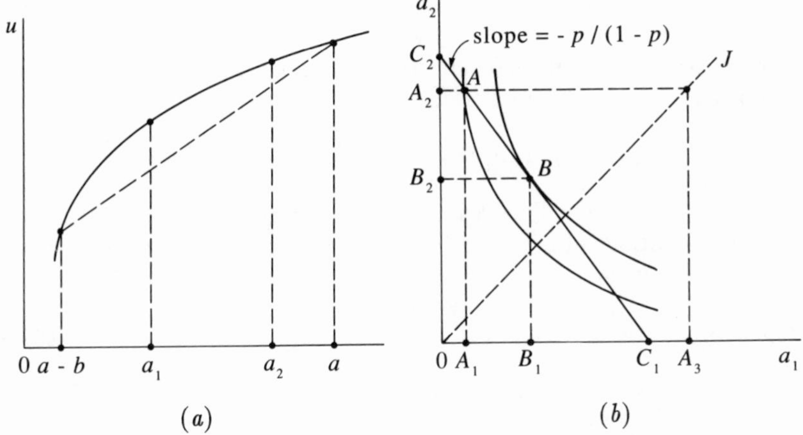

Figure 5.4: The demand for insurance

the insurance. In the risk neutral case, the individual will purchase the insurance ($x > 0$) depending on whether $\pi x > P$ (show why). In summary, the individual will purchase the insurance (irrespective of the values of πx and P) if and only if he or she is risk averse (that is, u is strictly concave).

Let $p \equiv P/x$. Then p signifies the price of insurance *per unit* of insurance coverage x. Assume that p is constant for different values of x. Assume also that p is exogenously given to each of the insured. The individual then chooses x so as to maximize his or her expected utility,

$$\phi(x) \equiv \pi u(a - b - px + x) + (1 - \pi)u(a - px).$$

Assuming $x^* > 0$ at optimum, the first-order condition $\phi'(x^*) = 0$ yields

$$\frac{\pi}{1 - \pi}\frac{u_1^*}{u_2^*} = \frac{p}{1 - p} \; (= \frac{P}{x - P}), \tag{30}$$

where $u_i^* \equiv u'(a_i^*)$, $i = 1, 2$. This means that the marginal rate of substitution between a_1 and a_2 weighted by their respective probabilities is equal to the premium per unit of the *net* insurance coverage. We may also compute

$$\phi''(x) = \pi u''(a_1)(1 - p)^2 + (1 - \pi)u''(a_2)p^2, \tag{31}$$

which is always negative, assuming that the individual is risk averse. Hence (30) furnishes a necessary and sufficient condition for a unique global maximum. Using (30) and the definition of R_a in (15), we may obtain the following relation from (31):

$$\phi''(x^*) = -(1-p)\pi u'(a_1^*)[(1-p)R_a(a_1^*) + pR_a(a_2^*)] < 0.$$

To obtain a graphic illustration of the above problem, we first observe that the definitions of p, a_1, and a_2 imply $p = (a - a_2)/(a_1 - a_2 + b)$, or

$$pa_1 + (1-p)a_2 = a - pb. \tag{32}$$

Needless to say, the a_1^* and a_2^* that satisfy (30) also satisfy (32). In fact, these a_1^* and a_2^* can also be obtained by choosing a_1 and a_2 to maximize $\pi u(a_1) + (1-\pi)u(a_2)$ subject to (32), $a_1 \geqq 0$, and $a_2 \geqq 0$. Figure 5.4*b* illustrates the individual's equilibrium described above, where point A signifies the "initial" point, that is, $A = (a - b,\ a)$, or $OA_1 = a - b$, $OA_2 = a$. The line C_1C_2 is drawn so as to pass through point A with slope equal to $-p/(1-p)$. It represents the locus of $(a_1,\ a_2)$ that satisfies (32), and it is called the **opportunity line**, as the individual can choose any value of a_1 and a_2 along this line.

The coordinate of point B is (a_1^*, a_2^*), and it is the optimum point for the individual. Since the slope of the indifference curve,

$$\{(a_1,\ a_2) : \pi u(a_1) + (1-\pi)u(a_2) = \pi u(a_1^*) + (1-\pi)u(a_2^*)\}, \tag{33}$$

is given by

$$\frac{da_2}{da_1} = -\frac{\pi}{1-\pi}\frac{u'(a_1)}{u'(a_2)},$$

condition (30) requires that the indifference curve be tangent to the opportunity line at point B. This is illustrated in figure 5.4*b*. Since the individual is risk averse, the indifference curves are strictly convex to the origin. Also, note that

$$OB_1 = a_1^* = a - b - px^* + x^*,\ OB_2 = a_2^* = a - px^*.$$

Thus we obtain

$$B_1A_1 = OB_1 - OA_1 = x^* - px^*\ A_2B_2$$
$$= OA_2 - OB_2 = px^* \equiv P^*,$$

where x^* and P^*, respectively, signify the demand for (gross) insurance coverage and the insurance premium. Let OJ be the ray from the origin whose slope is 45°. Then for any point along the OJ ray, we have $a_1 = a_2$, so that it signifies the locus of points for which the individual obtains the same assets. From the diagram, $OA_2 = OA_3$, so that

$$A_3A_1 = OA_3 - OA_1$$
$$= OA_2 - OA_1 = a - (a - b) = b.$$

Namely, A_3A_1 measures the amount of the loss if the accident occurs.

Now we introduce insurance companies. The *net* amount that an insurance company pays to the individual when the accident occurs is $x - P = (1 - p)x$ dollars. If the accident does not occur, the company receives $P = px$ dollars. The expected profit of the company is,

$$-\pi(1 - p)x + (1 - \pi)px.$$

Given competition in the insurance industry, these profits are forced to zero, that is,

$$\pi(1 - p) = (1 - \pi)p, \text{ or } \pi = p.$$

Under this assumption the company is said to charge an **actuarially fair premium**. For the insured, the insurance provides a **fair gamble** in the sense that its expected value is equal to zero. Substituting the above equation into (30), we obtain

$$u'(a - b - px^* + x^*) = u'(a - px^*). \tag{34}$$

Since $u'' < 0$, this implies

$$x^* = b. \tag{35}$$

Namely the insurance coverage x^* is equal to the loss b; that is, the individual will be completely insured against the loss (i.e., **full coverage**). In summary, we obtain proposition 5.2.

Proposition 5.2.

(i) The demand for insurance is positive (irrespective of π and p) if and only if the individual is risk averse.

(ii) The demand for insurance is determined by (30).

(iii) If the insurance company is willing to offer any insurance policy against loss at an actuarially fair premium, then the insured will choose a full coverage policy.[18]

Given the first order condition, which also ensures a unique global optimum, we can obtain the effect of changes in various parameters such as p, π, a, and the coefficient of absolute risk aversion by way of the usual comparative statics method. Such an analysis is left to the interested reader.

5.3.2 The Theory of the Firm

Consider a competitive firm that is able to sell any quantity of its output at the prevailing price p.[19] Let p be a random variable with known probability density function (p.d.f.), $\phi(p)$. No inventories may be held. A single output y is produced by a variable factor ("labor") and a fixed factor. Let w and x, respectively, be the price ("wage rate") and the input of the variable factor. Let π denote the profit of the firm (which should not be confused with probability π in the previous section). Assume that the profit of the firm is specified by

$$\pi = pf(x) - wx - a,$$

where a denotes the "fixed cost." Here, $f(x)$ denotes the production technology relating the variable input to the output, where it is assumed that $f(0) = 0$, and

$$f'(x) > 0, \ f''(x) < 0, \quad \text{for all } x \geqq 0.$$

Assume that the firm is competitive so that p and w are given exogenously to the firm. Assume also that the firm possesses a NM utility function u and chooses x to maximize the expected utility of profit,

$$E[u(\pi)] = E\{u[pf(x) - wx - a]\}$$

---

[18] An actuarially fair price, as stated in the text, is given by $p = \pi$, i.e., the premium per unit of coverage equals the probability of an accident. As Laffont (1989, p. 124) writes in this connection, "In practice, transaction costs (and the lack of competition) lead to an insurance premium that is greater than the actuarially fair price. ... In fact, these costs may be considerable."

[19] The exposition in this subsection follows Sandmo (1971); Hey (1979); and Sakai (1982).

$$= \int_o^\infty u[pf(x) - wx - a]\phi(p)dp,$$

subject to $x \geqq 0$.

The first-order condition for an optimum can be obtained in the usual way by differentiating this with respect to x and setting it equal to zero. Here, we need to apply the *rule of differentiation of integrals* (which we exposited in the previous chapter in connection with marginal cost pricing). It can readily be seen that this rule is important in the economics of uncertainty.

Omitting (*) to denote the optimum to avoid clutter, the first-order condition of the present problem is written as

$$E\{u'(\pi)[pf'(x) - w]\} = 0, \text{ or}$$

$$E[u'(\pi)pf'(x)] = E[u'(\pi)]w, \tag{36}$$

where we assume $x > 0$ at the optimum. The second-order sufficiency condition is satisfied, if the firm is risk averse, i.e., if $u'' < 0$, since

$$E\{u''(\pi)[pf'(x) - w]^2 + u'(\pi)pf''(x)\} < 0, \tag{37}$$

where we assume $u' > 0$.

Letting $\overline{p} \equiv E(p)$, the mean of the random variable p, we may rewrite (36) as

$$E[u'(\pi)(p - \overline{p})]f'(x) = E[u'(\pi)][w - \overline{p}f'(x)]. \tag{38}$$

On the other hand, since $E(\pi) = E[p\,f(x) - wx - a] = \overline{p}f(x) - wx - a$, we have

$$\pi - E(\pi) = (p - \overline{p})f(x).$$

Since $f(x) > 0$ by $x > 0$ at the optimum, we have

$$\pi \gtreqless E(\pi) \text{ as } p \gtreqless \overline{p}.$$

Hence, if and only if the firm is risk averse, we have

$$u'(\pi) \lesseqgtr u'(E\pi) \text{ as } p \gtreqless \overline{p}.$$

Then, if and only if the firm is risk averse, the following relation holds.

$$u'(\pi)(p - \overline{p}) \leqq u'(E\pi)(p - \overline{p}), \tag{39}$$

where the equality holds only when $p = \overline{p}$. Taking expectations, we have

$$E[u'(\pi)(p - \overline{p})] < u'(E\pi)E(p - \overline{p}) = 0,$$

where the equality to zero holds by the definition of mean. Hence the left-hand side of (38) is negative, so that

$$E[u'(\pi)][w - \overline{p}f'(x)] < 0.$$

Since $u' > 0$, we have $E[u'(\pi)] > 0$, so that

$$w < \overline{p}f'(x). \tag{40a}$$

If the uncertainty is removed and if p is replaced by $\overline{p}$, the optimum input is determined by

$$w = \overline{p}f'(x). \tag{40b}$$

Since $f'' < 0$, we may conclude that, for the risk averse firm, the equilibrium input and output under uncertainty are less than those for the corresponding certainty case.

To put this in a slightly different way, let p be written as

$$p = \overline{p} + \gamma\varepsilon, \tag{41}$$

where ε is a random variable with $E(\varepsilon) = 0$.[20] Substituting this into (38), we obtain

$$(\overline{p} - q)f'(x) = w, \quad \text{where } q \equiv -\gamma E[u'(\pi)\varepsilon]/E[u'(\pi)]. \tag{42}$$

By (42), we have $\overline{p} - q > 0$. Also, using (39) with (41), we may conclude that the firm is risk averse if and only if

$$u'(\pi)\gamma\varepsilon \leqq u'(E\pi)(p - \overline{p}),$$

with the equality holding only when $p = \overline{p}$. Taking expectations, we obtain

$$\gamma E[u'(\pi)\varepsilon] < u'(E\pi)E(p - \overline{p}) = 0. \tag{43}$$

[20] An increase in γ means a "stretching out" of the distribution about a constant mean, where the mean of p is equal to $\overline{p}$. When $\gamma = 0$, then $p = \overline{p}$ and uncertainty vanishes. Specifications such as (41) are often used in the literature.

Then recalling the definition of q, we can show from (43) that $q > 0$ if and only if the firm is risk averse.[21]

With $q > 0$, (42) means that, for the risk averse firm, input (and hence output) under uncertainty are less than those under certainty. This is the same conclusion as the one obtained earlier. Here, $\bar{p} - q > 0$ may be interpreted as the "effective price" of output under uncertainty, where q is interpreted as the "risk-bearing fee."[22]

Suppose now that x is a vector. For simplicity, assume $x = (x_1, x_2)$. Let $f(x)$ be the firm's production function. If price p prevails, the profit of the firm is written as

$$\pi = pf(x_1, x_2) - w_1 x_2 - w_2 x_2,$$

where w_i is the price of the ith factor ($i = 1, 2$). If x is a fixed factor, then, setting $a \equiv w_2 x_2$, we obtain the same model as the one discussed above. Thus, suppose that the firm chooses x_1 and x_2 to maximize the expected utility of profit. The first-order condition can be written as

$$E[u'(\pi)(pf_i - w_i)] = 0, \ i = 1, 2, \tag{44}$$

assuming $x_i > 0$, $i = 1, 2$, at the optimum, where $f_i \equiv \partial f / \partial x_i$, $i = 1, 2$. Substituting $p = \bar{p} + \gamma\varepsilon$ into (44), we obtain

$$(\bar{p} - q)f_i = w_i, \ i = 1, 2, \tag{45}$$

where q is the same as the one defined earlier. From (45) we may conclude that, under uncertainty, the "effective" value of each factor's marginal product is equal to the respective factor price. If constant returns to scale prevail, we have $f(x_1, x_2) = f_1 x_1 + f_2 x_2$ by Euler's equation for homogeneous functions. Then we obtain

$$(\bar{p} - q)f(x_1, x_2) = (\bar{p} - q)(f_1 x_1 + f_2 x_2) = w_1 x_1 + w_2 x_2.$$

Hence we have

$$E(\pi) \equiv \bar{p}y - w_1 x_1 - w_2 x_2 = qy, \tag{46}$$

where $y \equiv f(x)$. As observed earlier, this firm is risk averse if and only if $q > 0$. Then, from (46) we obtain

$$E(\pi) > 0. \tag{47}$$

[21] Similarly, we may assert that the firm is risk neutral (or a risk lover) if and only if $q = 0$ (or $q < 0$).

[22] Thus, the risk-bearing fee is positive ($q > 0$) if and only if the firm is risk averse. The term *risk-bearing fee* is from Sakai (1982).

This result can be contrasted to the usual conclusion that under certainty the long-run profit under constant returns to scale is zero. Inequality (47) states that, under uncertainty, the profit is positive (i.e., the profit is positive "on average"), and this is a direct consequence of the risk averse utility function.[23]

We may now summarize our results as follows.

Proposition 5.3. Assume that the price of output is the only random variable faced by a competitive firm that produces a single output.

(i) If the firm chooses the level of only one factor input, and if the firm is risk averse, the levels of input and output chosen under uncertainty are less than those under certainty.

(ii) Assume that the firm uses two inputs with constant returns to scale technology. Then the long-run expected profit for the risk averse firm is positive.

A number of interesting extensions have been made on the behavior of a firm under uncertainty. These extensions include studies in which (*a*) factor prices are uncertain, (*b*) the production function is uncertain due to "weather" or technological progress, or (*c*) the demand function is uncertain for a monopolistic firm. However, the basic method of analysis is similar to the above.

5.3.3 Portfolio Choice[24]

Consider an individual whose initial value of assets is denoted by A. Assume that there are two types of assets: one type yields no return

---

[23]It is argued that this justifies Frank Knight's (1921) contention that profits are reward for risk taking. See, for example, Sakai (1982, p. 42). More recently, however, Applebaum and Katz (1986, p. 528) argue that the effect of a mean preserving increase in price uncertainty on the output of individual firms "appears" to be ambiguous, while a mean preserving increase in price uncertainty reduces total *industry output*.

[24]The discussion here is largely indebted to Arrow (1970, chap. 3), which in turn is taken from Arrow (1965). Much of the modern theory of portfolio choice has been inspired by Tobin's important paper (1958) via the discovery that his theory is based on some restrictive assumptions. For example, his mean-value approach is valid only when the investor's utility function is quadratic, or the rates of return on the risky assets are normally distributed. Also, his "separation theorem" does not hold in general for the multiple risky security case (cf. Feldstein 1969). This "theorem" asserts that the investor's decision on portfolio choice can be separated from the choice between consumption and saving.

but it is riskless, and the other type yields a return with the rate of return r, where r is a random variable, which can be negative. The type 1 asset is called a **safe asset** and the type 2 asset is called a **risky asset**. Letting m and a, respectively, denote the individual's initial holdings of the type 1 and type 2 assets, the value of the individual's assets at the end of the current period (W) is written as

$$W \equiv m + a(1 + r).$$

For the sake of simplicity, assume that there are only two states of nature, S_1 and S_2. When S_1 occurs, $r = r_1 > 0$, and when S_2 occurs, $r = r_2 < 0$. Let π be the probability of S_1 occurring. Let W_i be the value of wealth when S_i occurs ($i = 1, 2$). Then we have

$$W_1 \equiv m + a(1 + r_1),\ W_2 \equiv m + a(1 + r_2).$$

Then letting $A \equiv m + a$, the value of the individual's initial wealth, we may rewrite this equation as

$$W_1 \equiv A + r_1 a,\ W_2 \equiv A + r_2 a. \tag{48}$$

The situation described above is equivalent to the following lottery:

$$(\pi;\ W_1,\ W_2) = (\pi;\ A + r_1 a,\ A + r_2 a).$$

The expected value of this lottery is

$$\begin{aligned} E(W) &\equiv \pi W_1 + (1 - \pi)W_2 \\ &= A + a[\pi r_1 + (1 - \pi)r_2] = A + aE(r). \end{aligned} \tag{49}$$

The expected utility can be written as

$$\pi u(W_1) + (1 - \pi)u(W_2) = \pi u(A + r_1 a) + (1 - \pi)u(A + r_2 a).$$

The individual chooses a (the amount of risky assets) to maximize the expected utility, that is, to maximize

$$\phi(a) \equiv \pi u(A + r_1 a) + (1 - \pi)u(A + r_2 a),$$

subject to $a \geqq 0$, while keeping the initial value of assets (A) constant. Assuming that $a^* > 0$, the first-order condition is written as $\phi'(a^*) = 0$. This can be rewritten as

$$\frac{\pi}{1 - \pi}\frac{u_1^*}{u_2^*} = -\frac{r_2}{r_1}\ (\equiv p), \tag{50}$$

where $u_i^* \equiv u'(W_i^*)$, $i = 1, 2$, and

$$W_1^* \equiv A + r_1 a^*, \ W_2^* \equiv A + r_2 a^*. \tag{51}$$

Condition (50) determines the optimal holding of risky assets (a^*). We may also compute

$$\phi''(a) = \pi r_1^2 u''(W_1) + (1 - \pi) r_2^2 u''(W_2),$$

which is always negative as long as the individual is risk averse (i.e., $u'' < 0$). Namely, the a^* determined by (50) furnishes a unique global maximum. We may note that condition (50) is analogous to (30) in the theory of insurance.

To obtain a graphic illustration, note that $(A - W_2)/(W_1 - A) = -r_2/r_1$ from (48), and note that this can be rewritten as

$$pW_1 + W_2 = (1 + p)A, \text{ where } p \equiv -r_2/r_1. \tag{52}$$

In fact, (50) can also be obtained by supposing that the individual chooses W_1 and W_2 so as to maximize $\pi u(W_1) + (1 - \pi)u(W_2)$ subject to (52), $W_1 \geqq 0$, and $W_2 \geqq 0$. Given an interior solution ($W_1^* > 0$, $W_2^* > 0$), the first-order condition yields (50), where W_1^* and W_2^* determined by (50) satisfy (52). In figure 5.5, the C_1C_2 line denotes the locus of (W_1, W_2)'s that satisfy (52), where the intercepts are given by

$$OC_1 = A(1 + p)/p, \ OC_2 = A(1 + p).$$

This line is analogous to the C_1C_2 line in figure 5.4*b* in the discussion of insurance, and it is the *opportunity line* of the present problem. Point A is obtained as the point of intersection between the opportunity line and the 45° line, OJ. Then, as is clear from (52), OA_1 ($= OA_2$) measures the initial value of assets (A). As is also clear from (48), at point A, the individual holds no risky assets ($a = 0$), and thus the line OJ is also called the **certainty line**.

The slope of the indifference curve,

$$\{(W_1, W_2) : \pi u(W_1) + (1 - \pi)u(W_2) = \text{ constant}\},$$

is given by

$$\frac{dW_2}{dW_1} = -\frac{\pi}{1 - \pi}\frac{u'(W_1)}{u'(W_2)}. \tag{53}$$

Then, as can be seen from (50), the optimum point B is obtained as the point in which the indifference curve is tangent to the opportunity line,

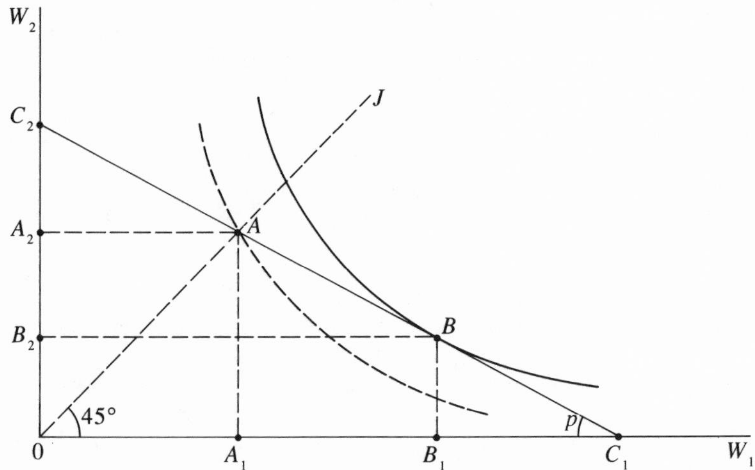

Figure 5.5: Optimum portfolio choice

as illutrated in figure 5.5. Note that

$$OB_1 = W_1^* \equiv A + r_1 a^*,\ OB_2 = W_2^* \equiv A + r_2 a^*.$$

We may also note

$$B_1 A_1 = r_1 a^*,\ A_2 B_2 = -r_2 a^*\ (> 0).$$

If $a^* > 0$, then $W_1^* > W_2^*$ so that $u_1^* < u_2^*$. Then from (50), we obtain $p(1 - \pi)/\pi < 1$. Thus,

$$E(r) \equiv \pi r_1 + (1 - \pi) r_2 > 0. \tag{54}$$

Conversely, if (54) holds, then $W_1^* > W_2^*$ so that $a^* > 0$. Thus, we obtain proposition 5.4.

Proposition 5.4. The risk averse individual holds risky assets if and only if the expected rate of return of such assets is positive.

In the preceding discussion, safe assets yield no return. It is possible that safe assets yield some return. In this case, letting i be the rate of return on such assets, we have

$$W_1 \equiv m(1+i) + a(1+r_1) \equiv m' + a' + a(r_1 - i),$$

$$W_2 \equiv m(1+i) + a(1+r_2) \equiv m' + a' + a(r_2 - i),$$

where $m' \equiv m(1+i)$ and $a' \equiv a(1+i)$. Then letting

$$A' \equiv m' + a',\ r_1' \equiv r_1 - i, \text{ and } r_2' \equiv r_2 - i,$$

we obtain

$$W_1' \equiv A' + r_1'a,\ W_2 \equiv A' + r_2'a. \tag{48'}$$

With these changes of notation, the rest of the analysis follows in exactly the same way as in the nonprime case with m and A, instead of m' and A'. Therefore, we proceed with our discussion by using m and A (i.e., by deleting the prime).

The optimal value of risky assets (a^*) depends on various parameters such as A, π, and r. The effect of a change in any one of these parameters can be analyzed by a routine comparative statics exercise. Here we illustrate such by considering a change in the initial size of the individual's wealth. Differentiating (50) and (52), with respect to A, we obtain

$$u''(W_1^*)dW_1^* = \alpha p u''(W_2^*)dW_2,$$

$$p dW_1^* + dW_2^* = (1+p)dA,$$

where $\alpha \equiv (1-\pi)/\pi$. From these two equations, we obtain

$$dW_1^*/dA = \alpha p(1+p)u''(W_2^*)/\Delta, \tag{55a}$$

$$dW_2^*/dA = (1+p)u''(W_1^*)/\Delta, \tag{55b}$$

where $\Delta \equiv [u''(W_1^*) + \alpha p^2 u''(W_2^*)]$. Clearly, $\Delta < 0$, $dW_1^*/dA > 0$, and $dW_2^*/dA > 0$ if and only if $u'' < 0$, or the individual is risk averse. From (48), we may note

$$(dW_1^*/dA) - (dW_2^*/dA) = (r_1 - r_2)(da^*/dA). \tag{56}$$

Substituting (55) into (56) and recalling (50) and the definition of R_a in (15), we may obtain

$$da^*/dA = \frac{-(1+p)\,u'(W_1^*)[R_a(W_2^*) - R_a(W_1^*)]}{\{\Delta(r_1 - r_2)\}}. \tag{57}$$

Then, assuming $u'' < 0$ and decreasing absolute risk aversion, $R_a' < 0$, we obtain

$$da^*/dA > 0,$$

since $W_1^* > W_2^*$ and $r_1 - r_2 > 0$. Using (55) and (56) as well as (50) and (51), and recalling the definition of R_r in (16), we may conclude:[25]

$$(A/a^*)(\partial a^*/\partial A) < 1 \text{ if and only if } R_r(W_1) > R_r(W_2).$$

Hence, assuming increasing relative risk aversion, $R_r' > 0$, we obtain

$$(A/a^*)(da^*/dA) < 1.$$

In summary, we obtain proposition 5.5.

Proposition 5.5. Assume that the individual is risk averse.

(i) Under the assumption of decreasing absolute risk aversion, an increase in the initial wealth (A) increases the investment in risky assets.

(ii) Under the assumption of increasing relative risk aversion, an increase in the initial wealth decreases the proportion of risky assets in total wealth and increases the proportion of safe assets.

These results are, in essence, due to Arrow (1965, Lecture 2; 1970, chap. 3). Subsequently, Cass and Stigliz (1970) show that Arrow's results do not generalize to the case of many risky assets. In particular, they give an example where an investor who can purchase one safe security and two risky securities invests a greater proportion of wealth into the two risky securities, even if his or her utility function exhibits increasing relative risk. However, they also show that Arrow's results do generalize for an important class of utility functions in which risky assets are held in fixed proportions, independent of wealth. Such utility functions are said to possess the **separation property**. Hart (1975) then establishes that the separation property is a necessary condition as well as a sufficient condition for the generalization of Arrow's results in the case of many risky assets. Namely, "given more than one risky security and a utility

[25] It can be shown that

$$(A/a^*)(da^*/dA) - 1 = [R_r(W_1^*) - R_r(W_2^*)]u'(W_1^*)/(a^*\Delta r_1).$$

We then recall $\Delta < 0$ if and only if $u'' < 0$.

function which does not possess the separation property, it is always possible to pick probability distributions for the returns of the risky securities so that the directions of change which Arrow established for the single risky security case are reversed" (p. 615). Hart (1975, p. 620) cautions us that "the class of utility functions which possess the separation property is very small." Sandmo (1977) then consider such a multisecurity problem from a fresh viewpoint, and concludes, "Indeed, one might raise the methodological question of whether comparative statics results ought not more fruitfully be made directly conditional on the signs and magnitudes of the wealth effect instead of more indirectly—and less meaningfully—on the form of the risk aversion functions" (p. 378).

5.3.4 Consumption and Savings Decision[26]

The classic treatise on the theory of saving is Irving Fisher's (1930) two period analysis. Although uncertainty is assumed away in his analysis of saving, it would provide the basic framework for the analysis under uncertainty. We shall thus briefly exposit Fisher's analysis.

Consider a consumer who faces a two-period, 1 (present) and 2 (future), horizon.[27] Let c_1 and c_2, respectively, denote present and future consumption. Let $u(c_1, c_2)$ represent his or her utility function, and let y_1 and y_2 denote his or her exogenous wage income for periods 1 and 2, respectively. Define savings (which may be positive, zero, or negative) in period 1 by

$$s \equiv y_1 - c_1. \tag{58}$$

Letting r be the real rate of interest, the individual's income for period 2 is equal to $y_2 + (1 + r)s$, so that we have

$$c_2 \leqq y_2 + (1 + r)s. \tag{59}$$

Combining (58) with (59), we have

$$(1 + r)c_1 + c_2 \leqq (1 + r)y_1 + y_2. \tag{60}$$

The individual is assumed to choose c_1 and c_2 to maximize $u(c_1, c_2)$ subject to the budget condition (60), where $c_1 \geqq 0$, and $c_2 \geqq 0$. To

[26] The discussion here follows Leland (1968), Sandmo (1969 and 1970), and Sakai (1982). See also Sandmo (1974), Hey (1979), and Laffont (1978). See also Sandmo (1985) for a useful survey of the topic.

[27] The analysis can easily be extended to T periods where $T > 2$.

solve this problem, we write its Lagrangian as

$$u(c_1, c_2) + \lambda[(1 + r)y_1 + y_2 - (1 + r)c_1 - c_2].$$

Assuming $c_1 > 0$ and $c_2 > 0$ at optimum, and ignoring the (*) to denote the optimum, the first-order conditions for this problem are written as

$$u_1 - \lambda(1 + r) = 0, \ u_2 - \lambda = 0, \tag{61a}$$

$$(1 + r)y_1 + y_2 - (1 + r)c_1 - c_2 \geqq 0, \tag{61b}$$

$$\lambda[(1 + r)y_1 + y_2 - (1 + r)c_1 - c_2] = 0, \tag{61c}$$

where $\lambda \geqq 0$ and where $u_i \equiv \partial u/\partial c_i > 0$, $i = 1, 2$. Note that (61a) can be rewritten as

$$u_1/u_2 = 1 + r. \tag{62a}$$

Since $\lambda > 0$ by (61a), we may rewrite (61b) as

$$(1 + r)c_1 + c_2 = (1 + r)y_1 + y_2. \tag{62b}$$

Equation (62a) is known as **Fisher's law** for the two-period problem. The term $(u_1/u_2 - 1)$ is called the **marginal rate of time preference**. Equation (62a) requires that this rate be equal to the real rate of interest.[28] Assuming that u is strictly quasi-concave, and noting that constraint (60) is linear, (62a) and (62b) are necessary and sufficient for a unique global maximum.

Equations (62a) and (62b) define the optimal values of c_1 and c_2 given the parameters as y_1, y_2, and r. Obtaining the effect of a change in any of these parameters on the optimal values of c_1 and c_2 are usual exercises in comparative statics. For example, by a routine exercise, we may obtain

$$\partial c_1/\partial y_1 = \frac{-(1 + r)[u_{12} - (1 + r)u_{22}]}{[u_{11} - 2(1 + r)u_{12} + (1 + r)^2 u_{22}]}, \tag{63}$$

[28] Equation (62a) is well-known. Paraphrasing the exposition by Gravelle and Rees (1981, p. 405), we may state this as follows. A \$1 reduction in c_1 reduces u by the marginal utility u_1. There will exist an increase in u_2 that will make the consumer just as well off as before the \$1 reduction. This compensation for the increase in c_1 is \$$(1 + \rho)$ and is defined by

$$u_1(c_1, c_2) = u_2(c_1, c_2)(1 + \rho).$$

Here, ρ is the consumer's subjective rate of interest, or his or her marginal rate of time preference. Under a competitive situation, ρ becomes equal to the real (market) rate of interest, r.

where $u_{ij} \equiv \partial^2 u/\partial c_i \partial c_j$, $i, j = 1, 2$. The sign of $\partial c_1/\partial y_1$ is, in general, indeterminate. However, in addition to $u_i > 0$ (nonsatiation), we may impose the following assumptions:

$$u_{ii} < 0, \; i = 1, 2, \text{ and } u_{12} (= u_{21}) \gtreqq 0. \tag{64}$$

Under these assumptions, we may assert, from (63), that $\partial c_1/\partial y_1 > 0$, that is, an increase in present income increases present consumption.

As observed earlier, under the assumption of $u_i > 0$, $\lambda > 0$, so that the budget condition holds with equality (62b). This in turn implies that (59) holds with equality at the optimum, i.e.,

$$c_2 = y_2 + (1 + r)s. \tag{59'}$$

In the literature, we often encounter the constraints being written in equality forms from the outset of the analysis. This can be justified on the ground that these equalities will hold in any case at the optimum under certain assumptions. In the present case, under the assumption of $u_i > 0$, equalities (62b) and (59′) hold eventually. Since procedure with equality constraints would ease our present exposition here, we henceforth proceed with equality constraints. We may first observe the way in which the exposition of the above intertemporal optimization problem is altered.

With (59′), we may observe that

$$u(c_1, c_2) = u[y_1 - s, \; y_2 + (1 + r)s] \equiv \Phi(s).$$

The consumer chooses s (saving) to maximize $\Phi(s)$. Ignoring the notation to indicate the optimum, the first-order condition is written as

$$\Phi'(s) = -u_1 + (1 + r)u_2 = 0,$$

which in turn yields to Fisher's law, (62a). We may also compute

$$\Phi''(s) = u_{11} - 2(1 + r)u_{12} + (1 + r)^2 u_{22}.$$

Under assumption (64), $\Phi''(s) < 0$, so that (62a) provides a necessary and sufficient condition for a unique global maximum.

We now introduce uncertainty into the model. Specifically, we assume that the future non-interest income y_2 is uncertain, where y_2 is a random variable with its probability density function being equal to $f(y_2)$. The uncertainty on y_2 is called **income risk**. The individual's expected utility function can be written as

$$E[u(c_1, c_2)] = E\{u[y_1 - s, y_2 + (1 + r)s]\}$$

$$= \int_Y u[y_1 - s, y_2 + (1 + r)s]f(y_2)dy_2 \equiv \phi(s), \quad (65)$$

where Y is the range of y . The individual chooses s to maximize $\phi(s)$. Again, ignore the notation that indicates optimum. Then recalling the rule of differentiation of integrals, the first-order condition for the optimum can be obtained from $\phi'(s) = 0$ as

$$E[u_1 - (1 + r)u_2] = 0.$$

This can equivalently be rewritten as

$$E(u_1)/E(u_2) = 1 + r. \quad (66)$$

This is an *uncertainty version of Fisher's law.* It states that the marginal rate of time preference under uncertainty, $E(u_1)/E(u_2) - 1$, is equal to the real rate of interest. We may also compute

$$\phi''(s) = E[u_{11} - 2(1 + r)u_{12} + (1 + r)^2 u_{22}].$$

Under assumption (64), $\phi''(s) < 0$, so that (66) furnishes the condition for a unique global maximum.

For simplicity, assume y_2 takes the following specific form:

$$y_2 = \overline{y}_2 + \gamma\varepsilon, \ \gamma > 0, \quad (67)$$

where $\overline{y}_2$ is the mean of y_2, and where ε is a random variable with $E(\varepsilon) = 0$. As mentioned earlier (see fn. 20), an increase in γ denotes a stretching out of the distribution about the constant mean, $\overline{y}_2$. When $\gamma = 0$, $y_2 = \overline{y}_2$ and the uncertainty vanishes. Now define the function θ by

$$\theta(s; y_1, \overline{y}_2, r, \gamma) \equiv E(u_1)/E(u_2) - 1, \quad (68)$$

which signifies the *marginal rate of time preference under income risk.* We may then compute

$$\partial\theta/\partial s = \{E(u_2)E[-u_{11} + (1 + r)u_{12}] - E(u_1)E[-u_{21} + (1 + r)u_{22}]\}/\{E(u_2)\}^2. \quad (69)$$

Since $\partial\theta/\partial s > 0$, we may assert that the optimal amount of saving under income risk (s^*) is uniquely determined by the intersection of the θ-curve and the r-line as illustrated in figure 5.6*a*.

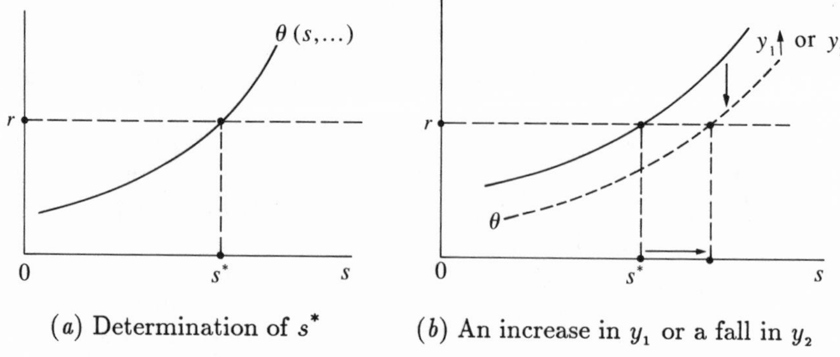

(a) Determination of s^*

(b) An increase in y_1 or a fall in y_2

Figure 5.6: Savings decisions under income risk

To obtain comparative statics results, we compute, for example,

$$\partial\theta/\partial y_1 = [E(u_2)E(u_{11}) - E(u_1)E(u_{21})]/\{E(u_2)\}^2 < 0, \tag{70a}$$

$$\partial\theta/\partial \overline{y}_2 = [E(u_2)E(u_{12}) - E(u_1)E(u_{22})]/\{E(u_2)\}^2 > 0. \tag{70b}$$

Hence an increase in y_1 or a fall in $\overline{y}_2$ causes a downward shift of the θ-curve as illustrated in figure 5.6*b*. This,in turn, increases the amount of saving s^*, as illustrated in figure 5.6*b*, so that $\partial s/\partial y_1 > 0$ and $\partial s/\partial \overline{y}_2 < 0$.

It can also be shown that[29]

$$\partial c_1/\partial y_1 > 0 \text{ and } \partial s/\partial y_1 > 0. \tag{71}$$

Namely, an increase in present income raises present consumption and present saving. This implies that the marginal propensity to save is between 0 and 1 since $(\partial c_1/\partial y_1) + (\partial s/\partial y_1) = 1$. Additionally, we may compute

$$\partial\theta/\partial r = \{E(u_2)E(u_{12}) - E(u_1)E(u_{22})\}/\{E(u_2)\}^2 > 0. \tag{72}$$

[29] From the usual exercise of comparative statics, we obtain

$$\partial s/\partial y_1 = E[u_{11} - (1 + r)u_{12}]/\phi'', \quad \partial c/\partial y_1 = (1 + r)E[-u_{12} + (1 + r)u_{22}]/\phi''.$$

Since $u_{11} < 0$, $u_{22} < 0$, $u_{12} \geqq 0$, and $\phi'' < 0$, we may conclude that $\partial s/\partial y_1 > 0$ and $\partial c_1/\partial y_1 > 0$.

Hence the θ-curve in figure 5.6 shifts up as a result of an increase in the interest rate r. However, the r-line also shifts up, and hence the effect of an increase in the interest rate on saving is indeterminate, which can also be confirmed by the usual comparative statics exercise.

To obtain the effect of an increase in the uncertainty of noninterest future income, recall (67) and *assume* that such an increase is captured by an increase in γ.[30] Differentiating (68) with respect to γ, we obtain

$$\partial\theta/\partial\gamma = \{E(u_2)E(u_{12}\varepsilon) - E(u_1)E(u_{22}\varepsilon)\}/\{E(u_2)\}^2.$$

Suppose that we can assume

$$E(u_{22}\varepsilon) > 0 \text{ and } E(u_{12}\varepsilon) \leqq 0. \tag{73}$$

Then we obtain $\partial\theta/\partial\gamma < 0$, so that the θ-curve in figure 5.6 shifts down when γ is increased. Namely, a precautionary demand for saving increases as income risk increases; or increased uncertainty about future income increases savings. Sandmo (1970, p. 353) quotes Boulding: "other things being equal, we should expect a man with a safe job to save less than a man with an uncertain job."

Condition (73), thus, plays an important role in obtaining comparative statics results. To obtain an understanding of (73), we consider the following function:

$$R_a(c_1, c_2) \equiv -u_{22}(c_1, c_2)/u_2(c_1, c_2). \tag{74}$$

This is similar to the Arrow-Pratt measure of absolute risk aversion, but it is different from it, since u now depends on two variables, c_1 and c_2. If we regard R_a as a function of c_2 alone, then the discussion of the coefficient of risk aversion in the previous section can be applied here without alteration (cf. hypothesis A). Boldly using the analogy of the one variable case, we assume that R_a is a decreasing function of c_2. Furthermore, when present consumption (c_1) increases, savings decrease and future income inclusive of interest income decreases. The individual then is more inclined to avoid uncertainty. Hence, R_a is an increasing, or at least a nondecreasing, function of c_1. In short, we may then assume

$$\partial R_a/\partial c_2 < 0 \text{ and } \partial R_a/\partial c_1 \geqq 0. \tag{75}$$

---

[30] That an increase in the variability of future income depends on γ is only an assumption made for the sake of simplicity. Although this assumption is made frequently, it may not hold. See Rothchild and Stiglitz (1971).

This assumption is introduced in Sandmo (1969), where he called

$$\partial R_a/\partial C_1 > 0$$

risk complementarity with a cautionary note. If the utility function is additive, i.e.,

$$u(c_1, c_2) = v_1(c_1) + v_2(c_2), \quad \text{then } R_a = -v_2''(c_2)/v_2'(c_2).$$

Hence, $\partial R_a/\partial c_1 = 0$ and $\partial R_a/\partial c_2 < 0$ reduces to the usual assumption of absolute risk aversion. It can be shown that assumption (75) implies (73).[31]

---

[31]See Sandmo (1970) and Sakai (1982). The proof runs as follows. From (59′) and (67), we have $c_2 = \bar{y}_2 + \gamma\varepsilon + (1+r)s$. Hence letting $\bar{c}_2 \equiv E(c_2)$, we obtain $c_2 - \bar{c}_2 = y_2 - \bar{y}_2 = \gamma\varepsilon$, so that

$$(*) \qquad c_2 - \bar{c}_2 \gtrless 0, \quad \text{as } \varepsilon \gtrless 0.$$

Since u_2 is a decreasing function with respect to c_2 (i.e., $u_{22} < 0$) by (64a),

$$u_2(c_1, c_2) \lessgtr u_2(c_1, \bar{c}_2) \quad \text{as } \varepsilon \gtrless 0.$$

Hence,

$$\varepsilon u_2(c_1, c_2) \leqq \varepsilon u_2(c_1, \bar{c}_2),$$

where the equality is obtained only when $\varepsilon = 0$. Taking expectations, we have

$$(**) \qquad E[\varepsilon u_2(c_1, c_2)] < E[\varepsilon u_2(c_1, \bar{c}_2)] = u_2(c_1, \bar{c}_2)E(\varepsilon) = 0.$$

On the other hand, since $\partial R_a/\partial c_2 < 0$ by (75), $(*)$ also implies

$$-u_{22}(c_1, c_2)/u_2(c_1, c_1) \lessgtr -u_{22}(c_1, \bar{c}_2)/u_2(c_2, \bar{c}_2), \quad \text{as } \varepsilon \gtrless 0.$$

This in turn implies

$$-\varepsilon u_{22}(c_1, c_2) \leqq -[u_{22}(c_1, \bar{c}_2)/u_2(c_1, \bar{c}_2)][\varepsilon u_2(c_1, c_2)],$$

where the equality follows only when $\varepsilon = 0$. Taking expectations, we obtain

$$-E[\varepsilon u_{22}(c_1, c_2)] \leqq -[u_{22}(c_1, \bar{c}_2)/u_2(c_1, \bar{c}_2)]E[\varepsilon u_2(c_1, c_2)].$$

Then recalling $E[\varepsilon u_2(c_1, c_2)] < 0$ from (**), we obtain

$$E[\varepsilon u_{22}(c_1, c_2)] > 0.$$

Similarly, from $\partial R_a/\partial c_1 \leqq 0$, we can show

$$E[\varepsilon u_{12}(c_1, c_2)] \leqq 0.$$

Next, we suppose that y_1 and y_2 are certain but that the real interest rate (or the "harvest rate") is uncertain due to, for example, inflation (or "weather"). The uncertainty on r is called **capital risk**, which is to be distinguished from the income risk (uncertainty or noninterest future income) discussed above. The problem of capital risk is also discussed by Sandmo (1970).[32] To simplify the exposition, we write r as

$$r = \bar{r} + \gamma\varepsilon, \ \gamma > 0, \tag{76}$$

which replaces (67). Here, $E(r) = \bar{r} =$ constant, and ε is a random variable with zero mean and its probability density function being given by $g(\varepsilon)$. Here, γ and ε should not be confused with the ones in (67). We assume $r > -1$, which is equivalent to assuming

$$\rho \equiv 1 + \bar{r} + \gamma\varepsilon > 0.$$

The individual chooses s to maximize

$$E\{u[y_1 - s, \ y_2 + (1 + \bar{r} + \gamma\varepsilon)s]\} \equiv \psi(s).$$

Again, ignoring the notation to indicate the optimum, the first-order condition $\psi'(s) = 0$ can be rewritten as

$$E[-u_1 + (1 + \bar{r} + \gamma\varepsilon)u_2] = 0.$$

This yields

$$E(u_1) = E(u_2) + \bar{r}E(u_2) + \gamma E(\varepsilon u_2).$$

Namely, we have

$$E(u_1)/E(u_2) - 1 = \bar{r} - \tau, \tag{77}$$

where τ is defined by

$$\tau \equiv -\gamma E(\varepsilon u_2)/E(u_2). \tag{78}$$

We may also compute

$$\psi''(s) = E(u_{11}) - 2E(\rho u_{12}) + E(\rho^2 u_{22}).$$

Under (64) and $\rho > 0$, $\psi'' < 0$ always. Hence, (77) furnishes a necessary and sufficient condition for a unique global maximum.

[32] Sandmo (1970) discusses both income risk and capital risk, whereas Leland (1968) discusses only income risk.

Using an argument similar to that used in footnote 31, we can show that $E(\varepsilon u_2) < 0$. This, in turn, implies that, τ, as defined in (78), is positive. Such a τ may be interpreted as the "risk-bearing fee" which is to be deducted from the real rate of interest. Namely, (77) states that the marginal rate of time preference under capital risk is equal to the "effective" rate of interest, $\bar{r} - \tau$, that is, the real rate of interest adjusted by the risk-bearing fee τ. Note that τ is analogous to the q defined in (42).

Denote again the marginal rate of time preference under capital risk by θ, that is,

$$\theta \equiv E(u_1)/E(u_2) - 1.$$

Then, partially differentiating θ with respect to s, we obtain

$$\partial\theta/\partial s = [E(u_2)E(-u_{11} + \rho u_{12}) - E(u_1)E(-u_{21} + \rho u_{22})]/[E(u_2)]^2.$$

With (64) and $\rho > 0$, we may conclude that $\partial\theta/\partial s > 0$. The optimal level of saving under capital risk (s^*) is determined by the intersection of the θ-curve and the $(\bar{r} - \tau)$-curve as illustrated in figure 5.7, where it can be shown that the sign of $\partial(\bar{r} - \tau)/\partial s$ can be either positive or negative.

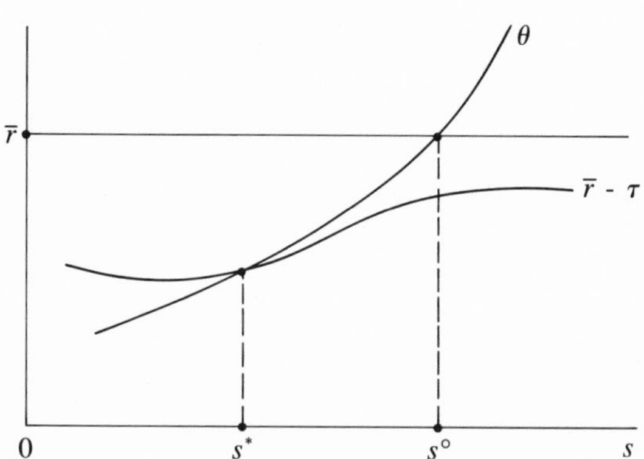

Figure 5.7: Savings under capital risk

As is clear from figure 5.7, the amount of saving under capital risk (s^*) is always less than that under certainty (s°), since $\bar{r} - \tau < \bar{r}$. We can obtain comparative statics results here by the usual procedure of differentiating (77), and such is left to the interested reader.

We now summarize some of the above results for the two-period problem.

Proposition 5.6.

(i) Under the income risk in which future noninterest income is uncertain,

(a) an increase in present income increases present consumption and present saving, so that the marginal propensity to save is between 0 and 1;

(b) an increase in the expected value of future noninterest income decreases saving;

(c) the effect of an increase in the real rate of interest on saving is uncertain; and

(d) an increase in uncertainty about future noninterest income *increases* saving under the assumption of risk complementarity.

(ii) Under the capital risk in which the real rate of return is uncertain, an increase in uncertainty *decreases* saving.

REMARK: Comparing statements (i*d*) and (ii), Sandmo (1970) highlights the distinction between income risk and capital risk.

5.4 Economics of Information

5.4.1 Asymmetry of Information, the Lemon Principle, and Signaling

Consider the market for used cars. Here, the sellers would have some knowledge about the quality of a car while the buyers do not (**asymmetry of information**).[33] Suppose that good cars and bad cars (lemons) are sold at the same price, assuming a buyer cannot tell the difference between a good car and a bad car. Consequently, the market is dominated by bad cars, and the price of a used car would be considerably lower than that of a new car. In such a case, the owner of a good car

[33] For a brief review of asymmetry of information, see Postlewaite (1987).

who does not want to sell his car at such a low price would be locked in. Bad cars thus drive out the good cars in the market because they sell at the same price as good cars.

The asymmetry of information problem described above is put forth in a seminal and exciting paper (1970) by Akerlof. The process which results in the market for used cars dominated by bad cars is often called the **lemon principle**. Needless to say, this phenomenon occurs in many other markets, even though the lemon principle in the used car market has become less acute with the advent of Japanese cars in the late 1970s, among which there are very few lemons (so that the resale values of these cars are quite high). In insurance and other markets, the lemon principle goes under the name of *adverse selection*, which will be exposited below.

The asymmetry of information problem has a number of other interesting applications. One important example may be signals and signaling. In the case of the used car market, the mechanic's appraisal provides a **signal** about the car's quality. To the extent that such signals exist, the price of a used car would be adjusted upward. There may be both informed consumers and uninformed consumers. Over time uninformed consumers can infer the value of the signal by observing the price, as the price must convey all the information available (assuming that there are people who purchase information). There are many circumstances under which the signal about the value of the commodity is *exogenously* supplied. The mechanic's appraisal in the used car market is one such example.

On the other hand, there are also many circumstances under which the signals about the values are *endogenously* supplied by members of the market. This is called **self-selection**. For example, in the labor market, education is often an important signal that conveys information about the quality of workers, and the workers are aware of this.[34]

---

[34]For a discussion of signaling, see Spence (1973), for example. Following him, consider a job market. As in most job markets, the employer is not sure of the productive capabilities of workers. Suppose there are two types of workers, type A and type B. The value of the marginal product of each type A worker is \$$a$ and that of each type B worker is \$$b$, where $a < b$. Assume that the employer cannot directly observe the marginal product prior to hiring. The employer is assumed to be risk neutral so that only the marginal product matters. Suppose that it is known from past experience that there is a strong correlation between an individual worker's ability and his or her level of education. Namely, let c_i be the cost of education (schooling) and assume that such is proportional to the level of education y, $c_i = k_i y$, $i = A, B$, where it is supposed that $k_A > k_B$. That is, the low ability person requires more costs in education than the high ability person to achieve a given level of education y. Since y is observable, the employer can offer a wage rate depending on his or her level of education. The question is whether the employer can successfully differentiate workers according to their capabilities by using their levels

Unfortunately, we do not have space to exposit all of these problems in detail here. Some important and illuminating readings can be found in Diamond and Rothchild (1989), for example. We now turn our attention to the asymmetry of information and moral hazard problem in the context of insurance markets.

5.4.2 Preventive Activity and Asymmetry of Information in Insurance

As in subsection 5.3.1, consider an individual who is thinking about purchasing an insurance policy.[35] As before, assume that there are only two states of nature, S_1 and S_2. In S_1, the individual suffers a loss of b dollars, and in S_2 suffers no loss. Let π be the probability of S_1 occurring. Let a be the initial value of the asset he or she wants to insure. Also, let x denote the amount that the insurance company pays (insurance coverage) if S_1 occurs, where P is the premium of such insurance. It will be assumed that the individual will be able to choose this level of insurance coverage x. Unlike our discussion in subsection 5.3.1, here we suppose that the insured can affect the probability of loss, π, by preventive activity.

Assume that the cost of preventive activity is measured in terms of dollars. Then letting z be the amount of such an expense, we have $\pi(z)$ where $\pi' < 0$ and $\pi'' > 0$. It is assumed that the preventive activity costs one dollar per unit and that the insurer cannot observe z. Then the problem for the insured is the same as that of making a decision on the lottery,

$$[\pi(z);\ a - b - z - P + x,\ a - z - P].$$

For concreteness, one may imagine automobile insurance, where the

---

of education. Spence asserts that the answer to this question can be affirmative, and this can produce **signaling equilibrium**, in which education is a **signal** and education costs are **signaling costs**. An employee here needs to think of himself as signaling, and he is only assumed to select signals to maximize the difference between wage offers and signaling costs. Spence (1973, p. 374) points out that the applications of the above signaling model can be quite wide, where he states, "I would argue further that a range of phenomena from selective admissions procedures through promotion, loans and consumer credit, and signaling status via conspicuous consumption lends itself to analysis with the same basic conceptual apparatus." For a good, brief survey of the theory of signaling, see Riley (1987).

[35] The discussion in this subsection mainly follows Pauly (1974). Shavell (1979) offers a similar model in which the cost of avoiding accidents is in utility units. See also Arrow (1963), Ehrlich and Becker (1972), Lippman and McCall (1981), and Laffont (1989).

probability of an accident depends on the level of activity that the insured takes to prevent accidents. There is an *asymmetry of information* concerning this that the insured knows about but the insurer does not know, and such an asymmetry of information is a key to the present formulation.

Following Pauly (1974), we consider the individual's problem of how much insurance to buy in two stages. First, he or she determines the value of z that maximizes the expected utility for each value of x. Then that person chooses the x that maximizes expected utility. Namely, in the first problem, the expected utility is treated as a function of z alone; that is,

$$\phi(z) \equiv \pi(z)u(a - b - z - P + x) + [1 - \pi(z)]u(a - z - P).$$

The individual chooses z to maximize $\phi(z)$ subject to $z \geqq 0$. Omitting $(*)$ to denote the optimum, we may write the first-order condition as

$$d\phi/dz = \pi'(z)[u(a_1) - u(a_2)] - [\pi(z)u'(a_1) + \{1 - \pi(z)\}u'(a_2)] \leqq 0, \tag{79a}$$

$$(d\phi/dz)z = 0,\ z \geqq 0, \tag{79b}$$

where $a_1 \equiv a - b - z - P + x$ and $a_2 \equiv a - z - P$.

If $x = b$ (full coverage), then $u(a_1) = u(a_2)$ so that $d\phi/dz < 0$, which in turn implies $z = 0$ (a corner solution). Namely, the individual with full coverage will not pay any attention to preventive activity. Also, it follows from (79a) that $d\phi/dz < 0$ for some values of x that are less than b. For such values of x, $z = 0$. On the other hand, for those values of x at which $z > 0$ at the optimum, conditions (79a) and (79b) are reduced to $d\phi/dz = 0$, that is,

$$\pi'(z)[u(a_1) - u(a_2)] = \pi(z)u'(a_1) + [1 - \pi(z)]u'(a_2). \tag{80}$$

This, in turn, determines z as a function of x, so that $z = z(x)$, where it is assumed that $z' < 0$.[36] The condition $z' < 0$ means that the individual will reduce the level of preventive activity as the insurance

[36] z' is obtained as

$$z' = \frac{[\pi u''(a_1) - \pi' u'(a_1)]}{[\pi''\{u(a_1) - u(a_2)\} + \{\pi u''(a_1) + (1 - \pi)u''(a_2)\}]}.$$

The denominator is always negative, but the numerator can be positive or negative since $\pi' < 0$.

coverage increases. If $z(x) = 0$, i.e., no preventive activity regardless of insurance coverage, then $z' = 0$ for such values of x.

Given that z is set at the level determined by (80) for each value of x, we have $z = z(x)$. The individual then determines the level of insurance coverage x to maximize his or her expected utility subject to $x \geqq 0$. Let $P = P(x)$ be the insurance premium schedule. With $z = z(x)$ and $P = P(x)$, the expected utility of the insured becomes a function of x alone, that is,

$$\psi(x) \equiv \pi[z(x)]u[a - b - z(x) - P(x) + x] + \{1 - \pi[z(x)]\}u[a - z(x) - P(x)].$$

We now come to the individual's *second problem*, in which x is chosen to maximize $\psi(x)$ subject to $x \geqq 0$. Assuming $x > 0$ at the optimum and omitting (*) to denote the optimum, the first-order condition, $\psi'(x) = 0$, yields

$$[\pi u'(a_1) + (1 - \pi)u'(a_2)](dP/dx) = \pi u'(a_1) - [\pi u'(a_1) + (1 - \pi)u'(a_2)]z' + \pi' z'[u(a_1) - u(a_2)]. \quad (81)$$

Given (80), the last two terms of the right-hand side of (81) cancel. Hence we obtain

$$dP/dx = \pi u'(a_1)/[\pi u'(a_1) + (1 - \pi)u'(a_2)]. \quad (82)$$

If the insurer were able to observe z, the premium could be made to vary according to z, which in turn affects π.[37]

[37] Although we have considered the present optimization problem in two steps following Pauly (1974), we can also consider it in one step. Namely, define $\Phi(z, x)$ by

$$\Phi(z, x) \equiv \pi(z)u[a - b - z - P(x) + x] + \{1 - \pi(z)\}u[a - z - P(x)],$$

and consider maximizing Φ with respect to z and x. When we have an interior solution ($z > 0$ and $x > 0$ at the optimum), the first-order conditions are written as

$$\partial\Phi/\partial z = \pi'[u(a_1) - u(a_2)] - [\pi u'(a_1) + (1 - \pi)u'(a_2)] = 0,$$
$$\partial\Phi/\partial x = \pi u'(a_1) - [\pi u'(a_1) + (1 - \pi)u'(a_2)]P'(x) = 0,$$

where $a_1 \equiv a - b - z - P(x) + x$ and $a_2 \equiv a - z - P(x)$ as defined in the text. Thus $\partial\Phi/\partial z = 0$ yields (82), and $\partial\Phi/\partial x = 0$ yields (84). We leave the interested reader to investigate the second-order condition of this problem. It appears that such a condition does not follow from the assumptions such as $\pi' < 0$, $\pi'' > 0$, $u' > 0$, and $u'' < 0$.

To examine the result here in a competitive setting, suppose that all individuals are identical in the sense that they will purchase identical amounts of insurance given a price schedule. Assume also that competition in the insurance industry forces the expected profits to zero, i.e., competition drives the premium to the actuarially fair one. Then, we have $-\pi(x - P) + (1 - \pi)P = 0$, or

$$P(x) = \pi[z(x)]x. \tag{83}$$

Therefore, $P' = \pi + \pi'z'x$. Substituting this into the left-hand side of (82), we obtain

$$\pi + \pi'z'x = \pi u'(a_1)/[\pi u'(a_1) + (1 - \pi)u'(a_2)] \equiv D(x), \tag{84}$$

where $D(x)$ signifies the demand schedule for insurance coverage x.

The insurance company does not know the individual's z. One may argue that, if the company can observe x, they should be able to infer z from $z(x)$, so that this company can adjust the insurance per unit of coverage. However, this does not work since the company only knows how much insurance it sold the individual. If the company increases the per unit premium according to x, the rational individual would only go to *other* companies, where the entry of firms to the insurance industry is free under the assumption of perfect competition.

The nonoptimality of competition arises precisely because the competitive $P'(\equiv dP/dx)$, the premium *per unit* of insurance, must be the same for all individuals. Since the insurance company does not know the level of z, it has to sell each *unit* of insurance at the same price, say p. Substituting this into (83), we obtain $p = \pi$, so that we get

$$p(= \pi) = D(x). \tag{85}$$

Note that π is clearly less than $\pi + \pi'z'x$ which appears on the left-hand side of (84), because $\pi' < 0$ and $z' < 0$. Hence, assuming that the demand schedule $D(x)$ is downwardsloping, the demand for insurance would become larger than the one determined by (84).[38] Namely, the competitive equilibrium can be characterized by an overproduction of insurance, that is, **over-insurance**. "In general there is no reason to expect competitive equilibrium to be optimal" (Pauly 1974, p. 51).

[38] To say this, we have implicitly assumed that the demand schedule for insurance is downward sloping, i.e., the right-hand side of (84) is a decreasing function with respect to x. In the present model, it appears that this need not be true, even if we assume decreasing absolute risk aversion ($R_a' < 0$, which implies $u''' > 0$). Then the downward sloping demand curve becomes simply an assumption.

In the problem we just considered, the insured knows the level of his or her preventive activity (z) and the insurer does not know about it. The latter implies that the insurance premium will not be affected by the level of z. Then the individual will be induced to lower the level of preventive activity as the insurance coverage increases. Namely, insurance induces the individual to lower the level of z when such a change does not alter the premium. Then the insurance company finds itself losing money. This is called the **moral hazard** problem.[39] The asymmetry of information plays an important role here, for if the insurance company can observe z, then the insurance premium can be varied according to the level of z, and there will be no moral hazard.[40]

Needless to say, insurance companies are not helpless in the face of the moral hazard problem. Two solutions are offered. One is incomplete coverage against loss, such as deductible policies. The second is observation by the insurer of the care taken. Both would give an individual

---

[39] Diamond and Rothchild (1989, p. 307) summarize this problem as follows.

> For many commodities, the cost of providing the commodity depends on the behavior of the purchaser. This is obviously true of insurance, where, for example, the expected cost of providing automobile insurance depends on the number of miles to be driven by the insured individual. A similar situation arises with products that come with guarantees, where the probability of a breakdown of the product within the guarantee period may depend on the way in which the product is used, or the amount that is used. If the supplier cannot observe the behavior of the purchaser, the price to be charged for the product cannot depend upon the behavior which affects costs. That is, automobile insurance does not generally depend on the number of miles to be driven.

It is generally noted that the term "moral hazard" is unfortunate, as it has unnecessary ethical connotations given that parties to contracts are not prevented from the standard maximization of utility. For this reason, Guesneri (1987) proposes the use of the term **hidden actions**, instead. Guesnerie (1987) contains a brief, useful survey of the topic.

[40] To investigate the moral hazard problem in insurance, Laffont (1989, pp. 125–27) specifies $P(x)$ to be equal to $\pi(z)x$. Then the problem of the insured is to choose z and x to maximize

$$\Psi(z, x) \equiv \pi(z)u[a - b - z - \pi(z)x + x] + [1 - \pi(z)][a - z - \pi(z)].$$

When an interior solution (i.e., $z > 0$ and $x > 0$ at the optimum) is ensured, the first-order conditions are written as

$$\partial\Psi/\partial z = 0 \text{ and } \partial\Phi/\partial x = 0,$$

where $\partial\Psi/\partial x = 0$ is obtained as

$$\pi(1 - \pi)[u'(a_1) - u'(a_2)] = 0,$$

or $a_1 = a_2$. This implies $x = b$, or full coverage. The major difficulty of this solution, which is the source of moral hazard here, is that the insurance company a motivation to prevent loss. If observation of care is either impossible or too expensive to be worthwhile, incomplete coverage is an optimal policy for the insurer, while, if the insurer can observe care with perfect accuracy, then an optimal insurance policy involves full coverage and care is observed *ex post*. If the insurer's observations are not perfectly accurate but can be made without cost, an optimal policy typically involves incomplete coverage, and other *ex ante* or *ex post* observations are of positive value (see Shavell 1979).

5.4.3 Adverse Selection

The asymmetry of information between the insurer and the insured with regard to the probability of casualty also causes an important problem, **adverse selection**, mentioned earlier. Suppose that the individuals can be classified into two groups by the probability of accidents, a high-risk group and a low-risk group. Let π_H and π_L , respectively, denote the probability of being in the high-risk and low-risk groups, where $\pi_H > \pi_L$. It is not essential that such probabilities depend on the level of care z. What is important here is that the insurer cannot distinguish between them, while individuals know their own risks. The insurer will obviously try to find ways of getting the low-risk people to reveal themselves by offering some deduction schemes and so on, which may have greater appeal to them. Suppose this fails. Then the basic policy will be most attractive to the high-risk people, which in turn drives up the insurance premium. Eventually, the low-risk people are chased out of the market,

---

cannot observe z, the level of self-protection by the insured. If instead, the insurance company sets a price p that is independent of z, then the problem is altered to the one of choosing z and x to maximize

$$\Gamma(z, x) \equiv \pi(z)u(a - b - z - px + x) + [1 - \pi(z)]u(a - z - px).$$

The first-order conditions of this problem are:

$$\partial\Gamma/\partial z = \pi'[u(a_1) - u(a_2)] - [\pi u'(a_1) + (1 - \pi)u'(a_2)] \leqq 0,$$

$$\partial\Gamma/\partial x = \pi' u(a_1) - p[\pi' u(a_1) + (1 - \pi)u'(a_2)] \leqq 0,$$

$z(\partial\Gamma/\partial z) = 0$, $x(\partial\Gamma/\partial x) = 0$, $z \geqq 0$, and $x \geqq 0$. The zero-profit condition, $\pi(x - px) = (1 - \pi)px$, requires $p = \pi$, in which case, $\partial\Gamma/\partial x = \pi(1 - \pi)[u'(a_1) - u'(a_2)]$. Hence, if $x > 0$ at the optimum, then $\partial\Gamma/\partial x = 0$, so that $u(a_1) = u(a_2)$, or $a_1 = a_2$. This, in turn, implies full coverage. Using $a_1 = a_2$, we obtain

$$\partial\Gamma/\partial z = -[\pi u'(a_1) + (1 - \pi)u'(a_2)] < 0.$$

Hence, with $z(\partial\Gamma/\partial z) = 0$, we must have $z = 0$ at the optimum. Namely, at the competitive equilibrium, the level of self-protection is zero. The price of insurance p is equal to $\pi(0)$.

and the insurance market will be dominated by the high-risk people. This is analogous to the lemon principle in the automobile case discussed earlier, in which the used car market is dominated by lemons. Noting the fact that people over 65 have great difficulty in buying medical insurance, and asking why the price rise does not match the risk, Akerlof (1970, pp. 492–93) states

> One answer is that as the price level rises the people who insure themselves will be those who are increasingly certain that they will need the insurance. ... The result is that the average medical condition of insurance applicants deteriorates as the price level rises—with the result that no insurance sales may take place at any price. This is strictly analogous to our automobile case where the average quality of used cars supplied fell with a corresponding fall in the price level.

This is also a *moral hazard* problem. *The asymmetry of information induces certain people to take advantage of it to the detriment of the other party without the other party knowing it.* The above examples of adverse selection necessarily involve moral hazard. On the other hand, adverse selection can occur without involving moral hazard. An interesting example of this is offered by Stiglitz and Weiss (1981) in the context of credit rationing.

They considered a competitive banking system in which the supply of loanable funds is an increasing function of the interest rate. Suppose that there are two types of firms, θ_1 and θ_2.[41] The θ_1-type firm undertakes an investment project θ_1, and the θ_2-type firm undertakes an investment project θ_2. Assume that both types of projects require the same amount of funds. Project θ_1 brings about $\$R_1$ to the firm if it is successful and \$0 if it fails, where the probability of the failure is q_1. On the other hand, project θ_2 brings about $\$R_2$ to the firm if it is successful and \$0 if it fails, where the probability of its failure is q_2. Assume that $q_1 < q_2$ and $R_1 < R_2$. Namely, project θ_1 has less probability of failure, but it brings less revenue in the case of success, as compared to project θ_2. Namely, the θ_1-type firm is a low-risk, low-return firm, while the θ_2-type firm is a high-risk, high-return firm. Each firm borrows $\$B$ with collateral $\$C$, where the rate of interest is equal to r. If project θ_i is successful, the θ_i-type firm receives $\$[R_i - (1 + r)B]$, and if it fails, the firm loses $\$C$.

[41] For concise and useful expositions of Stiglitz and Weiss (1981), see, for example, Nishimura (1989, pp. 254–57) and Wilson (1987).

The expected value of project θ_1 is

$$y_1(r) \equiv -q_1 C + (1 - q_1)\{R_1 - (1 + r)B\}.$$

Similarly, the expected value of project θ_2 for a given r is

$$y_2(r) \equiv -q_2 C + (1 - q_2)\{R_2 - (1 + r)B\}.$$

Assume that $(1 - q_1)R_1 < (1 - q_2)R_2$ and $B > C$, where the first relation states that project θ_2's expected revenue in the case of success is greater than that of project θ_1. Then we can show

$$y_1(r) < y_2(r), \quad \text{for each } r.$$

Let r^* and r^{**} be defined by

$$y_1(r^*) = 0 \quad \text{and} \quad y_2(r^{**}) = 0.$$

Then we have the following relations, depending on the current rate r.

$$\begin{aligned} r < r^* \quad & \Rightarrow \text{both projects will be undertaken,} \\ r^* < r < r^{**} \quad & \Rightarrow \text{only project } \theta_2 \text{ will be undertaken.} \end{aligned}$$

Let $z_i(r)$ be the expected revenue of the bank, if project θ_i is undertaken and if the rate of interest is equal to r. Then we have

$$z_1(r) \equiv q_1 C + (1 - q_1)(1 + r)B,$$

$$z_2(r) \equiv q_2 C + (1 - q_2)(1 + r)B.$$

Clearly, we have $z_1(r) > z_2(r)$, since $q_1 < q_2$ and $B > C$. Hence, in lending money, the bank would prefer project θ_1 to project θ_2. This is where the asymmetry of information arises. Suppose that the bank does not know which firms belong to which type. Each borrower requires the same amount of funds and is indistinguishable to the bank from any other borrower. If the bank raises the interest rate r, its revenue will, *ceteris paribus*, increase. However, if r is raised from the level below r^* to the level above it, $r^* < r < r^{**}$, then only type θ_2 firms remain. Namely, the market is dominated by the high-risk, high-returns firms, just like Akerlof's used car market is dominated by lemons. This is adverse selection due to asymmetry of information between the firms and the banks. However, this adverse selection involves no moral hazard.

Suppose that the bank knows by experience that $\alpha \cdot 100\%$ firms belong to θ_1 type and $(1 - \alpha) \cdot 100\%$ firms belong to the θ_2 type. Suppose further that the bank finances a total of n projects. Then the expected profit of the bank is

$$\pi(r) \equiv \alpha n z_1(r) + (1 - \alpha) n z_2(r) - nB.$$

As the interest rate r rises, the bank is willing to finance more projects (i.e., n rises). Also, $z_1(r)$ and $z_2(r)$ rise. Thus, $\pi(r)$ also rises initially. However, as r rises, eventually only the θ_2-type firms (the high-risk firms) remain, in which case $\pi(r)$ decreases accordingly, where we may recall $z_1(r) > z_2(r)$. Then the profit maximizing r for the bank can be below the market rate. By lowering the interest below the market clearing rate, and attracting the low-risk firms, it is possible for a bank to raise its expected rate of return. Since every borrower prefers the lower interest rate, the higher "market clearing" rate is not sustainable. The result is an equilibrium rate of return with an excess demand of loans, an equilibrium model with credit rationing.

This analysis of credit rationing has wide application to the **principal-agent problem.**[42] An **agent** is a person who is employed to act on behalf of another, called the **principal**. In any situation, the actions of an individual are not easily observable. A principal-agent problem then arises when the principal cannot precisely monitor the actions of the agent. The problem is how the principal can design a compensation system (a contract) that motivates the agent to act in his or her interest. Stiglitz and Weiss (1981) assert that the analysis of credit rationing "could apply equally well to any one of a number of principal-agent problems. For example, in agriculture the bank (principal) corresponds to the landlord and the borrower (agent) to the tenant while the loan contract corresponds to a rental agreement. ... The central concern in those principal-agent problems is how to provide the proper incentives for the agent. In general, revenue sharing arrangements such as equity finance, or share cropping are inefficient. Under those schemes ..., too little effort will be forthcoming from agents." (p. 407).

5.5 Concluding Remarks

The expected utility theory, despite criticisms, has been instrumental in producing a number of eye-opening results in economics. This has

[42]For an excellent, succinct, and brief exposition of the principal-agent problem, see Stiglitz (1987). See also Kotowitz (1987), where he cites *Wealth of Nations*. In Adam Smith, management is an agent, and the principal is the capitalist, in which Smith states, "Negligence and profusion ... must always prevail, more or less in the management of the affairs of such a company" (Smith 1776, p. 700).

also lead to interesting new developments in the economics of information. While the von Neumann-Morgenstern expected utility theory has a great advantage of being quite operational, we may note that there is one apparent shortcoming in its application. Namely, most of the results in the economics of uncertainty are based on the assumption that there is only one random variable, such as the one that can be expressed in terms of monetary units. When there is more than one random variable, the analysis becomes exceedingly difficult. This can be seen by simply noting that the procedure of taking expectation involves double or multiple integrals under such a circumstance, while if there is only one random variable, a simple integral will suffice in taking expectations. More importantly perhaps, a satisfactory extension of the Arrow-Pratt measures of risk aversion to the case of more than one random variable has not been obtained yet.

However, confining ourselves to the one variable case, expected utility theory has been able to produce many illuminating results, as we have seen in the discussion of the present chapter. Coupled with recent rapid developments in game theory and developments in other fields of economics such as industrial organization, there would be little doubt that the economics of uncertainty and information will continue to produce many more interesting results.

References

Akerlof, G. 1970. "The Market for Lemons: Qualitative Uncertainty and the Market Mechanism." *Quarterly Journal of Economics* 84 (August): 488–500.

Alchian, A. A. 1953. "The Meaning of Utility Meaurement." *American Economic Review* 43 (March): 26–53.

Allais, M. 1953. "Le Comportement de l'homme rationnel devant le risque Critique des postulates ex axiomes de l'ecole americaine." *Econometrica* 21 (October): 503–46.

Anscombe, F. J., and R. J. Aumann. 1963. "A Definition of Subjective Probability." *Annals of Mathematical Statistics* 34 (March): 199–205.

Applebaum, E., and E. Katz. 1986. "Measure of Risk Aversion and Comparative Statics." *American Economic Review* 76 (June): 524–29.

Arrow, K. J. 1963. "Uncertainty and Welfare Economics of Medical Care." *American Economic Review* 53 (December): 941–73. Reprinted in Arrow 1970 and also in Diamond and Rothchild 1989. The latter does not contain the appendix.

———. 1965. *Aspects of the Theory of Risk-Bearing.* Yrjö Jahnsson Lectures. Helsinki: Yrjö Jahnssoin Sattio.

———. 1970. *Essays in the Theory of Risk-Bearing.* Chicago: Markaham.

Bacharach, M. 1977. *Economics and the Theory of Games.* London: Macmillan.

Borch, K. H. 1968. *The Economics of Uncertainty.* Princeton, N. J.: Princeton University Press.

———. 1990. *Economics of Insurance.* Amsterdam: North-Holland.

Cass, D., and J. E. Stigliz. 1970. "The Structure of Investor Preferences and Asset Returns, and Separability in Portfolio Allocation: A Contribution to the Theory of Mutual Funds." *Journal of Economic Theory* 2 (June): 122–60.

Cowell, F. A. 1986. *Microeconomic Principles.* New York: Oxford University Press.

Deaton, A., and J. Muellbauer. 1980. *Economics and Consumer Behavior.* Cambridge: Cambridge University Press.

Diamond, P., and M. Rothchild, eds. 1989. *Uncertainty in Economics: Readings and Exercises.* Rev. ed. New York: Academic Press (1st ed. 1978).

Eatwell, J., M. Milgate, and P. Newman, eds. 1987. *The New Palgrave: A Dictionary of Econom-ics.* 4 vols. London: Macmillan.

Ehrlich, I., and G. S. Becker. 1972. "Market Insurance and Self-Protection." *Journal of Political Economy* 80 (July/August): 623–48.

Ellsberg, D. 1954. "Classic and Current Notions of 'Measurable Utility.'" *Economic Journal* 64 (September): 528–56.

Feldstein, M. S. 1969. "Mean-Variance Analysis in the Theory of Liquidity Preference and Portfolio Selection." *Review of Economic Studies* 36 (January): 5–12.

Fisher, I. 1930. *The Theory of Interest.* London: Macmillan.

Ford, J. L. 1983. *Choice, Expectation, and Uncertainty.* Oxford: Martin Robertson.

Friedman, M., and L. J. Savage, 1948. "The Utility Analysis of Choice Involving Risk." *Journal of Political Economy* 56 (August): 279–304.

Gravelle, H., and R. Rees. 1981. *Microeconomics.* London: Longman.

Green, H. A. J. 1978. *Consumer Theory.* New York: Academic Press.

Guesnerie, R. 1987. "Hidden Actions, Moral Hazard, and Contract Theory." In Eatwell, Milgate, and Newman 1987, 2: 646–50.

Hammond, P. J. 1987. "Uncertainty." In Eatwell, Milgate, and Newman 1987, vol. 4: 728–33.

Hart, O. D. 1975. "Some Negative Results on the Existence of Comparative Statics Results in Portfolio Theory." *Review of Economic Studies* 42 (October): 615–21.

Henderson, J. M., and R. E. Quandt. 1980. *Microeconomic Theory: A Mathematical Approach.* 3d ed. New York: McGraw-Hill.

Hey, J. D. 1979. *Uncertainty in Microeconomics.* New York: New York University Press.

Hirschleifer, J. 1965. "Investment Decision under Uncertainty: Choice-Theoretic Approaches." *Quarterly Journal of Economics* 79 (November): 509–36.

Hirshleifer, J., and J. G. Riley. 1979. "The Analytics of Uncertainty and Information - An Expository Survey." *Journal of Economic Literature* 17 (December): 1375–421.

Hosoe, M. 1987. *Economic Analysis of Uncertainty and Information* (in Japanese). Fukuoka, Japan: Kyushu University Press.

Kahneman, D., and A. Tversky. 1979. "Prospect Theory: An Analysis of Decision under Risk." *Econometrica* 47 (March): 263–91.

Kihlstrom, R. E., and L. J. Mirman. 1974. "Risk Aversion with Many Commodities." *Journal of Economic Theory* 8 (July): 361–88.

Kiritani, T. 1986. *Modern Theory of Asset Selection* (in Japanese). Tokyo: Toyo Keizai Shimpo-sha.

Knight, F. H. 1921. *Risk, Uncertainty, and Profit.* New York: Houghton Mifflin.

Kotowitz, Y. 1987. "Moral Hazard." In Eatwell, Milgate, and Newman 1987, 3: 549–51, 700.

Kreps, D. M. 1990. *A Course in Microeconomic Theory.* Princeton, N.J.: Princeton University Press

Laffont, J. J. 1989. *The Economics of Uncertainty and Information.* T rans. by J. P. Bonin and H. Bonin. Cambridge, Mass.: MIT Press.

Layard, P. R. G., and A. A. Walters. 1978. *Microeconomic Theory.* New York: McGraw-Hill.

Leland, H. E. 1968. "Savings and Uncertainty: The Precautionary Demand for Saving." *Quarterly Journal of Economics* 82, August: 465-73. Reprinted in Diamond and Rothchild 1989.

Lippman, S. A., and J. J. McCall. 1981. "The Economics of Uncertainty: Selected Topics in Probabilistic Methods." In *Handbook of Mathematical Economics*, ed. K. J. Arrow and M. D. Intriligator, 1: 211–84. Amsterdam: North-Holland.

Loomes, G., and R. Sugden. 1982. "Regret Theory: An Alternative Theory of Rational Choice under Uncertainty." *Economic Journal* 92 (December): 805–24.

———. 1983. "A Rationale for Preference Reversal." *American Economic Review* 73 (March): 428–32.

Luce, R. D., and Raiffa, H. 1957. *Games and Decisions.* New York: John Wiley and Sons.

Machina, M. J. 1982. "Expected Utility Analysis without the Independence Axiom." *Econometrica* 50 (March): 277–323.

———. 1987. "Expected Utility Hypothesis." In Eatwell, Milgate, and Newman 1987, 2: 232–39.

———. 1989. "Dynamic Consistency and Non-Expected Utility Models of Choice under Uncertainty." *Journal of Economic Literature* 22 (December): 1622–68.

Machina, M. J., and M. Rothchild. 1987. "Risk." In Eatwell, Milgate, and Newman 1987, 4: 201–06.

Malinvaud, E. 1977. *Leçons de théorie microéconomique.* 4th ed. Paris: Dunod. (The Japanese translation by T. Hayashi from the 4th ed. French original with translator's corrections of typos. Tokyo: Sobunsha, 1981. The English translation by A. Silvey from the 2d revised ed., Amsterdam: North-Holland.)

Marschak, J. 1950. "Rational Behavior, Uncertain Prospects, and Measurable Utility." *Econometrica* 18 (April): 111–41.

McCall, J. J. 1971. "Probabilistic Economics." *Bell Journal of Economics and Management Science* 2 (Autumn): 403–33.

McKenna, C. J. 1986. *The Economics of Uncertainty.* London: Wheatsheaf Books.

Nishimura, O. 1989. *Microeconomics* (in Japanese). Kyoto: Showado.

Okuno, M., and K. Suzumura. 1985. *Microeconomics I* (in Japanese). Tokyo: Iwanami.

Pauly, M. V. 1974. "Overinsurance and Public Provision of Insurance: The Roles of Moral Hazard and Adverse Selection." *Quarterly Journal of Economics* 8 (February): 44–54. Reprinted in Diamond and Rothchild 1989.

Pindyck, R. S., and D. L. Rubinfeld. 1989. *Microeconomics.* London: Macmillan.

Postlewaite, A. 1987. "Asymmetric Information." In Eatwell, Milgate, and Newman 1987, 1: 133–35.

Pratt, J. W. 1964. "Risk Aversion in the Small and in the Large." *Econometrica* 32 (January/February): 122–36. Reprinted in Diamond and Rothchild 1989.

Quirk, J. P. 1987. *Intermediate Microeconomics.* 3d ed. Chicago: Science Research Associates. (1st ed. 1976, 2d ed. 1983).

Riley, J. G. 1987. "Signaling." In Eatwell, Milgate, and Newman 1987, 4: 330–33.

Rothchild, M., and J. E. Stiglitz. 1970. "Increasing Risk I: A Definition." *Journal of Economic Theory* 2 (September): 225–43.

———. 1971. "Increasing Risk II: Its Economic Consequences." *Journal of Economic Theory* 3 (March): 66–84.

Sakai, Y. 1978 "A Simple General Equilibrium Model of Production: Comparative Statics with Price Uncertainty." *Journal of Economic Theory* 19 (December): 287–306.

———. 1982. *The Economics of Uncertainty* (in Japanese). Tokyo: Yuhikaku.

Sandmo, A. 1969. "Capital Risk, Consumption, and Portfolio Choice." *Econometrica* 37 (October): 586–99.

———. 1970. "The Effects of Uncertainty on Saving Decisions." *Review of Economic Studies* 37 (July): 353–60.

———. 1971. "On the Theory of the Competitive Firm Under Price Uncertainty." *American Economic Review* 65 (March): 65–73.

———. 1974. "Two-Period Models of Consumption Decision under Uncertainty." In *Allocation under Uncertainty: Equilibrium and Optimality*, ed. J. H. Drèze. New York: Macmillan.

———. 1977. "Portfolio Theory, Asset Demand, and Taxation: Comparative Statics with Many Assets." *Review of Economic Studies* 44 (June): 369–79.

———. 1985. "Effects of Taxation and Savings and Risk Taking." In *Handbook of Mathematical Economics*, ed. A. J. Auerbach and M. Feldstein, 1: 265–311. Amsterdam: North-Holland.

Savage, L. J. 1954. *Foundations of Statistics*. New York: John Wiley.

Schoemaker, P. J. H. 1982. "The Expected Utility Model: Its Various Purposes, Evidences and Limitations." *Journal of Economic Literature*, 20 (June): 529–63.

Shavell, S. 1979. "On Moral Hazard and Insurance." *Quarterly Journal of Economics* 93 (November): 541–62.

Silberberg, E. 1990. *The Structure of Economics*. 2d ed. New York: McGraw Hill (1st ed. 1978).

Sinn, H.-W. 1983. *Economic Decisions under Uncertainty*. Amsterdam: North-Holland.

Spence, M. 1973. "Job Market Signaling." *Quarterly Journal of Economics* 87, August: 355–74. Reprinted in Diamond and Rothchild 1989.

Stiglitz, J. E. 1987. "Principal and Agent." In Eatwell, Milgate, and Newman 1987, 3: 966–72.

Stiglitz, J. E., and A. Weiss. 1981. "Credit Rationing in Markets with Imperfect Information." *American Economic Review* 71 (June): 393–410.

Tobin, J. 1958. "Liquidity Preference as Behavior Towards Risk." *Review of Economic Studies* 25 (February): 65–86.

Varian, H. 1984. *Microeconomic Analysis*. 2d ed. New York: W. W. Norton.

von Neumann, J., and O. Morgenstern. 1953. *Theory of Games and Economic Behavior*. 3rd ed. Princeton, N.J.: Princeton University Press (1st ed. 1944, 2nd ed. 1949).

Wilson, C. 1987. "Adverse Selection." In Eatwell, Milgate, and Newman 1987, 1: 32–34.

Yaari, M. 1969. "Some Remarks on Measures of Risk Aversion and Their Use." *Journal of Economic Theory* 1 (October): 315–29. Reprinted in Diamond and Rothchild 1989.

Part 4

Differential Equations and Economic Analysis

CHAPTER 6

Elements of Differential Equations and Economic Applications

In recent years, it has become increasingly important to incorporate explicit dynamics in economic analysis. Many models, in which economists are content to a single period, have now incorporated explicit dynamics. The two tools that mathematicians have developed, differential equations and optimal control theory, are probably the most basic for economists analyzing dynamic problems. In the rest of the book, we study such tools with nontrivial economic applications.[1]

6.1 Basic Concepts and Existence of a Solution

Loosely speaking, a differential equation is an equation involving derivatives of unknown functions. For example, letting $\dot{x} \equiv dx/dt$, consider the following equation:

$$\dot{x}(t) = -ax(t), \tag{1}$$

where a is a positive constant, and $x(t)$ is a real-valued function defined in an open interval. Here $x(t)$ is the "unknown function" in the sense that its explicit form is unknown, or not specified a priori. Hence (1) is a differential equation.

More generally, we may consider the following equation:

$$\dot{x}(t) = f[t,\ x(t)], \tag{2}$$

where $x(t)$ is the "unknown function" and f is the known function. Hence, both functions f and x are real-valued where $t \in R$ and f is defined on an open interval $(\alpha,\ \beta)$ of R. Clearly, equation (1) is a special case of (2).

---

[1]The present chapter is adapted from Takayama (1980a, b).

If there is a function $\phi(t)$ such that, when it is substituted into (2), it reduces (2) to an identity in a certain open interval (α, β) in R, we call $\phi(t)$ a **solution** of (2) and the interval (α, β) the **domain** of the solution $\phi(t)$. Namely, $\phi(t)$ is a solution of (2) in the interval (α, β) if and only if

$$\dot{\phi}(t) = f[t, \phi(t)] \text{ for } \textit{all } t \in (\alpha, \beta). \tag{3}$$

For example, the function

$$\phi(t) = ce^{-at} \tag{4}$$

(where c is an arbitrary constant) is a solution of differential equation (1). The domain of this $\phi(t)$ is $R \equiv (-\infty, \infty)$. Indeed, we can easily observe

$$\dot{\phi}(t) = -ace^{-at} = -a\,\phi(t), \quad \text{for all } t \in R. \tag{5}$$

Namely, $\phi(t)$ specified by (4) reduces (1) to an identity for all $t \in (-\infty, \infty)$.

An even simpler example of (2) would be the following differential equation:

$$\dot{x} = 1, \tag{6}$$

whose solution is easily obtained as

$$\phi(t) = t + c,\ t \in R, \tag{7}$$

where c is an arbitrary constant.

Examples (1) and (6) indicate that the solution defined above is not, in general, unique. In fact, for both cases there can be infinitely many solutions, since c can be any arbitrary real number. On the other hand, if we are given the value of x as $x = x^{\circ}$ for $t = t^{\circ}$, the solution of either (1) or (6) becomes unique. For example, if $x = x^{\circ}$ for $t = 0$, the solution of (1) and (6) are, respectively, specified uniquely by

$$\phi(t) = x^{\circ}e^{-at}, \text{ and} \tag{4'}$$

$$\phi(t) = t + x^{\circ}. \tag{7'}$$

The value of the constant c is uniquely determined by such an "initial condition." We illustrate (7) and (7′) in figure 6.1. This is the solution of (6).

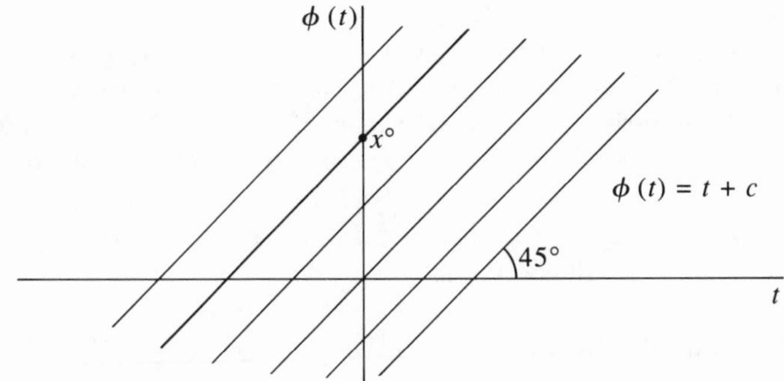

Figure 6.1: Illustration of solutions of (6)

Hence, one of the most important problems in the theory of differential equations is the question of whether or not there *exists* a solution passing through a given point $(t^\circ,\ x^\circ)$. Given such an existence, we are naturally concerned with whether or not such a solution passing through a given point $(t^\circ,\ x^\circ)$ is *unique*. In either of the differential equations (1) and (6), we can easily see that the solution that passes through an arbitrary given point $(t^\circ,\ x^\circ) \in R^2$ always exists and is unique.

In general, the problem of finding a solution of differential equation (2) that passes through a given point $(t^\circ,\ x^\circ)$ is called the **initial-value problem**, where $x(t^\circ) = x^\circ$ or $\phi(t^\circ) = x^\circ$ is called the **initial condition**. The function $\phi(t)$, which satisfies (3) with $\phi(t^\circ) = x^\circ$ where $t^\circ \in (\alpha,\ \beta)$, is called a **solution** of the initial-value problem for (2). The word *initial* reflects the fact that t° is often set equal to zero, signifying the initial time.

On the other hand, t° does not have to be zero. In the initial-value problem, it only suffices to specify a certain point $(t^\circ,\ x^\circ)$ to determine its solution and there is no need to restrict $t^\circ = 0$. For example, the solution of (1) is given by (4′) under the specification of $(0,\ x^\circ)$, that is, $x = x^\circ$ when $t = 0$. However, its solution can also be given by

$$\phi(t) = x^\circ e^{-a(t-t^\circ)}, \tag{4''}$$

under the specification of $(t^\circ,\ x^\circ)$, i.e., $x = x^\circ$ when $t = t^\circ$.[2]

[2]From (4), we obtain $x^\circ = ce^{-at^\circ}$ so that $c = x^\circ e^{at^\circ}$. Substituting this into (4)

We might also mention that although t is customarily taken to signify "time" (as the word "initial" suggests), this need not be the case. The theory of differential equations is a mathematical theory, and thus it is free from concepts (such as "time") used in various applications. On the other hand, since most applications interpret t as "time," it would facilitate the understanding of the theory if we follow such an interpretation. In this case (2) is taken to represent a *dynamic* or *evolutionary* process.

In (2) we assumed that both x and f are real-valued. More generally, they can be vector-valued. We may consider:

$$\dot{x}_i(t) = f_i[t, x_1(t), x_2(t), \ldots, x_n(t)], \; i = 1, 2, \ldots, n. \tag{8}$$

We call (8) a **system of n first-order differential equations**. In our discussion we confine ourselves to this type of differential equation. If the functions f_i's are independent of t (when $\partial f_i/\partial t \equiv 0$, for all i), then (8) is called **autonomous**.

In (2), the highest order of derivatives involved is one. We call such an equation a **first-order differential equation**. On the other hand, we may consider, for example,

$$\ddot{x}(t) = f[t, x(t), \dot{x}(t)], \tag{9}$$

where $\ddot{x}(t) \equiv d^2x/dt^2$. This is called a **second-order differential equation**. In general, the **order** of a differential equation is defined as the highest order of the derivative (of unknown functions) contained in it. We may observe that (9) can be converted to the type of equation described in (8). Defining $y(t)$ by $y(t) \equiv \dot{x}(t)$; we may rewrite (9) as

$$\dot{y}(t) = f[t, x(t), y(t)] \quad \text{and} \quad \dot{x}(t) = y(t), \tag{9'}$$

which is a system of two first-order differential equations. In a similar fashion, a differential equation of the nth order can be converted into a system of n first-order differential equations. We may note that in all of the above discussions, it is assumed that the "unknown function" $x(t)$ contains only one independent variable, or more specifically, $t \in R$, so that $\dot{x}(t)$ signifies the *total* derivative of $x(t)$. On the other hand, if t is a vector, then we shall, in general, have *partial* derivatives of the "unknown function," $x(t)$. In this case, the differential equation is called a **partial differential equation**, while the ones we discussed above, such as (2), (8), and (9), are called **ordinary differential equations**

---

yields (4″).

or simply, **differential equations**. We confine ourselves to ordinary differential equations.

We are now ready to provide a little more formal discussion. We shall do so by way of stating the most important theorem in the theory of differential equations. This theorem also clarifies some basic assumptions involved in dealing with differential equations.

Theorem 6.1 (Cauchy-Peano). Consider the system of differential equations given by (8), or more compactly,

$$\dot{x}(t) = f[t, x(t)], \tag{10}$$

where $x = (x_1, \ldots, x_n)$ and $f = (f_1, \ldots, f_n)$. Here $f : D \to R^n$ is a continuous function defined on $D \equiv T \times B$, where T is an open interval (a, b) in R, and B is an open subset of R^n. Assume that f is continuously differentiable with respect to x in B,[3] and let t° and x°, respectively, be points in T and B satisfying $x(t^\circ) = x^\circ$. Then there exists an R^n-valued function $\phi(t)$ defined on an open subinterval (α, β) of T such that $t^\circ \in (\alpha, \beta)$, and

(i) $\phi(t)$ is continuous in (α, β),

(ii) $\dot{\phi}(t) = f[t, \phi(t)]$, for all t in (α, β), except possibly for the elements of some countable subset of (α, β),

(iii) $\phi(t^\circ) = x^\circ$, and

(iv) if $\psi(t)$ is another function that satisfies conditions (i) through (iii) for some open subinterval (α', β') of T such that $t^\circ \in (\alpha', \beta')$,

then we have

$$\phi(t) = \psi(t), \quad \text{for all } t \in (\alpha, \beta) \cap (\alpha', \beta'). \tag{11}$$

REMARK: The function $\phi(t)$ that satisfies conditions (i) and (ii) of theorem 6.1 is called a **solution** of the system of differential equations (10), where $x(t^\circ) = x^\circ$ is the initial condition. Condition (iv) means that the solution that satisfies the initial condition is *unique*.

---

[3]Note that the continuous differentiability of f with respect to t is not assumed. The continuous differentiability of the function f with respect to x can be weakened to the condition called the "Lipschitz condition." On the other hand, this relaxation is not important for the present exposition and hence is omitted.

REMARK: Under the specified assumptions, theorem 6.1 establishes the existence of a unique solution $\phi(t)$ for a certain interval (α, β), given the initial condition. Note that the domain of the solution $\phi(t)$, the interval (α, β), is restricted to be a subset of T (which can be small). Namely, theorem 6.1 only provides a *local* existence theorem.

REMARK: Note that function f in differential equation (10) need not be defined on the entire space, $R \times R^n$, but rather it is defined on a certain open subset D. If $x = \phi(t)$ is a scalar-valued function, we can obtain a graphic representation of the solution path (t, x), where the solution paths are represented by curves in D in the $t - x$ space. While D can be the entire R^2 as in the case of figure 6.1, this need not be the case in general. D can be smaller than R^2. Note also that the initial point (t°, x°) must be in this set D. It is not an arbitrary point in R^2.

Theorem 6.1 ensures the existence of a unique solution in a certain interval of t given (t°, x°) under certain assumptions. The following examples illustrating the *nonuniqueness* or the *nonexistence* of a solution may be useful.

Example 6.1. Consider the following equation:[4]

$$\dot{x}(t) = f[x(t)] = x(t)^{2/3}, \quad \text{where } x \in R \text{ and } t \in R,$$

and let $t^\circ = 0$ and $x^\circ = 0$. Then both $\phi(t) = 0$ and $\phi(t) = (t/3)^3$ where $t \in R$ satisfy this equation, and by condition (iii), $\phi(t^\circ) = x^\circ$. The solution passing through (0, 0) is *not* unique. Clearly, the function f is *not* differentiable at $x = 0$, and hence it violates one of the assumptions of theorem 6.1.

Example 6.2. Consider the following equation:[5]

$$\dot{x}(t) = f[x(t)] = x(t)^2, \quad \text{where } x \in R \text{ and } t \in R.$$

Clearly, f is continuously differentiable in R. The solution of this equation that passes through point $t^\circ = 1$ and $x^\circ = 1$ can easily be obtained as $\phi(t) = -1/t$, where we may observe $\dot{\phi}(t) = 1/t^2$. On the other hand, the solution of this differential equation does *not* exist for $t^\circ = 0$. This example illustrates that theorem 6.1 does *not* ensure the *global* existence

[4] This example is adapted from Arnold (1978, pp. 14–15).

[5] This example is adapted from Yoshizawa (1967, pp. 3–4).

of a solution, i.e., the existence of a solution for *all* t for which $x(t)$ is defined.

An important classification of differential equations is according to whether they are linear or nonlinear. We say that the system of n differential equations (8) or (10) is **linear** if the function f is linear with respect to x, otherwise, f is **nonlinear**. The differential equations used in examples 6.1 and 6.2 are nonlinear. In general, a linear differential equation can be written in the form of

$$\dot{x}(t) = Ax(t) + u(t), \tag{12}$$

where $A \equiv [a_{ij}]$ is an $n \times n$ matrix and its elements a_{ij}'s are, in general, functions of t. Namely, $a_{ij} = a_{ij}(t)$, or $A = A(t)$. The function $u(t)$ is R^n-valued, and it is specified a priori. The function $u(t)$ is called a control function or a **forcing function**. If $u(t) \equiv 0$, then (12) is called **homogeneous**. If A is a constant matrix, that is, if the a_{ij}'s are all constants, then (12) is called **the system of linear differential equations with constant coefficients**. Equations (1) and (6) provide examples of homogeneous linear differential equations with constant coefficients. Note that the linearity of the function f neither implies nor requires the linearity of the solution $\phi(t)$ (cf. eq. 4).

For the system of linear differential equations, theorem 6.1 can be strengthened considerably. In other words, we have theorem 6.2.

Theorem 6.2. Suppose (10) in theorem 6.1 is given in the form of (12), where we assume that the functions $A(t)$ and $u(t)$ are continuous on T.[6] Let t° and x°, respectively, be points of T and B satisfying $x(t^\circ) = x^\circ$. Then there exists $\phi(x)$ such that

(i) $\phi(t)$ is continuous for all t in T,

(ii) $\dot{\phi}(t) = A\phi(t) + u(t)$, for all t in T,

(iii) $\phi(t^\circ) = x^\circ$, and

(iv) $\phi(t)$ which satisfies conditions (i) through (iii) is unique for all t in T.

REMARK: In other words, if the system of differential equations is linear, then the solution always exists as long as $A(t)$ and $u(t)$ are

[6]In this case, f is continuous in the (t, x)-space, and continuously differentiable in x.

continuous, and its existence is ensured for *all* t in T (i.e., it is global). Given the initial condition $(t^\circ,\ x^\circ)$, the solution is unique.

REMARK: For the system of n *linear* differential equations, it is possible to obtain a solution containing n arbitrary constants, from which all possible solutions follow by specifying the values for these constants via the "initial condition," $\phi(t^\circ) = x^\circ$. For example, all the solutions of (1) can be obtained by assigning the values for c in (4). In this sense, (4) and (7) are called the **general solutions** of (1) and (6), respectively. The solution obtained by assigning particular values to these constants is called a **particular solution**. Thus (4′) and (7′) are particular solutions of (1) and (6), respectively. On the other hand, for nonlinear equations the concept of a "general solution" may lose its meaning. Even if a solution containing n arbitrary constants may be found, it is still possible to find solutions which cannot be obtained by assigning values to these constants. Although this can readily be shown in examples 6.1 and 6.2, example 6.3 may also be useful in illustrating this.

Example 6.3. Consider the following simple nonlinear equation:

$$\dot{x}(t) = f[x(t)] = -x(t)^3, \quad \text{where } x \in R \text{ and } t \in R. \tag{13}$$

It can be shown easily that

$$\phi(t) = \{2(t + c)\}^{-1/2},\ t > -c \tag{14}$$

(where c is an arbitrary constant) is a solution. On the other hand,

$$\phi(t) = 0, \quad \text{for all } t \in R, \tag{14'}$$

is also a solution of (13), and yet this solution cannot be obtained by assigning a value to c in (14). We may note also that the solution of (13) is still unique given the initial condition $(t^\circ,\ x^\circ)$.[7]

REMARK: Discontinuities of f in (10) can arise at certain points in D. If t^* is such a point of discontinuity, then it is necessary to solve the equation separately for $t < t^*$ and for $t > t^*$. For instance, consider the following equation:

$$\dot{x}(t) = 1/t. \tag{15}$$

[7]Note that although x^3 can be defined for all x in R, $\phi(t)$ in (14) and (14′) cannot take any negative values. Corresponding to the restriction of t in a certain interval of R, $\phi(t)$ is also restricted to a subset of R. In this example, the set D in theorem 6.1 is not R^2, but rather it is restricted to a subset of R^2.

The solutions of this equation are written as,

$$\phi(t) = \log t + c, \quad \text{for } t > 0, \tag{16a}$$

$$\phi(t) = \log(-t) + c, \quad \text{for } t < 0, \tag{16b}$$

where c is an arbitrary constant. There are two solutions corresponding to two open intervals $(-\infty, 0)$ and $(0, \infty)$. We may recall that the solution of a differential equation defined in terms of theorem 6.1 (or theorem 6.2) is required to be a continuous function defined on a *certain* open interval such that it satisfies the given equation for all t in that interval. Note that $\phi(t)$ in (16) satisfies these properties, where $\phi(t)$ in (16a) and (16b) are, respectively, defined in the intervals $(0, \infty)$ and $(-\infty, 0)$, and discontinuous at $t = 0$.[8]

6.2 Stability

We consider the following system of first-order (autonomous) differential equations:

$$\dot{x}_i(t) = f_i[x_1(t), \ldots, x_n(t)], \; i = 1, \ldots, n. \tag{17}$$

More compactly, $\dot{x} = f(x)$, where f is a continuously differentiable function defined on an open subset D of R^n, and where t is in an open interval (a, b). Let x° be the value of x when $t = t^\circ$, and assume $x^\circ \in D$. We write the solution of differential equation (17) passing through (t°, x°) as $x(t; x^\circ)$, which is continuous with respect to x°.[9] We assume that the solution $x(t; x^\circ)$ exists and is unique.

---

[8]Needless to say, there can be more than one point of discontinuity. For example, the solution of the differential equation,

$$\dot{x}(t) = 2/(t^2 - 1),$$

is defined on the three intervals $(-\infty, -1)$, $(-1, 1)$, and $(1, \infty)$, where $t = -1$ and $t = 1$ are the points of discontinuity. The solution of this differential equation can be obtained as

$$\phi(t) = \log(t - 1) - \log(t + 1) + c, \; t > 1,$$

$$\phi(t) = \log(1 - t) - \log(t + 1) + c, \; -1 < t < 1, \text{ and}$$

$$\phi(t) = \log(1 - t) - \log[-(t + 1)] + c, \; t < -1.$$

[9]For the assumption of the continuity of $x(t; x^\circ)$ with respect to x°, see Kalman and Bertram (1960). In this connection, note that by definition of a solution, $x(t; x^\circ)$

An important concept in the theory of differential equations is that of "stability," which is a question of whether or not the solution $x(t, x^\circ)$ converges to a certain point called an "equilibrium point," as $t \to \infty$.

Definition 6.1. A constant vector x^* is called an **equilibrium (point)** of (17), if

$$f(x^*) = 0; \quad \text{that is,} \quad f_i(x^*) = 0, \; i = 1, 2, \ldots, n.$$

where x^* is the value of x in which x is stationary ($\dot{x} = 0$).

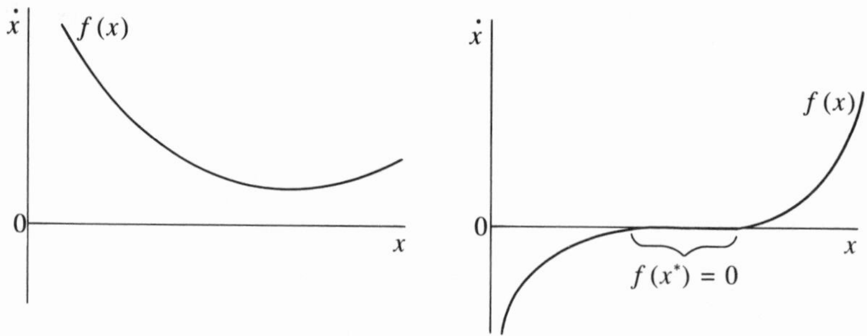

(a) Nonexistence of an equilibrium (b) Nonisolated equilibria

Figure 6.2: Nonexistence of an equilibrium and nonisolated equilibrium

In general, the equilibrium point may *not* exist; that is, there may *not* exist an x^* for which $f(x^*) = 0$. We illustrate this in figure 6.2a. Furthermore, when the equilibrium point exists, it may not be unique. There may be more than one x^* for which $f(x^*) = 0$. In fact, there can be infinitely many equilibrium points. If there exists a neighborhood about x^* in which there are no other equilibrium points, then x^* is called an **isolated** equilibrium point. In the nonlinear system, the equilibrium point may not even be isolated. In figure 6.2b, we illustrate the case in which there are infinitely many equilibrium points that are not isolated.

Assume that there exists an equilibrium point x^*, which is isolated. Then we may define the following concepts of stability.

---

is required to be *continuous* in t. Also note that the symbol ϕ, which was used to denote a *solution* in the previous section, is now replaced by x. This eases the notation and follows the usual convention in economics.

Definition 6.2. x^* is said to be **(asymptotically) locally stable**, if every solution starting sufficiently close to x^* converges to x^* as $t \to \infty$; that is, when $x(t;\ x^\circ) \to x^*$ as $t \to \infty$ for x° *sufficiently close* to x^*.[10]

Definition 6.3. x^* is said to be **(asymptotically) globally stable** if every solution converges to x^* as $t \to \infty$; that is, if $x(t;\ x^\circ) \to x^*$ as $t \to \infty$, regardless of the initial point x° (or regardless of whether or not x° is close to x^*).

Clearly, if x^* is globally stable, it is locally stable, but not vice versa. If x^* is not locally stable, it is called **unstable**. The word "asymptotically" in these definitions is often omitted in economics literature.[11] When it is obvious from the context whether a particular equilibrium point is locally or globally stable, we often omit the terms *locally* or *globally*.

To simplify the discussion, we now assume that x is a scalar and the function is a real-valued function ($n = 1$). The concept of stability is illustrated in figure 6.3. In figure 6.3a, there are three isolated equilibrium points, x^1, x^2, and x^3. It would be easy to see from this diagram that points x^1 and x^3 are asymptotically locally stable, whereas x^2 is unstable. Note that the stability property of a particular equilibrium point can be examined only by checking the sign of $f'(x^i)$ of the particular equilibrium point x^i [in which $f(x^i) = 0$]. x^i is asymptotically (locally) stable if $f'(x^i) < 0$, and it is unstable if $f'(x^i) > 0$. In figure 6.3a, $f'(x^1) < 0$, $f'(x^2) > 0$, and $f'(x^3) < 0$. Also note that the sign of $f'(x)$ for points other than the equilibrium points [i.e., the sign of $f'(x)$ for $x \neq x^i$] is not relevant in determining the stability property of the equilibrium point x^i, whereas the sign of $f'(x)$ at $x = x^i$ plays a crucial role. As illustrated in figure 6.3a, the $f(x)$ curve can "fluctuate" [and the sign of $f'(x)$ also fluctuates] *outside* the equilibrium points without affecting their stability property. In figure 6.3b, x^* is a unique equilibrium point which is asymptotically *globally* stable. Note that $f'(x^*) < 0$, and there is no definite sign of $f'(x)$ for $x \neq x^*$.

---

[10] Using the concept of a neighborhood, we may alternatively state the definition of local stability as: x^* is said to be **(asymptotically) locally stable** if there exists a neighborhood of x^*, $N(x^*)$, such that $x^\circ \in N(x^*) \subset D$ implies $x(t;\ x^\circ) \to x^*$ as $t \to \infty$.

[11] Mathematicians often use the term *stability* to mean what they call *Liapunov stability*. The **Liapunov stability**, roughly speaking, means that $x(t;\ x^\circ)$ remains bounded (but may or may not converge to x^* as $t \to \infty$), if x° is sufficiently close to x^*. In this case, the word *asymptotically* is important to distinguish asymptotic stability from (Liapunov) stability.

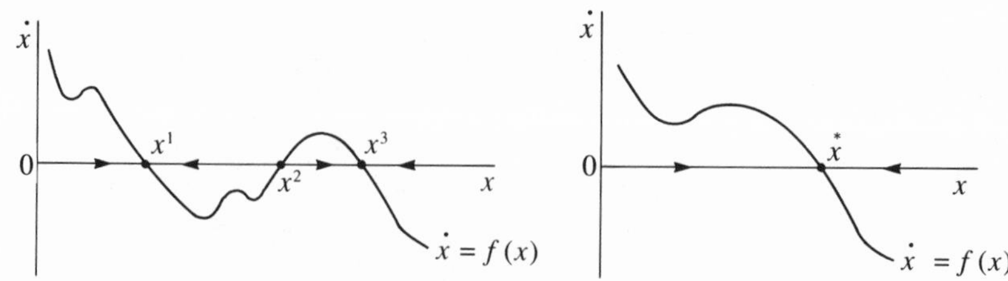

(*a*) Nonuniqueness and stability (*b*) Uniqueness and global stability

Figure 6.3: Nonuniqueness and the stability property of equilibria

When x is a scalar and f is real-valued, we may easily determine the stability property of equilibrium points by drawing a diagram like figure 6.3. This is called the **phase diagram** for the one-dimensional case. More specifically, the following conclusion should be apparent by drawing a diagram like figure 6.3.

Theorem 6.3. Let $\dot{x} = f(x)$, where $x \in R$, and let x^* be an isolated equilibrium point. Then x^* is asymptotically locally stable if $f'(x^*) < 0$, and unstable if $f'(x^*) > 0$, where $f'(x^*)$ is $f'(x)$ evaluated at x^*. If $f'(x^*) < 0$ for all x^* such that $f(x^*) = 0$, then x^* is unique and asymptotically globally stable.

Note that theorem 6.3 provides only a sufficient condition for stability and not a necessary condition. This is because x^* can be either stable or unstable when $f'(x^*) = 0$. This can easily be illustrated in figure 6.4*a* and *b*, in which $f'(x^*) = 0$; x^* is asymptotically globally stable in figure 6.5*a*, whereas x^* is unstable in figure 6.4*b*.

From theorem 6.3, we may readily obtain the following corollary.

Corollary. Let $\dot{x} = f(x)$, where $x \in R$, and let x^* be an isolated equilibrium point. Then ruling out the possibility of the "knife-edge case" of $f'(x^*) = 0$, x^* is asymptotically locally stable *if and only if* $f'(x^*) < 0$.

Returning to the general n-dimensional case of (17), or the *linear system* assoicated with (17), we first consider the special case in which the function f is linear. In particular, we consider the following *homogeneous*

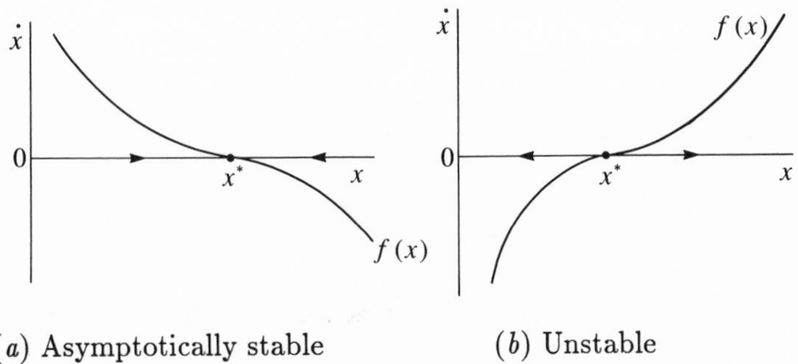

(*a*) Asymptotically stable (*b*) Unstable

Figure 6.4: The stability property when $f'(x^*) = 0$

system of linear differential equations,

$$\dot{x}(t) = Ax(t), \tag{18}$$

where $A \equiv [a_{ij}]$ is an $n \times n$ matrix with real entries, and where we assume A is nonsingular. Clearly, the origin, $x^* = 0$, is the unique (and hence *isolated*) equilibrium point of this system. Furthermore, as we remarked in theorem 6.2, the solution $x(t;\ x)$ for this system always exists for all t, and it is unique given the initial condition $(t^\circ,\ x^\circ)$.

Suppose that the linear system is given in the nonhomogeneous form

$$\dot{x}(t) = Ax(t) + b, \tag{19}$$

where A is again nonsingular and where b is a constant vector. The equilibrium point of (19) is obtained as $x^* = -A^{-1}b$, which is unique (and hence isolated).

For such a system, define $y(t)$ by $y(t) \equiv x(t) - x^*$. Then (19) can be written as

$$\dot{y}(t) = Ay(t), \tag{18$'$}$$

which has exactly the same form as (18). Since the behavior of the solution for (19) can completely be described by that of (18′) via $x = y - A^{-1}b$, it suffices to consider (18) or (18′) to investigate the properties of (19). The simplest example for (18) is the case in which A is a scalar ($n = 1$). Equation (4) provides such an example. For this case, the solution for (18) is (as discussed earlier) obtained as

$$x(t;\ x^{\circ}) = x^{\circ} e^{A(t - t^{\circ})}. \tag{4'''}$$

From this, we may conclude that the equilibrium point $x^* = 0$ is asymptotically globally stable if and only if $A < 0$ (ignoring the "knife-edge case" of $A = 0$). Needless to say, such a stability property can also be obtained by drawing a phase diagram, without obtaining the explicit solution, (4‴).

To study the stability property of nonlinear system (17), it is often useful to study its "linear counterpart." Let x^* be an isolated equilibrium point of nonlinear system (17), $\dot{x} = f(x)$. Since f is continuously differentiable, we have

$$f(x) = f(x^*) + A(x - x^*) + o(\| x - x^* \|),$$

where $A \equiv [a_{ij}]$ and $a_{ij} \equiv \partial f_i(x^*)/\partial x_j$, $i,\ j = 1,\ 2,\ \ldots,\ n$, and where $o(\cdot)$ is Landau's o (i.e., $\lim\ o(\| h \|)/\| h \| = 0$ as $h \to 0$). Since x^* is an equilibrium point, $f(x^*) = 0$, we have

$$f(x) = A(x - x^*) + o(\| x - x^* \|).$$

If the initial point x° and the solution $x(t;\ x^{\circ})$ is sufficiently close to x^*, then we may ignore the second term of the right-hand side of this equation (which amounts to ignoring the second-order or higher-order terms of Taylor's expansion). Then system (17) can be "approximated" by

$$\dot{x} = A(x - x^*), \tag{20}$$

which we call the **linear approximation system (LAS)** of (17) about x^*. Define $y(t)$ by $y(t) \equiv x(t) - x^*$. Then (20) is reduced to

$$\dot{y}(t) = Ay(t), \tag{20'}$$

which is formally identical to (18). Hence, the stability property of (20) can be studied by examining the results on the stability property of homogeneous linear system (18).

Theorem 6.4 highlights the role of the linear approximation system on the stability of the original nonlinear systems.

Theorem 6.4 (Liapunov). If x^* is asymptotically (globally) stable for system (20), then x^* is asymptotically locally stable for the original system (17), $\dot{x} = f(x)$.

Namely, the stability of the linear approximation system provides a *sufficient* condition for the asymptotic local stability of the original system.[12] We call the equilibrium point x^* **linear approximation stable** if it is asymptotically stable for its linear approximation system. Needless to say, the original system can contain more than one equilibrium point. Thus, theorem 6.4 is concerned with one of these isolated equilibrium points of the original system.

Note that the *converse* of theorem 6.4 is, in general, false. It is possible that x^* is a stable equilibrium point for the original system (17), while it is *not* for the LAS (20). The stability of the original system does *not* necessarily imply the stability of the LAS. Example 6.4 will be useful to illustrate this point.

Example 6.4. Consider the following differential equation:

$$\dot{x}(t) = \frac{-1}{5}[x(t) - x^*]^3, \; x \in R. \tag{21}$$

Clearly, x^* is the unique equilibrium point that is globally stable as can be seen from figure 6.5. On the other hand, note that the linear approximation system of (21) can be written as $\dot{x} = 0$. Then x^* is not an asymptotically stable equilibrium point for $\dot{x} = 0$, since the solution $x(t;\, x^\circ)$ for $x = 0$ is clearly equal to x° for all t and does not approach x^* whenever $x^\circ = x^*$. The equilibrium point x^* is not linear approximation stable.[13]

For the two-dimensional case ($n = 2$), the following result is well

[12] Theorem 6.4, in a slightly different form, is obtained by Liapunov (1907). Paraphrasing Kalman and Bertram (1970, p. 37), "it is common usage in engineering to consider only small derivatives from the equilibrium point by expanding f in a Taylor series about the equilibrium point and neglecting all higher order terms." Such a practice of examining the asymptotic local stability property has also become very popular in economics, especially after Samuelson's (1947) work. However, the justification of such a procedure in terms of the Liapunov theorem is often glossed over. See Kalman and Bertram (1960, example 9).

[13] A similar example is used in Takayama (1985, p. 308). For still another simple example, consider

$$\dot{x} = -x^3, \quad \text{where } x \in R.$$

Clearly, $x^* = 0$ is the unique equilibrium point, which is asymptotically globally stable. Let $f(x) \equiv -x^3$. Then $f'(x^*) = -3(x^*)^2 = 0$. Hence the linearized system of the above can be written as

$$\dot{x} = f'(x^*)(x - x^*) = 0; \quad \text{i.e., } \dot{x} = 0.$$

The equilibrium point of $\dot{x} = 0$ is again $x^* = 0$, but it is not asymptotically stable.

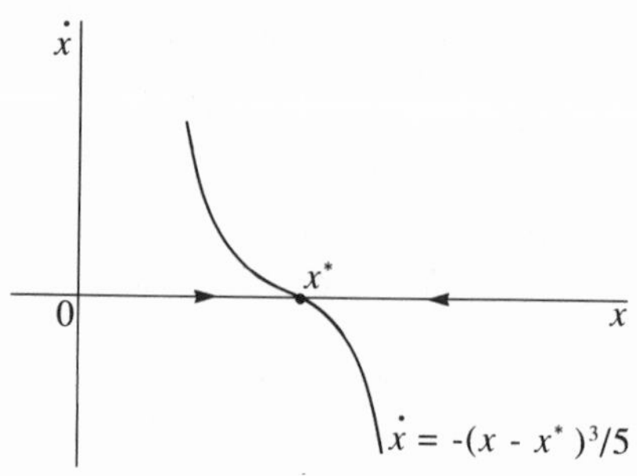

Figure 6.5: The stability of $\dot{x} = -(x - x^*)^3/5$

known and useful.

Theorem 6.5. Consider the following linear system

$$\begin{bmatrix} \dot{x}_1 \\ \dot{x}_2 \end{bmatrix} = \begin{bmatrix} a_{11} & a_{12} \\ a_{21} & a_{22} \end{bmatrix} \begin{bmatrix} x_1 \\ x_2 \end{bmatrix},$$

where the a_{ij}'s are constant real numbers, and where we assume that the coefficient matrix is nonsingular. Then the (unique) equilibrium point $x^* = 0$ (the origin) is asymptotically *globally* stable, *if and only if*

$$a_{11} + a_{22} < 0, \quad \text{and} \tag{22a}$$

$$a_{11}a_{22} - a_{12}a_{21} > 0. \tag{22b}$$

Note that conditions (22a) and (22b), respectively, specify the signs of the trace and the determinant of the coefficient matrix. Example 6.5 illustrates theorem 6.5.

Example 6.5. Consider the system

$$\begin{bmatrix} \dot{x}_1 \\ \dot{x}_2 \end{bmatrix} = \begin{bmatrix} -3 & -1 \\ -2 & -1 \end{bmatrix} \begin{bmatrix} x_1 \\ x_2 \end{bmatrix}.$$

Clearly, the equilibrium point of this system is the origin ($x_1 = x_2 = 0$). Since we have

$$(-3) + (-1) = -4 < 0 \text{ and } (-3)(-1) - (-1)(-2) = 1 > 0,$$

conditions (22a) and (22b) are satisfied; hence the origin (0, 0) is asymptotically globally stable by theorem 6.5.

Next, combining theorems 6.4 and 6.5, we may obtain the local stability result (theorem 6.6) for the two-dimensional *nonlinear* system.

Theorem 6.6. Consider the system of differential equations

$$\dot{x}(t) = f[x(t)],\ x = (x_1,\ x_2) \in R^2.$$

Let x^* be an isolated equilibrium point of this system. Then x^* is asymptotically *locally* stable, *if*

$$a_{11} + a_{22} < 0, \text{ and} \tag{22$'$a}$$

$$a_{11}a_{22} - a_{12}a_{21} > 0, \tag{22$'$b}$$

where $a_{ij} \equiv \partial f_i(x^*)/\partial x_j,\ i,\ j = 1,\ 2.$

Note that theorem 6.6 provides only a *sufficient* condition for the (asymptotic) *local* stability of an equilibrium point, whereas theorem 6.5 provides a *necessary and sufficient* condition for the (asymptotic) *global* stability of the (unique) equilibrium point. Condition (22′a) states that the trace of the Jacobian matrix of f evaluated at x^* is negative, and condition (22′b) states that the determinant of such a matrix is positive.

The Jacobian matrix of $f(x)$ evaluated at x^* may be written as

$$f'(x^*) = \begin{bmatrix} f_{11}(x^*) & f_{12}(x^*) \\ f_{21}(x^*) & f_{22}(x^*) \end{bmatrix} = \begin{bmatrix} a_{11} & a_{12} \\ a_{21} & a_{22} \end{bmatrix},$$

where $f_{ij} \equiv \partial f_i/\partial x_j,\ i,\ j = 1,\ 2.$ Conditions (22′a) and (22′b) may, respectively, be referred to as the **trace condition** and the **Jacobian determinant condition**. For the linear system, the coefficient matrix is nothing but the Jacobian matrix of $f(x)$. Hence, condition (22′) corresponds to condition (22).

Theorem 6.6 only provides a condition for local stability. Confining ourselves to the two-dimensional case, we have theorem 6.7 for global stability, which is due to Olech (1962).

Theorem 6.7 (Olech 1962). Given the nonlinear system,

$$\dot{x} = f[x(t)],\ x = (x_1,\ x_2) \in R^2,$$

its equilibrium point x^* is asymptotically globally stable, if

$$f_{11} + f_{22} < 0, \quad \text{for } all\ x, \tag{23a}$$

$$f_{11}f_{22} - f_{12}f_{21} > 0, \quad \text{for } all\ x, \text{ and} \tag{23b}$$

$$f_{11}f_{22} \neq 0 \text{ for } all\ x, \text{ or } f_{12}f_{21} \neq 0 \text{ for } all\ x, \tag{23c}$$

where $f_{ij} \equiv \partial f_i(x)/\partial x_j$, $i, j = 1, 2$.[14]

REMARKS:

(i) The a_{ij}'s in theorem 6.6 are the values of the f_{ij}'s evaluated at x^*. Clearly, conditions (22′a) and (22′b) are the "local" versions of conditions (23a) and (23b).

(ii) Note that both theorem 6.6 and 6.7 only provide sufficient conditions for stability. Thus, it is possible that the equilibrium point is stable even if these conditions are violated.

For the n-dimensional linear system, we have the following result.

Theorem 6.8. Consider the following linear system with constant coefficients:

$$\dot{x}(t) = Ax(t),\ x(t) \in R^n,$$

where $A = [a_{ij}]$ is an $n \times n$ matrix with real entries. Then its equilibrium point $x^* = 0$ (the origin) is asymptotically globally stable *if and only if* the real part of any eigenvalue of A is negative.

If A is symmetric and negative definite, then every eigenvalue of A is real and negative. Hence, a sufficient condition for the stability of $x^* = 0$ in theorem 6.8 is that A is symmetric and negative definite. We now wish to know the condition for all the eigenvalues of an arbitrary

---

[14]Write $f_{11}f_{22} \equiv \alpha(x)$ and $f_{12}f_{21} \equiv \beta(x)$. Then (23b) states $\alpha(x) - \beta(x) > 0$ for all x, whereas (23c) states that $\alpha(x) \neq 0$ for all x or $\beta(x) \neq 0$ for all x. One may conjecture whether (23c) is superfluous since (23b) seems to imply (23c). Although such a conjecture is correct for the linear system in which $\alpha(x)$ and $\beta(x)$ are constant regardless of x, this conjecture is *false* for the *nonlinear* system since α and β now depend on x. Namely, $\alpha(x) - \beta(x) > 0$ for all x does not necessarily imply that either $\alpha(x) \neq 0$ for all x or $\beta(x) \neq 0$ for all x. For instance, if $\alpha(x^\circ) = 0$, $\beta(x^\circ) < 0$, or if $\alpha(x^1) > 0$ and $\beta(x^1) = 0$, for some x° or x^1, (23b) can be satisfied, but (23c) cannot.

$n \times n$ matrix to have negative real parts. There is a famous condition to determine this, known as the **Routh-Hurwitz Theorem**. It deals with the roots of the characteristic equations, i.e., the eigenvalues.

Theorem 6.9. A *necessary and sufficient* condition is that all the roots of the equation

$$\alpha_0\lambda^n + \alpha_1\lambda^{n-1} + \ldots + \alpha_{n-1}\lambda + \alpha_n = 0$$

with real coefficients have negative real parts, which in turn holds *if and only if*

$$\alpha_1 > 0, \begin{vmatrix} \alpha_1 & \alpha_0 \\ \alpha_3 & \alpha_2 \end{vmatrix} > 0, \begin{vmatrix} \alpha_1 & \alpha_0 & 0 \\ \alpha_3 & \alpha_2 & \alpha_1 \\ \alpha_5 & \alpha_4 & \alpha_3 \end{vmatrix} > 0,$$

$$\ldots \begin{vmatrix} \alpha_1 & \alpha_0 & 0 & 0 & \ldots & \ldots \\ \alpha_3 & \alpha_2 & \alpha_1 & \alpha_0 & \ldots & \ldots \\ \alpha_5 & \alpha_4 & \alpha_3 & \alpha_2 & \ldots & \ldots \\ \ldots & \ldots & \ldots & \ldots & \ldots & \ldots \\ \ldots & \ldots & \ldots & \ldots & \ldots & \ldots \\ 0 & 0 & 0 & 0 & \ldots & \alpha_n \end{vmatrix} > 0. \quad (24)$$

Here, α_0 is taken to be positive (if $\alpha_0 < 0$, then multiply the equation by -1). Condition (24) is called the **Routh-Hurwitz condition**.

The power of theorem 6.9 is that it provides a *necessary and sufficient* condition for stability in a linear system when it is combined with theorem 6.8. To illustrate this, let $n = 2$, where the coefficient matrix is given by

$$\begin{bmatrix} a_{11} & a_{12} \\ a_{21} & a_{22} \end{bmatrix}.$$

The characteristic equation of this matrix is obtained as

$$\lambda^2 + \alpha_1\lambda + \alpha_2 = 0,$$

where $\alpha_1 \equiv -(a_{11} + a_{22})$, $\alpha_2 \equiv a_{11}a_{22} - a_{12}a_{21}$. The Routh-Hurwitz condition for the case of $n = 2$ is obtained from (24) as

$$\alpha_1 > 0 \text{ and } \alpha_1\alpha_2 > 0, \quad (24')$$

since $\alpha_0 = 1$. This is equivalent to $\alpha_1 > 0$ and $\alpha_2 > 0$. Hence, condition (24′) can equivalently be rewritten as

$$a_{11} + a_{22} < 0 \text{ and } a_{11}a_{21} - a_{12}a_{21} > 0.$$

This is precisely the same as stability condition (22) for the two-dimensional linear system.

For $n = 3$, the Routh-Hurwitz condition becomes

$$\alpha_1 > 0,\ \alpha_1\alpha_2 - \alpha_0\alpha_3 > 0,\ \alpha_3(\alpha_1\alpha_2 - \alpha_0\alpha_3) > 0.$$

This can easily be rewritten in equivalent form

$$\alpha_1 > 0,\ \alpha_2 > 0,\ \alpha_3 > 0,\ \alpha_1\alpha_2 - \alpha_0\alpha_3 > 0, \tag{24''}$$

since $\alpha_0 > 0$.

When $n \geqq 4$, the computation of the Routh-Hurwitz condition typically becomes very tedious unless we can use computers. This in turn often discourages the use of the Routh-Hurwitz condition in theoretical applications.

Suppose that instead of a linear system, we are given a *nonlinear* system,

$$\dot{x}(t) = f[x(t)], \quad \text{where } x(t) \in R^n.$$

In this case, we can obtain a *sufficient* condition for the asymptotic local stability of an (isolated) equilibrium point by using theorems 6.4, 6.8, and 6.9. Specifically, linearize this system about an (isolated) equilibrium point x^* to obtain the following linear approximation system:

$$\dot{x}(t) = A[x(t) - x^*],$$

where $A = [a_{ij}]$ and $a_{ij} \equiv \partial f_i(x^*)/\partial x_j$, $i, j = 1, 2, \ldots, n$. Then compute the characteristic equation of the matrix and examine the Routh-Hurwitz condition. Such a condition will provide a necessary and sufficient condition for the stability of the linear approximation system, and a sufficient (but *not* necessary) condition for the original system. As pointed out earlier, the stability of the *linear approximation system* is not necessary for the stability of the original system. Since there is a confusion in the literature on this point, this may have to be emphasized. This is especially the case when researchers wish to apply Samuelson's (1947) "correspondence principle" to analyze the comparative statics problem. Similarly, the Routh-Hurwitz condition, in general, does not provide a necessary condition for the (local) stability of the *original* nonlinear system. Hence, contrary to the usual practice, the Routh-Hurwitz condition as it is *cannot* be utilized in obtaining the information to determine comparative statics results.

Only when we know the *necessary* condition for the stability of the original nonlinear system (as is the case in the corollary to theorem 6.3 for the one-dimensional case), may we utilize the information of such a stability condition to ascertain the effect of a shift in a parameter on the equilibrium. For the two-dimensional case, theorem 7.10 in the next chapter provides the condition under which the stability criterion for the linear approximation system becomes *necessary* for the stability of the *original* system.

6.3 Economic Applications

6.3.1 The Stability of Competitive Equilibrium: the Walrasian Process[15]

Let x_i denote the market excess demand for the ith commodity ($i = 1, 2, \ldots, n+1$). If D_i and S_i, respectively, denote the market demand for and the market supply of the ith commodity, then $x_i \equiv D_i - S_i$. Let P_i be the price of the ith commodity ($i = 1, 2, \ldots, n+1$), and assume that x_i depends only on the P_i's; where

$$x_i = F_i(P_1, P_2, \ldots, P_n, P_{n+1}),\ i = 1, 2, \ldots, n+1, \tag{25}$$

or more compactly, $x = F(P)$, where $x = (x_1, \ldots, x_{n+1})$, etc. To honor the distinction between Walrasian and Marshallian stability (see fn. 40 later), we assume that the D_i's depend on P, but that S_i is constant for each i. A **competitive equilibrium** may then be defined by

$$F_i(P_1^*, \ldots, P_n^*, P_{n+1}^*) = 0,\ i = 1, \ldots, n+1, \tag{26}$$

or more compactly, $F(P^*) = 0$. The $(n+1)$ equations in (26) determine the equilibrium values of the $(n+1)$ prices, $P_1^*, \ldots, P_{n+1}^*$. Assume there exists a $P^* > 0$ such that $F(P^*) = 0$.

On the other hand, the price weighted sum of the market excess

[15]For surveys of the problem of the stability of a competitive equilibrium, see Negishi (1962), Hahn (1982), and Takayama (1985, chap. 3).

demands for all commodities must be identically equal to zero; that is,

$$P_1F_1(P) + \ldots + P_nF_n(P) + P_{n+1}F_{n+1}(P) \equiv 0. \tag{27}$$

Equation (27) is obtained by summing all the budget conditions of the economic agents (consumers, producers, and resource holders) in the economy, and it is called **Walras's Law**. Then one of the equations in (26) becomes superfluous, and thus the number of equations becomes less than the number of variables. However, this problem is avoided by simply noting that the excess demand function for each commodity is (positively) homogeneous of degree zero in all prices.[16]

Then letting $p_i \equiv P_i/P_{n+1}$, $i = 1, 2, \ldots, n$, we may define the function f_i by

$$f_i(p_1, p_2, \ldots, p_n) \equiv F_i(p_1, p_2, \ldots, p_n, 1),\ i = 1, 2, \ldots, n.$$

The $(n+1)^{\text{th}}$ commodity is called the **numéraire**. The competitive equilibrium is then defined in terms of the f_i's as

$$f_i(p_1^*, p_2^*, \ldots, p_n^*) = 0,\ i = 1, 2, \ldots, n, \tag{28}$$

or more compactly, $f(p^*) = 0$. The n equations in (28) are assumed to determine n equilibrium values of prices, $p_1^*, \ldots, p_n^*$. We assume there exists a $p^* > 0$ such that $f(p^*) = 0$, which we call a (**normalized**) **equilibrium price vector**. If p is not an equilibrium price vector, then $f_i(p) \neq 0$ for some or all i ($i = 1, 2, \ldots, n$). The value of the excess demand for the $(n+1)^{\text{th}}$ commodity, x_{n+1}, is obtained by using (27).

$$x_{n+1} = -[p_1f_1(p) + p_2f_2(p) + \ldots + p_nf_n(p)] \tag{27'}$$

Note that if p^* is an *equilibrium price vector*, then (27′) shows that $x_{n+1} = 0$. In other words, if the first n markets are in equilibrium, the $(n+1)^{\text{th}}$ market is automatically in equilibrium.

The (**Walrasian**) **stability problem** of a competitive equilibrium is concerned with the question of whether the price vector p, when it deviates from an equilibrium point p^*, will return to p^*. The fundamental premise imposed to study this problem is that an excess demand

---

[16] For each $i = 1, 2, \ldots, n+1$, we have

$$F_i(\alpha P_1, \ldots, \alpha P_{n+1}) = F_i(P_1, \ldots, P_{n+1}), \quad \text{for any } \alpha > 0.$$

This may be justified in terms of rationality of behavior. In other words, if the P_i's are measured in terms of some accounting unit (say, dollars), then changing the unit of measure should not affect each individual's behavior.

for the ith commodity raises the price of the ith commodity, and that an excess supply of the ith commodity lowers the price of the ith commodity. Following Samuelson's (1947) reformulation of the Walrasian stability problem, we may specify such a fundamental premise by the following system of differential equations:[17]

$$\dot{p}_i(t) = k_i f_i[p_1(t), p_2(t), \ldots, p_n(t)], \; i = 1, 2, \ldots, n, \tag{29}$$

where $\dot{p}_i$ denotes the derivative of p_i with respect to time (denoted by t), and where k_i signifies the **speed of adjustment** of the ith market (where k_i is assumed to be a positive constant). Let the initial condition of the above system be specified by $p = p^{\circ}$ when $t = 0$, and write the solution of the system as $p(t;\ p^{\circ})$. We assume that $p(t;\ p^{\circ})$ exists and is unique, and p^* for which $f(p^*) = 0$ is an *isolated* equilibrium point of system (29). Then the stability problem of a competitive equilibrium may be phrased as follows.

Given a p^* such that $f(p^*) = 0$,
will $p(t;\ p^{\circ}) \to p^*$ as $t \to \infty$?

This question becomes one of asymptotic *local stability* (of the system of differential equations) when we allow p° to be in a neighborhood of p^*. If p° is not restricted to a neighborhood of p^*, then the problem is that of asymptotic global stability.

To ease the exposition, we first assume that the number of commodities is equal to two (say, "agricultural goods" and "manufacturing goods," or "exportables" and "importables"), where the second commodity is designated as the numéraire. Then letting $f_1 = f$, (29) is simplified to

$$\dot{p}(t) = kf[p(t)], \; p \equiv P_1/P_2, \tag{30}$$

where p is a scalar. Let p^* be an (isolated) equilibrium price ratio of the two commodities where $f(p^*) = 0$. Then the stability question is analogous to the ones described in connection with figures 6.3 and 6.4, where x in these diagrams may be replaced by p. We then at once obtain the following result.[18]

[17] This system is interpreted to represent the "simultaneous *tâtonnement*." For the problem involved in the *tâtonnement* assumption in the stability analysis, see Takayama (1985, pp. 339–47).

[18] Walras, in his classic work, begins his analysis with a complete discussion of the

Proposition 6.1. In the two-commodity world of a nonnegative equilibrium, p^* is asymptotically locally stable if and only if $f'(p^*) < 0$, provided that we rule out the knife-edge case of $f'(p^*) = 0$. If $f'(p^*) < 0$ for any p^* for which $f(p^*) = 0$, then p^* is unique and asymptotically globally stable.

REMARK: $f'(p) < 0$ means an increase in the price of commodity 1 vis-à-vis commodity 2 lowers the excess demand of commodity 1.[19] If this holds for the relevant range of p, then the equilibrium price ratio (assuming it exists) is unique and asymptotically globally stable.

REMARK: The assumption of a two-commodity world is widely used in many studies on economic development, international trade, public finance, and so on. It is known to be a useful assumption to highlight important aspects of certain economic problems under a general equilibrium framework. The case of a three-commodity world contains interesting analytical problems and we postpone the discussion of such a case to the end of this chapter.

For the general n-commodity world, we may rewrite (29) as

$$\dot{p}(t) = Kf[p(t)], \tag{29'}$$

where K is the $n \times n$ diagonal matrix whose i^{th} diagonal element is $k_i > 0$. Let p^* be its isolated equilibrium point. The linear approximation system for (29) or (29′) may then be written as

$$\dot{p} = KA(p - p^*), \tag{31}$$

where $A = [a_{ij}]$, $a_{ij} \equiv \partial f_i(p^*)/\partial p_j$, $i, j = 1, 2, \ldots, n$. The question of local stability then boils down to the property of matrix A, which in turn is related to Hicks' (1939, 1946) study of stability. In fact, Hicks' condition for "perfect stability" is stated in terms of alternating signs of

two-commodity pure exchange economy (Walras 1954, pt. 2) and then systematically extends his analysis in several ways.

[19] For the demand side, this means that a relative increase in the price of commodity 1 will shift the demand away from commodity 1 into commodity 2, which in turn lowers the demand for commodity 1. This, then, will lower the excess demand for commodity 1, so that $f'(p) < 0$. Needless to say, the adverse income effect can increase the demand for commodity 1 when there is a relative increase in commodity 1's price (cf. the Hicks-Slutsky equation). In this case, the excess demand for commodity 1 may *increase* by a relative increase in commodity 1's price, i.e., $f'(p) > 0$.

principal minors of A. Samuelson (1947) shows that such a condition is neither necessary nor sufficient for the stability of the dynamic system (31) for the n-commodity case. In the 1958 volume of *Econometrica*, it was shown independently by Hahn, Negishi, and Arrow and Hurwicz, that p^* is an asymptotically globally stable equilibrium of the linear system (31) if $a_{ij} > 0$ for $i \neq j$. This implies that p^* is an asymptotically *locally* stable equilibrium for (29).[20]

In 1959, Arrow, Block, and Hurwicz obtained a major result on stability: p^* is an asymptotically *globally* stable equilibrium for (29), if $f_{ij} (\equiv \partial f_i / \partial p_j) > 0$ for all p and for *all* $i \neq j$. This assumption may be called **global gross substitutability**,[21] whereas this is contrasted to the assumption of $a_{ij} \equiv \partial f_i(p^*)/\partial p_j > 0$ for $i \neq j$, which may be called the assumption of **local gross substitutability**.[22] In spite of the landmark nature of the Arrow-Block-Hurwicz result, the assumption of gross substitutability for all commodities for the n-commodity world is too restrictive, and a number of attempts to relax this assumption have been published. Most of these attempts have not been too successful and attention has shifted to a computational algorithm to find an equilibrium price vector (e.g., Scarf 1974; Eaves and Scarf 1976; Scarf

[20] It now appears that the honor of first proving the stability of a competitive equilibrium goes to M. Allais. For this, Negishi (1989, p. 266) writes, "It was Allais . . . , who first demonstrated the convergence of Walrasian *tâtonnement* by assuming gross substitutability, . . . " Allais's work was published in 1943. Much prior to Allais's receiving the Nobel Prize in Economic Science in 1988, Negishi, in his excellent survey article on the stability of a competitive economy (1962, pp. 656–57), summarized Allais's contribution.

[21] Arrow, Block, and Hurwicz (1959) have presented an example of an individual's utility function that will give rise to a demand function which exhibits the global gross substitutability property. Their example is that individual i's utility function is given by

$$u_i(x_{i1}, x_{i2}, \ldots, x_{in}) = \sum_{j=1}^{n} \alpha_{ij} \log x_{ij},$$

$$\text{where } \sum_{j=1}^{n} \alpha_{ij} = 1, \ \alpha_{ij} > 0 \text{ for all } i \text{ and } j.$$

[22] To investigate the stability of competitive equilibrium, $\dot{p}_i = k_i f_i(p)$, $i = 1, 2, \ldots, n$, it is often postulated that $k_i = 1$ for all i "by a suitable choice of units of commodities," (e.g., Arrow and Hurwicz 1958; Arrow, Block, and Hurwicz 1959). As Lewis (1963) points out, "this implies a peculiar choice of units, and yet the stability result will not be affected as in the case in Arrow and Hurwicz (1958) and Arrow, Block, and Hurwicz (1959)."

1982). Hirota's (1981) work is a notable exception in this instance.

6.3.2 The Stability of Macroeconomic Equilibrium[23]

The Keynesian System. The well-known "Keynesian" (IS-LM) macroequilibrium system may be described by [24]

$$Y^* = E(Y^* - T, r^*) + G, \quad M/p = L(Y^*, r^*), \tag{32}$$

where Y = output, r = interest rate, E = consumption (C) plus investment (I), G = government expenditures, T = taxes minus transfer payments (net taxes), M = money supply, p = price level, and L = money demand. Here, G, T, M, and p are assumed to be fixed. The dynamic adjustment equations of this system can be written as

$$\dot{Y} = a[E(Y - T, r) + G - Y] \equiv f(Y, r), \tag{33a}$$

$$\dot{r} = b[L(Y, r) - M/p] \equiv g(Y, r), \tag{33b}$$

where a and b are positive constants signifying the speeds of adjustment of the respective markets. Clearly, (Y^*, r^*), which satisfies (32), is an equilibrium point of the system of differential equations, (33). As can easily be seen, the point (Y^*, r^*) is represented by the point of intersection of the IS and the LM curves.

To facilitate the analysis, we impose the following ("usual") assumptions:

$$0 < E_Y < 1, \; E_r < 0, \; L_Y > 0, \; L_r < 0, \quad \text{for all } (Y, r), \tag{34}$$

where $E_Y \equiv \partial E/\partial(Y - T)$, $E_r \equiv \partial E/\partial r$, etc. Under this assumption, the IS curve is downward sloping and the LM curve is upward sloping in

[23] This section is adapted from Takayama (1983). The stability of the IS-LM macro equilibrium is also discussed by Samuelson (1947), and Chang and Smyth (1972), for example. There is a considerable amount of literature that incorporates the government budget constraint into the basic IS-LM framework and the dynamics thus generated. For this, see Takayama (1980) and the literature cited therein.

[24] Whether or not the Hicksian (1937) IS-LM framework constitutes the correct interpretation of Keynes's *General Theory* has been controversial since the late 1960s. Hicks (1973) reported that Keynes himself accepted the Hicksian interpretation, and reproduced Keynes's letter to him dated March 31, 1937 (Hicks 1973, pp. 9–10). Keynes, responding to the IS-LM interpretation by Hicks, wrote, "I found it very interesting and really have next to nothing to say by way of criticism." Hicks concluded from this letter that "Keynes accepted the SI-LL diagram as a fair statement of his position" (1973, p. 10). On the other hand, Hicks goes on to say that "this is not a statement which I believe myself."

the usual manner, and hence the equilibrium point (Y^*, r^*), assuming its existence, is unique. Using (34), we may compute the Jacobian of (f, g) as

$$f_Y = a(E_Y - 1) < 0, \qquad f_r = aE_r < 0,$$

$$g_Y = bL_Y > 0, \qquad g_r = bL_r < 0, \tag{35}$$

for all (Y, r), where $f_Y \equiv \partial f/\partial Y$, $f_r \equiv \partial f/\partial r$, etc. From this, we may easily observe

$$f_Y + g_r < 0, \text{ for all } (Y, r), \tag{36a}$$

$$f_Y g_r - f_r g_Y > 0, \text{ for all } (Y, r), \text{ and} \tag{36b}$$

$$f_Y g_r \neq 0 \text{ and } f_r g_Y \neq 0, \text{ for all } (Y, r). \tag{36c}$$

Hence, all the assumptions of theorem 6.7 (Olech's theorem) are satisfied, so that we may obtain the subsequent result.[25]

Proposition 6.2. The "Keynesian" macro equilibrium point (Y^*, r^*) for (32) is asymptotically globally stable under the adjustment process defined by nonlinear system (33).

The Neoclassical System. The neoclassical system may be interpreted as the case in which Y is held constant (say, at the full employment level), while p fluctuates so as to bring about the equilibrium. The following two types of adjustment mechanisms are possible.

Type 1

$$\dot{p} = a[E(Y - T, r) + G - Y] \equiv \Phi(p, r), \text{ and} \tag{37a}$$

$$\dot{r} = b[L(Y, r) - M/p] \equiv \Psi(p, r). \tag{37b}$$

Type2

$$\dot{r} = a[E(Y - T, r) + G - Y] \equiv \phi(r, p), \text{ and} \tag{38a}$$

[25] There is an obvious weakness in the present proof of the proposition. Nowhere in the proof was it shown that the values of Y and r in the dynamic process stay in the positive orthant. It is simply assumed. As shown in the next chapter, we can examine this by way of a diagrammatical exposition of the trajectory.

$$\dot{p} = -b[L(Y, r) - M/p] \equiv \psi(r, p). \tag{38b}$$

Here $E + G - Y = (I + G - T) - (Y - T - C)$. Equation (37a) means that the excess demand for (resp. supply of) goods and services raises (resp. lowers) the price level, while (37b) describes the usual Keynesian adjustment process via the portfolio choice between money and bonds. Equation (38a) may be justified by the assumption that if the demand for new loanable funds like "credit" or loans ($= I + G - T$; i.e., private investment plus the government budget deficit) *minus* the supply of new loanable funds ($= Y - T - C$ = saving) is positive (resp. negative), then the interest rate rises (resp. falls).[26] This process may be associated with the **classical loanable funds theory**. On the other hand, (38b) may be justified by the assumption that an excess supply of (resp. demand for) cash balances decreases (resp. increases) the "value of money" ($1/p$) and hence increases (resp. decreases) p, where we may note that p is the relative price of goods and services vis-à-vis money.[27] More realistically,

---

[26]The following quotation from Ohlin (1937, pp. 224–25) might be relevant.

> The willingness of certain individuals to *increase* their holdings of various claims and other kinds of assets *minus* the willingness of others to reduce their corresponding holdings give the supply curves for the different kinds of new credit during the period. Naturally the quantities each individual is willing to supply depend on the interest rate. ...Similarly the total supply of *new* claims minus the reduction of the outstanding volume of *old* ones gives the demand—also a function of the rate of interest—for the different kinds of credit during the period. The prices fixed on the market for these different claims—and thereby the values of interest—are governed by supply and demand in the usual way.

Keynes (1937, p. 245) remarked, right after he quoted the preceding passage from Ohlin, that

> thus we are completely back again at the classical doctrine which Ohlin just repudiated—namely, that the rate of interest is fixed at the level where the supply of credit, in the shape of saving, is equal to the demand for credit, in the shape of investment.

From this controversy between Keynes and Ohlin, there have emerged famous discussions on "stocks and flows," which have been debated for the last fifty years or so. The present remark does not imply the intention to survey such a debate. Nor do we even wish to claim that the adjustment processes described in (37) and (38) are the correct representation of the neoclassical or Ohlin's theory. For a thorough discussion on this point, and stocks and flows, see Drabicki and Takayama (1979). Bertil Ohlin was a 1977 Nobel laureate in Economic Science.

[27]In the (Cambridge type) classical quantity theory of money, the demand for real cash balances does not depend on the interest rate. The interest rate per se cannot

however, the actual adjustment process may be a hybrid of the two types of processes.

Assuming again $E_r < 0$ and $L_r < 0$, we may determine the signs of the elements of the Jacobian matrices for the type 1 and the type 2 adjustment process as follows.

Type 1

$$\Phi_p = 0, \qquad \Phi_r = aE_r < 0,$$

$$\Psi_p = bM/p^2 > 0, \qquad \Psi_r = bL_r < 0, \text{ and} \tag{39}$$

Type 2

$$\phi_r = aE_r < 0, \qquad \phi_p = 0,$$

$$\psi_r = -bL_r > 0, \qquad \psi_p = -bM/p^2 < 0. \tag{40}$$

Thus we have

$$\begin{bmatrix} \Phi_p & \Phi_r \\ \Psi_p & \Psi_r \end{bmatrix} = \begin{bmatrix} 0 & - \\ + & - \end{bmatrix},$$

$$\begin{bmatrix} \phi_r & \phi_p \\ \psi_r & \psi_p \end{bmatrix} = \begin{bmatrix} - & 0 \\ + & - \end{bmatrix}. \tag{41}$$

The equilibrium point for the type 1 neoclassical system may be defined by

$$\Phi(p^*, r^*) = 0 \text{ and } \Psi(p^*, r^*) = 0,$$

while the equilibrium point for the type 2 neoclassical system may be defined by

$$\phi(\hat{r}, \hat{p}) = 0 \text{ and } \psi(\hat{r}, \hat{p}) = 0.$$

Using (41), we may assert that the equilibrium points, (p^*, r^*) for the type 1 process and $(\hat{r}, \hat{p})$ for the type 2 process, are unique (where

directly adjust the money market. Thus, it may be more reasonable to suppose the adjustment process is in the form of (38). The price level, instead of the interest rate, adjusts the money market. However, in the Keynesian world, we can view the money demand function to be chiefly determined by portfolio choice. In this case, (37) may be more appropriate. See Trevithick (1977, chap. 6).

we assume their existence). Also, using (41), we may easily assert that all three conditions of theorem 6.7 (Olech's theorem) are satisfied for both types of adjustment processes. Hence we may obtain the result in proposition 6.3.

Proposition 6.3.

(i) The equilibrium point (p^*, r^*) for the type 1 process is asymptotically globally stable.

(ii) The equilibrium point $(\hat{r}, \hat{p})$ for the type 2 process is also asymptotically globally stable.

As mentioned earlier, the adjustment process (38a) may be associated with the classical loanable funds theory. Strictly speaking, this may not be correct. More accurately, the excess demand for new loanable funds (F) may be written as

$$F \equiv [I + (G - T)] - [(Y - T - C) + (M/p - L)], \tag{42}$$

where C = consumption, I = investment, T = taxes minus transfer payments, and $M/p - L$ = the excess supply of real cash balances. To motivate (42), we may utilize an interpretation of Akerlof (1973), in which he assumes that the public's savings $(Y - T - C)$ are used solely for increasing its holdings of securities and that the excess supply of money $(M/p - L)$ is immediately channeled into the demand for securities (so that none of savings or $[M/p - L]$ goes to the purchase of securities). Thus the total supply for new loanable funds is equal to saving plus $(M/p - L)$; that is, $(Y - T - C) + (M/p - L)$, where Akerlof (1973) calls $(M/p - L)$ the "portfolio shift." Akerlof assumes that investment by firms (I) is financed exclusively through the issue of securities, and that the entire government budget deficit $(= G - T)$ is financed by printing securities. Thus, the total demand for new loanable funds is equal to $I + (G - T)$. In summary, the excess demand for new loanable funds can be written in the form defined by (42). Although all those assumptions used by Akerlof are not necessary to obtain the interpretation of (42) (see Drabicki and Takayama 1979), these would facilitate a useful interpretation of (42).

Recalling $E \equiv C + I$, we rewrite (42) as

$$F \equiv E + G + (L - M/p) - Y. \tag{43}$$

Assuming again $\dot{r} = aF$, where a is the speed of adjustment in the loanable funds market, we have

$$\dot{r} = a[E(Y - T, r) + G + L(Y, r) - M/p - Y]$$

$$\equiv \phi(r, p). \tag{44}$$

This would probably provide a more accurate representation of the adjustment process as compared to (38a). To complete our discussion, we may utilize the adjustment process (38b) to describe the movement of p as follows:

$$\dot{p} = -b[L(Y, r) - M/p] \equiv \tilde{\psi}(r, p). \tag{45}$$

The adjustment process described by (44) and (45) may be called the "*modified* type 2 neoclassical process."

The signs of the elements of the Jacobian matrix of this process may be determined as

$$\tilde{\phi}_r = a(E_r + L_r) < 0, \ \tilde{\phi}_p = aM/p^2 > 0,$$

$$\tilde{\psi}_r = -bL_r > 0, \ \tilde{\psi}_p = -bM/p^2 < 0, \tag{46}$$

for all (r, p). The equilibrium point of the modified type 2 process is again denoted by $(\hat{r}, \hat{p})$, which is defined by

$$\phi(\hat{r}, \hat{p}) = 0 \ \text{ and } \ \psi(\hat{r}, \hat{p}) = 0.$$

Using (46), and recalling Olech's theorem, we may easily obtain proposition 6.3′.

Proposition 6.3′. Assuming its existence, the equilibrium point $(\hat{r}, \hat{p})$ of the modified type 2 process is unique and it is asymptotically globally stable.

6.3.3 Neoclassical Growth Model

The well-known neoclassical growth model à la Solow (1956)[28] and Swan (1956) considers an economy that produces a single investment-consumption good. This economy can be described by the following system of five equations, in which the government sector and depreciation are ignored for the sake of simplicity. The system has the following equations:

---

[28] Robert Solow was the 1987 Nobel laureate in Economic Science.

$$Y = C + I, \tag{47a}$$

$$Y = F(N,\ K), \tag{47b}$$

$$\dot{K} = I, \tag{47c}$$

$$\dot{N}/N = n, \tag{47d}$$

$$C = (1 - s)Y, \tag{47e}$$

where Y = output, C = consumption, I = investment, F = the production function, N = labor, K = capital, and s = propensity to save.

Equation (47a) assumes equilibrium in the goods market, (47b) specifies the aggregate production function, (47d) assumes a constant rate of growth (n) of the population or labor force, and (47e) assumes that a constant proportion of output is saved. The fact that the same notation (N) is used in (47b) and (47d) implies the full employment of labor, while the fact that the same notation (K) is used in (47b) and (47c) implies the full employment of capital. The depreciation of capital, at least its explicit form, is ignored in (47). This system (47) pursues the behavior of the full employment equilibrium growth path.

Assuming constant returns to scale, (47b) may be rewritten as

$$y = f(k) \equiv F(1,\ k), \quad \text{where } y \equiv Y/N \text{ and } k \equiv K/N, \tag{48}$$

and we assume

$$f'(k) > 0,\ f(k) - kf'(k) > 0,\ f''(k) < 0 \text{ for all } k, \tag{49a}$$

$$f(0) = 0,\ f'(0) = \infty, \text{ and } f'(\infty) = 0. \tag{49b}$$

It can be shown easily that $f' = \partial F/\partial K$ (the marginal product of capital) and $f - kf' = \partial F/\partial N$ (the marginal product of labor), and that $f'' < 0$ if and only if $\partial^2 F/\partial K^2 < 0$ and $\partial^2 F/\partial N^2 < 0$.

Using (47a), (47b), (47c), and (48), we may observe

$$f(k) = Y/N = (C + I)/N = C/N + \dot{K}/N.$$

On the other hand, using $k \equiv K/N$ and (47d), we have $\dot{k} = \dot{K}/N - nk$. Thus we obtain

$$\dot{k} = f(k) - c - nk, \quad \text{where } c \equiv C/N. \tag{50}$$

This is the basic equation in the neoclassical aggregate growth model. The path in which $\dot{k} = 0$ is called a **steady state**. It can be shown from (47a), (47c), (47d), (48), and (50) that along the steady state, N, K, Y, C, and I all grow *at the same rate*, n. Thus the steady state is also called a **balanced growth path.**

In the Solow-Swan model, the model is closed by imposing the demand condition specified in the form of (47e). In other words, combining (50) with (47e), we obtain

$$\dot{k} = sf(k) - nk \equiv \phi(k), \tag{51}$$

which is the basic differential equation of the Solow-Swan neoclassical growth model. The (positive) equilibrium point k^* of this system is obtained by setting $\dot{k} = 0$ in (51) as

$$sf(k^*) = nk^*. \tag{52}$$

Let $k(t;\ k^\circ)$ be the solution of differential equation (51), where k° is the value of k when $t = t^\circ$. Suppose that the following condition is always satisfied at $k^* > 0$. We have

$$\phi'(k^*) = sf'(k^*) - n < 0. \tag{53}$$

Then recalling theorem 6.3, there exists a *unique* $k^* > 0$ that is asymptotically globally stable: namely, $k(t;\ k^\circ) \rightarrow k^*$ (where $k^* > 0$) as $t \rightarrow \infty$ regardless of the value of k° (as long as $k^\circ > 0$). Condition (53) may be called the **Solow-Swan condition**, and steady state k^* may be called a **Solow-Swan path**.

The existence of a unique $k^* > 0$ that is asymptotically globally stable can easily be illustrated diagrammatically, where the Solow-Swan condition (53) is satisfied under (49). Figure 6.6*a* indicates the unique existence of $k^* > 0$ under condition (49), where we may note condition (53) is satisifed. Figure 6.6*b* is the phase diagram for the present dynamic system. This illustrates the stability of k^*. From the diagram, it is clear that k increases over time if $k^\circ < k^*$, and k decreases over time if $k^\circ > k^*$, where k° is assumed to be positive. If $k^\circ = k^*$, then k remains at k°. Regardless of the initial value $k^\circ > 0$, $k(t;\ k^\circ)$ approaches k^* as $t \rightarrow \infty$. Thus, we may obtain the following result.

Proposition 6.4 (Solow, Swan). Under the specification of the present model, there exists a unique $k^* > 0$, which is asymptotically globally stable as long as $k^\circ > 0$.

REMARK: The nice stability property of proposition 6.4 breaks down by simply increasing the number of sectors from one to two. This was

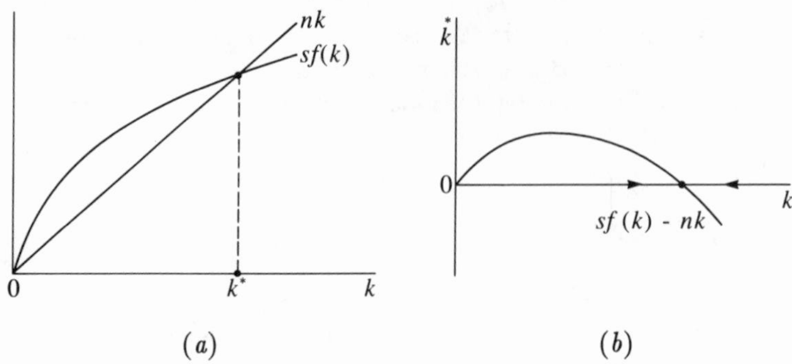

Figure 6.6: The Solow-Swan growth model

discovered independently by Uzawa (1961) and Takayama (1963). The gist of such discussions is summarized in Takayama (1972, pp. 65–68).

6.3.4 On the Phillips Curve

Since the 1960s, there has been a considerable amount of interest concerning the question of a seemingly systematic relation between the rate of inflation and the rate of unemployment. The focal point of such a discussion is the expectation augmented "Phillips curve" relation:

$$\pi = f(u) + \alpha\pi^e, \; f' < 0 \; \text{(and often } f'' < 0); \tag{54}$$

where π = the actual rate of inflation, u = the rate of unemployment, and π^e = the expected rate of inflation, and where α is a positive constant. The term $f(u)$ captures the spirit of the original Phillips curve relation (Phillips, 1958), where $f' < 0$ signifies a "trade-off" between price stability and a low unemployment rate (i.e., lowering u is bound to increase π, since $f' < 0$). The term $\alpha\pi^e$ captures a systematic shift of the Phillips curve due to a change in expectations on the rate of inflation. The role of the term $\alpha\pi^e$ has been emphasized since the late 1960s.[29] With a change in the expected rate of inflation (π^e), we ob-

[29] Using long-run data from the United Kingdom, Phillips (1958) reveals a systematic empirical relation between the rate of change of the wage rate ($\Delta w/w$) and the rate of unemployment. Using U.S. data for a much shorter period, Samuelson and Solow (1960) observed a similar relation between the rate of inflation and the rate of unemployment and called such a relation the "Phillips curve." Samuelson and Solow's

tain a different Phillips curve. This is shown in figure 6.7, where the $[\pi = f(u)]$ - curve represents the curve that corresponds to $\pi^e = 0$.

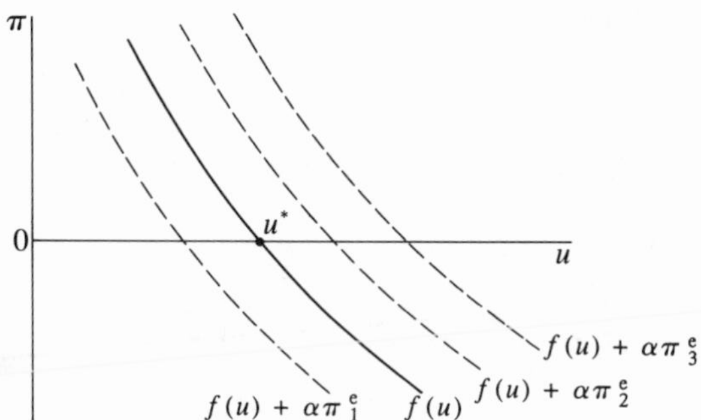

Figure 6.7: Expectation augmented Phillips curve

With regard to the mechanism of expectation formulation, we postulate the following **adaptive expectation formula.**[30]

$$\dot{\pi}^e = \beta(\pi - \pi^e), \tag{55}$$

where β is a positive constant. This means that if the actual rate of inflation exceeds the expected rate $(\pi > \pi^e)$, then the expectations are revised to increase the expected rate $(\dot{\pi}^e > 0)$. Conversely, if $\pi < \pi^e$,

---

study aroused a great deal of interest in the profession, resulting in refinements of the original Phillips and Samuelson-Solow relations by adding additional variables. In empirical studies since the late 1960s, it has become popular to include the term $\alpha\pi^e$ (where α is a positive constant) as the explanatory variable to explain *shifts* of the original Phillips curve relation, $\pi = f(u)$. Such studies have been prompted by a *simultaneous* increase in π and u since the late 1960s in the United States. A widespread belief in the stable relation of $\pi = f(u)$ with $f' < 0$ was then shaken (such a stable relation was indeed observed during most of the 1960s in the United States). See Santomero and Seater (1978) for a survey of the literature on this topic. The behavior of the Phillips curve in the 1970s and the 1980s should be most disappointing to those economists who adhere to *any* version of the Phillips curve. There are still many who believe it, however.

[30]In terms of the discrete time analogue, (55) can be written as

$$\pi_{t+1}^e - \pi_t^e = \beta(\pi_t - \pi_t^e), \tag{55'}$$

which facilitates the above interpretation. If we let $0 < \beta < 1$, (55′) is *equivalent*

then $\dot{\pi}^e < 0$, and the expectations are revised to decrease the expected rate. Suppose now that the government pursues a policy that attempts to maintain the rate of unemployment at a certain target level $\overline{u}$, and suppose further that such a policy is successful. To study the implications of such a governmental action, we set $u = \overline{u}$, and differentiate (54) with respect to time t to obtain

$$\dot{\pi} = \alpha\dot{\pi}^e.$$

Then recalling (55) and (54) in turn, we may observe

$$\dot{\pi} = \alpha\dot{\pi}^e = \alpha(\beta\pi - \beta\pi^e)$$

$$= \beta\{\alpha\pi - [\pi - f(\overline{u})]\} = \beta[f(\overline{u}) - (1 - \alpha)\pi].$$

Hence we obtain

$$\dot{\pi} = \beta[f(\overline{u}) - (1 - \alpha)\pi]. \tag{56}$$

Let π^* be the value of π that is obtained by setting $\dot{\pi} = 0$. π^* is obtained from

$$(1 - \alpha)\pi^* = f(\overline{u}). \tag{57}$$

The dynamic behavior of the solution $\pi(t;\ \pi^\circ)$ of differential equation (56) (where π° is the initial value of π) and the existence of the equilibrium rate π^* depend crucially on the relative magnitude of α and 1. If $\alpha = 1$, then π^* does not even exist unless $f(\overline{u}) = 0$. Hence if we accept the Phillips curve relation in the form of (54), the size of α becomes very important. In the late 1960s, many studies were published in an attempt to determine the magnitude of α empirically.[31]

Many early studies concluded that α was a fraction between 0 and 1, that is, $0 < \alpha < 1$. In this case, π^* uniquely exists, and it is asymptotically globally stable. The value of $\pi(t,\ \pi^\circ)$ approaches $\pi^* \equiv f(\overline{u})/(1 - \alpha)$, as $t \to \infty$ regardless of the initial value π°. This is

---

30 *cont.* to the postulate that expectations are formulated as

$$\pi^e_{t+1} = \beta\pi_t + \beta(1 - \beta)\pi_{t-1} + \beta(1 - \beta)^2\pi_{t-1} + \cdots.$$

Namely, π^e_{t+1} is formulated as a weighted sum of the past actual rate of inflation, where the weight structure is that of a geometric lag.

31 For example, Solow (1969) obtained the figures of $\alpha \cong 0.4$ or 0.6 for the United States, and $\alpha \cong 0.2$ for the United Kingdom. For a survey of the literature on this topic, see Santomero and Seater (1978, pp. 525–27). See also Solow (1976).

illustrated in figure 6.8. As is clear from the diagram, if $\pi(t;\ \pi^\circ) < \pi^*$, then $\dot{\pi} > 0$ and π increases over time; whereas if $\pi(t;\ \pi^\circ) > \pi^*$, then $\dot{\pi} < 0$ and π decreases over time. When $\pi = \pi^*$, $\dot{\pi} = 0$ by (56), so that

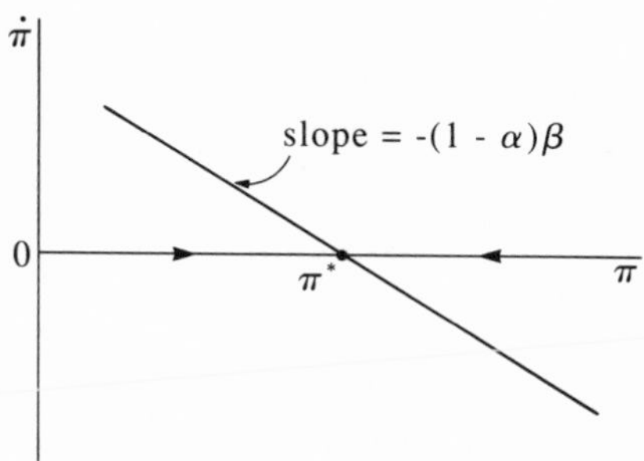

Figure 6.8: The phase diagram for (55) when $0 < \alpha < 1$

$\dot{\pi}^e = 0$ (since $\dot{\pi} = \alpha\dot{\pi}^e$). This in turn implies $\pi = \pi^e$ (= constant) by (55). Such a state in which the rate of inflation is accurately anticipated is called the *long-run* state in this line of the literature.

Friedman (1968) powerfully advocated that the value of α must theoretically be equal to 1.[32] This also conforms to Phelps's (1967) assertion. The view that $\alpha = 1$ has now also been supported by many economists.[33] (We may also note that our experiences of the 1970s and 1980s cast a doubt on the very existence of the "Phillips curve.") In any case, if α is indeed equal to unity, then the following important result follows from (54). In the state in which the actual rate of inflation is correctly anticipated (where $\pi = \pi^e$), then the rate of unemployment u is constant, *regardless of* the rate of inflation. Such a value of u is easily obtained from (54) as $f(u^*) = 0$. This u^* is called the **natural rate of**

---

[32] Milton Friedman was the 1976 Nobel laureate in Economic Science.

[33] One difficulty in obtaining conclusive evidence concerning the magnitude of α is that π^e is *not* observable. The adaptive expectation formula does provide a way to estimate π^e, and yet such a formula may not be acceptable as a rule for expectation formation. There is a direct estimate of the expected rate of inflation called the "Livingston data." However, its use in the present context may be questionable. Thus, Solow (1976) writes, "the Livingston series is a very noisy proxy for the expected rate of inflation."

unemployment.[34]

The rate of unemployment is independent of the rate of inflation in the long-run situation where $\pi = \pi^e$. Conversely, given the Phillips curve relation (54), this view [i.e., $f(u^*) = 0$ when $\pi = \pi^e$] necessarily implies that $\alpha = 1$. The basic underpinning of the view that $\alpha = 1$ is explained as follows. A change in monetary phenomena such as a change in the rate of inflation should not have any impact on real phenomena such as the rate of unemployment in the long run.[35]

Setting $\alpha = 1$ in (56), we have

$$\dot{\pi} = \beta f(\overline{u}). \tag{56'}$$

However, from $f' < 0$, we obtain

$$f(\overline{u}) \gtrless 0 \text{ according to whether } \overline{u} \lesseqgtr u^*.$$

Then from (56′) we may at once conclude that the rate of inflation π increases over time without limit if $\overline{u} < u^*$, and that π decreases without limit if $\overline{u} > u^*$.[36] If the government can actually successfully maintain the rate of unemployment at its target level $\overline{u}$, and if $\overline{u}$ is different from the natural rate u^*, then the economy must face either an ever-increasing

---

[34] This is often interpreted as the "full employment" rate of unemployment. Santomero and Seater (1978, p. 515) exposit it as follows.

> Because of market frictions and structural changes, unemployment is always positive. By implication, then, there will be unemployment even when the economy is in general equilibrium, defined as the absence of excess demand in each market or as the realization of all expectations. *The equilibrium rate of unemployment, commonly called the natural rate*, is determined by real phenomena such as market frictions. ... (italics added)

[35] Thus, the observed downward-sloping Phillips curve is an "illusion" only for the short-run situation in which variations in the rate of inflation are unexpected and can have real consequences, creating a downward-sloping (π, u) relation. In the long-run state in which the actual rate of inflation is correctly anticipated, such a relation disappears. Borrowing Solow's (1976, pp. 5–6) colorful words,

> Now it was argued that there could be no durable gearing between real things and the rate of change of monetary things. ... Money is a veil. ... In a word, the change in the price level is a veil. You might say; the rate of a change in a veil is a veil. ...

[36] Needless to say, if the rate of inflation becomes too large, the monetary economy collapses, and the analysis needs to be revised completely.

rate of inflation or deflation. Believers of this argument are then called **accelerationists.**[37]

In summary, we obtain the results in proposition 6.5.

Proposition 6.5. Suppose that the Phillips curve relation (54) and the adaptive expectation mechanism (55) hold, and suppose further that the government is successful in maintaining the rate of unemployment at a target level $\overline{u}$. Then

(i) if $0 < \alpha < 1$, there exists a unique equilibrium rate of inflation $\pi^* = f(u)/(1 - \alpha)$, which is asymptotically globally stable, and

(ii) if $\alpha = 1$, the only way to keep the rate of unemployment ($\overline{u}$) below the natural rate (u^*) is by continuously increasing the rate of inflation, where the natural rate of unemployment is determined by $f(u^*) = 0$.

Adaptive expectation mechanisms such as (55) have been attacked subsequently. Instead, the "rational expectation approach" has been powerfully advocated. The latter maintains that individuals' predictions should be consistent with the predictions of the model (i.e., expectations are self-fulfilling).[38] While the weaknesses of adaptive expectations are

---

[37]Solow (1976, p. 7) succinctly summarizes the accelerationist's view as follows.

> To maintain the new lower unemployment rate forever, it will be necessary to preserve forever the initial difference between the actual and expected rates of inflation, and the only way to do this, apart from mass hypnosis, is to have accelerating inflation, just fast enough so that expectations lag behind actuality by a fixed amount. For this reason, believers in this argument and in the existence of a natural rate of unemployment are often labeled "accelerationists."

[38]The exposition of the **macro rational expectation hypothesis** (or **new classical macroeconomics**) is beyond the scope of this book. For useful and illuminating expositions of this topic, see Shizuki and Mutoh (1981), Maddock and Carter (1982), Sheffrin (1983), Carter and Maddock (1984), Shaw (1984), and Lucas (1987), for example. Blinder (1987) provides an interesting comparison between J. M. Keynes and R. E. Lucas. At the outset, Blinder states, "We all know the old joke about the professor who uses the same questions year after year, but changes the answers. That joke encapsulates all too well what has happened in macroeconomics" (p. 130). In concluding the paper, he states, "...when Lucas changed the answers given by Keynes, he was mostly turning better answers into worse ones; ...modern Keynesian economics ...has a better claim to being 'scientific' than does new classical macroeconomics" (p. 136).

rather obvious,[39] the inverse relation between π and u may still be accepted *if* we can distinguish "uncertainty" as opposed to "risk" in the sense of Frank Knight, and if we believe that the world is characterized by "uncertainty." In fact, this appears to be the view taken by "monetarism mark I" as represented by Milton Friedman. See Hoover (1984) for an excellent discussion on the distinction between the two types of monetarism. As Hoover points out, there is an important difference with respect to the agent's ignorance of the future between "monetarism mark I" and "monetarism mark II" (see also Takayama 1986). However, if we argue that there is virtually no difference between risk and uncertainty in view of the von Neumann-Morgenstern axioms, monetarism mark II might make more sense, though it may divert more away from real world experiences.

The key distinction between the two versions of monetarism, then, is that mark I à la Friedman allows the "short-run" trade-off between the rate of inflation and the rate of unemployment but disallows such a trade off in the long run. In contrast to this, mark II does not allow such a trade-off even in the short run so that the Phillips curve should always be vertical at the natural rate of unemployment. The economy is then always at full employment according to mark II. "As with the neutrality of money, the new classicals deny even this short-run trade-off " (Hoover 1984, p. 62). Then, with regard to the mark II version and, to a certain extent, to the mark I version, the following comments by Modigliani (1977, p. 6) look very valid.

> The most glaring flow of MREH (macro rational expectation hypothesis) is its inconsistencies with the evidence: if it were valid, deviation of unemployment from the natural rate would have been small and transitory, in which case the *General Theory* would not have been written and neither would

---

[39] Write the adaptive expectations formula in a discrete time form as in (55′), which can equivalently be rewritten

$$\pi_{t+1}^{e} = \pi_t^{e} + \beta(\pi_t - \pi_t^{e}), \tag{55''}$$

where $\beta(\pi_t - \pi_t^e)$ can be interpreted as the term that corrects the prediction error. This formula means that the basis on which the correction of prediction error is made is π_t^e (the first term of the right-hand side of eq. 55″). When $\pi_t \neq \pi_t$, π_t^e is already known to be a wrong predictor at time t. Why then do people correct the prediction based on a wrong forecast? Also, the coefficient β of the correction term is constant regardless of the magnitude of $(\pi_t - \pi_t^e)$, the structure of the model, *etc.* Finally, the adaptive expectations formula uses *only* the past actual rates of inflation to predict π_{t+1}^e (recall fn. 30), and not any other information available up to and inclusive of time t.

> this paper. Sargent (1976) has attempted to remedy this flow by hypothesizing .... In other words, what happened to the United States in the 1930's was a severe attack of laziness.

Whether we use mark I or mark II, the behavior of real world economies appears to have little to do with either of them.

The Phillips curve relation has become very popular among some economists since the 1960s. However, it has been the long-held contention of the present author (since the early 1960s) that our economy is too complex to allow for such a simplistic explanation, and such also appears to have been the view of Professor Phillips himself. This criticism would apply equally to some studies of both accelerationists and nonaccelerationists. Even setting aside the usual question of the effects of such factors as the size of government budget deficits, the money supply, the balance of payments deficit, etc., on the Phillips curve, the reader may understand the point that is raised here by asking the following question: What is the effect of the rate of the exchange rate fluctuation, say, 5 percent or 500 percent (exogenous or endogenous, and anticipated or unanticipated) on the Phillips curve and on the "natural rate" of unemployment? In the 1970s and the 1980s, it has become increasingly difficult to detect the Phillips curve relation, whether we use the expectation augmented form or not, from the actual data. The Phillips curve is a ghost that has been haunting some economists (especially American economists) for some time. Many theoretical and empirical papers have been written assuming its existence. Perhaps, it is about time to discard it altogether.

6.3.5 Tobin's "Walras-Keynes-Phillips" Model: An Application of the Routh-Hurwitz Theorem

The discussion here is motivated by Tobin (1975). We begin our analysis by considering the following usual IS-LM macroequilibrium relation (where we omit the asterisk [*] to denote the equilibrium):

$$Y = E(Y - T, r - \pi^e) + G, \quad \text{and} \tag{58a}$$

$$M/p = L(Y, r), \tag{58b}$$

where Y = output, E = consumption plus investment, r = nominal interest rate, π^e = the expected rate of inflation, T = net taxes, G = government expenditures, M = money supply, p = price level, L = money demand, and where G, T, and M are assumed to be constant. The model described by (58a) and (58b) is basically the same as the one described in (32), except that π^e is implicitly taken to be an exogenously given constant in (32), and that p is no longer a constant in (58). In the present model, π^e shall be taken as endogenous. Note that $r - \pi^e$ signifies the real rate of interest. As in (32), we assume (34) concerning the signs of partial derivatives, where E_r is now defined as $\partial E/\partial(r - \pi^e)$.

Using this as a starting point, we can make a number of modifications so that the model approaches Tobin's (1975) models. A key feature in his models is that the goods market does not adjust quickly. We represent such an assumption as

$$\dot{Y} = \alpha[E(Y - T, r - \pi^e) + G - Y], \tag{59}$$

where α is a positive constant. Tobin (1975, p. 198) justifies the equation of this form by saying, "This implements the Keynesian view that in the very short run money wages and prices are set and output responds to variations of demand."[40]

In contrast to this, it is assumed that the money market adjusts very quickly by the fluctuation of interest rates and that (58b) holds for all t. Solving (58b) for r, we obtain

$$r = r(Y, p, M),$$

where

$$r_Y\,(\equiv \partial r/\partial Y) = -L_Y/L_r > 0, \; r_p\,(\equiv \partial r/\partial p) = -M/(p^2 L_r) > 0.$$

Using this we may define the function D by

$$D(Y, p, \pi^e) \equiv E[Y - T, r(Y, p, M) - \pi^e] + G,$$

[40] While many would agree that output adjusts more slowly than prices, it may be questionable whether (59) captures such an argument. While money wage rates may be slow to move (so-called "downward rigidity of money wage rate"), prices can move much more quickly and this may be all that is necessary to achieve the temporary equilibrium in the goods market. Secondly, there is a distinction between Walrasian vs. Marshallian stability, and it is not clear how Tobin interprets it. As Peter Newman (1965, pp. 106–8) points out, the common confusion on the point lies in the failure to distinguish clearly the theory of exchange from the theory of production. Both Marshall (1920) and Walras (1954) had theories of production as well as those of pure exchange, and both of them agreed that the Marshallian adjustment is explicitly designed for the theory of production, whereas the Walrasian price adjustment is more suited for the theory of exchange. Hence these concepts may not be compared in the same dimension. Discussing these in the same dimension contains a "serious substantive error of muddling up exchange with production" (Newman 1965, p. 107). For recent studies on the question of Walrasian vs. Marshallian stability, see Svenson (1984) and Ide and Takayama (1990, 1991a, b, and 1992a, b).

where

$$D_Y\,(\equiv \partial D/\partial Y) = E_Y - E_r L_Y/L_r,$$

$$D_p\,(\equiv \partial D/\partial p) = -E_r M/pL_r < 0, \quad \text{and}$$

$$D_{\pi^e}\,(\equiv \partial D/\partial \pi^e) = -E_r > 0.$$

We assume G and M are exogenously fixed. Since $E_Y < 1$, we have $D_Y - 1 = (E_Y - 1) - E_r L_Y/L_r < 0$, so that we have $D_Y < 1$. Substituting function D into (59), we may obtain the following adjustment equation of the goods market[41]

$$\dot{Y} = \alpha[D(Y, p, \pi^e) - Y]. \tag{60}$$

Following Tobin (1975), we assume that expectations on price changes (π^e) are formed in the adaptive way;

$$\dot{\pi}^e = \beta(\pi - \pi^e), \; \beta > 0, \tag{61}$$

which is the same as (55). Let Y^* be the full employment level of output. Y^* represents the level of output that corresponds to the natural rate of unemployment.

Finally, also following Tobin (1975), we postulate the following natural rate version of the Phillips curve:

$$\pi(\equiv \dot{p}/p) = \gamma(Y - Y^*) + \pi^e, \tag{62}$$

where γ is a positive constant. The system consisting of (60), (61), and (62) would capture the essence of what Tobin (1975) called the **WKP** (Walras-Keynes-Phillips) **model**. Whereas as our interpretation of (60) may be different from Tobin's, it is formally and qualitatively identical

---

[41] In standard macro textbooks, it is often assumed that adjustments to the equilibrium in the goods and money markets are sufficiently quick, so that we obtain the locus of (P, Y) combinations, which clears the goods market *and* the money market simultaneously for given values of exogenous variables. This is the **aggregate demand curve** relation à la Marschak (1951) and Brownlee (1950). In symbols, it may be expressed as

$$Y = Y(p;\, \pi^e), \quad \text{or } p = p(Y;\, \pi^e).$$

This is the locus of short-run equilibria of the goods *and* the money markets.

to Tobin's corresponding equation.[42] Also our (61) and (62) are identical to his. Hence, our system should perform in the same manner as Tobin's system.

Substituting (62) into (61), we obtain

$$\dot{\pi}^e = \beta\gamma(Y - Y^*). \tag{63}$$

The system of three differential equations, (60), (62), and (63), determines the time path of Y, p, π^e, given the initial condition. The equilibrium values of Y, p, and π^e are obtained by setting $\dot{Y} = \dot{p} = \dot{\pi}^e = 0$ in (60), (62), and (63). Note that at equilibrium we have $Y = Y^*$ and $p =$ constant (so that $\pi = \pi^e$). Namely, at equilibrium we have full employment and price stability. We denote the equilibrium value of p by p^*.

Linearizing (60), (62), and (63) about the equilibrium point, we obtain

$$\begin{bmatrix} \dot{Y} \\ \dot{p} \\ \dot{\pi}^e \end{bmatrix} = \begin{bmatrix} \alpha(D_Y - 1) & \alpha D_p & -\alpha E_r \\ \gamma p^* & 0 & p^* \\ \beta\gamma & 0 & 0 \end{bmatrix} \begin{bmatrix} Y - Y^* \\ p - p^* \\ \pi^e \end{bmatrix}, \tag{64}$$

where we may note $\pi^e = 0$ at equilibrium and $D_{\pi^e} = -E_r$, and where the partial derivatives, D_Y, D_p, and E_r are evaluated at the equilibrium point.

The characteristic equation of the coefficient matrix for (64) can be written as

$$\lambda^3 + a_1\lambda^2 + a_2\lambda + a_3 = 0; \tag{65}$$

$$a_1 \equiv -\alpha(D_Y - 1),\ a_2 \equiv -\alpha\gamma(D_p p^* - \beta E_r),$$
$$a_3 \equiv -\alpha\beta\gamma D_p p^*. \tag{66}$$

[42]Our model differs from that of Tobin's (1975) with respect to the procedure of obtaining (60). While he ignores the money markets, our (60) is obtained by juxtaposing the monetary equilibrium relation with the adjustment equation of the goods market assuming that the money market adjusts very quickly. Tobin (1975) introduces the wealth effect in the goods market, which we assume away for simplicity. Hence one may argue that our model is quite different from Tobin's. However, we may stress that our specification of the model, (64) with $D_Y < 1$, $D_p < 0$, and $D_{\pi^e} > 0$, is formally the same as Tobin's specification of the "goods market" in his WKP model (1975, eq. 2.1.1), with his specification of $E_Y < 1$, $E_p < 0$, and $E_{\pi^e} > 0$. Hence, analytically, our systems of differential equations should perform in a similar fashion as Tobin's.

The Routh-Hurwitz condition for stability [recall theorem 6.9 and condition (24″)] is written as

$$a_1 > 0,\ a_2 > 0,\ a_3 > 0,\ a_1 a_2 - a_3 > 0. \tag{67}$$

Condition a_2 is implied by the other conditions. Conditions $a_1 > 0$ and $a_3 > 0$ are satisfied by $D_Y < 1$ and $D_p < 0$. The remaining condition, $a_1 a_2 - a_3 > 0$, can be written as

$$D_p p^* - \beta E_r < -\beta D_p p^* / \alpha(D_Y - a)\ (< 0). \tag{68}$$

As McDonald (1980, p. 830) pointed out, there is a slip in Tobin's stability condition. Namely, Tobin's condition (1975, p. 199) can be written in terms of our notation as

$$D_p p^* - \beta E_r < 0, \tag{69}$$

and condition (68) is different from (69); that is, it is more stringent than condition (69).[43] In summary, we may obtain the conclusion in proposition 6.6.

Proposition 6.6. The equilibrium in Tobin's WPK model need not be stable.

In a nonstochastic model such as the present one, rational expectations amount to assuming "perfect myopic foresight," that is, $\pi = \pi^e$. Then (62) implies $Y = Y^*$. Thus, the economy must stay at the natural (or the full employment) level. With $Y = Y^*$, we have $p =$ constant by (62), so that we have $\pi = \pi^e = 0$. Setting $Y = Y^*$, $p = p^*$, and $\pi^e = 0$ in (60), we obtain

$$\dot{Y} = \alpha[D(Y^*, p^*, 0) - Y^*]. \tag{70}$$

Clearly, there is no guarantee that we will have

$$D(Y^*, p^*, 0) - Y^* = 0.$$

Let $D^* \equiv D(Y^*, p^*, 0)$. Then from (70), we may conclude that if $D^* > Y^*$, Y increases over time, and that if $D^* < Y^*$, Y decreases over

[43] Tobin's (69) is sufficient to ensure $a_2 > 0$, but it is not sufficient to ensure $a_1 a_2 - a_3 > 0$. Tobin (1975, p. 199) labels (69) "the critical *necessary* condition for stability" (italics added). Even if we correct (69) to (68) following McDonald (1980), this is still not quite accurate. Such a condition provides only a *sufficiency* condition for stability. The stability of the linear approximation system is, in general, only sufficient for the (local) stability of the original system (recall example 6.4).

time. Namely, if $\pi = \pi^e$, the equilibrium of Y in (70) is unstable.[44] This implies that the full employment state ($Y = Y^*$) can hardly be achieved under $\pi = \pi^e$. If people predict the future rate of inflation accurately, then the output level (Y) moves away from the full employment level (Y^*), once Y deviates from Y^*. This looks like a strang conclusion. In any case, Y cannot increase too much from the full employment value of Y^*. It is not clear what constitutes an upper bound for Y and what is the mechanism to stop Y from going up (or down) indefinitely.

Additional remarks on Tobin's WPK model may be in order. It is possible to see that his model imposes *two* adjustment equations, (60) and (62) for one market (i.e., the goods market). This might well be a cause of the somewhat strange implications of his model.[45] Also notice in Tobin's WKP model as specified above, the supply of money is assumed to be a constant, and yet the system consisting of (60), (62), and (63) is capable of producing inflation until its long-run equilibrium, at which $\pi = \pi^e = 0$, is achieved.

6.4 Competitive Equilibrium for the Three-Commodity Case

Here we consider a model of competitive equilibrium in which there are *three* commodities ("shelter," "clothing," and "food," or "exportables," "importables," and "nontradeables," etc.). Unlike (31) in subsection 6.3.1, we shall *not* consider the linear approximation system. Instead, assuming gross substitutability, here we shall prove the *global* stability of a competitive equilibrium. The present proof also illustrates the use of Olech's theorem (theorem 6.7). We shall then illustrate our discussion diagrammatically. Since such a diagrammatic technique, known as the **phase diagram technique**, has been widely used in economic analysis, the graphic method developed here should have broad applications in economics.

---

[44] Tobin (1975, p. 200) writes that when $\pi = \pi^e$, our system is "necessarily unstable." Although this conclusion coincides with ours, his justification seems to be false. He justifies this conclusion by using his (false) stability condition (69).

[45] As an alternative approach, one may hypothesize the aggregate demand relation (60″) à la Marschak (1951) and Brownlee (1950), and postulate the following adjustment equation:

$$\dot{Y} = \tilde{\alpha}[p(Y;\ \pi^e) - Y^*],\ \tilde{\alpha} > 0.$$

Since the money supply is fixed in the present model, we may set $\pi^e = 0$. Since $\partial p/\partial Y < 0$, the equilibrium of this adjustment equation is asymptotically globally stable.

As before, we let $x_i = F_i(P_1, P_2, P_3)$, $i = 1, 2, 3$, be the excess demand for the ith commodity. *Walras's law* can be written as

$$P_1F_1(P) + P_2F_2(P) + P_3F_3(P) \equiv 0, \quad \text{for all } P,$$

where $P = (P_1, P_2, P_3)$. Using the zero homogeneity of the excess demand functions, we may obtain

$$F_i(P_1, P_2, P_3) = F_i(p_1, p_2, 1) \;\; [\equiv f_i(p_1, p_2)], \; i = 1, 2, 3,$$

where $p_i \equiv P_i/P_3$, $i = 1, 2$. The dynamic adjustment process can be described by the differential equation,

$$\dot{p}_i = k_iF_i(p_1, p_2, 1) \;\; [\equiv k_if_i(p_1, p_2)], \; i = 1, 2, \tag{71}$$

where k_i, $i = 1, 2$, are positive constants, signifying the speeds of adjustment of the ith market. The **competitive equilibrium price vector** (p_1^*, p_2^*) is defined by

$$F_i(p_1^*, p_2^*, 1) = 0, \quad \text{or } f_i(p_1^*, p_2^*) = 0, \; i = 1, 2,$$

in which case the motion of prices become stationary. Thus, the competitive equilibrium price vector also signifies an equilibrium point of the system of differential equations (71). We assume that $p^* = (p_1^*, p_2^*)$ exists and that it is an isolated equilibrium point. Note that if the first two markets are brought into equilibrium or cleared, then the third market is automatically cleared by Walras's law.

Since $F_i(P)$, $i = 1, 2, 3$, are homogeneous of degree zero, we have, by using Euler's equation,

$$F_{i1}(P)P_1 + F_{i2}(P)P_2 + F_{i3}(P)P_3 \equiv 0, \; i = 1, 2, 3,$$

where $F_{ij} \equiv \partial F_i/\partial P_j$, $i, j = 1, 2, 3$. From this, we may at once obtain

$$F_{i1}p_1 + F_{i2}p_2 + F_{i3} \equiv 0, \; i = 1, 2, 3, \tag{72}$$

where $F_{ij} = F_{ij}(p_1, p_2, 1)$, $i, j = 1, 2$. From (72), we have

$$p_1/p_2 = -F_{12}/F_{11} - F_{13}/(F_{11}p_2), \quad \text{and} \tag{73a}$$

$$p_1/p_2 = -F_{22}/F_{21} - F_{23}/(F_{21}p_2). \tag{73b}$$

We now assume (global) gross substitutability in the sense that

$$F_{ij}(p, 1) > 0, \;\; \text{for all } p = (p_1, p_2), \; i \neq j, \; i, j = 1, 2. \tag{74}$$

This and (72) imply

$$F_{ii} < 0, \ i = 1, \ 2, \ 3, \ \text{for all } p.^{46} \tag{75}$$

Namely, the own-price effect must always be negative. Also (74) and (75) imply

$$p_1/p_2 > -F_{12}/F_{11}, \ p_1/p_2 < -F_{22}/F_{21}, \quad \text{for all } p. \tag{76}$$

This in turn implies

$$-F_{22}/F_{21} > -F_{12}/F_{11}, \quad \text{for all } p. \tag{77}$$

We are now ready to prove the result in proposition 6.7.

Proposition 6.7. Under (global) gross substitutability (74), the competitive equilibrium (p_1^*, p_2^*) is asymptotically globally stable under the dynamic adjustment process defined by (71).

Proof. By Olech's theorem, $p^* = (p_1^*, \ p_2^*)$ is asymptotically globally stable if

(*a*) $k_1F_{11} + k_2F_{22} < 0$ for all p,

(*b*) $k_1k_2(F_{11}F_{22} - F_{12}F_{21}) > 0$ for all p, and

(*c*) either $F_{11}F_{22} \neq 0$ for all p, or $F_{12}F_{21} \neq 0$ for all p.

Conditions (*a*) and (*c*) are clearly satisfied under gross substitutability, where we note (74) and (75). Condition (*b*) is also satisifed, since (77) can be rewritten as

$$F_{11}F_{22} - F_{12}F_{21} > 0, \quad \text{for all } p. \tag{77'}$$

(QED)

---

[46] Recall that $F_i(P) = D_i(P) - S_i$, $i = 1, \ 2, \ 3$, where D_i and S_i, respectively, denote the demand for and the supply of the ith commodity. We assume that S_i is constant for all i. Thus $F_{ij} > 0$, $i \neq j$ and $F_{ii} < 0$ may be interpreted as follows. An increase in the price of the jth commodity shifts the demand away from the jth commodity into the other commodities (so that $\partial D_j/\partial P_j < 0$ and $\partial D_i/\partial P_j > 0$, $i \neq j$). In terms of the Hicks-Slutsky equation, $\partial D_i/\partial P_j > 0$ precludes the possibility that the income effect is sufficiently large, as well as the possible adverse effect due to complementarity.

REMARK: Note that in this proof, the use of (73) via homogeneity plays a key role. Such a use of homogeneity to prove stability is borrowed from Drabicki and Takayama (1983).

The above discussion is also useful to obtain a graphic representation of the stability problem of a competitive equilibrium for the three-commodity case, we consider the (p_1, p_2)-plane. Define the $(F_i = 0)$-curve as the locus of (p_1, p_2) pairs in which $F_i(p_1, p_2, 1) = 0$, where we let $i = 1, 2$. To obtain the slope of the $(F_i = 0)$-curve, we differentiate $F_i = 0$ to obtain

$$F_{i1}dp_1 + F_{i2}dp = 0, \; i = 1, 2.$$

From this, the slopes of the two curves are easily obtained as

$$\left.\frac{dp_1}{dp_2}\right|_{F_1=0} = -\frac{F_{12}}{F_{11}} > 0, \quad \left.\frac{dp_1}{dp_2}\right|_{F_2=0} = -\frac{F_{22}}{F_{21}} > 0, \tag{78}$$

where the inequalities in (78) follow from gross substitutability, or from (74) and (75). Thus both curves are upward sloping on the (p_1, p_2)-plane. Furthermore, using (78), we may rewrite (76) as

$$\left.\frac{dp_1}{dp_2}\right|_{F_1=0} < \frac{p_1}{p_2}, \quad \left.\frac{dp_1}{dp_2}\right|_{F_2=0} > \frac{p_1}{p_2}. \tag{76'}$$

This means that the slope of the ray from the origin to any point on the $(F_1 = 0)$-curve is greater than the slope of the $(F_1 = 0)$-curve at that point, and that the slope of the $(F_2 = 0)$-curve at this point. This is illustrated in figure 6.9, where figure 6.9*a* and figure 6.9*b*, respectively, are concerned with the $(F_1 = 0)$-curve and the $(F_2 = 0)$-curve, and where broken lines signify various rays from the origin to the $(F_1 = 0)$-curve or to the $(F_2 = 0)$-curve.

The competitive equilibrium (p_1^*, p_2^*) defined by

$$F_i(p_1^*, p_2^*, 1) = 0, \; i = 1, 2,$$

can be described by the intersection of the $(F_1 = 0)$-curve and the $(F_2 = 0)$-curve. This is illustrated in figure 6.10, where point A signifies the competitive equilibrium.[47] Notice that to honor the relations in

---

[47] Differentiation of $F_3(p_1, p_2, 1) = 0$ yields

$$F_{31}dp_1 + F_{32}dp_2 = 0, \text{ or } dp_1/dp_2\Big|_{F_3=0} = -F_{32}/F_{31} < 0.$$

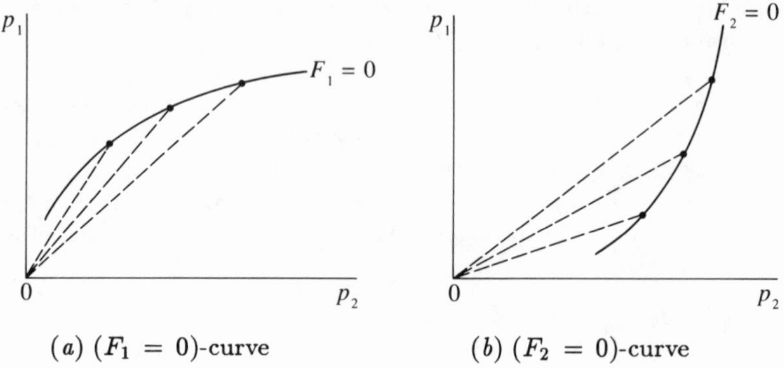

(*a*) ($F_1 = 0$)-curve (*b*) ($F_2 = 0$)-curve

Figure 6.9: ($F_1 = 0$)- **and** ($F_2 = 0$)**-curves**

(76′), the $0A$ ray in figure 6.10 must fall between the ($F_1 = 0$)- and the ($F_2 = 0$)-curves. Thus the ($F_1 = 0$)-curve must cut the ($F_2 = 0$)-curve from above at point A as illustrated. This then provides a diagrammatic proof of the existence of a unique competitive equilibrium under gross substitutability.[48] Needless to say, the existence of a competitive equilibrium is presupposed in proving the global stability result of proposition 6.7.

We now obtain a graphic representation of the dynamic behavior of (p_1, p_2), whose motion is described in (71). This is illustrated in figure 6.11. Note that the ($F_1 = 0$)-curve and the ($F_2 = 0$)-curve divides the nonnegative orthant of the (p_1, p_2) space into four regions. Since $F_{12} > 0$, we have $F_1 > 0$ to the right of the ($F_1 = 0$)-curve, and $F_1 < 0$ to the left of the ($F_1 = 0$)-curve. Hence $\dot{p}_1 > 0$ or p_1 increases over time to the right of the ($F_1 = 0$)-curve, and $\dot{p}_1 < 0$ or p_1 decreases over time to the left of the ($F_2 = 0$)-curve. Similarly, since $F_{22} < 0$, we have $F_2 < 0$ to the right of the ($F_2 = 0$)-curve, and $F_2 > 0$ to the left of the ($F_2 = 0$)-curve. Hence $\dot{p}_2 < 0$ or p_2 decreases over time to the right of the ($F_2 = 0$)-curve, and $\dot{p}_2 > 0$ or p_2 increases over time to the left of the ($F_2 = 0$)-curve. The direction of (p_1, p_2) is illustrated by the arrows

Thus the locus of (p_1, p_2) pairs in which $F_3 = 0$ is negatively sloped. Since $F_1 = 0$ and $F_2 = 0$ imply $F_3 = 0$, such a curve passes through point A.

[48]The use of relations like (76′) in establishing the existence and the uniqueness of a competitive equilibrium does not seem to be known in the literature. It has been clarified by Drabicki and Takayama (1983, p. 4).

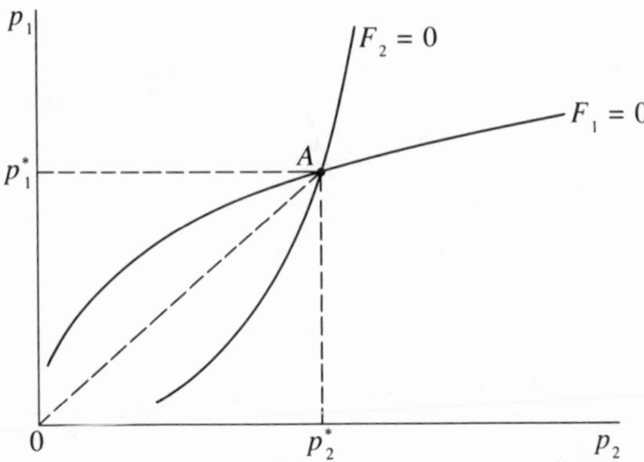

Figure 6.10: Existence and uniqueness of a competitive equilibrium

in the four regions defined by these two curves. Note that the dynamic behavior of (p_1, p_2) along each of these curves is obtained analogously. If the functions F_1 and F_2 are both linear, then the $(F_1 = 0)$- and the $(F_2 = 0)$-curves are straight lines. The dynamic behavior of such linear differential equations on the plane is well known, and we shall exposit it in the next chapter.

The equilibrium point A as illustrated in figure 6.11 is known as an "improper node." For the nonlinear system, it is known that the dynamic behavior of the solution of differential equations on the plane in a neighborhood of an equilibrium point can, except for some exceptional cases, be *approximated by* the dynamic behavior of the solution of its linear approximation system. This result is known as the **Poincaré theorem** (theorem 7.5), and figure 6.11 mimics the result of this theorem. The diagrammatic technique utilized here is quite useful in obtaining the graphic representation of the behavior of the solution of nonlinear systems for the two-dimensional case. Such a technique, known as the **phase diagram technique**, has been widely used in economic analysis.[49]

---

[49]The phase diagram technique was first introduced into economics by Marshall (1879) and adapted by Hicks (1939, 1946) to the stability analysis of a competitive market. Arrow and Hurwicz (1958) used the phase diagram technique more rigorously in their paper proving the global stability of the three-commodity economy.

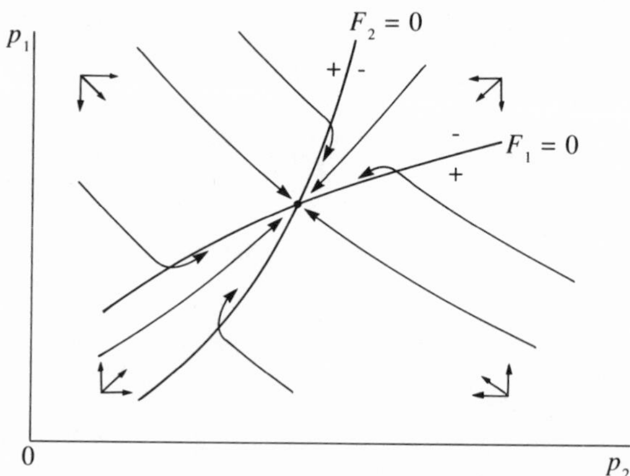

Figure 6.11: The dynamic behavior of $(p_1,\ p_2)$

References[50]

Akerlof, G. A. 1973. "The Demand for Money: A General Equilibrium Inventory Theoretic Approach." *Review of Economic Studies* 40 (January): 115–30.

Arnold, V. I. 1978. *Ordinary Differential Equations.* Trans. from the Russian original by R. A. Silverman. Cambridge, Mass.: MIT Press.

Arrow, K. J., H. D. Block, and L. Hurwicz. 1959. "On the Stability of the Competitive Equilibrium, II." *Econometrica* 27 (January): 32–109.

Arrow, K. J., and L. Hurwicz. 1958. "On the Stability of the Competitive

[50] There are many excellent textbooks on the theory of differential equations. Since it is not easy to list all of them, I only listed a few of them. For a slightly more complete list, see the references in the next chapter. Beltrami (1987) and Harris (1987) provide readable, fine discussions of dynamic models. Brock and Malliaris (1989) contains a good exposition of up-to-date materials that are useful to economists. In recent years, "chaos" has been attracting the interest of economists, physicists, and others. The exposition of the chaos theory is beyond the scope of this book. The interested reader is referred to Guckenheimer and Holmes (1983), Eckman and Ruelle (1985), Gleick (1987), Beltrami (1987), Baumol and Benhabib (1989), Devaney (1989), Brock and Malliaris (1989), Brock, Hsieh, and Le Baron (1991), and Benhabib (1992), for example. Gleick (1987) provides a non-technical and exciting reading of the topic. Beltrami (1987) and Devaney (1989) offer readable expositions. Guckenheimer and Holmes (1983) and Eckman and Ruelle (1985) are not easy for economists.

Equilibrium, I." *Econometrica* 26 (October): 522–52.

Baumol, W. J., and J. Benhabib. 1989. "Chaos: Significance, Mechanism, and Economic Applications." *Journal of Economic Perspectives* 3 (Winter): 77–105.

Beltrami, E. 1987. *Mathematics for Dynamic Modeling.* New York: Academic Press.

Benhabib, J. ed. 1992. *Cycles and Chaos in Economic Equilibrium*, Princeton, N.J.: Princeton University Press.

Blinder, A. S. 1987. "Keynes, Lucas, and Scientific Progress." *American Economic Review* 77 (May): 130–42.

Boyce, W. E., and R. C. DiPrima. 1986. *Elementary Differential Equations and Boundary Value Problems.* 4th ed. New York: Wiley (1st ed. 1964).

Brock, W. A., and A. G. Malliaris. 1989. *Differential Equations, Stability, and Chaos in Dynamic Economics.* Amsterdam: North-Holland.

Brock, W. A., D. A. Hseih, and B. Le Baron. 1991. *Nonlinear Dynamics, Chaos and Instability*, Cambridge, Mass.: MIT Press, 1991.

Brownlee, O. H. 1950. "The Theory of Employment and Stabilization Policy." *Journal of Political Economy* 62 (October): 412–24.

Carter, M., and R. Maddock. 1984. *Rational Expectations: Macroeconomics for the 1980s.* London: Macmillan.

Chang, W. W., and D. J. Smyth. 1972. "Stability and Instability of IS-LM Equilibrium." *Oxford Economic Papers* 24 (November): 372–84.

Devaney, R. L. 1989. *An Introduction to Chaotic Dynamical Systems.* 2d ed., Redwood City, Calif.: Addison-Wesley (1st ed. 1986).

Drabicki, J. Z., and A. Takayama. 1979. "The General Equilibrium Framework of Economic Analysis: Stocks and Bonds—With Special Application to Macroeconomic Models." In *General Equilibrium, Growth, and Trade*, ed. J. Green and J. Scheinkman, 355–401. New York: Academic Press.

————. 1983. "The Theory of Comparative Advantage in a Monetary World." *Southern Economic Journal* 50 (July): 1–17.

Eaves, C., and H. E. Scarf. 1976. "The Solution of Systems of Piecewise Linear Equations." *Mathematics of Operations Research* 1 (February): 1–27.

Eckman, J. P., and D. Ruelle. 1985. "Engodic Theory of Chaos and Strange Attractors." *Review of Modern Physics* 57, July: 617–56.

Friedman, M. 1968. "The Role of Monetary Policy." *American Economic Review* 58 (March): 1–17.

Gleick, J. 1987. *Chaos, Making a New Science.* New York: Viking.

Guckenheimer, J., and P. Holmes. 1983. *Nonlinear Oscillations, Dynamical Systems, and Bifurcations of Vector Fields.* New York: Springer-Verlag.

Hahn, F. 1982. "Stability." In *Handbook of Mathematical Economics*, vol. II, ed. K. J. Arrow and M. D. Intriligator, 749–93. Amsterdam: North-Holland.

Harris, M. 1987. *Dynamic Economic Analysis.* Oxford: Oxford University Press.

Hicks, J. R. 1937. "Mr. Keynes and the 'Classics': A Suggested Interpretation." *Econometrica* 5 (April): 147–59.

———. 1946. *Value and Capital.* 2d ed. Oxford: Clarendon Press (1st ed. 1939).

———. 1973. "Recollection and Documents." *Economica* 40 (February): 2–11.

Hirota, M. 1981. "On the Stability of Competitive Equilibrium and the Pattern of Initial Holdings: An Example." *International Economic Review* 22 (June): 461–67.

Hoover, K. D. 1984. "Two Types of Monetarism." *Journal of Economic Literature* 22 (March): 58–76.

Ide, T., and A. Takayama. 1990. "Factor Market Distortions and Variable Returns to Scale: Walrasian and Two Marshallian Criteria." Presented at the International Economics Symposium, University of Pennsylvania, November 17.

———. 1991a. "Variable Returns to Scale, Paradoxes, and Global Correspondence in the Theory of International Trade." In *Trade, Policy, and International Adjustments*, ed. A. Takayama et al, 108–54. San Diego: Academic Press.

———. 1991b. "Marshall-Lerner Condition Reconsidered." *Economics Letters* 35 (February): 201–7.

———. 1992a. "Variable Returns to Scale and Dynamic Adjustment: The Marshall-Lerner Condition Reconsidered," to appear in *General Equilibrium, Growth, and Trade. II. The Legacy of Lionel W. McKenzie*, ed. by M. Boldrin, R. Becker, R. W. Jones, and W. Thomson, San Diego: Academic Press.

———. 1992b. "Marshallian Stability and Economic Theory." Presented at the Midwest International Economics Conference (October), University of Pittsburgh.

Kalman, R. E., and J. E. Bertram. 1960. "Control System Analysis and Design via the 'Second Method' of Liapunov, I: Continuous Time System." *Journal of Basic Engineering* 82 (June): 371–93.

Keynes, J. M. 1937. "Alternative Theories of the Rate of Interest." *Economic Journal* 47 (June): 241–52.

Lewis, J. P. 1963. "Dimensions in Economic Theory." *Manchester School of Economics and Social Studies* 31 (September): 243–54.

Liapunov, A. M. 1907. "Problème général de la stabilité du mouvement." *Annales de la Faculté de Science de L'Université de Toulouse* 9: 203–24. Reprinted in *Annals of Mathematical Study*, no. 17 (1949). Princeton, N.J.: Princeton University Press.

Lucas, R. E. 1987. *Models of Business Cycles.* Yrjö Jahnsson Lectures. Oxford: Basil Blackwell.

McDonald, I. M. 1980. "On the Comparison of the Stability Implications of Marshallian and Walrasian Adjustment Schemes: A Note." *American Economic Review* 70 (September): 829–33.

Maddock, R., and M. Carter. 1982. "A Child's Guide to Rational Expectations." *Journal of Economic Literature* 20 (March): 39–51.

Marschak, J. 1951. *Income, Employment, and the Price Level (Notes on Lectures Given at the University of Chicago, Autumn 1948 and 1949).* Cowles Commission for Research in Economics. Reprinted (1965) by Augustus M. Kelley: New York.

Marshall, A. 1920. *Principles of Economics.* 8th ed. London: Macmillan (1st ed., 1890).

Modigliani, F. 1977. "The Monetarist Controversy Or, Should We Forsake Stabilization Policies," *American Economic Review* 67 (March): 1–19.

Negishi, T. 1962. "The Stability of a Competitive Economy: A Survey Article," *Econometrica* 30 (October): 635–69.

———. 1989. *History of Economic Theory.* Amsterdam: North-Holland.

Newman, P. 1965. *The Theory of Exchange.* Englewood Cliffs, N.J.: Prentice-Hall.

Ohlin, B. 1937. "Some Notes on the Stockholm Theory of Saving and Investments, II." *Economic Journal* 47 (June): 221–40.

Olech, C. 1963. "On the Global Stability of an Autonomous System on the Plane." In *The Contribution to Differential Equations*, ed. J. P. LaSalle and J. B. Diaz, 1:389–400. New York: Wiley.

Phelps, E. S. 1967. "Phillips Curves, Expectations of Inflation, and Optimal Unemployment Over Time." *Economica* 34 (August): 254–81.

Phillips, A. W. 1958. "The Relation between Unemployment and the Rate of Change of Money Wage Rate in the United Kingdom, 1861–1957." *Economica* 25 (August): 283–99.

Pontryagin, L. S. 1962. *Ordinary Differential Equations.* Trans. from the 1961 Russian original by L. Kascinskas and N. B. Counts. Reading, Mass.: Addison-Wesley.

Samuelson, P. A. 1947. *Foundations of Economic Analysis.* Cambridge, Mass.: Harvard University Press (enlarged ed. 1983).

Samuelson, P. A., and R. M. Solow. 1960. "The Problem of Achieving and Maintaining a Stable Price Level: Analytical Aspects of Anti-Inflation Policy." *American Economic Review* 50 (May): 177–94.

Santomero, A. M., and J. J. Seater. 1978. "The Inflation-Unemployment Trade-Off: A Critique of the Literature." *Journal of Economic Literature* 16 (June): 499–544.

Scarf, J. E. 1974. *The Computation of Economic Equilibria* (in collaboration with T. Hansen). New Haven, Conn.: Yale University Press.

———. 1982. "The Computation of Equilibrium Prices: An Exposition." In *Handbook of Mathematical Economics*, ed. K. J. Arrow and M. D. Intriligator, 2:1007–61. Amsterdam: North-Holland.

Shaw, G.K. 1984.*Rational Expectations: An Elementary Exposition.*Brighton, Sussex: Wheatsheaf.

Sheffrin, S. M. 1983. *Rational Expectations.* New York: Cambridge University Press.

Shizuki, T., and T. Mutoh. 1981. *Rational Expectations and Monetarism* (in Japanese). Tokyo: Nihon Keizai Shimbun-sha.

Simmons, G. F. 1972. *Differential Equations.* New York: McGraw-Hill.

Solow, R. M. 1956. "A Contribution to the Theory of Economic Growth." *Quarterly Journal of Economics* 70 (February): 65–94.

———. 1969. *Price Expectations and the Behavior of the Price Level.* Manchester: Manchester University Press.

———. 1976. "Down the Phillips Curve with Gun and Camera." In *Inflation, Trade, and Taxes: Essays in Honor of Alice Bourneuf*, ed. D. A. Besley, E. J. Kane, P. A. Samuelson, and R. M. Solow. Columbus, Ohio: Ohio State University Press.

Svenson, L. E. O. 1984. "Walrasian and Marshallian Stability." *Journal of Economic Theory* 34 (December): 391–379.

Swan, T. 1956. "Economic Growth and Capital Accumulation." *Economic Record* 32 (November): 334–61.

Takayama, A. 1963. "On a Two-Sector Model of Economic Growth: A Comparative Statics Analysis." *Review of Economic Studies* 30 (June): 95–104. This was completed in October, 1960, and included in his Ph.D. thesis, University of Rochester, March, 1962.

———. 1972. *International Trade: An Approach to the Theory.* New York: Holt, Rinehart, and Winston.

———. 1980a. "Olech's Theorem and the Stability of Macro Models." Lecture notes, Purdue Universty, February (a revision of the 1970 lecture notes at Purdue University).

———. 1980b. "Elements of Differential Equations." Lecture notes, Texas A & M University, March (a revision of the 1978 *lecture note* at the same university).

———. 1980c. "Does Monetary Policy Matter?" *Zeitschrift für die gesamte Staatswissenschaft.* 136 (Dezember): 593–616.

———. 1985. *Mathematical Economics.* 2d ed. New York: Cambridge University Press.

———. 1986. "The General Theory after Fifty Years: The Neoclassical Approach (A Partial View)." Presented at the annual meeting of the Eastern Economic Association, Philadelphia. Southern Illinois University Discussion Paper Series, No. 86-30.

Tobin, J. 1975. "Keynesian Models of Recession and Repression." *American Economic Review.* 65 (May): 195–202.

Trevithick, J. A. 1977. *Inflation: A guide to the Crisis in Economics.* Middlesex: Penguin Books.

Uzawa, H. 1961. "On a Two Sector Model of Economic Growth." *Review of Economic Studies* 29 (October): 40–47.

Walras, L. 1954. *Elements of Pure Economics.* Trans. W. Jaffé from the 1926 edition of the French original by W. Jaffé. London: Richard D. Irwin.

Yoshizawa, T. 1967. *Introduction to Differential Equations* (in Japanese). Tokyo: Asakura Shoten.

CHAPTER 7

Linear Differential Equations on the Plane and Elements of Nonlinear Systems

The study of linear differential equations for the two-dimensional case is important because many applications of differential equations are often two- dimensional, *and* because a number of key concepts such as "node," "saddle point," "spiral point," and "center" (which do not appear in one-dimensional problems) appear in two-dimensional problems. Also, the linear system for the two-dimensional case is often used as an approximation of the nonlinear system, and hence it is important to study the linear system, and understand the circumstances in which such an approximation is possible.

7.1 Linear Systems

Consider the systems of n first-order, linear differential equations with constant coefficients:

$$\dot{x}_i(t) = \sum_{j=1}^{n} a_{ij}x_j(t) + b_i,\ i = 1,\ 2,\ \ldots,\ n, \tag{1}$$

or more compactly,

$$\dot{x}(t) = Ax(t) + b, \quad \text{where } A \equiv [a_{ij}], \tag{2}$$

where the a_{ij}'s and b_j's are real numbers which are constants. Also assume that the x_i's are real numbers, and that A is nonsingular. The solution for this system is known to exist for all t in $(-\infty,\ \infty)$, and it is unique given the **initial condition**,

$$x_i(t^\circ) = x_i^\circ,\ i = 1,\ 2,\ \ldots,\ n. \tag{3}$$

The system of linear equations in (2) is the *homogeneous system* in which $b = 0$ and where

$$\dot{x}(t) = Ax(t). \tag{4}$$

Note that (2) can be rewritten in the form of (4), that is, $\dot{y} = Ay$ where $y \equiv x + A^{-1}b$. We henceforth confine most of our attention to (4).

Clearly (4) is satisfied by $x(t) = 0$ for all t, which is called the **trivial solution**. To obtain more useful, nontrivial solutions, write some specific solutions of (4) as

$$x^{(1)}(t),\ x^{(2)}(t),\ \ldots,\ x^{(k)}(t),\ \ldots \tag{5}$$

where $x^{(k)}(t)$ is an n-dimensional vector whose i^{th} element is $x_{ik}(t)$. Then we at once obtain the result in theorem 7.1.

Theorem 7.1. If $x^{(1)}(t)$ and $x^{(2)}(t)$ are solutions of (4), then their linear combination $c_1x^{(1)}(t) + c_2x^{(2)}(t)$ is also a solution, where c_1 and c_2 are arbitrary constants.

By repeated application of theorem 7.1 it follows that if $x^{(1)}(t)$, $x^{(2)}(t)$, ..., and $x^{(k)}(t)$ are some solutions of (4), then

$$c_1x^{(1)}(t) + c_2x^{(2)}(t) + \ldots + c_kx^{(k)}(t)$$

is also a solution for any constants $c_1, c_2, \ldots, c_k$.

Let $k = n$, and consider the $n \times n$ matrix $X(t)$ formed by this solution

$$X(t) \equiv [x^{(1)}(t),\ x^{(2)}(t),\ \ldots,\ x^{(n)}(t)] \equiv [x_{ij}(t)]. \tag{6}$$

The solutions $x^{(1)}(t)$, $x^{(2)}(t)$, ..., and $x^{(n)}(t)$ are said to be **linearly independent** for each t, if $X(t)$ is nonsingular for each t.[1] It can be shown that if $X(t)$ is nonsingular for *some* t, then $X(t)$ is nonsingular for

---

[1]In terms of matrix algebra, the n vectors $x^{(1)}$, $x^{(2)}$, ..., $x^{(n)}$, are said to be **linearly independent** if $c_1x^{(1)} + c_2x^{(2)} + \ldots + c_nx^{(n)} = 0$ holds only when $c_1 = c_2 = \ldots = c_n = 0$. On the other hand, these n vectors are said to be linearly dependent if there exists constants c_i's such that $c_i \neq 0$ for some i. The matrix $X \equiv [x^{(1)}, x^{(2)}, \ldots, x^{(n)}]$ is nonsingular, if and only if $x^{(1)}$, $x^{(2)}$, ..., $x^{(n)}$ are linearly independent. Or equivalently, the matrix X is nonsingular if and only if its determinant does not vanish. Thus, these two properties can also be used as the defining properties of a nonsingular matrix.

all t.[2] The determinant of $X(t)$ is called the **Wronskian**. The following theorem is fundamental in the theory of linear differential equations.

Theorem 7.2. If we find n specific solutions $x^{(1)}(t)$, $x^{(2)}(t)$, ..., $x^{(n)}(t)$ that are linearly independent for some t (i.e., whose Wronskian does not vanish for some t), then every solution of (4) can be expressed as a linear combination of these solutions, that is,

$$\phi(t) \equiv c_1 x_1^{(1)}(t) + c_2 x^{(2)}(t) + \ldots + c_n x^{(n)}(t), \tag{7}$$

in exactly one way.

The solution $\phi(t)$ given in (7) is called the **general solution**, and the constants c_1, c_2, ..., and c_n in (7) are usually specified by the n constants in (3), that is, the *initial condition*. With such a specification of the c_i's, the solution is called a **particular solution**. The concept of general solution is a conspicuous feature of *linear* differential equations. For the linear system such as (2), it is possible to obtain a solution containing n arbitrary constants from which all possible solutions follow by specifying values for these n constants. For *nonlinear* equations, this need not be the case. Even if a solution containing n arbitrary constants can be found, there may be other solutions that cannot be obtained by giving values of these n constants.[3]

7.2 Homogeneous Linear Systems on the Plane

We now focus our attention on the special case of the homogeneous linear system (4) in which $n = 2$. We consider the system:

$$\dot{x} = a_{11}x + a_{12}y, \qquad \dot{y} = a_{21}x + a_{22}y. \tag{8}$$

We assume that the coefficient matrix,

$$H \equiv \begin{bmatrix} a_{11} & a_{12} \\ a_{21} & a_{22} \end{bmatrix}, \tag{9}$$

is nonsingular.

To find a solution for (8), we may try

$$x = Ae^{\lambda t} \text{ and } y = Be^{\lambda t}, \tag{10}$$

[2] The matrix $X(t)$, when it is nonsingular, is known as a **fundamental matrix**.

[3] Recall Example 6.3 in the previous chapter.

where A, B, and λ are constants to be determined. The equations in (10) imply

$$\dot{x} = \lambda A e^{\lambda t} = \lambda x \text{ and } \dot{y} = \lambda B e^{\lambda t} = \lambda y. \tag{10'}$$

Substituting (10′) into (8), we obtain

$$(a_{11} - \lambda)x + a_{12}y = 0, \; a_{21}x + (a_{22} - \lambda)y = 0. \tag{11}$$

Substituting (10) into this, we obtain

$$(a_{11} - \lambda)A + a_{12}B = 0, \; a_{21}A + (a_{22} - \lambda)B = 0. \tag{12}$$

In matrix form, (12) becomes

$$\begin{bmatrix} a_{11} - \lambda & a_{12} \\ a_{21} & a_{22} - \lambda \end{bmatrix} \begin{bmatrix} A \\ B \end{bmatrix} = \begin{bmatrix} 0 \\ 0 \end{bmatrix}. \tag{13}$$

It is clear that $A = B = 0$ is the trivial solution of (13), which makes (10) the trivial solution of (8). On the other hand, (13) has nontrivial solutions whenever the determinant of the coefficient matrix vanishes, that is, whenever

$$\begin{vmatrix} a_{11} - \lambda & a_{12} \\ a_{21} & a_{22} - \lambda \end{vmatrix} = 0, \quad \text{or} \quad \det\,[H - \lambda I] = 0, \tag{14}$$

where I is the 2×2 identity matrix. Equation (14) is called the **eigen equation** or **characteristic equation**, and the roots of (14) are called the **eigenvalues**, **characteristic values**, or **characteristic roots**. The roots of (14) can be obtained by solving (14), or

$$\lambda^2 - p\lambda + q = 0, \tag{15}$$

where $p \equiv a_{11} + a_{22}$ and $q \equiv a_{11}a_{22} - a_{21}a_{12}$. That is,

$$\lambda^2 - (a_{11} + a_{22})\lambda + (a_{11}a_{22} - a_{21}a_{12}) = 0. \tag{15'}$$

The eigenvalues are then obtained as

$$\lambda = \frac{1}{2}\left[p \pm \sqrt{p^2 - 4q}\right]$$

$$= \frac{1}{2}\left[(a_{11} + a_{22}) \pm \sqrt{(a_{11} + a_{22})^2 - 4(a_{11}a_{22} - a_{21}a_{12})}\right]. \quad (16)$$

Write the two eigenvalues obtained in (16) as λ_1 and λ_2. Replace λ in (13) by λ_1, and write the resulting nontrivial solution as (A_1, B_1). Then

$$x = A_1 e^{\lambda_1 t}, \; y = B_1 e^{\lambda_1 t}, \quad (17)$$

is a nontrivial solution of the system (8). Similarly with λ_2, we find another nontrivial solution

$$x = A_2 e^{\lambda_2 t}, \; y = B_2 e^{\lambda_2 t}. \quad (18)$$

We might note that (12) or (13) can also be written as

$$\begin{bmatrix} a_{11} & a_{12} \\ a_{21} & a_{22} \end{bmatrix} \begin{bmatrix} A \\ B \end{bmatrix} = \lambda \begin{bmatrix} A \\ B \end{bmatrix}. \quad (19)$$

The nonzero vector (A, B) that has this property is known as an **eigenvector**.[4] It is clear that (A_1, B_1) is an eigenvector associated with λ_1, whereas (A_2, B_2) is an eigenvector associated with λ_2. Note also that if (A, B) is an eigenvector associated with eigenvalue λ, its constant multiple $(\theta A, \theta B)$ is also an eigenvector associated with λ (for any $\theta \neq 0$). If λ_1 and λ_2 are obtained by (16), and if $\lambda_1 \neq \lambda_2$, then the two eigenvectors associated with λ_1 and λ_2 are not proportional. Namely, there does not exist any θ such that $(A_1, B_1) = (\theta A_2, \theta B_2)$. To put it a different way, $A_1/B_1 \neq A_2/B_2$ if $\lambda_1 \neq \lambda_2$.

In order to obtain the general solution of the system (8), we have to obtain two linearly independent solutions (cf. theorem 7.2). Therefore, we are left with the task of determining whether or not the two solutions given in (17) and (18) are linearly independent. For this purpose, it is necessary to examine each of the three possibilities for λ_1 and λ_2. Since the expressions for λ_1 and λ_2 are given by (16), there are three possibilities: (*a*) λ_1 and λ_2 are real and distinct, (*b*) λ_1 and λ_2 are complex, and (*c*) λ_1 and λ_2 are real with $\lambda_1 = \lambda_2$.

---

[4]If the eigenvalue is zero for some (nonzero) eigenvector, then the coefficient matrix H must be singular (which is ruled out in the present exposition).

Distinct Real Roots

When the two roots, λ_1 and λ_2, are distinct real numbers, then it can be easily shown that (17) and (18) are linearly independent, and hence their linear combination

$$\begin{bmatrix} x \\ y \end{bmatrix} = c_1 \begin{bmatrix} A_1 e^{\lambda_1 t} \\ B_1 e^{\lambda_1 t} \end{bmatrix} + c_2 \begin{bmatrix} A_2 e^{\lambda_2 t} \\ B_2 e^{\lambda_2 t} \end{bmatrix}, \tag{20}$$

that is,

$$x = c_1 A_1 e^{\lambda_1 t} + c_2 A_2 e^{\lambda_2 t}, \; y = c_1 B_1 e^{\lambda_1 t} + c_2 B_2 e^{\lambda_2 t} \tag{21}$$

provides the general solution of the system (8). The values of c_1 and c_2 are determined by the initial condition, which in turn yields a particular solution that corresponds to it.

Example 7.1. In the case of the system

$$\begin{bmatrix} \dot{x} \\ \dot{y} \end{bmatrix} = \begin{bmatrix} 2 & 1 \\ 1 & 2 \end{bmatrix} \begin{bmatrix} x \\ y \end{bmatrix}. \tag{22}$$

Corresponding to (12), we obtain

$$(2 - \lambda)A + B = 0, \; A + (2 - \lambda)B = 0. \tag{23}$$

The characteristic equation here is written as

$$\begin{vmatrix} 2 - \lambda & 1 \\ 1 & 2 - \lambda \end{vmatrix} = 0, \quad \text{or} \quad \lambda^2 - 4\lambda - 3 = 0, \tag{24}$$

with roots $\lambda_1 = 3$ and $\lambda_2 = 1$. With $\lambda_1 = 3$, (23) becomes

$$-A + B = 0, \; A + B = 0. \tag{25}$$

A nontrivial solution of (25) is $A_1 = 1$ and $B_1 = -1$. Similarly, corresponding to $\lambda_2 = 1$, we find that $A_2 = 1$ and $B_2 = 1$. Hence the general solution of (22) is written as

$$\begin{bmatrix} x \\ y \end{bmatrix} = c_1 \begin{bmatrix} e^{3t} \\ -e^{3t} \end{bmatrix} + c_2 \begin{bmatrix} e^{t} \\ e^{t} \end{bmatrix}. \tag{26}$$

Namely, we have

$$x = c_1 e^{3t} + c_2 e^{t}, \; y = -c_1 e^{3t} + c_2 e^{t}. \tag{27}$$

Distinct Complex Roots

If λ_1 and λ_2 are distinct complex numbers, then they can be written in the form

$$\lambda_1 = a + ib, \; \lambda_2 = a - ib, \tag{28}$$

where $b \neq 0$, and where a and b are real numbers (recall eq. 16). In this case we expect the A's and B's obtained from (12) to be complex numbers. Corresponding to λ_1, we have $A_1 \equiv \alpha_1 + i\alpha_2$ and $B_1 = \beta_1 + i\beta_2$. Similarly, corresponding to λ_2, we have A_2 and B_2 that are, in general, complex numbers. Note that $\lambda_2 = \overline{\lambda}_1$ (the bar denotes a complex conjugate). Hence we can choose A_2 and B_2 as $A_2 = \overline{A}_1$ and $B_2 = \overline{B}_1$. Since the coefficients, a_{11}, a_{12}, a_{21}, and a_{22} are assumed to be real, taking complex conjugates of (12), we obtain

$$(a_{11} - \lambda)\overline{A}_1 + a_{12}\overline{B}_1 = 0, \; a_{21}\overline{A}_1 + (a_{22} - \lambda)\overline{B}_1 = 0.$$

We may therefore write the solutions corresponding to λ_1 and λ_2 as

$$x = A_1 e^{(a+ib)t}, \; y = B_1 e^{(a+ib)t}, \text{ and} \tag{29a}$$

$$x = \overline{A}_1 e^{(a-ib)t}, \; y = \overline{B}_1 e^{(a-ib)t}. \tag{29b}$$

From the elementary algebra of complex numbers, we have,

$$e^{i\theta} = \cos\theta + i\sin\theta, \tag{30}$$

for any real number θ. This is known as **Euler's formula.**[5]

[5]In the theory of complex numbers, the exponential function and the trigonometric functions of a complex number, z, are defined in terms of the following infinite series:

$$\begin{aligned} e^z &= 1 + \frac{z}{1!} + \frac{z^2}{2!} + \ldots + \frac{z^n}{n!} + \ldots \\ \cos z &= 1 - \frac{z^2}{2!} + \frac{z^4}{4!} - \ldots + (-1)^n \frac{z^{2n}}{(2n)!} + \ldots \\ \sin z &= z - \frac{z^3}{3!} + \frac{z^5}{5!} - \ldots + (-1)^n \frac{z^{2n+1}}{(2n+1)!} + \ldots \end{aligned}$$

Notice that these relations also hold when z is a real number. Letting $z = i\theta$ in these formulas, we obtain *Euler's formula*, as used in the text.

Hence we may rewrite (29a) as

$$x = A_1 e^{at}(\cos\ bt + i\ \sin\ bt),\ y = B_1 e^{at}(\cos\ bt + i\ \sin\ bt). \quad (31)$$

Recalling $A_1 = \alpha_1 + i\alpha_2$ and $B_1 = \beta_1 + i\beta_2$, we may rewrite (31) as

$$x = e^{at}[(\alpha_1\ \cos\ bt - \alpha_2\ \sin\ bt) + i(\alpha_1\ \sin\ bt + \alpha_2\ \cos\ bt)], \quad (32a)$$

$$y = e^{at}[(\beta_1\ \cos\ bt - \beta_2\ \sin\ bt) + i(\beta_1\ \sin\ bt + \beta_2\ \cos\ bt)]. \quad (32b)$$

Define the vectors u and v by

$$u \equiv \begin{bmatrix} \alpha_1\ \cos\ bt - \alpha_2\ \sin\ bt \\ \beta_1\ \cos\ bt - \beta_2\ \sin\ bt \end{bmatrix},$$

$$v \equiv \begin{bmatrix} \alpha_1\ \sin\ bt + \alpha_2\ \cos\ bt \\ \beta_1\ \sin\ bt + \beta_2\ \cos\ bt \end{bmatrix}. \quad (33)$$

Then (32a) and (32b) can be rewritten as

$$\begin{bmatrix} x \\ y \end{bmatrix} = e^{at}(u + iv). \quad (34)$$

Since this should provide a solution of (8), it is easy to see that

$$\begin{bmatrix} x \\ y \end{bmatrix} = e^{at}u, \text{ and } \begin{bmatrix} x \\ y \end{bmatrix} = e^{at}v \quad (35)$$

are real-valued solutions of (8). Furthermore, it can be shown that these two are linearly independent. Hence, the general solution is obtained as

$$\begin{bmatrix} x \\ y \end{bmatrix} = e^{at}(c_1 u + c_2 v). \quad (36)$$

Since we have already found the general solution, it is not necessary to consider (29b).

Example 7.2. In the case of the system[6]

$$\begin{bmatrix} \dot{x} \\ \dot{y} \end{bmatrix} = \begin{bmatrix} 1 & -1 \\ 5 & -3 \end{bmatrix} \begin{bmatrix} x \\ y \end{bmatrix}, \quad (37)$$

[6] This example is from Boyce and DiPrima (1977, pp. 313–15).

we have (cf. equation 12)

$$(1 - \lambda)A - B = 0,\ 5A - (3 + \lambda)B = 0. \tag{38}$$

The characteristic equation here is written as

$$\begin{bmatrix} 1 - \lambda & -1 \\ 5 & -3 - \lambda \end{bmatrix} = \lambda^2 + 2\lambda + 2 = 0, \tag{39}$$

which has the roots, $\lambda_1 = -1 + i$ and $\lambda_2 = -1 - i$. Nontrivial solutions of (38) for λ_1 and λ_2 are, respectively, obtained as

$$\begin{bmatrix} A_1 \\ B_1 \end{bmatrix} = \begin{bmatrix} 1 \\ 2 - i \end{bmatrix}, \text{ and } \begin{bmatrix} A_2 \\ B_2 \end{bmatrix} = \begin{bmatrix} 1 \\ 2 + i \end{bmatrix}. \tag{40}$$

Thus $\alpha_1 = 1$, $\alpha_2 = 0$, $\beta_1 = 2$, and $\beta_2 = -1$. Consider a solution,

$$\begin{bmatrix} x \\ y \end{bmatrix} = \begin{bmatrix} 1 \\ 2 - i \end{bmatrix} e^{(-1+i)t}. \tag{41}$$

Then, using Euler's formula, we rewrite this as

$$\begin{aligned} \begin{bmatrix} x \\ y \end{bmatrix} &= \begin{bmatrix} 1 \\ 2 - i \end{bmatrix} e^{-t}(\cos t + i \sin t) \\ &= \begin{bmatrix} e^{-t} \cos t \\ 2e^{-t} \cos t + e^{-t} \sin t \end{bmatrix} \\ &\qquad + i \begin{bmatrix} e^{-t} \sin t \\ -e^{-t} \cos t + 2e^{-t} \sin t \end{bmatrix} \end{aligned} \tag{42}$$

which corresponds to (31) and (32). Thus,

$$u = \begin{bmatrix} \cos t \\ 2 \cos t + \sin t \end{bmatrix}, \ v = \begin{bmatrix} \sin t \\ 2 \sin t - \cos t \end{bmatrix}. \tag{43}$$

Hence $e^{-t}u$ and $e^{-t}v$ constitute a set of real-valued solutions of (37), so that the general solution of (37) can be written as

$$\begin{bmatrix} x \\ y \end{bmatrix} = e^{-t}(c_1 u + c_2 v). \tag{44}$$

To verify that $e^{-t}u$ and $e^{-t}v$ are linearly independent, compute the determinant W (i.e., the Wronskian):

$$W \equiv \det\,[e^{-t}u,\ e^{-t}v]$$

$$= 2e^{-2t}(2\sin t\ \cos t - \cos^2 t - 2\sin t\ \cos t - \sin^2 t)$$

$$= -2e^{-2t}. \tag{45}$$

Since $W \neq 0$ for any t, it follows that $e^{-t}u$ and $e^{-t}v$ are linearly independent.

Equal Real Roots

When λ_1 and λ_2 have the same value λ, then (17) and (18) are not linearly independent. Hence, in order to construct the general solution, it is necessary to find a solution that is linearly independent of the solution:

$$x = Ae^{\lambda t},\ y = Be^{\lambda t}. \tag{46}$$

To find such a second solution, we look for a solution in the form of

$$x = (A_1 + A_2 t)e^{\lambda t},\ y = (B_1 + B_2 t)e^{\lambda t}. \tag{47}$$

It can be easily checked that (47) satisfies (8) [and hence it is a solution of (8)], and that (46) and (47) are linearly independent. It follows that the general solution can be written as

$$x = c_1 Ae^{\lambda t} + c_2(A_1 + A_2 t)e^{\lambda t},$$

$$y = c_1 Be^{\lambda t} + c_2(B_1 + B_2 t)e^{\lambda t}. \tag{48}$$

Namely,

$$\begin{bmatrix} x \\ y \end{bmatrix} = c_1 \begin{bmatrix} Ae^{\lambda t} \\ Be^{\lambda t} \end{bmatrix} + c_2 \begin{bmatrix} (A_1 + A_2 t)e^{\lambda t} \\ (B_1 + B_2 t)e^{\lambda t} \end{bmatrix}. \tag{48'}$$

The constants A_1, A_2, B_1, and B_2 are found by substituting (47) into (8). It can be shown that A_2 and B_2 are chosen in such a way that $A_2 = A$ and $B_2 = B$.

Example 7.3. In the case of the system[7]

$$\begin{bmatrix} \dot{x} \\ \dot{y} \end{bmatrix} = \begin{bmatrix} 3 & -4 \\ 1 & -1 \end{bmatrix} \begin{bmatrix} x \\ y \end{bmatrix} . \tag{49}$$

Corresponding to (12), we have

$$(3 - \lambda)A - 4B = 0, \; A - (1 + \lambda)B = 0. \tag{50}$$

The characteristic equation here is written

$$\lambda^2 - 2\lambda + 1 = 0, \quad \text{or} \quad (\lambda - 1)^2 = 0, \tag{51}$$

which has equal real roots, 1 and 1. With $\lambda = 1$, (50) becomes

$$2A - 4B = 0, \; A - 2B = 0, \tag{52}$$

which has a nontrivial solution $A = 2, \; B = 1$. So

$$x = 2e^t, \; y = e^t \tag{53}$$

is a nontrivial solution of (49). A second linearly independent solution in the form of (47) can be written as

$$x = (A_1 + A_2 t)e^t, \; y = (B_1 + B_2 t)e^t. \tag{54}$$

When this is substituted into (49), we obtain

$$(A_1 + A_2 t + A)e^t = 3(A_1 + A_2 t)e^t - 4(B_1 + B_2 t)e^t,$$

$$(B_1 + B_2 t + B)e^t = (A_1 + A_2 t)e^t - (B_1 + B_2 t)e^t,$$

which reduces to

$$(2A_2 - 4B_2)t + (2A_1 - A_2 - 4B_1) = 0,$$

$$(A_2 - 2B_2)t + (A_1 - 2B_1 - B_2) = 0.$$

Since these are identities that hold for all values of t, we must have

$$2A_2 - 4B_2 = 0, \quad 2A_1 - A_2 - 4B_1 = 0,$$

[7]This example and its subsequent exposition are from Simmons (1972, pp. 280–82).

$$A_2 - 2B_2 = 0, \quad A_1 - 2B_1 - B_2 = 0.$$

The two equations on the left have $A_2 = 2$ and $B_2 = 1$ as a nontrivial solution. Hence, the two equations on the right become

$$2A_1 - 4B_1 = 2, \; A_1 - 2B_1 = 1,$$

so that we may take $A_1 = 1$, $B_1 = 0$. Hence (54) can now be specified as

$$x = (1 + 2t)e^t, \; y = te^t. \tag{55}$$

Hence the general solution of (49) is written as

$$x = 2c_1e^t + c_2(1 + 2t)e^t, \; y = c_1e^t + c_2te^t. \tag{56}$$

It is easy to check that (53) and (55) are linearly independent.

The above discussion of the equal real roots case implicitly assumes away the case in which $a_{11} = a_{22} \neq 0$ and $a_{21} = a_{12} = 0$. Namely, it excludes the case when (8) is given by

$$\begin{bmatrix} \dot{x} \\ \dot{y} \end{bmatrix} = \begin{bmatrix} a_{11} & 0 \\ 0 & a_{11} \end{bmatrix} \begin{bmatrix} x \\ y \end{bmatrix}. \tag{57}$$

In this case, the characteristic equation is

$$\lambda^2 - 2a_{11}\lambda + a_{11}^2 = 0, \;\; \text{or} \;\; (\lambda - a_{11})^2 = 0, \tag{58}$$

so that $\lambda = a_{11}$. Substituting this (together with $a_{12} = a_{21} = 0$) into (12), we may at once conclude that the choice of A and B in (46) can be arbitrary. Note that (57) can also be written as

$$\dot{x} = a_{11}x, \qquad \dot{y} = a_{11}y, \tag{57'}$$

and the general solution of this is obviously

$$x = c_1e^{\lambda t}, \; y = c_2e^{\lambda t}, \;\; \text{where } \lambda = a_{11}, \tag{59}$$

instead of (48). In this case, the system is said to be **uncoupled** (since each of the two equations of (57′) can be solved independently).

7.3 Dynamic Behavior of the Solution on the Plane

In this section, we investigate the dynamic behavior of the solutions of systems of linear differential equations on the plane discussed in the preceding section. We have

$$\begin{bmatrix} \dot{x} \\ \dot{y} \end{bmatrix} = \begin{bmatrix} a_{11} & a_{12} \\ a_{21} & a_{22} \end{bmatrix} \begin{bmatrix} x \\ y \end{bmatrix}, \tag{8'}$$

Clearly, $(x, y) = (0, 0)$ is an *equilibrium point*, where $\dot{x} = \dot{y} = 0$. Assume that the coefficient matrix is nonsingular. The origin $(0, 0)$ is the only equilibrium point. As should be clear from the discussion in the preceding section, the dynamic behavior of the solution of (8′) critically depends on the eigenvalues of the coefficient matrix, λ_1 and λ_2. As a matter of fact, the discussion of the dynamic behavior involves more cases than those discussed previously. There are three major cases and two minor cases.

Unequal Real Roots of the Same Sign

Recall that the general solution for this case is given by

$$x = c_1 A_1 e^{\lambda_1 t} + c_2 A_2 e^{\lambda_2 t}, \ y = c_1 B_1 e^{\lambda_1 t} + c_2 B_2 e^{\lambda_2 t} \tag{20'}$$

where the A's and B's are constant. We begin by assuming both λ_1 and λ_2 are negative. Without loss of generality, we may assume $\lambda_1 < \lambda_2 < 0$. If both λ_1 and λ_2 are negative, it follows from (20′) that both x and y approach 0 as $t \to \infty$ (regardless of the initial condition). The equilibrium point $(0, 0)$ is asymptomatically globally stable. When $c_2 = 0$, we have from (20′),

$$x = c_1 A_1 e^{\lambda_1 t}, \ y = c_1 B_1 e^{\lambda_1 t}, \ \text{ so that } \ y = (B_1/A_1)x. \tag{60}$$

The solution trajectory (x, y) moves along the straight line,

$$y = (B_1/A_1)\,x,$$

on the $(x - y)$-plane, and it approaches $(0, 0)$, as $t \to \infty$, on this line (see fig. 7.1).[8] If $c_1 > 0$, the trajectory lies on one side of this line, and

[8]Such a plane is called a **phase plane**. A solution of the system (8), or its nonlinear counterpart, that satisfies a certain initial condition defines a curve on the phase plane. If such a solution (x, y) is not a constant, it is referred to as a **path** or a **trajectory**.

if $c_1 < 0$, it lies on the other side of this line. If $c_1 = 0$ instead, then we obtain, from (20′),

$$x = c_2 A_2 e^{\lambda_1 t}, \; y = c_2 B_2 e^{\lambda_1 t}, \quad \text{so that } \; y = (B_2/A_2)x. \tag{61}$$

The solution trajectory (x, y) moves along the straight line,

$$y = (B_2/A_2)\,x,$$

and it approaches $(0, 0)$ on this line as $t \to \infty$. If $c_1 \neq 0$ and $c_2 \neq 0$, then the solution trajectories are "curved" paths. From (20′), we may obtain

$$\frac{y}{x} = \frac{c_1 B_1 e^{\lambda_1 t} + c_2 B_2 e^{\lambda_2 t}}{c_1 A_1 e^{\lambda_1 t} + c_2 A_2 e^{\lambda_2 t}} = \frac{(c_1 B_1/c_2)e^{(\lambda_1 - \lambda_2)t} + B_2}{(c_1 A_1/c_2)e^{(\lambda_1 - \lambda_2)t} + A_2}\,. \tag{62}$$

Since $\lambda_1 < \lambda_2$ by assumption, it is clear that y/x approaches B_2/A_2 as $t \to \infty$. Therefore, all trajectories approach the origin and they are tangent to the $[y = (B_2/A_2)x]$-line except for one pair of trajectories approaching the origin along a different line, that is, the one whose slope

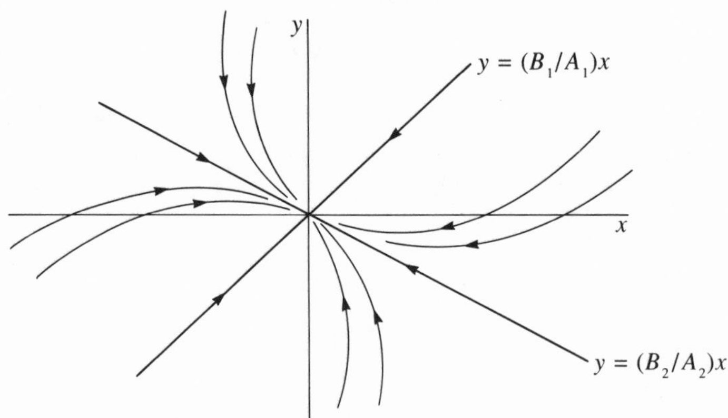

Figure 7.1: Improper node, $\lambda_1 \neq \lambda_2$

is B_1/A_1. This type of equilibrium point is called an **improper node** or simply a **node** (see fig. 7.1). A "proper node" will be discussed later.

When λ_1 and λ_2 are both positive, the situation is similar, except that the direction of motion on the trajectories is away from the equilibrium point (0, 0). Namely, every solution except for the solution ($x = 0$, $y = 0$ for all t) moves away from the origin, so that (0, 0) is unstable. When $\lambda_1 > \lambda_2 > 0$, the picture of the paths given in figure 7.1 remain unchanged, except that the arrows showing their directions are all reversed.

Real Roots of Opposite Signs

Without loss of generality, we may assume $\lambda_1 < 0 < \lambda_2$. The general solution for the case of real roots with opposite signs is again in the form of (20′), and we have specific solutions in the form of (60) and (61). Corresponding to (60) and (61), there are two pairs of paths that move along straight lines. Along the $[y = (B_1/A_1)x]$-line, x and y approach the origin as $t \to \infty$, since $\lambda_1 < 0$ in (60). On the other hand, along the $[y = (B_2/A_2)x]$-line, x and y move away from the origin. The arrows showing the direction of motion along this line are reversed compared to the case depicted in figure 7.1. See fig. 7.2.

When $c_1 \neq 0$ and $c_2 \neq 0$, the general solution (20′) represents curved paths. Since $\lambda_1 < 0$ and $\lambda_2 > 0$, the first term in the expression for x in (20′) converges to zero as $t \to \infty$, whereas the second term diverges away from zero to ∞ or $-\infty$ depending on whether $c_2A_2 > 0$ or $c_2A_2 < 0$. Hence as $t \to \infty$, x goes to ∞ or $-\infty$ depending on whether $c_2A_2 > 0$ or $c_2A_2 < 0$. Similarly, as $t \to \infty$, y diverges away from the origin depending on whether $c_2B_2 > 0$ or $c_2B_2 < 0$. When $c_1 \neq 0$ and $c_2 \neq 0$, none of the trajectories approaches the equilibrium point, (0, 0). Furthermore, from (62) and $\lambda_1 < 0 < \lambda_2$, it follows that each of the paths for this case is asymptotic to the $[y = (B_2/A_2)x]$-line when $t \to \infty$. Since (62) can also be written as

$$\frac{y}{x} = \frac{B_1 + (c_2B_2/c_1)e^{(\lambda_2-\lambda_1)t}}{A_1 + (c_2A_2/c_1)e^{(\lambda_2-\lambda_1)t}}, \tag{62'}$$

it follows that each of these paths is asymptotic to the $[y = (B_1/A_1)x]$-line when $t \to -\infty$. The equilibrium point for this case is called a **saddle point**. Figure 7.2 illustrates the qualitative behavior of the paths for the saddle point. Note that none of the paths except for the one on the $[y = (B_1/A_1)x]$-line converges to the origin, but rather diverges away from it as $t \to \infty$. Unless the initial point happens to lie on the $[y = (B_1/A_1)x]$-line, the dynamic path never approaches the equilibrium point. The $[y = (B_1/A_1)x]$-line is sometimes called the **stable branch**.

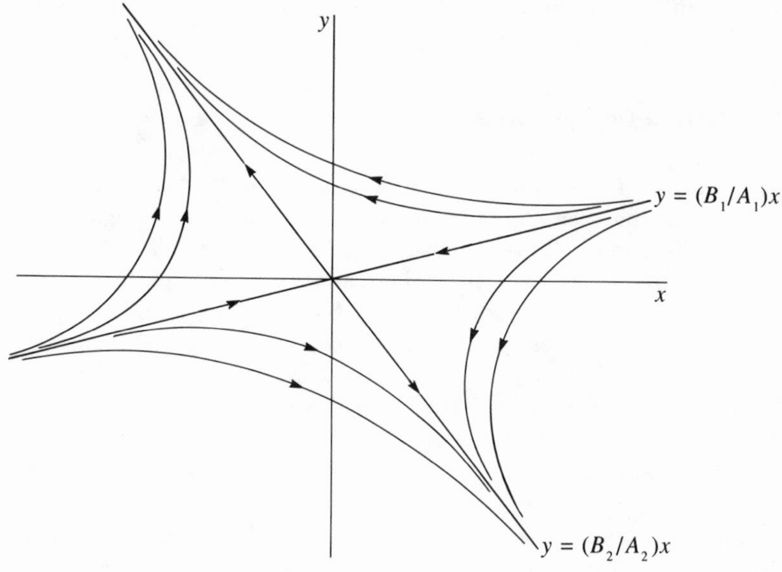

Figure 7.2: Saddle point, $\lambda_1\lambda_2 < 0$

Complex Roots (But Not Pure Imaginary)

In this case we can write λ_1 and λ_2 in the form of $a + ib$. We assume $a \neq 0$. The general solution for this case is given by

$$x = e^{at}[c_1(\alpha_1 \cos bt - \alpha_2 \sin bt) + c_2(\alpha_1 \sin bt + \alpha_2 \cos bt)], \quad (63a)$$

$$y = e^{at}[c_1(\beta_1 \cos bt - \beta_2 \sin bt) + c_2(\beta_1 \sin bt + \beta_2 \cos bt)], \quad (63b)$$

by virtue of (36) and (33). We first examine the case of $a < 0$. In this case, from (63), it follows immediately that $x \to 0$ and $y \to 0$ as

$t \to \infty$. The equilibrium point is asymptotically globally stable. We now show that the trajectories wind around the equilibrium point in a spiral manner.

To accomplish this we introduce the polar coordinates r and θ defined by

$$x = r \cos \theta \quad \text{and} \quad y = r \sin \theta. \tag{64}$$

Since $\theta = \tan^{-1}(y/x)$, we have

$$\dot{\theta} = (x\dot{y} - y\dot{x})/(x^2 + y^2), \tag{65}$$

where we may recall $d \tan^{-1} u/du = 1/(1 + u^2)$. We may note that $x^2 + y^2 = r^2$, and we may assume $x^2 + y^2 \neq 0$. Substituting (8) into (65) yields

$$\dot{\theta} = [a_{21}x^2 + (a_{22} - a_{21})xy - a_{12}y^2]/(x^2 + y^2). \tag{66}$$

Since the eigenvalues are complex in the present case, we have, from (16),

$$(a_{11} + a_{22})^2 - 4(a_{11}a_{22} - a_{21}a_{12}) = (a_{11} - a_{22})^2 + 4a_{21}a_{12} < 0. \tag{67}$$

From this, it follows that a_{21} and a_{12} have opposite signs. We first consider the case where $a_{21} > 0$ (so that $a_{12} < 0$). When $y = 0$ we have $\dot{\theta} = a_{21} > 0$ by virtue of (66). In fact, $\dot{\theta}$ can never be zero. To show this, suppose $\dot{\theta} = 0$. Then, from (66) it follows that

$$a_{21}x^2 + (a_{22} - a_{11})xy - a_{12}y^2 = 0, \quad \text{or}$$

$$a_{21}z^2 + (a_{22} - a_{11})z - a_{12} = 0, \quad \text{for some } z \equiv x/y.$$

But this implies

$$z = \frac{-(a_{22} - a_{11})^2 \pm \sqrt{(a_{22} - a_{11})^2 + 4a_{21}a_{12}}}{2a_{21}}.$$

Then z is a complex number by (67). Since x and y are real numbers, this is impossible. Thus $\dot{\theta}$ cannot be zero. Thus $\dot{\theta} = a_{21} > 0$ for $y = 0$ and $\dot{\theta} \neq 0$ for $y \neq 0$. $\dot{\theta}$ is always positive for $y = 0$ when $a_{21} > 0$. Similarly, $\dot{\theta}$ is always negative for $y = 0$ when $a_{21} < 0$. Since by (64),

x and y change sign infinitely often as $t \to \infty$, all paths must spiral into the origin (clockwise or counterclockwise depending upon whether $a_{21} < 0$ or $a_{21} > 0$). The equilibrium point in this case is called a **spiral point**, and is illustrated in figure 7.3. If $a > 0$, then from (63) we can at once conclude that the paths must diverge away from the origin as $t \to \infty$ (or approach the origin as $t \to -\infty$). So the equilibrium point is unstable. The graphic illustration for the case of $a > 0$ would be similar to figure 7.3, except that the direction of motion would be reversed.

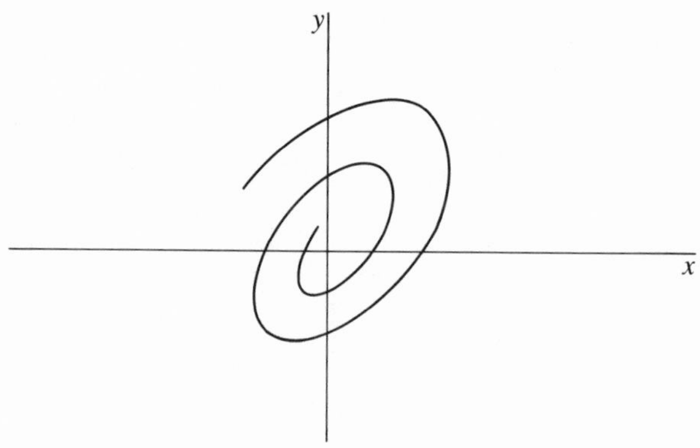

Figure 7.3: Spiral point, $\lambda_1 = a + ib$, $\lambda_2 = a - ib$.

Example 7.4. We consider the system

$$\dot{x} = -x + 2y, \; \dot{y} = -2x - y. \tag{68}$$

The eigenvalues of the coefficient matrix of this system can be obtained as

$$\lambda = -1 \pm 2i.$$

Constants, a and b in (63), take values -1 and 2, respectively. Since $a = -1$, each trajectory moves toward the equilibrium point, (0, 0), as $t \to \infty$. Since $a_{21} = -2 < 0$ in (68), the spiral trajectories move toward the origin clockwise. To obtain a graphic illustration, we first

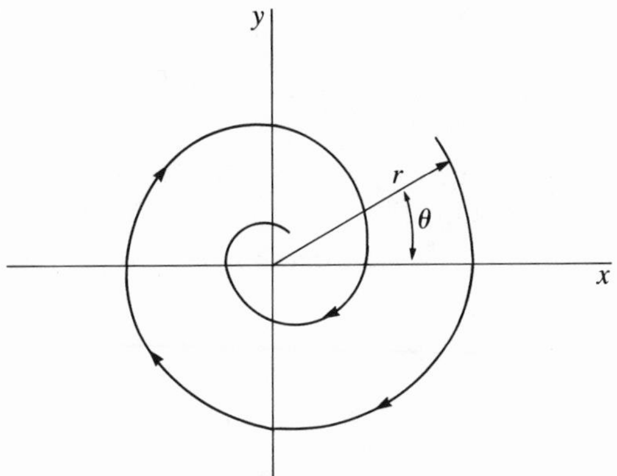

Figure 7.4: A spiral point

rewrite (68):

$$\frac{dy}{dx} = \frac{-2x - y}{-x + 2y}, \tag{69}$$

and introduce the polar coordinates r and θ defined by (64), where we have

$$r^2 = x^2 + y^2 \quad \text{and} \quad \theta = \tan^{-1}(y/x). \tag{70}$$

From (70), we obtain

$$r\frac{dr}{dx} = x + y\frac{dy}{dx}, \quad r^2\frac{d\theta}{dx} = x\frac{dy}{dx} - y,$$

so that we have

$$\frac{dr}{d\theta} = r\frac{x + y(dy/dx)}{x(dy/dx) - y}. \tag{71}$$

Substituting (69) into this and recalling $r^2 = x^2 + y^2$, we obtain

$$dr/d\theta = r/2. \tag{72}$$

Thus, (69) is rewritten in this very simple form. From (72), we have

$$r = ce^{\theta/2} \tag{73}$$

as the polar equation of the paths that represents a family of spirals. One such spiral is illustrated in figure 7.4. Note from (68) that $\dot{y} = -2x$ for $y = 0$. Along the x-axis, $\dot{y} \lesseqgtr 0$ depending on whether $x \gtreqless 0$. This confirms the clockwise direction of the motion.

In addition to the preceding three major cases, there are two other cases.

Pure Imaginary Roots

This is the case in which $\lambda = a \pm ib$, where $a = 0$ and $b \neq 0$. The general solution is again given by (63), except the exponential factor is now deleted. The trajectories neither approach the equilibrium point nor tend toward infinity as $t \to \infty$; they are no longer spirals. The motion is periodic in time and the trajectories are closed curves. The direction of motion around the closed curves is clockwise or counterclockwise, depending on whether $a_{21} < 0$ or $a_{21} > 0$.

These closed curves are actually ellipses. This can be proved by solving the differential equation,

$$\frac{dy}{dx} = \frac{a_{21}x_2 + a_{22}y}{a_{11}x_1 + a_{12}y}. \tag{74}$$

The equilibrium point, (0, 0), is called a **center**. We illustrate the trajectories for the case of $a_{21} > 0$ in figure 7.5.

Example 7.5. Consider the system

$$\dot{x} = -y, \ \dot{y} = x. \tag{75}$$

The eigenvalues can easily be obtained as $\lambda = \pm i$. Rewrite (75) as $dy/dx = -x/y$. Solving this differential equation, we obtain

$$x^2 + y^2 = c^2. \tag{76}$$

The trajectories are circles. Since $a_{21} = 1 > 0$ they move counterclockwise. This can also be confirmed directly from (75).

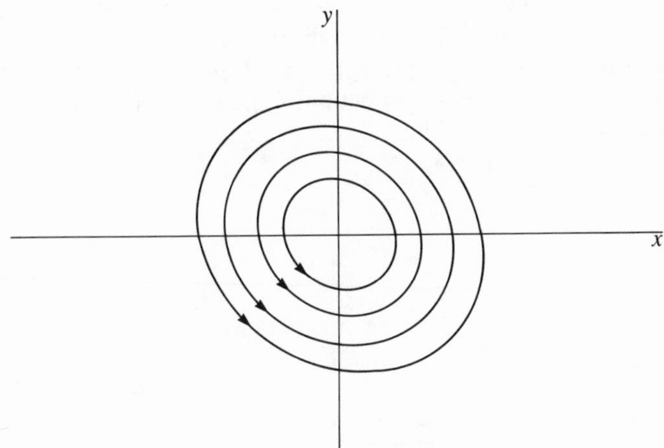

Figure 7.5: Center, $\lambda_1 = ib, \lambda_2 = -ib$

Equal Roots

Except for (57), the general solution in this case is given in the form of

$$x = c_1 A e^{\lambda t} + c_2(A_1 + At)e^{\lambda t}, \ y = c_1 B e^{\lambda t} + c_2(B_1 + Bt)e^{\lambda t},$$

where the A's and B's are definite constants and the c's are arbitrary constants. Therefore, all trajectories approach the origin or tend toward infinity as $t \to \infty$, depending upon whether $\lambda < 0$ or $\lambda > 0$. We assume $\lambda < 0$.

When $c_2 = 0$, we obtain the solutions,

$$x = c_1 A e^{\lambda t}, \ y = c_1 B e^{\lambda t}, \ \text{ so that } \ y = (B/A)x, \tag{77}$$

from (48′). Thus, there are two half-line paths in this case, each of which lies on the $[y = (B/A)x]$-line moving toward the origin as $t \to \infty$. For $c_2 \neq 0$, (48′) represents curved paths. From (48′), we may observe

$$\frac{y}{x} = \frac{(c_1/c_2)B + B_1 + Bt}{(c_1/c_2)A + A_1 + At}. \tag{78}$$

These trajectories approach the origin tangent to the $[y = (B/A)x]$-line, since $y/x \to B/A$ as $t \to \infty$ by L'Hospital's rule. To depict the trajectories, also observe $y/x \to B/A$ as $t \to -\infty$. These trajectories are illustrated in figure 7.6. The equilibrium point (0, 0) is again called an **improper node** or simply a **node**. When $\lambda > 0$, the situation remains the same, except the direction of the paths are reversed and the equilibrium point is unstable.

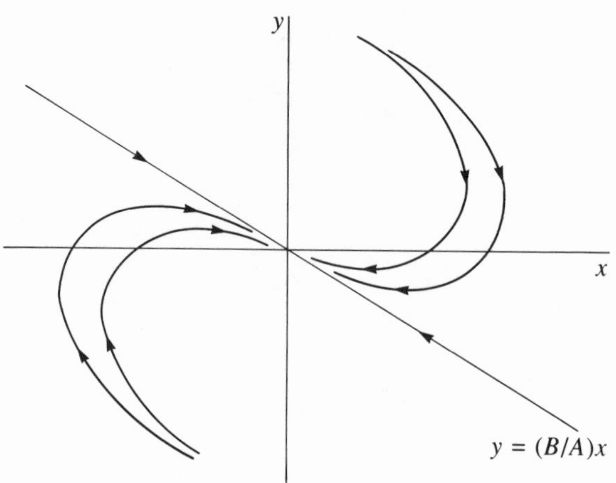

Figure 7.6: Improper node, $\lambda_1 = \lambda_2$

Finally, we examine a special case of the equal real roots case. We consider the system given by (57), or

$$\dot{x} = a_{11}x, \; \dot{y} = a_{11}y. \tag{57'}$$

In this case, $\lambda = a_{11}$, and the general solution is given by

$$x = c_1 e^{\lambda t}, \; y = c_2 e^{\lambda t}, \quad \text{where } \lambda = a_{11}, \tag{59}$$

as mentioned earlier. The trajectories approach the equilibrium point (the origin) or tend toward infinity as $t \to \infty$, depending on whether $\lambda (= a_{11}) < 0$ or $\lambda > 0$. We can easily observe

$$y/x = c_2/c_1. \tag{79}$$

Thus for $c_1 \neq 0$ and $c_2 \neq 0$, the trajectories are straight lines, $y = (c_2/c_1)x$. For $c_1 \neq 0$, $c_2 = 0$, the trajectories are on the x-axis, whereas they are on the y-axis when $c_1 = 0$ and $c_2 \neq 0$. These trajectories are illustrated in figure 7.7, where we assume $\lambda < 0$. When $\lambda > 0$, the situation remains the same except that the arrows are reversed. The equilibrium point (i.e., the origin) is called a **proper node** or a **stellar node**.

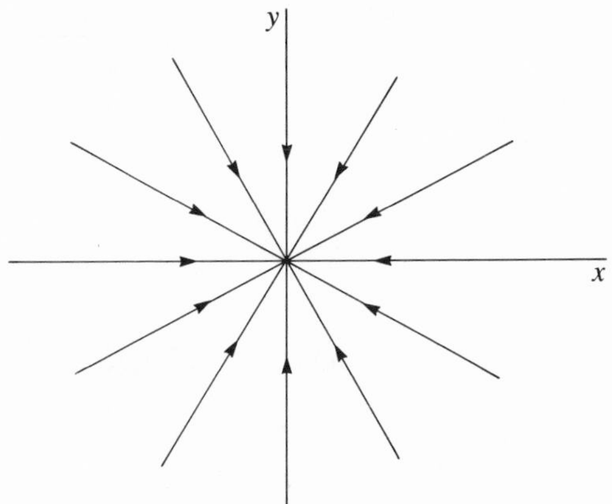

Figure 7.7: Proper node, $\lambda_1 = \lambda_2$

This exhausts all interesting cases. Some of the main results in the preceding discussion are obtained in Theorem 7.3.

Theorem 7.3.

(i) The equilibrium point (0, 0) of the linear system (8) is asymptotically (globally) stable, that is, $x \to 0$ and $y \to 0$ as $t \to \infty$, if and only if both eigenvalues have negative real parts.

(ii) Spiral trajectories are obtained if and only if the eigenvalues are complex numbers, but not pure imaginary. When the eigenvalues are pure imaginary, the trajectories are closed curves surrounding the origin.

(iii) The equilibrium point is a saddle point if and only if the eigenvalues are real and opposite in sign.

(iv) The equilibrium point is a node if and only if the eigenvalues are real and have the same sign (which includes the case of equal real roots).

Since the type of trajectories crucially depends on the eigenvalues, it may be worthwhile recalling their expression:

$$\lambda_1, \lambda_2 = \frac{1}{2}\left[(a_{11} + a_{22}) \pm \sqrt{(a_{11} + a_{22})^2 - 4(a_{11}a_{22} - a_{21}a_{12})}\right]. \quad (16)$$

From this we can easily observe

$$\lambda_1 + \lambda_2 = (a_{11} + a_{22}),\ \lambda_1\lambda_2 = a_{11}a_{22} - a_{21}a_{12}. \quad (80)$$

Recalling that H denotes the coefficient matrix of the linear systems (8), we may rewrite (80) as

$$\lambda_1 + \lambda_2 = \text{trace } H,\ \lambda_1\lambda_2 = \det H. \quad (80')$$

In fact, such a relation holds in general for an $n \times n$ matrix. Also note that this relation holds whether the eigenvalues are real or complex. Using (80′) and theorem 7.3, we can easily conclude the following.

Theorem 7.4. For the equilibrium point (0, 0) of the linear system (8), we may assert the following.

(i) the equilibrium point is asymptotically globally stable if and only if trace $H < 0$ and $\det H > 0$, where H is the coefficient matrix of (8).

(ii) The equilibrium is a saddle point if and only if $\det H < 0$.

REMARK: Statement (i) of the above theorem is the same as Theorem 6.5 in the previous chapter. The present discussion provides its proof. Statement (ii), though quite useful at times, is not well known in the literature.[9]

[9]The proof of (ii) goes as follows. If $q \equiv \det H < 0$, both eigenvalues must be real. Since $q = \lambda_1\lambda_2$, sign $\lambda_1 = -$sign λ_2, so that (0, 0) is a saddle-point. Conversely, if (0, 0) is a saddle-point, λ_1 and λ_2 are real and of the opposite sign, so that $q < 0$.

REMARK: Recently, among a certain group of economists, it has become popular to regard the saddle-point instability as stable. This is facilitated by focusing attention on the stable branch of saddle-like paths, as in the case of a famous paper by Sargent and Wallace (1973). The present author does not share this view.

All the important information concerning the pattern of the trajectories is contained in the trace and the determinant of the coefficient matrix. Thus letting

$$p \equiv \text{trace } H,\ q \equiv \det\ H; \quad \text{or}$$

$$p \equiv a_{11} + a_{22},\ q \equiv a_{11}a_{22} - a_{21}a_{12},$$

we recall that the characteristic equation can be rewritten in terms of p and q as

$$\lambda^2 - p\lambda + q = 0, \tag{15}$$

and the eigenvalues are obtained as

$$\lambda_1,\ \lambda_2 = \frac{1}{2}[p \pm \sqrt{p^2 - 4q}]. \tag{16'}$$

The locus of $(p,\ q)$ specified by $p^2 - 4q = 0$ defines a parabola on the $(p - q)$-plane (see fig. 7.8). In the region above this parabola, $p^2 - 4q < 0$, the roots are complex. In this region, the equilibrium point is a spiral point unless $p = 0$, while it is a center if $p = 0$ (and $q > 0$). On the other hand, in the region below this parabola, the roots are real. In particular, if $q < 0$, the equilibrium point is a saddle point. If $q > 0$ in the region below the parabola, the equilibrium point is a node. At any point on the parabola, we again obtain a node (which can be a proper node). Finally the equilibrium point is asymptotically stable if and only if $p < 0$ and $q > 0$. We may note that the possibility of $q = 0$ is ruled out as the coefficient matrix H is assumed to be nonsingular. The points raised in the present paragraph are summarized and illustrated in figure 7.8.

7.4 Nonlinear Systems

7.4.1 Local Behavior of the Trajectories on the Plane

Consider a nonlinear system,

$$\dot{x} = f_1(x,\ y),\ \dot{y} = f_2(x,\ y), \tag{81}$$

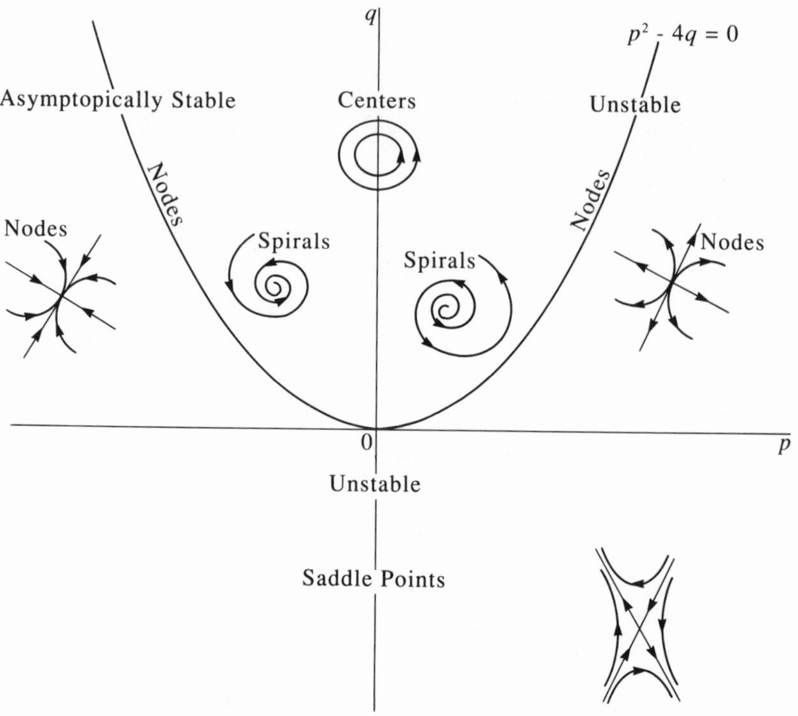

Figure 7.8: Patterns of trajectories

where f_1 and f_2 are assumed to be continuously differentiable. Furthermore, assume that the origin is an equilibrium point of (81), i.e.,

$$f_1(0, 0) = 0 \text{ and } f_2(0, 0) = 0. \tag{82}$$

Notice that the equilibrium point in the system (81) may not be unique. We therefore assume that there exists a neighborhood (or a circle) about the origin in which there are no other equilibrium points. The origin is an *isolated* equilibrium point.[10]

[10]In the case of the system of linear differential equations, the assumption that the coefficient matrix is nonsingular ensures the uniqueness of the equilibrium point. This, in turn, implies that the equilibrium point is isolated.

Now expand $f_1(x, y)$ and $f_2(x, y)$ in a Taylor series about the origin. Then we have

$$\dot{x} = a_{11}x + a_{12}y + f_1^{\circ}(x, y),\ \dot{y} = a_{21}x + a_{22}y + f_2^{\circ}(x, y), \tag{83}$$

where $a_{i1} \equiv \partial f_i(0, 0)/\partial x$ and $a_{i2} \equiv \partial f_i/\partial y$, $i = 1, 2$, and the functions $f_1^{\circ}(x, y)$ and $f_2^{\circ}(x, y)$ signify the second-order or higher order terms. From the differentiability of the functions f_1 and f_2, we have

$$f_1^{\circ}(x, y) = o(z),\ f_2^{\circ}(x, y) = o(z), \quad \text{where } z \equiv (x, y). \tag{84}$$

Here $o(z)$ is "Landau's o," that is,

$$o(z)/\| z \| \to 0 \text{ as } \| z \| \to 0.$$

Note that this implies $f_1^{\circ}(0, 0) = 0$ and $f_2^{\circ}(0, 0) = 0$, so that $(0, 0)$ is indeed an equilibrium point of (83). Assume that

$$a_{11}a_{22} - a_{21}a_{12} \neq 0. \tag{85}$$

The nonlinear system (81) that satisfies conditions (84) and (85) is sometimes called an **almost linear system** in the neighborhood of the equilibrium point (0, 0). (84) states that the functions f_1 and f_2 are well approximated by the linear functions $a_{11}x + a_{12}y$ and $a_{21}x + a_{22}y$, respectively.

It would now be natural to *conjecture* that the qualitative behavior of the paths of (81) near the equilibrium point is similar to that of the paths of the related linear systems:

$$\dot{x} = a_{11}x + a_{12}y,\ \dot{y} = a_{21}x + a_{22}y, \tag{86}$$

where the a_{ij}'s are taken from (83). Equation (86) takes the form that is identical to (8). The procedure for obtaining the linear system (86) from the nonlinear system (81) is called **linearization**. In theorem 7.5, we shall see that this conjecture is essentially true.[11]

---

[11] For simple expositions of this theorem, see, for example, Simmons (1972, pp. 325–27); and Boyce and DiPrima (1986, pp. 475–82). See also Hurewicz (1958, pp. 86–98); and Cesari (1959, pp. 156–63). Cesari (1959, p. 159) calls this theorem "Poincaré's *main result*." Incidentally, Simmons (1972) contains lively biographical notes on great mathematicians who have made significant contributions to the theory of differential equations. For Poincaré, see Simmons (1972, pp. 346–49), where Simmons writes, "Jules Henri Poincaré (1854–1912) was universally recognized at the beginning of the twentieth century as the greatest mathematician of his generation" (p. 346).

Theorem 7.5 (Poincaré). If the equilibrium point (0, 0) of (86) falls under any one of the three major classes described in section 7.3 (i.e., the cases of (*a*) unequal real roots of the same sign, (*b*) real roots of the opposite sign, or (*c*) complex roots with real parts), then the equilibrium point (0, 0) of (81), which is almost linear, is of the same type in a neighborhood of (0, 0).

Essentially, this theorem states that for x and y near zero, the nonlinear term $f_1^\circ(x, y)$ and $f_2^\circ(x, y)$ are small and do not affect the stability *and* the type of the equilibrium point as determined by its associated linear system, except for two cases: (*a*) roots that are pure imaginary, and (*b*) roots that are real and equal (multiple root). This is not a trivial theorem and the proof is not easy, although it is often taken for granted by economists. Furthermore, the theorem need not hold for the two remaining cases (equal real roots and pure imaginary roots), as stated in the theorem.

That (0, 0) is an equilibrium point of (81) is not as restrictive as it may look. For if $(x^*, y^*) \neq (0, 0)$ is an equilibrium point of (81), then defining u and v by $u \equiv x - x^*$ and $v \equiv y - y^*$, we may rewrite (83) as

$$\dot{u} = a_{11}u + a_{12}v + f_1^*(u, v), \; \dot{v} = a_{21}u + a_{22}v + f_2^*(u, v), \qquad (87)$$

where $f_1^*(u, v) \equiv f_1^\circ(u + x^*, v + y^*)$ and $f_2^*(u, v) \equiv f_2^\circ(u + x^*, v + y^*)$. Clearly, (0, 0) is an equilibrium point of (87), and it is isolated under (85). The linearization of (87) yields exactly the same linear system (86) except that the symbols x and y are replaced by u and v. When there is more than one equilibrium point for (81), we can study the qualitative behavior of the paths in a neighborhood of each equilibrium point in terms of the corresponding linear system obtained by the linearization of the original system (81) at that equilibrium point.

Given theorem 7.5, the result in theorem 7.6 is immediate.

Theorem 7.6. Let $n = 2$, where (86) is the linear system associated with (81), and the origin (0, 0) is an equilibrium point. Then the stability condition of (86), that is,

$$a_{11} + a_{22} < 0 \text{ and } a_{11}a_{22} - a_{21}a_{12} > 0,$$

is also *necessary* for (0, 0) to be locally stable for the *original* system (81), provided that the equilibrium point (0, 0) of (86) falls under any one of the three major classes described in section 7.3 [i.e., the case of

(a) unequal real roots of the same sign, (b) real roots of the opposite sign, or (c) complex roots with real parts].

Therefore, if we know that the "two remaining cases" (equal real roots—such as zero—and pure imaginary roots) are not obtained, then this stability condition, which also appears in chapter 6, is also *necessary* for the stability of the *original* system. This, in turn, enables us to use the correspondence principle by way of the linear approximation system, although it may not be easy to determine whether or not the solution belongs to the two remaining cases. The obvious method, which is not particularly uncommon among economists, is to simply assume that the solution does not belong to these two cases.

7.4.2 Stability of the Nonlinear System: Liapunov's Direct Method

We now turn to the discussion of stability for the *nonlinear* system for the n-dimensional case. The method is known as **Liapunov's second method**, or **direct method**, which is based on Liapunov (1907). The method is referred to as a "direct method" since no knowledge of the solution of the system of differential equations is required. Furthermore, Liapunov's (direct) method provides a more global type of information, such as the asymptotic stability of an equilibrium point. It is facilitated by constructing an auxiliary function, and it does rely on the linearization of the original nonlinear system.

Since Liapunov's method is not confined to the two-dimensional case, we consider the following system of n first-order nonlinear differential equations:

$$\dot{x} = f(x).^{12} \tag{88}$$

This system R is a compact form of

$$\dot{x}_i = f_i(x_1, x_2, \ldots, x_n),\ i = 1, 2, \ldots, n.$$

[12] As mentioned earlier, such a system is called an *autonomous system*. If the system is instead specified by

$$\dot{x} = f(x, t), \tag{88'}$$

it is called a *nonautonomous system*. x^* is said to be an **equilibrium point** of a nonautonomous system if $f(x^*, t) = 0$ for all t. There is also the Liapunov direct method that is applicable to establishing the stability of the equilibrium of nonautonomous systems.

Let the origin be an equilibrium point of (88), so

$$f(0) = 0. \tag{89}$$

The heart of Liapunov's direct method is to construct a real-valued function $V(x)$ in which x is governed by (88). We now state the major theorem.

Theorem 7.7 (Liapunov's Direct Method). Suppose that there exists a real-valued, continuously differentiable function $V(x)$ for the system (88) such that

(i) $V(x) > 0$ for all $x \neq 0$, and $V(0) = 0$,

(ii) $dV[x(t)]/dt < 0$ for all x that satisfy (88), and

(iii) $V(x) \to \infty$ as $\| x \| \to \infty$.

Then $x^* = 0$ is asymptotically globally stable, that is, $x(t) \to 0$ as $t \to \infty$, regardless of the initial condition.

The motivation of this theorem may be as follows.[13]

> Consider a physical system whose law of motion is given by (88). Interpret $V(x)$ as energy or potential energy associated with state x. If the rate of change of energy is negative for every possible state x, except for a single equilibrium point x^*, then the energy will continuously decrease until it reaches the minimum value $V(x^*)$, in which case any state x which is a perturbation from x^* will return to x^*.

The function $V(x)$ is called the **Liapunov function**. The real-valued, continuous function that has the property of condition (i) of theorem 7.7 is called **positive definite**. As an illustration of theorem 7.7, consider $\dot{x} = -x^3$, $x \in R$. Define the Liapunov function for this system by $V(x) \equiv x^2$. Conditions (i) and (iii) are trivially satisfied for $x \in R$. To show condition (ii) is also satisfied, simply observe $dV/dt = 2x\dot{x} = -2x^4 < 0$ for all $x \neq 0$. Hence the equilibrium point

---

[13]This motivation is adapted from Kalman and Bertram (1960), which is a lucid and clear-sighted exposition of stability theory and Liapunov's direct method. Many textbooks on differential equations also contain excellent expositions of Liapunov's direct method. See, for example, Lefschetz (1977, pp. 112–22); Simmons (1972, pp. 316–22); Boyce and DiPrima (1986, pp. 499–509); and Pontryagin (1962, sec. 26). See also Takayama (1985, pp. 347–58), and Henry (1987).

is asymptotically globally stable. In this example, it is not too difficult to find the Liapunov function. However, in more complicated problems, it could be very difficult to find a suitable Liapunov function.

In actual applications of Liapunov's method, the result from elementary algebra in theorem 7.8 is sometimes quite useful.

Theorem 7.8. Let the function $V(x, y)$ be given by

$$V(x, y) = ax^2 + bxy + cy^2. \tag{90}$$

Then we have $V(0, 0) = 0$, and

(i) $V(x, y) > 0$ for all $(x, y) \neq 0$, if and only if $a > 0$ and $4ac - b^2 > 0$.

(ii) $V(x, y) < 0$ for all $(x, y) \neq 0$, if and only if $a < 0$ and $4ac - b^2 > 0$.

The proof of this theorem is straightforward. The use of this theorem is illustrated by the following example from Boyce and DiPrima (1986, p. 507).

Example 7.6. Let the dynamic system be given by

$$\dot{x} = -x - xy, \ \dot{y} = -y - x^2 y. \tag{91}$$

Show that the origin $(0, 0)$ is asymptotically stable. We try the Liapunov function in the form of (90). Let us try $b = 0$. Then in order to have $V(x, y) > 0$ for all $(x, y) \neq (0, 0)$, we must have $a > 0$ and $c > 0$ by theorem 7.8. Also we have $V(x) \to \infty$ as $\| (x, y) \| \to \infty$. Furthermore, with $b = 0$, we have $V_x \equiv \partial V/\partial x = 2ax$ and $V_y \equiv \partial V/\partial y = 2cy$. Hence,

$$\begin{aligned} \dot{V}(x, y) &= V_x \dot{x} + V_y \dot{y} = 2ax(-x - xy) + 2cy(-y - yx^2) \\ &= -[2a(x^2 + x^2 y^2) + 2c(y^2 + x^2 y^2)] < 0, \end{aligned}$$

for all $(x, y) \neq (0, 0)$. Thus $V(x, y)$ satisfies all the conditions of theorem 7.7, so that $(0, 0)$ is asymptotically globally stable.

It is sometimes convenient to obtain a "local" version of theorem 7.7. To study asymptotic stability, it is often desirable to specify the region of stability, that is, the allowable deviation from the equilibrium point that the motion can dampen. Theorem 7.9 provides such a region.

Theorem 7.9. Suppose that there exists a continuously differentiable function $V(x)$ for the system (88) *and* a nonempty bounded domain D containing the origin, where $V(x) < K$ in D with the following properties:

(i) $V(x) > 0$ for all $x \neq 0$ and $V(0) = 0$, and

(ii) $dV[x(t)]/dt < 0$ for all $x(t) \neq 0$ satisfying (88).

Then every solution of (88) that starts at a point in D approaches the origin as $t \to \infty$.

7.4.3 Local Asymptotic Stability

Finally, it would be useful to study the *local* asymptotic stability of the equilibrium point for the nonlinear system. We again consider the linearization of (88). Taking a Taylor expansion of $f(x)$ about the origin (the equilibrium point), we obtain

$$\dot{x} = Ax + o(x), \quad \text{where } A \equiv [a_{ij}], \tag{92}$$

and $a_{ij} \equiv \partial f_i / \partial x_j$ evaluated at the origin. Assuming A is nonsingular, the origin is an isolated equilibrium point. Thus the linearization of (92) yields

$$\dot{x} = Ax. \tag{93}$$

The stability condition of the linear system (93) is well known. The two-dimensional case was discussed earlier. For the discussion for the n-dimensional case, see any textbook on differential equations. Using such a stability condition for a linear system and theorem 7.8, the following well-known result in theorem 7.10 can be obtained.

Theorem 7.10 (Liapunov). If $x^* = 0$ is stable for the linear system (93), then it is also locally asymptotically stable for the original nonlinear system (88). The solution $x(t;\ x^\circ,\ t^\circ)$ satisfying the initial condition $(x^\circ,\ t^\circ)$, approaches $x^* = 0$ as $t \to \infty$, provided that x° is in a certain neighborhood of the origin.

Although this theorem requires a nontrivial proof, many economists somehow take it for granted. The proof of this theorem, however, is immediate once we establish Lyapunov's direct method (theorem 7.7). See Kalman and Bertram (1960, pp. 383–84) for such a proof.

Exercises

The following set of exercises should be useful in facilitating the understanding of the material presented in this chapter.

(1) In each of the following problems, classify the equilibrium point (0, 0) (i.e., node, saddle point, spiral point, etc.), and determine whether it is asymptotically stable or unstable.

(a) $\dot{x} = 3x - 2y,\ \dot{y} = 2x - 3y$

(b) $\dot{x} = 2x - y,\ \dot{y} = x - y$

(c) $\dot{x} = y,\quad \dot{y} = 2x$

(d) $\dot{x} = x - 4y,\ \dot{y} = 4x - 7y$

(e) $\dot{x} = x - 3y,\ \dot{y} = 4x - 5y$

(f) $\dot{x} = 3x - 2y,\ \dot{y} = 4x - y$

Answer a, b, and c *without* explicitly obtaining the eigenvalues.

(2) Consider the following system of linear differential equations with constant coefficients,

$$\begin{bmatrix} \dot{x} \\ \dot{y} \end{bmatrix} = \begin{bmatrix} a_{11} & a_{12} \\ a_{21} & a_{22} \end{bmatrix} \begin{bmatrix} x \\ y \end{bmatrix},$$

where the coefficient matrix is assumed to be nonsingular.

(a) Let λ_1 and λ_2 be eigenvalues. Let $p \equiv a_{11} + a_{22}$ and $q \equiv a_{11}a_{22} - a_{21}a_{12}$.

(i) Obtain the expression for λ_1 and λ_2 in terms of p and q.

(ii) Assuming that λ_1 and λ_2 are real and distinct, write out the expression for the general solution of this system, where (A_1, B_1) and (A_2, B_2) are eigenvectors associated with λ_1 and λ_2, respectively.

(b) Clearly, the origin (0, 0) is the equilibrium point of the above system. What is the equilibrium point called in each of the following cases?

(i) λ_1 and λ_2 are real, distinct, and of the opposite signs.

(ii) λ_1 and λ_2 are real, distinct, and of the same sign.

(iii) λ_1 and λ_2 are complex (but not pure imaginary numbers).

(iv) λ_1 and λ_2 are pure imaginary numbers.

(c) State the necessary and sufficient condition for the equilibrium point to be a saddle point in terms of the a_{ij}'s.

(3) Consider the following system on the plane,

$$\dot{x} = x + y, \ \dot{y} = 4x - 2y.$$

(a) Obtain the expression for eigenvalues. What will be the equilibrium for this case (0, 0), a node, a stellar node, a spiral point, or a center? Is it asymptotically globally stable?

(b) Using the phase diagram technique, graphically illustrate the trajectory of the solution. Do not forget to obtain the two "key lines" to which the trajectors are asymptotic.

(c) The general solution of this system is obtained as

$$x = c_1 e^{-3t} + c_2 e^{2t}, \ y = -4c_1 e^{-3t} + c_2 e^{2t}.$$

What would be the values of c_1 and c_2, if the initial condition is given by $x = 1$ and $y = 1$ for $t = 0$?

(4) Consider each of the following systems on the plane and answer the same questions as (*a*), (*b*), and (*c*) of Question 3.

$$\dot{x} = -x + 2y, \ \dot{y} = -2x - y;$$

and

$$\dot{x} = 3x - 4y, \ \dot{y} = x - y.$$

References

There are many excellent textbooks and treatises on the theory of ordinary differential equations and the theory of linear and nonlinear systems, some of which are listed here.

Arnold, V. I. 1978. *Ordinary Differential Equations.* T rans. by R. A. Silverman. Cambridge, Mass.: MIT Press.

Boyce, W. E., and R. C. DiPrima. 1986. *Elementary Differential Equations and Boundary Value Problems.* 4th ed. New York: Wiley. (1st ed. 1965, 2d ed. 1969, 3d ed. 1977.)

———. 1986. *Elementary Differential Equations and Boundary Value Problems.* 4th ed. New York: Wiley.

Brock, W. A., and A. G. Malliaris. 1989. *Differential Equations, Stability, and Chaos in Dynamic Economics.* Amsterdam: North-Holland.

Cesari, L. 1959. *Asymptotic Behavior and Stability Problems in Ordinary Differential Equations.* Vol. 1b of *Ergebnisse der Mathematik und Ihrer Grenzgebiete.* Berlin: Springer Verlag.

Davies, T. V., and E. M. James. 1966. *Nonlinear Differential Equations.* Reading, Mass.: Addison-Wesley.

Hahn, W. 1967. *Stability of Motion.* New York: Springer Verlag.

Henry, C. 1987. "Lyapunov Function." In *The New Palgrave*, ed. J. Eatwell, M. Milgate, and P. Newman, Vol. 3, 256–59. London: Macmillan.

Hirsch, M. W., and S. Smale. 1974. *Differential Equations, Dynamic Systems, and Linear Algebra.* New York: Academic Press.

Hurewicz, W. 1958. *Lectures on Ordinary Differential Equations.* Cambridge, Mass.: MIT Press.

Kalman, R. E., and J. E. Bertram. 1960. "Control System Analysis and Design via the 'Second Method' of Liapunov, I: Continuous Time System." *Journal of Basic Engineering* 82 (June): 371–93.

Kaplan, W. 1958. *Ordinary Differential Equations.* Reading, Mass.: Addison-Wesley.

La Salle, J. P., and S. Lefshetz. 1961. *Stability by Liapunov's Direct Method with Applications.* New York: Academic Press.

Lefschetz, S. 1977. *Differential Equations: Geometric Theory.* New York: Dover Publications.(Based on the 2d ed. 1963.)

Liapunov, A. M. 1907. "Problème général de la stabilité du movement." *Annales de la Faculté de Science de L'Université de Toulouse* 9: 203–44. Reprinted in *Annals of Mathematical Study*, no. 17 (1949). Princeton, N.J.: Princeton University Press.

Petrovski, I. G. 1966. *Ordinary Differential Equations.* T rans. R. A. Siverman. Englewood Cliffs, N.J: Prentice-Hall.

Pontryagin, L. 1962. *Ordinary Differential Equations.* T rans. from the 1961 Russian original. Reading, Mass.: Addison-Wesley.

Simmons, G. F. 1972. *Differential Equations.* New York: McGraw-Hill.

Sargent, T., and N. Wallace. 1973. "The Stability of Models of Money and Growth with Perfect Foresight." *Econometrica* 41 (November): 1043–48. (Not a reference on differential equations per se.)

Takayama, A. 1985. *Mathematical Economics.* 2d ed. New York: Cambridge University Press. (Not a reference on differential equations per se.)

Yoshizawa, T. 1967. *Introduction to Differential Equations* (in Japanese). Tokyo: Asakura-Shoten.

CHAPTER 8

Macroequilibrium and Neoclassical Growth Models

In this chapter we illustrate more applications of the theory of differential equations to certain macroeconomic problems. The basic tools we use are phase diagram techniques, the theory of linear differential equations on the plane, and Poincaré's theorem.

8.1 Static Macroequilibrium and Its Stability[1]

A simple illustration of the applications to macro economics may be found in the stability of macroequilibrium discussed in chapter 6 (especially in connection with proposition 6.4). We describe the IS-LM macro adjustment process by

$$\dot{Y} = a[E(Y - T, r) + G - Y] \equiv \phi(Y, r), \tag{1a}$$

$$\dot{r} = b[L(Y, r) - M/p] \equiv \psi(Y, r), \tag{1b}$$

where Y = output, r = interest rate, E = consumption plus investment expenditures, G = government expenditures, T = taxes minus transfer payments, L = money demand, M = money supply, and p = price level. Here, G, M, p, and T are assumed to be fixed. The parameters a and b, respectively, signify the speeds of adjustment for the goods market and money market. The macroequilibrium may be defined by (Y^*, r^*) that satisfies

$$\phi(Y^*, r^*) = 0 \text{ and } \psi(Y^*, r^*) = 0, \tag{2}$$

[1]The macromodels described in this section (and in chap. 6) do not necesarrily reflect the author's view. These models, which are known to have certain virtues (as well as weaknesses), are taken up only to illustrate how particular tools in the theory of differential equations can be applied to problems in economics. See Takayama (1986).

which is nothing but the point of intersection of the IS and the LM curves.

To investigate the trajectory of (1), we impose the following assumptions:

$$0 < E_Y < 1,\ E_r < 0,\ L_Y > 0,\ L_r < 0,\quad \text{for all } Y \text{ and } r, \tag{3}$$

where $E_Y \equiv \partial E/\partial(Y - T)$, $E_r \equiv \partial E/\partial r$, etc. We may then compute

$$\phi_Y = a(E_Y - 1) < 0,\ \phi_r = aE_r < 0, \tag{4a}$$

$$\psi_Y = bL_Y > 0,\ \psi_r = bL_r < 0, \tag{4b}$$

for all Y and r, where $\phi_Y \equiv \partial\phi/\partial Y$, $\phi_r \equiv \partial Y/\partial r$, etc. If investment and consumption are completely inelastic, we have $E_r = 0$ so that $\phi_r = 0$. Also, under a **liquidity trap** we have $L_r \to -\infty$ so that $\psi_r \to -\infty$. Hence, for such polar cases we have

$$\phi_r = 0 \text{ and/or } \psi_r \to -\infty, \text{ as well as } \phi_Y < 0,\ \psi_Y > 0. \tag{4'}$$

The slopes of the $(\phi = 0)$-curve and the $(\psi = 0)$-curve may, respectively, be obtained as

$$\left.\frac{dr}{dY}\right|_{\phi=0} = -\frac{\phi_Y}{\phi_r} < 0,\ \left.\frac{dr}{dY}\right|_{\psi=0} = -\frac{\psi_Y}{\psi_r} > 0. \tag{5}$$

Thus under assumption (3), the $(\phi = 0)$-curve is downward sloping, and the $(\psi = 0)$-curve is upward sloping. This is illustrated in figure 8.1. These two curves, respectively, correspond to the familiar IS and LM curves. Also from (4), we may conclude that $\dot{Y} > 0$ (resp. $\dot{Y} < 0$) to the left (resp. right) of the $(\phi = 0)$-curve, and that $\dot{r} > 0$ (resp. $\dot{r} < 0$) to the right (resp. left) of the $(\psi = 0)$-curve.[2]

Consider the linear approximation system of (1):

$$\dot{Y} = \phi_Y^*(Y - Y^*) + \phi_r^*(r - r^*), \tag{6a}$$

$$\dot{r} = \psi_Y^*(Y - Y^*) + \psi_r^*(r - r^*), \tag{6b}$$

where the asterisk (*) signifies that the partial derivatives are evaluated at (Y^*, r^*).

[2]Note that $\phi_Y + \psi_r < 0$, $\phi_Y\psi_r - \psi_Y\phi_r > 0$, $\phi_Y\psi_r \neq 0$, and $\psi_Y\phi_r \neq 0$ for all (Y, r), if (4) holds. Using this, we showed the global stability of (Y^*, r^*) in chapter 6 (cf. Proposition 6.2). In Figure 8.1, (Y^*, r^*) is drawn as a spiral point. This need not be the case, as will become evident shortly.

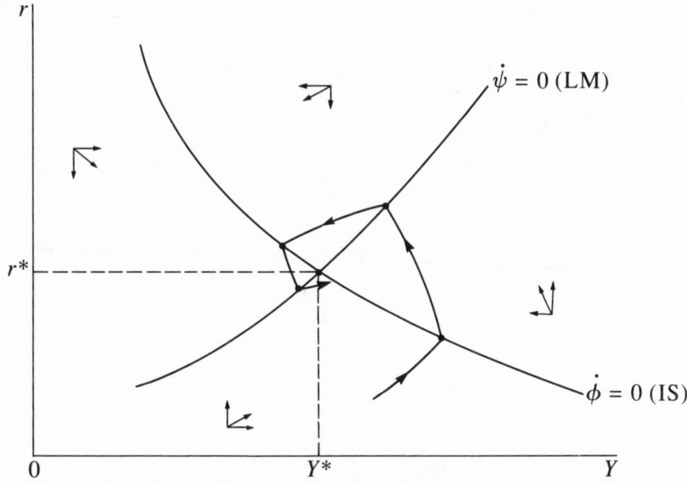

Figure 8.1: The adjustment path of static macro equilibrium: the case of a spiral point.

As discussed in the previous chapter, the shape of trajectories crucially depends upon the eigenvalues of the corresponding linear approximation system. We then write the characteristic equation of (6) as

$$\lambda^2 - \alpha\lambda + \beta = 0,$$

where

$$\alpha \equiv \phi_Y^* + \psi_r^* \text{ and } \beta \equiv \phi_Y^*\psi_r^* - \psi_Y^*\phi_r^*, \tag{7}$$

and the eigenvalues are obtained as

$$\lambda_1, \lambda_2 = \frac{1}{2}\left[\alpha \pm \sqrt{\alpha^2 - 4\beta}\right].$$

We may then observe

$$\alpha^2 - 4\beta = (\phi_Y^* + \psi_r^*)^2 - 4(\phi_Y^*\psi_r^* - \psi_Y^*\phi_r^*)$$

$$= (\phi_Y^* - \psi_r^*)^2 + 4\psi_Y^*\phi_r^*$$

$$= [a(1 - E_Y^*) - bL_r^*]^2 + 4abL_Y^*E_r^*.$$

Since $\alpha < 0$, λ_1 and λ_2 cannot be pure imaginary. Hence assuming away the knife-edge case of $\alpha^2 - 4\beta = 0$ (in which case we have multiple real roots), the behavior of the trajectory of (1) in a neighborhood of (Y^*, r^*) can be approximated by that of its linear approximation system (6) (cf. Theorem 7.5, Poincaré's theorem).[3] It is a *spiral point* if and only if

$$[a(1 - E_Y^*) - bL_r^*]^2 + 4abL_Y^*E_r^* < 0, \tag{8a}$$

and it is a *node* if

$$[a(1 - E_Y^*) - bL_r^*]^2 + 4abE_r^*L_Y^* > 0, \tag{8b}$$

where the eigenvalues are complex but not pure imaginary in the case of (8a), and they are real, distinct, and of the same sign in the case of (8b). Assuming that (8a) holds, we may illustrate the trajectory (Y, r) for (1) in figure 8.1, where (Y^*, r^*) is a *spiral point.*

The "Keynesians" tend to maintain a low magnitude of E_r (where $E_r = 0$ signifies completely interest-inelastic consumption and investment) and/or a high magnitude of L_r (where $L_r \to -\infty$ signifies the liquidity trap). Under such circumstances, inequality of (8b) is likely to hold, and the equilibrium point would be a *node.* When $E_r = 0$ the IS curve is vertical, while when $L_r \to -\infty$, the LM curve is horizontal. We may illustrate the adjustment paths of these two cases in figure 8.2, where the equilibrium point is asymptotically globally stable by using Olech's theorem.

On the other hand, the monetarists tend to assign a low value for the magnitude of L_r (where $L_r = 0$ signifies the classical quantity theory) and a high value for the magnitude of E_r. Under such circumstances, it is possible that (8a) is more likely to be satisfied, in which event the equilibrium point becomes a *spiral point* and the adjustment path shows a cyclical motion. Its graphic illustration is already indicated in figure 8.1. In summary, the behavior of the adjustment paths that satisfy (1) crucially depends on the magnitudes of the parameters specified in (3). From (8a), we may also conclude that the behavior of the adjust-

[3]We may note that the equilibrium point (Y^*, r^*) cannot be a saddle-point since $\beta > 0$.

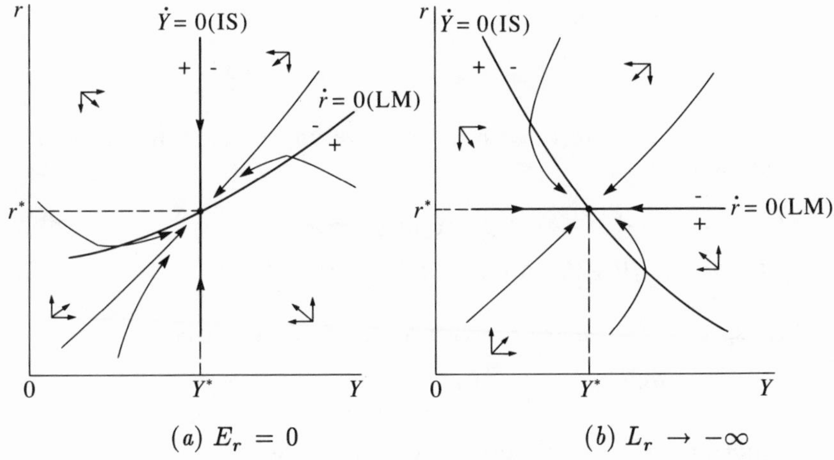

Figure 8.2: Keynesian adjustment paths: Extreme cases

ment path depends on the relative magnitudes of a and b, the speeds of adjustment.

We may summarize some of these results as follows.

Proposition 8.1. Under the monetarist inclination, the macroequilibrium point (Y^*, r^*) would be a spiral point, while under the Keynesian inclination it would be a *node*. The trajectories of these cases are illustrated in figure 8.2.

8.2 Money and Growth—Part 1[4]

Since Tobin's seminal work (1965) incorporating money into the Solow-Swan growth model, the "money and growth" model has been heavily discussed. Here we exposit the gist of such discussions. This, in turn, will provide a useful application of the theory of differential equations.

8.2.1 Model

We consider an aggregate economy producing a consumption-investment good (Y), using two factors, labor (N) and capital (K), under the tech-

[4]This section is based on Takayama (1979).

nology of constant returns to scale and diminishing returns. We write the production function of this economy as

$$Y = F(N, K), \quad \text{or} \quad y = f(k), \tag{9}$$

where $y \equiv Y/N$ and $k \equiv K/N$, and we impose the following usual assumptions

$$f'(k) > 0 \text{ and } f''(k) < 0 \text{ for all } k > 0; \tag{10a}$$

$$f'(0) = \infty, \ f'(\infty) = 0, \text{ and } f(0) = 0. \tag{10b}$$

We specify the demand function for nominal cash balances by[5]

$$L(pY, r, W^n) = \ell(pY, r)W^n. \tag{11}$$

The monetary equilibrium relation can be written as

$$M = \ell(pY, r)W^n, \tag{12}$$

where $M =$ the supply of nominal cash balances, $p =$ price level, $r =$ the nominal rate of return on physical assets, and $W^n =$ the nominal value of the public's (households and firms) net worth (or "wealth"). It would be reasonable to suppose

$$\ell_1 \equiv \partial\ell/\partial(pY) > 0, \ \ell_2 \equiv \partial\ell/\partial r < 0, \ 0 < \ell < 1. \tag{13}$$

Let z be the expected rate of price change and assume that it is equal to the actual rate of price change, that is, $z = \dot{p}/p \equiv \pi$, where the dot signifies the time derivative. This assumption is called **myopic perfect foresight**. (Such expectations are self-fulfilling, and under the nonstochastic framework, they are virtually equivalent to rational expectations.) Then we have

$$r = f'(k) + \pi, \tag{14}$$

assuming the full employment of resources. The nominal rate of return on physical assets (r) is equal to the marginal productivity of physical assets $f'(k)$ plus capital gains or losses from holding physical assets due to price changes (π). Assuming that physical assets and money (which

[5]Note that $(\partial L/\partial W^n)(W^n/L) = 1$ in (11): i.e., the wealth elasticity of the demand for nominal balances is assumed to be unity in (11). This assumption is often adopted in the "money and growth" literature including Tobin (1965). It will be dropped in the next section.

is here assumed to be Treasury money) are the only two assets in the economy, we may obtain

$$W^n \equiv pK + M. \tag{15}$$

The possible discrepancy of the two valuations of physical assets and current output is ignored following Tobin (1965) and much of the literature on this topic. Substituting (14) and (15) into (12), and noting that the function L is homogeneous of degree one with respect to pY and W^n in the absence of money illusion, we obtain

$$m = \ell[f(k),\ f'(k) + \pi](m + k), \tag{16}$$

where $m \equiv M/(pN)$, per capita real cash balances. We may rewrite (16) as

$$m = \lambda(k,\ \pi)k, \quad \text{where } \lambda \equiv \ell/(1 - \ell). \tag{17}$$

Also from $\ell_1 > 0$ and $\ell_2 < 0$, we obtain[6]

$$\lambda_k \equiv \partial\lambda/\partial k > 0, \quad \text{and } \lambda_\pi \equiv \partial\lambda/\partial\pi < 0. \tag{18}$$

Intuitively, $\lambda_\pi < 0$ means that a fall in the rate of inflation π raises the demand for money by making the holding of money more attractive vis-à-vis physical assets. Note that $(-\pi)$ signifies the real rate of return on money à la Irving Fisher.

Let C and I, respectively, be real consumption and real investment. Then, assuming away government expenditures on goods and services for simplicity, the equilibrium in the goods market can be written as

$$Y = C + I. \tag{19}$$

Following the literature on money and growth, we assume that investment is completely "passive" in the sense that "saving" ($= Y - C$) automatically brings forth an equal amount of investment. In other words, investment I adjusts automatically to maintain the equilibrium in the goods market.[7] Also, following much of the literature on this topic, we

---

[6]We may compute $\lambda_k = (\ell_1 f' + \ell_2 f'')/(1 - \ell)^2 > 0$ and $\lambda_\pi = \ell_2/(1 - \ell)^2 < 0$.

[7]Denote the net (real) taxes (taxes minus transfer payments) by T. Then the public's budget condition is written as

$$C + I + T + \dot{L}/p \equiv Y. \tag{*}$$

Let G be (real) government expenditures on goods and services. Then the government

assume that C is a constant fraction of (real) "disposable income" Y^D, that is,

$$C = (1 - s)Y^D, \; 0 < s < 1. \tag{20}$$

To obtain the expression for disposable income Y^D, we first observe

$$Y^D \equiv C + \dot{W}, \tag{21}$$

where $W \equiv W^n/p$ and the dot signifies the time derivative. Since $W \equiv W^n/p$ and $W^n \equiv pK + M$, we have $\dot{W} = \dot{K} + (\theta - \pi)M/p$, where $\theta \equiv \dot{M}/M$. Hence noting $\dot{K} = I$ by ignoring depreciation, and using (21), we obtain

$$Y^D \equiv C + I + (\theta - \pi)\dot{M}/p. \tag{22}$$

The rate of change of the money supply (θ) is an exogenous variable controllable by policy authorities. By substituting (19) into (22), we obtain the desired expression for Y^D,

$$Y^D = Y + (\theta - \pi)M/p. \tag{23}$$

---

budget condition can be written as

$$p(G - T) \equiv \dot{M}, \tag{**}$$

since there are no government bonds in the economy by assumption. Assume away G. Then (**) can be rewritten as

$$-T \equiv \dot{M}/p. \tag{**'}$$

In this economy, taxation is assumed away and government spending consists solely of transfer payments to the public that are financed by printing money. Adding the budget conditions of the public and the government, i.e., adding (*) and (**'), we obtain

$$Y \equiv C + I + (L - M)/p. \tag{***}$$

Hence if the monetary equilibrium is maintained over time (i.e., if $L = M$ for all time t), then $Y = C + I$. Conversely, if $Y = C + I$ for all t, we have $L = M$ for all t. The two equilibrium relations $Y = C + I$ and $L = M$ are *not* independent. In the literature, the equilibrium relation is usually specified by $L = M$. Then $Y = C + I$ follows automatically; i.e., it is *wrong* in this case to specify $Y = C + I$ as an equilibrium condition that is *independent of* $L = M$. That $Y = C + I$ automatically holds given $L = M$ is the true content of the statement that "investment is completely passive in the sense that saving ($Y - C$) automatically brings forth an equal amount of investment." This is a logical consequence of $L = M$, rather than an independent assumption, contrary to what is often stated in the literature.

This means that disposable income is equal to factor income Y plus real cash balances transfered to the public by the government ($\theta M/p = \dot{M}/p$) minus capital losses from holding cash balances due to inflation ($-\pi M/p$), where ($-\pi$) signifies the real rate of return on money.

Combining (19), (20), and (23), we obtain

$$I = sY - (1 - s)(\theta - \pi)M/p. \tag{24}$$

The basic accumulation equation of physical assets is given by $I = \dot{K}$. Assume that the population grows at a constant rate n, where $\dot{N}/N = n$. Then we can rewrite the accumulation equation of physical assets as

$$\dot{k} = I/N - nk. \tag{25}$$

Combining (24) and (25), we obtain

$$\dot{k} = sf(k) - (1 - s)(\theta - \pi)m - nk, \tag{26}$$

where $m \equiv M/(pN)$. Substituting (17) into (26), and dividing by k, we get

$$\dot{k}/k = \phi(k, \pi) \equiv h(k) - (1 - s)(\theta - \pi)\lambda(k, \pi) - n, \tag{27}$$

where $h(k) \equiv sf(k)/k$.

Next, from $m \equiv M/(pN)$, we arrive at

$$\dot{m}/m = \theta - \pi - n. \tag{28}$$

On the other hand, logarithmically differentiating (17), we have

$$\dot{m}/m = (\lambda_k \dot{k} + \lambda_\pi \dot{\pi})/\lambda + \dot{k}/k. \tag{29}$$

Hence, combining this with (27) and (28), we obtain

$$\dot{\pi} = \psi(k, \pi) \equiv a(k, \pi)[(\theta - \pi - n) - b(k, \pi)\phi(k, \pi)], \tag{30}$$

where $a(k, \pi) \equiv \lambda/\lambda_\pi < 0$ and $b(k, \pi) \equiv 1 + \lambda_k k/\lambda > 1$.

8.2.2 Steady State

Equations (27) and (30) constitute the system of differential equations from which the time path of (k, π) is determined. The steady-state value of $(k,\ \pi)$ is defined by setting $\dot{k} = \dot{\pi} = 0$ in (27) and (30):[8]

$$\phi(k^*,\ \pi^*) = 0 \quad \text{and} \quad \psi(k^*,\ \pi^*) = 0. \tag{31}$$

At the steady-state, we have

$$\pi^* = \theta - n, \tag{32}$$

so that $\dot{m} = 0$ by (28). At the steady-state, the capital-labor ratio, per capita real cash balances, and the rate of price change all become stationary. The steady-state value of m can easily be obtained once k^* and π^* are obtained from (31). Recall (17) as

$$m^* = \lambda(k^*,\ \pi^*)k^*. \tag{33}$$

Thus we may obtain the following result.

Lemma. At the steady-state at which k and π are stationary, m is also stationary.[9] The steady state value of price change (π^*) is equal to the rate of growth of the money supply (θ) minus the rate of population growth (n).

Next, substituting (32) into (27), we obtain

$$h(k) = [(1 - s)\lambda(k,\ \pi^*) + 1]n \tag{34}$$

in the steady-state, where $\pi^* = \theta - n$. Recalling $\lambda_k > 0$ and noting $h'(k) = -s(f - kf')/k^2 < 0$,[10] we may illustrate the steady-state value of k in figure 8.3. From figure 8.3, it is clear that the steady-state value of k is unique, if it exists. In this context, note $h(0) = \infty$ and $h(\infty) = 0$ as well as $h'(k) < 0$ for all $k > 0$. The existence of k^* is ensured as long as $\lambda(k,\ \pi^*)$ is defined for a sufficiently low value of k.

From (32), we can easily observe that an increase in θ increases the steady-state value of π. Since $\lambda_\pi < 0$, an increase in the steady-state value of π shifts the $[(1 - s)\lambda + 1]n$-curve in figure 8.3 down vertically.

---

[8] The notations ϕ and ψ in (31) should not be confused with the ϕ and ψ used in the previous section.

[9] Equation (17) can equivalently be written as

$$\pi = \pi(k,\ m),\ \pi_k > 0 \ \text{and}\ \pi_m < 0, \tag{17'}$$

where $\pi_k \equiv \partial\pi/\partial k = -(\lambda + \lambda_k k)/(\lambda_\pi k) > 0$ and $\pi_m \equiv 1/(\lambda_\pi k) < 0$.

[10] We may recall that $f - kf' = \partial F/\partial N$; i.e., $f - kf'$ signifies the marginal physical productivity of labor. From this we obtain $h' < 0$.

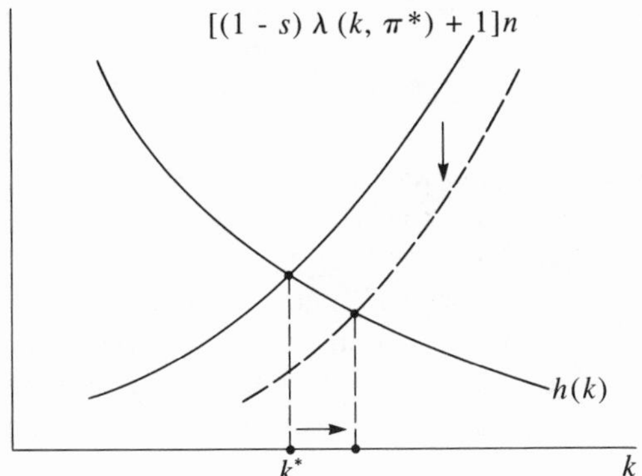

Figure 8.3: Steady-state value of k

More formally, differentiating (34) and recalling $d\pi = d\theta$ at the steady-state, we have

$$dk/d\theta = (1 - s)n\lambda_\pi/[h' - (1 - s)n\lambda_k] > 0, \tag{35}$$

since $h' < 0$, $\lambda_k > 0$, and $\lambda_\pi < 0$. Thus we derive the result in proposition 8.2.[11]

Proposition 8.2 (Tobin 1965). An increase in the rate of growth of the money supply increases the steady-state value of the capital-output ratio (k^*) as well as the steady-state value of the rate of price change (π^*).

This can be interpreted as follows. An increase in the rate of growth of the money supply lowers the real rate of return on money ($-\pi$), which in turn causes portfolio switching from money into physical assets by making holding money vis-à-vis physical assets less attractive. This implies that a change in the monetary variables induces a change in the real variables such as k, and it has surprised some economists who are used to thinking in terms of the neoclassical doctrine of the neutrality of money. On the other hand, the above proposition should be distinguished from the usual neutrality doctrine, which is concerned with the

[11] James Tobin was the 1981 Nobel laureate in Economic Science.

effect of a change in the *level* (rather than the rate of change) of nominal cash balances on real variables. Proposition 8.2 is thus often referred to as saying that money is *not* **superneutral** (instead of just neutral).

8.2.3 Stability and Instability

The preceding comparative statics exercise regarding the steady-state is not meaningful unless the steady-state is stable. Specifically, we need to investigate whether or not the time path of $(k,\ \pi)$ defined by the dynamic system of equations (27) and (30) will converge to the steady-state as time extends without limit. We investigate this question and the dynamic behavior of (k, π). For the latter, we construct a phase diagram on the $(k,\ \pi)$-plane. We assume that the value of θ is fixed at a certain level.

To investigate the dynamic behavior of the model, we compute the partial derivatives of the functions ϕ and ψ from (27) and (30) as

$$\phi_k \equiv \partial\phi/\partial k = h' - (1-s)n\lambda_k < 0, \tag{36a}$$

$$\phi_\pi \equiv \partial\phi/\partial\pi = (1-s)(\lambda - n\lambda_\pi) > 0, \tag{36b}$$

$$\psi_k \equiv \partial\psi/\partial k = -ab\phi_k < 0, \tag{37a}$$

$$\psi_\pi \equiv \partial\psi/\partial\pi = -a(1 + b\phi_\pi) > 0, \tag{37b}$$

where these partial derivatives are evaluated at the steady-state in which $\dot{k} = \dot{\pi} = 0$. In obtaining (36), we may recall $\theta - \pi = n$ when $\dot{k} = \dot{\pi} = 0$.

Observe from (36) and (37) that

$$\begin{aligned} J &\equiv \phi_k\psi_\pi - \psi_k\phi_\pi \\ &= -a\phi_k(1 + b\phi_\pi) + ab\phi_k\phi_\pi = -a\phi_k < 0. \end{aligned} \tag{38}$$

The Jacobian determinant evaluated at the steady-state is thus negative. From this we may conclude that the steady-state is a *saddle point* and, hence, it is unstable.

To determine the dynamic behavior of the $(k,\ \pi)$ path we now use the phase diagram technique. Define the $(\dot{k} = 0)$-curve as the locus of $(k,\ \pi)$ pairs along which $\phi(k,\ \pi) = 0$. Then its slope at the steady-state is determined as

$$\left.\frac{d\pi}{dk}\right|_{\dot{k}=0} = -\frac{\phi_k}{\phi_\pi} > 0. \tag{39}$$

Similarly, define the ($\dot{\pi} = 0$)-curve as the locus of (k, π) pairs along which $\psi(k, \pi) = 0$. Then its slope at the steady-state is found to be

$$\left.\frac{d\pi}{dk}\right|_{\dot{\pi}=0} = -\frac{\psi_k}{\psi_\pi} > 0. \tag{40}$$

Also using (38), we have

$$-\frac{\phi_k}{\phi_\pi} > -\frac{\psi_k}{\psi_\pi}, \quad \text{or} \quad \left.\frac{d\pi}{dk}\right|_{\dot{k}=0} > \left.\frac{d\pi}{dk}\right|_{\dot{\pi}=0} \tag{41}$$

at the steady-state. The ($\dot{k} = 0$)-curve is steeper than the ($\dot{\pi} = 0$)-curve at the steady-state. Combining this with (36) and (37), we can now construct the phrase diagram, figure 8.4. This illustrates the time path of (k, π). In figure 8.4, we illustrate the saddle-like behavior of trajectories. Unless the initial state is chosen appropriately, the dynamic path diverges away from the steady-state. A version of this result is obtained by Nagatani (1970). It is also recognized by Sidrauski (1967, p. 807).

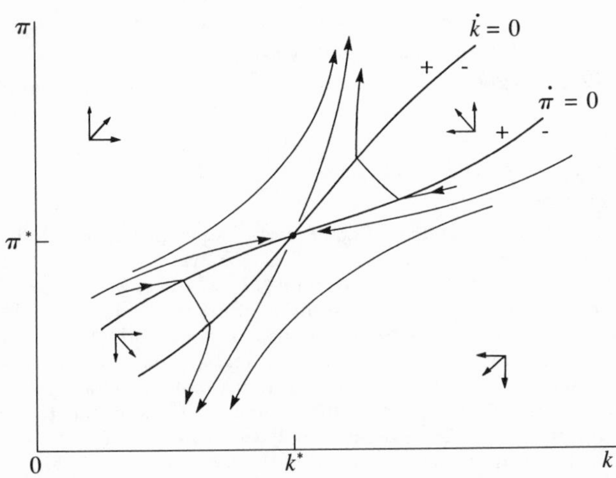

Figure 8.4: Dynamic behavior of (k, π)

Proposition 8.3. The steady-state defined by the dynamic system of (27) and (30) is a saddle point, and hence it is unstable.[12] The trajectory of $(k,\ \pi)$ is illustrated by figure 8.4.

This instability result seriously undermines the value of comparative statics exercises regarding the steady-state, such as proposition 8.2. A number of ways to remove this instability property have been suggested. One important way is to introduce *sluggish adjustment* in expectations (Sidrauski 1967). We now examine this approach. The heart of the approach is to introduce the *adaptive expectation mechanism:*

$$\dot{z} = \varepsilon(\pi - z), \tag{42}$$

where ε is a positive constant signifying the speed of adjustment of expectations and z signifies the expected rate of price change. Substitution of z for π in the previous system yields

$$m = \lambda(k,\ z)k, \tag{43}$$

$$\dot{k}/k = \phi(k,\ z) \equiv h(k) - (1 - s)(\theta - z)\lambda(k,\ z) - n, \tag{44}$$

$$\dot{z} = a(k,\ z)[(\theta - \pi - n) - b(k,\ z)\phi(k,\ z)], \tag{45}$$

where (43), (44), and (45), respectively, correspond to (17), (27), and (30). It is assumed that the monetary equilibrium relation (43) is maintained by the proper fluctuation of p on the lefthand side of (43), $m \equiv M/(pN)$. This in turn implies that (28) holds as it is.

From (42), we get $\pi = z + \dot{x}/\epsilon$. Substituting this into (45), we obtain

$$\dot{z} = \alpha\psi(k,\ z) \equiv \tilde{\psi}(k,\ z), \tag{46}$$

[12] As mentioned in the previous chapter, certain economists strongly believe that in a case like figure 8.4, the economy will always travel along the *stable branch* of saddle-like paths, so that the steady-state $(k^*,\ \pi^*)$ is always stable. This view has become popular since the Sargent-Wallace (1973) article dealing with monetary models similar to the one in the present discussion. Apparently, their justification is that the stable branch is the only "rational expectation" path. However, every path obtained as a solution of equations (27) and (30) should be a rational expectation path (See also Shiller 1978 and Gertler 1979). Surely, the steady-state that is unstable under certain restricted models need not imply that this is the case for every model. In fact, we shall show in the next section that the saddle-point instability completely vanishes when we introduce securities into the preset model. Furthemore, their use of the concept of "stability" differs from that in the tradition of the theory of differential equations. Unlike some economists, the author finds it unnecessary to redefine it in view of certain restricted economic models.

where $\alpha \equiv 1/(1 + a/\varepsilon)$ [$= \alpha(k, z)$], $a < 0$, and where $\psi(k, z) \equiv a[(\theta - z - n) - b(k, z)\phi(k, z)]$ as before. Equations (44) and (46) constitute the basic dynamic system under the expectation mechanism. Assume that expectations are sufficiently sluggish (i.e., ε is sufficiently close to zero) so that $\alpha < 0$. Then utilizing (36), we can at once observe

$$\phi_k < 0,\ \phi_z > 0;$$
$$\tilde{\psi}_k = \alpha\psi_k > 0,\ \tilde{\psi}_z = \alpha\psi_z < 0, \quad \text{for all } k \text{ and } z, \tag{47}$$

where these partials are evaluated for $\dot{k} = \dot{z} = 0$. Thus, we have, at the steady-state,

$$\phi_k + \tilde{\psi}_z < 0, \tag{48a}$$

$$\tilde{J} \equiv \phi_k\tilde{\psi}_z - \tilde{\psi}_k\phi_z = \alpha(\phi_k\psi_z - \psi_k\phi_z) > 0, \tag{48b}$$

for all k and z, and hence the steady-state is now asymptotically globally stable. The dynamic path of (k, z) can be illustrated by figure 8.5, where we utilize (47) and $J > 0$. From $J > 0$, we may obtain

$$-\frac{\phi_k}{\phi_z} > -\frac{\psi_k}{\psi_z}, \quad \text{or} \quad \left.\frac{dz}{dk}\right|_{\dot{k}=0} > \left.\frac{dz}{dk}\right|_{\dot{z}=0} \tag{49}$$

at the steady-state. It can be shown easily that the eigenvalues of the characteristic equation for the linear approximation system are real, distinct, and negative. Thus, (k^*, z^*) is a stable *node*, and we may obtain the result in proposition 8.4.

Proposition 8.4 (Sidrauski 1967). If expectations are sufficiently sluggish, then the steady-state is a node that is asymptotically globally stable. This, in particular, recovers the validity of proposition 8.2. The trajectory of dynamic system (44) and (46) is illustrated by figure 8.5.

The trouble with this adaptive expectation mechanism is the divergence between the actual rate of inflation (π) and the expected rate of inflation (z). In spite of the divergence, people commit the error of persistently following the rule of expectation formations that consistently provides wrongly predicted values. The coefficent ε in (42) is not obtained in a way that is consistent with the rational behavior of the public. Namely, ε appears to be totally *ad hoc.*[13]

---

[13]It can be shown that the adaptive expectation formula (42) is equivalent to assert

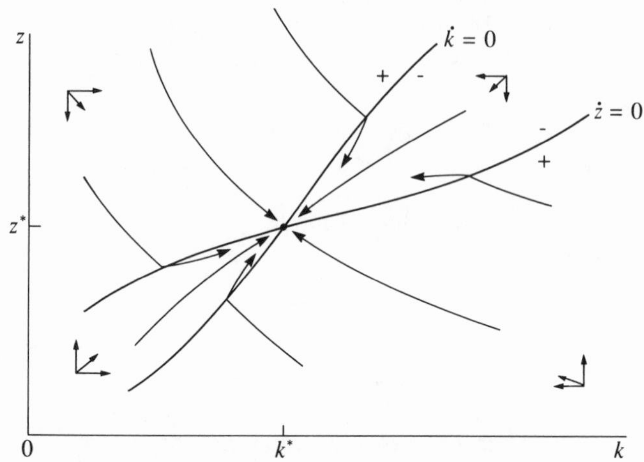

Figure 8.5: Stability under sluggish expectations

8.2.4 The Source of Instability

We may now return to the original instability result obtained under myopic perfect foresight ($\pi = z$) and investigate the source of instability. To this end, we first recall that the monetary equilibrium relation (17) can be rewritten as (recall fn. 9)

$$\pi = \pi(k,\ m), \quad \text{with } \pi_k > 0 \text{ and } \pi_m < 0. \tag{17'}$$

Using this and (28), we may define the function μ by

$$\dot{m}/m = \mu(k,\ m;\ \theta) \equiv \theta - \pi(k,\ m) - n.^{14} \tag{50}$$

---

that this expected rate of inflation is a weighted sum of the past (actual) rates of inflation with certain weights. It would be implausible to suppose that such weights are determined *exogenously* without any regard to certain fundamental conditions of the economy. It would be silly to suppose that one would expect the stock price of a certain company to be a weighted sum of its past prices with a fixed weight structure. The adaptive expectation hypothesis has a similar serious weakness.

Using (50), and defining $\mu_k \equiv \partial\mu/\partial k$ and $\mu_m \equiv \partial\mu/\partial m$, we obtain

$$\mu_k = -\pi_k < 0 \text{ and } \mu_m = -\pi_m > 0. \tag{51}$$

Here $\mu_m > 0$ means that the money accumulation equation (50) is unstable for each fixed k. This is illustrated in figure 8.6, where $\hat{m} = \hat{m}(k)$ is defined by

$$\pi(k, \hat{m}) = \theta - n. \tag{52}$$

Unless the initial value of m is equal to $\hat{m}$, m diverges away from $\hat{m}$. When m is equal to $\hat{m}$, π is equal to $\theta - n(\equiv \pi^*)$. When m diverges away from $\hat{m}$, π also diverges away from π^*.

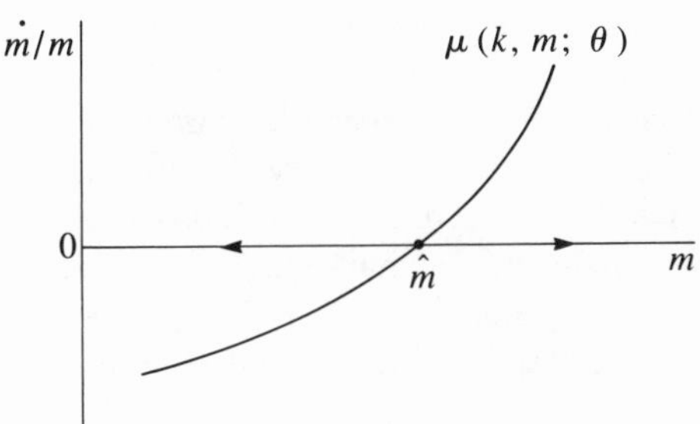

Figure 8.6: Instability of m for a fixed k

We may now examine more closely the cause of the instability of $\hat{m}$, as this is the source of the instability result obtained in section 8.2.3 under myopic perfect foresight. From (51), we at once see that the instability of $\hat{m}$ holds if and only if $\pi_m < 0$. Recalling that $\pi_m = 1/(\lambda_\pi k)$, we obtain $\pi_m < 0$ if and only if $\lambda_\pi < 0$, which in turn holds if and only if $\ell_2 < 0$ (see fn. 6). Specifically, $\pi_m < 0$ points to the fact that the demand

[14] Note that we may obtain the following equation by substituting (17′) into (26):

$$\dot{k} = sf(k) - (1 - s)[\theta - \pi(k, m)]m - nk.$$

Then the dynamic system may be described by this and (50), which in turn defines the trajectory of (k, m). This may be considered as an *alternative* description of the dynamic system, (27) and (30), which defines the trajectory of (k, π). It is immaterial to our results which system we adopt.

for money is a decreasing function with respect to the nominal rate of return on physical assets and, hence, to π, that is, $\lambda_\pi < 0$. The cause of the instability result obtained in section 8.2.3 is the fact that an *increase* in per capita real cash balances, m, must accompany a *fall* (instead of an increase) in the "rate of inflation," π, to maintain equilibrium in the money market, which in turn results in $\pi_m < 0$. Tobin (1965) calls $\pi_m < 0$ the **Wicksell effect**. A similar destabilizing process is analyzed in the context of the well-known **Wicksellian cumulative process.**

The preceding discussion points to the fact that the instability result (under rational expectations) is due to the equilibrium condition for money. Equation (17) alone is sufficient to determine the short-run equilibrium value of π for given values of k and m, and that $\lambda_\pi < 0$. As clarified in footnote 7, the equilibrium in the goods market is automatically ensured, once monetary equilibrium is achieved in the usual two-asset economy. Suppose now that we introduce the third asset, say interest-yielding securities, into the economy, in addition to money and physical assets, then equilibrium in the goods market cannot automatically be ensured by monetary equilibrium. The equilibrium rate of inflation (π) is then determined *simultaneously* by the *two* equilibrium conditions, one for the money market and the other for the goods market. In the next section, we shall systematically analyze such a three-asset model and show that the stability result can be obtained.

8.3 Money and Growth—Part 2[15]

8.3.1 Introduction

The analysis in section 8.2 is based on the model for an economy consisting of two assets, Treasury money and physical assets, and is characterized by three important properties:

(*a*) The expected rate of price change is always realized (perfect myopic foresight, or rational expectations).

---

[15]This section is based on Drabicki and Takayama (1984b), which is based on the assumption that the supply of money is exogenous. For an analysis that incorporates the banking sector and the endogeneity of the money supply, see Drabicki and Takayama (1984a). For the empirical plausibility of the "money supply" formula presented there, see Sims and Takayama (1985). This paper also contains the study on the demand for money. Most empirical studies have not successfully included both income and wealth as arguments of the money demand function due to multicollinearity. Sims and Takayama (1985) are successful in overcoming this difficulty.

(*b*) Individuals save a constant fraction s of their disposable income, or equivalently, consume a constant fraction $(1 - s)$ of their disposable income.

(*c*) The demand for money is always equal to its supply.

It was conjectured by Tobin that the steady-state of his model would be generally stable. However, as shown in the previous section, such a conjecture is false with the additional stipulation that:

(*d*) The money supply grows at a constant rate θ.

As discussed in section 8.2, it has been established that the steady state under (*a*)–(*d*) is a saddle point and, hence, unstable.

This instability result undermines the value of any comparative statics studies of the steady-state. Subsequently, various remedies for such an instability have been suggested in the literature. Sidrauski demonstrated in his paper (1967) that stability was possible if (*a*) was replaced with an adaptive expectations mechanism in which expectations adjust "sluggishly." While retaining assumptions (*a*)–(*c*), Burmeister and Dobell (1970, p. 185) showed that stability may be obtained if (*d*) is relaxed so as to allow the money stock to grow at a specified, nonconstant rate. Hadjimichalakis (1971a, 1971b) and Hadjimichalakis and Okuguchi (1979) have argued that instability may be removed by the proper relaxation of (*a*) and/or (*c*). In addition, stability is possible in the various so-called Keynes-Wicksell monetary growth models which relax assumption (*a*) and differ from the above in that they allow for planned savings to differ from planned investment (e.g., Rose 1966 and Stein 1966).

The relaxation of (*a*) has been subjected to serious criticism because it almost always accommodates irrational behavior, especially in the formation of expectations. A popular alternative approach à la Sargent and Wallace (1973) is to advocate initial "jumps" or impose certain terminal conditions to keep the economy on the *stable branch* of the saddle-like paths. However, this approach has a serious weakness from its ad hoc nature of ruling out the "deviant paths" (recall fn. 12).

The purpose of this section is to show that the stability of a monetary growth model is possible even if assumption *a* is retained. In particular, we show that stability is possible under assumptions (*a*)–(*d*), if a third asset, namely bonds, is introduced to the usual two-asset economy.[16]

[16] Needless to say, a good number of studies of money and growth include the bond market, but these violate some of the assumptions listed here (cf., e.g., Stein and Nagatani 1969; Fischer 1972; and Johnson 1976). For a clear exposition of the two-asset economy under consideration, see for example, Burmeister and Dobell (1970,

In particular, we consider an economy consisting of three assets, (Treasury) money, physical assets, and interest-yielding securities (or bonds). The supply of money is assumed to be completely controllable by the government. Also, we assume that all bonds are private bonds. A further analysis of a three-asset economy which explicitly incorporates the banking sector, the endogeneous nature of the money supply, government bonds, and government budget deficits or surpluses is carried out in Drabicki and Takayama (1984a).

As pointed out in section 8.2, in the two-asset model of money and physical assets, the rate of price change is determined by the money market alone in such a way that an expansionary monetary policy is necessarily deflationary. Such a consequence of the Wicksell effect is an unstable accumulation equation for per capita real cash balances. In turn, this contributes to, and results in, the instability of the entire system. When bonds are introduced as a third asset (and the three assets are imperfect substitutes for each other), another endogenous variable (the nominal rate of interest) enters the system and its equilibrium value is *simultaneously* determined with the equilibrium rate of price change by the money and goods markets. In such a case, we can show that an expansionary monetary policy is inflationary (at least in the steady-state). This can lead to a stable accumulation equation for the per capita real cash balances and an overall stable system. Our sufficient conditions for stability are quite weak compared with any sufficient conditions obtained in the literature.

8.3.2 Model and Momentary Equilibrium

We again assume that the homogeneous output Y is produced with fully employed labor N and capital K under a diminishing returns and constant returns to scale technology described by (9) and (10). In addition to physical capital, we now postulate that the economy contains two additional assets: money and bonds. All money is assumed to be government money. We also assume that all bonds are private (i.e., the government issues no bonds).[17] Let M and p, respectively, denote the nominal stock of money and the price level. In the absence of govern-

secs. 6–1 to 6–9) and Hadjimichalakis (1971a, "System A").

[17]For a notable example of such an assumption, see Patinkin (1965). Government bonds together with the banking sector are introduced systematically in Takayama and Drabicki (1976) and Drabicki and Takayama (1984a).

ment bonds, the public's real wealth (W) is given by[18]

$$W \equiv K + M/p. \tag{53}$$

Formally, this is the same as (15). Letting i and $\pi(\equiv \dot{p}/p)$, respectively, denote the nominal interest rate (on bonds) and the rate of inflation or price change, the monetary equilibrium condition may be specified as[19]

$$M = L[i,\ f'(k) + \pi,\ pY,\ pW],$$
$$L_1 < 0,\ L_2 < 0,\ L_3 > 0,\ 1 > L_4 > 0, \tag{54}$$

in which perfect myopic foresight is assumed. Here the introduction of i signifies that the portfolio choice involves bonds as well as money and physical assets. Under the usual homogeneity assumption of L, we may obtain, from (53) and (54),

$$m = L[i,\ f'(k) + \pi,\ f(k),\ k + m], \tag{54$'$}$$

where $m \equiv M/(pN)$ (per capita real cash balances).

The money supply is assumed to grow at a constant rate θ, that is,[20]

$$\dot{M}/M = \theta. \tag{55}$$

Equilibrium in the goods market is again specified by

$$Y = C + I, \tag{19}$$

where C and I, respectively, denote real consumption and investment. It is assumed that real consumption is a constant fraction of real disposable income Y^D, that is, $C = (1 - s)Y^D$ where $0 < s < 1$. Under the assumption of perfect myopic foresight, Y^D can be expressed as[21]

$$Y^D = Y + (\theta - \pi)M/p, \tag{23$'$}$$

[18]See Modigliani (1963, pp. 80–81) for the derivation of (53). See also Takayama and Drabicki (1976), Drabicki and Takayama (1984a), and Sims and Takayama (1985). These papers also incorporate the banking sector.

[19]Here the jth subscript denotes the partial derivative with respect to the jth argument, $j = 1,\ 2,\ 3$, and 4.

[20]As in sec. 8.2, it is assumed that the government makes no expenditures and collects no taxes, but simply prints money (which it transfers to the public) at a constant rate θ. This is a standard simplifying assumption in the money and growth literature.

[21]This is the expression obtained in sec. 8.2 for the no bond case. We obtain the same expression here by repeating a similar argument.

which is formally the same as (23). Unlike section 8.2, we do not assume that investment is "passive" in the sense that its quantity adjusts automatically to maintain equilibrium in the goods market. Rather, we assume that investment demand is given by[22]

$$I/N = z[i, f'(k) + \pi, y], \; z_1 < 0, \; z_2 > 0, \; 0 < z_3 < s. \tag{56}$$

Combining (19), (23′), and (56) with $C = (1 - s)Y^D$, we obtain

$$sf(k) = (1 - s)(\theta - \pi)m + z[i, f'(k) + \pi, f(k)], \tag{57}$$

where we recall $y = f(k)$. Equation (57) signifies the saving-investment equilibrium. The market clearing conditions (54′) and (57) determine (for given values of the parameters θ and s) the momentary equilibrium values of π and i as

$$\pi = \pi(k, m), \; i = i(k, m). \tag{58}$$

We postpone the task of determining the signs of the partial derivatives of the functions π and i to the appendix. Here we simply assert the basic result that, assuming the stability of momentary equilibrium, we have

$$\pi_k < 0, \; i_k > 0; \; \pi_m > 0, \; i_m < 0 \text{ if } \theta - \pi \geqq 0. \tag{59}$$

That is, an increase in the capital-labor ratio k (and hence the per capita output y) decreases the momentary equilibrium value of π and increases the corresponding value of i. On the other hand, an increase in per capita real cash balances increases the rate of inflation π and lowers the nominal rate of interest i if $\theta - \pi \geqq 0$. The result that $\pi_k < 0$ and $\pi_m > 0$ in (59), though it may look obvious, is completely opposite to the one obtained in (17′).

8.3.3 Long-Run Analysis

Let n be the rate of population growth (i.e., $n \equiv \dot{N}/N$), which is assumed to be a positive constant. Then we have $\dot{K} = I$ or $\dot{k} = z - nk$,

---

[22]The $0 < z_3 < s$ refers to the usual assumption that (as functions of income) the savings schedule is steeper than the investment schedule. Instead of (56), alternative investment demand functions may have been chosen without affecting our conclusions.

where we again assume away depreciation to ease the exposition. Utilizing (57) and (58) we obtain

$$\dot{k} = sf(k) - (1 - s)[\theta - \pi(k, m)]m - nk \equiv \dot{k}(k, m). \tag{60}$$

Differentiating $m \equiv M/(pN)$ and utilizing (58) yields

$$\dot{m} = [\theta - \pi(k, m) - n]m \equiv \dot{m}(k, m), \tag{50$'$}$$

which is formally the same as (50). Note that given the fixed values of the parameters θ, s, and n, conditions (60) and (50$'$) constitute a system of two differential equations in the unknowns k and m. The steady state of our system is defined by setting $\dot{k} = 0$ and $\dot{m} = 0$. In the steady-state, we again have

$$\pi^* = \theta - n. \tag{32$'$}$$

The steady-state rate of inflation, $\pi^* \equiv \pi(k^*, m^*)$, is equal to the rate of monetary expansion minus the rate of population growth.

We now study the dynamic behavior of the present system (60) and (50$'$). From (60) and (50$'$), and utilizing (59) and (32$'$), we may obtain:

$$\partial\dot{k}/\partial k = sf' - n + (1 - s)m\pi_k, \tag{61a}$$

$$\partial\dot{k}/\partial m = -(1 - s)(n - m\pi_m), \tag{61b}$$

$$\partial\dot{m}/\partial k = -m\pi_k > 0, \tag{62a}$$

$$\partial\dot{m}/\partial m = -m\pi_m < 0, \tag{62b}$$

where the partial derivatives are evaluated at the steady-state.

From (50$'$) and (62), the slope of the ($\dot{m} = 0$)-curve at the steady-state may be obtained as

$$\left.\frac{dm}{dk}\right|_{\dot{m}=0} = -\frac{\pi_k}{\pi_m} > 0 \tag{63}$$

Thus, the ($\dot{m} = 0$)-curve is upward sloping at the steady-state. The slope of the ($\dot{k} = 0$)-curve at the steady-state may be obtained from (60) and (61) as

$$\left.\frac{dm}{dk}\right|_{\dot{k}=0} = \frac{-[sf' - n + (1 - s)\, m\pi_k]}{(1 - s)(\pi_m m - n)}\,. \tag{64}$$

As shown in the appendix to this section, we have

$$\pi_m m - n > 0 \tag{65}$$

at the steady-state. Define k by $sf'(k) = n$. Then we have

$$sf'(k) \lesseqqgtr n \text{ according to whether } k \gtreqqless \bar{k}. \tag{66}$$

From (63) through (66), we may conclude

$$\left.\frac{dm}{dk}\right|_{\dot{k}=0} > \left.\frac{dm}{dk}\right|_{\dot{m}=0} > 0, \text{ as long as } k \geqq \bar{k}. \tag{67}$$

On the other hand, for $k \leqq \bar{k}$, it is possible to have

$$\left.\frac{dk}{dm}\right|_{\dot{m}=0} > \left.\frac{dm}{dk}\right|_{\dot{k}=0} \text{ and } \left.\frac{dm}{dk}\right|_{\dot{k}=0} \gtrless 0. \tag{68}$$

Thus, there can be more than one steady-state in the present system of (60) and (50′). Let (k^*, m^*) be one of them with $k^* \geqq \bar{k}$. Then from (67), the $(\dot{k} = 0)$-curve is upward sloping and steeper than the $(\dot{m} = 0)$-curve in a neighborhood of (k^*, m^*) as illustrated in figure 8.7. Let (k^{**}, m^{**}) be another steady-state. If k^{**} is sufficiently less than k, (68) is obtained instead of (67). In this case, the $(\dot{k} = 0)$-curve is flatter than the $(\dot{m} = 0)$-curve in a neighborhood of such a steady-state. Also from (61) and (62), we may conclude that $\dot{k} > 0$ (or $\dot{k} < 0$) to the left (or right) of the $(\dot{k} = 0)$-curve, and that $\dot{m} < 0$ (or $\dot{m} > 0$) to the right (or left) of the $(\dot{m} = 0)$-curve.

To obtain the stability property of a steady-state, we may compute the trace and the Jacobian determinant of the linear approximation system of (60) and (50′) as

$$\partial\dot{k}/\partial k + \partial\dot{m}/\partial m = sf' - n + (1 - s)m\pi_k - m\pi_m, \text{ and} \tag{69a}$$

$$(\partial\dot{k}/\partial k)(\partial\dot{m}/\partial m) - (\partial\dot{k}/\partial m)(\partial\dot{m}/\partial k)$$
$$= -m[(sf' - n)\pi_m + (1 - s)n\pi_k]. \tag{69b}$$

From (61) and (62), the derivatives are evaluated at a particular steady state. Let (k^*, m^*) be the steady-state at which $k^* \geqq \bar{k}$. Then from (69), we may at once obtain

$$\partial\dot{k}/\partial k + \partial\dot{m}/\partial m < 0, \tag{70a}$$

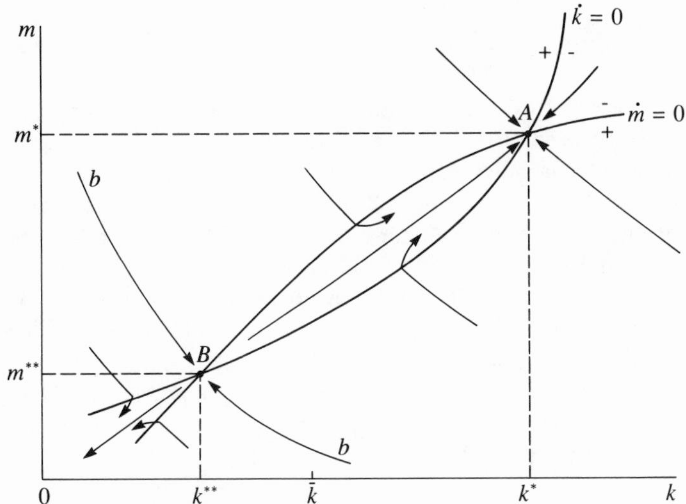

Figure 8.7: Dynamic path of $(k,\ m)$ with securities

$$(\partial\dot{k}/\partial k)(\partial\dot{m}/\partial m) - (\partial\dot{k}/\partial m)(\partial\dot{m}/\partial k) > 0, \tag{70b}$$

where the partial derivatives in (70) are evaluated at $(k^*,\ m^*)$. From this we may conclude that $(k^*,\ m^*)$ is asymptotically locally stable.

On the other hand, let $(k^{**},\ m^{**})$ be another steady-state at which

$$m[(sf' - n)\pi_m + (1 - s)n\pi_k] > 0. \tag{71}$$

Then the left-hand side of (69b) is negative, and $(k^{**},\ m^{**})$ is a saddle point and, hence, unstable. Also in this case, we have (68), and the $(\dot{k} = 0)$-curve is flatter than the $(\dot{m} = 0)$-curve in a neighborhood of $(k^{**},\ m^{**})$.

Using the preceding discussion, we may illustrate the dynamic path of $(k,\ m)$ in figure 8.7. In this diagram there are two steady-states, $A = (k^*,\ m^*)$ and $B = (k^{**},\ m^{**})$. Point A is asymptotically locally stable while point B is a saddle point. In figure 8.7, the economy always converges to the unique steady-state point, if the initial values of $(k,\ m)$

lie to the right of the locus bb. Here bb signifies the stable branch of the saddle-like paths, which leads to point B.

If we assume

$$sf' - n < 0, \quad \text{always in the steady-state,} \tag{72}$$

then the steady-state is unique and asymptotically globally stable. Condition (72) is the same stability condition that appears in the neoclassical growth model à la Solow and Swan where money and securities are assumed away. Recall condition (53) in chapter 6, in which we called such a condition the "Solow-Swan condition." Condition (72) also appears in the money and growth model by Hadjimichalakis and Okuguchi (1979). While this condition is sufficient to ensure stability in our model, it is not in the economy of Hadjimichalakis and Okuguchi (1979), which assumes away securities. Hadjimichalakis (1971b, p. 399) noted that condition (72) "is not a very drastic assumption. Since s is normally a small fraction, this condition is satisfied even if the steady-state k is substantially below the golden-rule k."

Proposition 8.5 (Drabicki and Takayama 1984b). The neoclassical growth model with money can have a stable steady-state under myopic perfect foresight, if interest-yielding securities are introduced into the model. In general, there can be more than one steady-state, and if the initial values of k and m exceed certain values, the steady-state is asymptotically stable. Furthermore, if condition (72) à la Solow and Swan is satisfied, then the steady-state is unique and asymptotically globally stable.

8.3.4 The Source of Stability

The preceding stability result provides a marked contrast with the usual (saddle-point) instability result. To study the source of our result, we may first note that our dynamic system, (60) and (50′), is identical in *form* to the ones used for the two-asset model.

This stability result stems from the fact that, in view of (62b)[resp. (61a) with (72) and $\pi_k < 0$], equation (50′) [resp. (60)] is stable for a *fixed* value of k (resp. m), whereas, in the usual two-asset models the equation corresponding to (50′) is unstable. Note that in our result, $\pi_k < 0$ and $\pi_m > 0$ (in the steady-state), plays a crucial role in obtaining the sign conditions for (61a) and (62b). Thus our result stabilizes the steady-state, while the usual result in the literature asserts $\pi_k > 0$ and $\pi_m < 0$ (in the steady-state), which in turn provides the source of instability. As mentioned earlier, the source of $\pi_m < 0$, that is, $L_2 < 0$, is called the "Wicksell effect" by Tobin (1965) and has been emphasized as the source of instability.

In summary, the source of our stability result then boils down to the difference in the sign conditions of π_k and π_m. This difference in turn stems from the fact that, under our specifications, the short-run equilibrium values of π and i are determined simultaneously by the money and the goods market equilibrium conditions. In contrast, in the usual literature on this topic, the momentary equilibrium value of π is determined by the money market alone.

8.3.5 Appendix to Section 8.3

In this appendix, we derive the results recorded in (59). To this end, we compute from the short-run equilibrium conditions (54′) and (57)

$$\pi_k = \{L_1[(s - z_3)f' - z_2 f''] + z_1(L_2 f'' + L_3 f' + L_4)\}/J, \tag{73a}$$

$$\pi_m = -[z_1(1 - L_4) + (1 - s)(\theta - \pi)L_1]/J, \tag{73b}$$

$$i_k = -\{[z_2 - (1 - s)m](L_2 f'' + L_3 f' + L_4) + L_2[(s - z_3)f' - z_2 f'']\}/J, \tag{73c}$$

$$i_m = \{[z_2 - (1 - s)m](1 - L_4) + (1 - s)(\theta - \pi)L_2\}/J, \tag{73d}$$

$$J \equiv [z_2 - (1 - s)m]L_1 - z_1 L_2. \tag{73e}$$

To obtain (59) from these, we appeal to the correspondence principle. We utilize the stability conditions for the *momentary* equilibrium, in which we hypothesize an adjustment process in which an excess demand for goods increases π and an excess demand for money increases i. That is,

$$d\pi/dt = \alpha\{(1-s)[f(k) + (\theta - \pi)m] + z[i, f'(k) + \pi, f(k)] - f(k)\} \equiv \Phi(\pi, i), \tag{74a}$$

$$di/dt = \beta\{L[i, f'(k) + \pi, f(k), k + m] - m\} \equiv \Psi(\pi, i), \tag{74b}$$

where t denotes time, α and β are positive constants, and where k and m are given. The necessary and sufficient conditions for the stability of the linear approximation system of (74) are

$$\Phi_\pi + \Psi_i < 0 \text{ and } \Phi_\pi \Psi_i - \Phi_i \Psi_\pi > 0, \tag{75}$$

where the partial derivatives appearing in (75) are evaluated at a particular momentary equilibrium point. By theorem 7.10, we may use (75) to obtain the signs for certain parameters and appeal to the correspondence principle. From (74), we may get

$$\Phi_\pi = \alpha[z_2 - (1 - s)m], \ \Phi_i = \alpha z_1 < 0, \tag{76a}$$

$$\Psi_\pi = \beta L_2 < 0, \ \Psi_i = \beta L_1 < 0, \tag{76b}$$

so that (75) may be rewritten as

$$\Phi_\pi + \Psi_i = \alpha[z_2 - (1 - s)m] + \beta L_1 < 0, \text{ and} \tag{77a}$$

$$\begin{aligned} \Phi_\pi \Psi_i - \Phi_i \Psi_\pi &= \alpha\beta\{[z_2 - (1-s)m]L_1 - z_1 L_2\} \\ &= \alpha\beta J > 0. \end{aligned} \tag{77b}$$

Since we assume $z_1 < 0$, $z_2 > 0$, $L_1 < 0$, and $L_2 < 0$, (77b) or $J > 0$ (i.e., the "Jacobian condition") requires that $z_2 - (1 - s)m < 0$ (which states that an increase in π must reduce the total demand for goods). This guarantees that (77a) or the "trace condition" will hold. Note also that (77b) requires that m be sufficiently bounded away from zero. $J > 0$ if and only if

$$m > (z_2 - z_1 L_2/L_1)/(1 - s) > 0. \tag{78}$$

Hence, under the "stability of momentary equilibrium assumption," that is, (77), the results in (59) follow easily from (73). Note that since (77) is stated without invoking the equilibrium condition for (73), (77) together with $\Phi_i \Psi_\pi \neq 0$ for all π and i ensure the asymptotic global stability of short-run equilibrium via Olech's theorem (theorem 6.7).

Note also that using (73b) and (73e), we can show

$$\pi_m m - n = \{z_1[nL_2 - (1 - L_4)m] - nz_2 L_1\}/J > 0,$$

for $\dot{m} = 0$ (i.e., $\theta - \pi = n$); $\pi_m m - n > 0$ is used signing dm/dk (for $\dot{k} = 0$).

References

Burmeister, E., and R. A. Dobell. 1970. "Money and Economic Growth." In *Mathematical Theories of Economic Growth*, New York: Macmillan.

Drabicki, J. Z., and A. Takayama. 1978. "Money, Growth, and the Stability of the Steady State under Myopic Perfect Foresight." *Economics Letters* 1(1): 51–54.

———. 1984a. "Money, National Debt, and Economic Growth." *Journal of Economic Theory* 33 (August): 356–67.

———. 1984b. "The Stability of a Neoclassical Monetary Growth Model." *Economic Studies Quarterly* 35 (December): 262–68.

Fischer, S. 1972. "Keynes-Wicksell and Neoclassical Models of Money and Growth." *American Economic Review* 62 (December): 880–90.

Foley, D. K., and M. Sidrauski. 1971. *Monetary and Fiscal Policy in a Growing Economy*. New York: Macmillan.

Gertler, M. 1979. "Money, Prices, and Inflation in Macroeconomic Models with Rational Inflationary Expectations." *Journal of Economic Theory* 21 (October): 222–34.

Hadjimichalakis, M. G. 1971a. "Equilibrium and Disequilibrium Growth with Money: The Tobin Models," *Review of Economic Studies* 38 (October): 457–79.

———. 1971b. "Money, Expectations, and Dynamics: An Alternative View." *International Economic Review* 12 (October): 381–402.

Hadjimichalakis, M. G., and K. Okuguchi. 1979. "The Stability of a Generalized Tobin Model." *Review of Economic Studies* 46 (January): 175–78.

Johnson, L. 1976. "Portfolio Adjustment and Monetary Growth." *Review of Economic Studies* 43 (October): 475–81.

Johnson, H. G. 1978. "Money in a Neo-Classical One-Sector Growth Model." In his *Selected Essays in Monetary Economics*. London: Allen and Unwin.

Modigliani, 0F. 1963. "The Monetary Mechanism and Its Interaction with Real Phenomena." *Review of Economics and Statistics* 45 (February): 79–107.

Nagatini, K. 1970. "A Note on Professor Tobin's 'Money and Economic Growth'." *Econometrica* 38 (January): 171–75.

———. 1978. "Money and Growth: An Introduction to the Theory of Dynamic Aggregate Behavior." Chap. 12. in *Monetary Theory*. Amsterdam: North-Holland.

Patinkin, D. 1965. *Money, Interest, and Prices*. 2d ed. New York: Harper and Row.

Rose, H. 1966. "Unemployment in a Theory of Growth." *International Economic Review* 7 (September): 260–82.

Sargent, T. J., and N. Wallace. 1973. "The Stability of Money and Growth with Perfect Foresight." *Econometrica* 41 (November): 1043–48.

Shiller, R. J. 1978. "Rational Expectations and the Dynamic Structure of Macroeconomic Models." *Journal of Monetary Economics* 4: 1–44.

Sidrauski, M. 1967. "Inflation and Economic Growth." *Journal of Political Economy* 75 (December): 796–810.

Sims, G. E., and A. Takayama. 1985. "On the Demand for and the Supply of Money: An Empirical Study." *Keio Economic Studies* 12: 1–26.

Stein, J. L. 1966. "Money and Capacity Growth." *Journal of Political Economy* 74 (October): 451–65.

Stein, J. L., and K. Nagatani. 1969. "Stabilization Policies in a Growing Economy." *Review of Economic Studies* 36 (April): 165–83.

Takayama, A. 1979. "Money and Growth: An Expository Note." *Lecture notes*, Texas A & M University, March.

———. 1986. "The General Theory after Fifty Years: The Neoclassical Approach (A Partial View)." *Discussion Paper Series*, no. 86–30. Carbondale: Southern Illinois University.

———. and J. Z. Drabicki. 1976. "On the Endogenous Supply of Money." *Keizai Kenkyu* (*Economic Review*) 27 (October): 336–48.

Tobin, J. 1965. "Money and Economic Growth." *Econometrica* 33 (October): 671–84. Reprinted with revisions in Tobin, J. 1971. *Essays in Economics: Macroeconomics*. Amsterdam: North-Holland, 133–45.

Part 5

Optimal Control Theory and Applications

CHAPTER 9

Elements of Optimal Control Theory and Applications

Optimal control theory is one of the most important tools of analysis. Although its use in dynamic problems is well known, the application is not confined to only this area. It is a modern version of the calculus of variations. The calculus of variations provided the fundamental mathematical method in finding the unifying principle in physics, reaching its culmination in the 1930s, especially at the University of Chicago. The advent of optimal control theory, especially via Pontryagin et al. (1962), Hestenes (1965), and others, caused great excitement in the academic profession, especially in science and engineering. Economic science is not an exception, where a large number of studies have been done in this field. Using the three remaining chapters, we shall study the gist of this tool and its applications to economics.

9.1 Pontryagin's Maximum Principle

Consider the problem of shooting a guided missile to intercept an airplane. The location of the missile at time t can be described by a three-dimensional, vector-valued function $x(t)$. The problem is to obtain the "optimal" trajectory $x(t)$ so that it maximizes or minimizes a certain objective. For example, the objective may be to minimize the time for the missile to reach the airplane. Clearly $x(t)$ can be "controlled" by a number of variables. For example, we may consider that the trajectory of the missile $x(t)$ is controlled by the fuel consumption of the missile at time t and the angle between the direction of thrust and the "flat" of the earth at time t.

These variables are, in general, denoted by an r-dimensional, vector-valued function $u(t)$. The function $x(t)$ is, in general, an n-dimensional, vector-valued function. The problem is to obtain the trajectory $x(t)$ by choosing a function $u(t)$ to maximize or minimize a certain objective. This problem is known as an **optimal control problem** and the theory for such a problem is called **optimal control theory**. Examples of optimal control are many and one can find many such examples in everyday life. Some problems are very complex and some are quite trivial (in the sense that the solution can be found easily). For example, a trivial problem is to minimize the time required to fill a bathtub with water by controlling the amount of water running from a faucet at each instant of time.[1] In economics also, there are many optimal control problems.

As currently formulated, optimal control theory is the result of important work by the famous Russian mathematician L. S. Pontryagin and his associates. This theory took over the classical theory of the calculus of variations. Inspired by this work, a number of important applications have been developed, and excellent textbooks that contain new results have been written (see Hestenes (1966); Berkovitz (1974); Young (1980); Macki and Strauss (1982); and Cesari (1983). The literature of the application of this technique to economic problems has also been expanding (see, for example, the literature cited in Kendrick (1981); see also Takayama (1974, 1985); Arrow and Kurz (1970); Pitchford and Turnovsky (1977); Kamien and Schwartz (1981, 1991); Sethi and Thompson (1981); Tu (1984); Seierstad and Sydsaeter (1987), and Brock and Malliaris (1989).[2]

The basic result of Pontryagin et al. (1962) is called **Pontryagin's maximum principle**. This principle is concerned with the necessary conditions for optimality. This condition is analogous to the maximization of the Lagrangian in the classical theory of constrained maximum or minimum. In this chapter, we give an expository account of the elements of optimal control theory in terms of Pontryagin's maximum principle, and illustrate it with some economic applications.

Consider the following system of n first-order differential equations,

$$\dot{x}_i(t) = f_i[x(t),\ u(t),\ t],\ i = 1,\ 2,\ \ldots,\ n, \tag{1}$$

where

$$x(t) = [x_1(t),\ x_2(t),\ \ldots,\ x_n(t)],\ u(t) = [u_1(t),\ u_2(t),\ \ldots,\ u_r(t)].$$

The f_i's, $x_i(t)$ and $u_k(t)$ are all real-valued functions. The boundary

---

[1] The opening exposition of this chapter is borrowed from Takayama (1985, p. 600).

[2] Since this is not a book that is dedicated to the exposition of optimal control theory, we shall focus our attention on the materials that would be most useful to economists. The reader who is interested in pursuing the subject further is referred to some of the books cited here.

conditions for (1) may be specified as

$$x_i(t^\circ) = x_i^\circ,\ i = 1,\ 2,\ \ldots,\ n. \tag{2}$$

If we specify the path of $u_k(t)$'s—say $u(t) = \overline{u}(t)$—then, assuming the uniqueness and the existence of a solution, we can completely specify the trajectory $x(t;\ x^\circ,\ t^\circ)$, as the solution path of (1) which satisfies (2). The Cauchy-Peano theorem (theorem 6.1), discussed in chapter 6, provides a set of sufficient conditions for the (local) existence and the uniqueness of a solution. The trajectory $x(t;\ x^\circ,\ t^\circ)$ clearly depends on the specification of $u(t)$.

In optimal control theory, we do not specify $u(t)$ ***a priori***, but rather we choose $u(t)$ from a set of functions—say, U—in order to maximize (or minimize) a certain target. For example, we may get the target as follows (where T is a fixed constant). We have

$$S = \sum_{i=1}^{n} c_i x_i(T), \tag{3}$$

and consider the problem of choosing $u(t) \in U$ so as to

Maximize S,

$$\text{Subject to } \dot{x}_i(t) = f_i[x(t),\ u(t),\ t],$$
$$\text{and } x_i(t^\circ) = x_i^\circ,\ i = 1,\ 2,\ \ldots,\ n, \tag{4}$$

where $u(t)$ is defined on some interval $t^\circ \leqq t \leqq T$. Once such a function, denoted by $u^*(t)$, is found, we should be able to find the corresponding function $x^*(t)$ as a solution of the system of differential equations (1) which satisfies the boundary condition.

In general, the variables $x_i(t)$, $i = 1,\ 2,\ \ldots,\ n$, that are assumed to be continuous in t, are called the **state variables**, and the variables $u_k(t)$, $k = 1,\ 2,\ \ldots,\ r$, are called the **control variables**.[3] When $u(t) \in U$, $u(t)$ is called an **admissible control function**. U is called the **set of admissible controls**. The range of $u(t)$ in U is denoted by $\overline{U}$,

[3]Note that the derivative of each state variable is in the constraint equations, but no derivatives of the control functions are involved either in the target function or in the constraint equations. This is sometimes used as a quick way to distinguish the state variables from the control variables.

and $\overline{U}$ is called the **control region**. We assume that U is restricted to the set where $u(t)$ is "piecewise continuous." By **piecewise continuous**, here we mean that a function is continuous except possibly at a finite number of points and that the discontinuity is limited to the **first kind**; that is, the left-hand and the right-hand limits are finite though they are not equal. It is allowed that the control region $\overline{U}$ be a closed set. In other words, $\overline{U}$ can incorporate a constraint such as

$$0 \leqq u(t) \leqq 1, \quad \text{for all } t.$$

In this case it is possible that $u(t) = 0$ or 1 for some t.

The f_i's are assumed to be continuous in each x_i, u_k, and t, and possess continuous partial derivatives with respect to each x_i and t. The range of $x(t)$ is denoted by X.[4] The boundary point (x°, t°) must be such that $x^{\circ} \in X$ and $x(t^{\circ}) = x^{\circ}$. It is required that $x(t)$ is continuous and have a piecewise continuous derivative. Although t often refers to *time* t in practical applications, this need not be the case, of course. However, following the usual convention, we may nickname t, "time" t.

We now state the basic theorem in this chapter. This theorem is concerned with the problem stated in (4), in which T is fixed, but $x(T)$ is *not* fixed *a priori.*

Theorem 9.1. Under the specification of problem (4), in order that $u^*(t)$ be a solution of the problem with the corresponding state variable $x^*(t)$, it is necessary that there exist a continuous, vector-valued function $p(t) \equiv [p_1(t), \ldots, p_n(t)]$, not vanishing simultaneously for each t,[5] such that

(i) $p(t)$ together with $x^*(t)$ and $u^*(t)$ solve the following **Hamilto-**

---

[4] X is assumed to be an open connected subset of R^n. A set X in R^n is said to be **connected** if it cannot be partitioned into two disjoint nonempty subsets of R^n which are open in X. Intuitively speaking, a set is connected if it is of "one piece" (but possibly with "holes").

[5] The phrase "not vanishing simultaneously" means that $p_1(t), \ldots,$ and $p_n(t)$ cannot vanish simultaneously, that is, $p(t) \equiv [p_1(t), \ldots, p_n(t)]$ is a non-zero vector. In this theorem and subsequent theorems on optimal control theory, $p(t)$, like $x(t)$, has piecewise continuous derivatives (as well as to be continuous) on the interval $[t^{\circ}, T]$. The possible discontinuities of $\dot{p}(t)$ and $\dot{x}(t)$ occur at the points of discontinuity of $u(t)$. This subtle point on $\dot{p}$ and $\dot{x}$ can safely be disregarded in most economic applications.

nian system,[6]

$$\dot{x}_i^* = \frac{\partial H^*}{\partial p_i},\ \dot{p}_i = -\frac{\partial H^*}{\partial x_i}\ ,\ i = 1,\ 2,\ \ldots,\ n, \tag{5}$$

where H, which is called the **Hamiltonian**[7], is defined by

$$H[x(t),\ u(t),\ t,\ p(t)] \equiv \sum_{i=1}^{n} p_i(t)\, f_i[x(t),\ u(t),\ t]\,; \tag{6}$$

(ii) The Hamiltonian is maximized with respect to $u(t)$, that is,

$$H[x^*(t),\ u^*(t),\ t,\ p(t)] \geqq H[x^*(t),\ u(t),\ t,\ p(t)],$$

$$\text{for all } u(t) \in U\,; \tag{7}$$

(iii) The following condition (called the **traversality condition**)[8] holds;

$$p_i(T) = c_i,\ i = 1,\ 2,\ \ldots,\ n\,; \tag{8}$$

(iv) $x_i(t^\circ) = \overset{\circ}{x}_i,\ i = 1,\ 2,\ \ldots,\ n.$

---

[6]The notations $\partial H^*/\partial x_i$ and $\partial H^*/\partial p_i$ mean that these partial derivatives are evaluated at $[x^*(t),\ u^*(t),\ t,\ p(t)]$.

[7]The following quotation from Simmons (1972, p. 77) may be of some interest to the reader. "One purpose of the mathematicians of the eighteenth century was to discover a general principle from which Newtonian mechanics could be deduced ... These facts and others suggested to Euler that nature pursues its diverse ends by the most efficient and economical means, and that a hidden simplicity underlies the apparent chaos of phenomena. It was this metaphysical idea that led him to create the calculus of variations as a tool for investigating such questions. Euler's dream was realized almost a century later by Hamilton." The Hamiltonian here captures its essence. William Rown Hamilton (1805–65) was an Irish mathematician and physicist. He "was a classic child prodigy ... At the age of three he could read English; at four he began Greek, Latin, and Hebrew; at eight he added Italian and French; at ten he learned Sanskrit and Arabic; and at thirteen he is said to have mastered one language for each year he lived. This forced flowering of linguistic futility was broken off at the age of fourteen, when he turned to mathematics, astronomy, and optics. At eighteen he published a paper correcting a mistake in Laplace's *Mécanique Céleste*; and while still an undergraduate at Trinity College in Dublin, he was appointed professor of astronomy at that institution and automatically became Astronomer Royal of Ireland." (Simmons, 1972, p. 387).

[8]We do not discuss the reason why (8) is called the *transversality condition.* For a good discussion of the transversality condition, see Pontryagin et al. (1962, chap. 1, sec. 2). See also Benveniste and Scheinkman (1982) and Araujo and Scheinkman (1983).

REMARK: Condition (ii), which requires that H be maximized, is the principal content of this theorem (and related theorems we shall discuss below). In view of this, these theorems are called the **maximum principle** by Pontryagin et al. (1962), and they are thus known as **Pontryagin's maximum principle**. Theorem 9.1 gives the necessary conditions for $u^*(t)$ to be optimal. It turns out that these conditions are also sufficient (for global optimum) if the f_i's are concave in x and u. An alert reader may have realized the similarity between this problem and the ordinary nonlinear programming discussed in chapter 2. The p_i's correspond to the Lagrangian multipliers, and H corresponds to the Lagrangian. The maximization of the Lagrangian is now converted to the maximization of the Hamiltonian. We may call the $p_i(t)$'s the **(Pontryagin) multipliers**. They are also called the **auxiliary variables** (Pontryagin et al. 1962) or the **costate variables**.

Note that (5) can be rewritten as

$$\dot{x}_i^* = f_i[x^*(t),\ u^*(t),\ t],\ \dot{p}_i = -\sum_{j=1}^{n} p_j\ (\partial f_j^*/\partial x_i),\ i = 1, \ldots, n,$$

where $\partial f_j^*/\partial x_i$ denotes $\partial f_j/\partial x_i$ evaluated at $[x^*(t),\ u^*(t),\ t]$. The system of equations (5) provides us with $2n$ first-order differential equations for $2n$ variables, $x_i(t)$, $p_i(t)$, $i = 1, 2, \ldots, n$. There are $2n$ boundary conditions, $x_i(t^\circ) = x_i^\circ$, $i = 1, 2, \ldots, n$; $p_i(T) = c_i$, $i = 1, 2, \ldots, n$ corresponding to these $2n$ equations. The role of the transversality condition (eq. 8) is thus to provide the additional boundary conditions. These $2n$ differential equations are not solvable unless the function $u(t)$ is specified. The role of condition (ii) is to specify the choice of $u(t)$. Once we find the path of $[x^*(t),\ u^*(t)]$ as the solution of the $2n$ differential equations that satisfies the $2n$ boundary conditions, we then obtain $x^*(T)$. Note that $x(T)$ is not specified *a priori* while T is fixed in the present problem. Corresponding to this, we obtain n additional conditions, $p_i(T) = c_i$, $i = 1, 2, \ldots, n$. We may call the pair $[x^*(t),\ u^*(t)]$ the **optimal pair** or the **solution pair**. The function $u^*(t)$ the **optimal control**, and the function $x^*(t)$ is called the **optimal trajectory**.

The target function as described in (3) is more general than it appears, as it includes the following integral target specification:

$$I \equiv \int_{t^\circ}^{T} f_\circ[x(t),\ u(t),\ t]dt. \tag{9}$$

To see this, define $x_\circ(t)$ by $\dot{x}_\circ \equiv f_\circ[x(t),\ u(t),\ t]$ with $x_\circ(t^\circ) = 0$. Then $I = x_\circ(T)$ is clearly a special case of (3). Hence the problem of maximizing I subject to $\dot{x}_\circ = f_\circ[x(t), u(t), t]$, (1), and (2), can be converted to the problem of maximizing $x_\circ(T)$ subject to (1), (2), and $x_\circ(t^\circ) = 0$. We can then immediately apply theorem 9.1. To this end, define the Hamiltonian by

$$\tilde{H}[x(t), u(t), t, p_\circ, p(t)] \equiv p_\circ f_\circ[x(t), u(t), t] + \sum_{i=1}^{n} p_i f_i[x(t), u(t), t].$$

Then (5), (7), and (8) are written as

$$\dot{x}_i^* = \frac{\partial \tilde{H}^*}{\partial p_i}, \quad \dot{p}_i = -\frac{\partial \tilde{H}^*}{\partial x_i}, \quad i = 0, 1, 2, \ldots, n, \tag{5'}$$

$$\tilde{H}[x^*(t), u^*(t), t, p_\circ, p(t)] \geqq \tilde{H}[x^*(t), u(t), t, p_\circ, p(t)], \tag{7'}$$

for all $u(t) \in U$, and

$$p_\circ(T) = 1, \; p_i(T) = 0, \; i = 1, 2, \ldots, n. \tag{8'}$$

Since $p_\circ(T) = 1$ and since $\dot{p}_\circ = 0$ by (5′), we have $p_\circ(t) = 1$ for all t. Hence, letting

$$\begin{aligned}\tilde{H} &= f_\circ[x(t), u(t), t] + \sum_{i=1}^{n} p_i f_i[x(t), u(t), t] \\ &\equiv H[x(t), u(t), t, p(t)],\end{aligned}$$

we may omit the case of $i = 0$ from (5′), (7′), and (8′), so that these can be rewritten as

$$\dot{x}_i^* = \frac{\partial H^*}{\partial p_i}, \quad \dot{p}_i = -\frac{\partial H^*}{\partial x_i}, \quad i = 1, 2, \ldots, n. \tag{5''}$$

$$H[x^*(t), u^*(t), t, p(t)] \geqq H[x^*(t), u(t), t, p(t)], \quad \text{for all } u(t) \in U. \tag{7''}$$

$$p_i(T) = 0, \; i = 1, 2, \ldots, n. \tag{8''}$$

Then (5″), (7″), and (8″) constitute a set of necessary conditions for $[x^*(t), u^*(t)]$ to be optimal for the problem of choosing $u(t) \in U$ so as to maximize the integral I in (9) subject to (1) and (2).

In the preceding discussion, we observed that the target in the integral form can be converted to a summation form S. Conversely, we can convert the target in the form of S in (3) to the integral form. To see this, note that

$$S \equiv \sum_{i=1}^{n} c_i x_i(T) = \int_{t^\circ}^{T} \sum_{i=1}^{n} c_i \dot{x}_i(t)dt + \sum_{i=1}^{n} c_i x_i(t^\circ).$$

Hence the maximization of S subject to (1) and (2) is equivalent to the maximization of the integral,

$$J \equiv \int_{t^\circ}^{T} f_\circ[x(t),\ u(t),\ t]dt, \quad \text{where } f_\circ \equiv \sum_{i=1}^{n} c_i f_i,$$

subject to (1) and (2).

Since $u_k(t)$ can be any piecewise continuous function, $u_k^*(t)$ may be such that

$$u_k^*(t) = 0 \quad \text{for } t^\circ \leqq t < \bar{t}, \text{ and}$$

$$u_k^*(t) = 1, \quad \text{for } \bar{t} \leqq t \leqq T.$$

Such a control is called the **bang-bang control**[9] and is often obtained in practical applications.

On the other hand, if u^* is in the interior of the control region $\overline{U}$ (or if $\overline{U}$ is an open set) and if each f_i is continuously differentiable in u (and H is continuously differentiable in u), then condition (ii) or (7) implies

$$\partial H^* / \partial u_k = 0, \ k = 1, 2, \ldots, n. \tag{7'''}$$

Conversely, if H is a concave function in the u_k's, then (7''') implies (7).

An Economic Application: Regional Allocation of Investment

To illustrate theorem 9.1, we consider the problem of regional allocation of investment as discussed by Takayama (1967 and 1985) which follows Rahman (1963 and 1966) and Intriligator (1964). Consider an economy

[9]If $u_k(t)$ hits the corner for a certain t and if it is in the interior for some other t, then such a control is called a **bang-coast control**. For example, if $0 \leqq u_k \leqq 1$, then the control, $u_k^*(t) = 0$ for $t^\circ \leqq t < \bar{t}$ and $0 < u_k^*(t) < 1$ for $\bar{t} \leqq t \leqq T$, is a bang-coast control. Note that bang-bang and bang-coast controls assume that the jump in control is "costless" or "inertia-less."

consisting of two regions(1 and 2), each producing one and the same output, Y (the "national product"). Assume that the output of each region Y_i ($i = 1, 2$) is produced with a fixed capital-output ratio so that we have

$$Y_i = b_i K_i, \ i = 1, 2,$$

where K_i denotes the stock of capital in region i. Following Rahman 1963, we consider the problem that the planning authority allocates the investment funds to the regions to maximize income of the whole economy at some given future terminal time T,

$$Y(T) \equiv Y_1(T) + Y_2(Y) \ [= b_1 K_1(T) + b_2 K_2(T)].$$

Since the investment funds (Z) for the two regions come from the savings accumulated in the whole economy, we have

$$Z = s_1 Y_1 + s_2 Y_2,$$

where the propensity to save s_i for each region is constant for all t and $0 < s_i < 1$, $i = 1, 2$. Defining g_i by $g_i \equiv b_i s_i$, we may rewrite this as

$$Z = g_1 K_1 + g_2 K_2.$$

Let $\beta = \beta(t)$ be the proportion of investment funds allocated to region 1. Clearly, $(1 - \beta)$ is the investment funds allocated to region 2. Then, ignoring depreciation of capital stock, we have the following equations:

$$\dot{K}_1(t) = \beta[g_1 K_1(t) + g_2 K_2(t)], \quad \text{and} \tag{10a}$$

$$\dot{K}_2(t) = (1 - \beta)[g_1 K_1(t) + g_2 K_2(t)]. \tag{10b}$$

Thus the problem formulated by Rahman (1963) is to choose $\beta(t)$ so as to

Maximize $b_1 K_1(T) + b_2 K_2(T)$,

Subject to (10), $0 \leqq 1$, $K_1(0) = K_1^\circ$, and $K_2(0) = K_2^\circ$.

This is a type of optimal control problem discussed in theorem 9.1. The state variables are $K_1(t)$ and $K_2(t)$, and the control variable is $\beta(t)$.

To solve this problem, we define the Hamiltonian for the present problem by

$$
\begin{aligned}
H &\equiv p_1\beta(g_1K_1 + g_2K_2) + (1-\beta)p_2(g_1K_1 + g_2K_2) \\
&= [\beta(p_1 - p_2) + p_2](g_1K_1 + g_2K_2).
\end{aligned}
$$

Omitting (*) which denotes optimality to avoid clutter, the Hamiltonian system consists of (10) and

$$\dot{p}_i = -\partial H/\partial K_i = -[\beta(p_1 - p_2) + p_2]g_i, \; i = 1,\ 2. \tag{11}$$

The transversality condition is given by

$$p_i(T) = b_i, \; i = 1,\ 2.$$

There are four differential equations in (10) and (11) corresponding to four variables $K_i(t)$ and $p_i(t)$, $i = 1, 2$, with four boundary conditions, $K_i(0) = K_i^\circ$ and $p_i(T) = b_i$, $i = 1, 2$. According to the maximum principle, we choose the control variable $\beta(t)$ to maximize H. Since $H = [\beta(p_1 - p_2) + p_2](g_1K_1 + g_2K_2)$, we at once obtain the following allocation rule of investment funds:

$$\beta(t) = 1 \text{ if } p_1(t) > p_2(t), \text{ and } \beta(t) = 0 \text{ if } p_1(t) < p_2(t).$$

Since (11) yields $\dot{p}_1/\dot{p}_2 = g_1/g_2$, we may obtain

$$p_1(t) - p_2(t) = \frac{g_1 - g_2}{g_2}\, p_2(t) + \frac{b_1b_2}{g_2}(s_2 - s_1),$$

by utilizing $p_i(T) = b_i$, $i = 1, 2$.

Hence if $g_1 > g_2$ and $s_2 > s_1$ (also for $g_1 = g_2$ and $s_2 > s_1$, *or* $g_1 > g_2$ and $s_2 = s_1$), $p_1(t) > p_2(t)$ for all t. Thus, $\beta(t) = 1$ for all t. In particular, if the saving rates in both regions are the same, we should invest all the funds in that region where the productivity of capital, b, is higher. Similarly, if the productivities are the same ($b_1 = b_2$), we should invest all the funds in the region where the savings rate is higher. This is also intuitively obvious. The analysis for the case of $g_1 > g_2$ and $s_1 > s_2$ is more difficult, and we shall omit it from the present exposition. The interested reader is referred to Takayama (1985, pp. 627–38) for a complete solution.

There are a number of difficulties in this problem. If, for example, $\beta(t) = 1$ for all t, people in region 2 are *disregarded* during the entire planning period. Although such a solution may be desirable from the planner's viewpoint, it need not be the case for the people in region 2.

Also, the specification of technology in the form of $Y_i = bK_i$ $(i = 1, 2)$ may be too simplistic. At least labor may have to be incorporated. Technology may then be specified by production functions $Y_i = F_i(N_i, K_i)$, where N_i signifies the labor force in region i. Imposing the usual neoclassical specification on F_i's, we would not obtain a "corner solution" such as $\beta(t) = 1$ for all t.

On the other hand, this problem is illustrative in a number of ways. For one thing, it is simple enough so that we can understand the nature of the solution fairly well, and yet it is not so easy as one may think. In fact, some economists erred in solving this problem. One reason why this problem is not easy is that it involves two state variables (instead of one). When the optimal control problem involves only one state variable, there is only one costate variable (i.e., Pontryagin multiplier), so that we obtain a system of two-dimensional differential equations, and the analysis of such a system is well known (cf. chap. 7). However, when there are two state variables, as in the above regional allocation of investment problem, this is no longer the case. The method obtained by Takayama (1967; 1985, pp. 627–38) can then be useful in analyzing the two-state variable problem. For a general discussion of this problem, see Pitchford (1977).

9.2 Various Cases

Theorem 9.1 is concerned with the case in which the time horizon (T) is fixed and the end-point $x(T)$ is *not* fixed *a priori* (it is determined from the solution of the problem). However, in many circumstances this may not be the case. For example, if the problem's goal is to minimize the time (T) to reach a certain target, then T is not specified *a priori;* it is, rather, obtained as a solution of the problem. Such a problem is called the **time optimal problem**. In general, we can formulate various problems depending, first, on whether or not the coordinates of the state vector $x(T)$ are fixed *a priori* and, second, on whether or not the "final time" (T) is fixed.

A few examples are now in order. In the problem of minimizing the time to fill a bathtub, the final state $x(T) = 100$ percent is fixed *a priori*, but the final time T is not specified; it is determined as a solution of the problem. In the problem of shooting a missile to intercept an airplane in a minimum amount of time, neither the final time T nor the final state $x(T)$ are specified *a priori*. They are determined as a part of the solution.

We now turn to a general consideration of such problems. First we discuss the case in which the terminal values of the state variables,

$x_i(T)$, $i = 1, 2, \ldots, n$, are fixed *a priori*. Next we consider the case in which the final time T is not fixed *a priori*.

(α) The Right-Hand End-Point $x(T)$ Specified

In this case, the transversality condition (8) is simply replaced by

$$x_i(T) = x_i^T,\ i = 1, 2, \ldots, n. \tag{12}$$

We lose n conditions by losing (8). Instead, we obtain n conditions by virtue of (12).[10]

(β) Final Time Open:

This is the case in which the "terminal time" T is not specified *a priori*. Since T is open, we have one additional degree of freedom in the system. Hence one additional equation is required, which is written as

$$H[x^*(T),\ u^*(T),\ T,\ p_\circ,\ p(T)] \equiv \sum_{i=0}^{n} p_i(T) f_i[x^*(T),\ u^*(T),\ T] = 0. \tag{13}$$

The system of differential equations, $\dot{x}_i = f[x(t),\ u(t),\ t]$, is said to be **autonomous**, if f does not depend on t explicitly, namely if it is written as

$$\dot{x} = f[x(t),\ u(t)];$$

otherwise it is called **nonautonomous**. For the autonomous system, (13) can be rewritten as

---

[10]In (12), *all* coordinates of the state vector $x(T)$ are fixed. Instead, if only some coordinates are fixed, i.e., if

$$x_i(T) = x_i^T,\ i = 1, 2, \ldots, n',\ n' < n, \tag{12'}$$

then we have

$$p_i(T) = c_i,\ i = n' + 1,\ n' + 2, \ldots, n. \tag{8'}$$

There are n equations in (12′) and (8′). These together with (2) [i.e., condition (iv) of theorem 9.1] provides $2n$ boundary conditions for $2n$ differential equations.

$$H[x^*(t),\ u^*(t),\ p_\circ,\ p(t)] \equiv \sum_{i=0}^{n} p_i(t) f_i[x_i^*(t),\ u^*(t)] = 0, \quad \text{for } all\, t. \qquad (14)$$

We are now ready to obtain variations of theorem 9.1. These are recorded in chapter 1 of Pontryagin et al. (1962). Note that they are essentially special cases of theorem 9.1 with the change of (5), (7), and (8) into (5″), (7″) and (8″) in section 9.1 and with the observation made at the beginning of section 9.2.

(A) Fixed Time with Fixed End Points Problem

We consider the following problem in which T and $x_i(T)$'s are fixed:

$$\underset{u(t)}{\text{Maximize}} \int_{t^\circ}^{T} f_\circ[x(t),\ u(t),\ t]dt$$

$$\text{Subject to } \dot{x}_i = f_i[x(t),\ u(t),\ t],\ i = 1,\ 2,\ \ldots,\ n,$$

$$\text{and } x_i(t^\circ) = x_i^\circ,\ x_i(T) = x_i^T,\ i = 1,\ 2,\ \ldots,\ n.$$

Theorem 9.2 (Pontryagin et al. 1962, pp. 67–68). In this problem, in order that $[x^*(t),\ u^*(t)]$ be optimal, it is necessary that there exist continuous functions $p_\circ,\ p_1(t),\ \ldots\ p_n(t)$, not vanishing simultaneously for each t, such that

(i) $x^*(t),\ u^*(t)$ and $p(t)$ solve the following Hamiltonian system,

$$\dot{x}_i^* = \frac{\partial H^*}{\partial p_i},\ \dot{p}_i = -\frac{\partial H^*}{\partial x_i},\ i = 1,\ 2,\ ,\ \ldots,\ n,$$

where

$$H[x(t),\ u(t),\ t,\ p_\circ,\ p(t)] \equiv p_\circ f_\circ[x(t),\ u(t),\ t] + \sum_{i=1}^{n} p_i(t) f_i[x(t),\ u(t),\ t];$$

(ii) $H[x^*(t),\ u^*(t),\ t,\ p_\circ,\ p(t)] \geqq [x^*(t),\ u(t),\ t,\ p_\circ,\ p(t)]$, for all $u(t) \in U$;

(iii) $p_\circ = \text{constant} \geqq 0$, for all t; and

(iv) $x_i(t^\circ) = \overset{\circ}{x}_i,\ x_i(T) = \overset{T}{x}_i,\ i = 1, 2, \ldots, n.$

As mentioned earlier, the phrase "not vanishing simultaneously" means that $[p_\circ(t), p_1(t), \ldots, p_n(t)]$ is a non-zero vector. Note that if we can show $p_\circ \neq 0$, then $p_\circ > 0$ by condition (iii), so that we can take $p_\circ = 1$ by normalization. In practical applications in economics, this is often the case. In much of the literature in economics, $p_\circ$ is thus often taken to be unity from the outset.

(B) Final Time Open with Fixed End-Point (Nonautonomous Case)

Consider the following problem:

$$\underset{u(t)}{\text{Maximize}} \int_{t^\circ}^{T} f_\circ[x(t), u(t), t]dt$$

$$\text{Subject to } \dot{x}_i = f_i[x(t), u(t), t],\ i = 1, 2, \ldots, n,$$

$$\text{and } x_i(t^\circ) = \overset{\circ}{x}_i,\ x_i(T) = \overset{T}{x}_i,\ i = 1, 2, \ldots, n.$$

Here, unlike the case (A), final time T is not specified *a priori*. For this case we have theorem 9.3.

Theorem 9.3 (Pontryagin et al. 1962, pp. 60–61). In this problem, in order that $[x^*(t), u^*(t)]$ be optimal, it is necessary that there exist continuous functions $p_\circ, p_1(t), \ldots, p_n(t)$, not vanishing simultaneously for each t, such that

(i) $x^*(t)$, $u^*(t)$ and $p(t)$ solve the following Hamiltonian system,

$$\dot{x}_i^* = \frac{\partial H^*}{\partial p_i},\ \dot{p}_i = -\frac{\partial H^*}{\partial x_i},\ i = 1, 2, \ldots, n,$$

where

$$H[x(t), u(t), t, p_\circ, p(t)] \equiv p_\circ f_\circ[x(t), u(t), t] + \sum_{i=1}^{n} p_i(t) f_i[x(t), u(t), t];$$

(ii) $H[x^*(t), u^*(t), t, p_\circ, p(t)] \geqq H[x^*(t), u(t), t, p_\circ, p(t)]$ for all $u(t) \in U$;

(iii) $H[x^*(T), u^*(T), T, p_\circ, p(T)] = 0$;

(iv) $p_\circ =$ constant $\geqq 0$, for all t; and

(v) $x_i(t^\circ) = x_i^\circ$, $x_i(T) = x_i^T$, $i = 1, 2, \ldots, n$.

Condition (iii) is added as a necessary condition because final time T is open.

(C) Time Optimal Problem (Nonautonomous Case)

Consider the following problem:

$$\underset{u(t)}{\text{Minimize}}\ T$$

$$\text{Subject to } \dot{x}_i = f_i[x(t), u(t), t],\ i = 1, 2, \ldots, n,$$

$$\text{and } x_i(t^\circ) = x_i^\circ,\ x_i(T) = x_i^T,\ i = 1, 2, \ldots, n.$$

Here the $x_i(t^\circ)$'s and the $x_i(T)$'s are both fixed but T is open.

The problem is called the **time optimal problem**, as it is concerned with minimizing the time for the transfer from a fixed point x_i° to another fixed point x_i^T satisfying a given set of differential equations, $\dot{x}_i = f_i[x(t), u(t), t]$, $i = 1, 2, \ldots, n$. Clearly this is a special case of the preceding problem (B) with $f_\circ[x(t), u(t), t] \equiv -1$ for all t. Hence, using theorem 9.3, we at once obtain theorem 9.4.

Theorem 9.4 (Pontryagin et al. 1962, p. 65). In this problem, in order that $[x^*(t), u^*(t)]$ be optimal, it is necessary that there exist continuous functions $p_1(t), \ldots, p_n(t)$, not vanishing simultaneously for each t, such that

(i) $x^*(t)$, $u^*(t)$ and $p(t)$ solve the Hamiltonian system,

$$\dot{x}_i^* = \frac{\partial H^*}{\partial p_i},\ \dot{p}_i = -\frac{\partial H^*}{\partial x_i},\ i = 1, 2, \ldots, n,$$

where

$$H[x(t), u(t), t, p(t)] \equiv \sum_{i=1}^{n} p_i(t) f_i[x(t), u(t), t];$$

(ii) $H[x^*(t), u^*(t), t, p(t)] \geqq H[x^*(t), u(t), t, p(t)]$, for all $u(t) \in U$;

(iii) $H[x^*(T), u^*(T), T, p(T)] \geqq 0$; and

(iv) $x_i(t^\circ) = x_i^\circ$, $x_i(T) = x_i^T$, $i = 1, 2, \ldots, n$.

REMARK: Condition (iii) follows from

$$p_\circ \geqq 0 \text{ and } -p_\circ + \sum_{i=1}^{n} p_i(T) f_i[x^*(T), u^*(T), T] = 0.$$

(D) Final Time Open with Fixed-End Points (Autonomous Case)

Consider the following problem:

$$(a) \quad \underset{u(t)}{\text{Maximize}} \int_{t^\circ}^{T} f_\circ[x(t), u(t)]dt$$

$$\text{Subject to } \dot{x}_i = f_i[x(t), u(t)],\ i = 1, 2, \ldots, n,$$

$$\text{and } x_i(t^\circ) = x_i^\circ,\ x_i(T) = x_i^T,\ i = 1, 2, \ldots, n.$$

Again T is not specified here. This is a special case of the problem considered for theorem 9.3. Owing to the problem condition's autonomous character, condition (iii) of theorem 9.3 is modified as

$$H[x^*(t), u^*(t), p(t)] = 0, \quad \text{for all } t,\ t^\circ \leqq t \leqq T. \tag{15}$$

The rest of theorem 9.3 holds as stated.

The time optimal problem for the autonomous case can be specified as:

$$(b) \quad \underset{u(t)}{\text{Minimize}}\ T$$

$$\text{Subject to } \dot{x}_i = f_i[x(t), u(t)],\ i = 1, 2, \ldots, n,$$

$$\text{and } x_i(t^\circ) = x_i^\circ,\ x_i(T) = x_i^T,\ i = 1, 2, \ldots, n.$$

This is a special case of the problem considered for theorem 9.4. Owing to the automomous character of the problem, condition (iii) of theorem 9.4 is modified as

$$H[x^*(t),\ u^*(t),\ p(t)] = \text{constant} \geqq 0,\ t^\circ \leqq t \leqq T. \tag{16}$$

Then we obtain theorem 9.5.

Theorem 9.5 (Pontryagin et al. 1962, pp. 19 and 20–21). The necessary conditions for $[x^*(t),\ u^*(t)]$ to be a solution of problem (D-*a*) are obtained by replacing condition (iii) of theorem 9.3 by condition (15), whereas the other conditions of theorem 9.3 hold as they are. The necessary conditions for $[x^*(t),\ u^*(t)]$ to be a solution of problem (D-*b*) are the same as those in theorem 9.4, except that condition (iii) is replaced by condition (16).

(E) Fixed Time with Variable Right-Hand End-Points Problem

We consider the following problem:

$$\underset{u(t)}{\text{Maximize}} \int_{t^\circ}^{T} f_\circ[x(t),\ u(t),\ t]dt$$

$$\text{Subject to } \dot{x}_i = f_i[x(t),\ u(t),\ t],\ i = 1,\ 2,\ \ldots,\ n,$$

$$\text{and } x_i(t^\circ) = \overset{\circ}{x_i},\ i = 1,\ 2,\ \ldots,\ n.$$

Here T is fixed but $x_i(T)$, $i = 1,\ 2,\ \ldots,\ n$, are open. Since $x_i(T)$'s are not fixed, we obtain the transversality condition, $p_i(T) = 0$, $i = 1,\ 2,\ \ldots,\ n$, instead. This problem is already discussed in connection with the target function (9).

Theorem 9.6 (Pontryagin et al. 1962, p. 69). In this problem it is necessary that there exist continous functions $p_1(t),\ p_2(t),\ \ldots,\ p_n(t^\circ)$, such that

(i) $x^*(t)$, $u^*(t)$ and $p(t)$ solve the following Hamiltonian system,

$$\dot{x}_i^* = \frac{\partial H^*}{\partial p_i},\ \dot{p}_i = -\frac{\partial H^*}{\partial x_i},\ i = 1,\ 2,\ \ldots,\ n,$$

where

$$H[x(t),\ u(t),\ t,\ p(t)] \equiv \sum_{i=1}^{n} p_i(t) f_i[x(t),\ u(t),\ t];$$

(ii) $H[x^*(t),\ u^*(t),\ t,\ p(t)] \geqq H[x^*(t),\ u(t),\ t,\ p(t)],$

for all $u(t) \in U$;

(iii) $p_i(T) = 0,\ i = 1,\ 2,\ \ldots,\ n$; and

(iv) $x_i(t^\circ) = \overset{\circ}{x}_i,\ i = 1,\ 2,\ \ldots,\ n.$

Theorems 9.1 through 9.6 are concerned with the necessary conditions for $[x^*(t), u^*(t)]$ to be optimal. If $f_\circ(x,\ u,\ t)$ and $f_i(x,\ u,\ t)$, $i = 1,\ 2,\ \ldots,\ n$, are all concave in x and u then these conditions are also sufficient for optimum (see Mangasarian 1966). In addition, if $f_\circ$ is strictly concave in x and u, the choice u and hence the optimal path is unique, i.e., we obtain theorem 9.7.

Theorem 9.7. If $f_\circ(x,\ u,\ t)$ and $f_i(x,\ u,\ t)$, $i = 1,\ 2,\ \ldots,\ n$, are all concave in x and u, then the set of necessary conditions stated in theorems 9.1 through 9.6 are also sufficient for optimum for their respective problems. In addition, if $f_\circ$ is strictly concave in x and u, then the optimal path is unique.

9.3 Two Illustrations

9.3.1 Calculus of Variations

Consider the integral:

$$J \equiv \int_a^b f[x(t),\ \dot{x}(t),\ t]dt,$$

where a and b are some constants, and where $x(t) = [x_1(t),\ \ldots x_n(t)]$. The classical calculus of variations problem is concerned with the problem of choosing $x(t)$ to maximize J subject to $x(a) = \alpha$ and $x(b) = \beta$. Letting $\dot{x} = u$, this question can be converted to the optimal control problem:

$$\underset{u(t)}{\text{Maximize}} \int_a^b f[x(t),\ u(t),\ t]dt$$

Subject to $\dot{x}_i = u_i$, $i = 1, 2, \ldots, n$, $x(a) = \alpha$, $x(b) = \beta$.

In this problem, both end points, $x(a)$ and $x(b)$, are fixed and final "time" T (which is equal to b) is fixed. Note, however, that there is no need to interpret t as time.

For this problem, we may apply theorem 9.2. Omitting (*) to denote the optimum for sake of simplicity, the set of necessary conditions for optimum for this problem can then be obtained as (18) through (21) below, where the Hamiltonian is defined by (17).

$$H = p_\circ f[x(t), u(t), t] + \sum_{i=1}^{n} p_i(t)u_i(t), \tag{17}$$

$$\dot{x}_i = \partial H/\partial p_i; \text{ i.e., } \dot{x}_i = u_i, \; i = 1, 2, \ldots, n, \tag{18}$$

$$\dot{p}_i = -\partial H/\partial x_i; \text{ i.e., } \dot{p}_i = -p_\circ(\partial f/\partial x_i), \; i = 1, 2, \ldots, n, \tag{19}$$

$$\partial H/\partial u_i = 0; \text{ i.e., } p_\circ \partial f/\partial u_i + p_i = 0, \; i = 1, 2, \ldots, n, \tag{20}$$

$$p_\circ = \text{ constant } \geqq 0. \tag{21}$$

Here we assume that control region $\overline{U}$ is an open set to obtain (20). This follows the assumption in the classical theory of calculus of variations.

We first show $p_\circ > 0$. To this end, suppose the contrary, $p_\circ = 0$. Then from (20), we have $p_i = 0$, $i = 1, 2, \ldots, n$. This contradicts that $p_\circ, p_1, \ldots, p_n$ cannot vanish simultaneously. Hence we must have, $p_\circ > 0$.

Letting $q_i \equiv p_i/p_\circ$, we then obtain, from (19) and (20),

$$\frac{\partial f}{\partial x_i} = -\dot{q}_i = \frac{d}{dt}\frac{\partial f}{\partial u_i}, \; i = 1, 2, \ldots, n.$$

Recalling $\dot{x}_i = u_i$, $i = 1, 2, \ldots, n$, we obtain

$$\frac{\partial f}{\partial x_i} = \frac{d}{dt}\frac{\partial f}{\partial \dot{x}_i}, \; i = 1, 2, \ldots, n. \tag{22}$$

This is the well-known formula in the classical theory of calculus of variations, and it is known as **Euler's equation.**[11]

---

[11] Modern optimal control theory is the outgrowth of the classical calculus of variations. Although the subject is old (some of such problems were solved by the ancient Greeks), it was launched as a coherent branch of mathematics by Euler in 1744.

Condition (22) with $x(a) = \alpha$ and $x(b) = \beta$ are necessary for optimum. Also, they are sufficient for optimum if $f(x, u, t)$ is concave in x and u. Thus we may obtain theorem 9.8.

Theorem 9.8 (*Euler's Equation*). In order that $x(t)$ maximizes the integral J defined above, subject to $x(a) = \alpha$ and $x(b) = \beta$, it is necessary that we have

$$\frac{\partial f}{\partial x_i} = \frac{d}{dt}\frac{\partial f}{\partial \dot{x}_i}, \; i = 1, 2, \ldots, n,$$

$x(a) = \alpha$, and $x(b) = \beta$. Furthermore, if $f(x, u, t)$ is concave in x and u, these necessary conditions are also sufficient for optimum.

REMARK: It is important to note that control region $\overline{U}$ is assumed to be an open set, which in turn allows an interior solution $\partial H/\partial u_i =$

About him, Simmons (1972, pp. 107–111) wrote with apparent admiration:

"Leonard Euler (1707–1783) was Switzerland's foremost scientist and one of the three greatest mathematicians of modern times (the other two being Gauss and Riemann). He was perhaps the most prolific author of all time in any field. The publication of his collected works was started in 1911, and it is estimated that more than 100 large volumes will ultimately be required for the completion of the project. His writings are models of relaxed clarity. He never condensed, and reveled in the rich abundance of ideas and the vast scope of his interests. The French physicist Arago ... remarked that 'He calculated without apparent effort, as men breathe, or as eagles sustain themselves in the wind.' He suffered total blindness during the last 17 years of his life; but ... he actually increased his already prodigious output of work.

Euler was a native of Basel and a student of Johann Bernoulli at the University, but he soon outstripped his teacher. His working life was spent as a member of the Academies of Science at Berlin and St. Petersburg. He was a man of broad culture, well versed in the classical languages and literatures ... many modern languages, physiology, medicine, botany, geography, and the entire body of physical science ...His personal life was as placid and uneventful as is possible for a man with 13 children.

Though he was not himself a teacher, Euler has had a deeper influence on the teaching of mathematics than any other man. This came about chiefly through his three great treatises: *Introductio in Analysin Infinitorum* (1748); *Institutiones Calculi Differentialis* (1755); and *Institutiones Calculi Integralis* (1768–1794). There is considerable truth in the old saying that all elementary and advanced calculus textbooks since 1748 are essentially copies of Euler or copies of copies of Euler. ... It was through his work that the symbols e, π, and i became common currency for all mathematicians, ... Among his other contributions to standard mathematical notations were sin x, cos x, the use of $f(x)$ for an unspecified function, and the use of $\sum$ for summation. ... The foundations of classical mechanics had been laid down by Newton, but Euler was the principal architect ...

Euler was the Shakespeare of mathematics—universal, richly detailed, and inexhaustible."

0, $i = 1, 2, \ldots, n$. In Pontryagin's maximum principle, $\overline{U}$, need not be an open set.

The simplest problem in the calculus of variations is probably the problem of finding the curves that join two fixed points on the plane with the minimum distance. Given the two points in figure 9.1, a curve joining A and B can be represented by $x(t)$ with $x(a) = \alpha$ and $x(b) = \beta$. Clearly, t does *not* represent "time" in this case.

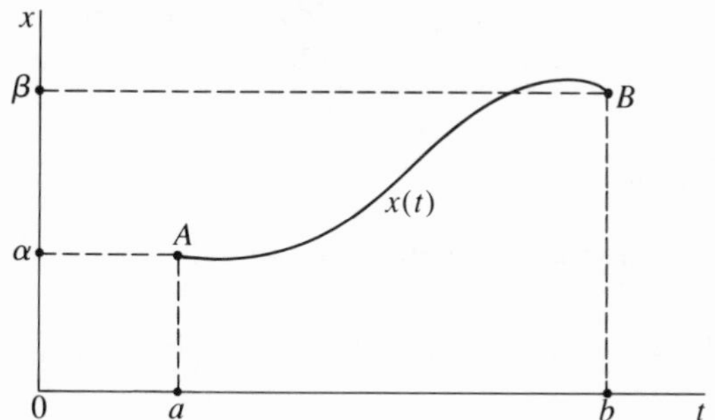

Figure 9.1: The minimum distance problem

Given an "arc" $x(t)$, the distance along each infinitesimal segment of $x(t)$ is given by

$$ds = \sqrt{(dt)^2 + (dx)^2} = \sqrt{1 + \dot{x}^2}\, dt.$$

Hence the distance between A and B along this arc can be computed as

$$J_D \equiv \int_a^b \sqrt{1 + \dot{x}^2}\, dt.$$

The problem then is finding a function ("arc") $x(t)$ so as to minimize J_D subject to $x(a) = \alpha$ and $x(b) = \beta$. The problem is called the **minimum distance problem**. The answer to this question is obviously the straight line joining A and B. This answer can be readily obtained without applying the calculus of variations technique. However, we can use this problem to illustrate the nature of such a technique.

To solve the minimum distance problem, let $f_D \equiv \sqrt{1 + \dot{x}^2}$. Then Euler's equation is written as

$$\frac{\partial f_D}{\partial x} = \frac{d}{dt}\left[\frac{\partial f_D}{\partial \dot{x}}\right] .$$

Since f_D contains no x, $\partial f_D/\partial x = 0$. Hence

$$\frac{\partial f_D}{\partial \dot{x}_2} = \frac{\dot{x}}{\sqrt{1 + \dot{x}^2}} = \text{constant}.$$

From this, we may obtain $\dot{x}(t) = c_1$ (constant), so that $x(t) = c_1 t + c_2$. Since $x(a) = \alpha$ and $x(b) = \beta$, we obtain

$$x(t) = \frac{\alpha - \beta}{a - b}t + \frac{a\beta - \alpha b}{a - b}.$$

This is the equation that denotes the desired straight line.

9.3.2 An Illustrative Problem by Pontryagin *et al.*

Following Pontryagin et al. (1962, pp. 22–26), we consider the time optimal problem:

$$\underset{u(t)}{\text{Minimize}} \;\; T$$

$$\text{Subject to } \dot{x} = y,\ \dot{y} = u,\ -1 \leqq u(t) \leqq 1,$$

$$\text{and } x(0) = x^{\circ},\ y(0) = y^{\circ},\ x(T) = 0,\ y(T) = 0, \quad (23)$$

where $(x, y) \in R^2$. We write the Hamiltonian for this problem as

$$H \equiv -p_o + p_1 y + p_2 u,$$

where p_o is a constant. Hence the Hamiltonian system can be written as

$$\dot{x}^* = \partial H^*/\partial p_1; \;\; \text{i.e.,} \dot{x}^* = y^*, \quad (24a)$$

$$\dot{y}^* = \partial H^*/\partial p_2; \;\; \text{i.e.,} \dot{y}^* = u^*, \quad (24b)$$

$$\dot{p}_1 = -\partial H^*/\partial x; \;\; \text{i.e.,} \dot{p}_1 = 0, \quad (25a)$$

$$\dot{p}_2 = -\partial H^*/\partial y; \ \text{i.e.,} \dot{p}_2 = -p_1. \tag{25b}$$

From (25), we may obtain

$$p_1 = c_1 \text{ and } p_2 = -c_1 t + c_2, \tag{26}$$

where c_1 and c_2 are some constants. The maximization of H yields

$$-p_0 + p_1 y^* + p_2 u^* \geqq -p_0 + p_1 y^* + p_2 u, \quad -1 \leqq u \leqq 1.$$

From this we obtain

$$u^*(t) = 1 \text{ if } p_2(t) > 0; \quad u^*(t) = -1 \text{ if } p_2(t) < 0.$$

For the rest of the analysis, we omit ($*$) for the sake of simplicity. For $u = 1$, we have $\dot{y} = 1$ from (24b), so that $y = t + s_2$. Then from $\dot{x} = y$, we obtain

$$x = \frac{1}{2}t^2 + s_2 t + s_1 = \frac{1}{2}(t + s_2)^2 + [s_1 - (s_2)^2/2], \text{ or}$$

$$x = \frac{1}{2}y^2 + s, \ s \equiv s_1 - (s_2)^2/2,$$

where s_1 and s_2 are constants of integration. For $u = -1$, we have $\dot{y} = -1$ from (24b), so that $y = -t + s_2'$. Then from $\dot{x} = y$, we may obtain

$$x = -\frac{1}{2}t^2 + s_2' t + s_1' = -\frac{1}{2}(-t + s_2')^2 + [s_1' + (s_2')^2/2], \text{ or}$$

$$x = -\frac{1}{2}y^2 + s', \ s' \equiv s_1' + (s_2')^2/2.$$

Thus we have

$$x = \frac{1}{2}y^2 + s, \ y = t + s_2, \ \text{ for } u = 1. \tag{27a}$$

$$x = -\frac{1}{2}y^2 + s', \ y = -t + s_2', \ \text{ for } u = -1. \tag{27b}$$

The equation $x = y^2/2 + s$ defines a family of parabolas.

From $\dot{x} = y$, x increases over time for $y > 0$ and x decreases over time for $y < 0$. Hence, during the time period for $u(t) = 1$, the phase points move clockwise along a parabola, $x = y^2/2 + s$, for some s.

Similarly, we may conclude that during the time period for $u(t) = -1$, the phase point also moves clockwise along a parabola, $x = -y^2/2 + s'$, for some s'.

The optimal trajectory is illustrated by figure 9.2 (which is borrowed from Pontryagin et al. 1962, p. 26). In figure 9.2, AO is the arc of parabola $x = y^2/2$ situated in the lower half-plane, and BO is the arc of the parabola $x = -y^2/2$ situated in the upper half-plane. If the initial point (x°, y°) is above the curve AOB, $u = -1$ until the phase point hits the arc AO, then $u = 1$ for the rest of time until it reaches the specified terminal point $[x(T) = 0$ and $y(T) = 0]$, the origin. Similarly if the initial point (x°, y°) is below the curve AOB, $u = 1$ initially until the phase point hits the arc BO, then $u = -1$ until it reaches the origin.

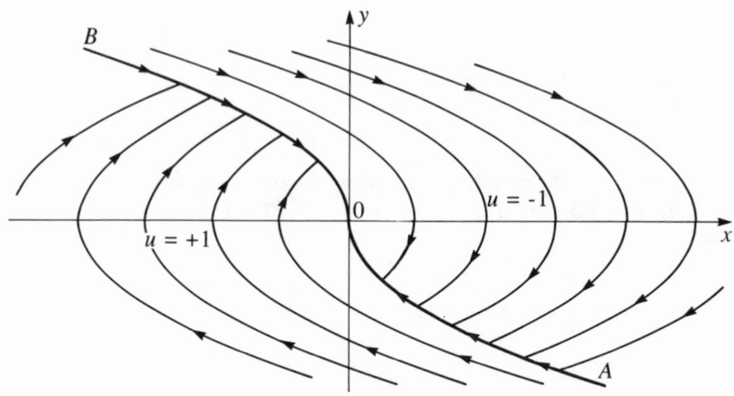

Figure 9.2: The optimal trajectory for (23)

Suppose that the initial point (x°, y°) is given by $x^\circ = 1$ and $y^\circ = 2$. Then initially, we have $u = -1$. Then using (27b) with $x^\circ = 1$ and $y^\circ = 2$, we may obtain, $s' = 3$ and $s'_2 = 2$, or

$$x = -y^2/2 + 3, \ y = -t + 2.$$

The phase point moves under the influence of $u = -1$, until it reaches the arc AO, or $x = y^2/2$. Then the value of u switches over and becomes equal to one right up to the instant of reaching the specified terminal point, the origin. So we have,

$$u(t) = -1,\ 0 \leqq t < t';\ u(t) = 1,\ t' \leqq t \leqq T,$$

where t' denotes the time at which the switch of u takes place.[12] The value of t' is obtained as $t' = 2 + \sqrt{3}$ from $y(t') = -\sqrt{3} = -t' + 2$. For $t' \leqq t \leqq T$, the phase point moves along the arc AO, $x = y^2/2$ under the influence of $u = 1$. Since $u = 1$, we have $y = t + s_2$ by (27a), so that $y(t') = -\sqrt{3} = t' + s_2 = (2 + \sqrt{3}) + s_2$. From this we obtain, $s_2 = -2 - 2\sqrt{3}$, or $y(t) = t - (2 + 2\sqrt{3})$ along arc AO from point $P = (3/2, -\sqrt{3})$ to the origin. Since $y(T) = 0 = T - (2 + 2\sqrt{3})$, $T = 2 + 2\sqrt{3}$, so that $T - t' = (2 + 2\sqrt{3}) - (2 + \sqrt{3}) = \sqrt{3}$. Namely, the required time for the phase point to move from point P to the origin is $\sqrt{3}$. The total time for the phase point to move from the initial point $(x^\circ, y^\circ) = (1, 2)$, to point P, and to the origin is given by, $t' + (T - t') = (2 + \sqrt{3}) + \sqrt{3} = 2 + 2\sqrt{3}$.

9.4 Optimal Growth Problem

In this section, we consider the optimal growth problem that has been discussed rather heavily in the 1950s and in the 1960s. This problem was solved in a more or less satisfactory way by Koopmans (1965) and Cass (1965). Here we discuss the problem to illustrate the optimal control technique.

Consider the neoclassical growth model given by

$$Y_t = C_t + I_t, \tag{28a}$$

$$Y_t = F(N_t, K_t), \tag{28b}$$

$$\dot{K}_t = I_t, \tag{28c}$$

$$\dot{N}_t/N_t = n, \tag{28d}$$

where Y_t = output, C_t = consumption, I_t = investment, F = production function, N_t = labor, K_t = capital, and n = the rate of population

[12] The coordinates of the switching point can be obtained as follows. Setting $-y^2/2 + 3 = x = y^2/2$, we obtain $y = -\sqrt{3}$. From $x = y^2/2$, we then have $x = 3/2$.

growth (assumed to be a constant). The subscript t denotes time. The depreciation of capital is assumed away to ease the exposition.[13]

Assume that F is homogeneous of degree one (constant returns to scale), so that we have

$$y_t = f(k_t), \text{ where } y_t \equiv Y_t/N_t \text{ and } k_t \equiv K_t/N_t.$$

We again impose the following usual assumptions:[14]

$$f'(k) > 0,\ f''(k) < 0 \text{ for all } k \geqq 0, \text{ and} \tag{29a}$$

$$f(0) = 0,\ f'(0) = \infty,\ f'(\infty) = 0. \tag{29b}$$

Under constant returns to scale, the four equations in (28) are reduced to:

$$\dot{k}_t = f(k_t) - nk_t - c_t, \tag{30}$$

where $c_t \equiv C_t/N_t$. As mentioned in chapter 6, (30) is the basic equation of the neoclassical aggregate growth model. Equation (30) specifies the **feasibility condition** for the present model. A path which satisfies (30) is called a **feasible path**. If, in addition, it satisfies the arbitrarily prescribed initial value k_o, it is called the **attainable path**. Note that (29) ensures the existence of a unique $\bar{k} > 0$ such that

$$f(\bar{k}) = n\bar{k}. \tag{31}$$

If we specify the demand behavior by

$$c_t = (1 - s)y_t,\ 0 < s < 1$$

(where s is a constant), then we may obtain, from (30),

$$\dot{k}_t = sf(k_t) - nk_t.$$

Then we can show that every attainable path converges to k_S, where k_S is uniquely defined by

$$sf(k_S) = nk_S, \text{ and } k_S > 0.$$

---

[13] Depreciation can be incorporated as follows. Let δ be the rate of depreciation and rewrite (28c) as $\dot{K}_t = I_t - \delta K_t$. This does not alter the present analysis in any essential way.

[14] Recall the discussion of the Solow-Swan growth model in chapter 6. In particular, we may note that $f' = \partial F/\partial K$ (the marginal product of capital), and that $f'' < 0$ if and only if $\partial^2 F/\partial N^2 < 0$ and $\partial^2 F/\partial K^2 < 0$.

Then from (30), we can show that given an arbitrarily specified initial value of $k_o > 0$, k_t that satisfies (30) approaches k_S as $t \to \infty$. This is the well-known result by Solow and Swan discussed in chapter 6.

The optimal growth problem asks a different question. Instead of specifying demand behavior, we ask: What is the necessary amount of consumption at each instant of time in order to maximize a certain target while satisfying feasibility condition (30) and an arbitrarily given initial value k_o? Such a problem was first asked and solved by Ramsey (1928). After a hiatus, this topic was heavily discussed in the 1950s and 1960s, producing important results by Cass (1965) and Koopmans (1965). Further efforts have been made and many more important results have been obtained.[15]

The target function considered by Cass (1965), Koopmans (1965), and others is

$$I \equiv \int_0^\infty u(c_t)e^{-\rho t}dt, \tag{32}$$

where u is a utility function associated with the "representative" individual in the society and ρ is the time discount factor. It is assumed that ρ is a positive constant.[16] We assume u is defined on $(0, \infty)$, is twice continuously differentiable, and

$$u'(c_t) > 0, \; u''(c_t) < 0, \quad \text{for all } c_t, \quad \text{and} \lim_{c_t \to 0} u'(c_t) = -\infty.$$

The last assumption represents "the necessity of avoiding extremely low levels of consumption per capita" (Cass 1965, p. 234).

Thus our problem is now to find the time path c_t to maximize the integral I defined in (32) subject to (30), $k_t \geqq 0$, $c_t \geqq 0$, and an arbitrarily given $k_o > 0$.

---

[15] For some of the literature from the 1950s and 1960s, see Takayama (1985, pp. 466–68). There are developments of this topic and related fields, notably "turnpike theory," often summarized under the name of "capital theory." For a recent survey of this topic, see McKenzie (1986), where he uses discrete time models. With continuous time models, important results are obtained, for example, in Benveniste and Scheinkman (1982), Araujo and Scheinkman (1983), and Becker, Boyd, and Sung (1989).

[16] This type of objective has been criticized by various authors "on the grounds that the pure rate of time preference should not be independent of the size and shape of the consumption profile." When preferences are time-additive as in the case of (32), this is "a direct consequence of the strong separability property by which the marginal rate of substitution for consumption at any two dates is independent of the consumption stream" (Becker, Boyd, and Sung 1989). Hicks (1965) gives an extended critique along these lines. We assume the target function in the form of (32) with a constant ρ only for the sake of simplicity.

The question thus formulated, however, sets an important problem. That is, how can we guarantee that I converges? If, for feasible paths with a prescribed $k_o > 0$, the integral does not converge (say, goes to ∞), this formulation becomes meaningless. The simplest way out of this difficulty is to assume that the utility function is bounded from above; due to satiation,[17] that is,

$$u(c_t) < \overline{u}, \quad \text{for all } c_t.$$

Then note that

$$I \equiv \int_0^\infty u(c_t)e^{-\rho t}dt \leqq \overline{u}/\rho.$$

With $k_o > 0$, it is possible to keep a positive level of consumption c_t which satisfies feasibility condition (30) for all t, so that I does not diverge away to $-\infty$.

We now turn to solving the maximization problem posed above. Note that k_t is the state variable and c_t is the control variable. Since it would be awkward to specify the value of $\lim k_t$ for $t \to \infty$ (in short, k_∞) in this problem, k_∞ is not a fixed *a priori*, and the relevant theorem would be a modification of theorem 9.6 that incorporates $T \to \infty$. Define the Hamiltonian by

$$H \equiv u(c_t)e^{-\rho t} + p_t[f(k_t) - nk_t - c_t],$$

where p_t is the (Pontryagin) multiplier. Then the following conditions are necessary for (k_t^*, c_t^*) to be optimal.

(i) (k_t^*, c_t^*) solve the following Hamiltonian system:

$$\dot{k}_t^* = \partial H^*/\partial p_t; \text{ that is, } \dot{k}_t^* = f(k_t^*) - nk_t^* - c_t^*, \tag{33a}$$

$$\dot{p}_t = -\partial H^*/\partial k_t; \text{ that is, } \dot{p}_t = -p_t[f'(k_t^*) - n]. \tag{33b}$$

[17] Actually, with some effort, this assumption can be weakened considerably. For this, recall $\overline{k}$ defined in (31). If $k_o > \overline{k}$, then from (30) $\dot{k}_t < 0$ for all t so as to maintain $c_t > 0$. Thus, $k_t < k_o$ for all t so that $f(k_t) < f(k_o)$ for all t. If $k_o \leqq \overline{k}$, we can show that for any attainable path, $k_t \leqq \overline{k}$ for all $t \geqq 0$ (by setting $c_t^* = 0$ for all t in (33a), which is called the **path of pure accumulation**). From these we can show that c_t, and hence $u(c_t)$, along any attainable path are bounded from above. If capital cannot be "eaten up" and current consumption should come from current output, this assertion can be obtained at once. We can show that this assertion can also be obtained without such an assumption. In the analysis in the text, we allow the possibility that capital is eaten up.

(ii) H is maximized with respect to $c_t \geqq 0$, that is,

$$H(k_t^*,\ c_t^*,\ t,\ p_t) \geqq H(k_t^*,\ c_t,\ t,\ p_t),$$

$$\text{for all } c_t \geqq 0 \text{ (for each } t\text{)},$$

which in turn requires

$$\partial H^*/\partial c_t \leqq 0 \ \text{ and } \ (\partial H^*/\partial c_t)c_t^* = 0, \ \text{ for each } t. \tag{34}$$

(iii) The transversality condition holds

$$\lim_{t\to\infty} p_t\, k_t^* = 0, \tag{35}$$

which replaces the following condition

$$\lim_{t\to\infty} p_t = 0. \tag{35$'$}$$

Although (35′) may look like a natural extension of $p_T = 0$ in theorem 9.6 for $T \to \infty$, it is known that (35′) does not hold in general and it should be replaced by (35).[18]

Conditions (33), (34), and (35) are also sufficient for $(k_t^*,\ c_t^*)$ to be optimal, since $u(t)$ and $[f(k_t) - nk_t - c_t]$ are concave in k_t and c_t.

Observe from (34),

$$\partial H^*/\partial c_t = u'(c_t^*)e^{-\rho t} - p_t \leqq 0 \ \text{ for all } t.$$

Hence if $c_t^* = 0$ for some t, then p_t is unbounded as $u'(0) = -\infty$. Since the multiplier must be bounded, this implies $c_t^* > 0$ for all t (an interior solution). Hence (34) is simplified to

$$\partial H^*/\partial c_t = 0, \ \text{ that is, } \ u'(c_t^*)e^{-\rho t} = p_t. \tag{36}$$

This equation, among others, clarifies the economic meaning of Pontryagin's multiplier (p_t) in the present context. Namely, p_t signifies the present value of the marginal (instantaneous) utility of consumption at time t. The magnitude of the loss of utility due to the sacrifice of one unit of consumption (which is then devoted to the accumulation of physical assets) at time t is measured by $u'(c_t)$, and hence its present value

[18] The transversality condition "at infinity" is a much debated question. See, for example, Arrow (1968a), Benveniste and Scheinkman (1982), Araujo and Scheinkman (1983), and Becker and Boyd (1988). The latter three analyzed this problem rigorously in a general framework.

is equal to $u'(c_t)e^{-\rho t}$. Thus, (36) implies that p_t signifies the "opportunity cost" (or the "shadow price") of accumulation. Note also that (36) implies $p_t > 0$ for all t as $u' > 0$ for all c_t.

The maximization of H with respect to c_t can be spelled out as

$$u(c_t^*)e^{-\rho t} + p_t[f(k_t^*) - nk_t^* - c_t^*] \geqq u(c_t)e^{-\rho t} + p_t[f(k_t^*) - nk_t^* - c_t],$$

for all $c_t \geqq 0$ (for each t). From this, we at once obtain, for each t,

$$[u(c_t^*) - u(c_t)]e^{-\rho t} \geqq p_t(c_t^* - c_t), \quad \text{for all } c_t \geqq 0.$$

This means that, for each t,

$$u(c_t^*) - u(c_t) \geqq 0, \quad \text{for all } c_t \geqq 0 \text{ such that } p_t c_t \leqq p_t c_t^*, \tag{37}$$

and

$$p_t c_t \leqq p_t c_t^*, \quad \text{for all } c_t \geqq 0 \text{ such that } u(c_t) \geqq u(c_t^*). \tag{38}$$

Relation (37) says that c_t^* maximizes utility u at each instant of time over those c_t's whose values do not exceed the value of the optimal consumption c_t^*. Thus (37) signifies the maximization of utility subject to the "budget condition." Relation (38) says that for the optimal consumption c_t^*, the consumption expenditure is minimized at each instant of time over those c_t's that would yield the level of utility that is higher than or equal to the one obtained from c_t^*. Relation (38) thus signifies the minimization of expenditures subject to utility constraint.

To ease notation, we drop the asterisk ($*$) that is used to denote the optimal path. Then (33a), (33b), (35) and (36) can be rewritten as

$$\dot{k}_t = f(k_t) - nk_t - c_t \tag{33'a}$$

$$\dot{p}_t = -p_t[f'(k_t) - n], \tag{33'b}$$

$$\lim_{t\to\infty} p_t k_t = 0, \text{ and} \tag{35''}$$

$$u'(c_t)e^{-\rho t} = p_t. \tag{36'}$$

Define q_t by

$$q_t \equiv p_t e^{\rho t}, \quad \text{so that } p_t = q_t e^{-\rho t}. \tag{39}$$

Using this, (36) can be rewritten as

$$u'(c_t) = q_t. \tag{40}$$

Thus, q_t signifies the current value of the marginal utility of consumption at time t, or the current opportunity cost of accumulation.[19] Solving (40) for c_t, we may obtain

$$c_t = c(q_t), \quad \text{where} \quad c' = 1/u'' < 0. \tag{41}$$

Using (33′a) and (41), we may define the function ϕ by

$$\dot{k}_t = \phi(k_t, q_t) \equiv f(k_t) - nk_t - c(q_t). \tag{42}$$

Also, from (39), we may observe

$$\dot{p}_t = \dot{q}_t e^{-\rho t} - \rho q_t e^{-\rho t} = (\dot{q}_t - \rho q_t)e^{-\rho t}, \quad \text{or}$$

$$\dot{p}_t/p_t = (\dot{q}_t/q_t) - \rho.$$

Hence we may rewrite (33′b) as

$$\dot{q}_t = -q_t[f'(k_t) - (n + \rho)] \equiv \psi(k_t, q_t). \tag{43}$$

In terms of q_t, the transversality condition (35″) may be rewritten as

$$\lim_{t\to\infty} q_t e^{-\rho t} k_t = 0. \tag{44}$$

Two differential equations (42) and (43) with two boundary conditions, (44) and a given $k_\circ$, completely specify the trajectory of (k_t, q_t). The steady state values of k and q (denoted by $\hat{k}$ and $\hat{q}$) are defined by

$$\phi(\hat{k}, \hat{q}) = 0 \quad \text{and} \quad \psi(\hat{k}, \hat{q}) = 0.$$

Since $f'' < 0$ for all k, the value of $\hat{k} > 0$ is uniquely determined by

$$f'(\hat{k}) = n + \rho. \tag{45}$$

---

[19] Equation (36′) or (40) is often referred to as the **Keynes-Ramsey rule** or the **Ramsey-Cass-Koopmans rule**. See Ramsey (1928, p. 7), Koopmans (1965), and Cass (1965).

Given $\hat{k}$, the steady state value of real per capita consumption ($\hat{c}$) is uniquely determined by

$$\hat{c} = f(\hat{k}) - n\hat{k},$$

by (33′a). This, in turn, uniquely determines $\hat{q}$ by (40). The path ($\hat{k}$, $\hat{c}$) is called the **modified golden rule path**.

For the dynamic system (42) and (43), we may compute

$$\phi_k(\equiv \partial\phi/\partial k_t) = f'(k_t) - n, \ \phi_q(\equiv \partial\phi/\partial q_t) = -c'(q_t), \tag{46a}$$

$$\begin{aligned}\psi_k(\equiv \partial\psi/\partial k_t) &= -q_t f''(k_t), \ \psi_q(\equiv \partial\psi/\partial q_t) \\ &= -[f'(k_t) - (n + \rho)].\end{aligned} \tag{46b}$$

The Jacobian determinant evaluated at the steady state ($\hat{k}$, $\hat{q}$) may then be obtained as

$$\hat{J} \equiv \hat{\phi}_k\hat{\psi}_q - \hat{\psi}_k\hat{\phi}_q = -\hat{\psi}_k\hat{\phi}_q = -\hat{q}f''(\hat{k})c'(\hat{q}) < 0.$$

From $\hat{J} < 0$, we may conclude that the steady state is a saddle point (see theorems 7.4 and 7.6). We now study the dynamic path of ($\hat{k}_t$, $\hat{q}_t$) in terms of the familiar phase diagram technique. First note that the value of k_t for which $\dot{q}_t = 0$ (or $\psi = 0$) is constant ($= \hat{k}$) by (43) regardless of the value of q_t. Also, since $\hat{\psi}_k = -\hat{q}f''(\hat{k}) > 0$ we may conclude that $\dot{q}_t > 0$ (resp. $\dot{q}_t < 0$) to the right (resp. left) of the ($\dot{q}_t = 0$)-line in the (k_t, q_t)-plane, where k_t is measured on the horizontal axis. This is illustrated in figure 9.3.[20]

The shape of the ($\dot{k}_t = 0$)-curve may be obtained from (42) as

$$\left.\frac{dq_t}{dk_t}\right|_{\dot{k}_t=0} = -\frac{\psi_k}{\psi_q} = \frac{f' - n}{c'}. \tag{47}$$

Let k^* be defined by

$$f'(k^*) = n. \tag{48}$$

The value of k^* is unique and $\hat{k} < k^*$, since $f'' < 0$. Let c^* be defined by

$$c^* \equiv f(k^*) - nk^*. \tag{49}$$

[20] Here the reader is asked to disregard the $\beta\beta$-curve (the dotted curve) and $\tilde{k}$. These concepts will be discussed later.

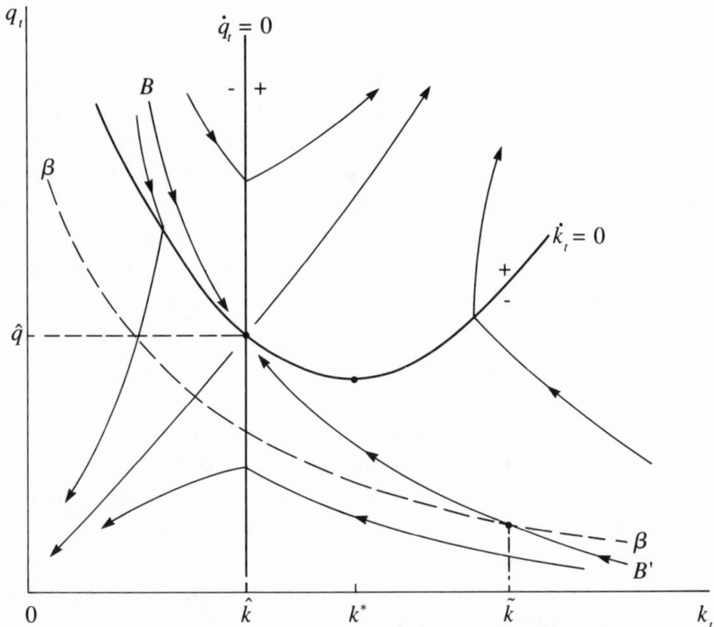

Figure 9.3: The dynamic behavior of $(k_t,\ q_t)$

The path $(k^*,\ c^*)$ is the familiar golden rule path.[21] Also, by the definition of k^* and $f'' < 0$, we have

$$f'(k_t) \gtrless n \text{ according to whether } k_t \lesseqgtr k^*. \tag{50}$$

[21] Consider a set of feasible paths for which k = constant for all t. Setting $\dot{k}_t = 0$ in (30), we obtain

(*) $\qquad c = f(k) - nk,$

where c is constant as k is constant. The path $(k,\ c)$ that satisfies (*) is called a **golden-age path** or a **balanced growth path**. Along such a path, N_t, K_t, C_t, Y_t, and I_t all grow at the same rate (n). A golden-age path that maximizes per capita consumption for each t is called the **golden rule path**. The maximization of $c = f(k) - n$ with respect to k at once yields (48), which states that the marginal product of capital is equal to the rate of population growth. This result on the golden rule path was obtained independently by various economists in different countries during 1961 and 1962. For specific references, see Takayama (1985, pp. 440–444).

Hence, using (47), (50), and $c' < 0$, we may conclude

$$\left.\frac{dq_t}{dk_t}\right|_{\dot{k}=0} \lesseqgtr 0 \text{ according to whether } k_t \lesseqgtr k^*. \tag{51}$$

Thus the $(\dot{k}_t = 0)$-curve is downward sloping for $k_t < k^*$, and it is upward sloping for $k_t > k^*$. This is also illustrated in figure 9.3. Also, from (46a), we may conclude that $\dot{k}_t > 0$ (resp. $\dot{k}_t < 0$) above (resp. below) the $(\dot{k}_t = 0)$-curve, as is illustrated in figure 9.3. The saddle-like behavior of (k_t, q_t) is also illustrated in figure 9.3.

Among infinitely many paths which satisfy (42) and (43), the ones which satisfy tranversality condition (44) and the prescribed initial value of the capital-labor ratio (k_o) are the optimal paths. It would be easy to see that the stable branches of the saddle-like paths (indicated by B and B' in fig. 9.3) satisfy these conditions. If $k_o < \hat{k}$, the optimal path is indicated by the B-curve, whereas if $k_o > \hat{k}$, the optimal path is indicated by the B'-curve. From the uniqueness of the optimal path implied by the strict concavity of function u, these are the only optimal paths. Note that along curves B and B' we always have $k_t > 0$ (as well as $q_t > 0$). The constraint $k_t \geqq 0$ imposed in the original maximization problem is automatically satisfied.

In summary, we may obtain proposition 9.1 along the line of results obtained by Ramsey (1928), Koopmans (1965), and Cass (1965).[22]

---

[22]Since the days when the optimal growth problem for an aggregative one-sector model was enthusiastically studied in the profession in the early 1960s, there has been an interest in the two-sector version of the optimal growth problem. Here, it may be worthwhile to sketch the gist of development in this problem. The interest in the two-sector formulation stems from the fact that two-sector models reveal certain fundamental issues concealed in the one-sector formulation (as in the case of two-sector versions of the Solow-Swan model). The pioneering study of the two-sector optimal growth problem is due to Srinivasan (1962, 1964); he assumed the capital intensity condition that the capital-labor ratio of the consumption good sector (k_C) is always greater than that of the investment good sector (k_I). Subsequently, Uzawa (1964) attempted to establish the Srinivasan theorem without such an assumption; he tried to prove the theorem for the two polar cases of $k_C > k_I$ and $k_I > k_C$ separately. In his fundamental paper (1970), Haque found Uzawa's analysis faulty, and wrote "we have noticed errors in his reasoning for each case" (p. 377). He continued, "The error in the case $k_C > k_I$ ... is immaterial since Srinivasan has dealt with this correctly, but the error in the case $k_I > k_C$ is serious." Uzawa misspecified the direction of motion of the demand and supply price of capital, which, subsequently, lead to an incorrect construction of the optimal path. In his paper, Haque first solved the problem considered by Srinivasan *without* assuming any capital intensity condition, and then likewise solved the problem considered by Uzawa. Haque solved the problem in full generality. (Haque's paper is not just comments on Uzawa's paper, but it resolves some fundamental issues). More recently, Uzawa (1989, pp. 522–60) ex-

Proposition 9.1. Given an arbitrary initial value $k_o > 0$, an optimal feasible path is unique and it converges to $(\hat{k}, \hat{q})$ monotonically. The optimal path is obtained as the stable branch of saddle-like paths, as illustrated in figure 9.3.

Proposition 9.1 can also be obtained in terms of a different phase diagram. For this purpose, we first observe, from (40):

$$\dot{q}_t = u'' \dot{c}_t \text{ so that } \dot{q}_t/q_t = u''\dot{c}_t/u'.$$

Then, using (43), we may obtain

$$\dot{c}_t = -(u'/u'') [f'(k_t) - (n + \rho)]. \tag{52}$$

This equation and (33a) constitute the dynamic system that specifies the time path of (k_t, c_t). By a routine exercise, the phase diagram for this system can be constructed, and it is illustrated in figure 9.4.[23]

Again the steady state is a saddle point, and the stable branches, B and B', of saddle-like paths are the unique optimal path. Figure 9.4 can be considered an alternative illustration of the optimal path, where the time paths of (k_t, c_t), instead of (k_t, q_t), are illustrated. Note that transversality condition (44) can be rewritten as

$$\lim_{t\to\infty} u'(c_t)e^{-\rho t}k_t = 0 \tag{44'}$$

by using (36). It is clear that the optimal path (k_t, q_t) as depicted by

---

posited the two-sector optimal growth model, in which he strangely ignored Hacque's work completely. Srinivasan, Uzawa, and Haque all assumed a linear objective function. The two-sector model under a nonlinear objective function was considered by Cass (in his unpublished Ph.D. dissertation at Stanford, 1965), where he, like Srinivasan, focused his attention on the case in which the consumption good sector is always more capital intensive than the investment good sector ($k_C > k_I$). A more comprehensive study considering both extreme cases ($k_C > k_I$ and $k_I > k_C$) was attempted by Hadley and Kemp (1971), but it unfortunately contained some serious errors. Drabicki and Takayama (1975) resolved the errors by Hadley and Kemp, and completely solved the problem under the nonlinear objective function. Furthermore, Drabicki and Takayama solved the two-sector optimal growth problem with *any capital intensity condition*. In contrast to this, all the previous authors writing on this problem considered only one or two of the polar cases of factor intensity assumption, and thus ignored the problem of factor intensity reversals altogether. What is more, Drabicki and Takayama did not confine themselves to the usual factor intensity reversals, but rather they allowed for identical capital intensities for *intervals* of the wage-rent ratio.

[23]Here the reader is again asked to disregard the dotted curve and $\tilde{k}$. These concepts will be discussed later.

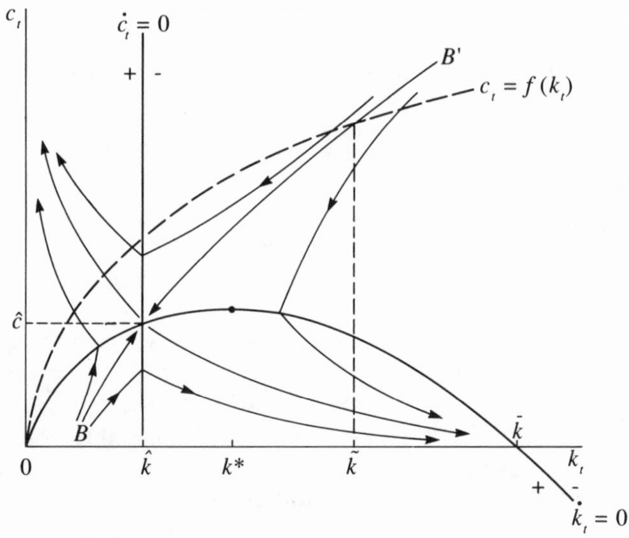

Figure 9.4: An alternative phase diagram for the optimal growth problem

the stable branch BB' in figure 9.4 satisfies this condition. Note also that $k_t \geqq 0$ along such a path.

REMARK: The discussion of the optimal growth problem by Ramsey (1928) rejects a positive discount rate ρ, as it appears in (32), by arguing that it is "unethical" to discount the utility of our descendants compared to the utility of ourselves. If $\rho = 0$, the integral defined in (32) does not necessarily converge. Instead of (32), Ramsey (1928) considered the integral in the form of

$$I_R \equiv \int_0^\infty [u(c_t) - \hat{u}]dt, \tag{32'}$$

where $\hat{u}$ is some reference path. Identifying $\hat{u}$ as $\hat{u} \equiv u(\hat{c})$, we may consider the problem of maximizing I_R subject to feasibility condition (30), $c_t \geqq 0$, $k_t \geqq 0$, and a given initial point condition $k_\circ$. The analysis of this problem would essentially be the same as above. We may then show that, given an arbitrary initial value of $k_\circ > 0$, the optimal path is unique and it converges to $\hat{k}$ monotonically. The optimal path may again be illustrated by the stable branch of saddle-like paths in figure 9.3 or in figure 9.4. Along such an optimal path, the integral I_R is convergent. Since $\rho = 0$, $\hat{k} = k^*$, that is, the modified golden rule path is equal to the golden rule path.

This analysis of the optimal growth path implicitly assumes that the current stock of capital (k_t) can be decumulated ("eaten up") at any desired rate. On the other hand, it may, in a sense, be more plausible to assume that investment, once in physical form, cannot be converted into consumer goods. Hence the economy cannot "eat up" the capital accumulated in the past.[24] Then the current consumption (c_t) comes only from the current output, $f(k_t)$. Mathematically, this amounts to imposing the condition[25]

$$c_t \leqq f(k_t). \tag{53}$$

The locus of (k_t, c_t) in which $c_t = f(k_t)$ is depicted as a dotted curve in figure 9.4. We may call such a locus the **boundary curve**.

In order to satisfy condition (53), the optimal path cannot lie above the boundary curve. Since along the ($\dot{k} = 0$)-curve we have

$$c_t = f(k_t) - nk_t,$$

and since along the boundary curve we have

$$c_t = f(k_t),$$

it is evident that the boundary curve must lie above the $\dot{k} = 0$ curve (as illustrated in fig. 9.4). Let $\tilde{k}$ signify the value of the capital-labor ratio determined by the intersection of the boundary curve and the stable branch, BB', of the saddle-like path. If the initial capital-labor ratio ($k_\circ$) does not exceed $\tilde{k}$, the optimal path would be the same as the one

---

[24]Such an assumption is called the **irreversibility of investment** by Arrow (1968b), where he analyzed the optimal growth problem with such a restriction.

[25]Let C_t and Y_t, respectively, denote the aggregate consumption and the aggregate output. Then, we may write the "feasibility condition" as

$$C_t + \dot{K}_t = Y_t.$$

The requirement, $\dot{K}_t \geqq 0$, then amounts to specifying

$$C_t \leqq Y_t,$$

from which (53) follows at once.

without (53). On the other hand, if $k_o > \tilde{k}$, k_t decreases over time *along the boundary curve*, so that c_t does not exceed $f(k_t)$, and after the point at which k_t reaches $\tilde{k}$, the optimal k_t moves along the BB'-curve toward $\hat{k}$.

This notion of the boundary curve can also be introduced in a (k_t, q_t) phase diagram such as figure 9.3. To see this, rewrite condition (53) as

$$\beta(k_t, q_t) \equiv f(k_t) - c(q_t) \geqq 0 \tag{54}$$

by using $c_t = c(q_t)$. The **boundary curve** is now defined as the locus of (k_t, q_t) such that $\beta(k_t, q_t) = 0$, and it is illustrated by the dotted curve $\beta\beta$ in figure 9.3. Since we have

$$\left.\frac{dq_t}{dk_t}\right|_{\beta=0} = f'/c' < 0 \tag{55}$$

the boundary curve is negatively sloped. Since $f' > 0$, (55) is satisfied in the region to the right of the boundary curve. Let $\tilde{k}$ (in fig. 9.3) signify the value of the capital-labor ratio determined by the intersection of the boundary curve and the stable branch BB' of the saddle-like paths. If the initial capital-labor ratio (k_o) does not exceed $\tilde{k}$, then the optimal path would be the same as the one without (54). On the other hand, if $k_o > \tilde{k}$, then the optimal k_t decreases *along the boundary curve*, and after the time point at which k_t reaches $\tilde{k}$, the optimal k_t moves along the BB'-curve toward $\hat{k}$. The analysis here is analogous to the one that we discussed earlier in terms of figure 9.4.

One question may arise in connection with this discussion of (53) and (54). Namely, how do we know the path along the boundary curve for $k_t > \tilde{k}$ is optimal? Although the answer to this question may be intuitively obvious, it requires a more formal analysis.[26]

References

Arrow, K. J. 1968a. "Applications of Control Theory to Economic Growth." In *Mathematics of the Decision Sciences*, pt. 2, ed. G. B. Dantzig and A. F. Veinott, 85–119, Providence, R.I.: American Mathematical Society.

[26] The problem can formally be stated as that of choosing c_t to maximize I, defined in (32), subject to (30), $c_t \geqq 0$, $k_t \geqq 0$, and (53), for all t for an arbitrary given specified value of k_0. The treatment of constraints such as (53) is discussed as the "g-constraint" in chap. 11.

———. 1968b. "Optimal Capital Policy with Irreversible Investment." In *Value, Capital and Growth: Papers in Honour of Sir John Hicks.*, ed. J. N. Wolfe, 1–19, Edinburgh: Edinburgh University Press.

Arrow, K. J., and M. Kurz. 1970. *Public Investment, the Rate of Return, and Optimal Fiscal Policy.* Baltimore, Md.: Johns Hopkins University Press.

Araujo, A., and J. A. Scheinkman. 1983. "Maximum Principle and Transversality Condition for Concave Infinite Horizon Economic Models." *Journal of Economic Theory* 30 (June): 1–16.

Becker, R. A., and J. H. Boyd III. 1988. "Recursive Utility and Optimal Capital Accumulation II: Sensitivity and Duality Theory." *Manuscript.*

Becker, R. A., J. H. Boyd III, and B. Y. Sung. 1989. "Recursive Utility and Optimal Capital Accumulation I: Existence," *Journal of Economic Theory* 47 (February): 76–100.

Benveniste, L. M., and J. A. Scheinkman. 1982. "Duality Theory for Dynamic Optimization Models of Economics: Continuous Time Case." *Journal of Economic Theory* 27 (June): 1–19.

Berkovitz, L. D. 1974. *Optimal Control Theory.* New York: Springer Verlag.

Brock, W. A., and A. G. Malliaris. 1989. *Differential Equations, Stability, and Chaos in Dynamic Economics.* Amsterdam: North-Holland.

Cass, D. 1965. "Optimum Growth in an Aggregative Model of Capital Accumulation." *Review of Economic Studies* 32 (July): 233–40.

Cesari, L. 1983. *Optimization: Theory and Applications.* New York: Springer Verlag.

Drabicki, J. Z., and A. Takayama. 1975. "On the Optimal Growth of the Two Sector Economy." *Keio Economic Studies* 12(1): 1–36.

Gelfand, I. M., and S. V. Fomin. 1963. *Calculus of Variations.* Trans. R. A. Silverman. Englewood Cliffs, N.J.: Prentice-Hall.

Hadley, G., and M. C. Kemp. 1971. *Variational Methods in Economics.* Amsterdam: North-Holland, chapter 6.

Haque, V. 1970. "Skeptical Noes on Uzawa's 'Optimal Growth in a Two-Sector Model of Capital Accumulation,' and a Precise Characterization of the Optimal Path." *Review of Economic Studies* 37 (July): 377–94.

Hesteness, M. R. 1965. "On Variational Theory and Optimal Control Theory." *Journal of SIAM Control* 3 (September): 23–48.

———. 1966. *Calculus of Variations and Optimal Control Theory.* New York: Wiley.

Hicks, J. R. 1965. *Capital and Growth.* Oxford: Oxford University Press.

Intriligator, M. S. 1964. "Regional Allocation of Investment: Comment." *Quarterly Journal of Economics* 78 (November): 659–62.

Kamien, M. I., and N. Schwartz. 1991. *Dynamic Optimization.* 2d ed. Amsterdam: North-Holland (1st ed. 1981).

Kendrick, D. 1981. "Control Theory with Applications to Economics." In *Handbook of Mathematical Economics*, ed. K. J. Arrow and M. D. Intriligator, vol. 1. Amsterdam: North-Holland.

Koopmans, T. C. 1965. "On the Concept of Optimal Economic Growth." In *The Econometric Approach to Development Planning*, Pontificiae Academiae Scientiarvm Scriptuvm Varia, 225–87; Discussion, 289–300. Amsterdam: North-Holland.

McKenzie, L. W. 1986. "Optimal Economic Growth, Turnpike Theorems, and Comparative Dynamics." In *Handbook of Mathematical Economics*, ed. K. J. Arrow and M. D. Intriligator, vol. 3. Amsterdam: North-Holland.

Macki, J., and A. Strauss. 1982. *Introduction to Optimal Control Theory.* New York: Springer Verlag.

Mangasarian, O. L. 1966. "Sufficient Conditions for the Optimal Control of Nonlinear Systems." *Journal of SIAM Control.* 4 (February): 139–52.

Pitchford, J. D. 1977. "Two State Variable Problems." In *Applications of Control Theory to Economic Analaysis*, ed. J. D. Pitchford and S. J. Turnovsky, 127–54, Amsterdam: North-Holland.

Pitchford, J. D., and S. J. Turnovsky, eds. 1977. *Applications of Control Theory to Economic Analysis.* Amsterdam: North-Holland.

Pontryagin, L. S., V. G. Boltyanskii, R. V. Gamkrelidze, and E. F. Mishchenko. 1962. *The Mathematical Theory of Optimal Processes.* Trans. from the Russian original by K. N. Trirogoff. New York: Interscience.

Rahman, M. A. 1963. "Regional Allocation of Investment." *Quarterly Journal of Economics* 77 (February): 26–39.

————. 1966. "Regional Allocation of Investment: Continuous Version." *Quarterly Journal of Economics.* 80 (February): 159–60.

Ramsey, F. P. 1928. "A Mathematical Theory of Saving." *Economic Journal* 38 (December): 543–59.

Sethi, S. P., and G. L. Thompson. 1981. *Optimal Control Theory Applications to Management Science.* Boston, Mass.: Martinus Nijhoff.

Seierstat, S., and K. Sydsaeter. 1987. *Optimal Control Theory with Economic Applications.* Amsterdam: North-Holland.

Simmons, G. F. 1972. *Differential Equations with Applications and Historical Notes.* New York: McGraw-Hill.

Srinivasan, T. N. 1964. "On a Two Sector Model of Growth." *Econometrica* 32 (July): 385–73 (Cowles Foundation Discussion Paper, 1962).

Takayama, A. 1967. "Regional Allocation of Investment: A Further Analysis." *Quarterly Journal of Economics* 81 (May): 330–37.

————. 1985. *Mathematical Economics*, 2d ed. New York: Cambridge University Press.

Troutman, J. L. 1983. *Variational Calculus with Elementary Convexity.* New York: Springer Verlag.

Tu, P. N. V. 1984. *Introductory Optimization Dynamics: Optimal Control with Economics and Management Science Applications.* Berlin: Springer Verlag.

Uzawa, H. 1964. "Optimal Growth in a Two-Sector Model of Capital Accumulation." *Review of Economic Studies* 31 (January): 1–24.

———. 1989. *Economic Analysis* (in Japanese). Tokyo: Iwanami.

Young, L. C. 1980. *Calculus of Variations and Optimal Control Theory.* New York: Chelsea Publishing.

CHAPTER 10

Infinite Horizon Optimization Control Problem and Applications

In applications of optimal control theory to economics, particular types of control problems are repeatedly used. Here, we are concerned with one of these. It is concerned with the problem in which the planning horizon is infinite, with the future being discounted. The left-hand end-point is fixed, and the right-hand end-point is left open. We obtain a general theorem, illustrate it in terms of a familiar problem (the optimal growth problem), and show a number of economic applications.

10.1 A General Theorem

We consider the problem of choosing $u(t)$ so as to

$$\text{Maximize} \int_0^\infty f_\circ[x(t),\ u(t),\ t]e^{-\rho t}dt$$

$$\text{Subject to } \dot{x}_i(t) = f_i[x(t),\ u(t),\ t],\ i = 1,\ 2,\ \ldots,\ n,$$

$$u_k(t) \geqq 0,\ k = 1,\ 2,\ \ldots,\ r, \text{ and } x(0) = x^\circ,$$

where ρ is a positive constant. It is assumed that the functions $f_\circ$'s and f_i's are continuously differentiable in the $(x,\ u,\ t)$-space. And the functions, $x_i(t)$'s, $0 \leqq t < \infty$, are continuous and $u_k(t)$'s, $0 \leqq t < \infty$, are piecewise continuous. Here $x(\infty)$ is not specified *a priori*. This type of optimization problem frequently appears in various applications of optimal control theory to economics.

Let $[x(t),\ u(t)]$ be optimal. Then it is necessary that there exist multipliers, $p_1(t),\ p_2(t),\ \ldots,\ p_n(t)$, such that the following conditions are satisfied.

(i) $p(t)$ together with $x(t)$ and $u(t)$ solve the Hamiltonian system

$$\dot{x}_i = \partial\tilde{H}/\partial p_i, \ i = 1, 2, \ldots, n, \tag{1}$$

$$\dot{p}_i = -\partial\tilde{H}/\partial x_i, \ i = 1, 2, \ldots, n, \tag{2}$$

where $\tilde{H}$ is defined by

$$\tilde{H}[x(t), u(t), t, p(t)]$$
$$\equiv f_\circ[x(t), u(t), t]e^{-\rho t} + \sum_{i=1}^{n} p_i(t)f_i[x(t), u(t), t]. \tag{3}$$

(ii) $\tilde{H}$ is maximized with respect to $u(t)$, subject to $u_k(t) \geqq 0$, $k = 1, 2, \ldots r$, that is,

$$\partial\tilde{H}/\partial u_k \leqq 0, \ u_k(\partial\tilde{H}/\partial u_k) = 0, \ k = 1, 2, \ldots, r. \tag{4}$$

(iii) The following transversality condition holds,

$$\lim_{t\to\infty} p_i(t)x_i(t) = 0, \ i = 1, 2, \ldots, n. \tag{5}$$

Conversely, if $f_\circ$ and f_i, $i = 1, 2, \ldots, n$, are all concave in x and u, and if there exist multipliers, $p_1, \ldots, p_n$, that satisfy (1), (2), (4), and (5) with $p_1 \geqq 0, \ldots, p_n \geqq 0$, then $[x(t), u(t)]$ are optimal. If, in addition, $f_\circ$ is strictly concave in x and u, then the optimal path is unique.

Define $q_i(t)$ by

$$q_i(t) \equiv p_i(t)e^{\rho t}, \quad \text{or} \quad p_i(t) = q_i(t)e^{-\rho t}. \tag{6}$$

In terms of $q_i(t)$, we may define function H by

$$H[x(t), u(t), t, q(t)]$$
$$\equiv f_\circ[x(t), u(t), t] + \sum_{i=1}^{n} q_i(t)f_i[x(t), u(t), t]. \tag{7}$$

Recalling (3), we may at once obtain,

$$H[x(t), u(t), t, q(t)] \equiv \tilde{H}[x(t), u(t), t, p(t)]e^{\rho t}. \tag{8}$$

The function H is called the **current value Hamiltonian**. Then (1), (4), and (5) can immediately be rewritten as

$$\dot{x}_i = \partial H/\partial q_i,\ i = 1,\ 2,\ \ldots,\ n, \tag{1'}$$

$$\partial H/\partial u_k \leqq 0,\ \ u_k(\partial H/\partial u_k) = 0,\ k = 1,\ 2,\ \ldots,\ r, \tag{4'}$$

$$\lim_{t\to\infty} q_i(t)e^{-\rho t}x_i(t) = 0,\ i = 1,\ 2,\ \ldots,\ n. \tag{5'}$$

Also, observing from (6), we have

$$\dot{p}_i = (\dot{q}_i - \rho q_i)e^{-\rho t}.$$

Then we may also obtain the following relations from (2) by using (8).

$$(\dot{q}_i - q_i)e^{-\rho t} = -\partial\tilde{H}/\partial x_i = -(\partial H/\partial x_i)e^{-\rho t},\ \text{ so that}$$

$$\dot{q}_i = \rho q_i - \partial H/\partial x_i,\ i = 1,\ 2,\ \ldots,\ n. \tag{2'}$$

In summary, we may obtain the following result.

Theorem 10.1. Let $[x(t),\ u(t)]$ be the solution of the maximization problem stated at the beginning of this section. Then it is necessary that there exist multipliers, $q_1(t),\ q_2(t),\ \ldots,\ q_n(t)$, such that the following conditions are satisfied.

(i) Let $q(t)$ together with $x(t)$ and $u(t)$ solve the Hamiltonian system,

$$\dot{x}_i = \partial H/\partial q_i,\ i = 1,\ 2,\ \ldots,\ n,\ \text{and} \tag{1'}$$

$$\dot{q}_i = \rho q_i - \partial H/\partial x_i,\ i = 1,\ 2,\ \ldots,\ n, \tag{2'}$$

where the current value Hamiltonian H is defined by

$$H[x(t),\ u(t),\ t,\ q(t)] \equiv f_\circ[x(t),\ u(t),\ t] + \sum_{i=1}^{n} q_i(t)f_i[x(t),\ u(t),\ t];$$

(ii) H is maximized with respect to u subject to $u_k(t) \geqq 0,\ k = 1,\ 2,\ \ldots, r$, that is,

$$\partial H/\partial u_k \leqq 0,\ u_k(\partial H/\partial u_k) = 0,\ k = 1,\ 2,\ \ldots,\ r; \tag{4'}$$

(iii) The following transversality condition holds,

$$\lim_{t\to\infty} q_i(t)e^{-\rho t}x_i(t) = 0,\ i = 1,\ 2,\ \ldots,\ n. \tag{5'}$$

Conversely, if $f_o(x, u, t)$ and $f_i(x, u, t)$, $i = 1, 2, \ldots, n$, are all concave in x and u, and if there exist multipliers, $q_1(t), \ldots, q_n(t)$, that satisfy (1′), (2′), (4′), and (5′) with $q_1 \geqq 0, \ldots, q_n \geqq 0$, then $[x(t), u(t)]$ are optimal. In addition, if f_o is strictly concave in x and u, then the optimal path is unique.

REMARK: Needless to say, the reader may choose any notations for the multipliers here, instead of the q_i's.

REMARK: If there is *no* constraint that requires $u_k(t) \geqq 0$, $k = 1, 2, \ldots, r$, for each t, then (4′) is rewritten as

$$\partial H/\partial u_k = 0,\ k = 1,\ 2,\ \ldots,\ r, \tag{4''}$$

provided that the optimal value of the u_k's are bounded. Also, if $u_k(t) > 0$ for all k and for all t *at optimum*, then (4′) can be restated as (4″). If H is linear with respect to u, and if admissible values of u_k are not bounded, then the values of u_k's that maximize H would be *unbounded*.

REMARK: If $x(t)$ is a scalar and if it is unique, the solution of this optimization problem is monotone (see Hartle 1987).

An Illustration: The Optimal Growth Problem

We first illustrate an application of theorem 10.1 in terms of the optimal growth problem that is familiar to us. Namely, we consider the optimal growth problem discussed in chapter 9. As noted earlier, the basic equation of the neoclassical aggregate growth model can be specified as

$$\dot{k}_t = f(k_t) - nk_t - c_t, \tag{9}$$

where k_t = the capital-labor ratio, n = the rate of population growth, c_t = per capita consumption, and $f(k_t)$ = the production function for per capita output.[1] Let $u(c_t)$ signify the utility function of the representative individual. The notation u should not be confused with the

[1]See chaps. 6 and 9. Note that variables k_t and c_t are functions of t (time).

control variable. We then consider the problem of choosing c_t to maximize $\int_0^\infty u(c_t)e^{-\rho t}dt$ subject to $\dot{k}_t = f(k_t) - nk_t - c_t$, $c_t \geqq 0$ for all t, and a given k_o, where ρ is a positive constant.[2] It is assumed that the following usual conditions are satisfied:

$$f' > 0,\ f'' < 0 \text{ for all } k_t > 0, \tag{10a}$$

$$f(0) = 0,\ f'(0) = \infty,\ f'(\infty) = 0, \text{ and} \tag{10b}$$

$$u' > 0,\ u'' < 0 \text{ for all } c_t > 0,\ u'(0) = \infty. \tag{10c}$$

Then $u(t)$ and $[f(k_t) - nk_t - c_t]$ are (strictly) concave in k_t and c_t.

The current value Hamiltonian for this problem may be defined as

$$H = u(c_t) + q_t[f(k_t) - nk_t - c_t],$$

where p_t is the multiplier associated with the state variable k_t. The control variable of this problem is c_t. Applying theorem 10.1 to this problem, we may at once observe that the following conditions are necessary and sufficient for a unique optimum:

$$\dot{k}_t = \partial H/\partial p_t, \text{ that is, } \dot{k}_t = f(k_t) - nk_t - c_t; \tag{11}$$

$$\dot{q}_t = \rho q_t - \partial H/\partial k_t, \text{ that is, } \dot{q}_t = -q_t[f'(k_t) - (n + \rho)]; \tag{12}$$

$$\partial H/\partial c_t \leqq 0, \text{ and } c_t(\partial H/\partial c_t) = 0, \text{ for all } t; \text{ and} \tag{13}$$

$$\lim_{t\to\infty} q_t e^{-\rho t}k_t = 0. \tag{14}$$

Assuming $u'(0) = \infty$, we have $c_t > 0$ for all t along the optimal path under condition $u'(0) = \infty$. Hence, (13) can be rewritten as

$$\partial H/\partial c_t = 0; \text{ that is, } q_t = u'(c_t). \tag{15}$$

From this we may derive

$$c_t = c(q_t),\ c' = 1/u'' < 0.$$

[2]There is an additional constraint, $k_t \geqq 0$ for all t. However, as in chap. 9, we may proceed by temporarily ignoring this constraint. We may then observe that the optimal path obtained in such a fashion indeed satisfies the constraint $k_t \geqq 0$ for all t.

Substituting this into (11), we may at once obtain

$$\dot{k}_t = f(k_t) - nk_t - c(q_t). \tag{16}$$

This and (12) constitute the basic dynamic system, which in turn determines the optimal path (k_t, q_t) given the initial value k_o and transversality condition (14). The rest of the analysis is the same as the one in chapter 9, where (15) and (16), respectively, correspond precisely to (40) and (42) in chapter 9. The optimal path of (k_t, q_t) is the same as the one illustrated by figure 9.3 in chapter 9. The monotonicity of optimal path k_t, which is due to the fact that k_t is a scalar and the uniqueness of a solution (see Hartle 1987), is apparent in figure 9.3.

10.2 Optimal Monetary Policy[3]

An important feature of the optimal growth problem discussed in the literature as exposited in the previous section and in chapter 9 is that it presupposes a centralized economy, in which the economic planner dictates to each consumer the amount of consumption (c_t) for each t. Another important feature is that money is assumed away. The purpose of this section is to investigate the optimal growth problem in the context of a *decentralized monetary* economy. We show, with a simple model, how optimal growth can be achieved via simple monetary policy. Although there are many varieties of monetary macro models under a decentralized framework in the literature, we have identified one model in which Cass-Koopmans type results for a nonmonetary centralized economy can be carried over. This model is based on the familiar neoclassical monetary growth model à la Tobin, that is exposited in section 2 of chapter 8. A key feature of this model is that the idea of Fisher's real rate of return on money and the Wicksellian cumulative process is juxtaposed with the Solow-Swan type of neoclassical aggregate growth model. This line of thought, developed in terms of descriptive models of a decentralized economy, is made applicable to the theory of optimal growth.

We again specify the feasibility path by

$$\dot{k} = f(k) - nk - c, \tag{9}$$

where the notation t denoting time is subsumed to avoid clutter. For simplicity, assume that per capita consumption (c_t) is a constant fraction

[3]This section is based on Drabicki and Takayama (1978). The extension of the analysis which incorporates the banking sector and the endogeneous nature of the money supply is obtained by Drabicki and Takayama (1983).

of per capita real disposal income (y^D),

$$c = (1 - s)y^D, \; 0 < s < 1. \tag{17}$$

Let p and M, respectively, signify the price level and the money supply, where we now use p to denote the price level instead of the Pontryagin multiplier. Then the expression for real disposable income (Y^D) under rational expectations may, as explained in section 8.2, be obtained as[4]

$$Y^D = Y + (\theta - \pi)M/p, \tag{18}$$

where Y = current real output, $\theta \equiv \dot{M}/M$ (the rate of monetary expansion) and $\pi \equiv \dot{p}/p$ (the rate of inflation). Letting N denote the labor force, we rewrite (18) as

$$y^D = f(k) + (\theta - \pi)m, \tag{18'}$$

where $y^D \equiv Y^D/N$ (real per capita disposable income) and $m \equiv M/(pN)$ (real per capita cash balances).

Letting K denote the stock of capital, we may specify the monetary equilibrium relation as

$$M = L[f'(k) + \pi, \; pY, \; M + pK],$$
$$L_1 < 0, \; L_2 > 0, \; 0 < L_3 < 1, \tag{19}$$

where it is assumed that the expected rate of inflation is equal to its actual rate. Since the money demand function L is homogeneous of degree one with respect to nominal income (pY) and the nominal value of wealth ($M + pK$), we may obtain, from (19),

$$m = L[f'(k) + \pi, \; f(k), \; m + k]. \tag{20}$$

Solve (20) for π to obtain[5]

$$\pi = \pi(k, m), \; \pi_k > 0 \text{ and } \pi_m < 0. \tag{21}$$

---

[4] To obtain (18), we assume that there are only two assets in the economy, Treasury money and physical assets, as in Tobin (1965). This assumption is also used to obtain (19). For an extension to the three-asset economy, see Drabicki and Takayama (1983).

[5] The expressions for π_k ($\equiv \partial\pi/\partial k$) and π_m ($\equiv \partial\pi/\partial m$) are obtained as follows:

$$\pi_k = -(L_1 f'' + L_2 f' + L_3)/L_1 > 0, \; \pi_m = (1 - L_3)/L_1 < 0.$$

Substituting (18′) and (21) into (17), we have

$$c = (1 - s)\{f(k) + [\theta - \pi(k, m)]m\}. \tag{22}$$

Combining this with (9), we obtain the first dynamic equation,

$$\dot{k} = sf(k) - nk - (1 - s)[\theta - \pi(k, m)]m. \tag{23}$$

Next, logarithmically differentiating $m \equiv M/(pN)$ and using $\dot{N}/N = n$, we may obtain

$$\dot{m} = (\theta - \pi - n)m.$$

Substituting (21) into this, we have

$$\dot{m} = [\theta - \pi(k, m) - n]m. \tag{24}$$

If the time path of θ is specified, (23) and (24) describe the motion of (k, m). If θ is a constant for all t, we may obtain the saddle-like behavior of (k, m).

In the present analysis, the monetary authority *chooses* the time path of θ so as to

$$\text{Maximize} \int_0^\infty u(c)e^{-\rho t}dt$$

Subject to (23), (24), and a given value of k_o,

where the expression for c is given by (22). To solve this problem, we define the current value Hamiltonian by

$$H \equiv u(c) + p_1\{sf(k) - nk - (1 - s)[\theta - \pi(k, m)]m\} + p_2[\theta - \pi(k, m) - n]m,$$

where p_1 and p_2 signify the (Pontryagin) multipliers, and where the expression for c is found in (22). Then we may conclude that the following conditions are necessary and sufficient for (k, m) to be uniquely optimal:[6]

$$\dot{k} = \partial H/\partial p_1, \quad \dot{m} = \partial H/\partial p_2; \tag{25}$$

[6] Here we need not restrict θ to a nonnegative number. Hence, the maximization of H with respect to θ simply yields $\partial H/\partial\theta = 0$, as indicated by (4″).

$$\dot{p}_1 = \rho p_1 - \partial H/\partial k; \tag{26a}$$

$$\dot{p}_2 = \rho p_2 - \partial H/\partial m; \tag{26b}$$

$$\partial H/\partial \theta = 0; \tag{27}$$

$$\lim_{t\to\infty} p_1 e^{-\rho t} k = 0; \text{ and} \tag{28a}$$

$$\lim_{t\to\infty} p_2 e^{-\rho t} m = 0. \tag{28b}$$

Note that (25) yields the same equations as (23) and (24). From (27), we obtain

$$(1 - s)u' = (1 - s)p_1 - p_2, \tag{29}$$

with $m > 0$. Also, from (26a) and (29), we get

$$\dot{p}_1 = (n + \rho)p_1 - (p_1 + p_2)f', \tag{30}$$

after some cancellations of terms. Also using (26b) and (29), we obtain

$$\dot{p}_2 = (n + \rho)p_2, \quad \text{or} \quad p_2 = p_2(0)e^{-(\rho + n)t}, \tag{31}$$

where $p_2(0)$ is the initial value of p_2. Combining this with (28b), we may obtain $p_2(0) = 0$, so that

$$p_2 = 0, \quad \text{for all } t. \tag{32}$$

This simply means that the shadow price of changing the supply of fiat money is zero (as it should be). Using (29) and (32), we may at once obtain the remarkable result,

$$u'(c) = p_1. \tag{33}$$

This is the same rule obtained in the context of the optimal growth problem for a centralized, moneyless economy (recall eq. 15 above). As we remarked in the previous chapter, (33) states the familiar Ramsey-Cass-Koopmans rule (or the Keynes-Ramsey rule) which equates the loss of marginal utility in giving up one unit of consumption to the shadow price of accumulation of physical assets (p_1). Condition (32) indicates the opportunity cost of monetary accumulation or decumulation is zero.

This reflects the fact that money can be printed or burned in furnaces with negligible costs.

Also, using (30) and (32), we get

$$\dot{p}_1 = -p_1[f'(k) - (n + \rho)], \tag{34}$$

which is the same as (12).

Using (22) and (23), we may obtain

$$\dot{k} = f(k) - nk - c. \tag{35}$$

Solving (33) for c, we arrive at

$$c = c(p_1), \; c' = 1/u'' < 0.$$

Substituting this into (35), we obtain

$$\dot{k} = f(k) - nk - c(p_1). \tag{36}$$

The optimal path of (k, p_1) can be specified by (34) and (36). The dynamic behavior of (k, p_1) is exactly the same as the one obtained in the standard literature (such as Cass 1965 and Koopmans 1965) for the centralized, moneyless economy when $\rho > 0$. It can again be illustrated by figure 9.3 in chapter 9. Since c is uniquely determined by (35) for each p_1, its dynamic behavior is identical to the one obtained in the standard Cass-Koopmans type model. Note that the time path of (k, p_1) is determined *independently* of m or of the monetary equation (24).

Setting $\dot{p}_1 = 0$ in (34), the following steady-state value of k is uniquely determined by

$$f'(k^*) = n + \rho. \tag{37}$$

Namely, the capital-labor ratio in the steady-state assumes the familiar *modified golden rule* path $\hat{k}$. Also, by setting $\dot{k} = 0$ and $\dot{m} = 0$ in (23) and (24), we obtain the following steady-state values of m and θ (denoted by m^* and θ^*):

$$m^* = [sf(k^*) - nk^*]/[(1 - s)n], \tag{38}$$

$$\theta^* = n + \pi^*, \tag{39}$$

where $\pi^* \equiv \pi(k^*, m^*)$. Real per capita consumption in the steady-state (c^*) is obtained from (22) and (39) as

$$c^* = (1 - s)[f(k^*) + nm^*].$$

Utilizing (38), we may rewrite this as

$$c^* = f(k^*) - nk^*. \tag{40}$$

The value of c^* is precisely the same as that obtained in the optimal growth literature.

We now summarize some of the results obtained in the above analysis.

Proposition 10.1.

(i) The optimal-growth path for the present monetary economy follows the familiar Ramsey-Cass-Koopmans rule (33).

(ii) The dynamic behavior of the optimal values of the capital-labor ratio (k), the shadow price of accumulation of physical capital (p_1), and real per capita consumption (c) is identical to the behavior found in standard literature (for $\rho > 0$), such as the Cass or Koopmans model where money is *not* introduced. The optimal trajectory of (k, p_1, c) in the present monetary economy is independent of the time path of per capita real cash balances (m), that is, the optimal monetary policy is "neutral."

(iii) The steady-state values of k and c are identical to those obtained in the standard Cass-Koopmans model for which $\rho > 0$. The steady-state rate of inflation (price change) is equal to the steady state value of monetary expansion (θ^*) minus the rate of population growth (n).

To obtain the optimal value of θ, we substitute the expression for c found in (22) into (33) and solve the resulting expression for θ to obtain

$$\theta = \theta(k, m, p_2).$$

Substituting this into (24), we may also obtain

$$\dot{m} = \dot{m}(k, m, p_1) = [\theta(k, m, p_1) - \pi(k, m) - n]m,$$

which specifies the motion of m.

In this analysis, we have assumed away interest-bearing securities and the endogenous nature of the money supply. It can be shown, however, that these complications do not alter the basic conclusion obtained in proposition 10.1 (see Drabicki and Takayama 1983).

10.3 Savings: Permanent Income Hypothesis

In this section, we analyze an individual's saving behavior.[7] In particular, we are interested in the classical Modigliani-Brumberg life-cycle hypothesis (1954)[8] and Friedman's permanent income hypothesis (1957).[9] There is a basic similarity between the two theories: both obtain savings/consumption behavior from an individual's explicit intertemporal choice based on a consistent utility function. In this respect, both theories are widely accepted in the literature. Since these two theories differ on some important aspects (cf. Modigliani 1990), here we focus on Friedman's permanent income hypothesis.

The basic feature of Friedman's theory is, as Farrell (1959, p. 679) once aptly put it, "the recognition that if an individual plans rationally to maximize his utility over his life, his consumption in any given year will depend not on his income in that year but on the resources of which he disposes." This notion is clearly in the tradition of Irving Fisher, for it captures the intertemporal nature of consumer's choice. Farrell (1959) calls this proposition "plausible but vague." He then offers a succinct

---

[7] This section is adapted from Takayama (1985b). This, in turn, is based on the author's lectures on macroeconomics at the University of Tokyo in the autumn of 1974, which have subsequently been repeated (with some modifications) in various universities.

[8] Franco Modigliani was the 1985 Nobel laureate in Economic Science.

[9] The historical development of Friedman's permanent income hypothesis and Modigliani-Brumberg's life-cycle hypothesis is rather dramatic. It begins with major forecasting errors, such as the one in predicting the volume of unemployment for the first quarter of 1946. The actual value was only 2.7 million instead of the predicted volume of 8.1 million (see Hagen 1947 for his reflections on his prediction errors). Similar predictions by Mosak and Smithies, which both appeared in the January 1945 issue of *Econometrica* are well known. Because of this forecasting error, a number of studies were produced with regard to the question of what should be the correct specification of the consumption function. In this connection, it also became clear that seemingly conflicting empirical evidence had to be reconciled in such an effort. Kuznets's data of 1869–1929 show a long-run stability of the average propensity to consume (APC); the Department of Commerce data show a short-run volatility of the marginal propensity to consume (MPC), and cross-section budget study data of 1901, 1917–19, 1935–36, 1941–42 show that the MPC is less than the APC, but this relation shifts to the right maintaining a constant APC. The first successful reconciliation effort was done by Duesenberry (1949). The "consumption function controversy" reached its peak with the publication of Modigliani and Brumberg's (1954) study and Friedman's (1957) study. For an excellent survey of the consumption function controversy beginning with the major forcasting errors of Hagen and others and culminating in the studies by Modigliani, Brumberg, and Friedman, see Shinohara (1958). See also Branson (1989, chap. 12). Both Modigliani and Friedman are Nobel laureates.

summary of this proposition in terms of the following two hypotheses:

(i) "*The Normal Income Hypothesis:* in any given period, an individual's current income ... affects his consumption ... only through its effect on his normal income ... [where the functional relation between consumption and normal income is independent of current income and assets]. (1959, p. 680)

(ii) "*The Proportionality Hypothesis:* for any individual, the relationship between his consumption and his normal income is one of proportionality." (1959, p. 681)

In terms of symbols, let c_o be current (i.e., time zero) real consumption and let y_o^* be permanent or normal (real) income. Then the "normal income hypothesis" can be written as

$$c_o = f(y_o^*),$$

where "transitory consumption" is assumed to be negligible. The proportionality hypothesis thus imposes a special functional form of the function f,

$$c_o = ky_o^*,$$

where the proportionality factor k, as Friedman (1957) puts it, depends on the interest rate, preferences, etc. We may rewrite this equation as

$$c_o = (1 - s)y_o^*, \tag{41}$$

where s signifies the propensity to save, and where we postulate that s depends on the real rate of interest. Since (41) captures both the normal income hypothesis and the proportionality hypothesis, (41) may be regarded as the key equation in the permanent income theory.

The purpose of the present section is then to indicate the circumstances under which the simple formula (41) can be obtained by the optimal control approach with the explicit recognition of an individual's rational behavior over time. Such a task will also indicate, by way of the assumptions made, the extent to which (41) holds.

We consider a consumer whose nominal income at time t (Y_t) consists of nominal wage income (W_t) and interest income from his or her assets (i_tA_t),

$$Y_t \equiv W_t + i_tA_t, \tag{42}$$

where A_t is the nominal value of interest-yielding assets at time t, and i_t is the nominal rate of interest.[10]

The consumer's income, Y_t, is allocated between consumption expenditures (C_t) and asset accumulation (A_t):

$$Y_t \equiv C_t + \dot{A}_t, \tag{43}$$

where the dot signifies the time derivative. Combining (42) and (43), we arrive at

$$\dot{A}_t \equiv W_t + i_t A_t - C_t. \tag{44}$$

Let p_t represent the price level at time t, and define the "real variables," a_t, w_t, and c_t, by

$$a_t \equiv A_t/p_t, \quad w_t \equiv W_t/p_t, \quad \text{and} \quad c_t \equiv C_t/p_t.$$

Then noting $\dot{a}_t \equiv \dot{A}_t/p_t - a_t\dot{p}_t/p_t$, we may rewrite (44) as

$$\dot{a}_t \equiv w_t + (i_t - \pi_t)a_t - c_t, \tag{45}$$

where $\pi_t \equiv \dot{p}_t/p_t$ signifies the expected rate of price change. Following Irving Fisher, let $r_t \equiv i_t - \pi_t$, signify the **real rate of interest** at time t. Thus, we may rewrite (45) as

$$\dot{a}_t \equiv w_t + r_t a_t - c_t. \tag{46}$$

The life-cycle hypothesis (and to a certain extent the permanent income hypothesis) typically considers a consumer whose life expectancy is finite. Although this is justified on obvious grounds, it involves a difficult problem where the pattern of optimal consumption then depends on the amount of the bequest, and the bequest utility must be associated with the utility of the heir, which in turn is associated with the utility of the heir's heir, and so on. This generates a problem involving an infinite chain of generations. Such a problem has been studied rather extensively in terms of the overlapping generation model à la Samuelson (1958), and recently the literature on this topic has further been expanded immensely. However, it is not clear how much insight we can obtain by this formulation about the permanent income hypothesis.

---

[10]The introduction of noninterest-yielding assets does not alter the essence of the present analysis. For simplicity, it is also assumed that the consumer's financial assets are of the nature of a savings account in the bank; i.e., they have a fixed money value with a variable interest rate. This is done to avoid the complications arising from capital gains or losses associated with consol-type bonds.

Furthermore, the analysis in terms of the overlapping generation model tends to become tedious and complex. To avoid such complications and yet to incorporate the infinite horizon aspect of consumer choice, it is often assumed that the life of a consumer is infinite, and this appears to follow the spirit of Friedman's permanent income hypothesis closely anyway. The theory considers a "representative consumer" whose life can be regarded as infinite (due to successive generations). Here we follow such a formulation. Thus letting c_t be the real consumption of our "representative consumer" at time t, we assume that his or her "lifetime" utility is given by

$$U \equiv \int_0^\infty u(c_t)e^{-\rho t}dt,$$

where $u' > 0$, $u'' < 0$ and $u'(0) = \infty$, and where ρ signifies the subjective rate of time discount, which is assumed to be a positive constant.[11]

The representative consumer then chooses the time path of c_t to maximize U subject to the asset accumulation equation (46), and the usual nonnegativity constraints on c_t, given the initial conditions. It is assumed that the consumer is "competitive" in the sense that he or she cannot affect the expected values of the price level p_t, the interest rate i_t, and wage income W_t.

To solve this optimization problem, we define the current value Hamiltonian H by

$$H(a_t,\ c_t,\ q_t) \equiv u(c_t) + q_t(w_t + r_t a_t - c_t),$$

where q_t is the multiplier. The solution to this optimal control problem may be obtained in a straightforward fashion. Among the set of necessary conditions for a unique interior solution,[12] we have the following equations.

$$\dot{a}_t = \partial H/\partial q_t, \text{ that is, } \dot{a} = w_t + r_t a_t - c_t; \tag{47a}$$

$$\dot{q}_t = \rho_t - \partial H/\partial a_t, \text{ that is, } \dot{q}_t = (\rho - r_t)q_t; \tag{47b}$$

$$\partial H/\partial c_t = 0, \text{ that is, } u'(c_t) = q_t; \tag{47c}$$

[11] As mentioned in connection with the optimal growth problem exposited in chapter 9, the assumption of a constant ρ imposes certain strong restrictions on the theory.

[12] An interior solution is obtained by assuming that $u'(0) = \infty$.

$$\lim_{t\to\infty} q_t e^{-\rho t} a_t = 0. \tag{47d}$$

Here we assume $c_t > 0$ for all t at optimum to obtain (47c). Due to the strict concavity of the function u and the linearity of constraint (46), these conditions are also sufficient for a unique optimum.

We first note the following equation from (47c):

$$\dot{q}_t = u''(c_t)\dot{c}_t. \tag{48}$$

Defining the **elasticity of marginal utility of consumption** by

$$\eta(c_t) \equiv -u''(c_t)c_t/u'(c_t) > 0, \tag{49}$$

we can rewrite (48) as

$$\dot{q}_t/q_t = -\eta(c_t)\dot{c}_t/c_t. \tag{50}$$

Combining this with (47b), we obtain

$$r_t = \rho + \eta(c_t)\dot{c}_t/c_t, \tag{51}$$

where the right-hand side of (51) signifies the "rate of time preference." Equation (51) is the key optimality condition for this problem.

To simplify the discussion, for the time being, we assume that the consumer expects that the real rate of interest, r_t, will be constant for all t, so that $r_t = r$. We may then rewrite (46) or (47a) as

$$\dot{a}_t - ra_t = w_t - c_t. \tag{46$'$}$$

Multiplying by e^{-rt} on both sides of (46′), we have

$$\frac{d}{dt}(a_t e^{-rt}) = (\dot{a}_t - ra_t)e^{-rt} = (w_t - c_t)e^{-rt}.$$

Since $d(a_t e^{-rt})/dt = (\dot{a}_t - ra_t)e^{-rt}$, we obtain

$$\frac{d}{dt}(a_t e^{-rt}) = (w_t - c_t)e^{-rt}.$$

Integrating both sides of this from 0 to ∞, we may observe

$$a_t e^{-rt}\Big|_0^\infty = \int_0^\infty (w_t - c_t)e^{-rt}dt.$$

From this we at once get

$$\int_0^\infty c_t e^{-rt} dt = a_o + \int_0^\infty w_t e^{-rt} dt \equiv a_o^*, \tag{52}$$

where a_o^* is the sum of the value of the consumer's present assets and the present value of all future wage income. Here, a_o^* signifies the real value of his or her total wealth. We assume that a_o^* is finite. Equation (52) thus signifies the **intertemporal budget condition**. In terms of a_o^*, we can now define his or her **permanent income** today (y_o^*) as[13]

$$y_o^* \equiv r a_o^*. \tag{53}$$

Namely, the value of the perpetuity that yields the income stream y_o^* is equal to $a_o^*(\equiv y_o^*/r)$ if the interest rate is r.

In the preceding discussion, we assumed $r_t = r$ for all t. In general, such an assumption may not be warranted. Skipping somewhat tedious computations,[14] we may obtain the following relation, which extends (52) to the case in which r_t is not constant:

$$\int_0^\infty c_t \exp\left(-\int_0^t r_s ds\right) dt = a_o + \int_0^\infty w_t \exp\left(-\int_0^t r_s ds\right) dt \equiv a_o^*. \tag{52'}$$

Note that (52′) reduces to (52) when r_t is constant. The permanent income, y_o^*, can again be defined by (53), where a_o^* is defined via (52′).

We now proceed with our discussion based on the assumption of a constant r_t. Also, we heroically assume that the elasticity of the marginal utility of consumption is constant,

$$\eta(c_t) \equiv \eta \quad \text{for all } t.$$

---

[13]This corresponds to Hicks's (1939, 1946) definition of income as the flow that would have to be consumed if wealth were to remain intact. As Yaari (1964, p. 312) noted, Friedman (1957) accepted Hicks's definition of income on the theoretical level (although "on the practical level he defines 'permanent income' in a somewhat different manner").

[14]To obtain (52′), multiply by

$$\exp\left(-\int_0^t r_s ds\right)$$

on both sides of (46′) (replacing r by r_t) and carry out a computation similar to the one used to obtain (52).

This is ensured if the utility function u is specified by

$$u(c_t) = \alpha c_t^{1-\eta} + \text{ constant}, 0 < \eta < 1, \text{ or} \tag{54a}$$

$$u(c_t) = \alpha \log c_t + \text{ constant, when } \eta = 1, \tag{54b}$$

where η is a constant. Such forms of the utility function often appear in the context of optimal growth models. For example, Goodwin (1961) and Stiglitz (1974) assume $\eta = 1$, whereas Tinbergen (1960, p. 482) quotes the figure from Ragnar Frisch's study of 1931, which says $\eta = 0.6$ for U.S. workers.[15] In the context of the individual's life-cycle model, such a formulation is used by Yaari (1964), Blinder (1974, p. 31), and others. Following Blinder, we may call the utility function in the form of (54), **isoelastic.**[16]

Assuming the isoelastic form of the utility function, we may simplify the optimal rule of consumption (51) as

$$r = \rho + \eta \dot{c}_t / c_t, \tag{51'}$$

from which we get

$$\dot{c}_t / c_t = \mu, \quad \text{where } \mu \equiv (r - \rho)/\eta.$$

This can easily be rewritten as[17]

$$c_t = c_0 e^{\mu t}. \tag{55}$$

Thus, consumption grows or shrinks depending on whether or not the real rate of interest r exceeds or falls short of the subjective discount rate ρ.[18]

---

[15] Ragnar Frisch and Jan Tinbergen were jointly awarded the first Nobel Prize in Economic Science in 1969 for work in econometrics.

[16] A justification of isoelastic utility functions is provided by Yaari (1964). Yaari's justification is critically discussed by Blinder (1974, pp. 31–32). Blinder (1974, p. 32) also claims that utility function (54) "has a long and venerable history in macroeconomics, since it is the basis of both Friedman's permanent income model [1957] and the life cycle model of Modigliani and Brumberg [1954]."

[17] Here c_0 signifies the optimal *current* real consumption that is obtained in the context of the present optimality condition (47).

[18] This result does not depend *per se* on the assumption that the utility function is isoelastic. The assumption of an isoelastic utility function imposes the restriction that the rate of expansion or contraction of consumption (i.e., $\dot{c}_t / c_t$) be a constant (μ).

This result is obtained by Yaari (1964, p. 309), and its economic interpretation is straightforward. For example, if $\rho > r$, "the household can improve its position by borrowing at the rate r in order to advance its consumption stream toward the present. Thus the optimal value of c_t would have to decline over time," (Blinder 1974, p. 30). The interpretation of the case for $\rho < r$ is analogous.

Since $\mu \equiv (r - \rho)/\eta$ by definition, and since ρ and η are assumed to be constants, μ is a function of r alone, that is, $\mu = \mu(r)$. A more revealing way of obtaining $\mu(r)$ may be to utilize (51′). We illustrate the determination of $\mu(r)$ by way of (51′) in terms of figure 10.1, where figures 10.1*a* and *b* illustrate the cases of $\rho > r$ and $\rho < r$, respectively.[19]

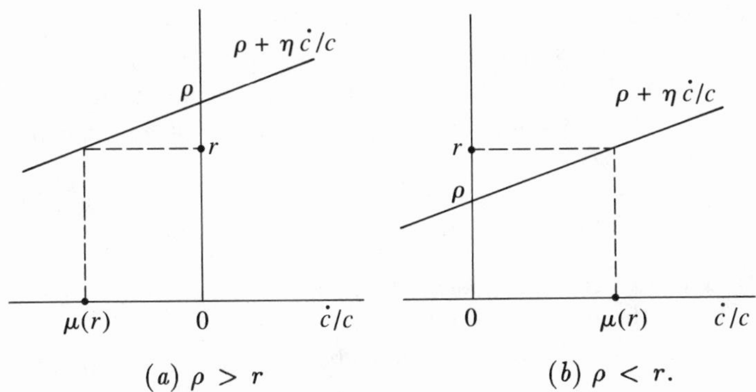

Figure 10.1: Determination of $\mu(r)$

Using (55), we may compute

$$\int_0^{\infty} c_t e^{-rt} dt = \int_0^{\infty} c_\circ e^{-(r-\mu)t} dt = \frac{c_\circ}{r - \mu}, \tag{56}$$

where it is important to note that we need to assume

$$r - \mu > 0, \tag{57}$$

to ensure that the integral in (56) converges and that the integral takes on a positive value. Note that if $r = \rho$ (in which case $\mu = 0$ and

[19] A similar diagram is obtained by Imai et al. (1972, p. 16), where they assume $r > \rho$. Following them, fig. 10.1 may be called the **Irving Fisher Diagram**.

$r > 0$), this condition is always satisfied. One may postulate a competitive mechanism that forces r to equal ρ in the long run, in which case real consumption stays stationary. However, we proceed here without imposing any such postulates.

Combining (56) with (52) and (53), we may now obtain

$$c_\circ = [1 - s(r)]y_\circ^*, \quad \text{where } s(r) \equiv \mu(r)/r. \tag{58}$$

This equation provides the relation that determines the optimal value of current consumption ($c_\circ$) from permanent income ($y_\circ^*$), defined in terms of (52) and (53). More importantly, (58) corresponds precisely to (41), that is, we have now obtained the key equation of the permanent income hypothesis. Note that the propensities to save and consume are, respectively, given by $s(r)$ and $[1 - s(r)]$, and that they depend on the real rate of interest, r. Also note that (58) implies that the (permanent) income elasticity of consumption is equal to unity.[20] By (53), this also means that the wealth elasticity of consumption is equal to unity.

Recalling the definition of $\mu \equiv (r - \rho)/\eta$, we may obtain the expression for $s(r)$ as

$$s(r) \equiv (1 - \rho/r)/\eta. \tag{59}$$

From (59), it is apparent that $ds(r)/dr > 0$, that is, the propensity to save increases as the real rate of interest increases.

At this point it may be useful to consider an extreme case in which wage income, w_t, is expected to be constant; that is, $w_t = w_\circ$ for all t. In this case, using the definition of $a_\circ^*$ in (52) and the definition of $y_\circ^*$ in (53), we get

$$y_\circ^* = ra_\circ + w_\circ \equiv y_\circ. \tag{60}$$

Namely, if the consumer expects that future wage income as well as the future real rate of interest will be constant, then permanent income is equal to current income. This relation must hold if the definition of permanent income should at all be tenable. Equation (60) shows that our definition of permanent income passes such a test. Furthermore, (60) also indicates that if we specify that current consumption depends on current income rather than on permanent income, it presupposes static expectations in the sense of our consumer expecting constant w_t and r_t for all future t.

---

[20] Yaari (1964, p. 313) states that "there exists empirical evidence to support this view," and subsequently offers an analysis exploring the implications of this view.

In this analysis, we required condition (57), i.e., $r - \mu > 0$. Recalling the definition of μ, we may easily conclude that (57) is satisfied if and only if

$$\rho > (1 - \eta)r. \tag{61}$$

Thus, a sufficient condition that (61) holds *and* consumption increases over time (that is, $\mu > 0$, or $r - \rho > 0$) is given by

$$r > \rho > (1 - \eta)r. \tag{62}$$

Recall the definition of $s(r)$ in (59), and assume $r > 0$. Then, $s > 0$ if and only if $r > \rho$, and $s < 1$ if and only if $\rho > (1 - \eta)r$. Namely, condition (62) is *necessary and sufficient* for $0 < s < 1$. Also note that $s < 1$ is required to ensure $c_o > 0$ (see eq. 58).

Some of the above results can be summarized in proposition 10.2.

Proposition 10.2. The permanent income hypothesis in the form of (41) or (58) can be obtained as the solution of the intertemporal choice of an individual, if the real rate of interest (r) stays constant. An increase in r raises the propensity to save. If the real rate of interest is not constant, then the permanent income hypothesis need not hold.

We may emphasize that (58), the key equation of the permanent income hypothesis, was obtained under the assumption of a constant real rate of interest ($r_t = r$). In general, if this assumption is violated, then we cannot obtain (58). Friedman's permanent income hypothesis may thus best fit the world in which the real rate of interest stays constant. If the rate of inflation (π_t) and the nominal rate of interest (i_t) move in such a way as to cause a fluctuation in the real rate of interest, then this discussion may require a major modification. In this context, it may be worthwhile to note that Friedman argues that the real rate of interest is fairly stable, at least in the long run (i.e., even though it demonstrates short-run fluctuations; see, for example, Friedman 1974, pp. 35–38 and 53–54).[21] Brunner and Meltzer (1974, p. 68), in their comments on this article, state that Friedman "assumes that real rates are constant and that market rates adjust rapidly to changes in anticipation." They then

[21] With regard to the stability of the real rate of interest, Friedman (1974, p. 37) notes, "We have interest rate data over very long periods of time, and these indicate that rates are very similar at distant times, if the times compared have similar price behavior (Gupta 1964). More recently, the Federal Reserve Bank of St. Louis has been estimating the 'real rate', and their estimates are remarkably stable despite very large changes in nominal rates."

say, "We know of no empirical evidence supporting these propositions." In this case, the preceding formulation of Friedman's permanent income hypothesis may be more pertinent to the "long-run state" in which anticipation is fully fulfilled, and such a state seems to be often at the heart of many of Friedman's works.

Finally, some concluding remarks are in order. We have shown how Friedman's relatively simple but insightful formulation of the permanent income hypothesis can be obtained by way of optimal control techniques in which the intrinsically intertemporal nature of consumer's choice plays a key role. In particular, we have shown (what may be considered) the key assertion of the permanent income hypothesis that current consumption is proportional to "permanent income," where the proportionality factor depends on the real rate of interest, if the underlying utility function is isoelastic. The optimal-control theory framework provides a structure that allows us to derive the key results. Consumption being proportional to "wealth" or "permanent income" emerges naturally from such a demonstration. Various assumptions made in the course of our analysis to obtain the conclusion indicates the extent to which the permanent income hypotheses can be vindicated.[22]

10.4 Investment [23]

Investment is a heavily debated topic in economics. Keynes's *General Theory* (1936) was instrumental in inspiring much of the debate in the modern theory of investment. Among such studies, Jorgenson's work on "neoclassical theory,"[24] the adjustment cost approach, and the theory of "Tobin's q" are important in formulating the modern theory of invest-

---

[22] We may note that this proportionality conclusion is analogous to the well-known result in the static-demand theory that under homothetic preferences the demand for each commodity is proportional to income and the proportionality factors depend on prices. Since we can always date commodities, the conclusion obtained in this section may not be too surprising. Namely, one may (somewhat loosely) argue that the permanent income hypothesis is just an application of the usual demand theory under homothetic preferences. However, this point obviously requires further careful scrutiny. In the usual demand theory, even the concept of "permanent income" is not clearly introduced.

[23] This section is adapted from Takayama (1987, 1991).

[24] Though it has been heavily criticized, the study of investment by Jorgenson and his associates in the 1960 s and the early 1970 s is important in inspiring later developments. An illustrative work would be Jorgenson (1967). He then wrote a series of survey articles on investment studies (e.g., Jorgenson 1971 and 1972). Jorgenson's theory has been incorporated in recent textbooks on investment (see Dornbusch and Fischer 1987, for example).

ment. In this section, we review these theories critically and conclude that unfortunately none of them is satisfactory, in spite of their obvious merits.

10.4.1 The "Neoclassical" Theory

Let K_t and I_t, respectively, signify the stock of capital and the flow of investment of an individual firm at time t. Then letting δ be the rate of depreciation, we have

$$\dot{K}_t = I_t - \delta K_t, \tag{63}$$

where $0 < \delta < 1$. It is assumed that the firm's output (Y_t) can be produced by capital (K_t) and labor (N_t), and that the firm's production function is assumed to be concave and is specified by

$$Y_t = F(N_t, K_t).$$

Letting p, w, and p_I, respectively, be the price of the firm's output, the wage rate, and the price of investment goods, we may write the net cash flow of the firm at time t as

$$R_t \equiv pY_t - wN_t - p_I I_t.$$

For the sake of simplicity, we assume that p, w, and p_I are exogenously given to the firm and that they stay constant for all t. Assuming a constant rate of discount (i), we may define the present value of the sum of cash flow for all future time by[25]

$$W \equiv \int_0^\infty R_t e^{-it} dt.$$

[25] The constant discount rate (i) may be interpreted as the nominal interest rate by which one can borrow or lend by any amount. It is assumed that i is exogeneously given to the firm and that the lending rate is equal to the borrowing rate. The latter assumption is often referred to as that of a **perfect capital market**. (The analysis for the case of imperfect capital markets is analogous, and hence can be omitted.) If i is not constant but varies over time, then e^{-it} in the expression for W is replaced by

$$e^{-\int_0^t i_s ds}.$$

Then we may obtain

$$W \equiv \int_0^\infty [pF(N_t, K_t) - wN_t - p_I I_t]e^{-it}dt. \tag{64}$$

The firm is to choose the streams of labor employment and investment, $\{N_t\}$ and $\{I_t\}$, so as to maximize W defined in (64) subject to (63), $N_t \geqq 0$, $K_t \geqq 0$, and the given initial capital stock ($K_\circ$). Note that gross investment I_t is allowed to be negative. The current value Hamiltonian for this problem can be defined by

$$H \equiv [pF(N_t, K_t) - wN_t - p_I I_t] + \lambda_t(I_t - \delta K_t), \tag{65}$$

where λ_t is the multiplier. Here I_t and N_t are the control variables and K_t is the state variable.

Then by theorem 10.1, we may conclude that the following conditions are necessary for optimum, and they are also sufficient for optimum since F is concave.

$$\dot{K}_t = \partial H/\partial \lambda_t, \text{ that is, } \dot{K}_t = I_t - \delta K_t; \tag{66a}$$

$$\dot{\lambda}_t = i\lambda_t - \partial H/\partial K_t, \text{ that is,}$$

$$\dot{\lambda}_t = (i + \delta) - pF_K, \text{ where } F_K \equiv \partial F/\partial K; \text{ and} \tag{66b}$$

$$\lim_{t\to\infty} \lambda_t e^{-it} K_t = 0, \tag{66c}$$

and that H is maximized with respect to N_t and I_t. The maximization of H with respect to N_t yields $\partial H/\partial N_t = 0$ assuming $N_t > 0$ at optimum. Thus we have

$$F_N = w/p, \text{ where } F_N \equiv \partial F/\partial N_t. \tag{67}$$

A bounded positive value of N_t at optimum can be obtained given the nonlinearity of H with respect to N_t, provided that proper restrictions are imposed on F.

Since the current value Hamiltonian defined in (65) can be rewritten as

$$H = pF(N_t, K_t) - wN_t - \delta\lambda_t K_t + (\lambda_t - p_I)I_t, \tag{68}$$

the maximization of H with respect to I_t yields

$$I_t \to \infty, \text{ if } \lambda_t > p_I; \quad I_t \to -\infty, \text{ if } \lambda_t < p_I, \tag{69}$$

and the value of I_t is indeterminate when $\lambda_t = p_I$. (69) states that the optimal value of I_t is unbounded.

Using essentially the same formulations as above, Jorgenson and his associates obtain

$$\partial H/\partial I_t = 0, \quad \text{that is,} \quad \lambda_t = p_I,$$

instead of (69). Unfortunately, this cannot be warranted since H is linear with respect to I_t, as we observed in (68). This constitutes a serious analytical difficulty in Jorgenson's work, although this does not deny the important contribution of his work where he obtains an explicitly dynamic formulation of investment and tests his theoretical finding in terms of real world data.

Condition (69) means that the firm would adjust to the desired stock of capital instantaneously. This, in particular, implies that there is no such thing as a "demand schedule" for investment. In fact, it reconfirms the contention by Lerner (1944) and Haavelmo (1961) in connection with the controversy surrounding Keynes's discussion of investment in terms of "marginal efficiency of capital." Their work both appeared prior to a series of works by Jorgenson and his associates on investment. Lerner and Haavelmo's contention may succinctly be summarized in the following quotation from Haavelmo (1961, p. 216):[26]

> What we should reject is the naive reasoning that there is a "demand schedule" for investment which would be derived from a classical scheme of producer's behavior in maximizing profit.

One way to carry out the analysis under the present framework is to let the bounds for I_t vary, namely,[27]

$$I_{\min} \leqq I_t \leqq I_{\max}.$$

Such an analysis is done by Takayama (1985a, pp. 688–97). As can easily be seen from (69), the investment rules for this case can be written as

$$I_t = I_{\max}, \ \text{if } \lambda_t > p_I; \quad I_t = I_{\min}, \ \text{if } \lambda_t < p_I,$$

[26] Trygve Haavelmo is the 1989 Nobel laureate in Economic Science.

[27] An obvious, simple candidate for $I_{\min}$ is 0: the restriction of $I_{\min} \geqq 0$ is often called the **irreversibility of investment** (see Arrow 1968). This means that the disinstallation of investment goods is very costly (if not prohibitively expensive). The (implicit) assumption that $I_{\min}$ and $I_{\max}$ are given exogenously may be *ad hoc*. For example, that $I_{\max}$ is determined by financial constraints imposed on a particular firm (see Niho and Musacchio 1983).

and the value of I_t is indeterminate when $\lambda_t = p_I$. Since λ_t can be interpreted as the shadow demand price of capital and p_I is the market price of capital, the economic interpretation of this rule is straightforward. The other optimality conditions, (66) and (67), hold as they are.

Assume that nonconstant returns to scale technology prevail and that (67) can be solved for N_t as

$$N_t = N(K_t,\ w/p).$$

Elsewhere (Takayama 1985a, pp. 691–94), it is shown that the optimal policy of the firm is to reach the desired stock of capital (K^*) as soon as possible, where N^* and K^* are determined by

$$F_N(N^*,\ K^*) = w/p, \text{ and} \tag{67'}$$

$$F_K(N^*,\ K^*) = (i + \delta)p_I/p. \tag{70}$$

Here $(i + \delta)p_I$ signifies the rent for capital. Thus (67′) and (70) are the famous marginal productivity rules. To see that $(i + \delta)p_I$ is the rent for capital, suppose that one unit of capital goods is rented with rent c. The physical quantity of one unit of capital goods at time t will decay to $e^{-\delta t}$; hence the rental payment will be $ce^{-\delta t}$. Therefore, if the capital good is rented for an infinite future, the present value of rent over all future time will be[28]

$$\int_0^\infty ce^{-\delta t}e^{-it}dt = \int_0^\infty ce^{-(i+\delta)t}dt = \frac{c}{i + \delta}\,. \tag{71}$$

The intertemporal arbitrage relation will equate this with the price of a unit of capital, so that

$$p_I = \frac{c}{i + \delta}, \quad \text{or} \quad c = (i + \delta)p_I. \tag{72}$$

Suppose that inflation takes place in the future, and also suppose that the rate of inflation ($\pi = \dot{p}/p$) is constant. In this case, the rental

---

[28]If the capital good is rented for a finite period of time, say T, then the intertemporal arbitrage relation is

$$p_I = \int_0^T ce^{-(i+\delta)t}dt + p_I e^{-(i+\delta)T}.$$

This yields the same relation as before, i.e., $c = (i + \delta)p_I$.

payment (in nominal terms) is equal to $ce^{\pi t}$ instead of c. Then (71) can be rewritten as

$$\int_0^\infty ce^{\pi t}e^{-\delta t}e^{-it}dt = \frac{c}{(i - \pi) + \delta}, \tag{71'}$$

where $(i - \pi)$ signifies the real rate of interest. The intertemporal arbitrage condition (72) can be rewritten accordingly as

$$c = [(i - \pi) + \delta]p_I. \tag{72'}$$

To ease the exposition, we henceforth assume $\pi = 0$.

The concept of c discussed above plays an important role in Jorgenson's theory of investment. Jorgenson calls this the **user cost of capital.**[29] It signifies the cost that a firm has to bear to obtain one unit of service from capital goods. With the rental possibility of capital, c is the rent of capital, which in turn equals $(i + \delta)p_I$ as shown in (72). When the firm wishes to purchase the capital good and install it in the firm instead of renting it, this definition of user cost still applies in the long-run state, as (70) indicates. Note that in these cases, the cost of installation as well as other costs are assumed away.[30] Note also that

---

[29] The concept of "user cost" is discussed in Keynes's *General Theory.* As a "preliminary" definition, he defined it as "the amounts which he [an entrepreneur] pays out to other entrepreneurs for what he has to purchase from them together with the sacrifice which he incurs by employing the equipment instead of leaving it idle," (1936, p. 23). Later (pp. 52–53), he gives a more "precise" definition of this concept. Apparently still dissatisfied with his own explanation, Keynes wrote an "Appendix on User Cost" (pp. 66–73). Although he states (p. 66), "A little reflection will show that all this is no more than common sense," one may find his exposition quite confusing. He could (or should) have explained the concept of user cost in a more streamlined manner. It requires a great deal of reading and rereading of the relevant portions of *General Theory* to be able to understand what Keynes meant (or should have meant) by this concept. For a useful exposition of Keynes's concept, see Uzawa (1984, pp. 131–58).

[30] The following well-known exposition, though it contains the difficulty of glossing over the distinction between p_I and p_K, is useful to obtain a further insight into the concept of user cost. Consider a firm that borrows p_I dollars at the beginning of the period. At the end of the period, the firm needs to return $(1 + i)p_I$ dollars. By p_I dollars, the firm is able to purchase one unit of the capital good. By the end of the period, one unit of capital becomes $(1 - \delta)$ unit, where δ is the rate of depreciation. Denote the price of the capital good at the end of the period by $(p_I + \Delta p_I)$, in which a change in p_I over time is allowed. Then the firm can sell one unit of the capital good purchased at the beginning of the period by $(1 - \delta)(p_I + \Delta p_I)$ at the end of the period. Suppose the firm receives the revenue of c dollars from the services of one unit of capital during the period. The firm obtains

$$c + (1 - \delta)(p_I + \Delta p_I) \text{ dollars}$$

in obtaining (70) and (72), the price variables such as p, p_I, and i are assumed to be constant. In real-world economies, these prices change from time to time. This may raise some concern on the emphasis on user cost in the sense of $(i + \delta)p_I$ in empirical literature.[31]

Suppose that the firm is in the long-run steady-state (N^*, K^*). Then, in view of (71) and (72), we immediately realize that (70) can be rewritten as

$$p_I = \int_0^\infty pF_K^* e^{-(i+\delta)t} dt, \tag{73}$$

where $F_K^* \equiv \partial F/\partial K_t$ evaluated at (N^*, K^*). This reminds us of the Keynesian rule of the marginal efficiency of capital. Equation (73) states that the demand for the stock of capital is determined by the equality between the unit price of capital and the present value of all future income from an additional unit of capital. Since (70) and (73) are equivalent, the Keynesian rule of the marginal efficiency of capital is similar to the neoclassical marginal productivity rule, if the firm is on the path (N^*, K^*). Therefore, we disagree with Jorgenson (1967, p. 152) and his associates' view: "Keynes's construction of the demand function for investment must be dismissed as inconsistent with the neoclassical theory of optimal capital accumulation."

On the other hand, as is well known, Keynes does *not* explicitly impose some of the preceding assumptions. Thus, Keynes obtained a rule

---

at the end of the period. Here the cost of disinstallation of capital (and other costs associated with selling it) at the end of the period is ignored. In a competitive market, the intertemporal arbitrage enforces the following equality:

$$(1 + i)p_I = c + (1 - \delta)(p_I + \Delta p_I).$$

Ignoring $\delta \Delta P_I$, this arbitrage condition reduces to

$$c = [(i - \Delta p_I/p_I) + \delta]\, p_I,$$

which corresponds to (72′). If p_I stays constant over the period ($\Delta p_I = 0$), then this equation can be simplified to

$$c = (i + \delta)p_I,$$

which corresponds to (72). In this discussion, we postulated that the firm borrows p_I dollars with interest rate i at the beginning of the period. If the firm has such funds to begin with and it does not have to borrow, the same analysis applies since the firm can lend p_I dollars and obtains $(1 + i)p_I$ dollars at the end of the period (assuming a perfect capital market). This is nothing but the usual concept of opportunity cost.

[31] Such a concept of user cost of capital abounds especially in recent empirical literature. Unfortunately, many of the empirical studies ignore the assumptions imposed to obtain the concept of user cost, $(i + \delta)p_I$.

that is less explicit than (73), that is,

$$p_K = \int_0^\infty Q_t e^{-(i+\delta)t} dt,$$

where Q_t is the "*expected* rate of return" on capital at time t. Here Q_t is the expected revenue minus the expected operating cost (not including the depreciation cost) per additional unit of capital, and p_K is the "supply price of capital-asset" (Keynes 1936, p. 135), which is different from p_I. It is assumed that probability density functions cannot be attached to the formation of expectations with regard to Q_t. All future prospects are "uncertain" in the sense of Frank Knight.[32] Setting aside this question, we emphasize the fact that capital goods are *not* of the type discussed previously where the "fixity" of capital is ignored. Such a "fixity" will cause a divergence between p_K and p_I. We shall obtain a more precise definition of p_K later in section 10.4.3.

It may be worthwhile to note that the values of N^* and K^* are equal to the ones determined by the static optimization problem of choosing N and K so as to maximize the profit

$$pF(N, K) - wN - cK.$$

In other words, the "long-run" solution (N^*, K^*) for the dynamic optimization problem is reduced to the one for the static optimization problem. The myopic rule is optimal after all, from the long-run viewpoint.

---

[32] This is often considered the fundamental aspect of Keynes's discussion on investment ("animal spirit") and, in fact, the basic theme underlying *General Theory*. Granting that there is an important element of truth in this, we ignore it in our discussion on investment to focus our attention on another important aspect, the "fixity of capital." Even if we agree that uncertainty in the Knightian sense is important in real world economies, we cannot agree with those "Fundamentalists" such as Joan Robinson and G. L. S. Shackle who believed that the Knightian uncertainty is "the very essence" of Keynes's theory. As a result of such a view, they insist on purging the concept of equilibrium altogether. In such a case, much of traditional economics is consequently bound to be denied. Yet they fail to offer any operationally useful, alternative propositions. This is hardly surprising: if human ignorance of the future is *chiefly* characterized by totally unpredictable "uncertainty," we cannot possibly obtain any useful propositions. From nothing, nothing can be produced. After all, if Keynes were to believe investment is chiefly due to a firm's "animal spirit," why does he develop his theory of marginal efficiency of capital and toil over such concepts as the user cost of capital?

10.4.2 The Adjustment Cost Approach

In the preceding analysis, it is assumed that the firm can increase or decrease its stock of capital without incurring installation or disinstallation costs and any other costs associated with it. Capital goods are rental goods (like rental cars) that are rented at a certain price for a given period of time and returned to the rental company. Although this is true for many firms, there are many instances where it is not the case. Steel firms do not rent revolving furnaces, and auto firms do not rent assembly lines. These firms have to build their capital stocks with certain installation costs and other costs as well. Should they decide to reduce the size of their plants or abolish them, they have to face certain disinstallation costs and other costs. This is often regarded as the fundamental aspect of capital goods, known as the "fixity of capital."

Emphasizing such frictional or adjustment costs involved in investment, Tobin (1967, p. 158) writes:

> Jorgenson's investment demand schedule cannot serve the analytical purposes for which such a schedule is desired, and one must look elsewhere for a determinant theory of investment. At the level of a single firm this may be derived from frictional or adjustment costs.

Although there are a number of ways to introduce the concept of "fixity of capital" into the firm's maximization problem, here we consider it as the costs per unit of gross *rising* with the investment rate. In particular, we replace $p_I I$ in the firm's objective function (64) by [33]

$$C_t = C(I_t), \tag{74}$$

where $C(0) = 0$, $C'(I_t) > 0$ for all I_t, and $C''(I_t) > 0$ for all $I_t > 0$.

The firm's maximization problem is altered by this modification. The firm is now to choose N_t and I_t so as to

$$\text{Maximize} \quad \int_0^\infty [pF(N_t,\ K_t) - wN_t - C(I_t)]e^{-it}\,dt$$

---

[33] Such a specification is due to Eisener and Strotz (1963); Lucas (1967a); Gould (1967); and Abel (1979), for example.

Subject to $\dot{K}_t = I_t - \delta K_t$, $N_t \geqq 0$, $K_t \geqq 0$ for all t,

and a given value of K_o.

The current value Hamiltonian for the problem can be defined by

$$H \equiv [pF(N_t, K_t) - wN_t - C(I_t)] + \lambda_t(I_t - \delta K_t), \tag{75}$$

where λ_t is the Pontryagin multiplier for the present problem. By theorem 10.1, we may then conclude that the following conditions are necessary and sufficient for a unique optimum, where we assume an interior solution and impose proper assumptions on F. The sufficiency is obtained given the convexity of function C and the concavity of function F.

The introduction of adjustment costs by way of function C makes H nonlinear with respect to I_t. This in turn enables us to obtain an interior solution, which avoids unbounded I_t. We then have:

$$\dot{K}_t = \partial H/\partial \lambda_t, \quad \text{that is,} \quad \dot{K}_t = I_t - \delta K_t; \tag{76a}$$

$$\dot{\lambda}_t = i\lambda_t - \partial H/\partial K_t, \quad \text{that is,} \quad \dot{\lambda}_t = (i + \delta)\lambda_t - pF_K; \tag{76b}$$

$$F_N = w/p; \tag{76c}$$

$$C'(I_t) = \lambda_t; \tag{76d}$$

$$\lim_{t \to \infty} \lambda_t e^{-it} K_t = 0. \tag{76e}$$

To obtain (76c) and (76d), we assume $N_t > 0$ and $K_t > 0$ for all t at optimum.

A further analysis of the problem is discussed in detail by Takayama (1985a, pp. 697–706). Here we sketch the manner in which we can carry out analysis beyond (76).[34] We assume that F is homogeneous of degree one (constant returns to scale), i.e., $F(N_t, K_t) = N_t f(k_t)$. We may impose the usual assumptions on f:

$$f' > 0 \text{ and } f'' < 0, \text{ for all } k_t; \ f(0) = 0, \ f'(0) = \infty, \ f'(\infty) = 0.$$

Then (76c) uniquely determines the value of $k^* \equiv K_t^*/N_t^*$, where k^* is a constant as long as w/p is constant. As before, define c by

[34] For the nonconstant-returns-to-scale case, see Takayama (1985a, pp. 699–701).

$c \equiv pF_K^* = pf'(k^*)$. Equation (76b) is then reduced to a simple linear equation,

$$\dot{\lambda}_t = (i + \delta)\lambda_t - c. \tag{77}$$

We now claim that the solution which satisifies the transversality condition (76e) is given by

$$\lambda_t = \frac{c}{i + \delta} \; (\equiv \lambda^*), \tag{78}$$

so that λ_t is a positive constant for all t. Clearly, (78) satisfies (77), and hence it is a solution of (77).

To show that it also satisfies the boundary condition (76e), we first combine (76d) and (78) to obtain

$$C'(I^*) = c/(i + \delta), \tag{79}$$

so that the optimal investment is a positive constant, that is, $I_t = I^*$ for all t.[35] Next, substituting $I_t = I^*$ into (76a), we obtain

$$\dot{K}_t = I^* - \delta K_t. \tag{80}$$

The solution to this linear differential equation can explicitly be obtained as

$$K_t = I^*(1 - e^{-\delta t})/\delta + K_\circ e^{-\delta t}. \tag{81}$$

Substituting (81) into

$$\lim_{t \to \infty} \lambda_t e^{-it} K_t = \lim_{t \to \infty} \lambda^* e^{-it} K_t,$$

we may observe that condition (76e) is satisfied. Thus we may conclude that (78) is a (particular) solution of (77) which satisfies the transversality condition (76e).

Since we have

$$I^*(1 - e^{-\delta t})/\delta = \int_0^t I^* e^{-\delta s} ds,$$

the first term of the right-hand side of (81) signifies the investment accumulated up to time t. The second term of the right-hand side of (81) is the initial capital stock left over at time t.

---

[35] To obtain $I^* > 0$ from (79), we assume $C'(0) < c/(i + \delta)$. Note that (79) corresponds to (72).

Since $C'' > 0$ and $f'' < 0$, we may easily obtain, from (79) and (76c),

$$\partial I^*/\partial i < 0,\ \partial I^*/\partial \delta < 0,\ \partial I^*/\partial p > 0,\ \text{ and } \partial I^*/\partial w < 0,$$

where we may recall $c \equiv pF_K$ and note that c increases as p increases or w decreases. Thus, investment demand decreases as interest rate, depreciation rate, or wage rate increases; it increases as the price of output rises.

Define $\hat{K}$ by $\hat{K} \equiv I^*/\delta$. Then we may rewrite (80) as

$$\dot{K}_t = \delta(\hat{K} - K_t). \qquad (80')$$

Interpreting $\hat{K}$ as the "long-run desired stock of capital," (80′) may be interpreted as the "response function," where the rate of response is equal to the rate of depreciation (δ). From (81), it is clear that K_t monotonically approaches $\hat{K}$ as $t \to \infty$, regardless of the value of the initial capital stock ($K_\circ$).

10.4.3 Tobin's q, the Value of the Firm, and Keynes's Rule of Marginal Efficiency of Capital

In an important paper (1969), Tobin introduced the concept of "q," which was later referred to as **Tobin's q**. Tobin's q has been attracting a great deal of attention since the late 1970s as *the* criterion for investment decisions. In his 1969 article, Tobin denotes the price of *currently* produced goods by p and the market price of *existing* capital goods by qp, where all goods are assumed to be homogeneous (see 1969, p. 326). Then q is the ratio of the market price of existing capital goods over the price of currently produced goods. Tobin, however, also pushes this concept a bit further by saying, "the *rate* of investment–the speed at which investors wish to increase the capital stock–should be related, if to anything, to q, the value of capital relative to its replacement cost" (1969, p. 330). He then argues that the "long-run equilibrium" condition "requires that capital be valued at its reproduction cost, i.e., $q = 1$" (p. 331).

In the 1969 article, Tobin also expresses the public's real physical assets by qK (e.g., p. 327). Namely, q here is *average* q, the ratio of the market value of existing capital to its replacement cost. However, it has then been generally agreed that the "q" which is relevent to investment decision is *marginal* q, the ratio of the market value of an *additional* unit of capital to its replacement cost. Tobin's 1969 article may be somewhat confusing in its distinction between the two q's, as the previous paragraph indicates. However, the importance of marginal q is made explicit in Tobin and Brainard (1977). In fact, they state the gist of the q theory succinctly, which is:

> The neoclassical theory of corporate investment is based on the assumption that the management seeks to maximize the present net worth of the company, the market value of the outstanding common shares. ... Clearly it is the q ratio *on the margin* that matters for investment: the ratio of the increment of market valuation to the cost of the associated investment. The crucial value for marginal q is 1, but this is consistent with average q values quite different from 1. ...(1977, pp. 242–43)

By the late 1970s, the q theory became quite popular, and Hall (1977, p. 85) called it "the major competitor to Jorgenson's theoretical framework," while he contended that the q theory was basically a neoclassical theory à la Jorgenson and his associates. On the other hand, Lovell stated that he was "struck by similarities between q theory and the neoclassical approach of Dale Jorgenson, Robert Hall, and others" (1977, p. 399), and continued to write,

> Neither approach works out the dynamics of the adjustment process within the context of a carefully articulated optimization framework that would specifically incorporate the process of expectation formation and adjustment costs.

There is also a series of works, notably by Abel (1979), Yoshikawa (1980), Hayashi (1982), Abel and Blanchard (1983), and Blanchard and Fischer (1989) that clarify that the q theory can indeed be derived from an intertemporal choice-theoretic framework. This framework explicitly takes account of adjustment costs associated with investment. The framework is then similar to that with adjustment costs discussed in the previous section. In this subsection, we first take up investment theory based on Hayashi (1982).

Since Hayashi's work is aimed at empirical investigation, it is quite tedious. For one thing, he allows for "depreciation allowance" per dollar of investment for tax purposes (his "D" function). It is further complicated by allowing nonconstant discount rate and corporate taxes. Although these generalizations are important, we assume these away in the following exposition to capture the gist of his theory. Also to ease the exposition, we assume all prices, p, p_I, and w, as well as i are constant over time.

While Hayashi's theory is based on the adjustment cost approach discussed above, he introduces such costs in the capital accumulation equation. Instead of using the usual equation,

$$\dot{K}_t = I_t - \delta K_t,$$

he modifies it as follows:[36]

$$\dot{K}_t = \Psi(I_t, K_t) - \delta K_t. \tag{82}$$

As Hayashi (1982, p. 216) puts it, "In this formulation, I units of gross investment do not necessarily turn into capital: only $\Psi \times 100$ percent of investment does ... Ψ is increasing and concave in I, Ψ drops sharply as I changes from 0 to negative, reflecting the irreversibility of investment." The Ψ function thus captures the spirit of the adjustment cost approach discussed earlier. He calls Ψ the "installation function," which is illustrated in figure 10.2. More specifically, we may (following Hayashi 1982) assume

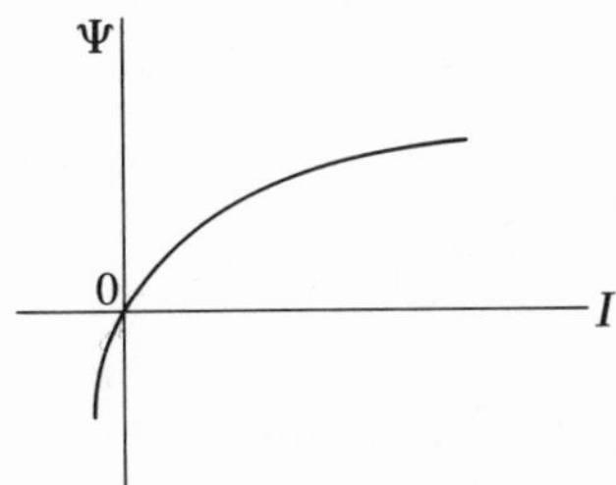

Figure 10.2: Illustration of the Ψ function

$$\Psi_I > 0,\ \Psi_{II} < 0, \quad \text{for all} \quad (I, K);\ \Psi(0, K) = 0, \quad \text{for all } K,$$

where $\Psi_I \equiv \partial\Psi/\partial I$ and $\Psi_{II} \equiv \partial^2\Psi/\partial I^2$. Furthermore, we may assume

$$0 < \Psi_I < 1 \text{ if } I > 0,\quad \Psi_I = 1 \text{ if } I = 0, \text{ and } \Psi_I > 1 \text{ if } I < 0,$$

[36] Hayashi (1982, p. 216) refers to Uzawa's (1968 and 1969) "Penrose function" in justifiying his Ψ function.

for all K. Jorgenson's specification amounts to specifying $\Psi_I = 1$ for all (I, K).

The firm is to choose the time paths of N_t and I_t so as to

$$\text{Maximize} \int_0^\infty [pF(N_t, K_t) - wN_t - p_I I_t]e^{-it}dt$$

Subject to (82), $N_t \geqq 0$, $K_t \geqq 0$, and given value of K_o.

The current value Hamiltonian for this problem can be written as

$$H \equiv [pF(N_t, K_t) - wN_t - p_I I_t] + \lambda_t[\Psi(I_t, K_t) - \delta K_t]. \tag{83}$$

Then the necessary conditions for (N_t, I_t, K_t) be optimal are given by (84a) through (84e) below. Since H is nonlinear with respect to N_t and I_t; we may assume that N_t and I_t are bounded. These conditions are also sufficient for an optimum, assuming that the functions F and Ψ are concave.

$$\dot{K}_t = \Psi(I_t, K_t) - \delta K_t; \tag{84a}$$

$$\dot{\lambda}_t = (i + \delta)\lambda_t - pF_K - \lambda_t \Psi_K, \text{ where } \Psi_K \equiv \partial\Psi/\partial K_t; \tag{84b}$$

$$F_N(N_t, K_t) = w/p; \tag{84c}$$

$$p_I = \lambda_t \Psi_I; \text{ and} \tag{84d}$$

$$\lim_{t\to\infty} \lambda_t K_t e^{-it} = 0, \tag{84e}$$

Here we again assume $N_t > 0$ and $I_t > 0$ for all t at optimum to obtain (84c) and (84d). The crucial assumption introduced by Hayashi is that the functions F and Ψ are homogeneous of degree one. This, in turn, is equivalent to specifying

$$F(N, K) = F_N N + F_K K, \quad \text{for all } N \text{ and } K, \text{ and} \tag{85a}$$

$$\Psi(I, K) = \Psi_I I + \Psi_K K, \quad \text{for all } I \text{ and } K. \tag{85b}$$

Next, we obtain:

$$\frac{d}{dt}\left(\lambda_t K_t e^{-it}\right) = (\dot{\lambda}_t K_t + \lambda_t \dot{K}_t - i\lambda_t K_t)\, e^{-it},$$

and we may observe:

$$\begin{aligned}
&\dot{\lambda}_t K_t + \lambda_t \dot{K}_t - i\lambda_t K_t \\
&\quad = -[(pF_K + \lambda_t \Psi_K)K_t - \lambda_t \Psi] && \text{(by 84a, b)} \\
&\quad = -[(pF - pF_N N_t) + \lambda_t(\Psi_K K_t - \Psi)] && \text{(by 85a)} \\
&\quad = [(pF - wN_t) + \lambda_t(\Psi_K K_t - \Psi)] && \text{(by 84d)} \\
&\quad = -\{(pF - wN_t) + \lambda_t[\Psi_K K_t - (\Psi_I I_t + \Psi_K K_t)]\} && \text{(by 85b)} \\
&\quad = -(pF - wN_t - p_I I_t). && \text{(by 84e)}
\end{aligned}$$

Thus along an optimal path, we have

$$\frac{d}{dt}\left(\lambda_t K_t e^{-it}\right) = -\left(pF - wN_t - p_I I_t\right) e^{-it}. \tag{87}$$

Integrating (86) from 0 to ∞ and using the transversality condition (84c), we obtain

$$\lambda_\circ K_\circ = V^*, \quad \text{where } V^* \equiv \int_0^\infty [pF - wN_t - p_I I_t] e^{-it} dt. \tag{88}$$

Note that V^* signifies the **value of the firm**. Under the homogeneity assumptions on F and Ψ, we are able to obtain a remarkably simple expression for the value of the firm, V^*.

Whether or not the value of the firm has a simple expression such as (88), we can understand the gist of Tobin's q theory in terms of the above work. Let V^* denote the value of the firm that is obtained on the basis of intertemporal choice. Then V^*, among other things, depends on the capital stock that the firm currently holds (i.e., $K_\circ$). Then $(\partial V^*/\partial K_\circ)$ measures an increase in the value of the firm by an additional unit of capital at time 0. If $(\partial V^*/\partial K_\circ)$ exceeds the market price of currently produced investment goods, p_I, then the firm is encouraged to push its investment further. Otherwise the firm would be discouraged. The magnitude of $(\partial V^*/\partial K_\circ)$ corresponds to what Keynes (1936, p. 135) calls the "supply price of capital-asset." In general, Tobin's **marginal** $\boldsymbol{q}$ (denoted by q_M) may then be defined by

$$q_M \equiv (\partial V^*/\partial K_\circ)/p_I. \tag{89}$$

His investment criterion is simply determined by whether or not q_M exceeds unity. Thus Tobin and Brainard (1977, p. 238) state:

> Economic logic indicates that a normal equilibrium value of q is 1 for reproducible assets which are in fact being reproduced, and less than 1 for others. Values of q above 1 should stimulate investment, in excess of requirements for replacement and normal growth, and values of q below 1 discourage investment.

In contrast to (89), Tobin's **average** $\boldsymbol{q}$ (denoted by q_A) can be defined by

$$q_A \equiv V^*/(p_I K_\circ). \tag{90}$$

Hence *if* Hayashi's homogeneity assumption, (85), is satisfied, we may obtain the following remarkable result from (88) through (90):

$$q_M = q_A, \tag{91}$$

where (88) plays a crucial role in obtaining (91). Equation (91) states that marginal q is equal to average q, provided that the production function and the installation function are both homogeneous of degree one. We may call this **Hayashi's theorem.**[37]

As Hayashi (1982, p. 214) emphasizes, "the 'q' theory is not operational as long as q is not observable." What is relevant to investment decision in Tobin's theory is *marginal* q and not average q. However, we can only observe average q, and not marginal q. Hayashi then continues to write, "Empirical works based on the 'q' theory have utilized average q as a proxy for marginal q" as represented by von Furstenberg (1977). Hayashi's theorem thus provides a remarkable bridge between theoretical and empirical studies. Based on this theorem, Hayashi then proceeds with an empirical study. There is one difficulty in his procedure. Nowhere does he empirically test the plausibility of his homogeneity assumption (85). Suppose that this assumption is not warranted in real-world economies. Then his empirical study has little meaning. Thus there is a dilemma in Hayashi's study. To pursue his empirical investigation, he needs the homogeneity assumption, as it enables him to obtain the measure of marginal q (i.e., $q_M = q_A$), and yet the plausibility of his empirical results depends on the empirical validity of such

[37] Note that in the formulation by Hayashi, the homogeneity assumptions play a key role in obtaining $q_M = q_A$. In Yoshikawa's formulation (1980), we can again obtain $q_M = q_A$ given his homogeneity assumptions. A general theorem underlying these two formulations is then recognized by Rose (1981), who obtains useful theorems on optimal control theory in a remarkably simple fashion.

an assumption.[38]

In fact, there may even be a theoretical difficulty in his homogeneity postulate. To examine this, we assume that F and Ψ are indeed both homogeneous of degree one, and briefly examine its theoretical implications. By using the homogeneity of Ψ, we may define the function ψ by

$$\psi(z_t) \equiv \Psi(z_t,\ 1)K_t, \quad \text{where } z_t \equiv I_t/K_t, \tag{92}$$

where we may assume

$$\psi' > 0,\ \psi'' < 0 \ \text{ for all } z;$$

$$\psi'(0) = 1,\ 0 < \psi' < 1 \ \text{ for } z > 0, \text{ and } \ \psi' > 1 \ \text{ for } z < 0.$$

Also, let $F(N_t,\ K_t) \equiv N_t f(k_t)$ as before. Then conditions (84a) through (84e) can be rewritten as:

$$\dot{K}_t = [\psi(z_t) - \delta]K_t; \tag{93a}$$

$$\dot{\lambda}_t = [(i + \delta) - \psi(z_t) + z_t\psi'(z_t)]\lambda_t - pF_K; \tag{93b}$$

$$F_N = w/p; \tag{93c}$$

$$p_I = \lambda_t\psi'(z_t); \quad \text{and} \tag{93d}$$

$$\lim_{t\to\infty} \lambda_t e^{-it} K_t = 0. \tag{93e}$$

Also k and hence pF_K are constant by virtue of (93c), $F_N = f(k) - kf'(k)$, and $F_K = f'(k)$.

Solving (93d) for z_t as

$$z_t = g(\lambda_t), \quad \text{where } g'(\lambda_t) = -\psi'/\lambda_t\psi'' > 0. \tag{94}$$

Substituting this into (93a) and (93b), we may obtain

$$\dot{K}_t = \{\psi[g(\lambda_t)] - \delta\}K_t, \text{ and} \tag{95a}$$

[38] The q theory has been introduced in recent macro textbooks. See, for example, Branson (1989, pp. 305–7), where he noted that the link between marginal q and average q can be "complex." He then points out that these two can move in the *opposite* direction!

$$\dot{\lambda}_t = \{(i + \delta) - \psi[g(\lambda_t)] + g(\lambda_t)\psi'[g(\lambda_t)]\} - c, \tag{95b}$$

where $c \equiv pF_K$. Equations (95a) and (95b) define the time path of (K_t, λ_t), given the boundary conditions (93e) and $K_\circ$. After somewhat tedious analysis, we can show that either K_t increases without limit or K_t shrinks to zero (see Semba 1989). Namely, either Hayashi's firm expands without a limit, or it disappears! It can be shown that this difficulty can be avoided if the Ψ function is not homogeneous of degree one. The homogeneity of Ψ facilitates an empirical investigation via Hayashi's theorem, but a theoretical difficulty accompanies it.

To forestall possible misunderstanding, we might note that there is nothing wrong with the concept of the value of the firm and the definitions of q_M and q_A in (89) and (90). The difficulty in Hayashi's paper is that he fails to pursue the implication of the homogeneity of function Ψ.

Next, let us obtain the value of the firm and its implication for the adjustment cost model discussed in the previous subsection. Recall that the optimality conditions are presented in (76a) through (76e). Also, recall that F is homogenous of degree one, that along an optimal path $k_t = k^*$ (= constant), $I_t = I^*$(= constant), and $c \equiv pF_K(1, k^*)$, and that the time path of capital stock is given by (81). Then observe:

$$\begin{aligned}
V^* &\equiv \int_0^\infty [pF(N_t, K_t) - wN_t - C(I^*)]e^{-it}dt \\
&= \int_0^\infty [pF_K(1, k^*)K_t - C(I^*)]e^{-it}dt \\
&= \int_0^\infty \{c[I^*(1 - e^{-\delta t})/\delta + K_\circ e^{-\delta t}] - C(I^*)\}e^{-it}dt \\
&= (cI^*/\delta)\int_0^\infty e^{-it}dt - c(I^*/\delta - K_\circ)\int_0^\infty e^{-(i+\delta)t}dt \\
&\qquad - C(I^*)\int_0^\infty e^{-it}dt \\
&= [cI^*/\delta - C(I^*)]/i - c(I^*/\delta - K_\circ)/(i + \delta) \\
&= \frac{c}{i + \delta}K_\circ + \frac{c\delta}{(i + \delta)i}\hat{K} - \frac{C(I^*)}{i},
\end{aligned}$$

where $\hat{K} \equiv I^*/\delta$.

From this, an increase in the value of the firm by an additional unit of capital at time 0 (i.e., $\partial V^* / \partial K_\circ$) can readily be computed as

$$\partial V^* / \partial K_\circ = c/(i + \delta) \; (\equiv \lambda^*). \tag{96}$$

where we may note that I^* is independent of $K_\circ$ by (79). Namely, λ^* signifies the marginal increase in the value of the firm by an additional unit of capital at time 0. That is, $(\partial V^* / \partial K_\circ)$ is equal to the value of the Pontryagin multiplier (λ) at time 0. Using (79), we may obtain

$$\partial V^* / \partial K_\circ = C'(I^*) = c/(i + \delta). \tag{97}$$

The first equality of (97) states that investment (I^*) is pushed to the point at which the marginal increase in the value of the firm by an additional unit of capital is equal to the marginal adjustment cost due to investment.

As pointed out earlier, $(\partial V^* / \partial K_\circ)$ can be interpreted as what Keynes (1936, p. 135) calls the "supply price of capital-asset" (p_K). Then we may obtain from (96)

$$p_K = \int_0^\infty c e^{-(i+\delta)t} dt \;\; [= c/(i + \delta)]. \tag{98}$$

Since one unit of capital produces the income stream of $c = pF^*_K$, and since one unit of capital acquired at $t = 0$ will decay to $e^{-\delta}$ at time t, the right-hand side of (98) signifies the present value of the total income stream obtained from one unit of capital acquired at $t = 0$. Equation (98) thus signifies **Keynes's rule of marginal efficiency of capital**, which equates the supply price of capital to the present value of all future income streams. It is important to distinguish (98) from (73): p_I in (73) is replaced by p_K in (98). The distinction between p_K and p_I is important since it stems from the "fixity of capital" or adjustment costs involved in investment. From (98), we may conclude that *Keynes's rule of marginal efficiency of capital is consistent with investment that is obtained from the intertemporal decision-making process of a firm, in which we also obtain the proper understanding of the supply price of capital.*

Substituting (76a) and (76b) into (86) and recalling the homogeneity of the function F and (76c), we may also observe:

$$\begin{aligned}\frac{d}{dt}\left(\lambda_t K_t e^{-it}\right) = &\left\{\left[(i + \delta)\lambda_t - pF_K\right] K_t \right.\\ &\left. + \lambda_t(I_t - \delta K_t) - i\lambda_t K_t\right\} e^{-it}\end{aligned}$$

$$= (-pF_K K_t + \lambda_t I_t)e^{-it}$$

$$= (pF - wN_t - \lambda_t I_t)e^{-it}.$$

Integrating this from 0 to ∞, we get

$$\lambda_\circ K_\circ = \int_0^\infty (pF - wN_t - \lambda^* I^*) e^{-it} dt, \tag{99}$$

where we may recall $\lambda_\circ = \lambda_t = \lambda^* = c/(i + \delta)$ and $I_t = I^*$ for all t. Notice that the right-hand side of (99) is *not* the value of the firm in the sense of Hayashi (1982). Also, in the present case, marginal q is *not* equal to average q.

Finally, we may examine whether "Tobin's q rule" is tenable as an investment criterion. The q rule states that investment is pushed up to the point at which marginal q is equal to unity. Recalling (89) and (97), we may obtain

$$q_M = C'(I^*)/p_I. \tag{100}$$

When $q_M = 1$, we then have

$$p_I = C'(I^*). \tag{101}$$

On the other hand, it would be plausible to suppose

$$C'(0) = p_I. \tag{102}$$

That is, the marginal adjustment cost is equal to the purchase price of capital when the rate of investment is zero. Since $C'' > 0$ for all I, (101) and (102) are inconsistent with each other, except for the case of $I^* = 0$. These considerations then suggest the need for further investigation of the q theory. Namely, if (101) is to determine the investment demand I^*, then I^* must be zero by (102). One way to get out of this difficulty might be to abandon the premise that investment is pushed to the point at which $q_M = 1$. Then, from the first relation of (100), we may conclude that $I^* \gtreqless 0$ depending upon whether $q_M \gtreqless 1$. This then determines whether the level of investment is positive or negative, but it does *not* determine the magnitude of investment. Then, contrary to the usual belief, the q rule is unsatisfactory as a theory that determines the *magnitude* of investment demand. A similar argument can also be made in terms of the installation function (Ψ) approach.

We now summarize some of the results obtain in this section.

Proposition 10.3.

(i) If there exist no adjustment costs of investment, optimum investment would be unbounded. In this case there is no such thing as "demand schedule" for investment, and Jorgenson's theory of investment contains a serious difficulty.

(ii) With the introduction of adjustment costs, there exists a demand schedule for investment, and it is a decreasing function of interest rate, depreciation rate, and wage rate, and an increasing function of output price.

(iii) Tobin's q theory captures an important aspect of investment à la the value of the firm, and it is consistent with the dynamic theroy of investment via adjustment costs. However, it is unsatisfactory as a theory to explain the magnitude of investment.

(iv) Keynes' concept of "supply price of capital-asset" (p_K) can be defined by an increase in the value of the firm per additional increase in capital ($\partial V^* / \partial K_\circ$). His theory of marginal efficiency of capital can then be vindicated as a dynamic theory of investment à la the adjustment cost approach.

References

Abel, A. 1979. *Investment and the Value of Capital.* New York: Garland.

Abel, A., and O. J. Blanchard. 1983. "An Intertemporal Model of Saving and Investment." *Econometrica* 51 (May) 675–92.

Arrow, K. J. 1968. "Optimal Capital Policy with Irreversible Investment." In *Value, Capital, and Growth: Papers in Honour of Sir John Hicks.* ed. J. N. Wolfe, 1–19, Edinburgh: Edinburgh University Press.

Blanchard, O. J., and S. Fischer. 1989. "Consumpton and Investment: Basic Infinite Horizon Models." In *Lectures in Macroeconomics*, 37–90. Cambridge, Mass.: MIT Press, 37–90.

Blinder, A. S. 1974. *Toward an Economic Theory of Income Distribution.* Cambridge, Mass.: MIT Press.

Branson, W. H. 1989. *Macroeconomic Theory and Policy.* 3d ed. New York: Harper and Row.

Brunner, K., and A. H. Meltzer. 1974. "Friedman's Monetary Theory." In *Milton Friedman's Monetary Framework: A Debate with his Critics.* ed. R. J. Gordon, 63–89, Chicago: University of Chicago Press, 63–89.

Burmeister, E., and R. A. Dobell. 1970. *Mathematical Theories of Economic Growth.* New York: Macmillan.

Cass, D. 1965. "Optimum Growth in an Aggregate Model of Capital Accumulation." *Review of Economic Studies* 32 (July): 233–40.

Dornbusch, R., and F. Fischer. 1987. *Macroeconomics.* 4th ed. New York: McGraw-Hill.

Drabicki, J. Z., and A. Takayama. 1978. "Money, Inflation, and Optimal Economic Growth." *Economics Letters* 1(1): 55–58.

————. 1983. "An Optimal Monetary Policy in an Aggregate Neoclassical Model of Economic Growth." *Journal of Macroeconomics* 5 (Winter): 53–74.

Duesenberry, J. S. 1949. *Income, Saving, and the Theory of Consumer Behavior.* Cambridge, Mass.: Harvard University Press.

Eisner, R., and R. H. Strotz. 1963. "Determinants of Business Investment." In *Impacts of Monetary Policy*, ed. D. B. Suits et al. Englewood Cliffs, N.J.: Prentice-Hall.

Farrell, M. J. 1959. "The New Theories of the Consumption Function." *Economic Journal* 69 (December): 678–96.

Fisher, I. N. 1930. *The Theory of Interest.* New York: Macmillan.

Foley, D. K., and M. Sidrauski. 1971. *Monetary and Fiscal Policy in a Growing Economy.* New York: Macmillan.

Friedman, M. 1957. *A Theory of the Consumption Function.* Princeton, N.J.: Princeton University Press.

————. 1974. "A Theoretical Framework for Monetary Analysis." In *Milton Friedman's Monetary Framework: A Debate with His Critics*, ed. R. J. Gordon, 1–62. Chicago: University of Chicago Press.

Goodwin, R. M. 1961. "The Optimal Growth Path for an Underdeveloped Economy." *Economic Journal* 71 (December): 756–74.

Gould, J. P. 1968. "Adjustment Costs in the Theory of Investment of the Firm." *Review of Economic Studies* 35 (January): 47–55.

————. 1969. "The Use of Endogenous Variables in Dynamic Models of Investment." *Quarterly Journal of Economics* 83 (November): 580–99.

Haavelmo, T. 1961. *A Study in the Theory of Investment.* Chicago: University of Chicago Press.

Hagen, E. E. 1947. "The Reconversion Period: Reflection of a Forecaster." *Review of Economics and Statistics* 29 (May): 756–74.

Hahn, F. H., and R. C. O. Matthews. 1964. "The Theory of Economic Growth: A Survey." *Economic Journal* 74 (December): 779–902.

Hall, R. E. 1977. "Investment, Interest Rates, and the Effects of Stabilization Policies." *Brookings Papers on Economic Activity* 1: 61–103.

Hall, R. E., and D. W. Jorgenson. 1971. "Application of the Theory of Optimum Capital Accumulation." In *Tax Incentives and Capital Spending*, ed. G. Fromm, 9–60, Washington, D.C.: Brookings Institution.

Hartle, R. F. 1987. "A Simple Proof of the Monotonicity of the State Trajectories in Autonomous Control Problems." *Journal of Economic Theory* 42 (February): 211–15.

Hayashi, F. 1982. "Tobin's Marginal and Average *q*: A Neoclassical Interpretation." *Econometrica* 50 (January): 213–24.

Hicks, J. R. 1946. *Value and Capital.* 2d ed. Oxford: Clarendon Press (1st ed. 1939).

Imai, K., H. Uzawa, R. Komiya, T. Negishi, and Y. Murakami. 1972. *Price Theory III* (in Japanese). Tokyo: Iwanami.

Jorgenson, D. W. 1963. "Capital Theory and Investment Behavior." *American Economic Review* 53 (May): 247–59.

———. 1965. "Anticipations and Investment Behavior." In *Brookings Quarterly Econometric Model of the United States*, ed. E. Kuh, G. Fromm, and L. R. Klein. Amsterdam: North-Holland.

———. 1967. "The Theory of Investment Behavior." In *Determinants of Investment Behavior*, ed. R. Ferber. New York: NBER.

———. 1971. "Econometric Studies of Investment Behavior: A Survey." *Journal of Economic Literature* 9 (December): 1111–47.

———. 1972. "Investment Behavior and the Production Function." *Bell Journal of Economics and Management Science* 3 (Spring): 220–51.

———. 1974. "Investment and Production: A Review." In *Frontiers of Quantitative Economics*, ed. M. D. Intriligator and D. A. Kendrick, 2: 341–75, Amsterdam: North-Holland.

Keynes, J. M. 1936. *General Theory of Employment, Interest, and Money.* London: Macmillan.

Koopmans, T. C. 1965. "On the Concept of Optimal Economic Growth." In *The Econometric Approach to Development Planning.* Amsterdam: North-Holland.

Lerner, A. P. 1944. *The Economics of Control: Principles of Welfare Economics.* New York: Macmillan.

———. 1965. "On Some Recent Developments in Capital Theory." *American Economic Review* 55 (May): 284–95.

Lovell, M. C. 1977. "Comments and Discussion of von Furstenberg's Paper." *Brookings Papers on Economic Activity* 2: 398–401.

Lucas, R. E. 1967a. "Adjustment Costs and the Theory of Supply." *Journal of Political Economy* 75, August: 321–34.

———. 1967b. "Optimal Investment Policy and the Flexible Accelerator." *International Economic Review* 8 (February): 78–85.

Lutz, F., and V. Lutz. 1951. *The Theory of Investment of the Firm.* Princeton, N.J.: Princeton University Press.

McLaren, K., and R. Cooper. 1980. "Intertemporal Duality: Application to the Theory of the Firm." *Econometrica* 48 (November): 1755–62.

Modigliani, F. 1975. "The Life-Cycle Hypothesis of Saving of Twenty Years Later." In *Contemporary Issues in Economics*, ed. M. Parkin. Manchester: Manchester University Press.

———. 1990. "Frisch Lecture." The Sixth World Congress of Econometric Society, Barcelona, Spain, August 24.

Modigliani, F., and R. E. Brumberg. 1954. "Utility Analysis and Consumption Function: An Interpretation of Cross Section Data." In *Post-Keynesian Economics*, ed. K. K. Kurihara, 388–436, New Brunswick, N.J.: Rutgers University Press.

Morrison, C. J. 1986. "Structural Models of Dynamic Factor Demands with Negative Expectations: An Empirical Assessment of Alternative Expectation Specifications." *International Economic Review* 27 (June): 365–86.

Morrison, C. J., and E. R. Berndt. 1981. "Short-Run Labor Productivity in a Dynamic Model." *Journal of Econometrics* 16 (August): 339–65.

Nagatani, K. 1970. "A Note on Professor Tobin's Money and Economic Growth." *Econometrica* 38 (January): 171–75.

Niho, Y. and R. A. Musacchio. 1983. "Effects of Regulation and Capital Market Imperfections on the Dynamic Behavior of a Firm." *Southern Economic Journal* 49 (January): 625–36.

Ramsey, F. P. 1928. "A Mathematical Theory of Saving." *Economic Journal* 38 (December): 543–59.

Rose, H. 1981. "Shadow Prices in Intertemporal Plans under Constant Returns to Scale." *Economics Letters* 8: 35–37.

Samuelson, P. A. 1958. "An Exact Consumption-Loan Model with or without the Social Contrivance of Money." *Journal of Political Economy* 66 (December): 467–82.

Semba, K. 1989. "Reconsiderations of Investment Theory" (in Japanese) *Aoyama Gakuin Seikei Ronshu* 14 (October): 73–95.

Shinohara, M. 1958. *Consumption Functions* (in Japanese). Tokyo: Keiso Shobo.

Stiglitz, J. E. 1974. "Growth with Exhaustible Natural Resources: Efficient and Optimal Economic Growth." *Review of Economic Studies* 41: 123–37.

Summers, L. H. 1981. "Taxation and Corporates Investment: A q-Theory Approach." *Brookings Papers on Economic Activity* 1:67–140.

Takayama, A. 1971. "A Note on Marginal Efficiency of Capital and Marginal Productivity of Capital." *Lecture notes*, Purdue University, February.

———. 1985a. *Mathematical Economics.* 2d ed. New York: Cambridge University Press.

———. 1985b. "Permanent Income Hypothesis: An Optimal Theory Approach to a Classical Macro Thesis." *Journal of Macroeconomics* 7 (Summer): 347–62.

———. 1987. "Chapter 7: Investment Demand." *Lecture notes*, Southern Illinois University, October.

———. 1991. "Investment Demand: A Survey." *Osaka Economic Papers* 40 (March): 115–40.

Tinbergen, J. 1960. "Optimum savings and Utility Maximization over Time." *Econometrica* 28 (April): 481–89.

Tobin, J. 1965. "Money and Economic Growth." *Econometrica* 33 (October): 671–84.

———. 1967. "Comment." In *Determinants of Investment Behavior*, ed. R. Ferber. New York: NBER.

———. 1968. "Notes on Optimal Monetary Growth." *Journal of Political Economy* 76 (July/August): 833–59.

———. 1969. "A General Equilibrium Approach to Monetary Theory." *Journal of Money, Credit and Banking* 1 (February): 15–29.

Tobin, J., and W. Brainard. 1977. "Asset Markets and the Cost of Capital." In *Economic Progress, Private Values, and Public Policy: Essays in Honor of William Fellner*, ed. B. Belassa and R. Nelson, 235–262, Amsterdam: North-Holland.

Treadway, A. B. 1969. "What is Output? Problems of Concept and Measurement." In *Production and Productivity in the Service Industries*, ed. V. Fuchs. New York: Columbia University Press.

———. 1971. "On the Rational Multivariate Flexible Accelerator." *Econometrica* 39 (September): 845–55.

———. 1974. "The Global Optimal Flexible Accelerator." *Journal of Economic Theory* 7 (January): 17–39.

Tsiang, S. C. 1969."A Critical Note on the Optimum Supply of Money." *Journal of Money, Credit, and Banking* 9 (May): 266–80.

Uzawa, H. 1966. "An Optimal Fiscal Policy in an Aggregate Model of Economic Growth." In *The Theory and Design of Economic Development*, ed. I. Adelman and E. Thorbeck. Baltimore, Md.: University of Maryland Press.

———. 1968. "The Penrose Effect and Optimum Growth." *Economic Studies Quarterly* 19 (March): 1–14.

———. 1969. "Time Preference and the Penrose Effect in a Two Class Model of Economic Growth." *Journal of Political Economy* 77 (July/August): 628–52.

———. 1984. *Reader's Guide to Keynes' "General Theory"* (in Japanese). Tokyo: Iwanami.

von Furstenburg, G. 1977. "Corporate Investment: Does Market Valuation Matter in the Aggregate?" *Brookings Papers on Economic Activity* 2: 349–97.

Yaari, M. E. 1964. "On the Consumer's Lifetime Allocation Process." *International Economic Review* 5 (September): 304-317.

Yoshikawa, H. 1980. "On the 'q' Theory of Investment." *American Economic Review* 70 (September): 739–43.

———. 1984. *Studies on Macroeconomics* (in Japanese). Tokyo: University of Tokyo Press.

CHAPTER 11

Extensions of Optimal Control Themes

11.1 The Main Theorem

So far, the major constraint in the optimal control problem is given by a system of differential equations,

$$\dot{x}_i = f_i[x(t),\ u(t),\ t],\ i = 1,\ 2,\ \ldots,\ n, \tag{1}$$

where $x(t) = [x_1(t),\ \ldots,\ x_n(t)]$ and $u(t) = [u_1(t),\ \ldots,\ u_r(t)]$. Although this remains a key form of constraints, it often becomes necessary to consider other forms of constraints. Here we take up some important ones: namely, the "g-constraint" and the "integral constraint," and (in this section) we discuss the question of how optimal control theorems are affected by these constraints. In subsequent sections, we then illustrate the results under such constraints via applications: in particular, section 11.2 is concerned with the consumer's lifetime allocation process, section 11.3 discusses the isopermetric problem, and section 11.4 analyzes spatial pricing.[1]

g-Constraints

One important form of constraint is given by

$$g_j[x(t),\ u(t),\ t] \geqq 0,\ j = 1,\ 2,\ \ldots,\ m', \tag{2a}$$

$$g_j[x(t),\ u(t),\ t] = 0,\ j = m' + 1,\ \ldots,\ m. \tag{2b}$$

We refer to constraints in the form of (2) as the **g-constraints**. It requires that $[x(t),\ u(t)]$ be in a certain region defined by (2). Equation (2a) allows for the possibility of

$$g_j[x(t),\ u(t),\ t] > 0,$$

[1] This chapter is adapted from Takayama (1978).

for some t and some j, where (2b) disallows such a possibility. (2a) deals with inequality constraints and (2b) deals with equality constraints.

Example 11.1. Recall the optimal growth problem discussed in chapter 10, in which the economic planner is to choose the path of per capita consumption so as to

$$\text{Maximize} \int_0^\infty u(c_t)e^{-\rho t}dt$$

$$\text{Subject to } \dot{k}_t = f(k_t) - nk_t - c_t, \text{ and a given } k_o.$$

Suppose we require that capital cannot be "eaten up" so that current consumption must come from current output. This requires the following constraint,

$$c_t \leqq f(k_t),$$

which is a constraint in the form of (2a).

Integral Constraints

Another form of constraint is written as

$$I_k \equiv \int_0^T h_k[x(t),\ u(t),\ t] \geqq 0,\ k = 1,\ 2,\ \ldots,\ \ell'. \tag{3a}$$

$$I_k \equiv \int_0^T h_k[x(t),\ u(t),\ t] = 0,\ k = \ell' + 1, \ldots, \ell. \tag{3b}$$

These are called **integral constraints**. Constraint (3a) allows the possibility of $I_k > 0$ for some k and for some t, whereas T in these integrals can be fixed, open, or ∞. This type of constraint is seen, for example, in the problem of individual savings where the individual consumer's budget constraint may be imposed over the lifetime period instead of each instant of time.

We now consider the problem of choosing $u(t) \in U$ so as to

$$\text{Maximize} \int_0^T f_o[x(t),\ u(t),\ t]dt + \psi[x(T)]$$

Subject to (1), (2), (3), and $x(0) = x^{\circ}$(fixed),

where T is assumed to be fixed, and $x(T)$ is *not* fixed *a priori*. The values $x(0)$ and 0 in the above problem can, respectively, be replaced by $x(t^{\circ})$ and t°. The discussion is analogous to the one presented below.

In this problem, the ψ function is to assign the utility on the remaining stock $x(T)$ at the end of planning horizon T. If $\psi \equiv 0$, then the optimal path would be to leave no assets at T, that is, $x(T) = 0$. All the functions, $f_{\circ}, f_1, \ldots, f_n, \psi, g_1, g_2, \ldots, g_m, h_1, \ldots, h_{\ell}$, are assumed to be continuously differentiable on a set X of the points in the (x, u, t)-space. Given $u(t) \in U$, X is determined by the relevant constraints. It should be apparent that the problem thus stated encompasses a wide class of questions that appear in economics as well as in science and engineering. Here we may note that the problem can be transformed into other forms in which T is open or ∞, and $x(T)$ is open, as is observed in chapter 9.

Before stating our main theorem, theorem 11.1, which provides the characterization of the optimum, we must state the "rank condition" reported in Hestenes (1965 and 1966).

Rank Condition. The $s \times r$ matrix,

$$\left[\frac{\partial g_E}{\partial u}\right],$$

has rank s along the optimal trajectory, where E is the set of indices in which g_j's are *effective* at optimum, that is,

$$E \equiv \{j : g_j[x(t), u(t), t] = 0\},$$

along the optimal trajectory $[x(t), u(t)]$, and s is the number of these effective constraints. Note that this rank condition imposes restrictions only on the "g-constraints," that is, (2a) and (2b), and no restrictions on the f_i's and h_k's. This rank condition is somewhat (but not completely) analogous to the classical rank condition in the theory of ordinary nonlinear programming (see chap. 2, and Takayama 1985, p. 98). Assuming this rank condition, we are now ready to state theorem 11.1, which we may call **Hestenes' theorem** (cf. Hestenes 1965 and 1966).

Theorem 11.1. Suppose that the arc,

$$z \equiv [x(t), u(t)],\ 0 \leqq t \leqq T,$$

is a solution of the current maximization problem. Then there exist multipliers,

$$p_\circ,\ p_i(t),\ q_j(t),\ \lambda_k,\ i = 1, \ldots, n,\ j = 1, \ldots, m,\ k = 1, \ldots, \ell,$$

not vanishing simultaneously on $0 \leqq t \leqq T$, such that the following relations hold for each t:

$$\dot{x}_i = \frac{\partial L}{\partial p_i},\ \dot{p}_i = -\frac{\partial L}{\partial x_i},\ i = 1, 2, \ldots, n, \tag{4}$$

where L is the **generalized Hamiltonian** defined by

$$\begin{aligned} &L[x(t),\ u(t),\ t,\ p_\circ,\ p(t),\ q(t),\ \lambda] \\ &\quad \equiv p_\circ f_\circ[x(t),\ u(t),\ t] + \sum_{i=1}^{n} p_i(t) f_i[x(t),\ u(t),\ t] \\ &\qquad + \sum_{j=1}^{m} q_j(t) g_j[x(t),\ u(t),\ t] + \sum_{k=1}^{\ell} \lambda_k h_k[x(t),\ u(t),\ t], \end{aligned} \tag{5}$$

$$\frac{\partial L}{\partial u_i} = 0,\ i = 1, 2, \ldots, r, \tag{6}$$

$$q_j(t) \geqq 0,\ g_j[x(t),\ u(t),\ t] \geqq 0, \tag{7a}$$

$$q_j(t) g_j[x(t),\ u(t),\ t] = 0,\ j = 1, 2, \ldots, m', \tag{7b}$$

$$g_j[x(t),\ u(t),\ t] = 0,\ j = m' + 1, \ldots, m, \tag{7c}$$

$$\lambda_k \geqq 0,\ \lambda_k I_k = 0,\ k = 1, 2, \ldots, \ell',$$

$$I_k = 0,\ k = \ell' + 1, \ldots, \ell, \text{ and} \tag{8}$$

$$\frac{\partial \psi}{\partial x_i(T)} = p_i(T),\ i = 1, 2, \ldots, n, \text{ (transversality condition)} \tag{9}$$

where the u_i's are assumed to be bounded.

Theorem 11.2.[2] Conversely, if $f_\circ(x, u, t)$, $f_i(x, u, t)$, $i = 1, 2, \ldots, n$, $g_j(x, u, t)$, $j = 1, 2, \ldots, m$, and $h_k(x, u, t)$, $k = 1, 2, \ldots, \ell$, are

[2]The proof of this theorem is obtained in Takayama (1985, pp. 660–64). The concavity of functions, $g_1, \ldots g_m$, can be relaxed to quasi-concavity.

all concave and differentiable in x and u for each t, and if the function $\psi[x(T)]$ is concave and differentiable in $x(T)$, then the set of necessary conditions in (4) through (9) are also *sufficient* for optimality, provided that $p_\circ = 1$ and $p_i(t) \geqq 0$, $i = 1, 2, \ldots, n$, for all t. If either $f_\circ$ is strictly concave in x and u, or ψ is strictly concave in $x(T)$, the optimal path is unique.

REMARK: Note that $\dot{x}_i = \partial L/\partial p_i \,(i = 1, 2, \ldots, n)$ in condition (4) reduces to the differential equation constraint (1). Also, using (4) through (7), we may obtain[3]

$$\frac{dL}{dt} = \frac{\partial L}{\partial t}. \tag{10}$$

REMARK: From condition (6) of theorem 11.1, we can also assert that, along the optimal path, the function $H(x, u, t, p_\circ, p, \lambda)$ is maximized with respect to u for all (x, u, t) satisfying $g_j(x, u, t) \geqq 0$, $j = 1, 2, \ldots, m'$, and $g_j(x, u, t) = 0$, $j = m' + 1, \ldots, m$, where the function H is defined by[4]

$$\begin{aligned} &H[x(t),\ u(t),\ t,\ p_\circ,\ p(t),\ \lambda] \\ &\quad \equiv p_\circ f_\circ[x(t),\ u(t),\ t] + \sum_{i=1}^{n} p_i(t) f_i[x(t),\ u(t),\ t] \\ &\qquad\qquad + \sum_{k=1}^{\ell} \lambda_k h_k[x(t),\ u(t),\ t]. \end{aligned} \tag{11}$$

---

[3] To obtain (10), first observe

$$\begin{aligned} \frac{dL}{dt} &= L_x \cdot \dot{x} + L_u \cdot \dot{u} + L_t + L_p \cdot \dot{p} + L_q \cdot \dot{q} \\ &= L_x \cdot f + L_t - f \cdot L_x + g \cdot \dot{q} = L_t + g \cdot \dot{q}, \end{aligned} \tag{10'}$$

by using (4), (5), and (6), where L_x, L_u, L_p, and L_q denote the gradient vectors of L with respect to x, u, p, and q, and $L_t \equiv \partial L/\partial t$. If $g_j = 0$, then $g_j \dot{q}_j = 0$. On the other hand, if $g_j > 0$ on some interval, then $q_j g_j = 0$ in condition (7) implies $g_j = 0$ (constant), so that $g \cdot \dot{q} = 0$. Then, $dL/dt = \partial L/\partial t$ follows from (10′).

[4] If we add the asterisk (∗) to signify the optimal trajectory of $[x(t), u(t)]$ and the corresponding specification of the multipliers, this may be more clearly stated as

$$H[x^*(t),\ u^*(t),\ t,\ p_\circ^*,\ p^*(t),\ \lambda^*] \geqq H[x^*(t),\ u(t),\ t,\ p_\circ^*,\ p^*(t),\ \lambda^*], \tag{11'}$$

for all $u(t) \in U$ satisfying $g_j[x^*(t), u(t), t] \geqq 0$, $j = 1, 2, \ldots, m'$ and $g_j[x^*(t), u(t), t] = 0$, $j = m' + 1, \ldots, m$.

The function H is referred to as the **Hamiltonian** for the present problem. When the "g-constraints" (that is, conditions 2a and 2b) are absent, then the function L in theorem 11.2 (defined in eq. 5) reduces to the simple Hamiltonian function H. In this case the maximization of L subject to the g-constraints reduces to the unconstrained maximization of H.

REMARK: It is important to note that the function g_j's contain u explicitly. If this is not the case, i.e., if $g_j = g_j[x(t), t]$, then the optimal path can "jump." Such constraints are known as the **bounded state variable constraints** (see for example, Hestenes 1966, chap. 8; Funk and Gilbert 1970; Russak 1970; and Seierstad and Sydsaeter 1977).

Note that in this formulation of the problem, we supposed that the terminal stock $x_i(T)$'s are *not* fixed *a priori*, while T remains fixed. On the other hand, we may often encounter the problem in which the terminal stock $x_i(T)$'s are fixed *a priori*, that is,

$$x_i(T) = x_i^T, \; i = 1, 2, \ldots, n, \tag{12}$$

where x_i^T signifies the predetermined value of $x_i(T)$, $i = 1, 2, \ldots, n$. In this case, the transversality condition (9) no longer holds and we instead have (12). Note that we lose n conditions by dropping (9), we now add n new conditions by virtue of (12).

In practical applications, the "non-negativity constraints,"

$$u_i(t) \geqq 0, \quad \text{for some } i\text{'s}, \tag{13}$$

often appear. Although such restrictions can be incorporated as a part of the constraints in the form of $g_j \geqq 0$, it would usually be simpler, if we merely define the function L *leaving out* the constraints in the form of $g_i = u_i \geqq 0$, and rewrite condition (6) of theorem 11.1 as

$$\frac{\partial L}{\partial u_i} \leqq 0 \text{ and } \frac{\partial L}{\partial u_i} u_i = 0, \quad \text{for such } i\text{'s}, \tag{6$'$}$$

where we assume that the u_i's are bounded. It is also possible that the only important (or relevant) g-constraints take the form of $u_i \geqq 0$. In this case, (6′) is further simplified to

$$\frac{\partial H}{\partial u_i} \leqq 0 \text{ and } \frac{\partial H}{\partial u_i} u_i = 0, \quad \text{for such } i\text{'s}, \tag{6$''$}$$

where the u_i's are assumed to be bounded. Furthermore, in the literature, researchers often impose the conditions that would ensure the "interior solution," that is, $u_i(t) > 0$ (for all t) at the optimum for all i's whenever the u_i's are restricted by the constraints, $u_i \geqq 0$. In this case, (6″) is still further simplified as

$$\frac{\partial H}{\partial u_i} = 0, \quad \text{for such } i\text{'s.} \tag{6'''}$$

In actual applications to economics, the rank condition à la Hestenes is usually satisfied. Furthermore, we can, from the context of a particular given problem, often safely set $p_\circ = 1$. Hence it is more or less customary in economics that no justification is given for setting $p_\circ = 1$ and no examination of the rank condition occurs. In the subsequent analysis, we follow such a practice, although it may not be accurate. In our examples below, this should cause no difficulty.

11.2 Consumer's Lifetime Allocation Process: Finite Horizon Case

Consider an individual whose planning horizon (or lifetime) is T, which is finite.[5] His or her real income and consumption expenditures at time t are, respectively, denoted by y and $c(t)$, where y is assumed to be constant. Assume that all assets are held in the form of interest-yielding securities; the accumulation (or decumulation) equation of assets $a(t)$ is given by[6]

$$\dot{a}(t) = y + ra(t) - c(t), \tag{14}$$

where r signifies the real rate of interest, which is assumed to be constant.

---

[5] This problem is first discussed by Yaari (1964) without the explicit use of optimal control theory. Since Yaari's pioneering work, there have been a number of extensions of the problem. Recall that the infinite horizon formulation is discussed in chap. 10. The present exposition is influenced by the method used by Hu (1978), which provides an important application of the present problem to the question of social security. See also Phillip (1974).

[6] Note that $a(t)$ can be negative. A negative $a(t)$ signifies the net amount of debt. Notice also that (14), by allowing the possibility of borrowing, implicitly assumes that the consumer's lending rate and borrowing rate are equal. The relaxation of this assumption is often seen in the literature.

We assume that the consumer's lifetime utility is given by[7]

$$U \equiv \int_0^T u[c(t)]e^{-\rho t}dt + \psi[a(T)]e^{-\rho T}, \tag{15}$$

where $\rho > 0$ is the subjective rate of discount, while $u(c)$ signifies the (instantaneous) utility of consumption, and ψ signifies the utility of his or her bequest. Here $u(c)$ should not be confused with control variables. We assume that the functions u and ψ are monotone increasing and strictly concave, that is,

$$u' > 0,\ u'' < 0,\ \psi' > 0, \text{ and, } \psi'' < 0. \tag{16}$$

Furthermore, we assume

$$u'(0) = \infty, \tag{17}$$

which means that the individual has a strong incentive to avoid very low consumption. Although the specification of the bequest function ψ can be *ad hoc* due to the infinite chain of generations, we do not get into this question. Our problem may thus be only illustrative, while the present formulation facilitates the comparison of the present case with the infinite horizon case discussed in the previous chapter.

The individual chooses the time path of his consumption $c(t)$ and his terminal wealth $a(T)$ to maximize lifetime utility, U, subject to the asset accumulation equation (14), the nonnegativity constraints $c(t) \geqq 0$ for all t, and the prescribed value of his initial wealth, $a(0) = a_\circ$. Clearly, $a(T)$ is the state variable and $c(t)$ is the control variable for this problem. The Hamiltonian for this problem can be written as

$$\tilde{H} \equiv u[c(t)]e^{-\rho t} + p(t)[y + ra(t) - c(t)]. \tag{18}$$

Then, the necessary (and sufficient) conditions for the unique optimum are written as[8]

$$\dot{a}(t) = \partial\tilde{H}/\partial p, \text{ that is, } \dot{a}(t) = y + ra(t) - c(t), \tag{19}$$

[7]One question that may arise in the context of (15) is that of whether the individual can leave a negative amount of assets when he dies at time T, i.e., whether $a(T)$ can be negative. If his children or someone else is willing to pay his debt, and if he does not mind this, $a(T)$ can be negative. The question of whether $a(T)$ can be negative is incorporated in the function ψ. The difficulty of such a formulation is that the magnitude of such a debt can be arbitrary or *ad hoc*.

[8]The sufficiency follows from the strict concavity of u and the linearity of the right-hand side of (14). The strict concavity of u ensures the uniqueness of optimum path.

$$\dot{p}(t) = -\partial\tilde{H}/\partial a, \quad \text{that is,} \quad \dot{p}(t) = -p(t)r, \tag{20}$$

$$\partial\tilde{H}/\partial c \leqq 0 \quad \text{and} \quad (\partial\tilde{H}/\partial c)c(t) = 0, \quad \text{for each } t, \text{ and} \tag{21}$$

$$p(T) = \psi'(a_T)e^{-\rho T}, \quad \text{where} \quad a_T \equiv a(T). \tag{22}$$

Note that (19) is the same as (14). That is, along the optimal path, constraint (14) must be satisfied. Since it can easily be shown that (17) enables us to ensure $c(t) > 0$ for all t, (21) yields

$$\partial\tilde{H}/\partial c = 0, \quad \text{that is,} \quad u'[c(t)]e^{-\rho t} = p(t). \tag{23}$$

The economic interpretation of these results are similar to the interpretation obtained for the infinite horizon problem discussed earlier. In (23), it is clear that $p(t)$ signifies the present value of the marginal utility of consumption at time t. The magnitude of the loss due to the sacrifice of one unit of consumption (which is devoted to his or her wealth accumulation, saving) at time t is measured by $u'[c(t)]$, and hence its present value is equal to $u'[c(t)]e^{-\rho t}$. Thus (23) means that $p(t)$ signifies the opportunity cost of accumulation (saving). Note also that (20) can be written as

$$\dot{p}(t)/p(t) = -r, \tag{20$'$}$$

namely, $-\dot{p}/p$ is equal to the rate of return from holding assets (i.e., the interest rate). Recalling the interpretation of $p(t)$ as the shadow price of saving, (20′) then signifies the intertemporal arbitrage condition (for a particular individual).

Next, define $q(t)$ by

$$q(t) \equiv p(t)e^{\rho t}, \text{ so that } p(t) = q(t)e^{-\rho t}. \tag{24}$$

Then observe

$$\dot{p} = \dot{q}e^{-\rho t} - \rho q e^{-\rho t} = (\dot{q} - \rho q)e^{-\rho t},$$

so that

$$\dot{p}/p = \dot{q}/q - \rho. \tag{25}$$

Hence we may rewrite (20) or (20′) as

$$\dot{q}(t)/q(t) = \rho - r. \tag{26}$$

Differential equation (26) yields the explicit form of $q(t)$, that is,

$$q(t) = q_{\circ}e^{(\rho-r)t}, \quad \text{where} \quad q_{\circ} \equiv q(0). \tag{27}$$

Since we may rewrite (22) as $q(T) = p(T)e^{\rho T} = \psi'(a_T)$, we have from (27),

$$q_{\circ}e^{(\rho-r)T} = \psi'(a_T). \tag{28}$$

Also, we may rewrite (23) as

$$u'[c(t)] = q(t). \tag{29}$$

Note that this implies $q(t) > 0$ for all t.

Optimality conditions (20), (21), and (22) are now rewritten as (26), (29), and (28), respectively, and (26) in turn is reduced to (27). These, together with (14) or (19), we may specify as the optimal path. The procedure of converting p to q is exactly the same as the one that is used in the previous chapter to obtain theorem 10.1. As done before, we may define the current value Hamiltonian by

$$H \equiv u[c(t)] + q(t)[y + ra(t) - c(t)], \tag{16'}$$

and we may obtain (26), (29), and (28) directly.

Define the function ϕ as the inverse function of u', and we rewrite (29) as

$$c(t) = \phi[q_{\circ}e^{(\rho-r)t}], \quad \text{where} \quad \phi' = 1/u'' < 0, \tag{30}$$

by using (27). From (30), we may conclude that the individual increases (resp. decreases) his consumption monotonically over his lifetime if and only if the real rate of interest exceeds (resp. falls short of) his subjective discount rate. This conclusion corresponds to the one obtained for the infinite horizon problem in the previous chapter. For the finite horizon problem, see Yaari (1964, p. 309), where he assumes away the bequest motive. Note that if $r < \rho$, consumption monotonically decreases over time.

Next note that the integration of the (instantaneous) budget equation (14) yields

$$\int_0^T c(t)e^{-rt}dt + a_t e^{-rT} = a_{\circ} + \int_0^T ye^{-rt}dt, \tag{31}$$

which signifies the lifetime budget condition of the individual. Requiring this condition for *every point* in his or her lifetime[9] amounts to specifying

$$\int_0^t c(s)e^{-rs}ds + a(t)e^{-rt} = a_\circ + \int_0^t ye^{-rs}ds. \tag{32}$$

Differentiation of (32) in t yields (14).

Define the function Y by

$$Y(y,\ r,\ a_\circ) \equiv a_\circ + \int_0^T ye^{-rt}dt = a_\circ + (1 - e^{-rT})y/r, \tag{33}$$

where Y signifies the "lifetime income" of the individual. From (33), we may at once obtain

$$\partial Y/\partial a_\circ > 0, \quad \text{and} \quad \partial Y/\partial y > 0, \tag{34}$$

as is expected.

By substituting (33) and (30) into (31) we may define the function a_T by

$$\begin{aligned} a_T &= \{Y(y,\ r,\ a_\circ) - \int_0^T \phi[q_\circ e^{(\rho-r)t}]e^{-rt}dt\}e^{rT} \\ &\equiv a_T(q_\circ,\ y,\ a_\circ,\ \rho,\ r). \end{aligned} \tag{35}$$

Then, we can easily obtain the following relations:

$$\partial a_T/\partial q_\circ > 0,\ \partial a_T/\partial y > 0, \tag{36a}$$

$$\partial a_T/\partial a_\circ > 0,\ \partial a_T/\partial \rho > 0. \tag{36b}$$

To obtain the initial value of the multiplier $q_\circ$, we rewrite (28) as

$$q_\circ = \psi'[a_T(q_\circ,\ y,\ a_\circ,\ \rho,\ r)]e^{(r-\rho)T} \equiv q_\circ(y,\ a_\circ,\ \rho,\ r), \tag{37}$$

by using (35). Then by virtue of (36), we have

$$\partial q_\circ/\partial y < 0,\ \partial q_\circ/\partial a_\circ < 0,\ \ \partial q_\circ/\partial \rho < 0. \tag{38}$$

---

[9] Since $a(t)$ can be negative, this requirement is not as restrictive as it may sound. Then $a(T) > 0$ is not optimum, since one can always increase consumption (and thus satisfaction) by making $a(T) = 0$.

Using the function $q_\circ$ defined in (37) together with (30), we may define the function ϕ^* by

$$c(t) = \phi[q_\circ(y, a_\circ, \rho, r)e^{(\rho-r)t}] \equiv \phi^*(y, a_\circ, \rho, r, t). \tag{39}$$

Since $\phi' < 0$, we may conclude from (38),

$$\partial\phi^*/\partial y > 0, \quad \text{and} \quad \partial\phi^*/\partial a_\circ > 0. \tag{40}$$

Thus, an increase in income or the initial wealth increases the consumption for each t.

Finally, we may consider this problem by supposing that the individual has no bequest motive. In this case, we may require that

$$a(T) = 0. \tag{41}$$

This means that the individual cannot die with a debt $[a(T) \not< 0]$. Except that (28) is replaced by (41), the other optimality conditions (14), (26), and (29) hold as they are. Thus, (31) also holds, whereas (35) should be rewritten as

$$0 = a_T(q_\circ, y, a_\circ, \rho, r). \tag{42}$$

Solving this for $q_\circ$, we may define the function $q_\circ^*$ as

$$q_\circ = q_\circ^*(y, a_\circ, \rho, r). \tag{43}$$

Then, recalling (36), we may obtain

$$\partial q_\circ^*/\partial y < 0, \ \partial q_\circ^*/\partial a_\circ < 0, \ \partial q_\circ^*/\partial\rho < 0. \tag{38$'$}$$

Substituting (43) into (30), we obtain

$$c(t) = \phi[q_\circ^*(y, a_\circ, \rho, r)e^{(\rho-r)t}] \equiv \phi^*(y, a_\circ, \rho, r, t), \tag{39$'$}$$

where we have

$$\partial\phi^*/\partial y > 0, \ \partial\phi^*/\partial a_\circ > 0. \tag{40$'$}$$

To obtain further insight into the problem, we may explicitly specify the utility function by

$$u(c) = \log\ c. \tag{44}$$

In this case, (30) can be written as

$$c(t) = e^{(r-\rho)t}/q_\circ. \tag{45}$$

Hence (35) is written as

$$\begin{aligned} a_T &= [Y(y,\ a_\circ,\ r) - \frac{1}{q_\circ}\int_0^T e^{-\rho t}dt]e^{rT} \\ &= [Y(y,\ a_\circ,\ r) - (1 - e^{-\rho T})/(\rho q_\circ)]e^{rT}. \end{aligned} \tag{46}$$

We consider the case in which there is no bequest motive and a_T is specified to be zero. Equation (46) with $a_T = 0$ defines the function $q_\circ^*$ as

$$q_\circ = (1 - e^{-\rho T})/[\rho Y(y,\ a_\circ,\ r)] \equiv q_\circ^*(y,\ a_\circ,\ \rho,\ r).$$

Substituting this into (45), we may define the function Φ^* by

$$\begin{aligned} c(t) &= e^{(r-\rho)t}\rho Y/(1 - e^{-\rho T}) \\ &\equiv \Phi^*(y,\ a_\circ,\ \rho,\ r), \quad \text{where } Y = Y(y,\ a_\circ,\ r). \end{aligned} \tag{47}$$

Then recalling $\partial Y/\partial y > 0$ and $\partial Y/\partial a_\circ > 0$, we obtain

$$\partial\Phi^*/\partial y > 0,\ \partial\Phi^*/\partial a_\circ > 0. \tag{48}$$

11.3 Isoperimetric Problem

Ancient Greeks proposed the problem of finding the closed curve (on the plane) of given length which encloses the greatest area. This problem is known as the *isoperimetric problem.* The solution is known to be a circle. It turns out that this problem can be considered as a calculus of variation problem in which the restriction of a "given length" yields a constraint in the form of an integral. Thus, the calculus of variation problems with *integral constraints* are often called **isoperimetric problems**. Interpreting these in such a general fashion, there are many "isoperimetric problems" in economics, as integral constraints often appear in economic problems. Instead of considering such examples, here we consider the proper isoperimetric problem, that is, the kind considered by the ancient Greeks. We consider a problem that is slightly degenerated. We shall find the curve of a given length joining the two points (0, 0) and (1, 0), in the $(t,\ x)$ coordinate, which lies above the t-axis and encloses the maximum area between itself and the t-axis. Namely, we wish to find the curve $x(t)$ so as to

$$\text{Maximize} \int_0^1 x(t)dt$$

$$\text{Subject to} \int_0^1 \sqrt{1 + \dot{x}^2}\, dt = a, \text{ and}$$

$$x(0) = 0,\ x(1) = 0. \tag{49}$$

Here t obviously does *not* signify "time." Although this is a standard problem in the textbooks of classical calculus of variations and may be solved more easily by such a technique,[10] here we solve this problem by using the optimal control technique. This will illustrate how to go about dealing with isoperimetric problems using the optimal control technique.

To solve this problem, we define $u(t)$ by $u(t) \equiv \dot{x}(t)$, and convert the problem to an optimal control problem of $u(t)$ so as to

$$\text{Maximize} \int_0^1 x(t)dt$$

$$\text{Subject to } \dot{x} = u,$$

$$\int_0^1 (a - \sqrt{1 + u^2})dt = 0,^{11} \tag{50}$$

and (49). The (generalized) Hamiltonian of this problem can be specified as

$$L \equiv x(t) + p(t)u(t) + \lambda\left[a - \sqrt{1 + u(t)^2}\right], \tag{51}$$

where p and λ are the multipliers, and λ is a constant independent of t.

---

[10] For the exposition of the isoperimetric problems from the standpoint of classical calculus of variations, see, for example, Gelfand and Fomin (1963); Hadley and Kemp (1971); and Simmons (1972).

[11] Instead of (50), we may consider the inequality constraint in the form of

$$\int_0^1 (a - \sqrt{1 + u^2})dt \geqq 0. \tag{50$'$}$$

In this case, the curve is required not to exceed the given length a. Theorem 11.1 enables us to investigate such a problem. The solution, as can be expected, is the same as the one given by (50).

The necessary conditions for optimum for this problem can be written as[12]

$$\dot{x} = \partial L/\partial p, \quad \text{that is,} \quad \dot{x} = u, \tag{52a}$$

$$\dot{p} = -\partial L/\partial x, \quad \text{that is,} \quad \dot{p} = -1, \tag{52b}$$

$$\partial L/\partial u = 0, \quad \text{that is,} \, p = \lambda u/\sqrt{1 + u^2}, \tag{52c}$$

and (49). Combining (52b) and (52c), we get

$$\frac{d}{dt}\left(\frac{\lambda u}{\sqrt{1 + u^2}}\right) = -1,$$

which can be integrated as

$$\frac{u}{\sqrt{1 + u^2}} = \frac{c_1 - t}{\lambda}, \tag{53}$$

where c_1 is the integration constant. Recalling $u = \dot{x}(t)$, and integrating (53) again, we obtain

$$(t - c_1)^2 + (x - c_2)^2 = \lambda^2. \tag{54}$$

Needless to say, (54) is the equation of a circle with radius λ and with the center at (c_1, c_2). Note that when $a < 1$, the solution of the problem does not exist (cf. Fig. 11.1). Hence we must require $a \geqq 1$. Furthermore, when $a > \pi/2$, the arc does not remain for $t \in [0, 1]$, but extends into the region in which $t < 0$ and $t > 1$, in which case the above integrals lose their meaning. Namely, we require

$$1 \leqq a \leqq \pi/2.$$

We may now illustrate the solution of the present problem for different values of a in figure 11.1.

The constants c_1 and c_2 in (54) are determined by substituting the boundary conditions $x(0) = 0$ and $x(1) = 0$ into (54). They are determined by

$$c_1^2 + c_2^2 = \lambda^2, \; (1 - c_1)^2 + c_2^2 = \lambda^2.$$

[12] Since the terminal end-point is specified as $x(1) = 0$ in the present problem, we do not have the transversality condition.

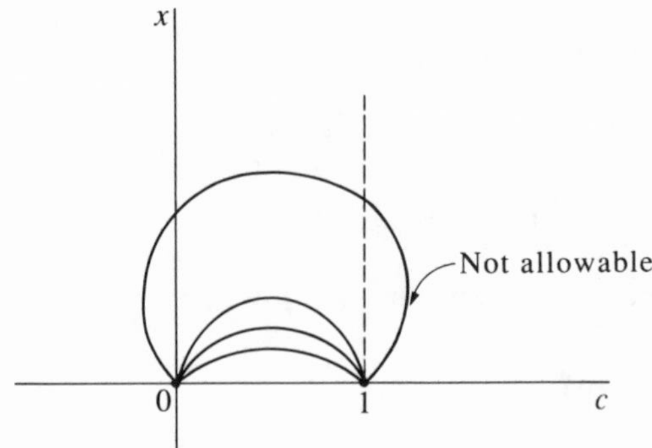

Figure 11.1: Isoperimetric problem

Thus we have

$$c_1 = 1/2, \; c_2 = \sqrt{\lambda^2 - 1/4}.$$

From (52c) and (53), we may compute

$$p = -(t - 1/2),$$

where we may use $c_1 = 1/2$. Also, differentiation of (54) yields

$$u = -(t - c_1)/(x - c_2),$$

where we recall $\dot{x} = u$ and $\lambda =$ constant. Substituting this into (53) and using (54), we obtain

$$\sqrt{1 + u^2} = \frac{\lambda}{\sqrt{\lambda^2 - (t - c_1)^2}}. \tag{55}$$

Integrating this over [0, 1], and using (50), we may determine the value of λ, which in turn determine the value of c_2.[13]

[13]The integration of the right-hand side of (55) yields

$$\int \frac{1}{\sqrt{1 - z^2}} dz = \arcsin z,$$

11.4 Spatial Pricing Problem

Although t, in optimal control theory, is often used to signify "time" in practical applications, this does not have to be the case, as exemplified in the previous section. In economic applications, the variable t can also refer to "Mr. t" in the continuum trader model, or "income" in the taxation model, and so forth. Some such applications are seen in El-Hodiri (1971, pp. 122–26) and Mirrlees (1971), for example. Here we shall use the ***spatial pricing problem*** as such an example, in which t refers to "location t." We consider both the profit maximizing and the welfare maximizing problems of a monopolistic competitive firm.[14]

Consider a monopolistic competitive firm whose product is sold up to a finite distance, T, from the firm. The firm is subject to two costs, production and transportation costs. Let $\tau(t)$ signify the unit transport costs, where t denotes the distance away from the firm. We assume $\tau(0) = 0$. Let $p(t)$ be the delivered price at location t, and let $y[p(t)]$ be the demand function where we assume $y'(\equiv dy/dp) < 0$. That the firm can charge different prices according to locations implies price discrimination. It is assumed that such price discrimination is economically *and* institutionally feasible. Let $Y(T)$ signify the total quantity sold over the entire market-space. Namely, it is defined by

$$Y(T) \equiv \int_0^T y[p(t)]dt, \tag{56}$$

where T denotes the market boundary distance away from the firm. Although it may be desirable to treat T as an economic variable, here we simply assume that it is predetermined by institutional or physical reasons. With the total production $Y(T)$, we denote total production costs by $C[Y(T)]$. Needless to say, total output (which is equal to the total quantity demanded) depends on the firm's pricing policy, $p(t)$, over its market-space.

The firm chooses $p(t)$ so as to maximize its total profits over its

---

where $z \equiv (t - 1/2)/\lambda$.

[14] The analysis in this section can more simply be carried out in terms of the usual nonlinear programming theory (see the appendix to this section). The present discussion is only for the sake of illustration; we hope to show that general theorems presented in section 11.1 can be applied to different branches of economics. This section is also adapted from Takayama (1978). The writing of this lecture note was inspired by conversations with Mark Fratrik.

market-space,

$$\pi \equiv \int_0^T \{p(t)y[p(t)] - \tau(t)y[p(t)]\}dt - C[Y(T)],$$

subject to

$$\dot{Y}(t) = y[p(t)]. \tag{57}$$

We may note that (57) is obtained by differentiating (56) with respect to T, and that the integration of (57) over $[0, T]$ yields (56). This is an optimal control problem, where $Y(t)$ is the state variable and $p(t)$ is the control variable.

To facilitate the solution of this problem, we consider the inverse demand function,

$$p(t) = P[y(t)], \tag{58}$$

where P is the inverse function of $y(p)$, so that $P' \equiv dP/dy = 1/y' < 0$. With this, the problem of choosing $p(t)$ is converted to that of choosing $y(t)$ so as to maximize

$$\pi = \int_0^T \{P[y(t)]y(t) - \tau(t)y(t)\}dt - C[Y(T)],$$

subject to $\dot{Y}(t) = y(t)$. Here the state and the control variables are $Y(t)$ and $y(t)$, respectively. The Hamiltonian of this problem can readily be defined by

$$H \equiv P[y(t)]y(t) - \tau(t)y(t) + q(t)y(t), \tag{59}$$

where $q(t)$ is the multiplier associated with the constraint (57), $\dot{Y} = y$. Then the necessary conditions for an interior solution can be written as[15]

$$\dot{Y} = \partial H/\partial q, \quad \text{that is,} \quad \dot{Y}(t) = y(t), \tag{60a}$$

$$\dot{q} = -\partial H/\partial Y, \quad \text{that is,} \quad \dot{q}(t) = 0, \tag{60b}$$

$$\partial H/\partial y = 0, \quad \text{that is,} \quad P'y + P - \tau + q = 0, \quad \text{and} \tag{60c}$$

[15]Assuming the total revenue function (net of transport costs), $[p(y)y - \tau y]$, is concave in y and the cost function C is concave in Y, this set of necessary conditions is also sufficient for optimum. If either of these functions is strictly concave, then the optimum is unique.

$$-C'[Y(T)] = q(T), \quad \text{where} \quad C' \equiv dC/dY. \tag{60d}$$

Note that (60d) corresponds to (9), signifying the transversality condition of the present problem.

From (60b) and (60d), we at once obtain

$$q(t) = \text{constant} = -c^* \quad \text{for all } t, \tag{61}$$

where $c^* \equiv C'[Y(T)]$ at optimum. The multiplier $q(t)$ is constant regardless of location and it signifies the negative of marginal cost of production. Noting that $(P'y + P)$ signifies the marginal revenue for the market at location t, $MR(t)$. Equation (60c) implies

$$MR(t) = \tau(t) + c^*, \tag{62}$$

where the right-hand side of (62) is the marginal total cost of transportation and production. When transport costs are ignored, that is, $\tau(t) \equiv 0$, (62) reduces to the familiar rule of $MR = MC$ for a "spaceless monopoly," where MC only refers to the marginal cost of production. Namely, (62) is an extension of the usual $MR = MC$ rule to the spatial monopoly case.

To obtain further insight into the problem, we define the elasticity of demand $\eta(t)$ for the market at location t by

$$\eta(t) \equiv -y'P/y, \quad \text{so that} \quad \eta(t) = -P/(P'y) > 0. \tag{63}$$

Namely, η signifies the usual demand elasticity of the ratio of the percentage change in the quantity demanded per percentage change in the price. Using (60c), (61), and (63), we obtain

$$p(t) = \frac{\tau(t) + c^*}{1 - 1/\eta(t)}. \tag{64}$$

Here we require[16]

$$1 - 1/\eta(t) > 0 \quad \text{for all } t, \tag{65}$$

[16]The elasticity condition, $1 - 1/\eta > 0$ (or equivalently, $\eta > 1$), is the usual condition that is required for a monopolistic firm. It is easy to show that this condition is equivalent to the condition that the marginal revenue must be positive at optimum.

in order to have $p(t) > 0$ for all t. With (65), we have $0 < 1/\eta(t) < 1$ for all t. If we ignore transport costs, as in the usual price theory textbooks, (64) reduces to

$$p(t) = \frac{c^*}{1 - 1/\eta(t)}. \tag{66}$$

The firm will charge a higher price at the location whose demand elasticity is lower. That is,

$$p(t_0) < p(t_1), \quad \text{whenever } \eta(t_0) > \eta(t_1). \tag{67}$$

This is the standard result in the theory of price discrimination. Equation (64) thus extends this well-known result of price discrimination to the spatial monopoly case.

Suppose $\eta(t) = \text{constant}$ for all t. In this case, $p(t)$ a simple linear function of $\tau(t)$, as is illustrated in figure 11.2*a*. The price of the product at the location of the firm is obviously denoted by $p(0)$. If $\eta = \text{constant}$, then $p(0) = c^*/(1 - 1/\eta)$, assuming $\tau(0) = 0$. Hence we obtain

$$p(t) - p(0) = \frac{\tau(t)}{1 - 1/\eta} > \tau(t). \tag{68}$$

This inequality states that the transport cost charged by the firm, $p(t) - p(0)$, is higher than the actual transport costs incurred, $\tau(t)$. This is illustrated in figure 11.2*b*.

Differentiating (64) and letting $\varepsilon(t) \equiv 1/\eta(t)$, we obtain

$$\dot{p}(t) = (\tau' + p\varepsilon')/(1 - \varepsilon), \tag{69}$$

where $\tau' \equiv d\tau/dt$ and $\varepsilon' \equiv d\varepsilon/dt$. Since $1 - \varepsilon > 0$ by (65), we may conclude from (69) that the necessary and sufficient condition for $\dot{p} > 0$ (i.e., the delivered price increases as the distance from the firm increases) is

$$\tau' + p\varepsilon' > 0. \tag{70}$$

It would be reasonable to assume $\tau' > 0$, for all t, that is, the transport costs increase as the distance from the firm increases. Then a sufficient condition for $\dot{p} > 0$ is given by

$$\varepsilon' \geqq 0, \quad \text{that is } \eta' \leqq 0, \tag{71}$$

where $\eta' \equiv d\eta/dt$. Thus, if the demand elasticity is constant for all locations, or if it decreases as distance increases, then the firm will charge

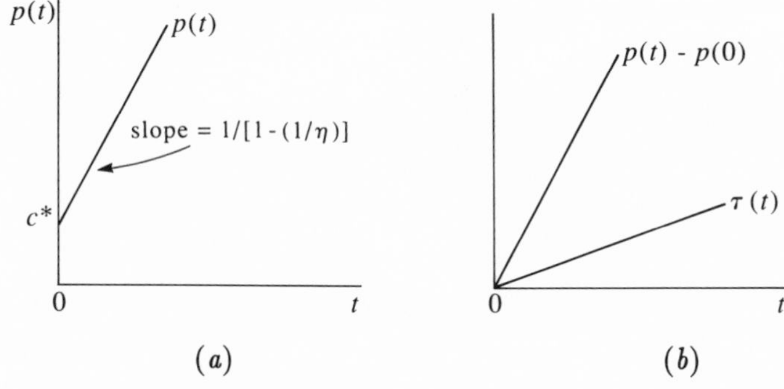

Figure 11.2: Pricing policy for a spatial monopoly: constant demand elasticity case

a higher delivered price for the customer whose distance from the firm is greater (i.e., $\dot{p} > 0$). Greenhut and Ohta (1975, p. 94) assert that "demand curves of decreasing elasticities are probably empirically the most realistic curves," while they provide no references to empirical studies that support their assertion.

On the other hand, if we allow the possibility of $\eta' > 0$, the paradoxical phenomenon of $\dot{p} < 0$ can occur. If the demand elasticity increases as distance increases, then it is possible that the firm will charge a lower delivered price for the customers whose distance from the firm is greater. However, this "paradox" is not hard to understand. For the case in which the transport cost can be ignored, the price should be lower for the customers whose distance from the firm is greater, since its demand elasticity is larger by assumption (i.e., $\eta' > 0$). This corresponds to the case of usual price discrimination. Needless to say, the transport cost can be significant, and it increases as distance increases.

This paradox (or more precisely, antinomy) occurs when the price reduction due to an increase in the demand elasticity outweighs an increase in the transport cost. This reminds us of the theory of dumping in international trade, where "dumping" here is defined as the practice of charging a lower price in the foreign market compared to the domestic market. Dumping can occur when the demand elasticity (of the home product) is sufficiently more elastic in the foreign market compared to the domestic market.[17]

---

[17]Actually, to show why dumping can be profitable for this case, we do not need

Finally, we may investigate the case in which this spatial monopoly is required to maximize "social welfare." Assume that social welfare is measured in terms of the sum of the consumers' surplus over the entire market-space plus the profits of the firm. Recall that $p(t) = P[y(t)]$ signifies the inverse demand curve and denote the area under the demand curve by $F(y)$,

$$F(y) \equiv \int_0^y P(y^*)dy^*. \tag{72}$$

Then total social welfare is measured by

$$W \equiv \int_0^T \{F[y(t)] - \tau(t)y(t)\}dt - C[Y(T)]. \tag{73}$$

The firm is then required to choose $y(t)$ so as to maximize W subject to $\dot{Y}(t) = y(t)$.

To solve this problem, define the Hamiltonian, H, by

$$H \equiv F[y(t)] - \tau(t)y(t) + q(t)y(t), \tag{74}$$

where $q(t)$ is the multiplier associated with the present maximization problem and should be distinguished from $q(t)$ for the profit maximizing firm discussed earlier. The necessary conditions for an interior solution can be written as

$$\dot{Y} = \partial H/\partial q; \quad \text{that is, } \dot{Y}(t) = y(t), \tag{75a}$$

$$\dot{q} = -\partial H/\partial Y; \quad \text{that is, } \dot{q} = 0, \tag{75b}$$

$$\partial H/\partial y = 0; \quad \text{that is, } F'[y(t)] - \tau(t) + q(t) = 0, \text{ and} \tag{75c}$$

$$-C'[Y(T)] = q(T). \tag{75d}$$

These conditions are also sufficient for an optimum if the demand curve is downward sloping, that is, if $P'(y) < 0$.

---

optimal control theory. It suffices to consider only two markets, domestic and foreign. (Needless to say, dumping is *prohibited internationally* although price discrimination over different regions are usually permissible within one country.) In comparing the domestic and foreign prices in the definition of dumping, the foreign price is usually defined as the FOB price, which does not include the transport cost (as well as the insurance premium for shipping) between the domestic and foreign markets.

From (75b) and (75d), we get

$$q(t) = \text{constant} = -c^*, \quad \text{where } c^* \equiv C'[Y(T)], \tag{76}$$

which is the same condition as that obtained for the profit-maximizing firm, i.e., (61). From the definition of F in (72), note that $F'(y) = P(y) = p(t)$. Hence, from (75c) and (76), we get

$$p(t) = \tau(t) + c^*. \tag{77}$$

The optimum delivered price (optimum from the viewpoint of social welfare) is equal to the transport cost plus the *MC* of production (c^*). Since $\tau(0) = 0$, we have $p(0) = c^*$. Thus the price at the firm's location is equal to c^*, which corresponds to the usual result of *marginal cost pricing* for a "spaceless" (welfare-maximizing) monopoly. The difference between the delivered price and the transport cost, $p(t) - \tau(t)$, is known as the **mill price**. Equation (77) says that the mill price is constant and equal to the *MC* of production for the welfare-maximizing firm. The transport cost that the firm charges its customers, $p(t) - p(0)$, will be exactly equal to the actual transport cost $\tau(t)$. Furthermore, recalling (65), we may observe

$$\frac{\tau(t) + c^*}{1 - 1/\eta(t)} > \tau(t) + c^*. \tag{78}$$

So the delivered price at the same location will be higher in the case of the profit-maximizing firm compared to the welfare-maximizing firm, if c^* is constant.

In reality, the firm is often allowed to pursue its private profit motive, while it is regulated that the transport costs charged customers is equal to the actual transport cost, so that the mill price must be kept constant. This requirement is known as **mill pricing**. The firm is required to honor

$$p(t) - m = \tau(t) \tag{79}$$

that is, $p(t) = m + \tau(t)$, where $m = p(0)$ signifies the *mill price*. In this case, the firm's profit function can be rewritten as

$$\begin{aligned} \pi &= \int_0^T \{P[y(t)]y(t) - \tau(t)y(t)\}dt - C[Y(R)] \\ &= \int_0^T my(t)dt - C[Y(R)]. \end{aligned} \tag{80}$$

We now consider the problem of choosing $y(t)$ to maximize π subject to $\dot{Y} = y$. Again define the Hamiltonian, H, by

$$H \equiv my(t) + q(t)y(t), \tag{81}$$

where $q(t)$ is the multiplier associated with the problem. The necessary (and sufficient) conditions for an interior solution can be written as

$$\dot{Y} = \partial H/\partial q; \quad \text{that is, } \dot{Y}(t) = y(t), \tag{82a}$$

$$\dot{p} = -\partial H/\partial Y; \quad \text{that is, } \dot{q}(t) = 0, \tag{82b}$$

$$\partial H/\partial y = 0; \quad \text{that is, } m + q(t) = 0, \quad \text{and} \tag{82c}$$

$$-C'[Y(T)] = q(T). \tag{82d}$$

From (82), we can easily obtain

$$-q(t) = c^{*} = m, \tag{83}$$

where $c^{*} \equiv C'[Y(T)]$ is constant for all t. Substituting (83) into (79), we obtain

$$p(t) = \tau(t) + c^{*}, \tag{84}$$

which would be exactly the same pricing policy for the welfare-maximizing firm obtained in (77). The present method of regulation, that is, mill pricing, also achieves the social optimum, *provided that* m is set equal to c^{*}. The rule of $m = c^{*}$ states that the mill price is equal to the marginal cost of production. Hence it is an application of the marginal cost pricing rule.

Appendix to Section 11.4: Spatial Pricing Problem and Nonlinear Programming

In this appendix, we shall show that all the results obtained in section 11.4 via the optimal control formulation can, in fact, be obtained much more easily by the usual nonlinear programming technique as exposited in chapter 2.[18] This, then, illustrates that two important tools, nonlinear programming and optimal control theory, are closely related, and it is

[18] This appendix is again from Takayama (1978).

often a matter of convenience which of the tools we use to analyze a particular economic problem.

Consider a monopolistic firm that sells its product to n, well-defined regional markets. Let p_i be the delivered price for the ith market, and let y_i be the demand for the product in the ith market ($i = 1, 2, \ldots, n$). The inverse demand function is specified by $p_i(y_i)$, where $p_i' \equiv dp_i/dy_i < 0$ (downward-sloping demand curve). Let τ_i be the unit cost of transportation to the ith market.

Then the firm's total profit is specified by

$$\pi \equiv \sum_{i=1}^{n} [R_i(y_i) - \tau_i y_i] - C(\sum_{i=1}^{n} y_i), \tag{85}$$

where $R_i(y_i) \equiv p_i(y_i)y_i$ and C signifies the total cost function. It is supposed that the firm maximizes its profit, π. Assuming $y_i > 0$ for all i at optimum, the profit maximization condition is readily obtained as

$$\partial\pi/\partial y_i = 0, \quad \text{that is,} \quad R_i' = \tau_i + c^*, \; i = 1, 2, \ldots, n, \tag{86}$$

where $c^* = C'(\sum_{i=1}^{n} y_i)$ evaluated at optimum, and $R_i' \equiv dR_i/dy_i$. This condition simply states that the *MR* is equal to the *MC* of transportation and production for each market. The usual *MR* = *MC* rule is a special case of (86) in which $\tau_i \equiv 0$, for all i.

Define the demand elasticity of the ith market (in the usual fashion) as

$$\eta_i \equiv -(dy_i/dp_i)(p_i/y_i) = -p_i/(P_i' y_i) > 0.$$

We may rewrite (86) as

$$p_i = \frac{\tau_i + c^*}{1 - \varepsilon_i}, \quad \text{where } \varepsilon_i \equiv 1/\eta_i, \; i = 1, 2, \ldots, n. \tag{87}$$

Note that $p_i > 0$ requires

$$1 - \varepsilon_i > 0, \quad \text{so that} \quad 0 < \varepsilon_i < 1, \tag{88}$$

for each i. This condition ($1 - \varepsilon_i > 0$) is equivalent to requiring the *MR* for the ith market to be positive. If we ignore transport costs, as is the case in the usual price theory textbooks, (87) reduces to

$$p_i = c^*/(1 - \varepsilon_i). \tag{87'}$$

From this we may readily conclude

$$p_i > p_j, \quad \text{whenever} \quad \eta_i < \eta_j. \tag{89}$$

The firm will charge a higher price at the location whose demand elasticity is lower. As mentioned earlier, this is a standard result in the theory of price discrimination.

Suppose that the demand elasticity for each region is the same, that is, $\eta_i = \eta$ (so that $\varepsilon_i = \varepsilon$) for all i. Then we have, from (87) and (88),

$$p_i - p_o = \tau_i/(1 - \varepsilon) > \tau_i, \; i = 1, 2, \ldots, n, \tag{90}$$

where $p_o \equiv c^*/(1 - \varepsilon)$. Here it is assumed that $\tau_i = 0$ in the place in which the firm is located. The value of p_o is obtained from (87) by setting $\tau_i = 0$. The inequality in (90) states that the transport cost charged by the firm, $p_i - p_o$, is higher than the actual transport cost incurred (τ_i).

Now let us return to the case in which demand elasticities can differ from one market to another. Using (87), simple calculation yields

$$p_j - p_i = \frac{[(1 - \varepsilon_i)\Delta\tau + (c^* + \tau_i)\Delta\varepsilon]}{(1 - \varepsilon_i)(1 - \varepsilon_j)}, \quad \text{for all} \quad i, \; j, \tag{91}$$

where $\Delta\tau \equiv \tau_j - \tau_i$ and $\Delta\varepsilon \equiv \varepsilon_j - \varepsilon_i$. Assume that the distance of the jth market from the firm is greater than that of the ith market, that is, $\Delta\tau > 0$. Then, from (91), we may at once conclude

$$p_j - p_i > 0, \quad \text{if} \quad \eta_j \leqq \eta_i, \tag{92}$$

where we may note $\eta_j \leqq \eta_i$ implies $\Delta\varepsilon \geqq 0$. Namely, if the demand elasticity is constant for all locations, or if it decreases as distance increases, then the firm will charge a higher delivered price for the customers whose distance from the firm is greater.

If we allow the possibility that the elasticity increases as distance increases, the "paradoxical" phenomenon may occur; that is, in such a case it is possible that the firm will charge a lower delivered price for the customer whose distance from the firm is greater. However, the paradox is not hard to understand. For the case in which transport costs are ignored, the price should be lower for the customers whose distance from the firm is greater, if its demand elasticity is larger. On the other hand, the transport cost can be significant, and it increases as distance increases. This "paradox" occurs when the price reduction due to an increase in the demand elasticity outweighs an increase in the transport cost. Again, this result is analogous to "dumping" in international trade in which the firm finds it profitable to discriminate against domestic customers in favor of foreign customers. As mentioned earlier (cf. fn. 17), this sort of dumping, though it is permitted domestically, is prohibited internationally.

Now suppose that this firm is required to maximize "social welfare," where social welfare is measured in terms of the consumers' surplus over the entire market, plus the profit of the firm. The area under the ith demand curve is defined by

$$F_i(y_i) \equiv \int_0^{y_i} p(y_i^*)dy_i^*. \tag{93}$$

Then total social welfare is measured by

$$W \equiv \sum_{i=1}^{n} [F_i(y_i) - \tau_i y_i] - C(\sum_{i=1}^{n} y_i). \tag{94}$$

The firm is required to choose y_i (which is equivalent to choosing p_i) so as to maximize W.

Assuming again $y_i > 0$ for all i at optimum, the necessary conditions for optimum states

$$\partial W/\partial y_i = 0, \quad \text{that is, } p_i = \tau_i + c^*,\ i = 1, 2, \ldots, n, \tag{95}$$

where we may note $F_i' = p_i$. Since $p_i' < 0$ by assumption, W is concave in they y_i's, so that (95) is also sufficient for global maximum. Condition (95) states that the optimum delivered price (optimum from the viewpoint of social welfare) is equal to the transport costs (τ_i) plus the marginal cost of production (c^*). Note that the delivered price at the firm's location for this welfare-maximizing monopoly is obtained by setting $\tau_i = 0$, that is, $p_o = c^*$. This corresponds precisely to the well-known result of *marginal cost pricing* for the "spaceless monopoly." Since $0 < \epsilon_i < 1$ by (88), we have

$$(\tau_i + c^*)/(1 - \varepsilon_i) > \tau_i + c^*, \tag{96}$$

where we assume that the MC of production (c^*) is constant. In view of (87) and (95), (96) states that the delivered price to the same market will be higher in the case of the profit-maximizing firm compared to the welfare-maximizing firm.

In reality, the firm is often allowed to pursue its private profit motive, while it is regulated that the transport cost charged to customers is equal to the actual transport cost τ_i, so that the difference between the delivered price and the transport cost, $p_i - \tau_i$ (which is the *mill price*) is being kept constant. Namely, the firm is required to honor

$$p_i - m = \tau_i \tag{97}$$

(that is, $p_i = m + \tau_i$), where m signifies the mill price. In the case of *mill pricing*, the firm's profit function (85) is rewritten as

$$\pi = \sum_{i=1}^{n} [(m + \tau_i)y_i - \tau_i y_i] - C(\sum_{i=1}^{n} y_i)$$
$$= mY - C(Y), \quad \text{where } Y \equiv \sum_{i=1}^{n} y_i. \tag{98}$$

The firm chooses y_i to maximize π.

Again assuming $y_i > 0$ at optimum, the optimality condition is written as

$$m = C'(Y). \tag{99}$$

By virtue of (97), this condition is exactly the same as condition (95) for the welfare-maximizing firm. Mill pricing achieves a social optimum, if the mill price is set equal to the marginal cost of production.

References

El-Hodiri, M. A. 1971. *Constrained Extrema: Introduction to the Differentiable Case with Economic Applications.* Berlin: Springer Verlag.

Funk, J. E., and E. G. Gilbert. 1970. "Some Sufficiency Conditions for Optimality in Control Problems with State Space Constraints." *SIAM Journal on Control* 8 (November): 498–504.

Gelfand, I. M., and S. V. Fomin. 1963. *Calculus of Variations.* Trans. from the Russian original by R. A. Silverman. Englewood Cliffs, N.J.: Prentice-Hall.

Greenhut, M. L., and H. Ohta. 1975. *Theory of Spatial Pricing and Market Areas.* Durham, N.C.: Duke University Press.

Hadley, G., and M. C. Kemp. 1971. *Variational Methods in Economics.* Amsterdam: North-Holland.

Hestenes, M. R. 1965. "On Variational Theory and Optimal Control Theory." *SIAM Journal on Control* 3 (September): 23–48.

———. 1966. *Calculus of Variations and Optimal Control Theory.* New York: Wiley.

Hu, S. C. 1978. "On the Dynamic Behavior of the Consumer and the Optimality Provision of Social Security." *Review of Economic Studies* 14 (October): 437–45.

Mirrlees, J. A. 1971. "An Exploration in the Theory of Optimum Income Taxation." *Review of Economic Studies* 38 (February): 175–208.

Phillip, L. 1974. *Applied Consumption Analysis*, Amsterdam: North-Holland. See esp. chap. 10.

Russak, B. 1970. "On Problems with Bounded State Variables." *Journal of Optimization Theory and Applications* 5 (February): 114–57.

Seierstad, A., and K. Sydsaeter. 1977. "Sufficient Conditions in Optimal Control Theory." *International Economic Review* 18 (June): 367–91.

Simmons, G. F. 1972. *Differential Equations.* New York.: McGraw-Hill.

Takayama, A. 1978. "Optimal Control Themes: Part II." Lecture notes. Texas A & M University.

———. 1985. *Mathematical Economics.* 2d ed. New York: Cambridge University Press.

Yaari, M. E. 1964. "On the Consumer's Lifetime Allocation Process." *International Economic Review* 5 (September): 304–17.

Appendices

APPENDIX A

Elements of Linear Algebra

Linear algebra or matrix algebra is a very useful tool for analysis in economic theory. It has also been used heavily in econometrics. In this appendix, we assemble some elements of this topic, especially those used in economic theory. Although this book does not use *all* the material presented, the material here is purported to provide a useful summary of this tool.

A.1 Matrices and Basic Operations

Let $a_{ij} \in R$, $i = 1, 2, \ldots, m$, $j = 1, 2, \ldots, n$, and consider the following ordered rectangular array of the a_{ij}'s,

$$A \equiv \begin{bmatrix} a_{11} & a_{12} & \cdots & a_{1n} \\ a_{21} & a_{22} & \cdots & a_{2n} \\ \cdots & \cdots & \cdots & \cdots \\ \cdots & \cdots & \cdots & \cdots \\ a_{m1} & a_{m2} & \cdots & a_{mn} \end{bmatrix},$$

or simply $A \equiv [a_{ij}]$. Such an array is called a **matrix (over the real field) of order m by n**, which is often written as $m \times n$. It is possible to consider an array $[a_{ij}]$ where the a_{ij}'s are complex numbers. However, in this book we assume that the a_{ij}'s are all real numbers. Two matrices A and B are said to be **equal** (denoted by $A = B$) if they are of the same order and $a_{ij} = b_{ij}$ for all i and j. The matrix A is called a **square matrix** if $m = n$. Let $A = [a_{ij}]$ and $B = [b_{ij}]$ be two matrices of the same order. We define the **summation** (or **addition**) of two matrices by component-wise addition; that is, if $C = [c_{ij}]$ denotes the summation of two matrices, A and B (i.e., $C = A + B$), then C is obtained by

$$c_{ij} \equiv a_{ij} + b_{ij}, \quad \text{for all } i \text{ and } j. \tag{1}$$

Let α be a scalar (real number). Then we define **scalar multiplication** by component-wise multiplication; that is,

$$\alpha A \equiv [\alpha a_{ij}], \quad \text{where } A = [a_{ij}]. \tag{2}$$

For example, if $\alpha = 3$, and

$$A = \begin{bmatrix} 1 & 2 \\ 3 & 4 \end{bmatrix}, \quad \text{then } 3A = \begin{bmatrix} 3 & 6 \\ 9 & 12 \end{bmatrix}.$$

From (1) and (2), it follows that the difference of two matrices A and B, denoted by $C = A - B$, is obtained by

$$c_{ij} = a_{ij} - b_{ij}, \quad \text{for all } i \text{ and } j.$$

Let A, B, and C be three matrices of the same order, and let α and β be scalars. Then given the rules of addition and scalar multiplication defined by (1) and (2), we can easily show:

$$A + B = B + A. \qquad \text{(commutative law)} \tag{3}$$

$$(A + B) + C = A + (B + C). \qquad \text{(associative law)} \tag{4}$$

$$\alpha(A + B) = \alpha A + \alpha B. \qquad \text{(distributive law)} \tag{5}$$

$$(\alpha + \beta)A = \alpha A + \beta A. \qquad \text{(distributive law)} \tag{6}$$

If all the elements of matrix A are zero, we call A the **zero matrix**. We denote the zero matrix simply by 0: that is, we use the same notation as a scalar zero (or vector zero). This should not cause much confusion since the meaning of 0 is usually obvious from the context. For the zero matrix 0, we have, from the rule of addition (1),

$$A + 0 = 0 + A = A. \tag{7}$$

Consider the set S of all $n \times n$ (square) matrices over the real field. It is easy to see that S is closed under addition, defined by (1), and scalar multiplication, defined by (2). Also, from (3) through (7), it is easy to show that S satisfies all the defining properties of a linear space. Hence S is a linear space.

We may summarize some of the results in theorem A.1.

Theorem A.1 Define the rules of (matrix) addition and scalar multiplication by equations (1) and (2), respectively. Then we have properties

(3) through (7), where the relevant matrices need not be square but must be of the same order. In particular, the set of all square matrices of the same order forms a linear space.

Matrix Multiplication

We now define the multiplication of two matrices. Let A be an $m \times n$ matrix and let B be an $n \times k$ matrix. Then the product, matrix $C = AB$, is an $m \times k$ matrix of which the ith element is defined by

$$c_{ih} \equiv \sum_{j=1}^{n} a_{ij}b_{jh},\ i = 1,\ 2,\ \ldots,\ m,\ h = 1,\ 2,\ \ldots,\ k. \tag{8}$$

Namely, the ith element of the product matrix is obtained by multiplying the elements of the ith row of the first matrix (A) by the corresponding elements of the jth column of the second matrix (B) and summing over all terms. This is **matrix multiplication**. Such a rule of multiplication is possible if and only if the number of columns of A is equal to the number of rows of B. For example, if

$$A = \begin{bmatrix} a_{11} & a_{12} & a_{13} \\ a_{21} & a_{22} & a_{23} \end{bmatrix}, \text{ and } B = \begin{bmatrix} b_{11} & b_{12} \\ b_{21} & b_{22} \\ b_{31} & b_{32} \end{bmatrix},$$

then AB is a 2×2 matrix,

$$AB = \begin{bmatrix} a_{11}b_{11} + a_{12}b_{21} + a_{13}b_{31} & a_{11}b_{12} + a_{12}b_{22} + a_{13}b_{32} \\ a_{21}b_{11} + a_{22}b_{21} + a_{23}b_{31} & a_{21}b_{12} + a_{22}b_{22} + a_{23}b_{32} \end{bmatrix}.$$

Since the number of columns of the first matrix must be equal to the number of rows of the second matrix in order to make matrix multiplication meaningful, it is possible that we cannot define the product of two matrices BA even if we can define the product AB. On the other hand, if the two matrices are of order $m \times n$ and $n \times m$, then both products, AB and BA, exist. Clearly, AB and BA are of different orders if $m \neq n$. Thus, $AB \neq BA$ if $m \neq n$. If both matrices are square and of the same order, then both products exist and will be of the same order, but *not necessarily* equal. Many such examples are given in matrix algebra textbooks. The following example is from Gantmacher (1959, I, p. 7).

Example A.1.

$$\begin{bmatrix} 1 & 2 \\ 3 & 4 \end{bmatrix} \begin{bmatrix} 2 & 0 \\ 3 & -1 \end{bmatrix} = \begin{bmatrix} 8 & -2 \\ 18 & -4 \end{bmatrix}, \text{ but}$$

$$\begin{bmatrix} 2 & 0 \\ 3 & -1 \end{bmatrix} \begin{bmatrix} 1 & 2 \\ 3 & 4 \end{bmatrix} = \begin{bmatrix} 2 & 4 \\ 0 & 2 \end{bmatrix}.$$

In other words, in general $AB \neq BA$; that is, matrix multiplication is not *commutative*. In the matrix product AB, A is called the **premultiplier** and B is called the **postmultiplier**. If $AB = BA$, then the matrices A and B are called **permutable** or **commuting**. Assuming that the relevant products of two matrices can be defined, the following relations can be shown directly from the definition of matrix multiplication (8).

$$(AB)C = A(BC). \qquad \text{(associative law)} \quad (9)$$

$$A(B + C) = AB + AC. \qquad \text{(distributive law)} \quad (10)$$

$$(A + B)C = AC + BC. \qquad \text{(distributive law)} \quad (11)$$

Let $A = [a_{ij}]$ be a square matrix. A is said to be a **symmetric matrix**, if $a_{ij} = a_{ji}$ for all i and j. A is said to be a **diagonal matrix**, if its off-diagonal elements are all zero, that is, if $a_{ij} = 0$ for all $i \neq j$. Clearly, every diagonal matrix is symmetric. A diagonal matrix is said to be the **identity matrix** or the **unit matrix** (which we denote by I), if all its diagonal elements are equal to unity. Although we do not explicitly specify the order of I, it should usually be obvious from the context. For example, if A is an $n \times n$ matrix, then the I in AI is also an $n \times n$ matrix. For the identity matrix, we have

$$AI = IA = A. \quad (12)$$

A.2 Transposes, Vectors, Simultaneous Equations, and Nonsingular Matrices

The **transpose** of a matrix A (which is not necessarily square) is defined to be the matrix obtained from A by interchanging the rows and columns, and it is denoted by A' (or A^T). Namely, if $A = [a_{ij}]$, then $A' = [a_{ji}]$. For example,

$$A = \begin{bmatrix} a_{11} & a_{12} & a_{13} \\ a_{21} & a_{22} & a_{23} \end{bmatrix}, \quad A' = \begin{bmatrix} a_{11} & a_{21} \\ a_{12} & a_{22} \\ a_{13} & a_{23} \end{bmatrix}.$$

It is also easy to see that $I' = I$.

With regard to the transpose of matrices, we have the following useful results that are easy to prove:

$$(AB)' = B'A'. \tag{13}$$

$$\text{If } A'A = 0, \text{ then } A = 0. \tag{14}$$

$$A = (A')'. \tag{15}$$

$$(A + B)' = A' + B'. \tag{16}$$

An n-dimensional vector $x \in R^n$ may be viewed as an $n \times 1$ matrix, and such an $n \times 1$ matrix is called an (n-dimensional) **column vector**. It may be written as

$$x = \begin{bmatrix} x_1 \\ x_2 \\ \cdot \\ \cdot \\ \cdot \\ x_n \end{bmatrix}.$$

The transpose of x is given by $x' = (x_1, x_2, \ldots, x_n)$, and it can be viewed as a $1 \times n$ matrix. Such a $1 \times n$ matrix is called an (n-dimensional) **row vector**.

Unless otherwise specified, or unless it is obvious from the context, we shall view a particular vector (say, x) as a column vector (and x' denotes a row vector) in our discussion of matrix algebra. Thus, for example, if A is an $m \times n$ matrix, then Ax is an m-dimensional column vector where x is an n-dimensional column vector. The (Euclidian) inner product $x \cdot y$ defined in section A.1 can also be written as

$$x \cdot y = x'y = y'x.$$

Since vectors can be regarded as special cases of matrices, the rules of the transpose of matrices, (13) through (16), also apply here. For example, since $Ix = x$ and $I = I'$, we have, in view of (12),

$$Ix = x, \text{ and } x'I = x'. \tag{12'}$$

Also, letting A be an $m \times n$ matrix, and letting x and y, respectively, be n-dimensional and m-dimensional vectors, we have, using (9) and (13),

$$y \cdot (Ax) = y'(Ax) = (Ax)'y = (x'A')y = x'(A'y) = x \cdot (A'y).$$

In short, we have the following useful rule:

$$y \cdot (Ax) = y'(Ax) = x'(A'y) = x \cdot (A'y). \tag{17}$$

Although using the prime (′) notation to denote the transpose is very convenient, it has one difficulty. It can be confused with derivatives of a function.[1] For this reason, $x \cdot x$ is often preferred to $x'x$ in order to denote the Euclidian inner product. On the other hand, when it is obvious from the context that the use of the prime does not involve derivatives and that it will ease the reading, we shall use the prime to denote the transpose.

One caution may be in order here. When we regard vectors as special cases of matrices, the multiplication of two vectors will yield different results depending on whether we interpret them as column or row vectors. This may be illustrated by example A.2.

Example A.2.

$$(x_1, x_2)\begin{bmatrix} y_1 \\ y_2 \end{bmatrix} = x_1y_1 + x_2y_2,$$

$$\begin{bmatrix} x_1 \\ x_2 \end{bmatrix}(y_1, y_2) = \begin{bmatrix} x_1y_1 & x_1y_2 \\ x_2y_1 & x_2y_2 \end{bmatrix}.$$

The former signifies the Euclidean inner product of x and y, while the latter does not.

We now consider the following system of simultaneous equations:

$$\begin{array}{ccccccccccc} a_{11}x_1 & + & a_{12}x_2 & + & a_{13}x_3 & + & \cdots & + & a_{1n}x_n & = & b_1, \\ a_{21}x_1 & + & a_{22}x_2 & + & a_{23}x_3 & + & \cdots & + & a_{2n}x_n & = & b_2, \\ \cdots & & \cdots & & \cdots & & \cdots & & \cdots & & .. \\ \cdots & & \cdots & & \cdots & & \cdots & & \cdots & & .. \\ a_{m1}x_1 & + & a_{m2}x_2 & + & a_{m3}x_3 & + & \cdots & + & a_{mn}x_n & = & b_m. \end{array} \tag{18}$$

In terms of matrix notation, this system can compactly be written as

$$Ax = b, \tag{18'}$$

[1] To avoid such confusion, some writers use notation such as x^T (instead of x') to denote the transpose of x. The difficulty of such a notation is that algebraic manipulations involving vectors and matrices often get crowded with the superscript T and may look messy. We wish to avoid such clutter.

where $A = [a_{ij}]$ is an $m \times n$ matrix, and where x and b are column vectors with $x' = (x_1, x_2, \ldots, x_n)$ and $b' = (b_1, b_2, \ldots, b_m)$.

It is important to note that the use of matrix notation greatly simplifies the writing of simultaneous equations. Note also that the definition of matrix multiplication in terms of (8) is essential in facilitating such a simplification. Even setting aside all important and useful results in matrix algebra, such a notational simplification by itself should be of great value.

We may summarize some of these results in theorem A.2.

Theorem A.2. Define the rule of matrix multiplication by (8). Then we have properties (9) through (14). In addition, the system of simultaneous equations (18) can be compactly written as (18′). For additional properties of the transpose of matrices, we have rules (15) and (16).

Nonsingular Matrices

Let A be a *square* matrix, and let I be the identity matrix of the same order. Suppose that there exist square matrices X and X^* of the same order such that

$$AX = X^*A = I.$$

Then we have, recalling (9) and (12),

$$X = IX = (X^*A)X = X^*(AX) = X^*I = X^*,$$

so that we must have $X = X^*$. We call such an X the **inverse matrix** of A. Note that the inverse matrix, if it exists, is unique.

To see this, let X and Y be two inverse matrices of A; that is,

$$AX = XA = I \text{ and } AY = YA = I.$$

But we may then observe, again recalling (9) and (12),

$$X = XI = X(AY) = (XA)Y = IY = Y,$$

so that X must be equal to Y. We denote the inverse matrix of A by A^{-1}. If A has an inverse, A is called **nonsingular**; A is **singular** otherwise. If A is nonsingular, we have

$$AA^{-1} = A^{-1}A = I. \tag{19}$$

It would be easy to see that inverses exist for some matrices, as the following example indicates:

$$A = \begin{bmatrix} 1 & 0 \\ 0 & 2 \end{bmatrix}, \; A^{-1} = \begin{bmatrix} 1 & 0 \\ 0 & 1/2 \end{bmatrix}.$$

Also, it is easy to see that not every matrix has an inverse; that is, not every matrix is nonsingular. For example, neither of the following matrices has an inverse. Here both A and B are singular.[2]

$$A = \begin{bmatrix} 1 & 0 \\ 0 & 0 \end{bmatrix}, \text{ and } B = \begin{bmatrix} 1 & 2 \\ 2 & 4 \end{bmatrix}. \tag{20}$$

To see this, compute

$$AX = \begin{bmatrix} x_{11} & x_{12} \\ 0 & 0 \end{bmatrix}, \; BX = \begin{bmatrix} x_{11} + 2x_{21} & x_{12} + 2x_{22} \\ 2x_{11} + 4x_{21} & 2x_{12} + 4x_{22} \end{bmatrix},$$

$$\text{where } X = \begin{bmatrix} x_{11} & x_{12} \\ x_{21} & x_{22} \end{bmatrix}.$$

Clearly, AX cannot be the identity matrix, so that A does not have an inverse. Also, if BX is the identity matrix, then we must have,

$$x_{11} + 2x_{21} = 1, \; 2x_{11} + 4x_{21} = 0,$$

$$x_{12} + 2x_{22} = 0, \; 2x_{12} + 4x_{22} = 1,$$

which is impossible, so that B is also singular.

Let A be a nonsingular matrix and consider the system of simultaneous equations (18′), $Ax = b$. Premultiplying A^{-1} on both sides of this equation, we at once obtain

$$x = A^{-1}b.$$

Since the inverse matrix A^{-1} is unique, the solution x for $Ax = b$ is unique.

For nonsingular matrices, the following results are useful and easy to prove:

$$A = (A^{-1})^{-1}, \tag{21}$$

[2]One may easily check that two columns (or rows) of matrix A or B in (20) are linearly dependent. This, in turn, confirms that these matrices are singular.

$$(AB)^{-1} = B^{-1}A^{-1}. \tag{22}$$

A.3 Linear Independence, Rank, and Linear Subspaces

To probe more deeply into the nature of nonsingular matrices, it is necessary to discuss the concept of the "rank" of a matrix. First, we recall the concept of linear independence discussed in section A.2. Consider k vectors, $x^1, x^2, \ldots, x^k$, in R^n. We may say that these vectors are **linearly independent** if, for $\alpha_j \in R$, $j = 1, 2, \ldots, k$,

$$\alpha_1 x^1 + \alpha_2 x^2 + \ldots + \alpha_k x^k = 0 \text{ implies}$$

$$\alpha_1 = \alpha_2 = \ldots = \alpha_k = 0.$$

Also, we may say that these k vectors are **linearly dependent** if

$$\alpha_1 x^1 + \alpha_2 x^2 + \ldots + \alpha_k x^k = 0 \text{ for some } \alpha_j \neq 0, \quad j = 1, 2, \ldots, k.$$

Let $A = [a_{ij}]$ be an $m \times n$ matrix. We define the **column rank** of A as the largest number of linearly independent columns, and the **row rank** of A as the largest number of linearly independent rows. It can be shown that the row rank and the column rank of any $m \times n$ matrix are, in fact, equal, and this result is known as the **Rank Theorem**.

Theorem A.3 (*rank theorem*). For any (rectangular) matrix A, the column rank and the row rank are equal.

This theorem enables us to simply refer to the **rank** of A. The zero matrix has zero rank, and it can be easily shown that the transpose of A has the same rank as A, which we may denote as

$$\text{rank } A' = \text{rank } A.$$

To discuss the inverse of matrices, we confine ourselves to square matrices. Let A be an $n \times n$ matrix. Then it can be shown that A is nonsingular if and only if the rank of A is equal to n (in which case A is said to have **full rank**). From this it follows easily that the transpose of a nonsingular matrix is nonsingular. In addition, it is the case that

$$(A')^{-1} = (A^{-1})'. \tag{23}$$

Also, we can easily show that a diagonal matrix is nonsingular if and only if all its diagonal elements differ from zero, and that if A is a nonsingular diagonal matrix whose i^{th} diagonal element is a_{ii}, then A^{-1} is also a diagonal matrix whose i^{th} diagonal element is equal to $(1/a_{ii})$.

We may now summarize some of the results concerning the inverse of square matrices in theorem A.4.

Theorem A.4.

(i) A matrix is nonsingular, if and only if it has full rank; and if it is nonsingular, then its inverse is unique.

(ii) If A is nonsingular, then $Ax = b$ allows for a unique solution, $x = A^{-1}b$.

(iii) Nonsingular matrices conform to properties (21) through (23).

(iv) If A is a diagonal matrix whose i^{th} diagonal element is $a_{ii} \neq 0$, then A is nonsingular and A^{-1} is a diagonal matrix whose i^{th} diagonal element is given by $(1/a_{ii})$.

Linear Subspaces and Ranks

A subset V of a *linear space* X (for its definition, recall L1–L8 of chap. 1) that satisfies the following two conditions is called a **linear subspace** of X, if

(i) $x, y \in V$ implies $x + y \in V$, and

(ii) $x \in V$ implies $\alpha x \in V$ for all $\alpha \in R$.

That is, V is a subset of X that is closed under addition and scalar multiplication. It can be shown easily that V satisfies all the axioms for a linear space, and hence it is also a linear space. Let x° be a point in X. Then $\{\alpha x^{\circ} : \alpha \in R\}$ is a linear subspace of X. Also, the set $\{0\}$ consisting of the zero vector alone is a subspace, and X itself is a subspace of X: the two subspaces $\{0\}$ and X are sometimes called **trivial subspaces**.

Since a linear subspace V of X itself is a linear space, the concepts such as linear independence and basis are also relevant here. If the k vectors, $x^1, x^2, \ldots, x^k$, are linearly independent in V and if any vector in V can be represented as a linear combination of these vectors, then these k vectors are said to form a **basis** of V, and the number of such vectors (here k) is called the **dimension** of V, which we may denote by

$$\dim V = k.$$

For example, the dimension of $\{\alpha x^\circ : \alpha \in R\}$ is equal to one. Although the theory of linear subspaces like the theory of linear spaces can be developed quite extensively without restricting X to be R^n (the Euclidian space), we assume $X = R^n$ to ease the present discussion.

Let $A = [a_{ij}]$ be an $m \times n$ rectangular matrix. Define the set K by

$$K \equiv \{y : y = Ax,\ x \in R^n\}$$

Then K is a subset of R^n. Since y^1, $y^2 \in K$ implies $y^1 + y^2 \in K$, and since $y \in K$ implies $\alpha y \in K$ for all $\alpha \in R$, K is a linear subspace of R^n. If the rank of A is equal to k, then there are k linearly independent column vectors in A. It is easy to see that any y in K can be represented as a linear combination of k column vectors. Hence this dimension of K is equal to k, or

$$\dim K = \text{rank } A. \tag{24}$$

Next define the set N (called the **null space** of A) by

$$N \equiv \{x : Ax = 0,\ x \in R^n\}.$$

It can easily be shown that N is a linear subspace of R^n. A fundamental result concerning the null space of A is

$$\dim N + \text{rank } A = n \quad (\text{i.e., } \dim N = n - \text{rank } A).^3 \tag{25}$$

The following relations on the ranks of matrices are well known and useful. They can be obtained by utilizing the concept of a subspace.

$$\text{rank } AA' = \text{rank } A, \tag{26}$$

$$\text{rank } AB \leqq \text{minimum } \{\text{rank } A,\ \text{rank } B\}, \tag{27}$$

$$\text{rank } AB = \text{rank } A, \text{ if } B \text{ is nonsingular,}^4 \text{ and} \tag{28}$$

---

[3]If, in particular, A is a square matrix (an $n \times n$ matrix), then A is nonsingular if and only if rank $A = n$ by theorem A.5. Hence by (25), we may conclude that A is nonsingular if and only if the null space N of A has rank zero. N consists of the zero vector alone.

$$\text{rank } (A + B) \leqq \text{ rank } A + \text{ rank } B, \tag{29}$$

where matrices A and B, except for B in (28), need not be square. In general, the rank of AB *cannot* uniquely be determined by the ranks of A and B. The results in theorem A.5 can be obtained, and they are often useful.

Theorem A.5.

(i) The dimension of $K \equiv \{y : y = Ax, \ x \in R^n\}$ is equal to the rank of A.

(ii) The dimension of the null space of an $m \times n$ matrix A is equal to n minus the rank of A; that is, (25) holds.

(iii) For the ranks of matrices, we have (26) through (29).

Statement (ii) or (25) turns out to be quite useful in economics. This may be illustrated by example A.3.

Example A.3 (Cost Minimization). Consider the usual problem of cost minimization, in which a competitive firm chooses a factor input combination $x \in R^n$ to minimize $w \cdot x$ subject to $f(x) \geqq y$, $x \geqq 0$ where w = factor price vector, y = the target level of output, and $f(x)$ = the production function, and where w and $y(> 0)$ are given parameters. The solution of this problem x^*, in general, depends on w and y, and hence can be expressed as, $x^* = x(w, y)$. The quantity $\partial x_i / \partial w_j$ measures the effect of a change in the jth factor price upon the demand for the ith factor when output is held constant. Consider an $n \times n$ matrix $S \equiv [\partial x_i / \partial w_j]$. Then S signifies the substitution matrix of the cost minimization problem, where we may note $S = S(w, y)$. Since the problem of choosing (αx) to minimize $w \cdot (\alpha x)$ subject to $f(x) \geqq y$ and $x \geqq 0$ yields the same solution as this problem for any $\alpha \in R$ and $\alpha > 0$, we have $x(\alpha w, y) = x(w, y)$ for any such positive α. The value of $x(w, y)$ is (positively) homogeneous of degree zero in w. Hence, by

[4] As a corollary to this, we may assert that all nonsingular matrices of the same order have the same rank. For if A and B are two matrices of the same order, and if rank $A = n_1$ and rank $B = n_2$, then by (28), rank $AB = n_1$, and rank $AB = n_2$ so that $n_1 = n_2$.

Euler's equation for homogeneous functions, we have

$$\sum_{j=1}^{n} \frac{\partial x_i}{\partial w_j} w_j = 0, \ i = 1, 2, \ldots, n.$$

Namely, we have $Sw = 0$ for all w. Thus, S is a singular matrix, or rank $S \leqq n - 1$. The null space of S is defined by

$$N \equiv \{z : Sz = 0, \ z \in R^n\}.$$

Assume that $z'Sz < 0$ for all nonzero z not proportional to w (i.e., ***Samuelson's regularity condition*** which is introduced in chap. 3). This condition and $Sw = 0$ imply that $N = \{z : z = \alpha w, \ \alpha \in R\}$. Hence the rank of N is equal to one. Then by (25), the rank of S is equal to $n - 1$. From this we may also conclude that the rank of the $(n - 1) \times (n - 1)$ matrix obtained from S by deleting the nth columns and the nth row (or any one of its columns and the corresponding row) is equal to $n - 1$, so that such a matrix is nonsingular.

A.4 Matrices as Linear Transformations[5]

To obtain a further insight into matrix algebra, it is important to recognize a matrix as a representation of a linear transformation and not simply an array of numbers. In fact, the basic rules of matrix algebra, such as the rules of addition, scalar multiplication, and matrix multiplication, and relations such as (26) through (29) follow naturally from such a recognition. Furthermore, this recognition will bridge the theory of matrix algebra with the theory of linear transformations (or operators) which are more profound and richer in results than the former.

Let X and Y be two linear spaces over the real field. The reader may (without loss of generality of the argument here) assume that $X = R^n$ and $Y = R^m$. Consider a transformation (or a mapping) T that associates each element x of X with an element y of Y; that is,

$$T : X \to Y, \ \text{with} \ T(x) = y.$$

Transformation T is said to be a **linear transformation**, if it satisfies the following two conditions:

---

[5]This section can be skipped, if the reader so desires. The topic here may be more difficult. For good expositions of the topic, see Shilov (1977, pp. 78–82); and Halmos (1958, pp. 55–68), for example.

(i) $T(x^1 + x^2) = T(x^1) + T(x^2)$, for all $x^1,\ x^2 \in X$, and

(ii) $T(\alpha x) = \alpha T(x)$, for all $\alpha \in R$ and $x \in X$.

From conditions (i) and (ii), it follows easily that

$$T(\alpha_1 x^1 + \alpha_2 x^2 + \ldots + \alpha_k x^k) = \alpha_1 T(x^1) + \alpha_2 T(x^2) + \ldots + \alpha_k T(x^k),$$

for any $\alpha_i \in R$ and $x^i \in X$, $i = 1, 2, \ldots, k$. For example, $T : R^n \to R^m$ defined by $y = T(x) = Ax$ (where A is an array of $m \times n$ scalars $[a_{ij}]$) is a linear transformation.[6]

The fundamental properties of linear transformations may be stated as follows: associated with any linear transformation, $T : X \to Y$, there exists an array of scalars $[a_{ij}]$ (which we have called a "matrix"), and such an association is one-to-one, where X and Y are assumed to be finite dimensional.

To proceed with the proof of this statement, let X and Y, respectively, be n- and m-dimensional, and let $e \equiv \{e^1,\ e^2,\ \ldots,\ e^n\}$ be some fixed basis of X and let $f \equiv \{f^1,\ f^2,\ \ldots,\ f^m\}$ be some fixed basis of Y. Let $T : X \to Y$ be a linear transformation. Since any vector in Y can be expressed as a linear combination of the basis vectors, $f^1,\ f^2,\ \ldots,\ f^m$, we have

$$T(e^j) = a_{1j} f^1 + a_{2j} f^2 + \ldots + a_{mj} f^m,\ j = 1, 2, \ldots, n, \tag{30}$$

for some scalars a_{ij}'s. The $m \times n$ array of these coefficients thus obtained is called the **matrix associated with linear transformation** $\boldsymbol{T}$ (relative to the bases e and f) which we denote by $A(e,\ f)$. Note that $A(e,\ f)$ is the same as the $m \times n$ array of numbers $A = [a_{ij}]$. Note, however, that this definition does not define "matrix," rather it defines "the matrix associated with a linear transformation." Also note that $A(e,\ f)$ is determined in terms of certain bases or **coordinate systems**, e and f, in which the *ordering* as well as the elements of each basis are important.

[6]Let b be a nonzero m-dimensional vector. Then it can be shown easily that $T(x) = Ax + b$ is *not* a linear transformation. Since $y = Ax + b$ is conventionally called a "linear function" and since "function" and "transformation" are used synonymously, this is rather unfortunate. [Transformation $T(x) = Ax + b$ is known as a **linear affine** or **affine**]. However, as mentioned earlier, it does not seem worthwhile to makea fuss about this point. The reader should easily be able to discern the distinction from the context. The only caution we took here is that we used the notation T to denote a linear transformation instead of the usual functional notations such as $f,\ g,\ \phi$, etc.

In terms of the basis e, an arbitrary vector x in X can be written as

$$x = x_1 e^1 + x_2 e^2 + x_3 e^3 + \ldots + x_n e^n,$$

for some scalars x_i's. If $e^1 = (1, 0, \ldots, 0)$, $e^2 = (0, 1, 0, \ldots, 0)$, $\ldots$, and $e^n = (0, 0, \ldots, 0, 1)$, then $x = (x_1, x_2, \ldots, x_n)$. Let $y = T(x)$ and write y in terms of the basis f in Y as

$$y = y_1 f^1 + y_2 f^2 + \ldots + y_m f^m.$$

Then we may observe

$$\begin{aligned} y &= \sum_{i=1}^{m} y_i f^i = T(x) = T(x_1 e^1 + \ldots + x_n e^n) \\ &= \sum_{j=1}^{n} x_j T(e^j) = \sum_{j=1}^{n} x_j (a_{1j} f^1 + \ldots + a_{mj} f^m) \\ &= \sum_{i=1}^{m} (a_{i1} x_1 + \ldots + a_{in} x_n) f^i. \end{aligned}$$

Comparing coefficients of the vector f^i, we obtain

$$y_i = a_{i1} x_1 + a_{i2} x_2 + \ldots + a_{in} x_n, \; i = 1, 2, \ldots, m.$$

The coefficient matrix of this system is nothing but the matrix $A(e, f)$. Therefore, we may conclude that the matrix $A(e, f)$ associated with the linear transformation T completely determines the result of applying T to any vector x in X.

Conversely, given an array of $m \times n$ scalars, $[a_{ij}]$ (which we denote by A as before), we may define a linear transformation $T : X \to Y$, and we can further show that the matrix $A(e, f)$ associated with T is exactly equal to $[a_{ij}]$, that is, $A(e, f) = A$. To show this, given an array of scalars $A = [a_{ij}]$, we consider an arbitrary vector x in X given by

$$x = x_1 e^1 + x_2 e^2 + \ldots + x_n e^n,$$

for some scalars x_i's, and define $T : X \to Y$ by

$$T(x) = y_1 f^1 + y_2 f^2 + \ldots + y_m f^m,$$

where the coefficients, $y_1, y_2, \ldots, y_m$, are *determined by*

$$y_i \equiv \sum_{j=1}^{n} a_{ij}x_j, \; i = 1, 2, \ldots, m, \quad \text{that is, } y = Ax.$$

It is easy to see that such a transformation is linear. Furthermore, letting the vector e^1 have components $x_1 = 1, x_2 = 0, \ldots, x_n = 0$, we have

$$T(e^1) = a_{11}f^1 + a_{21}f^2 + \ldots + a_{m1}f^m.$$

Similarly, we have

$$T(e^j) = a_{1j}f^1 + a_{2j}f^2 + \ldots + a_{mj}f^m, \; j = 1, 2, \ldots, n,$$

which is the same as (30), $A = A(e, f)$. Thus, given $A = [a_{ij}]$, we have constructed a linear transformation $T : X \to Y$, and the matrix associated with $T(A(e, f))$ is shown to be equal to A.

In summary, we have theorem A.6.

Theorem A.6. Given fixed bases, $\{e^1, e^2, \ldots, e^n\}$ of X and $\{f^1, f^2, \ldots, f^m\}$ of Y, there exists, by way of (30) or equivalently by $y = Ax$, a one-to-one correspondence between the linear transformation $T : X \to Y$ and an $m \times n$ array of scalars $A = [a_{ij}]$, and the matrix associated with T, $A(e, f)$, is equal to A.

Thus, matrix $A = [a_{ij}]$, an array of scalars as defined at the outset of this appendix, may be referred to as the "matrix representation" of some linear transformation. Given theorem A.6, if we define addition, scalar multiplication, product, etc., of linear transformations properly, the results obtained from these definitions must be completely analogous to the ones obtained earlier in terms of $[a_{ij}]$, an array of scalars.[7]

Define the addition, scalar multiplication, and product of linear trans-

[7]Recall that linear spaces X and Y on which the linear transformation is defined are assumed to be finite dimensional. When X and Y are infinite dimensional, we do not have any decent analogue of the concept of matrix, an array of scalars $[a_{ij}]$. Furthermore, most of the important results on linear transformations can be shown without the use of the concept of matrix. Thus the theory of matrix algebra simply becomes a special case of the theory of linear transformations (operators) in which X and Y are finite dimensional. Based on this, Halmos (1958) developed a textbook on the theory of matrix algebra in terms of the theory of linear transformation on finite dimensional linear spaces.

formations, T_1, T_2, $T : X \to Y$, by[8]

$$(T_1 + T_2)(x) = T_1(x) + T_2(x), \quad \text{for all } x \in X, \tag{1'}$$

$$(\alpha T)(x) = \alpha[T(x)], \quad \text{for all } \alpha \in R \text{ and } x \in X, \text{ and} \tag{2'}$$

$$(T_1 \circ T_2)(x) = T_1[T_2(x)], \quad \text{for all } x \in X. \tag{8'}$$

Then we can show that $(T_1 + T_2)$, (αT) and $(T_1 \circ T_2)$ are linear transformations from X into Y, and that the matrix representations of these linear transformations in (1′), (2′) and (8′) satisfy rules (1), (2) and (8) defined earlier for matrices, that is, arrays of scalars. It is also easy to see that the identity matrix I is the matrix representation of the identity transformation $I : X \to X$ defined by $I(x) = x$, and that the zero matrix of order $m \times n$ is the matrix representation of the zero transformation that maps every vector x in X into the zero vector in Y. It can be shown that all the results such as (3) through (7) and (9) through (12) established earlier, hold as they are for the matrix representations of linear transformations (for fixed basis vectors).

In summary, we can establish a corollary to theorem A.6.

Corollary. The one-to-one correspondence between a linear transformation T and a matrix A (an array of scalars $[a_{ij}]$) preserves addition, scalar multiplication, product, and zero.

Let $T : X \to X$. T is a linear transformation X into itself, and let $I : X \to X$ be the identity transformation. Namely, $Ix = x$ for all x in X. Suppose that there exists linear transformation S, $S^* : X \to X$, such that

$$TS = S^*T = I.$$

Then we can easily show that $S = S^*$ and that such an S is unique. When such an S exists, we say that T is **invertible**, and denote such an S by T^{-1}. Then we obviously have

$$TT^{-1} = T^{-1}T = I.$$

[8]Two linear transformations, T_1, $T_2 : X \to Y$, are said to be **equal** (written as $T_1 = T_2$), if $T_1(x) = T_2(x)$ for every x in X. The transformation $T_1 \circ T_2$ in (8′) is the "composite transformation" of T_1 and T_2. It corresponds to a composite function. Since the definition of matrix multiplication by (8) holds for the matrix representations of T_1, T_2, and $(T_1 \circ T_2)$ when $(T_1 \circ T_2)$ is defined by (8′), the definition (8) may be considered a natural consequence of the fact that a matrix is a one-to-one representation of linear transformation.

Clearly, T^{-1} is also a linear transformation from X into itself. We can also show that T is invertible if and only if its matrix representation is nonsingular. Assuming T is invertible, the matrix representation of T^{-1} corresponds to the inverse of the matrix representation of T.

A.5 Determinants and Partitioned Matrices

A.5.1 Determinants, Laplace Expansion, and Cramer's Rule

Given any *square* matrix A, we can associate a *scalar* quantity called the **determinant** of A, which we may denote by det A or $|A|$. For example, the reader should have encountered:

$$\begin{vmatrix} a_{11} & a_{12} \\ a_{21} & a_{22} \end{vmatrix} = a_{11}a_{22} - a_{12}a_{21}.$$

To study the rule of such an association, we consider an $n \times n$ matrix $A = [a_{ij}]$, and consider any product of n elements that appear in different rows and different columns of A. This product contains just one element for each row and for each column (thus no elements appear twice in a particular product). We may write such a product in the following form:

$$a_{i_1 1}a_{i_2 2} \dots a_{i_n n}. \tag{31}$$

For the first element of this product, we can always choose the element appearing in the first column of A. Hence the first element of the product can be written as $a_{i_1 1}$. Similarly, for the second element of the product, we can always choose the element appearing in the second column of A and thus it can be written as $a_{i_2 2}$. Repeating this, we may write a typical product in the form of (31). Since no elements can appear in the product twice, the integers

$$i_1, i_2, \dots, i_n$$

must be all different, and thus represent some *permutation* of n integers, $1, 2, 3, \dots, n$.[9] For example,

$$\{1, 2, 4, 3\}, \ \{4, 3, 1, 2\}, \ \{1, 3, 2, 4\},$$

[9] More precisely, by a **permutation** of the integers, $1, 2, \dots, n$, we mean a one-to-one mapping (π) that assigns each such integer to another one of such integers so that π is also onto). To say that π is one-to-one means that $\pi(i) = \pi(j)$ can happen only when $i = j$.

are permutations of $\{1, 2, 3, 4\}$. By an **inversion** in $\{i_1, i_2, \ldots, i_n\}$, we mean an arrangement of two indices such that the larger index comes before the smaller index. We denote the number of inversions by $N(i_1, i_2, \ldots, i_n)$. For example, in the permutation $\{1, 2, 4, 3\}$, there is only one inversion (4 before 3), and in the permutation $\{4, 3, 1, 2\}$, there are five inversions (4 before 3, 4 before 1, 4 before 2, 3 before 1, and 3 before 2). Hence,

$$N(1, 2, 4, 3) = 1, \; N(4, 3, 1, 2) = 5.$$

If the number of inversions in the sequence $\{i_1, i_2, \ldots, i_n\}$ is even, we put the plus sign before the product (31); and if the number is odd, we put a minus sign before the product, thus we rewrite the product as

$$(-1)^{N(i_1, i_2, \ldots, i_n)} \cdot (a_{i_1 1} a_{i_2 2} \ldots a_{i_n n}). \tag{31'}$$

Take the summation of the products in the form of (31′) over all possible permutations of $\{1, 2, \ldots, n\}$ (with no repetitions). We then have

$$\sum (-1)^{N(i_1, i_2, \ldots, i_n)} \cdot (a_{i_1 1} a_{i_2 2} \ldots a_{i_n n}). \tag{32}$$

Such a sum is formally defined as the **determinant** of A (denoted by $|A|$ or det A). There are, as is well known, $n!$ terms in such a sum. If A is an $n \times n$ matrix, the **order** of det A is said to be equal to n, and the elements a_{ij} of matrix A are also called the **elements** of det A.

Using this definition of the determinant, we may, in a straightforward way, obtain the following rules concerning determinants (for the proofs, see any textbook of matrix algebra):

$$|A'| = |A|, \tag{33}$$

Interchanging any two columns (or rows) of A changes the sign of the determinant of A, (34)

The determinant of a matrix with two identical rows (or columns) is equal to zero, (35)

$$|AB| = |A|\,|B|, \quad \text{if } A \text{ and } B \text{ are square matrices,} \tag{36}$$

$$|A^{-1}| = 1/|A|, \quad \text{and} \tag{37}$$

If every element of *one* row (or column) of A is multiplied by a scalar α to yield a new matrix B, then we have $|B| = \alpha|A|$. (38)

Hence from (38) if *every* element of A is multiplied by α, then $|\alpha A| = \alpha^n |A|$. Note that (33), (34), (36), and (38) follow directly from the definition of a determinant. Results (35) and (37), respectively, follow readily from (34) and (36).

Consider an $n \times n$ matrix $A = [a_{ij}]$. If we simultaneously delete a row and a column from A, then the remaining elements form a matrix of order $n - 1$. The determinant of such a matrix is called a **minor** of A. If we delete the ith row and the jth column, the minor thus obtained is denoted by Δ_{ij}. For example,

$$\Delta_{11} = \begin{vmatrix} a_{22} & a_{23} & \dots & a_{2n} \\ a_{32} & a_{33} & \dots & \dots \\ \dots & \dots & \dots & \dots \\ \dots & \dots & \dots & \dots \\ a_{n2} & a_{n3} & \dots & a_{nn} \end{vmatrix}.$$

Define A_{ij} by

$$A_{ij} \equiv (-1)^{i+j} \Delta_{ij}.$$

Then A_{ij} is called the **cofactor** of the element a_{ij} of the determinant $|A|$. Clearly, we have

$$A_{11} = \Delta_{11},\ A_{12} = -\Delta_{12},\ A_{13} = \Delta_{13},\ A_{23} = -\Delta_{23}.$$

From this, we may obtain the following rule, called the **(Laplace) rule of expansion of cofactors** (or simply, the **Laplace expansion**).

$$\begin{aligned} |A| &= a_{i1}A_{11} + a_{i2}A_{i2} + \dots + a_{in}A_{in}, \\ &= a_{1j}A_{ij} + a_{2j}A_{2j} + \dots + a_{nj}A_{nj}, \end{aligned} \tag{39}$$

for any $j = 1, 2, \dots, n$. For example, we have

$$\begin{vmatrix} a_{11} & a_{12} & a_{13} \\ a_{21} & a_{22} & a_{23} \\ a_{31} & a_{32} & a_{33} \end{vmatrix} = a_{11} \begin{vmatrix} a_{22} & a_{23} \\ a_{32} & a_{33} \end{vmatrix} - a_{12} \begin{vmatrix} a_{21} & a_{23} \\ a_{31} & a_{33} \end{vmatrix} + a_{13} \begin{vmatrix} a_{21} & a_{22} \\ a_{31} & a_{32} \end{vmatrix}.$$

From (39) we can easily show that a determinant is unchanged in value when a constant multiple of any other row or column is added to any row or column. We can also show that matrix A is nonsingular if and only if $|A| \neq 0$. Assuming that A is nonsingular, from (39) we may also obtain the next rule for the inversion of a matrix:

$$A^{-1} = \left[\frac{A_{ji}}{|A|}\right] = \frac{1}{|A|}[A_{ji}]. \tag{40}$$

The matrix $[A_{ji}]$ is called the **adjoint** of A. Namely, to obtain the adjoint of A, form a new matrix where a_{ij} is replaced by its cofactor A_{ij}, and then transpose this new matrix.

Example A.4.

$$\text{For } A = \begin{bmatrix} 1 & 2 \\ 3 & 4 \end{bmatrix},$$

$$A_{11} = 4,\ A_{12} = -3,\ A_{21} = -2,\ A_{22} = 1,$$

$$|A| = 1 \cdot 4 - 2 \cdot 3 = -2, \text{ and}$$

$$A^{-1} = \frac{-1}{2}\begin{bmatrix} 4 & -2 \\ -3 & 1 \end{bmatrix} = \begin{bmatrix} -2 & 1 \\ \frac{3}{2} & -\frac{1}{2} \end{bmatrix}.$$

Write the system of simultaneous equations as $Ax = b$, where A is an $n \times n$ matrix and b is an n-dimensional column vector whose i^{th} element is b_m. Assuming that A is nonsingular, the solution of this system can be uniquely written as

$$x = A^{-1}b, \text{ or}$$

$$x_j = \frac{1}{|A|}(b_1 A_{1j} + b_2 A_{2j} + \ldots + b_n A_{nj}),\ j = 1, 2, \ldots, n,$$

which can readily be rewritten as

$$x_j = D_j/|A|,\ j = 1, 2, \ldots, n, \tag{41}$$

where D_j is the determinant obtained from $|A|$ by replacing its jth column by b; that is,

$$A = \begin{bmatrix} a_{11} & \cdots & a_{1j} & \cdots & a_{1n} \\ a_{21} & \cdots & a_{2j} & \cdots & a_{2n} \\ \cdots & \cdots & \cdots & \cdots & \cdots \\ \cdots & \cdots & \cdots & \cdots & \cdots \\ a_{n1} & \cdots & a_{nj} & \cdots & a_{nn} \end{bmatrix},$$

$$D_j \equiv \begin{vmatrix} a_{11} & \cdots & b_1 & \cdots & a_{1n} \\ a_{21} & \cdots & b_2 & \cdots & a_{2n} \\ \cdots & \cdots & \cdots & \cdots & \cdots \\ \cdots & \cdots & \cdots & \cdots & \cdots \\ a_{n1} & \cdots & b_n & \cdots & a_{nn} \end{vmatrix} .$$
$$\text{(j)}$$

Equation (41) is the well-known **Cramer's rule.**

Theorem A.7. For the determinant defined as above, we have (33) through (38), the Laplace rule of expansion of cofactors (39), the inverse rule (40), and Cramer's rule (41).

A.5.2 Partitioned Matrices and Determinants

Since a matrix is a rectangular array of scalars, we may partition it into submatrices. For example,

$$A = \left[\begin{array}{ccc|c} a_{11} & a_{12} & a_{13} & a_{14} \\ a_{21} & a_{22} & a_{23} & a_{24} \\ \hline a_{31} & a_{32} & a_{33} & a_{34} \end{array}\right]$$

may be partitioned to give four submatrices,

$$A_{11} = \begin{bmatrix} a_{11} & a_{12} & a_{13} \\ a_{21} & a_{22} & a_{23} \end{bmatrix}, \; A_{12} = \begin{bmatrix} a_{14} \\ a_{24} \end{bmatrix},$$

$$A_{21} = \begin{bmatrix} a_{31} & a_{32} & a_{33} \end{bmatrix}, \; A_{22} = \begin{bmatrix} a_{34} \end{bmatrix},$$

and A may then be written as

$$A = \begin{bmatrix} A_{11} & A_{12} \\ A_{21} & A_{22} \end{bmatrix} .$$

These A_{ij}'s should not be confused with cofactors.

The basic rules of addition and multiplication still apply to partitioned matrices. For example,

$$\begin{bmatrix} A_{11} & A_{12} \\ A_{21} & A_{22} \\ A_{31} & A_{32} \end{bmatrix} + \begin{bmatrix} B_{11} & B_{12} \\ B_{21} & B_{22} \\ B_{31} & B_{32} \end{bmatrix} = \begin{bmatrix} A_{11}+B_{11} & A_{12}+B_{12} \\ A_{21}+B_{21} & A_{22}+B_{22} \\ A_{31}+B_{31} & A_{32}+B_{32} \end{bmatrix} ,$$

where each A_{ij} is of the same order as the corresponding B_{ij}, and

$$\begin{bmatrix} A_{11} & A_{12} \\ A_{21} & A_{22} \end{bmatrix} \begin{bmatrix} B_{11} \\ B_{21} \end{bmatrix} = \begin{bmatrix} A_{11}B_{11} + A_{12}B_{21} \\ A_{21}B_{11} + A_{22}B_{21} \end{bmatrix}$$

where the partitioning of rows of B into B_{11} andB_{21} should conform to the partitioning of the columns of A so that the matrix multiplication is specified in the right-hand side of the above equation.

From this and the Laplace rule of expansion, it follows easily that if

$$A = \begin{bmatrix} A_{11} & A_{12} \\ A_{21} & A_{22} \end{bmatrix}, \tag{42}$$

where A_{11} and A_{22} are square matrices (not necessarily of the same order) and where A_{12} and A_{21} are square matrices, *and* if either $A_{12} = 0$ or $A_{21} = 0$, then we have

$$|A| = |A_{11}|\ |A_{22}|. \tag{43}$$

Let A be a partitioned matrix in the form of (42), and assume that A_{11} and A_{22} are nonsingular. Then we can show the following useful rule

$$\begin{aligned} |A| &= |A_{11}|\ |A_{22} - A_{21}A_{11}^{-1}A_{12}| \\ &= |A_{22}|\ |A_{11} - A_{12}A_{22}^{-1}A_{21}|. \end{aligned} \tag{44}$$

Clearly, (43) follows as a special case of (44) in which $A_{12} = 0$ and/or $A_{21} = 0$.

A.6 Eigenvalues, Eigenvectors, and Symmetric Matrices

Let $A = [a_{ij}]$ be an $n \times n$ matrix. Suppose there exists an $x \in R^n$ and $\lambda \in R$ such that

$$Ax = \lambda x,\ x \neq 0; \tag{45}$$

then we say that λ is an **eigenvalue** or **characteristic root** (or, simply **root**) of A. The vector x is called an **eigenvector** or **characteristic vector** (associated with λ).[10] Since we can equivalently rewrite $Ax = \lambda x$ as

$$(\lambda I - A)x = 0, \tag{45'}$$

[10] Eigenvectors are required to be *non*zero, since the zero vector trivially satisfies the defining equation $Ax = \lambda x$. On the other hand, an eigenvalue can be zero.

we can immediately see that if λ is an eigenvalue, then (45′) has a solution $x \neq 0$, so that $(\lambda I - A)$ must be singular; that is,

$$\phi(\lambda) \equiv |\lambda I - A| = 0, \tag{46}$$

where $|\lambda I - A|$ is the determinant of $(\lambda I - A)$. Conversely, if λ is a solution of (46), then (45′) has a nonzero solution x. Namely, (45′) and (46) are equivalent. Equation (46) is called the **characteristic equation** or **eigenequation** (of A).

Example A.5.

(i) $A = \begin{bmatrix} 1 & 1 \\ 1 & 1 \end{bmatrix}$, $\phi(\lambda) = \begin{bmatrix} \lambda - 1 & -1 \\ -1 & \lambda - 1 \end{bmatrix} = \lambda(\lambda - 2) = 0;$

hence, $\lambda = 0$, and 2.

(ii) $A = \begin{bmatrix} 1 & 0 \\ 0 & 1 \end{bmatrix}$, $\phi(\lambda) = \begin{bmatrix} \lambda - 1 & 0 \\ 0 & \lambda - 1 \end{bmatrix} = (\lambda - 1)^2 = 0;$

hence, $\lambda = 1$ (double root).

When $A = [a_{ij}]$ is an $n \times n$ matrix, the characteristic equation can equivalently be written

$$\phi(\lambda) = \lambda^n + \alpha_1 \lambda^{n-1} + \ldots \alpha_{n-1}\lambda + \alpha_n = 0, \tag{47}$$

where the α_i's are functions of the a_{ij}'s. The characteristic equation is a polynomial. By the **fundamental theorem of algebra**, the nth order polynomial has n (not necessarily distinct) roots. Each root is not necessarily a real number; it can be a complex number. Hence an eigenvector is not necessarily a real vector; that is, its element can be a complex number. When $n = 2$, there are two eigenvalues, λ_1, λ_2. It is possible that $\lambda_1 = \lambda_2$ ("double root") in which case we say that the **multiplicity** of the root is equal to 2. In general, if λ_i is an eigenvalue of A with multiplicity m_i, and if there are altogether k distinct eigenvalues of A, then we have

$$m_1 + m_2 + \ldots + m_k = n, \text{ and } m_1, m_2, \ldots, m_k \leqq n.$$

When the multiplicity of a particular eigenvalue λ of A is equal to one, then λ is called a **simple root**.

Example A.6. Let $n = 2$. Then the characteristic equation can be written as

$$\lambda^2 + \alpha_1 \lambda + \alpha_2 = 0,$$

where $\alpha_1 \equiv -(a_{11} + a_{22})$, $\alpha_2 \equiv a_{11}a_{22} - a_{12}a_{21}$, and where we may note that α_2 is the determinant of A. From this quadratic equation, the eigenvalues are obtained as

$$\lambda = \frac{1}{2}\left[-\alpha_1 \pm \sqrt{(\alpha_1^2 - 4\alpha_2)}\right].$$

Write the two eigenvalues as λ_1 and λ_2. Clearly λ_1 and λ_2 can be real (when $\alpha_1^2 - 4\alpha_2 \geq 0$) or complex (when $\alpha_1^2 - 4\alpha_2 < 0$). When $\alpha_1^2 - 4\alpha_2 = 0$, we have $\lambda_1 = \lambda_2$ (double root). Note that if λ_1 and λ_2 are complex roots, they are complex conjugates for each other. Letting a and b be real numbers, they can be written in the form of

$$\lambda_1 = a + ib, \text{ and } \lambda_2 = a - ib,$$

where $i \equiv \sqrt{-1}$. Example A.6 plays an important role in chapter 7.

For characteristic equation (47), we can easily show that

$$\alpha_1 = -(a_{11} + a_{22} + \ldots + a_{nn}), \ \alpha_n = |A|, \tag{48}$$

which may be confirmed in terms of example A.6. In general, letting $A = [a_{ij}]$ be an $n \times n$ matrix, the sum of its diagonal elements, $a_{11} + a_{22} + \ldots + a_{nn}$, is called the **trace** of A, which is denoted by trace A. From (48), we can assert that $(-\alpha_1)$ is the trace of A.

Note that if $x \neq 0$ is an eigenvector, that is, if $Ax = \lambda x$, then θx (for any nonzero real number θ) is also an eigenvector associated with the same eigenvalue θ. Furthermore, it is possible that two distinct vectors x and y for which $x \neq \theta y$ for any $\theta \in R$ (one is not a scalar multiple of the other) can be the eigenvectors associated with the *same* eigenvalue. In general, an $n \times n$ matrix A may *not* have n distinct eigenvalues, and yet A can have n linearly independent eigenvectors. The reader may check the validity of this statement by examining the 2×2 *identity* matrix. On the other hand, the eigenvectors that correspond to distinct eigenvalues are all distinct.

Some of the useful results on eigenvalues and eigenvectors, which are well known in matrix algebra, are summarized in theorem A.8. Note that statements (vi) through (viii) require that a particular matrix be symmetric (i.e., $a_{ij} = a_{ji}$ for all i and j). Λ in statements (v) and (vii) of the theorem is the diagonal matrix defined by

$$\Lambda \equiv \begin{bmatrix} \lambda_1 & 0 & \cdot & \cdot & \cdot & \cdot & \cdot & 0 \\ 0 & \lambda_2 & & & & & & \cdot \\ \cdot & & \cdot & & & & & \cdot \\ \cdot & & & \cdot & & & & \cdot \\ \cdot & & & & \cdot & & & \cdot \\ \cdot & & & & & \cdot & & \cdot \\ 0 & 0 & \cdot & \cdot & \cdot & \cdot & \cdot & \lambda_n \end{bmatrix}. \tag{49}$$

Theorem A.8. Let A be an $n \times n$ matrix.

(i) If $\lambda_1, \lambda_2, \ldots, \lambda_n$ are the eigenvalues of A (not necessarily distinct), then we have

$$\text{trace } A = \lambda_1 + \lambda_2 + \ldots + \lambda_n, \; |A| = \lambda_1 \lambda_2 \ldots \lambda_n, \tag{50}$$

(ii) The number of nonzero eigenvalues of A is equal to the rank of A.

(iii) Let $\lambda_1, \lambda_2, \ldots, \lambda_n$ be the eigenvalues of A (not necessarily distinct) and let $x^1, x^2, \ldots, x^n$ be the corresponding eigenvectors. Then the eigenvalues of A^k, for any (positive or negative) integer k, are given by $\lambda_1^k, \lambda_2^k, \ldots, \lambda_n^k$, and the corresponding eigenvectors are given by $x^1, x^2, \ldots, x^n$. In particular, the eigenvalues of A^{-1} are $1/\lambda_1, \ldots, 1/\lambda_n$.

(iv) If $\lambda_1, \lambda_2, \ldots, \lambda_k$ $(k \leqq n)$ are *distinct* eigenvalues of A, then the corresponding eigenvectors, $x^1, x^2, \ldots, x^k$, of these k eigenvalues are linearly independent.

(v) If the n eigenvalues, $\lambda_1, \lambda_2, \ldots, \lambda_n$, of A are all *distinct*, then A can be **diagonalized** in the sense that[11]

$$P^{-1}AP = \Lambda, \tag{51}$$

where $P \equiv [x^1, x^2, \ldots, x^n]$ is an $n \times n$ matrix, and where $x^1, x^2, \ldots, x^n$ are the corresponding (column) eigenvectors of these eigenvalues.[12]

---

[11] P is nonsingular (so that P^{-1} exists), since the n eigenvalues are all distinct so that their corresponding eigenvectors are linearly independent by statement (i).

[12] Notice that $Ax^i = \lambda_i x^i$ by definition. If we let A' be the transpose of A, then

(vi) If A is *symmetric*, then all of its eigenvalues are real numbers, and (hence) every element of A's eigenvectors is a real number.

(vii) Let $\lambda_1, \lambda_2, \ldots, \lambda_n$, be the (not necessarily distinct) eigenvalues of A and let $x^1, x^2, \ldots, x^n$ be their corresponding eigenvectors. Then if A is *symmetric*, we can choose these $x^1, x^2, \ldots, x^n$ in such a way that A can be diagonalized as

$$P'AP = \Lambda, \tag{52}$$

where $P = [x^1, x^2, \ldots, x^n]$, and the x^i's are orthogonal for each other, that is, $x^i \cdot x^j = 0$, for all $i \neq j$.[13]

(viii) If the eigenvalues of A are all zero and if A is a *symmetric* matrix, then A is the zero matrix.

REMARK: A square matrix P is said to be an **orthogonal matrix**, if

$$P'P(= PP') = I. \tag{53}$$

An orthogonal matrix is always nonsingular, and we have $P^{-1} = P'$. Furthermore, the determinant of an orthogonal matrix is equal to either 1 or -1.[14] The matrix P in statement (vii) of theorem A.8 is an orthogonal matrix, since $x^i \cdot x^j = 0$ for all $i \neq j$, and since we can choose the x_i's in such a way that $x^i \cdot x^i = 1$ for all i. Equations (51) and (52) are

---

we have $A'y^i = \lambda_i y^i$ for each λ_i, $i = 1, 2, \ldots, n$. If $\lambda_i \neq \lambda_j$, then we can show, $x^i \cdot y^j = y^i \cdot x^j = 0$ $(i \neq j)$, while $x^i \cdot y^i \neq 0$. Hence, if $\lambda_1, \lambda_2, \ldots, \lambda_n$ are all distinct as in the present case, then we have

$$x^i \cdot y^j = 0,\ y^i \cdot x^j = 0,\ i \neq j,\ x^i \cdot y^i \neq 0,\ i, j = 1, 2, \ldots, n.$$

[13]If A is symmetric, then $A = A'$. Then $Ax^i = \lambda_i x^i$ implies $A'x^i = \lambda_i x^i$. Hence, from fn. 12, we have $x^i \cdot x^j = 0$ if $\lambda_i \neq \lambda_j$. (The eigenvectors corresponding to two distinct eigenvalues of a symmetric matrix are always orthogonal to each other.) Notice that statement (vii) does not require that all eigenvalues are distinct. If, in particular, one of A's eigenvalues, say λ, has multiplicity $\alpha > 1$, then there are α distinct eigenvectors corresponding to such a λ. These are orthogonal to each other, provided that A is symmetric.

[14]Postmultiplying both sides of $P'P = I$ by P^{-1}, $P' = P^{-1}$ follows at once. Taking the determinant of both sides of $P'P = I$ and recalling (33) and (36), we can easily conclude $|P| = 1$ or -1.

called the **spectral decompositions** of A.[15]

A.7 Negative or Positive Definite Matrices

Let $A = [a_{ij}]$ be an $n \times n$ matrix (over the real field) not necessarily symmetric, and let $x \in R^n$ be a column vector. Then consider a real-valued function $Q(x)$ defined on R^n by

$$Q(x) \equiv x'Ax \; (= \sum_{i=1}^{n} \sum_{j=1}^{n} a_{ij}x_i x_j). \tag{54}$$

As mentioned in chapter 1, $Q(x)$ is called a **(real) quadratic form.** We repeat the following definition from chapter 1.

Definition. Let $Q(x) = x'Ax$ be a quadratic form.

(i) A is said to be a **positive definite**, if $Q(x) > 0$ all x except $x = 0$, and A is said to be a **negative definite**, if $Q(x) < 0$ for all x, except $x = 0$.

(ii) A is said to be **positive semidefinite** if $Q(x) \geqq 0$ for all x, and A is said to be **negative semidefinite**, if $Q(x) \leqq 0$ for all x.

Theorem A.9 relates these concepts of (negative or positive) "definiteness" to eigenvalues, where statement (iii) follows from statements (i) and (ii) and from the fact that none of the eigenvalues of a nonsingular matrix is zero.

Theorem A.9. Let A be an $n \times n$ symmetric matrix and $Q(x) \equiv x'Ax$.

(i) A is positive definite (resp. negative definite), if and only if every eigenvalue of A is positive (resp. negative).

(ii) A is positive semidefinite (resp. negative semidefinite), if and only if every eigenvalue of A is nonnegative (resp. nonpositive).

---

[15] We may rewrite (51) and (52), respectively, as

$$A = \sum_{i=1}^{n} \lambda_i x^i \cdot y_i \quad \text{and} \quad A = \sum_{i=1}^{n} \lambda_i x^i \cdot x^i,$$

where y^i is the ith column of P^{-1}.

(iii) If A is positive (resp. negative) semidefinite, *and* if A is nonsingular, then A is positive (resp. negative) definite.

REMARK: If A is positive or negative definite, then none of its eigenvalues are zero. Hence by statement (ii) of theorem A.8, A is nonsingular. By statement (vii) of theorem A.8 every symmetric matrix can be *diagonalized* as (52). Namely, there exists an orthogonal matrix P such that $P'AP = \Lambda$, where $P'P = PP' = I$. Then letting $y \equiv Px$ (which is called an **orthogonal transformation** of x), we may observe

$$x'Ax = (Px)'PAP'(Px) = y'\Lambda y.$$

Thus we may rewrite $Q(x) \equiv x'Ax$ as[16]

$$x'Ax = \lambda_1 y_1^2 + \lambda_2 y_2^2 + \ldots + \lambda_n y_n^2. \tag{55}$$

From this, statements (i) and (ii) of theorem A.9 hold at once.

Example A.7. Recall the problem of cost minimization discussed in example A.3. As before, let $x^* = x(w, y)$ be a solution of the problem; $x(w, y)$ signifies the vector of factor demand functions. Let $S \equiv [\partial x_i/\partial w_j]$ be the $n \times n$ substitution matrix. S is symmetric, and it is a singular matrix by $Sw = 0$, and the rank of S is equal to $n - 1$ under Samuelson's regularity condition. As mentioned earlier, this condition states that $z'Sz < 0$ for all z *not proportional to* w. This almost asserts that S is negative definite, but *not quite* due to the emphasized clause. In fact, S *cannot* be negative definite as it is singular, so that S negative semidefinite. Since rank $S = n - 1$, the $(n - 1) \times (n - 1)$ matrix obtained by deleting the nth row and the nth column is negative definite by statement (iii) of theorem A.9. Denote such a matrix by $\tilde{S}$. Then $z'\tilde{S}z < 0$ for *all* $(n - 1)$ dimensional non-zero vector z. Let $x_{ij} \equiv \partial x_i/\partial w_j$. Then by statement (ii) of theorem 1.3 in

---

[16] If A is positive definite, then $\lambda_i > 0$ for all i by statement (i) of theorem A.9. Hence, we may assert that if A is positive definite then there exists a nonsingular $n \times n$ matrix C such that

$$z'Az = z_1^2 + z_2^2 + \ldots + z_n^2, \text{ where } z \equiv Cx,$$

and where $z_i = y_i\sqrt{\lambda_i}$. Similarly, we may also assert that if A is *negative* definite, then there exists a nonsingular matrix C such that

$$z'Az = -(z_1^2 + z_2^2 + \ldots + z_n^2).$$

chapter 1, we have

$$x_{11} < 0, \begin{vmatrix} x_{11} & x_{12} \\ x_{21} & x_{22} \end{vmatrix} > 0, \begin{vmatrix} x_{11} & x_{12} & x_{13} \\ x_{21} & x_{22} & x_{23} \\ x_{31} & x_{32} & x_{33} \end{vmatrix} < 0 \ldots .$$

Furthermore, in $z'\tilde{S}z < 0$, let $z' = (0, \ldots, 1, \ldots, 0)$; that is, z is the $(n - 1)$ dimensional column vector whose elements are all zero except for the ith element. Then we obtain $x_{ii} < 0$. Since the choice of i can be arbitrary, this holds for all $i = 1, 2, \ldots, n - 1$. Also, since interchanging the nth row and the nth column of A by (say) the first row and the first column will not affect this discussion (which amounts to saying that reassigning a particular number to a particular commodity does not affect the discussion), we may also assert $x_{nn} < 0$. Thus, we have

$$x_{ii} \equiv \partial x_i / \partial w_i < 0, \quad \text{for all } i = 1, 2, \ldots, n.$$

The change in the ith factor price always reduces the demand for the ith factor for all $i = 1, 2, \ldots, n$; that is, the own-price effect is always negative.

One of the most important questions on inequalities of quadratic form is to determine the sign of $Q(x) \equiv x'Ax$ when x is constrained by $Bx = 0$, where B is an $m \times n$ matrix. Such a question appears in the classical theory of optimization, which has become familiar to economists since Hicks's *Value and Capital* (1946) and Samuelson's *Foundations* (1947). To answer the above question, assume $n > m$ and define the following submatrices of A and B, for $k = m + 1, m + 2, \ldots, n$.

$$A_k \equiv \begin{bmatrix} a_{11} & \cdot & \cdot & \cdot & \cdot & \cdot & a_{1k} \\ a_{21} & \cdot & \cdot & \cdot & \cdot & \cdot & a_{2k} \\ \cdots & \cdot & \cdot & \cdot & \cdot & \cdot & \cdots \\ \cdots & \cdot & \cdot & \cdot & \cdot & \cdot & \cdots \\ \cdots & \cdot & \cdot & \cdot & \cdot & \cdot & \cdots \\ a_{k1} & \cdot & \cdot & \cdot & \cdot & \cdot & a_{kk} \end{bmatrix}, \quad \text{and}$$

$$B_{m,k} \equiv \begin{bmatrix} b_{11} & \cdot & \cdot & \cdot & \cdot & \cdot & b_{1k} \\ \cdot & & & & & & \cdot \\ \cdot & & & & & & \cdot \\ \cdot & & & & & & \cdot \\ \cdot & & & & & & \cdot \\ b_{m_1} & \cdot & \cdot & \cdot & \cdot & \cdot & b_{mk} \end{bmatrix}.$$

Note that there are $(n - m)$ A_k's and $(n - m)$ $B_{m,k}$'s. Furthermore, define the following $n - m$ *bordered determinants*, C_k's (where C_k being bordered by $B_{m,k}$) by

$$|C_k| \equiv \det \begin{bmatrix} 0 & B_{m,k} \\ B_{m,k} & A_k \end{bmatrix}, \quad k = m + 1, \ m + 2, \ \ldots, \ n,$$

where $B'_{m,k}$ is the transpose of $B_{m,k}$, and 0 is the $m \times m$ matrix whose entries are all zero. $|C_k|$ is an $(m + k) \times (m + l)$ determinant. Then we have theorem A.10.[17]

Theorem A.10. Let A be symmetric and $B_{m,m}$ be nonsingular (rank $B = m$). Then

(i) $x'Ax < 0$ for all $x \neq 0$ such that $Bx = 0$, if and only if $(-1)^k C_k > 0$, $k = m + 1, \ m + 2, \ \ldots, \ n$;

(ii) $x'Ax > 0$ for all $x \neq 0$ such that $Bx = 0$, if and only if $(-1)^m C_k > 0$, $k = m + 1, \ m + 2, \ \ldots, \ n$.

References

Debreu, G. 1952. "Definite and Semidefinite Quadratic Forms." *Econometrica* 20 (April): 295–300.

Gantmacher, F. R. 1959. *The Theory of Matrices.* Trans. from the Russian original *Theoriya Matrits* by K. A. Hirsch. 2 vols. New York: Chelsea Publishing Co.

Hadley, G. 1969. *Linear Algebra.* Reading, Mass: Addison-Wesley.

Halmos, P. R. 1958. *Finite Dimensional Vector Spaces.* Princeton, N.J.: van Nostrand.

Hicks, J. R. 1946. *Value and Capital.* 2d ed. Oxford: Clarendon Press.

Mann, H. B. 1943. "Quadratic Forms with Linear Constraints." *American Mathematical Monthly* 50 (August–September): 430–33.

Marcus, M. and H. Minc. 1964. *A Survey of Matrix Theory and Matrix Inequalities.* Boston: Allyn and Bacon.

[17]For the proof, see Mann (1943) and Debreu (1952). In statement (i), the sign of $|C_k|$ depends upon k; thus statement (i) says that the last $(n - m)$ successive principal minors of the bordered matrix C_n alternate signs. In statement (ii), the sign of $|C_k|$ depends upon m; thus statement (ii) says that the last $(n - m)$ successive principal minors of C_n all have the identical sign, $(-1)^m$.

Samuelson, P. A. 1947. *Foundations of Economic Analysis.* Cambridge, Mass.: Harvard University Press.

Shilov, G. E. 1977. *Linear Algebra.* Trans. R. A. Silverman from the Russian original. New York: Dover Publishing.

APPENDIX B

Seven Kinds of Concavity and Quasi-Concave Programming: A Survey of Some Results and Extensions

There are a number of studies that relate various concepts of concavity such as Ponstein (1967); Mangasarian (1969); Newman (1969); and Diewert, Avrel, and Zang (1979). The present study in a sense follows the same spirit.[1] We present seven kinds of concavity and quasi-concavity and show the relationship among them. Most of the relations are known, and yet we find it useful to obtain our relations. These relations, in turn, put the seven concepts of concavity in proper perspective. The known relations are included to make our exposition as streamlined as possible. With the perspective thus obtained, we consider the quasi-concave programming problem. This problem is considered in an important work by Arrow and Enthoven (1961), and then by Mangasarian (1969). We shall highlight the importance of pseudo-concavity in this context (this follows Mangasarian 1969 and Martos 1975). The concept of pseudo-concavity is introduced by Mangasarian (1965).

B.1 Seven Kinds of Concavity[2]

Let f be a real-valued function defined on a convex set X in R^n. Then the following definitions of five kinds of concavity are well known.

Definition B.1. Function f is said to be **quasi-concave** if[3]

$f(x) \geqq f(x^{\circ})$ implies

[1] This appendix is based on Ide and Takayama (1988). Many concepts here are introduced in chapter 2.

[2] Corresponding to seven kinds of concavity discussed here, there are seven kinds of convexity, which can be obtained by simply putting minus (−) signs in front of the relevant functions. The relations analogous to the ones obtained here can also be obtained for these seven kinds of convex functions.

[3] The symbox ∀ reads "for all."

$$f[\theta x + (1 - \theta)x^\circ] \geqq f(x^\circ),\ \forall\, x,\, x^\circ \in X,\ 0 \leqq \theta \leqq 1. \qquad (1)$$

Definition B.2. Function f is said to be **explicitly quasi-concave** if it is quasi-concave *and* if

$$f(x) > f(x^\circ) \text{ implies } f[\theta x + (1 - \theta)x^\circ] > f(x^\circ),$$

$$\forall\, x,\, x^\circ \in X,\ x \neq x^\circ,\ 0 < \theta \leqq 1. \qquad (2)$$

Definition B.3. Function f is said to be **strictly quasi-concave** if

$$f(x) \geqq f(x^\circ) \text{ implies } f[\theta x + (1 - \theta)x^\circ] > f(x^\circ),$$

$$\forall\, x,\, x^\circ \in X,\ x \neq x^\circ,\ 0 < \theta < 1. \qquad (3)$$

Definition B.4. Function f is said to be **concave** if

$$f[\theta x + (1 - \theta)x^\circ] \geqq \theta f(x) + (1 - \theta)f(x^\circ),$$

$$\forall\, x,\, x^\circ \in X,\ 0 \leqq \theta \leqq 1. \qquad (4)$$

Definition B.5 Function f is said to be **strictly concave** if [4]

$$f[\theta x + (1 - \theta)x^\circ] > \theta f(x) + (1 - \theta)f(x^\circ),$$

$$\forall\, x,\, x^\circ \in X,\ x \neq x^\circ,\ 0 < \theta < 1. \qquad (5)$$

With regard to explicit quasi-concavity, the result in lemma B.1 is from Karamardian (1967).

[4] This definition of strict quasi-concavity is different from the one introduced by Ponstein (1967) and discussed by Mangasarian (1969). His "strict quasi-concavity" corresponds to our explicit quasi-concavity, whereas our strict quasi-concavity corresponds to his "unnamed concavity." The concept (with its term) of explicit quasi-concavity was introduced by Martos (1967) and further discussed by Thompson and Parke (1973). Our seven kinds of concavity correspond to the seven kinds of concavity discussed in Ponstein (1967), with the difference in naming explicit quasi-concavity and strict quasi-concavity.

Lemma B.1. If f is upper-semicontinuous,[5] then (2) implies the quasi-concavity of f.

Proof. See Karamardian (1967); Mangasarian (1969, p. 139), and Martos (1975, pp. 45–46). Hence in particular, if f is continuous, (2) implies the quasi-concavity of f. The results in the following remark are well known and indicate the importance of explicit quasi-concavity and strict quasi-concavity.

REMARK: Let S be a convex subset of X.

(i) If f is explicitly quasi-concave, then every local maximum of f in S is also a *global* maximum.

(ii) If f is strictly quasi-concave, then every local maximum of f in S is also a *unique global* maximum.

The results in theorems B.1 and B.2 are obvious from the definitions.

Theorem B.1. Every explicitly quasi-concave function is quasi-concave, and every strictly quasi-concave function is explicitly quasi-concave (and hence quasi-concave). The converse of these statements need not hold.

Theorem B.2. Every concave function is explicitly quasi-concave, and every strictly concave function is strictly quasi-concave (and hence explicitly quasi-concave). The converse of these statements need not be true.

In practical applications, f is often assumed to be a *differentiable* function defined in an open convex set X in R^n. We focus our attention on such a case. Denote the gradient vector of f by f_x, and if it is evaluated at, say x°, denote it by f_x°, that is, $f_x^\circ \equiv f_x(x^\circ)$. The following two concepts of concavity for the differentiable case are important.

Definition B.6. Function f is said to be **pseudo-concave** if

$f(x) > f(x^\circ)$ implies

$$f_x^\circ \cdot (x - x^\circ) > 0, \ \forall\, x,\ x^\circ \in X,\ x \neq x^\circ, \tag{6}$$

[5]For the concept of upper-semicontinuity, see Takayama (1985, p. 239), for example.

where the dot $(\cdot)$ signifies the Euclidian inner product. By taking the contrapositive of (6), the equation can equivalently be stated as

$$f_x^\circ \cdot (x - x^\circ) \leqq 0 \quad \text{implies}$$

$$f(x) \leqq f(x^\circ), \forall\, x,\, x^\circ \in X,\, x \neq x^\circ. \tag{6'}$$

Definition B.7. Function f is said to be **strictly pseudo-concave** if

$$f(x) \geqq f(x^\circ) \quad \text{implies}$$

$$f_x^\circ \cdot (x - x^\circ) > 0, \forall\, x,\, x^\circ \in X,\, x \neq x^\circ. \tag{7}$$

Similarly, (7) can equivalently be stated as

$$f_x^\circ \cdot (x - x^\circ) \leqq 0 \quad \text{implies}$$

$$f(x) < f(x^\circ), \forall x,\, x^\circ \in X,\, x \neq x^\circ. \tag{7'}$$

For the differentiable case, the derivative properties of various kinds of concavity in lemma B.2 are well known.

Lemma B.2.

(i) Function f is concave if and only if

$$f_x^\circ \cdot (x - x^\circ) \geqq f(x) - f(x^\circ), \forall\, x,\, x^\circ \in X. \tag{8}$$

(ii) Function f is strictly concave if and only if

$$f_x^\circ \cdot (x - x^\circ) > f(x) - f(x^\circ), \forall\, x,\, x^\circ \in X,\, x \neq x^\circ. \tag{9}$$

(iii) Function f is quasi-concave if and only if

$$f(x) \geqq f(x^\circ) \quad \text{implies}$$

$$f_x^\circ \cdot (x - x^\circ) \geqq 0, \forall\, x,\, x^\circ \in X. \tag{10}$$

There does not seem to be a simple characterization of a differentiable, explicitly quasi-concave function in terms of the gradient of the function such as above (see Mangasarian 1969, p. 140).

Theorem B.3 relates the two concepts of pseudo-concavity to the two concepts of concavity. The statements in theorem B.3, except for the one that involves strict pseudo-concavity, are shown in Mangasarian (1969, pp. 144–45).

Theorem B.3.

(i) Every strictly concave function is strictly pseudo-concave.

(ii) Every concave function is pseudo-concave.

(iii) The converse of statements (i) and (ii) need not hold.

(iv) Strict pseudo-concavity is neither necessary nor sufficient for concavity.

Proof: Statements (i) and (ii) are obvious from (6) through (9). To show statement (iii), it suffices to give the following example, attributed to Mangasarian (1965; 1969, p. 145).

Example B.1. Let $f: R \to R$, which is defined by

$$f(x) = x + x^3.$$

Clearly f is not concave on R for $x > 0$. However, it is pseudo-concave on R because $f'(x) = 1 + 3x^2 > 0$, and

$$\begin{aligned} f_x^\circ(x - x^\circ) \leqq 0 \Rightarrow x - x^\circ \leqq 0 \Rightarrow x^3 \leqq (x^\circ)^3 \\ \Rightarrow f(x) \leqq f(x^\circ). \end{aligned}$$

(Note that this function is also pseudo-convex.) Another example may be useful. Let $f: R \to R$, which is defined by

$$\begin{aligned} f(x) &= 0.5x^2 + 0.5, \quad \text{for } x \geqq 1, \\ &= x, \quad \text{for } -1 \leqq x \leqq 1, \\ &= -0.5x^2 - 0.5, \quad \text{for } x \leqq -1. \end{aligned} \tag{11}$$

This function is continuously differentiable for x in R. It is easy to see that (7) is satisfied, so that f is strictly pseudo-concave (and hence pseudo-concave), whereas f is not concave for $x > 1$. To show statement (iv), it suffices to show that concavity need not imply strict pseudo-concavity. To this end, we consider example B.2.

Example B.2. Let $f : R \to R$, which is defined by, $f(x) = 1$, $\forall x \in R$. f is clearly concave. However $f'(x) = 0$ for all x, and hence f cannot be strictly pseudo-concave. (QED)

We now relate the two concepts of pseudo-concavity to explicit quasi-concavity and strict quasi-concavity.

Theorem B.4.[6] Every pseudo-concave function is explicitly quasi-concave, whereas the converse need not hold.

Proof. To show the first statement, let $f(x) > f(x^\circ)$, x, $x^\circ \in X$, $x \neq x^\circ$. Suppose that f is not explicitly quasi-concave. Then by (2) we have

$$F(\theta) \equiv f[\theta x + (1 - \theta)x^\circ] \leqq f(x^\circ) = F(0),\ 0 \leqq \theta < 1.$$

This implies $F'(0) \leqq 0$. Since $F'(0) = f_x^\circ \cdot (x - x^\circ)$, we have, $f_x^\circ \cdot (x - x^\circ) \leqq 0$. This contradicts the pseudo-concavity of f. To show that the converse need not hold, consider example B.3.

Example B.3. Let $f : R \to R$ be defined by $f(x) = x^3$. Clearly f is strictly quasi-concave and hence explicitly quasi-concave. Letting $x^\circ = 0$ and $x = 1$, it is easy to see $f_x^\circ(x - x^\circ) = 0$. (QED)

Theorem B.5. Every strictly pseudo-concave function is strictly quasi-concave, whereas the converse need not hold.

Proof. The proof is analogous to that of theorem B.4, and hence can be omitted.

Example B.3 also offers an example for which the converse need not hold. Recalling (7), we may obtain the following result from theorem B.5.

Corollary. Function f is strictly quasi-concave, if (7) holds.

The converse of this corollary need not hold. To see this, again consider example B.3 and note $f_x(0) = 0$.

Denoting "concavity," "strict concavity," "pseudo-concavity," "strict pseudo-concavity," "explicit quasi-concavity," "strict quasi-concavity,"

[6]This theorem is from Mangasarian (1965). Our proof is somewhat simpler than his proof.

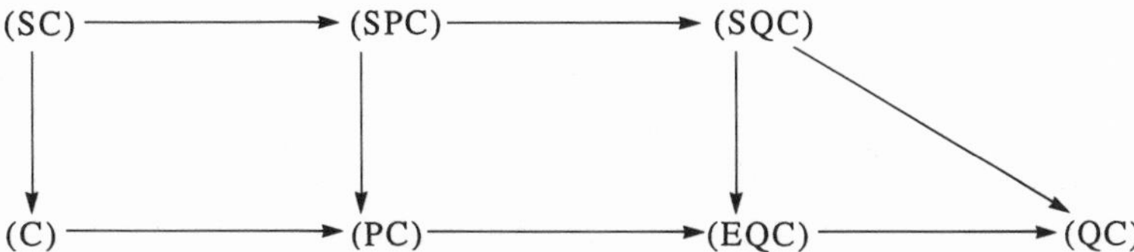

Figure B.1: Logical connections among seven kinds of concavity

and "quasi-concavity," by (C), (SC), (PC), (SPC), (EQC), (SQC), and (QC), respectively, we may schematically illustrate the logical connections of these concepts as obtained in theorems B.1–B.5 by figure B.1. All implications are represented by single arrows. Implications not so represented are not true in general. Figure B.1 shows that the class of quasi-concave functions is the largest class considered and the strictly concave case is the smallest.

B.2 The Role of Nonvanishing Gradients

Let $f(x)$ be a real-valued continuously differentiable function defined on an open convex set X in R^n, and let f_x be its gradient vector. In this section we investigate some implications of $f_x \neq 0$ to the relationship among various concepts of concavity. In applications to economics, for example, if we interpret $f(x)$ to be an individual's utility function, $f_x \neq 0$, is satisfied when the consumer is not satiated for at least one commodity. If we interpret $f(x)$ to be a production function, then $f_x \neq 0$ is satisfied when the marginal productivity of at least one factor is positive. Hence, condition $f_x \neq 0$ would be important in the application of quasi-concave programming results to problems in economics and other fields.

One result that we shall obtain in this section can be stated as in theorem B.6.

Theorem B.6. Assume that $f_x \neq 0$ for all $x \in X$. Then the following three properties of f are equivalent:

(i) $f(x)$ is quasi-concave,

(ii) $f(x)$ is explicitly quasi-concave, and

(iii) $f(x)$ is pseudo-concave.

Let x° be some point in X and assume $f_x^\circ \neq 0$. A key concept in this section is the set,

$$P(x^\circ) \equiv \{x \in X : f_x^\circ \cdot (x - x^\circ) = 0\}. \tag{12}$$

This signifies the hyperplane tangent to the upper level set

$$L(x^\circ) \equiv \{x \in X : f(x) \geqq f(x^\circ)\},$$

at x°. We first prove the result in lemma B.3.

Lemma B.3: Let $f(x)$ be a quasi-concave function on X. Assume that $f_x^\circ \neq 0$ for some $x^\circ \in X$. Then we have

$$f(x) \leqq f(x^\circ), \quad \text{for all} \quad x \in P(x^\circ). \tag{13}$$

Proof. Suppose the contrary. Namely, suppose that there exists an $x \in P(x^\circ)$ such that $f(x) > f(x^\circ)$. Since f is continuous, we can choose $h \in R^n$ in such a way that $(x + h) \in X$ and

$$f(x + h) \geqq f(x^\circ). \tag{14}$$

Furthermore, since $f_x^\circ \neq 0$, we can choose such an h to satisfy $f_x^\circ \cdot h < 0$. Define z by $z \equiv x + h$. Then we may observe

$$f_x^\circ \cdot (x - x^\circ) = f_x^\circ \cdot (z - h - x^\circ) = f_x^\circ \cdot (z - x^\circ) - f_x^\circ \cdot h = 0.$$

Thus we have

$$f_x^\circ \cdot (z - x^\circ) < 0. \tag{15}$$

Since f is quasi-concave, taking the contrapositive of (10), (15) implies $f(z) < f(x^\circ)$. This contradicts (14). (QED)

Using lemma B.3, we may prove the result in theorem B.7.

Theorem B.7. Let $f(x)$ be a quasi-concave function on X. Assume

$$f_x \neq 0 \quad \text{for all} \quad x \in X. \tag{16}$$

Then f is pseudo-concave.

Proof. Suppose that f is not pseudo-concave. Then from (6), there exist $x^{\circ}, x^{1} \in X$ with $x^{\circ} \neq x^{1}$ such that

$$f(x^{1}) > f(x^{\circ}) \text{ and } f_x^{\circ} \cdot (x^{1} - x^{\circ}) = 0, \tag{17}$$

where the possibility of $f_x^{\circ} \cdot (x^{1} - x^{\circ}) < 0$ is precluded by the quasi-concavity of f. Equation (17) means $x^{1} \in P(x^{\circ})$ and yet $f(x^{1}) > f(x^{\circ})$, which contradicts (13). (QED)

REMARK: The converse of theorem B.7 need not hold. To show this, consider example B.4.

Example B.4. Let $f : R \to R$ be defined by $f(x) = -x^2$. Since f is (strictly) concave, it is pseudo-concave (and quasi-concave). However, $f_x(0) = 0$.

Since every pseudo-concave function is explicitly quasi-concave by theorem B.4, and since every explicitly quasi-concave function is quasi-concave, theorem B.6 follows at once from theorem B.7. Theorem B.7 clarifies the role of $f_x \neq 0$ on the relation between quasi-concavity and pseudo-concavity. We shall now clarify the role of $f_x \neq 0$ on the relation between strict quasi-concavity and strict pseudo-concavity. The analysis can be similar to the preceding by proving results analogous to lemma B.3 and theorem B.7 in similar ways. Corresponding to $P(x^{\circ})$ defined in (12), we now define

$$\overline{P}(x^{\circ}) \equiv \{x \in X : f_x^{\circ} \cdot (x - x^{\circ}) = 0, \ x \neq x^{\circ}\}. \tag{12$'$}$$

Lemma B.4. Let $f(x)$ be a *strictly* quasi-concave function on X, and let $f_x^{\circ} \neq 0$ for some $x^{\circ} \in X$. Then we have

$$f(x) < f(x^{\circ}), \text{ for all } x \in \overline{P}(x^{\circ}). \tag{13$'$}$$

Proof. Suppose that there exists an $x \in \overline{P}(x^{\circ})$ such that $f(x) \geqq f(x^{\circ})$. Since f is strictly quasi-concave, we have, by definition,

$$f(x) \geqq f(x^{\circ}) \text{ implies}$$

$$f(\overline{x}) > f(x^{\circ}), \ \forall\, x, \ x^{\circ} \in X, \ x \neq x^{\circ}, \ 0 < \theta < 1,$$

where $\overline{x} \equiv \theta x + (1 - \theta)x^{\circ}$. By observing

$$f_x^{\circ} \cdot (\overline{x} - x^{\circ}) = \theta f_x^{\circ} \cdot (x - x^{\circ}) = 0,$$

by definition of $\overline{x}$, we may conclude that $\overline{x} \in \overline{P}(x^{\circ})$. Since f is continuous and $f_x^{\circ} \neq 0$, we may choose $h \in R^n$ in such a way that $x + h \in X$,

$$f(x + h) \geqq f(x^{\circ}) \text{ and } f_x^{\circ} \cdot h < 0, \tag{18}$$

as in the proof of lemma B.3. Let z be defined by $z \equiv \overline{x} + h$. Then we may observe

$$0 = f_x^{\circ} \cdot (\overline{x} - x^{\circ}) = f_x^{\circ} \cdot (z - h - x^{\circ}) = f_x^{\circ} \cdot (x - x^{\circ}) - f_x^{\circ} \cdot h.$$

Since $f_x^{\circ} \cdot h < 0$ by (18), we have

$$f_x^{\circ} \cdot (z - x^{\circ}) < 0.$$

Since f is quasi-concave, taking the contrapositive of (10), $f_x^{\circ} \cdot (z - x^{\circ}) < 0$ implies $f(z) < f(x^{\circ})$, which contradicts $f(z) \leqq f(x^{\circ})$ in (18).(QED)

From lemma B.4, we may obtain the result in theorem B.8.

Theorem B.8: Let $f(x)$ be a *strictly* quasi-concave function on X, and assume (16). Then f is strictly pseudo-concave.

Proof. Suppose the converse; that is, suppose that there exist x°, $x^{1} \in X$, $x^{\circ} \neq x^{1}$ such that

$$f(x^{1}) \geqq f(x^{\circ}) \text{ and } f_x^{\circ} \cdot (x^{1} - x^{\circ}) = 0, \tag{17$'$}$$

where the possibility of $f_x^{\circ} \cdot (x^{1} - x^{\circ}) < 0$ is precluded by the quasi-concavity of f. But since f is strictly quasi-concave with (16) by assumption, we have (13′) by lemma B.4. This contradicts (17′). (QED)

Combining this with theorem B.5, we at once obtain the following result.

Corollary: Given (16), that is, given that $f_x \neq 0$ for all $x \in X$, f is strictly quasi-concave if and only if it is strictly pseudo-concave.

Various concepts of concavity are global concepts. In the context of our later discussion on quasi-concave programming, it would be convenient to define certain "local" concepts.

Definition B.6′. Function f is said to be **locally pseudo-concave at $\mathbf{x}^{\circ}$** if $f_x^{\circ} \neq 0$ and

$$f(x) > f(x^{\circ}) \Rightarrow f_x^{\circ} \cdot (x - x^{\circ}) > 0, \; \forall\, x \in X \text{ with } x \neq x^{\circ}. \tag{6$''$}$$

Definition B.7′. Function f is said to be **locally strictly pseudo-concave at x°** if

$$f(x) \geqq f(x^\circ) \Rightarrow f_x^\circ \cdot (x - x^\circ) > 0, \ \forall\, x \in X \ \text{ with } x \neq x^\circ. \quad (7'')$$

Going through the proofs of theorems B.7 and B.8, we can readily see that these theorems can be extended as follows.

Theorem B.7′. Let $f(x)$ be a quasi-concave function on X. Assume

$$f_x^\circ \neq 0 \text{ for some } x^\circ \in X. \quad (16')$$

Then f is locally pseudo-concave at x^1.

Theorem B.8′. Let $f(x)$ be a strictly quasi-concave function on X, and assume (16′). Then f is locally strictly pseudo-concave at x°.

B.3 Quasi-Concave Programming

Let f, g_1, g_2, ..., g_m be real-valued, continuously differentiable, *quasi-concave* functions defined in R^n. Consider the problem of choosing $x \in R^n$ so as to

(**QCP**) Maximize $f(x)$,

$$\text{Subject to } g_1(x) \geqq 0, \ \ldots, \ g_m(x) \geqq 0, \text{ and } x \geqq 0.$$

This problem is known as a **quasi-concave programming problem** (QCP) and it is discussed by Arrow and Enthoven (1961).[7] The set S, defined by

$$S \equiv \{x \in R^n : g_1(x) \geqq 0, \ g_2(x) \geqq 0, \ldots, g_m(x) \geqq 0, \ x \geqq 0\},$$

is the constraint set of this problem. Let x° be a solution of (QCP), which we write as:

---

[7] Arrow and Enthoven's work (1961) is repeatedly exposited in a number of places with innovative remarks and improvements. See, for example, Mangasarian (1969, pp. 151–52), Murata (1977, pp. 317–20, and pp. 322–23); and Uekawa and Kimura (1987, pp. 81–88). However, the substance of Arrow and Enthoven's work remains as the standard reference. An important generalization in terms of a pseudo-concave objective function, is accomplished by Mangasarian (1969, pp. 151–52). See also Martos (1975, pp. 125–26).

(**M**) There exists an x° that maximizes $f(x)$ subject to $x \in S$.

Let $g = (g_1, g_2, \ldots, g_m)$ and $\lambda = (\lambda_1, \lambda_2, \ldots, \lambda_m)$. Define the Lagrangian (in the usual way) as

$$\Phi(x, \lambda) \equiv f(x) + \lambda \cdot g(x).$$

Then the first-order condition (**FOC**) can be stated as:

(**FOC**) There exists an (x°, λ°), $x^\circ \geqq 0$, $\lambda^\circ \geqq 0$, such that

$$\Phi_x^\circ \leqq 0,\ \Phi_x^\circ \cdot x^\circ = 0,\ g(x^\circ) \geqq 0,\ \lambda^\circ \cdot g(x^\circ) = 0, \tag{19}$$

where Φ_x° denotes the gradient vector of Φ with respect to x, evaluated at (x°, λ°). Let g_x° be the Jacobian matrix of g, evaluated at x°, so that g_x° is an $m \times n$ matrix. As is well known, we may then rewrite $\Phi_x^\circ \leqq 0$ and $\Phi_x^\circ \cdot x^\circ = 0$ as

$$f_x^\circ + \lambda^\circ g_x^\circ \leqq 0, \quad \text{and} \quad (f_x^\circ + \lambda^\circ g_x^\circ) \cdot \mathbf{x}^\circ = \mathbf{0},$$

respectively, where the rule of multiplication for $\lambda^\circ g_x^\circ$ should be self-evident.

Needless to say, (FOC) need not imply condition (M). Arrow and Enthoven (1961) offer the following remarkable result, which is discussed in chapter 2.

Theorem B.9. (FOC) implies condition (M) if any one of the following conditions is satisfied, where $f_{x_i}^\circ \equiv \partial f(x^\circ)/\partial x_i$:

(i) $f_{x_i}^\circ < 0$ for some i,

(ii) $f_{x_i}^\circ > 0$ for some "relevant i,"

(iii) $f_x^\circ \neq 0$, and f is twice continuously differentiable (i.e., $f \in C^2$), and

(iv) f is concave,

where the ith coordinate variable x_i is said to be a **relevant variable**, if there exists an $\overline{x}$ in the constraint set S such that $\overline{x}_i > 0$.

REMARK: Note that conditions (i), (ii), and (iii) require only the quasi-concavity of f.

One may think that the concavity of f is too restrictive, whereas he or she is willing to accept the quasi-concavity of f. In this section, we investigate how far we can go. Recalling figure B.1, we may easily see that the concept, which comes next after quasi-concavity, is explicit quasi-concavity or strict quasi-concavity. However, it is plain that this does not work as the following result shows.

REMARK: (FOC) need not imply (M), if f is explicitly quasi-concave, or if f is strictly quasi-concave.

To prove this, it suffices to give the following example.

Example B.5. Let $f : R \to R$, which is defined by

$$f(x) = (x - 1)^3.$$

Note that f is strictly quasi-concave and hence explicitly quasi-concave. Assume that there are no g constraints. Then $x^\circ = 1$ satisfies (FOC), whereas $x^\circ = 1$ is not a solution of (QCP).

The concept that comes after explicit quasi-concavity or strict quasi-concavity in figure B.1 is pseudo-concavity or strict pseudo-concavity. We now show the following result. The first statement is obtained by Mangasarian (1969, pp. 151–53).

Theorem B.10. Assume that $g_1, \ldots, g_m$ are all quasi-concave.

(i) If f is pseudo-concave, then (FOC) implies (M).

(ii) If f is strictly quasi-concave, then (FOC) implies (M), and x° furnishes a unique global maximum.

Proof. Following Arrow and Enthoven (1961), we consider the following identity.

$$f_x^\circ \cdot (x^1 - x^\circ) = (f_x^\circ + \lambda^\circ g_x^\circ) \cdot (x^1 - x^\circ) - (\lambda^\circ g_x^\circ) \cdot (x^1 - x^\circ). \quad (20)$$

Assume that x° satisfies (FOC) and $x^1 \in S$. Then, $(f_x^\circ + \lambda^\circ g_x^\circ) \cdot (x^1 - x^\circ) \leqq 0$. Namely, the first term of the right-hand side of (20) is nonpositive. If $\lambda_j^\circ = 0$, the jth component of the second term vanishes. If $\lambda_j^\circ > 0$, then $g_j(x^\circ) = 0$ by (FOC). Since $x^1 \in S$, $g(x^1) \geqq 0$. Since $g_j(x)$ is quasi-concave for all j, we have

$$g_{j_x}^\circ \cdot (x^1 - x^\circ) \geqq 0, \quad \text{for all } j \quad (21)$$

by (10), where g_{j_x} is the gradient vector of g_j. Thus we may obtain $-(\lambda^{\circ} g_x^{\circ}) \cdot (x^1 - x^{\circ}) \leqq 0$. The second term of the right-hand side of (20) is nonpositive. Thus we have

$$f_x^{\circ} \cdot (x^1 - x^{\circ}) \leqq 0. \tag{22}$$

Since f is pseudo-concave, we obtain, from (22) and (6′),

$$f(x^{\circ}) \geqq f(x^1), \quad \text{for all } x^1 \in S. \tag{23}$$

This finishes the proof of statement (i). To show statement (ii), let f be strictly pseudo-concave. Then we may obtain, from (7′),

$$f(x^{\circ}) > f(x^1) \text{ for all } x^1 \in S. \tag{24}$$

Since every strictly pseudo-concave function is strictly quasi-concave, the uniqueness follows at once from (24).[8] (QED)

REMARK: The assumption that $g_1, \ldots, g_m$ are all quasi-concave can be relaxed to the assumption that the constraint set S is convex. This occurs because if $S \equiv \{x \in R^n : g_1(x) \geqq 0, \ldots, g_m(x) \geqq 0, x \geqq 0\}$ is convex, then we have

$$g_{j_x}^{\circ} \cdot (x - x^{\circ}) \geqq 0, \quad \text{for all } x \in S, \tag{25}$$

for all the constraints for which we have $g_j(x^{\circ}) = 0$. This result can be used in lieu of (21) of the preceding proof. To show (25), first observe that, by the convexity of S, we have, for $x^1 \in S$,

$$g_j[(1 - \theta)x^{\circ} + \theta x^1] \geqq 0, \ 0 \leqq \theta \leqq 1, \quad \text{for all } j$$

where $g_j(x^1) \geqq g_j(x^{\circ}) = 0$. Let $G_j(\theta) \equiv g_j[(1 - \theta)x^{\circ} + \theta x^1]$. Then $G_j(\theta) \geqq g_j(x^{\circ}) = G_j(0)$. Thus $G_j'(0) \geqq 0$. Hence differentiating $G_j(\theta)$ and setting θ equal to zero, we have

$$g_j(x) \geqq g_j(x^{\circ}) \Rightarrow g_{j_x}^{\circ} \cdot (x^1 - x^{\circ}) \geqq 0, \quad \text{for all } j. \tag{26}$$

Finally, we relate Mangasarian's theorem (theorem B.10) to the Arrow-Enthoven theorem (theorem B.9). Since every concave function

[8] Suppose not: let x° and x^* both satisfy (FOC). Then define $\bar{x}$ by $\bar{x} \equiv \theta x^{\circ} + (1 - \theta)x^*$, $0 < \theta < 1$. $\bar{x} \in S$, since the g_j's are all quasi-concave so that S is convex. Using the strict quasi-concavity of f, $f(\bar{x}) > f(x^{\circ}) = f(x^*)$, which contradicts (17).

is pseudo-concave by theorem B.3, it is clear that Mangasarian's theorem takes care of condition (iv) of the Arrow and Enthoven theorem. Hence, it suffices to focus our attention on conditions (i) through (iii) of the Arrow and Enthoven theorem to relate theorems B.9 and B.10. We may then recall our results obtained in section B.2.

Going through the proof of theorem B.10, we may readily obtain the result in theorem B.11.

Theorem B.11. Assume that the constraint set S is convex. If f is locally pseudo-concave at x°, then (FOC) implies (M), where (FOC) and (M) are defined in terms of x°.

Recalling theorem B.7′, this result can at once be restated as theorem B.12.

Theorem B.12. Assume that the constraint set S is convex. If f is quasi-concave and if condition (16′) holds, then (FOC) implies (M), where (FOC) and (M) are defined in terms of x°.

Condition (16′), $f_x^\circ \neq 0$, generalizes conditions (i), (ii), and (iii) of the Arrow-Enthoven theorem (theorem B.9). In particular, we are able to remove the concept of "relevant variables" in the Arrow-Enthoven theorem.

References

Arrow, K. J., and A. C. Enthoven. 1961. "Quasi-Concave Programming." *Econometrica* 29 (October): 779–800.

Diewert, W. E., M. Avrel, and I. Zang. 1979. "Nine Kinds of Quasi-concavity and Concavity." Discussion Paper no. 79–29. University of British Columbia.

Ide, T., and A. Takayama. 1988. "Seven Kinds of Concavity and Quasi-Concave Programming: A Survey of Some Results and Extensions." Discussion Paper Series, no. 88–8. Southern Illinois University at Carbondale.

Karamardian, S. 1967. "Duality in Mathematical Programming." *Journal of Mathematical Analysis and Applications* 20 (November): 344–58.

Mangasarian, O. E. 1965. "Pseudo-Convex Functions." *SIAM Journal on Control* 3: 281–90.

———. 1969. *Nonlinear Programming.* New York: McGraw-Hill.

Martos, B. 1967. "The Direct Power of Adjacent Vertex Programming Methods." *Management Science*, ser. A, 12 (November): 241–52.

———. 1975. *Nonlinear Programming: Theory and Methods.* Amsterdam: North-Holland.

Murata, Y. 1977. *Mathematics for Stability and Optimization of Economic Systems.* New York: Academic Press.

Newman, P. 1969. "Some Properties of Convex Functions." *Journal of Economic Theory* 1 (October): 291–314.

Ponstein, J. 1967. "Seven Kinds of Convexity." *SIAM Review* 9 (January): 115–99.

Takayama, A. 1985. *Mathematical Economics.* 2d. ed. New York: Cambridge University Press.

Thompson, W. A., Jr. and D. W. Parke. 1973. "Some Properties of Generalized Concave Functions." *Operations Research* 21 (January/February): 305–13.

Uekawa, Y., and Y. Kimura. 1987. *Economic Theory* (in Japanese). Tokyo: Toyo Keizai Shimpo-sha.

APPENDIX C

Consumer's Surplus[1]

C.1 Introduction

The concepts of consumer's surplus have a long history, and have been used widely in applied economics. Yet, on the theoretical level, economists have not been able to reach a significant consensus.[2] The concept in terms of the "Marshallian triangle" originates with Dupuit (1844), and was popularized by Marshall (1890, 1920) in which he duly recognized the importance of the constancy of the marginal utility of income (1920, p. 842). In *Value and Capital* (1939), Hicks proposed to interpret consumer's surplus in terms of "compensating variations." Henderson (1941) pointed out that such measures are different from Marshall's concept unless the income effect of demand is negligible. Hicks (1941, 1942, 1943, 1945, and 1956) produced a famous set of studies on the subject, in which he placed central importance on his concepts of compensating and equivalent variations to measure welfare changes of a consumer. Hicks (1941, p. 166) remarked, "consumer's surplus is not a mere economic plaything, a *curiosum*. It is the foundation of an important branch of Economics." Sono (1943) published an important (although virtually unnoticed outside of Japan) study, in which he duly emphasized Dupuit's contribution. Samuelson (1942; 1947, pp. 195–97) did not like the concepts of consumer's surplus at all. Yet they remain an important

[1]This appendix is based on Takayama (1982, 1984, and 1987).

[2]Assuming that consumers are alike and that their utilities can be added up, Marshall summed the individual consumer's surpluses in a market to obtain an aggregate welfare measure, and in his practical use of the concept he placed the apostrophe in consumers' surplus after the s. With the advent of the new welfare economics and the rejection of interpersonal comparison of utilities, it has become more customary to discuss the concept in terms of a single consumer, i.e., *consumer's surplus*. Yet, even confined to a single consumer, this concept has generated substantial debate. Here, we confine ourselves to a single consumer to obtain the proper perspective of the literature.

tool of analysis for applied economists. In fact, the debate has become more heated recently, producing various interesting works especially after the 1970s.[3] Useful surveys on this topic are provided, for example, by Currie, Murphy, and Schwitz (1971); Chipman and Moore (1976); Ng (1980, chap. 4); Just, Hueth, and Schmitz (1982); Chipman (1982); G. McKenzie (1983); Boadway and Bruce (1984); and Takayama (1982, 1984, and 1987).[4] In the course of these discussions, Mohring (1971) and Silberberberg (1972 and 1990) duly emphasized the importance of line intergrals and path dependence in the discussion of consumer's surplus, which was also recognized by Hotelling (1938) and Sono (1943). The formulation of the concepts of consumer's surplus with a more complete discussion of line integrals and path independence was done by Chipman and Moore (1976 and 1980), who then related the evaluation of the relevant line integral to the constancy of the marginal utility of income utilizing Samuelson's (1942) important work.

In this appendix, we shall assemble various different threads of discussions on this topic in a systematic and transparent fashion so as to dispel some of the confusions on this topic and to obtain a clear understanding of the framework of analysis. We shall show that the welfare measure, if it is defined properly, is always independent of path, so that path independence is not really a problem. We shall then illustrate our approach in terms of the constancy of marginal utility of income. We shall show that the Marshallian measure is indeed a correct measure of welfare change under such a circumstance. Willig (1976 and 1979) believed the Hicksian measures of compensating and equivalent variations are the correct measures and that they can be approximated by the Marshallian measure. We show that the discrepancy between the Marshallian and the Hicksian measures can be very large (can be even infinitely large). Furthermore, Willig does not offer a satisfactory justification of why the Hicksian measures are the correct measures. G. McKenzie (1983) argued that the concept of equivalent variations is the right one. We show that this also has difficulties.

---

[3]See, for example, Katzner (1970, pp. 152–55); Harberger (1971); Mohring (1971); Silberberg (1972; 1978, pp. 350–56); Burns (1973); Bergson (1975); Hause (1975); Cicchetti, Fisher and Smith (1976); McKenzie and Pearce (1976 and 1982); Seade (1978); Willig (1976, and 1979); Hausman (1981); Morey (1984); G. McKenzie (1983); and Takayama (1984).

[4]Suzumura (1985) cites 181 references on this topic.

The Marshallian Triangle and Path Independence

Before we finish the introductory section, it would be useful to familiarize ourselves with the concepts of the Marshallian triangle and path independence. Consider a consumer who chooses a consumption bundle $x = (x_1, x_2, \ldots, x_n)$ to maximize a real-valued utility function $u(x)$ subject to the budget constraint $p \cdot x (\equiv \sum p_i x_i) \leqq Y$ and $x \geqq 0$, where $Y > 0$ is his or her (nominal) income and $P = (P_1, P_2, \ldots, P_n)$ is a nominal price vector. The consumer is assumed to be a price-taker. For simplicity, we assume that $P_i > 0$, and $u_i (\equiv \partial u / \partial x_i) > 0$ for each i at the optimum (local nonsatiation), and that $u(x)$ is twice continuously differentiable. Then assuming an interior solution (i.e., $x_i > 0$ for all i at the optimum), the first-order condition for an optimum is given by

$$u_i(x) = \lambda P_i,\ i = 1, 2, \ldots, n, \quad \text{and} \quad P \cdot x = Y, \tag{1}$$

where λ is the Langrangian multiplier. Clearly, $\lambda > 0$ at optimum. Assuming that u is strictly quasi-concave, (1) furnishes a necessary and sufficient condition for a unique global maximum. The $(n+1)$ equations in (1) determine $\lambda(P, Y)$ and the *demand functions* of n commodities,

$$x_i = x_i(P_1, P_2, \ldots, P_n, Y) = x_i(P, Y),\ i = 1, 2, \ldots, n,$$

which are homogeneous of degree zero in P and Y. Let $Q^\circ = (P^\circ, Y^\circ)$ and $Q^1 = (P^1, Y^1)$, respectively, signify the "initial" and the "terminal" situations. Consider a single price change, that is,

$$P_1^\circ \neq P_1^1,\ P_i^\circ = P_i^1,\ i = 2, 3, \ldots, n,\ Y^\circ = Y^1.$$

Marshall then argued that the welfare impact of such a price change can be measured by the trapezoid to the left of the demand curve of commodity 1. This is the famous concept of consumer surplus by Marshall, following Dupuit (1844).[5] In figure C.1*a*, the downward-sloping curve denotes the demand curve for commodity 1.[6]

When its price is OA, the consumer's surplus is measured by the "triangle" $AA'C$.[7] When its price is raised to OB by taxes, etc., then the

[5]This concept of consumer surplus did not originate with Marshall; he apparently developed the notion after reading the works of A. A. Cournot around 1868, and was also aware of Dupuit's now well-known work (1844). See Dooley (1983) and Whitaker (1975).

[6]Needless to say, the choice of commodity 1 is arbitrary: i.e., we call any commodity which is under our concern "commodity 1."

[7]Marshall (1920, p. 124) states, "The excess of the price which he would be willing

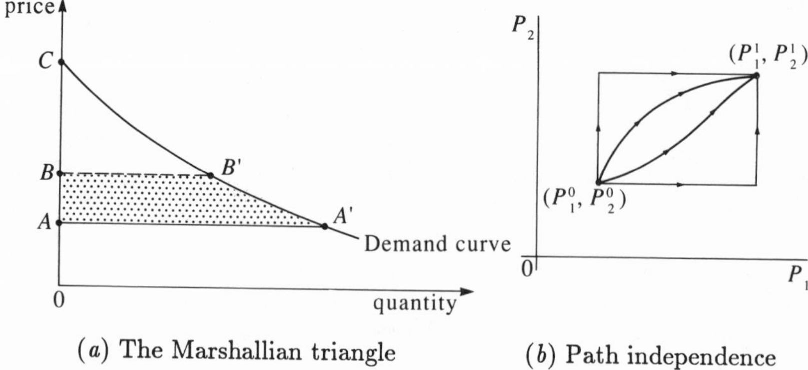

(*a*) The Marshallian triangle (*b*) Path independence

Figure C.1: Consumer's surplus

loss to the consumer is measured by the shaded trapezoid area $ABB'A'$. Similarly, if the price falls from OB to OA, the consumer gains by the amount of $ABB'A'$.[8] Noting that $OA = P_1^\circ$ and $OB = P_1^1$, the trapezoid area, $ABB'A'$ determined by Marshallian triangle, can simply be written as

$$T \equiv -\int_{P_1^\circ}^{P_1^1} x_1(P_1,\ P_2^\circ,\ \ldots,\ P_n^\circ,\ Y^\circ)dP_1. \tag{2}$$

to pay rather than going without the thing, over that which he actually does pay is the economic measure of surplus satisfaction. It may be called *consumer's surplus.*" He goes on to say, "It is obvious that the consumer's surplus derived from some commodities are much greater than from others. ... Good instances are matches, salt, a penny newspaper, or a postage stamp."

[8]If the demand does not have a finite intercept with the price axis (i.e., if OC is not finite), then the triangular area can be infinitely large. This is the case when the utility function is given by the Cobb-Douglas form, for example. Marshall (1920, pp. 841–42) was aware of such a problem. Even in this case, the trapezoid area $ABB'A'$ is finite. Notice also that the trapezoid area $ABB'A'$ cannot measure the welfare change if any other prices or the consumer's income change, for such changes shift the demand curve. Marshall is clearly aware of it. On the other hand, Walras (1954) is very critical of this concept for this very reason, where he states for example, "Unfortunately, all these statements are erroneous, and Dupuit's theory is no improvement on J. B. Say's. ... In general, the maximum pecuniary sacrifice which a consumer is willing to make to obtain a unit of product depends not only on the utility of product in question, but also on the utility of all other products in the market, and, finally, on the consumer's means. ... We may, therefore, ... definitely reject all Dupuit's statements in his memoirs ..." (1954, pp. 445–46).

Here, the minus is attached to reflect that a price rise causes a loss to the consumer. We call (2) the **Dupuit-Marshall measure**, or simply the **D-M measure**.

Although the definition in (2) is quite simple, it begs more questions than it answers. In general, x_1 depends on the prices of *other* commodities *and* income. If income and the price of any other commodity change, then the demand curve will shift so that T is no longer well defined. In a sequel to the aforementioned work, Hicks introduced the four concepts of consumer's surplus, all of which are different from the Dupuit-Marshall concept. Among the four concepts, compensating and equivalent variations have attracted the most attention. As Hicks now puts it (1981, p. 115), the chief motive of introducing these four concepts is to "extend the analysis to cover cases in which more than one price is changing."[9] On the other hand, where more than one price is changing, a new problem arises. This is the problem of whether or not the welfare measure, whatever its definition, is independent of a particular path that prices change. That there can be (infinitely) many paths that prices can take can be illustrated in figure C.1*b*. It is then natural to hope that consumer's surplus, however it is defined, takes a unique value regardless of the paths of price change. The same problem can arise when income changes (say, by income tax) even if only one price changes. This is the problem of **path independence**.

Silberberg (1972) followed the Dupuit-Marshall tradition and defined consumer's surplus for the multiprice changing case by the following line integral (connecting P° to P^{1}),[10]

$$T = -\int_{P^{\circ}}^{P^{1}} \sum_{i=1}^{n} x_i(P, Y^{\circ})dP_i, \tag{2'}$$

which reduces to the D-M measure when $P_i^{\circ} = P_i^1$, $i \neq 1$. He then found that the path independence condition requires the homotheticity of all demand functions, x_i's. In contrast to such a conclusion, it can easily be shown that compensating and equivalent variations automatically satisfy the path independence condition (e.g., Willig 1979; Suzumura 1985). Furthermore, these Hicksian measures, though based on ordinal utility, provide monetary (say, dollar) measures. They are "simple, unambiguous, and allocatively operative within a Pareto context." (Mishan

[9] I am indebted to Professor Hicks for pointing this out to me.

[10] A quick exposition of line integrals can be made as follows. Let $f(x, y)$ and $g(x, y)$ be real-valued functions on R^2. Consider a curve defined by $y = \phi(x)$; $a = \phi(A)$ and $b = \phi(B)$ can then be obtained as

1977, p. 1). We call these Hicksian measures the ***H* measures**.

C.2 Some Basics

Here we collect the materials that are necessary for later discussions. All of these materials are discussed in chapter 3. We assume that the demand functions, $x_i(P, Y)$, $i = 1, 2, \ldots, n$ and the associated Lagrangian multiplier $\lambda(P, Y)$ are continuously differentiable. Then we obtain the *Hicks-Slutsky equation:*[11]

$$\partial x_i/\partial P_j = S_{ij} - x_j(\partial x_i/\partial Y), \; i, \; j = 1, 2, \ldots, n, \tag{3}$$

where S_{ij} is the net substitution effect. As discussed in chapter 3, the $n \times n$ matrix $S \equiv [S_{ij}]$ is known as the *net substitution matrix* or the *Slutsky matrix*. Define function U by

$$U(P, Y) \equiv u[x(P, Y)]. \qquad (\textit{indirect utility function})$$

Clearly, $U(P, Y)$ is homogeneous of degree zero. We assume that it is twice continuously differentiable. Applying the envelope theorem, we

---

10 *cont.*

$$\int_A^B f(x, y)dx + g(x, y)dy = \int_A^B f[x, \phi(x)]dx + g[x, \phi(x)]\phi'(x)dx.$$

In general, the value of this integral depends on a particular path $\phi(x)$, in which case the line integral is said to be **path dependent**. If the integral is independent of a particular path, then it is called **path independent**. The necessary and sufficient condition for path independence is given by

$$\partial f(x, y)/\partial y = \partial g(x, y)/\partial x, \quad \text{for all } x \text{ and } y.$$

The topic of line integral and path independence is seen in most textbooks on advanced calculus. For a good exposition see, for example, Apostol (1957).

[11] In this connection, the following remark by Dooley (1983, pp. 29–30) might be of interest: "Pareto's derivation is mathematically identical to Slutsky's equation, as E. Slutsky ... generously acknowledged. Both Pareto and Slutsky published their papers in *Giornale degli economisti*, one of the leading journals in economics at that time. Pareto's work also had an independent influence on the value theory of Hicks ... , although Hicks did not recognize that Pareto's solution is equivalent to Slutsky's equation." One implication of the Hicks-Slutsky equation is that the demand curve need *not* be downward sloping. For this, Dooley (1983, p. 30) writes, "Pareto's work was reviewed by Sanger (1895) in the *Economic Journal*, and Marshall ... cited Sanger's review in the footnote to the new section on the Giffen good, which was inserted in the third edition of Marshall's *Principles*. While Marshall gave credit to Sir R. Giffen for observing that the demand curve for bread could be positively sloped, no one has ever located Giffen's observation at least to the satisfaction of G. J. Stigler ...."

may readily obtain, for all relevant (P, Y),

$$\partial U(P, Y)/\partial P_i = -\lambda(P, Y)x_i(P, Y) < 0, \ i = 1, 2, \ldots, n, \quad \text{(4a)}$$

$$\partial U(P, Y)/\partial Y = \lambda(P, Y) > 0, \ \text{and} \quad \text{(4b)}$$

$$\partial U(P, Y)/\partial P_i + x_i \partial U(P, Y)/\partial Y = 0, \ i = 1, 2, \ldots, n. \quad \text{(*Roy's identity*) (4c)}$$

Dual to the above problem, we may consider the problem of choosing an x to minimize expenditure $P \cdot x$ subject to $u(x) \geqq u$ and $x \geqq 0$. Let $x^*(P, u)$ be the solution of this problem (the *compensated demand function*), and let $e(P, u) \equiv P \cdot x^*(P, u)$ (the *minimum expenditure function*). Then letting $S^* \equiv [x^*_{ij}] \equiv [\partial x^*_i/\partial P_j]$, S^* is symmetric and negative semidefinite.

Major propositions of duality theory that are pertinent to the present topic are:

$$Y = e[P, U(P, Y)], \ x(P, Y) = x^*[P, U(P, Y)], \quad \text{(5a)}$$

$$x[P, e(P, u)] = x^*(P, u), \ \text{and} \quad \text{(5b)}$$

$$U[P, e(P, u)] = u. \quad \text{(5c)}$$

Note that proposition (5b), which follows from (5a), yields (3) upon differentiation in p_j where $S_{ij}(P, Y) \equiv x^*_{ij}[P, U(P, Y)]$. Thus we may conclude that matrix S is also symmetric and negative semidefinite. Furthermore, we have: $\partial e/\partial P_j = x^*_j(P, u)$, Shephard's lemma.

C.3 Computing the Hicksian Measures

We shall discuss the H measures, compensating and equivalent variations. According to Hicks (e.g., 1956, p. 177); also Willig (1976, p. 590), the **compensating variation** is the amount by which one would have to increase (or reduce) a person's income to make him just as well off after a change in prices as he had been in the initial situation. The compensating variation, which we shall denote by C, can then be defined in symbols as:

$$U(P^\circ, Y^\circ) = U(P^1, Y^\circ + C), \quad \text{(6)}$$

or $C = e[P^1, U(P^\circ, Y^\circ)] - Y^\circ$ by (5c). Given P° and P^1, the individual is better off compared to his or her initial situation if and only if Y^1 –

$Y^\circ > C$. On the other hand, the **equivalent variation** is defined as the amount of change in income which would have exactly the same effect upon a person's utility as a price change. Denoting this by E, it can then be defined in symbols as:

$$U(P^1, Y^\circ) = U(P^\circ, Y^\circ - E), \tag{7}$$

or $E = Y^\circ - e[P^\circ, u(P^1, Y^\circ)]$ by (5c). We may illustrate C and E diagrammatically in figure C.2, where we assume that P_i = constant for all i except 1.

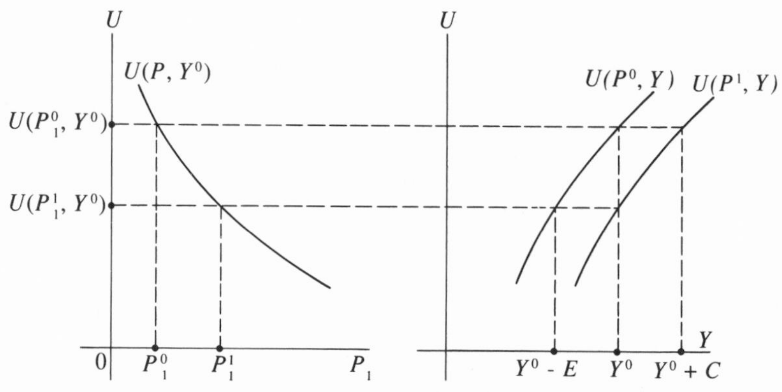

Figure C.2: Compensating and equivalent variations

An obvious difficulty of the H measures is that they cannot be computed from empirical data since U is not observable. To overcome this, Willig (1976) argues that under certain assumptions, the D-M measure can be used as an approximation of the H measures. For him, the H measures are the "correct" welfare measures. Seade (1978) obtains "workable" formulas to compute the H measures directly by assuming that all Engel curves are linear (which corresponds to Gorman's quasi-homotheticity). Hausman (1981) abandons such an assumption, and attempts to obtain exact formulas to compute the H measures by assuming that the observed demand functions are linear or log linear. G. McKenzie and Pearce (1976 and 1982) and G. McKenzie (1983) propose yet another approach to compute the H measures, in which the Taylor expansion of the marginal utility of income plays an important role in their method.

Vartia (1983) also proposes an ingenious method to compute the H measure. By recalling Shephard's lemma and (5b), we may obtain

$$\frac{de}{dt} = \sum_{i=1}^{n} x_i[P(t),\ e]\ \frac{dP_i(t)}{dt},\ \text{since}\ \frac{de(P,\ u^\circ)}{dt} = \sum_{i=1}^{n} \frac{\partial e}{\partial P_i}\ \frac{dP_i}{dt}.$$

This can be viewed as an ordinary differential equation, in which $e(t)$ is the unknown function. Vartia proposed three algorithms to obtain the numerical solution of this differential equation. His "main algorithm" is then related to the Harberger (1971) welfare indicator. Nagatani (1984) pointed out that two of Vartia's methods are essentially the same as those used in Houthakker's well-known paper (1950) on revealed preference, and his "main algorithm" is not particularly superior to the other two algorithms.

The recent popularity of the H measures, as indicated above, seems to be based on the ordinalist revolution, for which Hicks (1946, p. 18) wrote, "The quantitative concept of utility is not necessary to explain market phenomena. Therefore, on the principle of Occam's razor, it is better to do without it." However, as Pareto was already well aware, this does not imply that utility cannot be cardinal (see Chipman 1976). The ordinalist stance has also been shaken since the work of von Neumann and Morgenstern (1953) under risk-taking circumstances. Following Georgescu-Roegen (1952), Chipman (1976, p. 76) also puts this in a metaphor by saying, "Just because the equilibrium of a table is determined by three of its legs, we are not required by any scientific principle to assume that actual tables have only three legs, especially if direct observation suggests that they may have four."[12]

Regardless of which stance we adopt, we still see another important shortcoming in the H measures. In the literature, we do not see any convincing arguments as to why these measures can be the "correct" welfare

[12]In this connection, it may be useful to recall Samuelson's intellectual evolution from a staunch ordinalist in the early period to a reluctant cardinalist in the middle period, and "to the most recent period, in which cardinalist measurement is accepted as having a valid rule in certian well-defined uses." See Chipman (1982, pp. 32 and 59–63). In this connection, confining specifically to consumer's surplus, Bergson's (1975, p. 43) refusal to apply the principle of Occam's razor should be worth noting, where he writes, "I have ventured to urge here ... that such a further application of Occam's razor is inappropriate." Pareto's position is also quite different from Hicks and many other recent ordinalists. While he was clearly aware of the fact that the measurement or the cardinality of utility is not essential to the explanation of economic equilbrium, he continued to believe that utility was, in principle, capable of measurement. See Chipman (1976, pp. 76–80).

measures, nor do we see a clear discussion regarding which one of the H measures we should choose when the discrepancy of these measures becomes great. Furthermore, the H measures assume that the consumer's income stays constant. The question can be asked with regard to how we should modify the H measures to incorporate income changes. This is not a trivial question.

The discussion of consumer's surplus refers to a single consumer. Suppose that more than one person is involved. We may, in concluding this section, ask the question whether we can use the sum of compensating variations ($\sum C$) as a measure of the gain or loss of the group as a whole. Putting this question in the following way, "can we say if $\sum C > 0$, gainers can more than compensate losers, and the change in prices will at least lead to a potential Pareto improvement?" Boadway (1974) discovered that the answer to this question is negative. Since it is very tempting to give an affirmative answer to the above question, Ng (1980, p. 96) calls Boadway's discovery the **Boadway Paradox**.

C.4 The Correct Welfare Measure

To find the welfare impact of changes from Q° to Q^1 where $Q \equiv (P, Y)$, we first observe the following obvious relation:

$$dU = \sum_{i=1}^{n} U_i\, dP_i + U_Y\, dY,\ U_i \equiv \partial U/\partial P_i,\ U_Y \equiv \partial U/\partial Y.$$

It would then be natural to *define* the welfare impact of changes in prices and income (denoted by ΔU) in terms of the following **line integral**:

$$\Delta U \equiv \int_{Q^\circ}^{Q^1} \left(\sum_{i=1}^{n} U_i dP_i + U_Y dY\right). \tag{8}$$

An important question here is: how do we know that the line integral on the right-hand side of (8) is independent of the path connecting Q° to Q^1? However, this problelm can easily be resolved by recalling the following well-known mathematical result (e.g., Apostol 1957, pp. 280–81 and 292).

Lemma C.1. Let $f(x)$ be continuously differentiable in an open convex subset D of the Euclidian space R^n. Then the line integral,

$$I = \int_{A}^{B} f_1(x)dx_1 + \ldots + f_n(x)dx_n,\ f_i \equiv \partial f/\partial x_i, \tag{9}$$

connecting every pair of end points, A and B, in D by a piecewise smooth curve[13] is independent of path and I has a unique value, $I = f(A) - f(B)$.

Applying this to (8), we may at once conclude that ΔU is unique, that is,

$$\Delta U = U(Q^1) - U(Q^\circ), \tag{10}$$

and that the line integral in (8) connecting every end point Q° and Q^1 by a piecewise smooth curve is independent of the path. Also, ΔU is homogeneous of degree zero in $Q \equiv (P, Y)$, so that ΔU is invariant with respect to changes in the unit of measurement of Q.

Furthermore, by a well-known mathematical result (e.g., Apostol 1957, p. 293), the path independence of the line integral in (8) implies

$$\frac{\partial}{\partial P_j}\frac{\partial U}{\partial P_i} = \frac{\partial}{\partial P_i}\frac{\partial U}{\partial P_j} \quad \text{and}$$

$$\frac{\partial}{\partial P_i}\frac{\partial U}{\partial Y} = \frac{\partial}{\partial Y}\frac{\partial U}{\partial P_i}, \quad i,\ j = 1,\ 2,\ \ldots,\ n, \tag{11}$$

for all P and Y. This is satisfied since U is twice continuously differentiable (so that its Hessian matrix is symmetric). We may also assert that (11) is *sufficient* (as well as necessary) for the path independence of the line integral in (8).[14]

---

[13]In general, we have the following definitions. Let $x(t) = [x_1(t), \ldots, x_n(t)]$ be a continuous vector-valued function defined on a closed interval $[a, b]$. The image of $[a, b]$ under $x(t)$ is said to be a **curve** described by x. If $x(a) = x(b)$, the curve is said to be **closed**, and if $x(a) \neq x(b)$, it is called an **arc**. If $x(t)$ is continuously differentiable, the curve is said to be **smooth**. If the curve itself is not smooth, but is composed of a finite number of arcs, each of which is smooth, it is termed **piecewise smooth**. If $x(t)$ is one-to-one, then the curve is called **simple**. Namely, a simple curve is the one in which it never "crosses" on a half open interval $[a, b)$. Piecewise smooth curves are always simple.

[14]In general, we may assert the following mathematical result. Let $h_i(x)$, $i = 1, \ldots, n$, be continuously differentiable real-valued functions on an open convex subset D of the Euclidian space R^n. The the line integral,

$$I \equiv \int_A^B h_1(x)dx_1 + h_2(x)dx_2 + \ldots + h_n(x)dx_n,$$

connecting every pair of end points, A and B, in D by a piecewise smooth simple curve in D is independent of path if and only if

(*) $\partial h_i(x)/\partial x_j = \partial h_j(x)/\partial x_i,\ i \neq j,\ i,\ j = 1,\ 2,\ \ldots,\ n.$

To obtain the economic interpretation of (11), we obtain, by recalling (3) and (4),

$$\frac{\partial x_i}{\partial P_j} + x_j \frac{\partial x_i}{\partial Y} = \frac{\partial x_j}{\partial P_i} + x_i \frac{\partial x_j}{\partial Y}, \; i, \; j = 1, \; 2, \; \ldots, \; n. \tag{12}$$

In view of (3), this condition is clearly equivalent to $S_{ij} = S_{ji}$, that is, the symmetry condition of the Slutsky matrix. Note also that this condition provides the integrability condition of demand functions.[15] Thus, the existence of a utility function, whether it is ordinal or cardinal, almost trivially implies the path independence of our welfare measure, and

---

Given this theorem, we may also assert that the twice continuous differentiability of U is *sufficient* (as well as necessary) for the independence of path. The necessity of condition (*) for the independence of path in this theorem is not difficult to show (e.g., Apostol 1957, theorems 10–38 and 10–45), in which the convexity of D is not required. Its sufficiency requires an additional restriction such as the simple connectedness or the convexity of D. Most advanced calculus textbooks show sufficiency by assuming $n = 2$. Apostol (1957, theorems 10–48) also shows sufficiency without requiring $n = 2$, but requires D to be an open interval (which is really sufficient for our purpose). When D is not restricted to an open interval, the proof becomes much more difficult, requiring an n-dimensional extension of Green's (or Stokes's) theorem.

[15] See, for example, Samuelson (1950); Antonelli (1971); and Hurwicz (1971) for the (local) integrability problem. The symmetry condition of the Hicks-Slutsky matrix $[S_{ij}]$ provides "mathematical integrability," which, as Hurwicz (1971) pointed out, should be distinguished from the condition of "economic integrability." More specifically, the symmetry of $[S_{ij}]$ is necessary and sufficient for mathematical integrability, while the negative semidefiniteness of $[S_{ij}]$ is sufficient for economic integrability. In this connection, it may be worthwhile to recall the evolution of Samuelson's thinking in this context. As is well known, Samuelson (e.g., 1938) rejected the concept of utility in his early period . His *Weak Axiom of revealed preference* purports to construct the demand theory directly from the observed relation between demand and price-income pairs, thus "dropping off the last vestiges of utility analysis" (Samuelson 1938, p. 662). This is because Samuelson could not find a convincing economic interpretation of the symmetry of the Hicks-Slutsky matrix: the Weak Axiom only provides $[S_{ij}]$ to be negative semidefinite but not symmetric. Houthakker's landmark work in (1950) changed the entire picture. The symmetry was shown to follow from his Strong Axiom, which in turn attaches an economic meaning to the symmetry. This then prompted Samuelson's (1950) work on integrability, which purports to investigate the problem of recovering the utility function from the observed demand function. This may be contrasted with Samuelson's earlier writing (Samuelson 1938, p. 68) in which he states, "Concerning the question of integrability, I have little to say. I *cannot* see it is really an important problem" (italics added). It is subsequently established that the Strong Axiom is equivalent to the preference hypothesis (e.g., Richter 1966). Also, Hurwicz and Richter (1971) shows that "Ville's axiom" provides exactly what is needed above the Weak Axiom in order to yield the Strong Axiom (which is equivalent to the Slutsky symmetry condition). This in turn appears to provide the long sought economic interpretation of the symmetry condition (see Chipman 1982, pp. 32–49).

conversely, the path independence condition requires the integrability condition, which in turn ensures the recoverability of a utility function. In summary, we have:

Theorem C.1. The line integral in (8) is independent of path, *and* (as a result of it) we have $\Delta U = U(Q^1) - U(Q^\circ)$. The measure ΔU is unique depending only on Q^1 and Q°, and it is invariant with respect to changes in the unit of measurement of the P_i's and Y.

We are now ready to proceed with our analysis. Substituting (4a) and (4b) into (8), we obtain the following fundamental formula:

$$\Delta U = \int_{Q^\circ}^{Q^1} \sum_{i=1}^{n} (-\lambda x_i) dP_i + \lambda dY. \tag{13}$$

From this it is clear that ΔU depends on λ, where $\lambda = \partial U / \partial Y$ signifies the **marginal utility of income** (**MUI**). Since λ, in general, depends on both P and Y, we need some assumptions, such as the "constancy" of λ, to carry out the integration in (13) and obtain useful conclusions. In fact, Marshall (1920, p. 842) was clearly aware of the importance of the assumption of the constant MUI. Marshall also realized that λ is not a strict constant, but it is only *approximately* constant.[16] Unfortunately, however, the "constancy" of MUI is subject to different interpretations.[17]

One natural interpretation is that it is constant for all values of P and Y. However, this is impossible since U_Y is homogeneous of degree -1 in P and Y (see Samuelson 1942).[18] As Samuelson (1942) also pointed

[16] Marshall (1920, p. 132, fn. 1) states, "In mathematical language the neglected elements would generally belong to the *second order quantities* ..." (italics added); see also Marshall (1920, p. 842).

[17] The constancy of marginal utility of income (or money) caused a big controversy: Dooley (1983, p. 30) states, "Marshall's treatment of the marginal utility of money as a constant has generated perhaps more comment than any of his special assumptions." Dooley then sketches this controversy and argues that Marshall was confused on this problem.

[18] Let $f(x)$ be a function on R^n, which is homogeneous of degree m. Then each $f_i (\equiv \partial f / \partial x_i)$ is homogeneous of degree $(m - 1)$. This follows from Euler's theorem for homogeneous functions (theorem 1.7). Since $\lambda(P, Y) = \partial U(p, Y)/\partial Y$ by (4b) and since U is homogeneous of degree zero, λ is homogeneous of degree -1. To show that $U_Y = \lambda(P, Y)$ *cannot* be constant, suppose the contrary: i.e., assume $\lambda(P, Y) = a$, where a is a real number independent of P and Y. Then using the fact that λ is homogeneous of degree -1, we have

$$a = \lambda(\alpha P, \alpha Y) = \lambda(P, Y)/\alpha = a/\alpha, \quad \text{for any } \alpha.$$

out, there are two other important interpretations of the constancy of MUI. One interpretation is that it is invariant with respect to changes in all prices, that is,

$$U_Y(P, Y) = \gamma(Y), \quad \text{for all } P \text{ and } Y. \tag{14}$$

According to Samuelson (1942), this assumption was made implicitly by Marshall.

Since (14) implies that the demand functions are homothetic, we may, following Chipman and Moore (1976), call the interpretation in terms of (14), **the case of homothetic demands**. The second important interpretation is that MUI is independent of income and the prices of all goods except one commodity (the numéraire commodity). Namely,

$$U_Y(P, Y) = \gamma^*(P_n). \tag{15}$$

For reasons we shall explain later, we call this case **the case of vertical Engel curves**. Hicks (1941, 1946, 1956, etc.) interpreted Marshall's assumption of the constancy of MUI in the sense of (15), and such a specification is also widely used in the literature.[19]

We now illustrate our approach via (13) by using two alternative interpretations concerning the "constancy" of MUI, where Roy's identity is useful in proving lemmas C.2 and C.3.

The only a that satisfies this equation is 0, and this contradicts $\lambda > 0$.

[19]Still another interpretation is by Pareto, who argues that Marshall's assumption of the constancy of MUI amounts to saying that the price elasticity of the commodity under concern is equal to unity (Dooley 1983, p. 32). Although Pareto apparently conceded that this may be true for a minor commodity like nutmeg, he then rejected the constancy assumption as counterfactual. How convinced Pareto was on the non-constancy of MUI is indicated by his letter, dated September 15, 1907, which was offered by Georgescu-Roegen (1968, p. 176):

> *One cannot consider as constant* the ophelimity of money. And we return to the usual refrain: in that manner one does not take account of the independence of phenomena. The Marshalls and the Edgeworths obstinate themselves in the error, so as not to confess that in the polemic with Walras they had been wrong. Those English gentlemen believe that outside England and Germany there are only asses, I say that the English proposition of the constancy of the [marginal] utility of money is an *assininity*. This proposition is fundamental. If the Marshall & Co. are right, I am wrong and vice versa. *And with people who persist in saying such ineptitudes*, I *do not intend to associate in any manner*. I cannot speak clearer than this.

(a) The Case of Homothetic Demands: Interpretation of (14)

Since the line integral (13) is independent of path, we may choose the path of integration in which Y is held constant at Y° along the integration with respect to P_i's. Then using (14), we may rewrite (13) as

$$\Delta U = -\gamma^{\circ} \int_{P^{\circ}}^{P^1} \sum_{i-1}^{n} x_i(P, Y^{\circ}) dP_i + \int_{Y^{\circ}}^{Y^1} \gamma(Y) dY, \tag{16}$$

where $\gamma^{\circ} \equiv \gamma(Y^{\circ})$. If in addition, P_i is constant for all i except $i = 1$, and if income is kept constant ($Y^{\circ} = Y^1$), then (16) becomes

$$\Delta U = -\gamma^{\circ} \int_{P^{\circ}}^{P_1^1} x_1(P_1, P_2^{\circ}, \ldots, P_n^{\circ}, Y^{\circ}) dP_1 = \gamma^{\circ} T, \tag{16'}$$

where T is defined in (2). Equation (16′) states that the ΔU of a price change is equal to γ° times the area defined by the Marshallian trapezoid. Choosing the unit of measurement of Y° properly, we may set $\gamma^{\circ} = \gamma(Y^{\circ}) = 1$. Thus, we have obtained a justification for the Dupuit-Marshall measure. Also, when income stays constant, (16) reduces to (2′) with $\gamma^{\circ} = 1$, which in turn justifies the Silberberg (1972) measure.

The difficulty here is that ΔU then depends on the measure of the unit of income, while ΔU in (16) should be independent of it by theorem C.1. To resolve this difficulty, the following result is important.

Lemma C.2 (Samuelson, 1942).[20] Constancy of MUI in the sense of (14) implies

$$\gamma(Y) = a/Y, \quad \text{where } a \equiv \gamma(1), \tag{17}$$

and each demand function is *homothetic*, that is, $x_i(P, Y) = \xi_i(P)Y$. Furthermore, (14) holds if and only if $u(x)$ can be written in the form

---

[20] Equation (17) follows immediately from the (−1) homogeneity of U_Y. The homotheticity can be proved by differentiating Roy's identity (4c) with respect to Y, utilizing (16), and obtaining the desired Euler equation. To show that (18) is sufficient for (14), simply observe

$$\begin{aligned} Y &= \sum P_i x_i = \sum (u_i/\lambda) x_i = \sum (c_1 \phi_i / \lambda\phi) x_i = (c_1/\lambda\phi) \sum \phi_i x_i \\ &= c_1 \phi/\lambda\phi = c_1/\lambda, \end{aligned}$$

so that $\lambda = c_1/Y$, where $\phi_i \equiv \partial\phi/\partial x_i$, and where $u_i = \lambda P_i$. The proof here is simpler than those in the literature.

of

$$u(x) = c_1 \log \phi(x) + c_2, \tag{18}$$

where $\phi(x)$ is homogeneous of degree one and c_1 and c_2 are some constant (with $c_1 = a$).

Note that $u(x)$ in (18) is *not* ordinal as it *cannot* be replaced by any strictly increasing transformation of itself.[21] Using (16), (17) and $x_i = \xi_i(P)Y$, we may readily observe

$$\Delta U = a \log Y^1/Y^\circ - a \int_{P^\circ}^{P^1} \sum_{i=1}^{n} \xi_i(P) dP_i, \tag{19}$$

where $a \equiv \gamma(1)$ is a pure constant. Equation (19) simplifies the formula obtained by Katzner (1970) and Chipman and Moore (1976). From (19), we may conclude that U is unique up to an increasing linear transformation of itself, and hence U is cardinal,[22] and hence ΔU is also cardinal, where $\gamma(1)$ serves as the "measuring stick" for cardinality.

When income and prices (except p_1) are kept constant, (19) is reduced to

$$\Delta U = -\int_{P_1^\circ}^{P_1^1} \xi_1(P_1, P_2^\circ, \ldots, P_n^\circ) dP_1, \tag{19'}$$

where we set $\gamma(1) = 1$ by the proper choice of units. This corresponds to the D-M measure except that x_1 is replaced by ξ_1. We may now summarize some of these results in theorem C.2.

Theorem C.2. If the margial utility of income is constant in the sense of (14), then ΔU is measured by (19), where we may set

---

[21] If $u(x) = \phi(x)$, we have

$$Y = \sum P_i x_i = \sum (u_i/\lambda) x_i = \sum (\phi_i x_i)/\lambda = \phi/\lambda = u/\lambda,$$

so that $\lambda = U(P, Y)/Y$. From this and (4b), we obtain $\partial\lambda/\partial Y = 0$, which is impossible.

[22] Namely, if a_1 and a_2 are two constant values of $\gamma(1)$, then clearly ΔU in terms of a_1 is a constant multiple of ΔU in terms of a_2, which implies U is unique up to an increasing linear transformation of itself, and hence U is cardinal. This is similar to the fact that temperature is cardinal, where the Fahrenheit degree is an increasing linear transformation of the centigrade degree by $F = (9/5)C + 32$.

$a = \gamma(1) = 1$. The utility measure ΔU is cardinal, where $\gamma(1)$ is the "measuring stick," and ΔU is independent of the choice of the unit of measurement of the P_i's and Y.

Homothetic demands mean that Engel curves are all straight lines from the origin. There have been numerous budget studies that negate this assertion (at least globally), and this is often used to reject the constancy of MUI in the sense of (14). However, it may be possible to assume homothetic demands with (14) as a *local* approximation of true demand functions in the range of the price-income change from (P°, Y°) to (P^1, Y^1), and it is a testable hypothesis, which we may call **local homotheticity**.[23] In our daily life, we often hear statements such as "Mr. Jones spends 3 percent of his income for his electric bill, 5 percent on gasoline, 20 percent for food ..." Such a statement often (implicitly) presupposes local homotheticity.

To forestall misunderstandings, we may point out that although (14) implies homothetic preferences, the converse does not necessarily hold. In other words, (14) specifies only a special class of homothetic preferences, as is clear from (18). To illustrate this, consider the utility function of two goods $u(x_1, x_2)$. If $u(x_1, x_2) = \log x_1 x_2$, then we may obtain $\lambda = 2/Y$ in which case (14) is satisfied. On the other hand, if $u(x_1, x_2) = x_1 x_2$, then we may obtain $\lambda = Y/(2P_1 P_2)$, in which case (14) is *not* satisfied. Yet both utility functions $\log x_1 x_2$ and $x_1 x_2$ are homothetic and yield the *same* demand functions $x_i = Y/2P_i$, $i = 1, 2$. Note that $u = \log x_1 x_2 = 2 \log x_1^{1/2} x_2^{1/2}$ satisfies (18), while $u = x_1 x_2$ does not. This example would not be surprising from the cardinalist stance. Also, this indicates that our theorem C.2 has a far reaching implication: that is, it can provide a basis for a scientifically legitimate theory of measurable utility.

---

[23]The cardinality of ΔU implied by local homotheticity is rather eye-opening, as it provides a basis for a scientifically legitimate theory of measurable utility. Namely, if the marginal utility of income is independent of prices, i.e., if (14) holds in a neighborhood of observation, then ΔU is cardinal. The following quote from Chipman (1982, p. 51) may be relevant to this point:

> More important is the general point that there exists restrictive hypothesis concerning consumer behavior ... that could serve as a basis for measuring utility in much the same way that physicists find it convenient to measure temperature.

As Chipman goes on to argue, the assumption marginal utility of income is independent of prices is a "proposition that carries strong empirical implications concerning consumer's preferences, which can be verified or refuted by observations on his market demand behavior" (1982, p. 52).

Example C.1. Suppose the utility function is given by (18), and furthermore

$$\phi(x) \equiv x_1^{\alpha_1}, x_2^{\alpha_2}, \ldots, x_n^{\alpha_n}, \quad \alpha_i > 0 \text{ for all } i, \text{ and } \sum_{i=1}^{n} \alpha_i = 1.$$

In this case, demand functions are homothetic and obtained as

$$x_i = \alpha_i Y/P_i, \; i = 1, 2, \ldots, n,$$

so that $\xi_i(P) = \alpha_i/P_i$. Consider the construction of a hydroelectric dam that lowers the price of electricity from P_1° to P_1^1. Assume that this project is financed by levying a lump sum tax which reduces the income of our consumer from $\$Y^\circ$ to $\$Y^1$. Assume, for simplicity, that all *other* prices stay constant. This project's welfare impact on the consumer may be computed, using (19), as

$$\Delta U = \log Y^1/Y^\circ - \alpha_1 \log P_1^1/P_1^\circ.$$

where we set $\gamma(1) = 1$ by the choice of units. Hence, $\Delta U > 0$ if and only if $Y^1/Y^\circ > (P_1^1/P_1^\circ)^{\alpha_1}$. For example, if P_1 falls by 10 percent so that $P_1^1/P_1^\circ = 0.9$, and the consumer's income is \$16,000 with $\alpha_1 = 0.03$, then the maximum amount that the consumer is willing to pay for the project may be computed as[24]

$$Y^\circ - Y^1 = [1 - (.9)^{.03}]Y^\circ = \$50.49.$$

(b) The Case of Vertical Engel Curves: Interpretation of (15)

Lemma C.3 (Samuelson 1942). Under condition (15), we have[25]

$$\gamma^*(P^n) = b/P_n, \quad \text{where } b \equiv \gamma^*(1), \text{ and} \tag{20a}$$

[24] Simply set $\Delta U = 0$. This amount (\$50.49) corresponds to the Hicksian compensating variation. The median family income in the United States in 1977 was \$16,009. The average share of the electricity bill in the budget among U.S. families is about 3 percent. If Mr. A spends approximately 3 percent of his income for electricity (which is a local homotheticity), and if his income is \$16,000, then one may argue that this consumer saves approximately \$16,000 × 0.03 ×0.01 = \$48 by the 10 percent reduction of his electric bill. This amount is not far from \$50.49 obtained above.

[25] Equation (20a) follows immediately from the (-1) homogeneity of U_Y. Equation (20b) be shown easily by differentiating Roy's identity (4c) with respect to Y.

$$\partial x_i(P, Y)/\partial Y = 0, \; i =, 2, \ldots, n - 1. \tag{20b}$$

Furthermore, (15) holds if and only if $u(x)$ can be written as[26]

$$u(x) = c_1 \Psi(x_1, x_2, \ldots, x_{n-1}) + (c_1 x_n + c_2), \tag{21}$$

where c_1 and c_2 are some constants (with $c_1 = b > 0$); see also Sono (1943, p. 94).

Equation (20b) means that a change in income Y does not affect the demand for any commodities except one commodity, commodity n. For $n = 2$, this means that the Engel curves are straight lines parallel to the axis of the numéraire commodity (commodity 2). The case of (15) was thus referred to as the case of *vertical Engel curves*, where commodity 2 is measured on the vertical axis. This case was popularized by Hicks (1946, pp. 38–41), in which all commodities except commodity 1 are grouped together as a single "commodity." The assumption of vertical Engel curves is often justified for a commodity such as tea or salt, in which a person's expenditure on that commodity is a small part of his or her whole income.

We now proceed with our analysis by setting $P_n = 1$. Letting p_i be the *normalized* price of commodity i and $p = (p_1, p_2, \ldots, p_{n-1})$, we obtain, from (20b),

$$x_i = h_i(p), \; i = 1, 2, \ldots, n - 1, \tag{22a}$$

$$x_n = h_n(p, y) \equiv y - \sum_{i=1}^{n-1} p_i h_i(p), \tag{22b}$$

where y is the income in terms of commodity n. Combining (13), (20a), and (22), we obtain

$$\Delta U = b(y^1 - y^\circ) - b \int_{p^\circ}^{p^1} \sum_{i=1}^{n-1} h_i(p)\, dp_i. \tag{23}$$

Clearly, ΔU in (23) is independent of the choice of unit in measuring Q. As in (19), the utility measures U and ΔU are again cardinal, where $b \equiv \gamma^*(1)$, instead of $a \equiv \gamma(1)$ is the "measuring stick" for cardinality.

---

[26] To show that (21) implies (15), simply recall $u_n = \lambda P_n$, and note $u_n = c_1$ from (21). Then we have $P_n = c_1$, so that (15) holds. Note that $c_1 = b \equiv \gamma^*(1)$.

If $n = 2$, (23) can be simplified, by setting $b = 1$ by the choice of units, as

$$\Delta U = (y^1 - y^\circ) - \int_{p_1^\circ}^{p_1^1} h_1(p)dp_1. \tag{23$'$}$$

This corresponds to the formula obtained by Sono (1943, p. 95). If income is constant, this can further be reduced to

$$\Delta U = -\int_{p_1^\circ}^{p_1^1} h_1(p)dp_1. \tag{23$''$}$$

This corresponds to the D-M measure except that x_1 and P_1 are replaced by h_1 and p_1, respectively. In summary, we have:

Theorem C.3. Under the assumption of vertical Engel curves, (15), ΔU is measured by (23), and it is cardinal and is independent of the choice of the unit in measuring P and Y. The "measuring stick" for cardinality is $\gamma^*(1)$.

C.5 Hicksian Measures under Constancy of Marginal Utility of Income

We now relate the two concepts of the Hicksian welfare measures, C and E defined in (6) and (7), to the constancy of MUI. If λ is constant in the sense of (14), we have formula (19). Then defining A and τ by

$$A \equiv \int_{P^\circ}^{P^1} \sum_{i=1}^{n} x_i(P, Y^\circ)dP_i = Y^\circ \int_{P^\circ}^{P^1} \sum_{i=1}^{n} \xi_i(P)dP_i, \tag{24a}$$

$$\tau \equiv A/Y^\circ, \tag{24b}$$

we may easily obtain[27]

$$C = Y^\circ(e^\tau - 1). \tag{25}$$

Note that if all the prices except P_1 are kept constant, A defined in (24) measures the familiar area defined by the Marshallian trapezoid area:

$$A = \int_{P_1^\circ}^{P_1^1} \xi_i(P_1, P_2^\circ, \ldots, P_n^\circ)Y^\circ dP_1. \tag{24$'$}$$

[27] See Takayama (1984, p. 616).

Likewise, the equivalent variation may be obtained from (19) and (27) as[28]

$$E = Y^{\circ}(1 - e^{-\tau}). \tag{26}$$

Then we may *unequivocally* conclude, for $P^{\circ} \neq P^{1}$,[29]

$$E < A < C. \tag{27}$$

Example C.2. We use the same utility function considered in example C.1. Assume that all prices except that of commodity 1 are fixed, and that income Y is held constant. Then letting $z \equiv \Delta P_1/P_1^{\circ}$, where $\Delta P_1 \equiv P_1^1 - P_1^{\circ}$, we may compute:[30]

$$\overline{C} = (1 + z)^{\alpha_1} - 1, \tag{28a}$$

$$\tau = \alpha_1 \log (1 + z), \tag{28b}$$

$$\overline{E} = 1 - (1 + z)^{-\alpha_1}, \tag{28c}$$

where $\overline{C} \equiv C/Y^{\circ}$, $\tau \equiv A/Y^{\circ}$, and $\overline{E} = E/Y^{\circ}$.

This example also shows that if z is sufficiently close to zero, we can see from (28) that C, A, and E can all be approximated by $\alpha_1 z Y^{\circ}$. On the other hand, if z is not sufficiently close to zero, then the discrepancies of these three measures can be large. In particular, if $P_1^1 \to \infty$, as in the Marshallian triangle, then we may readily obtain, from (28),[31]

$$E \to Y^{\circ}, \; A \to \infty, \; C/A \to \infty.$$

Namely, the discrepancies among E, A, and C can be very large as z gets large.[32] Hence, if we claim that C and E are the correct measures

---

[28] See Takayama (1984, p. 617).

[29] Chipman and Moore (1980, p. 945) obtained a similar relation by imposing a certain restrictive assumption. What is argued here is that such a restriction can be completely dispensed with (see Takayama 1984, pp. 617–18).

[30] See Takayama (1984, p. 619).

[31] To show $C/A \to \infty$ as $z \to \infty$, simply apply L'Hospital's rule to $C/A = [(a + z)^{\alpha_1} - 1]/[\alpha_1 \log(1 + z)]$.

[32] However, for such a large change in P_1, the assumption of homothetic demands, which we take as a local approximation would be likely to break down.

(as in Willig 1976, Hausman 1981, and others), then we are forced to confront the difficulty that the discrepancies between the "correct" measures can be infinitely large, *even* in a "restrictive" situation in which (14) is imposed.

We may now summarize some of these results in theorem C.4.

Theorem C.4. If the marginal utility of income is constant in the sense of (14), then $-A/Y^{\circ}$ measures the true welfare change due to price changes with income constant, and we always have $E < A < C$. When $|A|$ is sufficiently small, the degree of over- and under-estimations of A by C and E are of a second-order smallness. On the other hand, if $|A|$ is large, neither E nor C approximates A well; the discrepancies can be quite large.

To illustrate further the weakness of the Hicksian measures, consider a (single) price rise from P_1° to P_1^1, in which case the compensating variation can be illustrated by $P_1^{\circ}AB'P_1^1$ as in figure C.3, where DD' is the ordinary demand curve and AB' is the compensated one (passing through A). Note that DD' is flatter than AB' as long as the income effect is positive (as in the present case). Now suppose that the price rise takes place in two steps from P_1° to P_1' to P_1^1. Then the compensating variation would be the shaded area, $P_1^{\circ}AC'P_1'$ plus $P_1'CB''P_1^1$ in figure C.3. Thus, it depends on the number of steps taken in a particular price rise. Similarly, the equivalent variation also depends on the number of steps for a particular price change.[33] On the other hand, if we regard the price rise from P_1° to P_1^1 as consisting of a large number of steps, the compensating and the equivalent variations would both be close to the D-M measure, $P_1^{\circ}ABP_1^1$. Since we wish to require that the welfare measure be invariant with respect to the number of steps taken, this discussion also indicates the weakness of the H measures.[34]

Finally, if the constancy of MUI is interpreted in the sense of (15), then we may easily obtain the following well-known result:[35]

$$E = A = C.$$

[33] For a price rise from P_1° to P_1^1, the equivalent variation is measured by $P_1^1BEP_1^{\circ}$, where BE is the compensated demand curve passing through point B.

[34] The diagrammatical exposition here is due to Mishan (1977, pp. 14–18), which is repeated by Ng (1980, pp. 90–92). Hause (1975) and G. McKenzie (1983) favor the use of equivalent variation. However, even from the discussion via fig. C.3 alone, we may conclude that this cannot be correct.

[35] See Takayama (1984, p. 621).

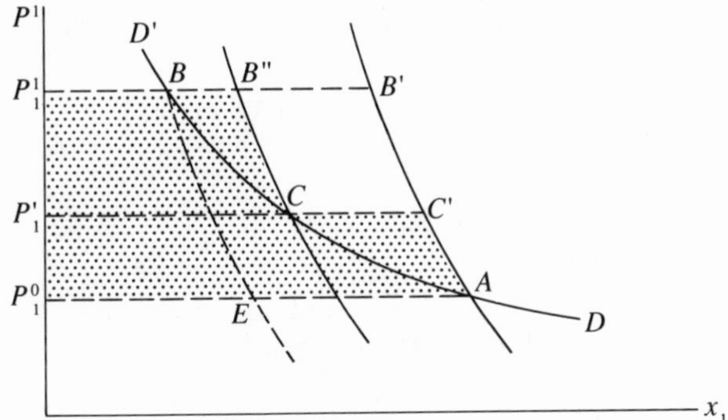

Figure C.3: The Dupuit-Marshall measure and compensating variation

Namely, for the vertical Engel curve case, these three welfare measures all coincide. This result is hardly surprising, since the income effect is zero for this case, so that the compensated and the uncompensated demand curves coincide, and we may recall figure C.3.

Concluding Remarks

With the presence of income effect in the demand functions, H measures *cannot*, in general, be the correct welfare measures, whereas the D-M measure (with proper modifications) provides the correct welfare measure for a single price change assuming the approximate constancy of MUI. Also, with the constancy of MUI, (indirect) utility can be cardinal, which conforms with the cardinalist stance of Marshall.

We may also point out, however, that there *can* be other interesting cases in which we can carry out the computation of our welfare measure formula (13) without assuming the constancy of MUI (which may be too stringent an assumption for some readers). Here we only *illustrated* such a computation for historically important cases.[36]

[36] We may also note that there is a close relation between the theory of consumer's surplus and that of index numbers (see, for example, Rader 1976; Bruce 1977; Vartia 1983; and Suzumara 1985). The parallel study of both topics can be quite fruitful, though it appears that much work remains to be done in this context.

References

Apostol, T. M. 1957. *Mathematical Analysis.* Reading, Mass.: Addison-Wesley.

Antonelli, G. B. 1971. "On the Mathematical Theory of Political Economy." Trans. from the Italian original by J. S. Chipman and A. P. Kirman. In Chipman et al. 1971, 333–60.

Bergson, A. 1975. "A Note on Consumer's Surplus." *Journal of Economic Literature* 13 (March): 38–44.

Boadway, R. W. 1974. "The Welfare Foundation of Cost-Benefit Analysis." *Economic Journal* 84 (December): 926–39.

Boadway, R., and N. Bruce. 1984. *Welfare Economics.* Oxford: Basil Blackwell.

Bruce, N. 1977. "A Note on Consumer's Surplus, the Divisia Index, and the Measurement of Welfare Change." *Econometrica* 45 May: 1033–38.

Burns, M. E. 1973. "A Note on the Concept and Measure of Consumer's Surplus." *American Economic Review* 63 (June): 335–44.

Chichetti, C. J., A. C. Fisher, and V. K. Smith. 1976. "An Economic Evaluation of a Generalized Consumer Surplus Measure: The Mineral King Controversy." *Econometrica* 64 (November): 1259–76.

Chipman, J. S. 1976. "The Paretian Heritage." *Cahiers Vilfredo Pareto, Revue europenne des sciences sociales* 14: 65–171.

———. 1982. "Samuelson and Consumption Theory." In *Samuelson and Neoclassical Economics*, ed. G. R. Feiwel. Boston: Kluweiz Nijhof.

Chipman, J. S., L. Hurwicz, M. K. Richter, and H. F. Sonnenschein, eds. 1971, *Preferences, Utility, and Demand.* New York: Harcourt, Brace and Jovanovich.

Chipman, J. S., and J. C. Moore. 1976. "The Scope of Consumer's Surplus Arguments." In *Evolution, Welfare and Time in Economics: Essays in Honor of Nicholas Georgescu-Roegen*, ed. A. M. Tang, F. M. Westfield, and J. S. Worley, 69–123, Lexington, Mass.: D. C. Heath.

———. 1980. "Compensating Variation, Consumer's Surplus and Welfare." *American Economic Review* 70 (December): 933–49.

Currie, J. H., J. A. Murphy, and A. Schwitz. 1971. "The Concept of Economic Surplus and Its Use in Economic Analysis." *Economic Journal* 81 (December): 741–99.

Dixit, A., and P. A. Weller. 1979. "The Three Consumer's Surpluses." *Economica*, n.s. 66 (May): 121–29.

Dooley, P. C. 1983. "Consumer's Surplus: Marshall and His Critics." *Canadian Journal of Economics* 16 (February): 26–38.

Dupuit, J. 1844 [1969]. "On the Measurement of the Utility of Public Works." Trans. R. H. Barback. In *Readings in Welfare Economics*, ed. K. J. Arrow and T. Satovsky, 255:83, Homewood, Ill.: Richard D. Irwin.

Georgescu-Roegen, N. 1952. "A Diagrammatic Analysis of Complementarity." *Southern Economic Journal* 19 (July): 1–20.

———. 1968. "Revisiting Marshall's Constancy of Marginal Utility of Money." *Southern Economic Journal* 35 (October): 176–81.

Harberger, A. C. 1971. "Three Basic Postulates for Applied Welfare Economics: An Interpretative Essay." *Journal of Economic Literature* 9 (September): 785–87.

Hause, J. C. 1975. "The Theory of Welfare Cost Measurement." *Journal of Political Economy* 83 (December): 1145–82.

Hausman, J. A. 1981. "Exact Consumer's Surplus and Deadweight Loss." *American Economic Review* 71 (September): 662–76.

Henderson, A. 1941. "Consumer's Surplus and the Compensating Variation." *Review of Economic Studies* 8 (February): 117–21.

Hicks, J. R. 1939. *Value and Capital.* 1st ed. Oxford: Clarendon Press, (2d ed. 1946).

———. 1941. "The Rehabilitation of Consumer's Surplus." *Review of Economic Studies* 8 (February): 108–16.

———. 1942. "Consumer's Surplus and Index Numbers." *Review of Economic Studies* 9 (Summer): 126–37.

———. 1943. "The Four Consumer's Surpluses." *Review of Economic Studies* 11 (Winter): 31–41.

———. 1945–46. "The Generalized Theory of Consumer's Surplus." *Review of Economic Studies* 13: 68–74.

———. 1956. *A Revision of Demand Theory.* Oxford: Clarendon Press.

———. 1981. "The Four Consumer's Surpluses." In *Wealth and Welfare: Collected Essays on Economic Theory*, 1:114–32, Oxford: Basil Blackwell.

Hicks, J. R., and R. G. D. Allen. 1934. "A Reconsideration of the Theory of Value." *Econometrica* 1 (February and May): 52–76, 196–219.

Hotelling, H. 1938. "The General Welfare in Relation to the Problems of Taxation and of Railway and Utility Rates." *Econometrica* 6 (April): 242–69.

Houthakker, H. S. 1950. "Revealed Preferences and the Utility Function." *Economica* 17 (May): 159–74.

Hurwicz, L. 1971. "On the Problem of Integrability of Demand Functions." In Chipman et al., 1971, 174–214.

Hurwicz, L., and M. K. Richter. 1971. "Ville Axiom and Consumer Theory." *Econometrica* 47 (May): 603–19.

Just, R. E., D. L. Hueth, and A. Schmitz. 1982. *Applied Welfare Economics and Public Policy.* Englewood Cliffs, N.J.: Prentice-Hall.

Katzner, D. W. 1970. *Static Demand Theory.* New York: Macmillan.

McKenzie, G. W. 1979. "Consumer's Surplus Without Apology: Comment." *American Economic Review* 69 (June): 465–74.

———. 1983. *Measuring Economic Welfare.* New York: Cambridge University Press.

McKenzie, G. W., and I. F. Pearce. 1976. "A New Operational Procedure for Evaluating Economic Policies." *Review of Economic Studies* 43 (October): 465–68.

———. 1982. "Welfare Measurement—A Synthesis." *American Economic Review* 72 (September): 669–82.

Marshall, A. 1920. *Principles of Economics.* 8th ed. London: Macmillan. (1st ed. 1890).

Mishan, E. J. 1960. "A Survey of Welfare Economics, 1939–1959." *Economic Journal* 70 (June): 197–265.

———. 1977. "The Plain Truth about Consumer Surplus." *Zeitschrift für Nationalökonomie* 37: 1–24.

Mohring, H. 1971. "Alternative Welfare and Loss Measures." *Western Economic Journal* 9 (December): 349–68.

Morey, E. R. 1984. "Confuser Surplus." *American Economic Review.* 74 (March): 163–73.

Nagatani, H. 1984. "Algorithms for the Hicksian Measures of Consumer's Surplus: Professor Houthakker Reevaluated" (in Japanese). *Osaka University Economics (Osaka Daigaku Keizaigaku)* 34: 135–46.

Ng, Y. K. 1980. *Welfare Economics.* New York: Wiley.

Rader, T. 1976. "Equivalence of Consumer Surplus, the Divisia Index of Output, and Eisenberg's Addilog Social Utility." *Journal of Economic Theory* 13 (August): 58–66.

Richter, M. K. 1966. "Revealed Preference Theory." *Econometrica* 34 (July): 635–45.

Samuelson, P. A. 1938. "A Note on the Pure Theory of Consumer's Behavior." *Economica*, n.s. 5 (February): 61–71.

———. 1942. "Constance of the Marginal Utility of Income." In *Studies in Mathematical Economics and Econometrics: In Memory of Henry Schultz*, ed. O. Lange, F. McIntyre, and T. O. Yatema, 75–91, Chicago: University of Chicago Press.

———. 1947. *Foundations of Economic Analysis.* Cambridge, Mass.: Harvard University Press (enlarged ed., 1983).

———. 1950. "The Problem of Integrability in Utility Theory." *Economica*, n.s. 17 (November): 355–85.

Seade, J. K. 1978. "Consumer's Surplus and Linearity of Engel Curves." *Economic Journal* 88 (September): 479–96.

Silberberg, E. 1972. "Duality and the Many Consumer's Surpluses." *American Economic Review* 62 (December): 942–52.

———. 1990. *The Structure of Economics*. 2d ed. New York: McGraw-Hill (1st ed. 1978).

Sono, M. 1943. "On Dupuit's Relative Utility from the Point of View of Choice Theory" (in Japanese). *Economic Essays (Keizai Ronso)* 57: 88-97.

Suzumura, K. 1985. "Consumer's Surplus and Welfare Evaluation" (in Japanese) *Economic Review (Keizai Kenkyu)* 36 (January): 53–66

Takayama, A. 1982. "On Consumer's Surplus." *Economic Letters* 10: 35-42.

———. 1984. "Consumer's Surplus, Path Independence, Compensating and Equivalent Variations." *Zeitschrift für die gesamte Staatswissenschaft* 140 (Dezember): 594–625.

———. 1987. "Consumer Surplus." In *The New Palgrave*, ed. J. Eatwell, M. Milgate, and P. Newman, 1: 607–13. London: Macmillan.

Vartia, Y. O. 1983."Efficient Methods of Measuring Welfare Change and Compensated Income in Terms of Ordinary Demand Functions." *Econometrica* 51 (January): 79–98.

von Neumann, J., and O. Morgenstern. 1953. *Theory of Games and Economic Behavior*. 3rd ed. Princeton, N.J.: Princeton University Press. (1st. ed. 1944, 2nd ed. 1949).

Walras, L. 1954. *Elements of Pure Economics*. Trans. from the 1926 version by W. Jaffé. Homewood, Ill.: Richard D. Irwin.

Whitaker, J. K., ed. 1975. *The Early Economic Writings of Alfred Marshall, 1867–1890*. Vol. 2. New York: Free Press.

Willig, R. D. 1976. "Consumer's Surplus Without Apology." *American Economic Review* 66 (September): 589–97.

———. 1979. "Consumer's Surplus Without Apology, Reply." *American Economic Review* 69 (June): 469–74.

Indices

Name Index

Abbott, M. 211
Abel, A. 522, 526
Acton, J. R. 234
Afriat, S. N. 132, 139
Akerlof, G. A. 306, 313, 314, 354
Alchian, A. A. 261, 268
Allais, M. 269, 270, 349
Allen, R. G. D. 142, 145, 151, 178, 181
Anderson, R. K. 106, 137, 163, 171
Anscombe, F. J. 258
Antonelli, G. B. 632
Apostol, T. M. 52, 626, 630, 632
Applebaum, E. 290
Araujo, A. 455, 479
Arnold, V. I. 330
Arrow, K. J. 93, 94, 95, 96, 97, 102, 107, 117, 152, 174, 197, 224, 235, 257, 273, 278, 279, 281, 290, 295, 296, 301, 307, 316, 349, 375, 452, 479, 487, 517, 605, 615, 616, 617, 618, 619
Ashenfelter, O. 211
Aumann, R. J. 258
Averch, H. A. 212, 215, 217, 219, 234
Avrel, M. 605

Bacharach, M. 265
Bailey, E. E. 219
Bator, F. M. 236
Battalio, R. 211
Baumol, W. J. 212, 213, 376
Becker, G. S. 307
Becker, R. A. 477, 479
Beltrami, E. 376
Benhabib, J. 376
Benveniste, L. M. 455, 477, 479
Berg, S. V. 201, 221
Bergson, A. 235, 622, 629
Berkovitz, L. D. 452
Berndt, E. R. 150, 155, 156, 173
Bernoulli, J. 470
Bertram, J. E. 333, 339, 412, 414
Blackorby, C. 139, 152, 156
Blanchard, O. J. 526
Blinder, A. S. 212, 364, 510, 511
Bliss, G. M. 111
Block, H. D. 349
Boadway, R. A. 236, 622, 630
Boiteux, M. 221, 234
Borch, K. H. 257, 281
Borts, G. H. 219
Boulding, K. 301
Boyce, W. E. 390, 409, 412, 413
Boyd III, J. H. 477, 479
Brainard, W. 526, 529
Branson, W. 504, 531
Brock, W. A. 376, 452
Brown, R. J. 150, 152
Brownlee, O. H. 367, 370
Bruce, N. 236, 622, 643
Brumberg, R. E. 504, 510
Brunner, K. 513
Buchanan, J. M. 221
Burmeister, E. 437
Burns, M. E. 622
Burstein, M. 190

Carathéodory, C. 111, 130
Carter, M. 363
Cass, D. 295, 475, 477, 481, 484, 485, 498, 501, 502, 503
Cauchy, A. L. 22, 27, 329, 453
Cesari, L. 409, 452
Chang, W. W. 350
Chao, C. C. 150, 156, 157
Chenery, H. B. 152
Chipman, J. S. 622, 629, 632, 634, 636, 637, 640

Christensen, D. O. 150, 152
Christensen, L. R. 155, 157, 173
Cicchetti, C. J. 622
Coase, R. 235, 236, 237, 242, 245, 246
Cobb, C. W. 31, 151, 153, 214, 624
Cournot, A. A. 623
Cowell, F. A. 257
Crew, M. A. 201, 219, 221
Currie, J. H. 622

Danzig, G. B. 111
Darrough, M. N. 173
Deaton, A. 211, 257, 279
Debreu, G. 235, 603
Devaney, R. L. 376
Diamond, P. 257, 307, 311
Diewert, W. E. 137, 153, 173, 605
DiPrima, R. C. 390, 409, 412, 413
Dirichlet, P. G. L. 30
Dixit, A. K. 75
Dobell, R. A. 437
Dooley, P. C. 623, 626, 633, 634
Dornbusch, R. 514
Douglas, P. H. 31, 151, 153, 214, 624
Drabicki, J. Z. 352, 354, 373, 374, 436, 438, 439, 444, 485, 498, 499, 503
Drèze, J. H. 201, 234
Duesenberry, J. N. 504
Dupuit, J. 197, 621, 623, 624, 625, 643

Eaves, C. 349
Eckman, J. P. 376
Edgeworth, F. Y. 634
Ehrlich, I. 307
Eichhorn, W. 163
Eisner, R. 522
El-Hodiri, M. A. 106, 213, 215, 557
Engel, E. 628, 634, 637, 639, 640
Enthoven, A. C. 95, 96, 97, 102, 107, 174, 605, 615, 616, 617, 618, 619
Euler, L. 112, 289, 389, 455, 469, 470, 472, 635

Färe, R. 100, 139, 148
Farrell, M. J. 504
Feldstein, M. S. 290
Ferguson, C. E. 188, 190, 193, 195, 196
Fischer, S. 437, 514, 526
Fisher, A. C. 622
Fisher, I. N. 296, 297, 298, 425, 498, 504, 506, 511
Fomin, S. V. 554
Ford, J. L. 257
Førsund, F. R. 148
Fratrik, M. 557
Friedman, M. 187, 193, 271, 361, 504, 505, 506, 509, 510, 513, 514
Frisch, R. 159, 510
Funk, J. E. 546
Fuss, M. 152, 153

Gantmacher, F. R. 575
Gelfand, I. M. 554
Georgescu-Roegen, N. 629, 634
Gertler, M. 432
Giffen, R. 146, 188, 190, 192, 626
Gilbert, E. G. 546
Gleick, J. 376
Goldman, A. J. 110
Goodwin, R. M. 510
Gorman, W. M. 628
Gould, J. P. 522
Gravelle, H. 297
Green, H. A. J. 257, 280
Green, L. 211
Greenhut, M. L. 561
Guckenheimer, J. 376
Guesnerie, R. 311

Haavelmo, T. 517
Hadjimichalakis, M. G. 437, 438, 444
Hadley, G. 485, 554
Hagen, E. E. 504
Hahn, F. 345, 349
Hall, R. E. 136, 526
Halmos, P. R. 585, 588
Hamilton, W. R. 455
Hammond, P. J. 265
Hanoch, G. 158, 162, 211
Haque, W. 484, 485
Harberger, A. C. 622, 629
Harris, M. 376
Hart, O. D. 295, 296
Hartle, R. F. 496, 498
Hatta, T. 163, 170
Hause, J. C. 622, 642
Hausman, J. A. 622, 628, 642
Hayashi, F. 526, 527, 528, 530, 532, 534

Heckman, J. 211
Helpman, E. 162
Henderson, A. 621
Henderson, J. M. 190, 211, 257
Henry, C. 412
Hestenes, M. R. 75, 111, 451, 452, 543, 546
Hey, J. D. 257, 281, 286, 296
Hicks, J. R. 101, 111, 125, 131, 138, 142, 143, 145, 152, 175, 187, 190, 198, 206, 208, 212, 235, 348, 350, 372, 375, 477, 509, 602, 621, 622, 625, 626, 627, 629, 639
Hirota, M. 350
Hirschleifer, J. 221, 257, 280
Hobson, E. W. 42
Holmes, P. 376
Homma, M. 236
Hoover, K. D. 364
Hosoe, M. 257
Hotelling, H. 136, 137, 197, 622
Houthakker, H. S. 170, 172, 221, 629, 632
Hsieh, D. A. 376
Hu, S. C. 547
Hueth, D. L. 622
Hurewicz, W. 409
Hurwicz, L. 93, 94, 102, 106, 117, 174, 224, 349, 375, 632
Hurwitz, A. 343, 344, 345, 365, 369

Ide, T. 148, 157, 161, 162, 200, 201, 366, 605
Imai, K. 236, 511
Intriligator, M. 75, 458

Johnson, L. 437
Johnson, L. O. 212, 215, 217, 219, 234
Jorgenson, D. W. 153, 173, 514, 517, 520, 522, 526, 535
Joskow, P. L. 201
Just, R. E. 622

Kagel, J. 211
Kahn, A. E. 219
Kahneman, D. 268, 270
Kaldor, N. 205, 235
Kalman, R. E. 333, 339, 412, 414
Kamien, M. I. 452
Karamardian, S. 606
Karlin, S. 145
Katz, E. 290
Katzner, D. W. 622
Kemp, M. C. 485, 554
Kendrick, D. 452
Keynes, J. M. 351, 352, 353, 363, 365, 368, 422, 423, 437, 481, 501, 514, 517, 519, 520, 521, 525, 529, 533, 535
Kihlstrom, R. E. 275
Killingsworth, M. R. 212
Kimura, Y. 615
Kleindorfer, P. R. 201, 219, 221
Klevorick, A. K. 212, 213
Knight, F. H. 205, 258, 290, 364, 521
Koopmans, T. C. 475, 477, 481, 484, 498, 501, 502, 503
Kotowitz, Y. 315
Kreps, D. M. 257
Krugman, P. R. 162
Kudoh, K. 245
Kuhn, H. W. 84, 105, 106
Kurz, M. 452
Kuznets, S. 504

L'Hospital, G. F. 641
Laffont, J. J. 257, 281, 286, 296, 307, 311
Lagrange, J. L. 84, 106, 112
Lancaster, K. 121
Landau, E. 409
Lange, O. 235
Lau, L. J. 148, 153, 154, 173
Layard, P. R. G. 211, 257
Le Baron, B. 376
Le Châtelier, H. L. 163, 171
Ledyard, J. O. 236
Lefschetz, S. 412
Leland, H. E. 296, 303
Lerner, A. P. 235, 517
Lewis, J. P. 349
Liapunov, A. M. 335, 338, 411, 412, 413, 414
Lippman, S. A. 257, 281, 307
Littlechild, S. 234
Loomes, G. 268
Lucas, R. E. 363, 522
Luce, R. D. 265
Luenberger, N. G. 75

Machina, M. J. 265, 268
Macki, J. 452
Maddock, R. 363
Malinvaud, E. 257
Malliaris, A. G. 376, 452
Mangasarian, O. L. 75, 85, 468, 605, 606, 607, 608, 609, 610, 615, 617, 618, 619
Mann, H. B. 603
Manning, G. 234
Marino, A. 166
Marschak, J. 367, 370
Marshall, A. 146, 150, 345, 366, 375, 621, 623, 624, 625, 626, 633, 634, 643
Martos, B. 605, 606, 607, 615
McCall, J. J. 257, 281, 307
McDonald, I. M. 369
McFadden, D. 152, 153
McKenna, C. J. 257, 281
McKenzie, G. W. 622, 628, 642
McKenzie, L. W. 135, 137, 140 ,145, 235, 477
Meade, J. E. 236
Menger, C. 134
Metzler, A. H. 513
Minhas, B. 152
Mirman, L. J. 275
Mirrlees, J. A. 557
Mishan, E. J. 235, 625, 642
Mitchell, M. 234
Modigliani, F. 364, 439, 504, 510
Mohring, H. 234, 622
Moore, J. C. 622, 634, 636, 640
Morey, E. R. 622
Morgenstern, O. 257, 259, 262, 265, 268, 316, 364, 629
Morishima, M. 152, 212
Morrison, C. J. 150
Mosak, J. D. 193, 504
Muelbauer, J. 211, 257, 279
Mundlak, Y. 152, 153
Munkres, J. R. 8
Murata, Y. 615
Murphy, J. A. 622
Musacchio, R. A. 517
Musgrave, R. A. 211
Mutoh, T. 363

Nagatani, H. 629
Nagatani, K. 188, 190, 193, 431, 437
Negishi, T. 146, 345, 349
Nelson, J. R. 201
Newman, P. 366, 605
Newton, I. 470
Ng, Y. K. 622, 630, 642
Niho, Y. 517
Nikaido, H. 104, 111
Nishimura, O. 257, 313

Occam, W. 629
Oettli, W. 163
Ohlin, B. 236, 352
Ohta, H. 162, 561
Okuguchi, K. 437, 444
Okuno, M. 145, 257
Olech, C. 341, 354, 356, 370, 422
Otani, Y. 163, 166

Panzar, J. C. 201, 221, 234
Pareto, V. 237, 625, 626, 629, 630, 634
Parke, D. W. 606
Patinkin, D. 438
Pauly, M. V. 307, 308
Peano, G. 329, 453
Pearce, I. F . 622, 628
Phelps, E. S. 361
Phillip L. 547
Phillips, A. W. 358, 359, 363, 364, 365, 368
Pigou, A. C. 235, 236
Pindyck, R. S. 257
Pitchford, J. D. 452
Poincaré, J. H. 375, 409, 422
Pollak, R. A. 168, 170, 171
Ponstein, J. 605, 606
Pontryagin, L. S. 412, 451, 452, 455, 456, 461, 463, 464, 465, 467, 471, 472, 474
Portes, R. D. 188, 195, 196
Postlewaite, A. 305
Pratt, J. W. 257, 273, 277, 278, 301, 316
Primont, D. 139
Puu, T. 188, 190, 192

Quandt, R. E. 190, 211, 257
Quirk, J. P. 257

Rader, T. 643

Rahman, M. A. 458, 459
Raiffa, H. 265
Ramsey, F. P. 477, 481, 484, 486, 501, 503
Rees, R. 297
Reymond, D. B. 42
Richter, M. K. 632
Riley, J. G. 257, 307
Robbins, L. 235
Robinson, R. 521
Rose, H. 437, 530
Rothchild, M. 257, 265, 301, 307, 311
Routh, E. J. 343, 344, 345, 369
Roy, R. 134, 137, 171, 172, 176, 627, 635
Rubinfeld, D. L. 257
Ruelle, D. 376
Russak, B. 546
Russell, R. R. 139, 152, 156

Saijo, T. 138
Sakai, Y. 188, 190, 192, 257, 270, 276, 281, 286, 289, 290, 296, 302
Samuelson, P. A. 101, 111, 125, 130, 131, 132, 133, 134, 135, 141, 143, 149, 163, 165, 166, 170, 171, 174, 187, 190, 193, 198, 339, 344, 349, 350, 358, 359, 506, 585, 601, 602, 621, 622, 629, 632, 633, 634, 635, 638
Sandmo, A. 281, 286, 296, 301, 302, 303, 305
Sanger, G. C. 626
Santomero, A. M. 359, 360, 362
Sargent, T. J. 365, 407, 432, 437
Savage, L. J. 258, 271
Saving, T. R. 188, 190, 193, 195, 196
Say, J. B. 624
Scarf, H. E. 349
Scheinkman, J. A. 455, 477, 479
Schmitz, A. 622
Schoemaker, P. J. H. 257
Schwartz, H. A. 22
Schwartz, N. 452
Schwitz, A. 622
Scitovsky, T. 211, 236
Seade, J. K. 622, 628
Seater, J. J. 359, 360, 362
Seierstad, A. 452, 546
Semba, K. 532
Sen, A. K. 197
Sethi, S. P. 452
Shackle, G. L. S. 521
Shavell, S. 307, 311
Shaw, G. K. 363
Sheffrin, S. M. 363
Shephard, R. W. 135, 137, 138, 143, 147, 148, 149, 153, 155, 156, 174, 177, 180, 192, 193, 194, 195, 196, 627
Sherman, R. 234
Shiller, R. J. 432
Shilov, G. E. 585
Shinohara, M. 504
Shizuki, T. 363
Sicilian, J. 166
Sidrauski, M. 431, 432, 433, 437
Silberberg, E. 145, 163, 257, 622, 625, 635
Simmons, G. F. 409, 412, 455, 470, 554
Sims, G. E. 156, 436, 439
Sinn, H. W. 257
Slater, M. 92, 93, 97, 102, 107
Slutsky, E. 138, 144, 145, 175, 206, 208, 212, 348, 372, 626, 632
Smale, N. 83
Smith, A. 235, 240, 315
Smith, V. 622
Smithies, A. 504
Smyth, D. J. 350
Solow, R. M. 152, 355, 357, 358, 359, 360, 361, 362, 363, 423, 444, 476, 477, 484, 498
Sono, M. 621, 622, 640
Spence, M. 306, 307
Srinivasan, T. N. 484, 485
Starrett, D. A. 221
Stein, J. L. 219, 437
Steiner, P. O. 221, 226, 227, 234
Stigler, G. J. 146, 187, 626
Stiglitz, J. E. 236, 295, 301, 313, 315, 510
Strauss, A. 452
Strotz, R. H. 522
Sugden, R. 268
Sung, B. Y. 477
Suzumura, K. 145, 257, 622, 625, 644
Svensson, L. E. O. 366
Swan, T. 355, 357, 358, 423, 444, 476, 477, 484, 498

Sydsaeter, K. 452, 546
Syrquin, M. 188, 190, 192, 193

Takayama, A. 48, 75, 77, 86, 92, 93, 103, 105, 106, 111, 121, 125, 131, 132, 134, 136, 137, 145, 148, 150, 156, 157, 161, 162, 163, 171, 183, 198, 200, 201, 206, 212, 213, 214, 215, 217, 219, 221, 235, 239, 325, 339, 345, 347, 350, 352, 354, 358, 366, 373, 374, 412, 419, 423, 436, 438, 439, 444, 452, 458, 460, 477, 483, 485, 498, 499, 503, 504, 514, 517, 518, 523, 541, 543, 544, 557, 564, 605, 607, 621, 622, 640, 641, 642
Taylor, B. 50, 338
Thompson, G. L. 452
Thompson, W. A., Jr. 606
Tinbergen, J. 510
Tobin, J. 170, 290, 365, 366, 368, 369, 370, 423, 425, 429, 436, 437, 445, 498, 499, 522, 525, 529, 530, 534, 535
Trevithick, J. A. 353
Tschirhart, J. 201, 221
Tu, P. N. V. 452
Tucker, A. W. 84, 105, 106, 110
Turnovsky, S. J. 452
Turvey, R. 234
Tversky, A. 268, 270

Uekawa, Y. 615
Uzawa, H. 93, 94, 102, 106, 107, 117, 152, 174, 224, 358, 484, 485, 519, 527

Varian, H. R. 145, 162, 257
Vartia, Y. O. 629, 643
Vickery, W. 201
Ville, J. 632
Viner, J. 187, 201
von Furstenberg, G. 530
von Neumann, J. 257, 259, 262, 265, 268, 316, 364, 629

Wallace, N. 407, 432, 437
Walras, L. 345, 346, 347, 348, 365, 366, 368, 370, 624, 634
Walters, A. A. 211, 257
Weierstrass, K. 36, 42
Weiss, A. 313, 315
Westfield, F. M. 219
Whitaker, J. K. 623
Wicksell, K. 436, 437, 438, 445, 498
Wilansky, A. 18
Williamson, O. E. 221, 222, 226, 227
Willig, R. D. 201, 622, 625, 627, 628, 642
Wilson, C. 313
Wiseman, J. 234
Wood, D. O. 156

Yaari, M. E. 280, 509, 510, 511, 547, 550
Yabushita, S. 245
Yoshikawa, H. 526, 530
Yoshizawa, T. 330
Young, L. C. 452

Zajac, E. E. 213, 217
Zang, I. 605
Zellner, A. 180

Subject Index

Boldface page numbers indicate the principal explanation or definition of the entry.

AC (*see* Average cost)
AC-curve (*see* Average cost curve)
Accelerationists **363**
Accumulation equation of physical assets 427, 527, 547, 548
Actuarially fair premium **285**, 310
Adaptive expectations **359**, 363, 364, 432, 433, 434, 437
Adjustment mechanism (*see* Adjustment process)
Adjustment process 351–355
Admissable control function **453**
Adverse income effect 210
Adverse selection 306, **312**–315
  in credit rationing 313–315
Affine transformation (*see* Linear affine transformation)
Aggregate demand curve **367**
Aggregate production function **356**
Allais's paradox **269**
Allen partial elasticity of factor substitition (*see* Elasticity of substitution)
Animal spirit 521
Arc **631**
Arrow's impossibility theorem 197
Arrow-Enthoven condition **107**
Arrow-Enthoven theorem **95**–96, 102, 174, 618–619
Arrow-Hurwicz-Uzawa condition **94**, 106
Arrow-Hurwicz-Uzawa theorem **93**, 97, 102, 117, 174, 224
  rank condition in **94**
Arrow-Pratt measure of risk aversion (*see* Coefficient of risk aversion)
Asymmetry of information
  in lemon principle **305**–307
  in insurance 307–312
  in credit rationing 313–315
  in principal-agent problem 315
Auxiliary variables (*see* Multipliers in optimal control theory)
Average cost **126**, 201, 202, 203, 204, 205
Average cost curve **126**, 143, 158, 187, 194, 195, 196, 200, 201, 202, 203, 204, 205
  monotone decreasing 204
  U-shaped 143, 158, 194, 196, 201, 202, 203, 204
Average propensity to consume 504
Averch-Johnson effect **212**, 217, 219, 234
Axiom of extension **5**
Axiom of specification **4**

Balanced growth path **357**, **483**
Bang-bang control **458**
Bang-coast control **458**
Bathtub problem 452
Behavior toward risk *generally* 271–273
  risk averse **271**–275, 280, 282–283, 285, 287 288, 289, 290, 292, 293, 294, 295
  risk lover **271**, 282, 289
  risk neutral **271**, 282, 289, 306
Bequest function 548
Bequest motive 550, 552, 553
Binary relation
  complete 258–**259**
  ordering **259**
  partial quasi-ordering **259**
  reflexive **258**
  total **259**
  transitive **258**, 263

Boadway paradox **630**
Bordered determinant **603**
Bordered Hessian condition **116**, 118–120, 129
Bordered Hessian determinant **64**
Bordered Hessian matrix **64**, 98, **116**, 117, 128, 130, 170, 188, 193, 195
Boundary curve **487–488**
Bounded **13**
Bounded above **13**
Bounded below **13**
Bounded state variable constraints **546**
Budget line 63, 99
Budget set **82**

Calculus of variations 451, 452, 468–472
Capital risk **303**, 305
Capital-labor substitution 219
Carathéodory-Samuelson theorem **130**
Cardinal utility **267**, 636, 637, 639, 640, 643
Cartesian product **6**, 53
Cauchy sequence **27**
Cauchy-Peano theorem **299**, 453
Cauchy-Schwartz inequality **22**–23
Center 383, **402**
Certainty equivalent under risk **273**
Certainty line under risk **292**
CES function **152**, 153, 156
Chain rule **45**
Characteristic equation **386**, 393, 394, 433, 596, 597
Characteristic root (*see* Eigenvalue)
Characteristic value (*see* Eigenvalue)
Characteristic vector (*see* Eigenvector)
Characterization of optimum by first-order condition 85–103
Characterization of optimum by saddle-point condition 103–111
Class (*see* Set)
Classical optimization theory *generally* 111–120
  comparison to nonlinear programming 117–120
  effective constraints in 113–114
  equality constraints in 111
  first-order condition in **112**–115, 117–119
  Lagrangian in 112, 117
  local maximum condition in **111**–115, 117
  rank condition in **113**–117, 128, 130
  second-order necessary condition in **114**–115, 117, 128
  second-order sufficient condition in **114**–117, 120, 128–130
Closed interval **7**
Coase theorem *generally* 235–247, **245**
Cobb-Douglas function 31, 60, 62, 151, 153, 154, 214, 624
Coefficient of risk aversion *generally* 273–278, 316
  absolute risk aversion **274**, 276–277, 281, 301
  relative risk aversion **274**, 276–277
Cofactor **592**, 593, 594
Collection (*see* Set)
Comparative advantage 202
Comparative dynamics **125**
Comparative statics **125**–131
Compensated change in income **146**
Compensated demand curve 642, 643
Compensated demand function **143**, 627
Compensated price effect 210
Compensating variations 621, **627**, 630, 638, 642
Competitive equilibrium 235, **345**, 347, 349, 373, 374
  existence of 374
  price vector **346**, 349, **371**
  uniqueness of 374
Competitive industry 200
Complements
  of goods **146**, 372
  of inputs **142**, 157
Complete monopoly 196
Complex linear space (*see* Linear space with complex field)
Composite function theorem **45**
Compound lottery **258**–260
Compound prospect (*see* Compound lottery)
Concave function 52–60, **53**, 87, 92, 93, 94, 95, 96, 212, 215, 266, 496, 515, 516, 545, 558, **606**, 607, 608, 609, 610, 611, 613, 616, 617, 618
  strictly **53**–56, 58–60, 87, 96, 174, 271, 272, 275, 277, 282, 468, 508,

548, 558, **606**, 607, 608, 609, 610, 611, 613
Concavity condition **107**
Condition (A-E) (*see* Arrow-Enthoven condition)
Condition (A-H-U) (*see* Arrow-Hurwicz-Uzawa condition)
Condition (BHC) (*see* Bordered Hessian condition)
Condition (Conc) (*see* Concavity condition)
Condition (Conv) (*see* Convexity condition)
Condition (FOC) (*see* First-order condition)
Condition (LM) (*see* Local maximum condition)
Condition (lm) (*see* Local minimum condition)
Condition (M)(*see* Global maximum condition)
Condition (m) (*see* Global minimum condition)
Condition (R) (*see* Rank condition in classical optimization theory)
Contition (RC) (*see* Regularity condition)
Condition (S) (*see* Slater's condition)
Condition (SONC) (*see* Second-order necessary condition in classical optimization theory)
Condition (SOSC) (*see* Second-order sufficiency condition in classical optimization theory)
Condition (SP) (*see* Saddle-point condition)
Constant returns to scale **49**, 143, **150**, **158**, **159**–161, 204, 289, 290, 356, 523
Constraint qualifications **93**
Consumer's budget constraint 542
Consumer's choice **78**, 82, 98–101, 143–147, 171, 176
Consumer's demand function 172
Consumer's intertemporal choice 212
Consumer's lifetime allocation process 541, 547–553
Consumer's lifetime utility **548**
Consumer's surplus **198**, 221–222, 567, 621–647
Continuous function **29**–31, 35–36, 76–77, 83, 266, 329 412, 607, 612, 614
  piecewise **454**, 458
  uniformly **29**
  upper-semi 607
Control function **331**
Control region **454**
Control variable **453**, 459, 548, 558
Convex combination **52**, 83
Convex function 52–60, **54**, 94, 523
  strictly **54–55**, 57, 59–60, 271, 275, 281, 282
Convexity condition 106–**107**
Coordinate **7**
Coordinate system **586**
Corner solution **89**, 99, 101, 102
Cosine law in trigonometry **21**
Cost function **112**, 135, 140, 176, 178, 188, 197
  concavity of **140**, 164
  homogeneity of degree one **140**, 154
Cost minimization **78**, 101–103, 125–126, 134–135, 140–143, 151, 157, 164, 173, 176, 178, 189, 190, 197, 217, 584–585, 601
  Lagrangian multiplier in **135**, 164, 167
Costate variables (*see* Multipliers in optimal control theory)
Cramer's rule **594**
CRS (*see* Constant returns to scale)
Curve **631**, 632
  closed 402, **631**
  piecewise smooth **631**
  simple **631**
  smooth **631**

D-M measure (*see* Dupuit-Marshall measure)
Daeyang Prize 201
Decentralized monetary economy 498
Decreasing absolute risk aversion (hypothesis A) 275, **277** 295, 301, 310
Decreasing returns to scale **150**, **158**, **159**–161, 202, 204
Demand function 623, 625, 627, 634, 636, 637, 638
  compensated 627

homothetic 625, 634, 636, 637, 638
Derivative **40–44**, **42**
first-order **49**, **51**
k^{th} order **49**
left-hand **41**
partial **43**
right-hand **41**
second-order **49**, **51**
second-order partial **50**
Determinant 340, 341, 590–595, **591**, 592, 596, 597, 599, 603
order of **591**
elements of **591**
Differentiable function **40–44**, **42**, 57, 607
continuously **44**, 46, 48, 85, 89, 132, 176, 189, 329 330, 333, 408, 414, 458, 493, 543, 609, 611, 626, 631
k times **50**
three-times continuously 278
twice **50**
twice continuously **50**, 59, 65, 95, 135, 153, 191, 273, 277, 477, 616, 623, 626, 631, 632
Differential equation(s) *generally* 325–418
almost-linear system **409**
(asymptotically) globally stable **335**–336, 338–339, 341–342, 348, 351, 354, 357, 370, 372, 395, 399, 405–406, 412–413, 420, 422, 433, 446
(asymptotically) locally stable **335**–336, 339, 341, 344, 347–349, 410, 414
autonomous system of **328**, 411, 462, 466–467
domain of the solution **326**
equilibrium **334**–342, 347, 349, 351, 353–355, 371 395–414
existence of solution 325, **329**–331
first-order **328**
general solution of **332**, 385, 388, 390, 392, 394–395, 397, 402–404
homogeneous system of **331**, 336, 338, 383
initial condition 326, **327**, 329, 332, 347, 383, 388, 395, 414
initial-value problem **327**
instability of equilibrium in **335**
isolated equilibrium **334**, 336, 337, 341, 347, 371 408
Liapunov stable **335**
linear **331**
linear system **331**, 336–337, 338, 342, 343, 344, 405, 406, 409, 410, 414
linearly independent solutions **384**, 392, 393
nonautonomous system of **411**, 462, 464–466
nonexistence of solution 330, 335
nonhomogeneous system of 337
nonlinear **331**, 332
nonlinear system **331**, 338, 341, 342, 344, 351, 375, 407–414
nonuniqueness of solution **330**, 336
ordinary **328**
partial **328**
particular solution of **332**, 385, 388
periodic motion 402
second-order **328**
solution of 325–**327**, 329–334, 384, 385, 386, 387, 388, 390, 391, 393, 394, 395, 396
speed of adjustment **347**
stability condition 410–411
trivial solution of **384**, 386
uncoupled system of **394**
uniqueness of solution **329**, 331–332, 337, 339, 357
Differentiation
of inner product 52
of integrals 198, **200**, 287
of quadratic forms 52
Discontinuous function **29**–30
Dirichlet's **30**
of the first kind **30**, 454
Disposable income 426–427, 437
Distance function 138
Dot product (*see* Euclidean inner product)
Downward rigidity of money wage rate 366
DRS (*see* Decreasing returns to scale)
Duality 137–139
Duality relations **137**
Duality theorem **137**
Dumping 561–562, 567

Dupuit-Marshall measure 622, **625**, 628, 635, 640 642, 643
Dynamic behavior of the solution on the plane *generally* 395–407
  complex roots (not pure imaginary) 398–402, 410
  complex roots (pure imaginary) 402–403, 405, 410, 411
  equal roots 403–405, 410, 411
  real roots of opposite signs 397–398, 406, 410
  unequal real roots of same sign 395–397, 406, 410

Economics of information 305–316
Economics of uncertainty 357–321
  continuity axiom **259**, 263, 267
  independence axiom **261**–262, 263, 268–270
  linearity property **265**
  monotonicity property **262**, 263, 264
  order-preserving property **265**–266
Education as signal 306
Effective rate of interest 304
Eigen equation (*see* Characteristic equation)
Eigenvalue 343, **386**–387, 395, 399, 400, 405–406, 407, 433, **595**–600
  multiplicity of **596**, 599
  simple root **596**
Eigenvector **387**, **595**–600
Elasticity of demand 193, **231**, 232, 559, 560, 561 565, 566
  constant 560, 566
  decreasing 561
  increasing 561
Elasticity of factor substitution **151**–157, 178, 181
Elasticity of marginal utility of consumption **508**, 509
Engel curve 628, 637 (*see* also Vertical Engle curve)
Envelope theorem 131–137, **132**, 164, 188, 626
  maximum value function in **132**
Equivalent variations 621, **628**, 641, 642
Euclidean distance **19**
Euclidean inner product **18**, 577, 578, 608
Euclidian norm **20**
Euclidian space 13–**24**
Euler equation
  for homogenous functions **49**, 289, 371, 585
  in calculus of variations **469**–470, 472, 635
Euler-Lagrange theorem 112–113
Euler's formula connecting the exponential and trigonometric functions **389**, 391
Euler's theorem for homogeneous functions **48**
Evaluating vector **108**
Exhaustion of product problem **49**
Expansion effect (*see* Scale effect)
Expansion path **133**, 161, 162, 163, 177
Expected rate of return on capital 521
Expected utility 270, 271, 280, 282, 283, 286, 289, 291, 299, 308, 309, 315
Expected utility hypothesis *generally* 257–270
Expected utility property **265**
Expected utility theorem **264**
Expenditure elasticity of a factor **195**
Expenditure function **143**–144, 627
  concavity of 144
  homogeneity of degree one 144
Expenditure minimization problem **143**
Exponential function 389
External diseconomies 235
External economies 235
Externalities 235, 237–242

Factor demand function **103**, 153, 192
Factors of Production
  E-K complementarity 156
  E-L substitutability 156
Fair gamble **285**
Fair-rate-of-return constraint 212
Fair-rate-of-return regulation 218, 234
Family (*see* Set)
First-order condition (for optimum) 85–103, **88**, 91–100, 101–102, 104, 106–108, **112**–119, 130, 174, 196, 198, 213, 215, 224, 230, 238–241, 283, 287, 289, 291, 292, 298, 303,

309, 311, 312, 616, 617, 618, 619, 623
Fisher's law **297**–299
uncertainty version of **299**
Fixed coefficient technology 234
Fixed costs 205
Fixity of capital 521, **522**, 533
Flexible functional forms 152
Forcing function (*see* Control function)
Free competition 240
Full capacity 225–228
Full employment 351, 356, 362, 370, 424
Function **10**–12
bijection (*see* one-to-one correspondence)
composite **12**
constant **11**
domain of **10**
graph of **11**
image of **10**, 12
injection (*see* one-to-one)
inverse **11**, 48
inverse image of **12**, 35
monotone increasing 275, 548
multivalued **11**
nowhere continuous 30
nowhere differentiable 42
of class $C^{(k+1)}$ **50**
one-to-one **11**, 590
one-to-one correspondence **11**
onto **10**
range of **10**
real-valued **10**
set-valued **11**
single-valued **11**
solvability of 47
value of **10**
Fundamental equation in value theory (*see* Hicks-Slutsky equation)
Fundamental equation of comparative statics **128**
Fundamental matrix **385**
Fundamental theorem of algebra **596**

g-constraint 489, **541**, 546
Geometric lag 360
Get-rich-quick effect **270**
Giffen good **146**, 626
Giffen input 190, 192
Giffen paradox 146, 188
Global maximum **86**–88, 119, 174, 286, 292, 297, 298, 299, 303, 607, 617
unique 116, 286, 292, 297, 298, 299, 303, 607, 617
Global maximum condition **86**–89, 91–93, 97–98, 104–108, 616, 617, 618, 619
Global minimum **86**
Global minimum condition **86**
Golden-rule path 444, 482, **483**, 487, 502
modified **482**, 487, 502
Golden-age path (*see* Balanced growth path)
Goldman-Tucker theorem **110**,
Goods market equilibrium 445
Greatest lower bound (*see* Infimum)
Green's theorem 632
Gross substitutability 349–350, 370, 371, 372, 373, 374
global **349**, 372
local **349**

H measure (*see* Hicksian measure)
Hamiltonian **455**, 457, 460, 469, 495, 497, 500, 507, 516, 523, 528, 544, 546, 548, 550, 554, 558, 562, 564
current value **495**, 497, 500, 507, 516, 523, 528, 550
generalized **544**, 554
Hamiltonian system **454–455**, 463, 464, 465, 467 472, 478, 495
Hayashi's homogeneity assumption **482**, 530, 531
Hayashi's theorem in investment theory **530**, 532
Hessian matrix **51**, 58, 96, 117, 128, 135, 154, 165, 168, 174, 224, 631
negative definite 174, 224
negative semidefinite 164, 168
symmetry of 135, 154, 631
Hestenes's theorem **543**
Hicks-Slutsky equation 131, 144–**145**, 175, 206, 209, 212, 348, 372, 626
Hicks-Slutsky matrix (*see* Substitution matrix in consumption)
Hicksian demand function (*see* Compensated demand function)

Hicksian measure of welfare change 622, 625–**626**, 627–630, 640–643
computation of 627–630
H measure (*see* Hicksian measure of welfare change)
Hidden actions **311**
Homogeneous linear system on the plane *generally* 385–394
distinct complex roots 389–392
distinct real roots 388–389
equal real roots 392–394
Homogeneous function 49, 144, 150, 210, 214, 289, 371, 425, 476, 499, 523, 528, 532, 585, 623, 631, 634, 635, 639
of degree m **49**, 633
of degree -1 633, 635, 638
of degree one 144, 150, 214, 425, 476, 499, 523, 528, 532
of degree zero 584, 623, 626, 631, 633
Homothetic demand **634**, 635–638, 641
Homothetic function **147**–151, 155, 161, 177, 625, 634, 636, 638
Homothetic preferences 514, 637
Hotelling's lemma **136**, 137
Hotelling's symmetry relation **136**, 137
Hyperplane 612

Implicit function theorem **46**–47, 99, 127
Improper node (*see* Node)
Income effect **145**, 642, 643
Income elasticity of consumption 512
Income risk **298**–300, 303, 305
Income-leisure choice **206**–212
budget condition in 206
Increasing relative risk aversion (hypothesis B) **277**, 295
Increasing returns to scale **150**, **157**, **158**, **159**–162, 202, 204
local measure of 162–163
Indifference curve **56**, 62–63, 64, 81, 82, 98, 99
under risk **280**–281, 284
Indifference surface (*see* Indifference curve)
Indirect utility function **133**, 172, 176
addilog form of **172**
Inferior good **146**, 209
Inferior input **146**, **190**–191, 193, 196
Infimum **13**
Inflection point **92**
Inner product (*see* Euclidean inner product)
Inner product space **18**
Insurance 281–290, 292, 307–313
Insurance coverage 282, 283, 284, 285, 307, 308, 310, 311, 312
full coverage **285**, 308, 312
Insurance premium 282, 284, 285, 309, 310, 311, 312
Integrability
economic 632
mathematical 632
necessary and sufficient condition for mathematical integrability 632
sufficient condition for economic integrability 632
Integral constraints **542**, 553
Intertemporal arbitrage condition 519–520, 549
Intertemporal budget condition **509**
Intertemporal decision-making process of a firm 533
Inverse demand function 213, 565
Inverse function theorem **48**
Investment *generally* 514–535
adjustment cost approach 522–525
irreversibility of **487**, 517, 527
neoclassical theory 515–522
passive 425, 440
IRS (*see* Increasing returns to scale)
Irving Fisher diagram **511**
IS curve 350, 420, 422
IS-LM 350
IS-LM macroequilibrium 350, 365
Isoelastic utility function **510**
Isoperimetric problem 541, **553**–556

Jacobi's theorem 170
Jacobian determinant condition **341**
Jacobian matrix **45**, 47–48, 95, 112, 132, 170, 341, 351, 352, 430, 442
nonsingularity of 42–43, 48
Jensen's inequality **272**
Joint profit maximization 239

Keynes-Ramsey rule **481**, 501, 503
Keynesian 422, 423
Knife-edge case 336, 348, 422

Knightian uncertainty 521
Kuhn-Tucker-Lagrange condition **106**

L'Hospital's rule 641
Labor supply curve *generally* 206–212
  backward-bending 207–208, 210–211
  upward-sloping 207, 210–211
Lagrangian 84, **88**, 90, 91, 92, 96, 98, 101, 104, 109, 112, 117, 127, 130–131, 133, 136, 224, 230, 238, 297, 452, 456, 616
Lagrangian multiplier **88**, 109, 132, 134, 164, 167, 188, 212, 224, 623, 626
  interpretation of 134
Landau's o-symbol **43**, 409
Laplace expansion **592**, 594, 595
Laplace rule of expansion of cofactors (*see* Laplace expansion)
Law of demand **146**
LAS (*see* Linear approximation system)
Le Châtelier-Samuelson principle **163**–171
Least upper bound (*see* Supremum)
Lemon principle **306**, 313, 314
LeS principle (*see* Le Châtelier-Samuelson principle)
Level set (*see* Indifference curve)
Liapunov function **412**–413
Liapunov's direct method 411–414
Liapunov's theorem **338**, 414
Liapunov's second method (*see* Liapunov's direct method)
Life-cycle hypothesis 504, 506
Lifetime budget condition **551**
Lifetime income **551**
Limit of a function **28**
  left-hand **29**
  right-hand **29**
Line integral 625, **630**, 631, 633
Linear affine (*see* Linear affine transformation)
Linear affine transformation **266**–267, 586
Linear algebra 573–604
Linear approximation stable 339
Linear approximation system **338**, 370, 411, 420–421, 433, 442, 446
Linear differential equation on the plane 383–418, 419
Linear homogeneous function (*see* Homogeneous function of degree one)
Linear programming **79**, 83, 108–111
  duality theorem **110**
  dual problem in **110**
Linear space 14–18, **15**, 582, 585
  associative law in **14**
  basis for 16–**17**, **582**
  commutative law in **14**
  dimension of **17**, **583**, 584
  distributive laws in **14**
  finite dimensional **17**
  infinite dimensional **17**
  origin of **15**
  orthogonal basis for **24**
  with complex field **16**
Linear subspace **582**–583
  trivial **582**
Linear transformation **585**–590, 636
  addition of **588**
  equality of **589**
  invertible **589**, 590
  product of **588**–589
  scalar multiplication of **588**
Linearization **409**–410
Liquidity trap **420**, 422
Livingston data 361
LM curve 350, 420, 422
Loanable funds 313, 354
Loanable funds theory **352**, 354
Local homotheticity **637**
Local maximum **86**–88, 111, 117, 118, 119, 607
Local maximum condition **86**–89, 91–95, 97, 106–108, **111**–115, 116, 128
Local minimum **86**
Local minimum condition **86**
Local nonsatiation **98**
Logical statement 8–10
  conclusion **8**
  contrapositive **9**
  contrapositive argument **9**
  converse **9**
  hypothesis **8**
  logical quantifier **10**
  (logically) equivalent statements **9**

necessary and sufficient condition **9**
necessary condition **9**
negation **10**
quantifier **10**
sufficient condition **9**
vacuously true statement **8**
Logical connections among seven kinds of concavity 611
Long-run desired stock of capital 525
Long-run marginal cost 164
Long-run price elasticity of variable demands **167**
Long-run rate of unemployment 361
Long-run supply elasticity **167**
Long-run total cost 165
Loss principal (à la C. Menger) 134
Lower bound **13**

Macro adjustment processes 350–355, 419–423
Macro rational expectation hypothesis 363, 364
Macroequilibrium
Keynesian system 350–351
neoclassical system 351–355
Mangasarian's theorem 618–619
Mapping (*see* Function)
Marginal adjustment cost of investment 534
Marginal cost **126**, 135, 142, 157, 169, 187, 188, 193 196, 198, 199, 200, 201, 202, 203, 204, 205, 229, 231, 559, 564, 565, 568
Marginal cost curve **126**, 187, 188, 192, 194, 195, 199, 200, 201, 202, 203, 204
Marginal cost pricing 196–201, **199**, 229, 287, 563 564, 567
Marginal efficiency of capital 517, 525, **533**, 535
Marginal product 58
Marginal productivity rules 518
Marginal propensity to consume 504
Marginal propensity to save 305
Marginal rate of substitution 177, **207**–208, 283
Marginal rate of time preference **297**, 299, 304
under capital risk **304**
under income risk **300**

Marginal revenue 196, 231, 559, 560, 565
Marginal revenue product 214, 218
Marginal revenue product curve 218
Marginal utility of consumption 58, 99, 481, 549
negative 99
Marginal utility of income **133**, 621, 622, 628, **633**–643
constancy of 621, 622, 633–637, 640–643
Marginal utility of money (*see* Marginal utility of income)
Market failure 236, 240
Market solution 240
Marshallian adjustment 366
Marshallian demand function **99**
Marshallian measure of welfare change (*see* Dupuit-Marshall measure)
Marshallian stability 345, 366
Marshallian trapezoid **635**, 640
Marshallian triangle 621, 623–626, 641
Matrix(ces) 45, **573**–603
addition of **573**, 574
adjoint of **593**
as linear transformations 585–590, **586**
associative law **574**, 576
column rank of **581**
commutative law **574**
commuting **576**
diagonal **576**, 582, 598
diagonalization of **598**
distributive law **574**, 576
equality of **573**
full rank of **581**
identity **576**, 580, 589, 597
inverse **579**, 580, 581, 582, 590
linearly dependent columns in 580
linearly dependent rows in 580
minor of **592**
multiplication of **575**–576, 595
nonsingular 84, 129, 340, 384, 385, 395, 407, 414, **579**, 580, 581, 582, 584, 585, 590, 593, 595, 598, 599, 600, 601, 603
null space of **583**, 585
orthogonal **599**
permutable **576**
post multiplier in **576**

premultiplier in **576**
rank of **581**–584, 585
rank theorem of **581**
row rank of **581**
rule of the inversion of 593
scalar multiplication of **574**
singular 387, 580, 585, 601
spectral decomposition **600**
square **573**, 574, 576, 579, 581, 582, 583, 590, 591, 595, 599
summation of (*see* addition of)
symmetric 130, 135, 146, 154, 342, **576**, 597, 599, 600, 601, 603, 627, 631, 632
trace of 340, 341, **597**
transpose of **576**, 577, 578, 579, 581, 593, 598, 603
unit **576**
zero **574**, 582, 589
Matrix algebra (*see* Linear algebra)
Maximum element **13**
Maximum principle (see Pontryagin's maximum principle)
MC (*see* Marginal cost)
MC-curve (*see* Marginal cost curve)
Mean-value approach 290
Measure for returns-to-scale 150
Measuring stick for cardinality 636, 637, 640
Metric **19**
Metric space **19**
triangular inequality in **19**
symmetry in **19**
Mill price **563**, 564, 568
Mill pricing **563**, 568
Minimum cost function (*see* Cost function)
Minimum distance problem **471**–472
Minimum element **13**
Minimum expenditure function (*see* Expenditure function)
Minimum wage legislation 219
Monetarism mark I 364
Monetarism mark II 364
Monetarists 422
Monetary equilibrium 368, 424, 426, 434, 440, 445, 446
Monetary policy
deflationary 438
inflationary 438
Money 350, 365, 366, 368, 419, 423, 425, 426, 428, 429, 430, 438, 498, 499, 503
neutrality of 429
superneutrality of **430**
Money and growth model 423–447
Drabicki-Takayama's extension of 436–447
Tobin's 423–436
Monopolistic competitive firm 557
Monopoly 196, 565
Monopsony 223
Moral hazard 307, **311**, 313
Mormons 100
MUI (*see* Marginal utility of income)
Multipliers in optimal control theory **456**, 478, 479, 493, 494, 495, 497, 499, 500, 507, 523, 533, 544, 545, 551, 554, 558, 562, 564
Myopic perfect foresight **424**, 436, 439, 444

Necessary and sufficient condition for optimal control 468, 470, 479, 497, 500, 507–508, 516, 523, 528, 545, 548
Necessary and sufficient condition in nonlinear programming 89, 92–93, 95, 97, 98, 102, 109
Necessary condition in nonlinear programming (*see* First-order condition)
Necessary condition for optimal control 454, 457, 465, 467, 468, 469, 470, 478, 493, 495, 507, 516, 528, 545, 548, 555, 558
Negative definite **37**–40, 59, 129, 174, 224, 342, **600**, 601 602
Negative semidefinite **37**–40, 58–59, 129, 130, 164, 168, **600**, 601, 602
Neighborhood of a point **34**, 86
Neoclassical growth model 356–358, 419–448, 475, 476, 496, 498
Neoclassical technology 234
Net substitution **145**
Net substitution matrix (*see* Substitution matrix)
New classical macroeconomics (*see* Macro rational expectation hypothesis)

Newtonian mechanics 455
NM utility function **264**, 266, 267, 271, 274, 275, 277, 286
examples of 278–281
Node 375, 383, **396**, 404, 407, 422, 433
Nominal rate of return on physical assets 424, 436
Nonhuman workers 212
Nonlinear programming *generally* 75–120, **78**
choice variable (*see* decision variable)
constraint function **77**, 83, 96
constraint set **75**, 77, 80–81, 86–87, 93
decision variable **75**, 80, 119
effective constraints **82**
equality constraint 84–85
feasible set (*see* constraint set)
inconsistent constraints **80**
ineffective constraints **82**
inequality constraint 85
interior solution 99, 102, 113, 208
maximand function **75**, 89, 96
mixed constraints **85**
nonnegative constraint **77**, 84, 119
objective function (*see* maximand function)
optimum point (*see* solution)
rank condition **94**–95
solution **75**–76, 81–84
unique solution **75**, 84, 87
Nonlinearities on the budget condition 212
Non-market interdependence of economic agents (*see* Externalities)
Nonmonetary centralized economy 498
Nonnegative orthant **80**, 104
Nonsatiation 208, 298
Nonstorable good 219
Nonvanishing gradients in quasi-concave programming 611–615
Normal good 209
Normal income hypothesis **505**
Normal input **190**–191, 196
Normalized price 639
Normed linear space **20**
triangular inequality in **20**
Normed vector space (*see* Normed linear space)
Numéraire **346**, 634, 639

Occam's razor 629
Olech's theorem 341–342, 354, 355, 370, 422
Open ball **34**
radius of **34**
Open interval **7**
Operator (*see* Function)
Opportunity cost **134**, 224
Opportunity cost of accumulation **480**, 481, 549
Opportunity line under risk **284**, 292
Optimal control theory *generally* **451**–569
existence of solution 453
infinite horizon *generally* 493–540
not vanishing simultaneously **454**, 463, 464, 465, 469
optimal control **456**
optimal pair **456**
rank condition in **543**, 547
solution pair (*see* optimal pair)
uniqueness of solution 453
Optimal growth path 487, 503
Optimal growth problem 475–489, 496–498, 542
attainable path **476**
feasible condition for **476**, 487
feasible path **476**, 498
path of pure accumulation **478**
two-sector 484
Optimal monetary policy 498–504
Optimal pricing policy **233**–234
Outcomes (in a prospect) **258**, 259, 264, 268
Output elasticity of the demand for a factor **193**, 195
Over-insurance **310**
Overlapping generation model 506
Own-price effect 602

Pareto optimum 235, **239**–242, 244–245, 247
Partitioned matrices 594–595
Passus coefficient (*see* Scale elasticity)
Path (*see* Trajectory)
Path independence 623–626, **625**, 631, 632, 633
Peak-load problem 219–235
firm-peak case 227–229, 233
profit-maximizing monopoly 230–234

shifting-peak case 226, 228–229, 232
welfare-maximizing monopoly 221–229
Perfect capital market **515**, 520
Perfect myopic foresight (*see* Myopic perfect foresight)
Perfect stability 348
Permanent income **509**, 512, 514
Permanent income hypothesis 504–514
Permutation **590**–591
inversion in **591**
Phase diagram **336**, 357, 361, 486
Phase diagram technique **370**, **375**, 419, 430, 482
Phase plane **395**
Phillips curve 358–365, 367
expectation augmented 360–365
Pigouvian solution 236
Pigouvian tax-cum-subsidy scheme 237, 240
Planned investment 437
Planned savings 437
Planning model **78**
Poincaré's theorem **375**–376, 410, 419, 422
Polar coordinates 401
Pontryagin multipliers (*see* Multipliers in optimal control theory)
Pontryagin's maximum principle 451–461, **456**, 471
Pontryagin's theorem **467**
Portfolio choice 290–296, 439
Portfolio shift 354
Portfolio switching 429
Positive definite **37**–40, 59, 412, **600**, 601
semidefinite **37**–40, 59, **600**, 601
Positive definite function **412**
Pratt's theorem **274**
Preference ordering 258–259
Preventive activity under risk 307–312
Price discrimination 560, 561, 562, 566
Principal **315**
Principal-agent problem **315**
Private profit maximization 240
Probability density function 286
Production externality 237
Production function 57–58, 213
concavity of 58
Production isoquant **56**
Profit maximization 135–137, 188, 190, 217
Lagrangian in 136
Profit maximization condition 241, 243, 565
Profit maximizing firm 562, 567
Propensity to save 512
Proper node 396, **405**
Proportionality hypothesis **505**
Prospect **258**, 259, 272
Pseudo concave function **607**, 609, 610, 611, 612, 613, 615, 617, 618, 619
locally **614**, 615, 619
locally strictly **615**, 619
strictly **608**, 609, 610, 611, 613, 614, 617, 618
Pure exchange economy 348

Quadratic form 36–40, **37**, 180, 600, 602
Quantity theory of money 352
Quasi-concave function 60–65, **60**, 80–81, 87–88, 95, 102, 118, 119, 544, **605**, 606, 607, 608, 611, 612, 613, 614, 615, 616, 617, 618, 619
explicitly **61**–64, **606**, 607, 608, 610, 611, 613, 617
strictly **60**–65, 93, 96–98, 118, 119, **606**, 607, 610, 611, 613, 614, 615, 617, 618, 623
Quasi-concave programming 95–98, **615**–619
Quasi-convex function **60**, 81
explicitly **60**
strictly **60**
Quasi-fixed factor **150**, 164, 167, 170
Quasi-ordering
complete **259**
partial **259**
total **259**
Quasi-saddle-point condition **106**

Ramsey-Cass-Koopmans rule (*see* Keynes-Ramsey rule)
Rate of depreciation 476, 515, 519, 525
Rate of inflation 358, 359, 361, 364, 370, 433–434, 436, 439, 440
actual 359, 433
expected 358, 359, 433, 434

Rate of interest 296, 297, 299, 304, 305, 352, 365, 419, 439, 440, 506, 547
nominal 366, 439, 440, 506
real 296, 297, 299, 304, 305, **506**, 548
stability of real rate 513
Rate of time preferences **508**
Rate of unemployment 358, 360, 361, 362, 363, 364
long-run 361
natural **361**–362, 363, 365
Rational expectations 363, 364, 424, 432, 436, 499
Rational number **8**
Rationing 170–171
Real rate of return on money 425, 429
Regional allocation of investment 458–461
Regressive factor (*see* Inferior input)
Regret theory 268
Regularity condition 138–**139**, 147
Regulatory constraints 212–219
behavior of the firm under 212–219
Relative risk premium **277**
Relevant variable **95**, 616, 619
Returns to scale, its concept 150, 157–163
Revealed preference
strong axiom of 632, 633
weak axiom of 632
Risk aversion function 296
Risk-bearing fee **289**, 304
Risk complementarity **302**
Risk premium 272, **273**, 277, 281
Risky asset **291**–295
Risky security 296
Root (*see* Eigenvalue)
Routh-Hurwitz condition **343**–345, 368
Routh-Hurwitz theorem **343**, 365–370
application of 365–370
Roy's identity **134**, 137, 172, 176, 627, 634, 635, 638

Saddle point in nonlinear programming **103**–111
saddle-point characterization 83, 137
saddle-point condition 85, 104–108, **105**
Saddle point in differential equations 383, **398**, 405, 407, 422, 430, 432, 443, 482, 485
Safe asset **291**, 293
Samuelson's reciprocity relation **135**
Samuelson's regularity condition **141**, 166, 169, 189, 585, 601
Saving-investment equilibrium 440
Savings decisions
under no risk 296–299
under capital risk 302–304, 305
under income risk 299–302, 304–305
Scalar **14**
Scale coefficient **159**
Scale diseconomies 204
Scale economies 204–205
Scale effect **189**–190, 192
Scale elasticity **159**
Scale factor (*see* Scale coefficient)
Second-order condition (for optimum) 98, 99, 287, 309
Second-order differentiable approximation **153**
Seemingly unrelated regression 181
Self-fulfilling expectations 363, 424
Self-selection **306**
Sensitivity analysis **125**–181
Separable cost function **147**, 155, 176
Separation property **296**
Separation theorem 290
Sequence **25**–29, 36
bounded **26**
Cauchy **27**
convergent **25**–28
convergent subsequence **36**
limit inferior of **27**
limit of **25**, 28, 36
limit point of **26**, 28
limit superior of **27**
of real numbers **26**
subsequence of **26**, 36
terms of **25**
values of **25**
Series 27–**28**
absolutely convergent **28**
infinite **28**
partial sum of **28**
Set **4**–8
boundary of **34**
boundary point of **34**
bounded **35**–36
closed **32**–33, 36

compact **35**, 76, 83
complement of **6**
connected **454**
convex **52**–53, 54, 55, 56–58, 80–81, 87, 95, 605, 607, 611, 618, 619, 631
coordinate **7**
derived **34**
difference between **5**
disjoint **5**
element of **4**
empty **5**
equality of **5**
finite **4**
index **7**
infinite **4**
interior of **34**
interior point of **34**
intersection of **5**
linear sum of **53**
nonintersecting (*see* disjoint)
of all ordered n-tuples of real number **14**
open **32**–33, 57–58, 611, 631
open kernel of (*see* interior of)
proper subset **5**
sequential compactness of **36**
subset **5**
union of **5**
Set of admissable controls **453**
Seven kinds of concavity (global concepts) 605–611
Shadow price (*see* Opportunity cost)
Shadow demand price of capital **518**
Shephard (-McKenzie) lemma (*see* Shephard's lemma)
Shephard duality 138, 153
Shephard duality theorem 138–139
Shephard's lemma **135**–136, 137, 148, 153, 155, 156, 174, 177, 180, 188, 192, 193, 194, 195, 196, 627
Shephard-Samuelson theorem **143**, 160, 174
Short-run price elasticity of variable input demands **167**
Short-run supply elasticity **167**
Short-run total costs 165
Sidrauski's theorem **433**
Signals **306**–307
endogenously supplied 306
exogenously supplied 306
job market signaling 306
signaling costs **307**
signaling equilibrium **307**
Simple lottery **260**
Simplex method **83**
Slater's condition **92**–94, 97, 102, 105
Slater's counterexample **91**–92
Sluggish adjustment 432
Sluggish expectations 433, 437
Slutsky equation (*see* Hicks-Slutsky equation)
Slutsky matrix (*see* Substitution matrix in consumption)
Slutsky symmetry condition 632
Social discount rate 223
Social optimum (*see* Pareto optimum)
Social welfare 197, 230, 562, 567
Solow-Swan condition **357**, 444
Solow-Swan growth model (*see* Neoclassical growth model)
Solow-Swan path **357**
Solow-Swan theorem **357**
Solution pair (*see* Optimal pair)
Source of instability 434–436
Source of stability 444–445
Spaceless monopoly 559, 563, 567
Spatial monopoly 559, 561, 562
Spatial pricing problem *generally* 557–568
spatial pricing problem and nonlinear programming 564–568
spatial pricing problem and optimal control theory 557–564
Spiral point 383, **400**, 422
Srinivasan theorem 485
Stable branch (of saddle like paths) **397**, 407, 432 437, 484, 485, 487, 488
Stability of competitive equilibrium
general formulation of 345–350
three-commodity case 370–376
Stability of macroeconomic equilibrium
dynamic behavior of trajectories 419–423
Keynesian system 350–351
neoclassical system 351–355
State variable **453**, 454, 459, 461, 548
States (*see* States of nature)
States of nature **257**

States of the world (*see* States of nature)
Static demand theory 514
Static Macroequilibrium 419–423
Steady state **356**, 427–433, 437, 441, 442, 443, 444, 482, 485, 502, 503
  asymptotically global stability 444
  unique 444
Stellar node (*see* Proper node)
Stocks and flows 352
Stoke's theorem (*see* Green's theorem)
Subjective rate of discount 550
Substitutes
  of goods **146**
  of inputs **142**, 151, 157
Substitution effect in production **189**–190, 192
Substitution matrix in consumption 131, 138, **146**, 164, 175, 209, 601, 626, 627, 632
  negative semidefiniteness of 146, 175, 209, 627, 632
  singularity 601
  symmetry of 146, 601, 627, 632
Substitution matrix in production **140**–141
  negative semidefiniteness of 141
  symmetry of 140–141
Successive principle minors **39**, 116, 603
Sufficient condition in nonlinear programming **95**, 116, 224
Sufficient condition for optimal control 468, 470, 479, 508, 516, 528, 545, 548
Superior input **195**–196
Supply price of capital asset 521, 530, 533, 535
Supremum **13**
Supremum principle **13**
System of simultaneous equations 578, 580, 593

Tâtonnement 347, 349
  simultaneous 347
  Walrasian 349
Taylor's expansion 338, 628
Taylor's expansion formula **50**
Theory of exchange 366
Theory of production 366
Theory of the firm under risk 286–290
Three-asset economy 436, 438
Tobin's q 525–535
  average q 525, **530**–531, 534
  marginal q 525–526, **529**–531, 534
Topological space **33**
Topology **33**–34
  discrete **34**
  indiscrete **34**
Total cost 221–222
Total profit **232**–233
Total revenue **198**, 221–222
Total revenue function **197**
Total social benefit **223**
Trace condition **341**
Trade-off between price stability and a low employment 358
Trajectory **395**, 396, 397, 399, 400, 402, 403, 404, 405, 406, 408, 420, 421, 431, 432, 433, 435, 451, 456, 474, 481, 543
  optimal 451, **456**, 474, 543
Transcendental logarithmic function (*see* Translog function)
Transformation **8** (*see also* Function)
  composite **589**
  monotonic 266
  orthogonal **601**
Transitory consumption 505
Translog cost function 153–154, 178
Translog reciprocal utility function **173**
Transversality condition **455**, 460, 467, 479, 481, 484, 485, 494, 496, 498, 524, 544, 546, 555, 559
Trigonometric function 55, 389
Turnpike theory 477
Two-asset economy 436, 437

Unbounded **13**
Uncertainty 258, 364
Upper bound **13**
Upper contour set (*see* Upper level set)
Upper level set **56**, 612
User cost of capital 519–521
Utility function 63, 98–99, 126, 144, 637, 638
  homothetic 637
Utility maximization **126**–131, 144
  consumer's choice in 126

first-order condition in 127, 130, 133
Lagrangian in 127, 130, 133
Lagrangian multiplier in 133

Value of the firm 525, 529, 533, 535
Various cases of Pontragin's maximum principle 461–463
final time open with fixed end-points (autonomous system) 466–467
final time open with fixed end-points (non-autonomous system) 464–465
fixed time with fixed end-points 463–464
fixed time with variable right-hand end-points 467–468
time optimal problem **461**, 465–466
Vectors **13**–24, 44, 577
addition of **14**
angle between **22**
column **577**, 578, 593, 600, 602
difference of **14**
dimension of **14**
gradient **44**, 132, 545, 611, 616
linear combination of **16**, 582, 586
linear dependence of **16**, 581
linear independence of **16**, 581, 583
i^{th} coordinate of **14**
orthogonality of **23**
row **577**, 578
scalar multiplication of **14**
zero **15**, 595

Vector inequalities 85
Vector space (*see* Linear space)
Vertical Engel curve **634**, 638–640, 643
Ville's axiom 632
vNM utility function (*see* NM utility function)
von Neumann-Morgenstern axioms 364
von Neumann-Morgenstern theorem 262–264
von Neumann-Morgenstern utility function (*see* NM utility function)

Walras's law **346**, 371
Walras-Keynes-Phillips model à la Tobin 365–370, **367**
Walrasian adjustment 366
Walrasian stability 345, 366
Walrasian stability problem **346**–347
Weierstrass theorem **36**, 76, 83
Welfare maximizing firm 563, 564, 567, 568
Welfare maximizing monopoly 567
Wicksell effect **436**, 445
Wicksellian cumulative process **436**
WKP model (*see* Walras-Keynes-Phillips model)
Wronskian **385**

Young's theorem **52**